RHODES

RHODES

By
J. G. LOCKHART
and
THE HON. C. M. WOODHOUSE

HODDER AND STOUGHTON

Printed and bound in Great Britain
for Hodder and Stoughton Ltd.,
St. Paul's House, Warwick Lane, London, E.C.4
by Richard Clay and Company, Ltd.,
Bungay, Suffolk

CONTENTS

LIST OF ILLUSTRATIONS

NOTE ON SOURCES

THE most recent and comprehensive bibliography of sources on South African history will be found in the revised edition (1963) of Volume VIII of the *Cambridge History of the British Empire*. So far as Rhodes is concerned, every work and virtually every reference of importance, up to the date of publication (1952), is listed in *A Bibliography of Cecil John Rhodes*, published by the Central African Archives, Salisbury, Southern Rhodesia. This indispensable work has made it unnecessary to include a full bibliography here, which would be largely a reproduction of it; and the comparatively few items that have needed to be added to it in the course of the succeeding ten years are readily indicated below. It only remains to acknowledge my debt to the *Bibliography* and to the staff of the Central African Archives who produced it. They also gave valuable help in correspondence with Mr. Lockhart and myself in response to enquiries. To Mr. E. E. Burke, the compiler of the *Bibliography*, and Mr. T. W. Baxter, the present Director of the Archives, we have been particularly indebted.

In giving references to the sources used in the following notes, the practice adopted has been to be sparing of references to well-known works already published. Exceptions have been made for those works to which recourse would not ordinarily be made for the study of Rhodes's life, and also for substantial quotations—for instance those from his speeches, collected in 1900 by "Vindex". The works specially used for particular chapters are indicated in the notes to those chapters. Few specific references are given to the following general works, which have been used in greater or less degree throughout:

Biographical

Baker, Herbert: *Cecil Rhodes by his Architect* (Oxford, 1938)
Clark, G. N.: *Cecil Rhodes and his College* (Oxford, 1953)
Currey, Ronald: *Rhodes—a Biographical Footnote* (Cape Town, 1956)
Fuller, T. E.: *The Right Honourable Cecil Rhodes* (London, 1910)
Gross, Felix: *Rhodes of Africa* (London, 1956)
Hensman, Howard: *Cecil Rhodes: a study of a career* (Edinburgh, 1901)

"Imperialist": (J. R. Maguire): *Cecil Rhodes; with personal reminiscences by Dr. Jameson* (London, 1897)

Jourdan, Philip: *Cecil Rhodes: his private life by his private secretary* (London, 1910)

Le Sueur, Gordon: *Cecil Rhodes, the Man and his Work* (London, 1913)

Lockhart, J. G.: *Cecil Rhodes* (London, 1933)

McDonald, J. G.: *Rhodes: a Life* (London, 1927)

Maurois, André: *Cecil Rhodes* (London, 1953)

Michell, Lewis: *The Life of the Rt. Hon. Cecil John Rhodes, 1853–1902* (London, 1910)

Millin, Sarah Gertrude: *Rhodes* (London, 1933; revised edition, 1953)

Plomer, William: *Cecil Rhodes* (London, 1933)

Stead, W. T.: *The Last Will and Testament of Cecil John Rhodes* (London, 1902)

Stent, Vere: *A Personal Record of Some Incidents in the Life of Cecil Rhodes* (Cape Town, 1924)

"Vindex" (the Rev. F. Verschoyle): *Cecil Rhodes: his Political Life and Speeches, 1881–1900* (London, 1900)

Williams, Basil: *Cecil Rhodes* (London, 1921)

Historical and General

Cambridge History of the British Empire, vol. III (1959)

Cambridge History of the British Empire, vol. VIII (revised, 1962)

De Kiewiet, C. W.: *A History of South Africa, Social and Economic* (Oxford, 1950)

Hailey, Lord: *An African Survey Revised, 1957* (Oxford, 1958)

Halévy, Elie: *Imperialism and the Rise of Labour* (London, new edition, 1951)

Hanna, A. J.: *The Story of the Rhodesias and Nyasaland* (London, 1960)

Hattersley, A. F.: *South Africa, 1652–1933* (London, 1933)

Hofmeyr, J. H.: *South Africa* (London, 1931)

Keppel-Jones, Arthur: *South Africa* (London, 1949)

Macmillan, W. M.: *Bantu, Boer and Briton* (London, 1929)

Newton, A. P.: *Select Documents relating to the Unification of South Africa* (London, 1924)

Robinson, R., and J. Gallagher, with A. Denny: *Africa and the Victorians* (London, 1961)

Sillery, A.: *The Bechuanaland Protectorate* (Oxford, 1952)

Walker, E. A.: *A History of Southern Africa* (London, revised
    edition, 1957)
Williams, Basil: *Botha, Smuts and South Africa* (London, 1946)
Worsfold, W. B.: *The Union of South Africa* (London, 1912)

The above works are referred to, where necessary, by the
author's name.

In addition, substantial use has been made of the Rhodes
Papers in the Library of Rhodes House, Oxford, by permission
of the Trustees. These papers have been examined by some previous biographers, notably Sir Lewis Michell and Professor Basil
Williams, but some of the material in them was either overlooked
or withheld from publication for reasons of discretion. Examples
of what was overlooked are some items of correspondence relating
to the Jameson Raid, all of which were previously supposed to
have been either destroyed or at least removed from the Rhodes
Papers. An example of what was withheld for reasons of discretion is the collection described as the Radziwill Papers, including some letters purporting to have been written by Rhodes to
Princess Radziwill in 1900–1. The more interesting of these
items are contained in the Appendices to this book.

The Rhodes Papers properly so called were formerly the
property of the British South Africa Company, which gave them
to the Rhodes Trustees. They are carefully filed and indexed in
three series: A—outgoing letters; B—outgoing telegrams; C—
incoming letters and telegrams. Unfortunately, but naturally, the
incoming correspondence is far more voluminous and less interesting than the outgoing. Still more unfortunately, it only
begins to be copious from the year 1897, because the bulk of
Rhodes's papers up to the end of 1896 were destroyed in the fire
at Groote Schuur in December of that year. This misfortune has
aggravated the natural tendency in the life of any celebrated man,
that his later years are the better documented. It is some comfort
to know that the losses in the fire of 1896 may not have been too
disastrous, because the first editor who indexed the papers has
recorded that it was not Rhodes's normal habit in any case to
keep copies of outgoing letters and telegrams before 1897.

The break in the continuity of the Rhodes Papers in 1896 happens fortuitously to coincide fairly closely with the division of
labour between the two authors of this book. Mr. Lockhart's
work ended with his lamented death when he had reached the
early months of 1896: he had in fact completed up to Chapter 18

inclusive, though I have made substantial additions to Chapters 16–18 inclusive. In the main, therefore, Mr. Lockhart had not used the more systematically organised and indexed of the Rhodes Papers, particularly the incoming letters and telegrams from 1897. This chance division accounts for the fact that the later chapters appear to be more lavishly annotated with references to the Rhodes Papers.

The division is not absolute, however. The indexed incoming correspondence reaches back earlier than 1897, though it is intrinsically less interesting than the outgoing. There are also other collections of papers relating to Rhodes which have not, like the Rhodes Papers proper, been gathered together in a single collection. Among them are included, for instance, Rhodes's Wills and correspondence relating to them; a number of early letters; and an interesting collection of letters received by Lord Elton, then General Secretary of the Rhodes Trust, in response to a letter published in the press in 1955, inviting personal recollections of Rhodes. The simplest way of indicating such papers seemed to be to give the references under which they will be found in the catalogue of Rhodes House Library, prefixed by the initials "R.H.L." —thus for example: R.H.L. MSS. Afr. s. 115, f. 59. I have been greatly helped in compiling these references by the skill and care of the Rhodes House Librarian, Mr. L. B. Frewer, whose knowledge of the collections in his charge has been invaluable.

In addition to all the above material, there are other specific collections relevant to the biography of Rhodes in the Library at Rhodes House. The following are the most important of them:

The *Cowan Papers*, collected for a projected biography, which was never completed, and bought by the Trustees. They contain little on Rhodes himself, but are a valuable source for the early history of the family.

The *Le Sueur Papers*, collected by Rhodes's secretary, Gordon Le Sueur, for his biography, and bought by the Trustees.

The *Maund Papers*, consisting of 24 articles written by E. A. Maund for private circulation in his old age, during the early 1920's. They are valuable only for the period of the negotiation of the mining concessions in Southern Rhodesia, in which Maund himself played a part.

The *Michell Papers*, collected by Sir Lewis Michell for his biography. They include a number (more than 30) of papers abstracted from the Rhodes Papers properly so called, where they are recorded in the index.

The *Radziwill Papers*, consisting of Princess Radziwill's correspondence with Rhodes, Stead, Hawksley and others in 1900–1, together with a section of her diary and an account of her trial for forgery in 1902. They contain some information on the political background of the Boer War years, but are rendered extremely unreliable by the Princess's notorious inability to distinguish truth and fiction.

The *Basil Williams Papers*, consisting of note-books and correspondence in the course of the preparation of Basil Williams's biography.

Most of the above papers were examined by Mr. G. F. Metcalfe in 1947–48, and the business papers listed below by Mr. Charles Wilson in 1956, but they have not otherwise been studied as a whole or used for biographical purposes since Professor Basil Williams wrote his biography in 1921. Other scholars have, however, used relevant parts of the papers for particular studies, e.g. Dr. Roland Oliver in his *Sir Harry Johnston and the Scramble for Africa*, and Sir Theodore Gregory in his *Ernest Oppenheimer and the Economic Development of Southern Africa*. The files which have been generally available in the past are those containing the outgoing letters (A and B) and the following files of incoming letters and telegrams:

C.1: Administration
C.2A: The Cape, to 1895
C.2B: The Cape, 1896–1902
C.3A: Charters, 1889–91
C.3B: Charters, 1892–6
C.16: Miscellaneous
C.25: Delagoa Bay
C.26: Groote Schuur
C.27: Personal, Political and Business
C.28: Personal
C.29: Index

The following files of incoming correspondence have not hitherto been made generally available by the Trustees:

C.4: Charter (Home Board)
C.5: Charter (Cape)

C.6:   Cold Storage
C.7A: De Beers Mines, 1890–96
C.7B: De Beers Mines, 1897–1902
C.8:   Farms
C.9:   Finance
C.10: Goldfields
C.11: Hawksley
C.12: Immigration
C.13: Inyanga
C.14: McDonald
C.15: Michell
C.17: Ngami Trek
C.18: Northern Rhodesia
C.19: Rhodesia
C.20: Rhodesia Railways
C.21: Syfret, E.R.
C.22: Transcontinental Telegraph
C.23: Transvaal
C.24: Wernher, Beit & Co.

The above, as will be seen, mainly cover business matters. If they contain any particularly guilty secrets, I have been unable to detect them. More interesting, though much more difficult to assess, are the *Radziwill Papers*, which have also been withheld from study hitherto. I am grateful to the Trustees for allowing me to see all this material for the first time, though I cannot encourage readers to expect any sensational revelations from it. The only remarkable discovery I can claim is the full text of the earliest of the famous "missing telegrams" of the Jameson Raid period. What is chiefly remarkable about it is that it has not been noticed before, although it is not in one of the hitherto "reserved files" but in one that has been open to inspection for many years; and it is even recorded in the index, though not in terms that would readily lead to its identification as such. A note on it will be found in Appendix A.

Among the papers at Rhodes House there are, of course, a great many documents which have been quoted, in full or in part, in previous biographies of Rhodes or other works. It seemed unnecessary to reproduce them again textually in a new biography, even at the expense of a loss of "definitiveness", since they are so readily accessible elsewhere. To have included them in full would have needlessly enlarged the size of the present volume, without adding anything new to the portrait of Rhodes. A reference, or a brief excerpt has seemed, in most cases, to be sufficient.

References and sources are given at the end of each chapter. Detailed references are confined, in the main, to new sources, that is to say, to the Rhodes Papers. To have given references in detail to all the standard works that have been consulted would have necessitated, if carried to its logical conclusion, a reference for practically every sentence in the book. In order to reduce the load to a minimum, the aim has been to concentrate references as much as possible; and when a paragraph needs several, the practice usually followed is to give one collective reference at the end of it. Unless such a practice is adopted, most readers are apt to lose interest by the time sentences have been raised to the power of 120 or more; and that would be a matter for regret.

One final confession of failure has also to be made. When Mr. Lockhart died, the later part of his typescript was unrevised, and in some cases the references given by him were sketchy. It has proved impossible, despite the combined efforts of Mr. Frewer and myself, to verify the source of every item of new material contained in his later chapters, particularly Chapter 14, although there is no doubt that it derives principally from Mr. Lockhart's researches in the Rhodes House Papers.

In conclusion, I should like to express my thanks to Sir Robert Tredgold, Mr. T. W. Baxter, Mr. A. F. Madden, Mr. E. T. Williams and Mr. L. B. Frewer, who have read the whole of the work and made most valuable comments and suggestions; and to Professor Carroll Quigley and Professor Joseph Baylen, with both of whom I have had discussions and correspondence on particular points. I am also indebted to Messrs. Edward Arnold (Publishers) Ltd., who have given permission for the long extract from Mr. Ian Colvin's *Life of Jameson* at the beginning of Chapter 6; and to the Warden and Fellows of New College, Oxford, for permission to quote from the *Milner Papers*.

C. M. W.

INTRODUCTION

THE main purpose of this new biography of Cecil Rhodes has been to make full use of the Rhodes Papers at Rhodes House, Oxford, which are the principal subject of the preceding Note. The portrait of Rhodes which emerges, though not very different from before, is perhaps a little sharper in focus and in detail, in contrast to the fuzzy aura of hero-worship with which his admirers blurred the outline, or to the black and menacing shadow over Africa evoked by his enemies. It is a little easier, too, in many cases to find rational motives for his actions in place of the mystical vision or the unscrupulous cynicism which have sometimes been used to explain everything: or rather one should say "in addition to" that vision and that cynicism, for Cecil Rhodes had an ample measure of both. Perhaps one thing also emerges more clearly from the totality of the Rhodes Papers: that those who hated him most were those who knew him least, and those who most admired and loved him were those who knew him best. Of course, the judgment of either side may be discounted and derided, but it is well to be clear about the facts.

W. T. Stead, the brilliant journalist of liberal imperialism, perceived the fact long ago. Immediately after Rhodes's death in 1902, he wrote:[1]

> The few who knew him loved him. The majority, to whom he was unknown, paid him their homage, some of their admiration, and others of their hate. And it must be admitted that the dread he inspired among those who disliked him was more widespread than the affection he commanded from those who came within the magic of his presence.

Stead's judgment has been notably and continuously confirmed in the last sixty years. For the biographies of Rhodes have, in the nature of things, been written less and less by people who knew him personally; and they have also grown by and large progressively more critical. On the other hand, when a last round-up was made in 1955 by Lord Elton of personal reminiscences of Rhodes by those still living who had even the slightest personal contact with him, the fairly numerous responses, slight though

17

they were in substance, showed hardly a single note of hostility towards him, or even of criticism.

It is true that these posthumous tributes came almost exclusively from people of little importance in his life, who saw him, if at all, from a great distance and from far below. He was always a good leader of humble servants who subordinated their wills entirely to his own. He was at his magnanimous best in dealing with the young or the little man. No harsh criticism of him need be expected from those who never attempted to cross his path, or were never in a position to do so. But a different opinion of him was formed by some of those contemporaries who had a personality as strong as his own, and different principles or conflicting ambitions. The list of those who became his severest critics and enemies, in many cases after once pinning their hopes to his greatness, is long and formidable. It includes, among fellow-pioneers in Africa, such names as Lord Lugard, Sir Harry Johnston, the Reverend John Mackenzie, Sir Charles Warren and of course Paul Kruger. Among politicians at the Cape, it includes W. P. Schreiner, J. X. Merriman and Jan Hofmeyr. Among writers and journalists, it includes Henry Labouchere, Wilfred Scawen Blunt, Olive Schreiner and her husband, S. C. Cronwright; and even his admirers, W. T. Stead and F. E. Garrett, were often fiercely critical of him. Among the political figures at Westminster his most devoted admirers were not of the highest calibre—for instance George Wyndham and Reginald Brett (later Lord Esher). Although Lord Rosebery and Joseph Chamberlain and Parnell were captivated by interest in some of his ideas, against them have to be set the stern disapproval of Sir William Harcourt, Sir Michael Hicks-Beach, Sir Henry Campbell-Bannerman and most of the Establishment of the day. Rosebery and Milner became devotees of Rhodes only after his death. Gladstone and Salisbury were both impervious to his magic.

Yet it would not be accurate to say that Rhodes's admirers were weaker personalities in contrast to the men and women of vigour and imagination equal at least to those of his antagonists, if not his own, who were among his most devoted partisans. Dr. Jameson, with all his faults, was no spineless weakling; nor was Lord Grey nor Sir William Milton, his lieutenants in Rhodesia; nor were missionaries like Father Coillard and John Moffat, nor men of action like Frederick Selous and Johan Colenbrander, nor financiers like Alfred Beit and Lord Rothschild. Many men began as his enemies and were converted to friendship, or at least to

alliance with him: Barney Barnato at Kimberley, for instance, and
several of the rival concession-hunters in the North. Even Lord
Milner was near to conversion when Rhodes died, and became one
of his Trustees. Among women too Rhodes had his devoted
partisans who were certainly neither weak nor sentimental:
Flora Shaw, for instance, who was torn between admiration for
him and a still stronger feeling for Frederick Lugard; and old
Mrs. Schreiner, who remained loyal to him until the last, in
opposition to her own son and daughter; not to mention the
women who went north in the wake of the pioneers in 1891.

Such divisions of opinion about Rhodes in his lifetime have
been reflected among students of Africa since his death. For good
or ill—and it can be and is still endlessly argued which pre-
dominates—he left an indelible mark on innumerable aspects of
African life: the relations of black and white men and of Dutch
and British colonists; the drawing of frontiers, the evolution of
the Union, the development of Rhodesia, the growth of industry
and communications; and agriculture, education and the arts also
bear his impress. Men's judgments on his qualities might differ:
indeed, they did, and still do, diametrically; but there could be no
disputing the magnitude of his personality and its impact on the
world. He was greatly hated and greatly loved. It was in character that he should be both hated and loved, for his personality
was full of contradictions: indifference towards Rhodes was an
impossibility. And it was also in character that both the hatred
and the love should be on a grand scale, for everything about
Rhodes, every action and reaction, was magnified many times
beyond natural size. It was a curious chance that the very name
which he bore invited the incredibly apt nickname of the Colossus.
The colossal and the contradictory—these are the indispensable
clues to his personality.

The colossal was something that everyone recognised about
him at first impact. His plans were always on an immense scale:
to monopolise the diamond industry, to paint the map of Africa
red, to restore the United States to an enlarged British Empire, to
"square the Pope", to found a secret society which should control
the world, to annex the planets, even, in a moment of frustration
and euphoria combined. "Men are ruled by their foibles,"
Milner wrote of him early in their acquaintance, "and Rhodes's
foible is size." Everyone with whom his conversations are on
record has reported the same preoccupation with the grand scale.
"I like the big and the simple, the barbaric, if you like," he told

his architect, Herbert Baker. "My ruling purpose is the extension
of the British Empire," he told Bramwell Booth, the founder of
the Salvation Army. Even his downfall was on a heroic scale,
and caused his friend and colleague, W. P. Schreiner, to adjure
him not to give way to pettiness: "You must go on living your
life on big lines." It was inconceivable to his contemporaries that
a Rhodes "cut down to size" could, or would wish to, survive.

The contradictoriness of his character was less obvious to most
of them, perhaps partly because, as a former secretary, H. L.
Currey, correctly explained:[2]

> He does not want any living man to know him. His life
> and interests seem mapped out into squares; and the man who
> is concerned with Square 6 must know nothing of Square 7.

Many of his companions were simple and unsophisticated men,
bachelors like himself, who did not seek to probe beneath the
surface. But those who saw more deeply into his character, if
they did not always divine the contradictions in it, were at least
perturbed by the contradictory emotions which he evoked in
them. Labouchere, for instance, at one time described him as "an
Empire jerry-builder . . . a mere vulgar promoter masquerading
as a patriot, and the figurehead of a gang of astute Hebrew
financiers with whom he divided profits". Labby grilled Rhodes
mercilessly at the Select Committee of Enquiry into the Jameson
Raid in 1897, and yet called him afterwards "an entirely honest,
heavy person"; and after his death Labby admitted that Rhodes
probably never cared for money, "except for the power it gave",
and that he stood out head and shoulders above all his associates.

Olive Schreiner, too, the brilliant authoress of *The Story of an
African Farm*, was perpetually torn between contempt and admiration for him. When she first met Rhodes, about 1890, she said she
felt "a kind of mysterious affinity with him" and added that:[3]

> He is even higher and nobler than I expected; but our
> friends are so different (that) we could never become close
> friends. He spoke to me more lovingly and sympathetically
> of *An African Farm* than anyone has ever done.

Even after opposing his native policy, especially over the Strop
Bill in 1894, she declared that "she still believed in his greatness";
and even after the Jameson Raid, she refused commissions to write
articles attacking him. But she attacked him bitterly on her own
account in *Trooper Peter Halket of Mashonaland*, and rejoiced in the

hatred felt for him by the Boers in 1899. Her affection for her husband, S. C. Cronwright, was first engaged by the vigour with which he attacked Rhodes in the press. She was reported to have said that nothing would give her greater pain than that her name should be mentioned in connection with Rhodes in any way whatever, though the source of the story records that she had just been having lunch with him. On the news of his death, she wrote to a friend that "it was a greater shock to me than I could have believed possible". Sir Edmund Gosse wrote after her death that "her feelings of alternate attraction and repulsion to and from Cecil Rhodes were violent to the last degree".

Olive Schreiner's ambivalence towards Rhodes may be partly attributed to the fierce extravagance of her own personality, but it was also an accurate reaction of feminine intuition to the contradictions in Rhodes's character. A more sober assessment which confirms hers is to be found in the autobiography of Rhodes's political colleague, James Rose Innes, later Chief Justice of the Union and perhaps the most reliable contemporary witness, who saw Rhodes with critical generosity, safely this side idolatry. Rhodes was not a simple character, he wrote: he was "full of contradictory qualities whose divergencies were accentuated by the scale of his personality". Rosebery, on the other hand, thought just the opposite. Nobody, he declared, when unveiling the tablet in the Examination Schools at Oxford to commemorate the foundation of the Rhodes Scholarships, had ever been more slandered in his lifetime than Rhodes, "whose life was simplicity itself".

The verdict must go with Rose Innes rather than Rosebery. Those who saw only the simplicity of Rhodes's character saw only one facet of it, which was all he intended them to see. But if we accept each particular judgment as honest, and put them all together, their independent testimonies in fact compose an infinitely complex character. Rhodes was hot-tempered, dictatorial, cynical, vindictive, humourless, moody, impatient, quarrelsome; he was a hard task-master, he never forgot an injury, he readily broke anyone whom he could not use. He was also frank, generous, considerate, sentimental, conciliatory, boyish, romantic, shy; he was kind to the young, fair to his adversaries, especially if they stood up to him, and ready to admit himself in the wrong. All these qualities are abundantly testified by stories told by his contemporaries. It is interesting that his friend Sir Thomas Fuller and his secretary Gordon Le Sueur use the same anecdote as illustrations of his readiness to turn away hostility by a conciliatory gesture and of his habit of "squaring" enemies by the use of his money. But it is too simple an explanation that different witnesses saw the same qualities in different lights. The contradictions were there and were real; and why not? Most people are a complex of contradictions: it is only when a man is built on the grand scale that they become too glaring to overlook.

In his public life, the most striking contrast in Rhodes's character was between the nobility of his ends and the ruthless cynicism of the means which he often used to pursue them. He discerned his ideals in quotations from Aristotle, Marcus Aurelius and John Ruskin; he called upon Rudyard Kipling and Stead to formulate them into words, and Herbert Baker and Watts in visual works of art; he loved to lose himself in contemplation, sometimes in the vast spaces of the *veld*, more often on the slopes of Table Mountain, which he would speak of as his church. He had a passion for creative activity with a strong taste for history and antiquity. Even in the most critical year of his life, 1895, his correspondence about the Bechuanaland Protectorate and the Jameson Raid is intermingled with letters to an agent in Rome about old African maps, or chiding subordinates in Rhodesia for damaging the ancient monuments. The ruins of Zimbabwe and the temples of upper Egypt fascinated him, but most of all he felt inspired by the classical civilisation of Greece and Rome. Gibbon's *Decline and Fall of the Roman Empire* was among his favourite books, along with the *Meditations* of Marcus Aurelius; he wanted young South African artists to be trained in the sunlight and culture of the Mediterranean; he even planned to erect replicas of Doric temples at Kimberley and Cape Town. His passion for education was renowned, and Oxford was one of the abiding loves of his life. His ambitions to unite South Africa under the Union Jack, to revive the British Empire, to reconcile Boer and Briton, to create a tolerable life for the African native, were all in themselves honourable and selfless. Even his passion for making money was no more than part of the grand design. Yet with so much good intention in his visionary heart, he appeared to be quite insensitive to the unscrupulous and sometimes despicable means which he adopted to achieve his ends.

The gulf between his ideals and some of his practices is the more remarkable because of his own immense abilities. He could have achieved everything that would have satisfied a normal man's ambition without recourse to sharp practice. He had marvellous powers of persuasion, whether in the seemingly interminable monologues which mesmerised hard-headed business associates like Alfred Beit and Barney Barnato, or in the hardly less interminable speeches, made without notes or preparation from his prodigious memory, which bewitched the shareholders of his many companies and Boers and Britons alike in his political audiences. He had a magical capacity to inspire loyalty and enthusiasm. Witness the remark of E. S. Grogan, who as a young man walked along Rhodes's route from the Cape to Cairo and wrote a book about the journey, for which Rhodes contributed an introduction: "I am one of the thousands of young men who, but for Rhodes's influence, would be walking up and down Piccadilly thinking of their collars." Another such was young Hubert Hervey, killed in Matabeleland in 1896, whose dying wish was to see Rhodes for the last time—a wish that was fulfilled—and who said as he was carried off the field of battle: "Who knows but that I may soon be pegging out claims for England in Jupiter?" Such was the effect on men of the magnetism of Rhodes's vision. But he also excelled all his contemporaries in South Africa in every field of practical endeavour: as a businessman, as a statesman, as a pioneer of under-developed territories, as a reconciler of the white races. Why then did he have to resort to dishonourable short cuts to the achievement of his visions?

There is no simple answer, but there were many contributory reasons. A major one was the impatience induced by failing health and a growing awareness of it. There was also his natural taste for power, both acquiring and exercising it over his fellow-men; his predilection for judging the value of everything by the criterion of utility alone; his conviction that his judgment was always right; and a certain bluntness of his moral sense, encouraged by the sycophantic satellites who gathered round him in his later years as his power grew. These are familiar defects which have been observed by everyone who has ever written about Rhodes. To them two others, less familiar, can perhaps be added: an unexpected shortsightedness of his lofty vision, and an exasperating childishness, as of a schoolboy who never grew up. These are all aspects of a single character, not isolated defects: they interacted upon each other, and to illustrate one with examples is often to illustrate others as well. Like the colours of a spectrum, they shade into each other; but again like the colours of a spectrum, they can be distinctly seen.

The impatience which grew on Rhodes in his later years was

not a feature of his youth. When he was growing cotton in Natal, or building up the amalgamation of the diamond mines, or planning the Union of South Africa by economic links, he was deeply conscious of the need for gradual consolidation and organic growth. Impatience came partly with success and partly with illness—the years 1894–95 being crucial in both cases. Success gave him far more to do than one man could manage; he was never able to organise an efficient staff or secretariat; he was casual about correspondence and administration and bored with all paper-work—the obverse of the marvellous memory for facts and figures which made every speech such a *tour-de-force*. The relatively few letters he wrote were ill-expressed and often misleading in meaning, because he was in too much of a hurry to make himself clear. The sense of urgency increased as he began to realise that his days were numbered. They had been numbered, indeed, when he first went to South Africa as a boy, but the healthy life in a good climate had postponed the danger for many years until he reached the summit of power in 1894. Then persistent illness dogged him—malaria, influenza, heart attacks, severe falls from his horse. He began to realise that a lifetime was too short for his chosen work, and to look for short cuts.

The taste for power, which hardly needs emphasis, was there from the first. No one could have reached Rhodes's eminence without it. Innumerable anecdotes illustrate it. He once chided General Gordon for having refused to accept a present of a roomful of gold when he was in China, arguing that it was impossible to carry out one's ideas without money to back them. "Money is power," he declared, "and what can one accomplish without power?" He saw power in his diamonds too, though for some reason of which he did not give a very clear account, he found it more difficult to assess the power implicit in a gold-mine. He wanted Africa "all red"; he wanted to influence the Parliament at Westminster through contributions of money, first to Parnell's Irish Nationalists (provided that they would accept Home Rule within a federal Empire) and later to the Liberal Party (provided they would not withdraw from any conquered territory); he even wanted to control posterity through his secret society, based first upon his money and later on, no longer a secret, upon his educational trust.

It must be emphasised that when Rhodes spoke of power, he meant power to do good: to promote the good of his fellow-men and his native country. But of course he was himself the judge of what was good for them, and he used a utilitarian rather than a moral criterion. He used it, indeed, quite unscrupulously by moral standards. "Every man has his price", whether or not he used the words himself (which has been denied by his most devoted secretary, Philip Jourdan), is an accurate translation of his belief that money meant power. So did many other things, whether intrinsically admirable or not. Snobbery meant power, for instance: he had a weakness for royalty, duchesses and titled officers; and he argued that the safest way to ensure that one of his out-posts of empire should not be surrendered by a craven government was to name it after a Royal Duke. Religion and education also meant power. He financed both on a generous scale, provided he could be sure that the end-product would be useful. Missionaries could count on liberal funds if they were good pioneers of the British flag; so could schoolmasters, if their main object was to produce useful citizens and not, to quote his Will, "what I call a loafer". Even patriotism must not be a mere sentiment: the British flag earned his praise on one occasion because it was Britain's best commercial asset. "He looks upon men as machines," Reginald Brett once wrote of him, and added: "this is not very penetrating". It was unusually penetrating on the part of Brett.

The imputation of shortsightedness now comes as no surprise. Rhodes has constantly been praised as a man of vision; and so he was, both in his inspired guesses about the future, and in his plans for moulding mankind to meet it. A sufficient example of the first is his saying that tariffs would be the politics of the next hundred years, or that race was beginning to replace religion as the great divider of mankind; of the second, his plan to promote international peace through a scheme of educational interchange. But he also had fatal blind-spots. He entirely failed to foresee how his conception of the world was going to be falsified, both in the short term and the long, by developments which were already implicit in the world around him. The idea of knitting Africa together in a network of British-controlled communications was magnificent; but his telegraph line was to be superseded within a generation by the wireless, and his railway within half a century by the aeroplane. True, no one else foresaw these developments either, although Marconi telegraphed by wireless across the Atlantic in Rhodes's lifetime and the Wright brothers flew within two years of his death. But Rhodes, great visionary though he was and preoccupied with communications, saw no farther than the potentialities of the bicycle and the cablegram.

Even more fatal in the long run was his blindness to the future course of human relations. He staked his political career on the reconciliation of Boer and Briton in South Africa, and then destroyed the possibility of it by the Jameson Raid. Worse still, he never appreciated the damage that he had done. One direct consequence of his folly was, of course, the Boer War; but another was the rise to power of the Afrikaner Nationalists, who finally reversed the verdict of the Boer War by carrying the Union out of the Commonwealth in 1961. Moreover, the rise of the Nationalists meant not only the prolongation of the tension between Boer and Briton, but also the prolongation of the humiliating oppression of the native Africans. Rhodes claimed to be the most enlightened promoter of Bantu progress as well as of Anglo-Boer reconciliation, and so in a sense he was; but he was fatally wrong in thinking that it was possible to be consistently and whole-heartedly both. His attitude in each case cannot be divested of an air of expediency, not to say hypocrisy, which his enemies rightly sensed.

Rhodes would probably have been unmoved by charges of inconsistency in these matters. As men so diverse as Jan Hofmeyr, General Gordon, W. T. Stead and Milner all independently detected, he regarded himself as virtually infallible and able to override the rules binding ordinary men. Napoleon Bonaparte was one of his favourite characters in history, a taste which he shared with Nietzsche's Superman and Dostoevsky's Raskolnikov. Why should he worry about consistency? Like Walt Whitman, he could say:

> Do I contradict myself?
> Very well then I contradict myself.
> (I am large, I contain multitudes).

He lived, in fact, in a dream world in which everything would come right in the end, however improbable it might seem, thanks to his genius. He hated to be brought down to earth by smaller minds. These were the psychological marks of a mentality that was in some respects conspicuously childish.

There were other marks of it as well. One was his curiously undeveloped handwriting, sprawling vast and scarcely legible across the notepaper, sometimes barely a dozen words to the page. The language and thoughts of his letters are often no less childish

and they evoked a corresponding quality in the replies of some
of those to whom he wrote. The same was true of much of his
behaviour among intimate cronies. He enjoyed the simplest of
family games, as well as billiards and bridge; he liked to mix
either with the very young, with whom he could romp and quarrel
as if he were their own age, or with much older people—especially
motherly women like old Mrs. Schreiner or Mrs. Koopmans de
Wet—who made him feel youthful. "I am a boy! Of course I
shall never grow old!" he was heard to exclaim as late as 1900,
when he was in his forty-eighth year and within two years of his
death. Yet in fact he was prematurely aged, with the appearance
of a man of sixty when he was still in his early forties. In the last
years of his life, the harsh reality broke through his boyish optimism, and he passed from youth to age almost overnight.

No doubt the weaknesses of Rhodes's character would have
been less damaging if he had had a good wife. His nature craved
and needed family life; but his restless energy, coupled perhaps
with scruples about his precarious health, denied him the satisfaction of it except for transitory substitutes. Marriage would
have softened the asperity, even brutality, of some of his dealings
with other men. Better care would have been taken of his precarious health. It would also have protected him from the malice
of disappointed admirers, like Olive Schreiner, or scheming
adventuresses, like Princess Radziwill. His relations with women
were peculiar, in no sinister sense of the term. Those who knew
him best strenuously denied allegations of immorality against him,
as they did also, and undoubtedly with equal truth, allegations of
intemperance. They did not trouble to deny, because only a later
and more vindictive generation chose to make the fashionable
calumny of a life-long bachelor, that he was a homosexual. It
might seem hardly worth commenting on an accusation which
was never made in Rhodes's lifetime, nor would it be if some of
those who later wrote about him had not chosen to imply that
there was something abnormal about his emotional friendships
with other men. Certainly there was nothing sinister about them,
nor did any of his contemporaries comment on them in that sense.
If evidence were wanted that such ideas occurred to no one in his
lifetime, it might perhaps be found in the story recorded by a
woman whose services were once offered to him as a secretary.[4]
"I don't want a secretary," he replied. "Can't you find me a nice
English boy?" No reasonable person could imagine those words
being uttered by a man who was a homosexual, unless he was a

flagrant exhibitionist, which no one has ever suggested of Rhodes. He abhorred, too, any kind of indecent talk or joking.

His sentimental relations were governed by the twin facts that he was naturally kind and deeply reserved. He preferred, in his youth, women against whom no protection was necessary: either older women, or unattractive girls as shy as himself, such as those he habitually chose as dancing partners in the early days at Kimberley, saying that in any case he only danced for exercise. There is no reason to doubt his later explanation that he was quite simply too busy to seek a wife in his youth, and that marriage would have distracted him from his ambitions. Those ambitions also provided him with all the emotional outlet that his energy required. He erected a barrier of bachelors round himself as a protection against more normal emotional entanglements, and much resented any defections from their number into matrimony. His feelings towards many of them were undoubtedly emotional, which is not to say that they were perverse.

There are many touching stories of his kindness to young men, ranging from the occasion at Groote Schuur when he hastily changed back from evening dress into his rumpled working clothes in order that a young guest might not be the only one at his table informally dressed, to the tragic and tender climax of his devotion to Neville Pickering on his death-bed. Towards young Pickering it would be hard to say whether his feelings were rather those of David to Jonathan or those of David to Absalom. But the episode is certainly one of the noblest in his life, and it is note-worthy that from that episode also grew the fateful devotion of Rhodes and Jameson. Towards men of his own generation, like Dr. Jameson, Alfred Beit, Sir Charles Metcalfe and Rochfort Maguire, he was the most loyal of friends; but it was the younger generation that engrossed his affections. He treated his young secretaries—all men—with almost exaggerated generosity, until one or two of them abused it and earned no more than an ironic rebuke. He once sent a young sailor, H. Palk, whom he had met on a ship, to W. T. Stead to be trained as a secretary, and the result justified the gamble. On one of his farms he employed a junior manager, referred to as "philosopher Ross", whom nothing would induce him to dismiss, useless though he became ("exertion will kill him," he wrote to J. G. McDonald).[5] Johnny Grimmer, Karri Davis, young Philip Jourdan and others became his inseparable companions. No woman's company could take their place.

Yet he was certainly not in any conventional sense a woman-hater, as he assured Queen Victoria in an unusually courtierly phrase: how could he hate a sex to which Her Majesty belonged? He enjoyed the society of his friends' wives, who could have no designs on him. He treated young girls with an almost fatherly kindness, and he showed once a momentary glimpse of regret at having never married when he wrote, on an unknown topic, to a fellow-member of the Cape Assembly:[6] "I would be guided very much by what my wife desired." The simplest explanation of the facts is the most likely, and that was his own. He simply had other preoccupations which clashed with matrimony. And if it is true that a wife would have saved him from some of his self-inflicted disasters, it is also true that a married Cecil Rhodes might well never have been the subject of a biography at all.

Such a thought would perhaps have set Rhodes's mind to work on the favourite exercise which he called "looking to the comparative". The exercise was simple: when things looked bad, Rhodes would remind himself how much worse they might be in other circumstances, or how tedious life might be without the stimulus of shocks and setbacks. The classic example of "doing the comparative", as he sometimes colloquially called it, occurred at one of the most depressing moments in Rhodes's life, in December 1896. The fiasco of the Jameson Raid was less than a year behind; he had resigned all his public positions; his devoted friend Jameson was a convicted criminal, and his brother Frank had been forced to resign his commission after being sentenced to death and reprieved; the rebellion of the Matabele in Rhodesia was barely quelled, that of the Mashona was still in progress, and the task of reconstruction had still to be broached; and to crown all, his beloved home at the Cape, Groote Schuur, had been razed to the ground by fire. Rhodes chose this time to awaken his friend Albert Grey from his sleep one night in Bulawayo to ask him whether he had ever considered how fortunate he was to be alive and in good health and to have been born an Englishman, when so many millions of other human beings had had no such luck.

The familiar anecdote illustrates many of the qualities in Rhodes's character that have been outlined here: the exuberance, the boyishness that had also an element of childishness in it, the pride in patriotism, the readiness to accept things as they came, the determination never to let his soaring imagination be weighed down by mundane circumstances. Perhaps hours of solitary brooding had preceded the thunderclap of simplicity which he wanted to communicate to his friend before the inspiration faded. This was the kind of contemplative thought that prompted the question Rudyard Kipling records—"What's your dream?"—or the touching and characteristic letter which he wrote to Stead on 14 August 1891. It is a long and important letter, much of which Stead later embodied in *The Last Will and Testament of Cecil J. Rhodes*, but one excerpt will here suffice:[7]

'. . . they are calling the new country Rhodesia that is from the Transvaal to the South end of Tanganyika the other name is Zambesia. I find I am human and should like to be living after my death still perhaps if that name is coupled with the object of England everywhere and united the name may convey the discovery of an idea which ultimately led to the cessation of all wars and one language throughout the world . . ."

"That is my thought," Rhodes might have concluded if he were making a speech. "My thought" was one of his favourite expressions, summing up in the simplest terms the outcome of hours of exalted brooding on the slopes of Table Mountain or the flat expanse of the *veld*, where he could be, as he put it, "alone with the Alone". Though often expressed in mystical terms, his thoughts were generally down to earth and practical. Indeed, the very process of thinking was itself a practical occupation in his eyes, or at any rate he chose to represent it so: thus, to his brother, Frank, who once complained he had been bored, having nothing to do and nothing to read, Rhodes's indignant retort was: "Couldn't you *think*?" The books which he preferred, too, were those that led to "thoughts": Winwood Reade's *The Martyrdom of Man*, for instance, with its popularised version of Darwinism; or F. Marion Crawford's *An American Politician*, which had a strong influence on his political ideas; or Gibbon's *Decline and Fall of the Roman Empire*, which set him thinking, like the monuments of Egypt, about the transitoriness of human power; or Dean Farrar's *Seekers after God*.

Best of all was the *Meditations* of Marcus Aurelius, which was as full of thoughts as *Hamlet* of quotations. Rhodes kept a copy almost always with him, though once or twice he lent it to specially favoured friends, so that they could see from his annotations the passages which most impressed him. His own copy, which was to have passed to his young Australian friend, Karri Davis, could not be found after his death, but two marked duplicates survive, one at Rhodes House and the other in the possession of his niece, Miss Georgia Rhodes. Curiously enough, the marked passages are not identical in the two copies, perhaps because they are based on loans of the original at different dates. But they have one point in common, that the passages marked are generally those which have a practical application to the right conduct of a man's daily life. In neither copy, however, is there any verbal annotation in addition to the side-lines and underlinings. Here too Rhodes's communings with his own soul were inarticulate.

His devotion to the *Meditations* of Marcus Aurelius was genuine, and was not merely a sentimental nostalgia for the classics he studied at Oxford. "Remember always that you are a Roman" was one of his favourite quotations, and Rhodes liked to be reminded of his facial resemblance to busts of certain Roman Emperors. He preferred the Roman virtues to the Greek. No doubt he regarded Marcus Aurelius as an embodiment of the former, perhaps forgetting that he had written his *Meditations* in Greek. (Rhodes pursued his classical studies after taking his degree in translation only, and once spent an enormous sum on having Gibbon's sources translated into English for his benefit, by an arrangement with Hatchard's book-shop.) But although he sedulously marked the more practical moralisings of the Emperor, there were two kinds of passages which specially attracted him: those that were concerned with the brevity and transitoriness of human life, and those that inculcated a habit of retirement into contemplation. He was not in the normal sense a religious man, but meditation was the nearest he came to religion.

"Live as on a mountain" was another of his favourite phrases from Marcus Aurelius. Perhaps when he underlined it he had in mind his own saying that to him a mountain was a church—in particular Table Mountain. The Archbishop of Cape Town at his funeral denied that he should be called an irreligious man merely because he never went to church. President Kruger held the contrary view, that because he never went to church it was impossible to come to any agreement with him. It deserves mention that both Kruger and Rhodes often quoted the Bible; but Kruger's quotations were derived almost exclusively from the Old Testament, which described the sort of world he desired to live in, and Rhodes's mainly from the New. There was generally, too, a strong element of cynicism in Rhodes's Biblical quotations, as when he declared that his favourite story was the parable of the importunate widow, or when he compared a Chancellor of the Exchequer to the wealthy young man who would not follow Christ's advice to sell all his possessions and give the proceeds to the poor. Rhodes's own judgment on himself was that he was an agnostic, though he was prepared to take an even chance on the existence of God. If it be true that he derived the word "agnostic" from "the Latin *agnosco*—I do not know", then, despite his Oxford degree, he could claim to share with Shakespeare the distinction of having small Latin and less Greek.

Once he emerged from his contemplative reveries, his ideas were fixed and unassailable, however obscure the reasoning which lay behind them. Thus, his musings on the possibility of God's existence convinced him that if God did exist, which he was prepared to accept for the sake of argument, it must be His intention that Rhodes should paint the map of Africa red. The invincible tenacity with which Rhodes stuck to such conclusions was recognised by men as stubborn as himself: General Gordon and Barney Barnato, to name but two. There is a terrifying simplicity about these fanatical convictions, which is reminiscent of the relentless faith of Oliver Cromwell; and in this respect, if no other, Rhodes was pitted against a man of the same character in President Kruger. It is perhaps hardly surprising that to Oswald Spengler, Rhodes appeared as the herald of a new age of Caesars and a forerunner of Fascism, though it must be remembered that to Spengler those were not terms of reproach. Spengler's vision of the new age looks a good deal less convincing in the 1960's than it may have done thirty or forty years ago; but one can never tell.

History has a way of presenting a different appearance according to the distance in time from which it is examined. South African history provides particularly striking illustrations. It was possible thirty or forty years ago for historians to record that the British won the second Anglo-Boer War in 1902, and healed the wounds in 1905 by a magnanimous settlement. Neither judgment would stand today. For the Boer War did not end, in the view of the extreme Afrikaner Nationalists, in 1902. It ended rather in 1961, when South Africa withdrew from the Commonwealth, and it ended in the triumph of Krugerism; and in the longer run, perhaps more important than the struggle for power between the two white races is the struggle between the white and black Africans, which was overlooked in the first settlement and still left unresolved in the second. All this has relevance to the life of Rhodes, although it all took place after his death. For even if hostile critics may have exaggerated the blame attributable to him for the Boer War, he cannot be acquitted of having contributed to the triumph of Krugerism sixty years later. In mitigation the best that can be said is that if he had lived another ten years, he might have redeemed his terrible errors by helping to procure a different political settlement: for instance, a federal Union instead of a unitary state, and one in which the fate of the native Africans was not left open, at the mercy of the Afrikaner extremists.

But biography and history are concerned with the facts as they were, and not as they might have been. The facts about Rhodes are complex, and final judgment can still not be made. The mark that he made on African history was indelible, both for good and ill. The mark that he made after his death on the educational links of the Commonwealth and the English-speaking world has done much to redress the balance in his favour, thanks to the wisdom of his Trustees as well as to his own brilliant but erratic vision. He was a man of colossal ability and tragic defects; perhaps a man born out of his time. Such a man would perhaps have been judged to be born out of his time whenever he had lived. But whereas he would himself have claimed to be born before his time, and would have welcomed Spengler's endorsement of that claim, the truth is perhaps rather that he was born too late. On any calculation, the tide of British imperialism turned to ebb within a generation of his death. He failed to foresee it, and not even his superhuman energies could have prevented the turn of the tide.

Olive Schreiner called him, after his death, "a great might-have-been". But that too is a mistake. Rhodes was what he was, with all his faults and his great qualities, his vision and his blindness, his sincerity and his cynicism, his simplicity and complexity, his capacity for inspiring the deepest love and the deepest hate. He achieved what he achieved, including his failures, and he could have done nothing else. There was nothing else he might have been, except Cecil John Rhodes.

Notes

[1] Stead, 51
[2] Currey, 21.
[3] Hobman, *Olive Schreiner*, 48.
[4] R.H.L. MSS. Afr. t. 10, f. 162.

[5] R.H.L. Micr. Afr. 413, f. 14 (Palk); Rhodes Papers, A. 80, 82, 151 (Ross).
[6] Rhodes Papers, B. 209.
[7] R.H.L. Micr. Afr. 413, f. 18. p. 15.

CHAPTER ONE

THE BOY

A VISITOR, calling upon the Vicar of Bishop's Stortford in the middle sixties of the last century, might, as he entered the little semi-detached Vicarage, have noticed the presence or, more probably, the absence of one member of the numerous family of the Vicar, Mr. Francis William Rhodes. Possibly someone would remark that the third son, Cecil, was in the garden, and the visitor, if he had had the curiosity to go out and look for him, might have seen a slender, frail-looking, untidy boy of thirteen or fourteen sitting on a gate and gazing across the sloping meadows to the River Stort, then a navigable stream. Cecil, on the rare occasions in later life when he spoke of his childhood, would tell how, sitting on that gate, with the smell of malt about him from the maltings at the bottom of the garden, he would watch the barges passing up and down the river and was led by the sight of them to wonder what was happening in that greater world outside Bishop's Stortford, what golden hopes and mighty purposes possessed the men in it, and what a boy like Cecil Rhodes ought to be planning to try to do with his life.

If we are to discover the kind of man he became, we may well start with the boy on the garden gate at the Vicarage on the London Road; for there he first dreamed of the world and of the place in it which should one day be his. Sometimes he would run indoors and tell his father of his thoughts.

"My father," he once confided to a friend and companion of his later years, Sir James McDonald,[1] "frequently, and I am now sure wisely, demolished many of my dreams as fantastical, but when I had rebuilt them on more practical lines, he was ready to listen again. He never failed to put his finger on the weak spots, and his criticisms soon taught me to consider a question from every possible point of view."

The dreams and schemes of a boy of thirteen are usually fantasies, but those of Cecil Rhodes would one day come near to the truth. They were the fantasies of a boy whose feet were firmly on the ground even when his head was in the stars.

*　　*　　*

An unpublished record of the family of Rhodes by a Mr. Charles Cowan, preserved in the papers at Rhodes House, traces it from a shadowy origin in the village of Whitmore, between Stafford and Crewe, to the red granite cenotaph in the old churchyard of St. Pancras, where five generations of the family are commemorated. "My ancestors," Rhodes was fond of saying, "were keepers of cows"—an origin through which he would one day claim kinship with the South African farmers he was to know so well. To have roots in the soil, and better still, to belong to the landed gentry, were always important to him.

In 1601 the name first appears in the Parish Registers of Whitmore. There or thereabouts the Rhodes's farmed till, at the beginning of the eighteenth century, one William Rhodes, a prosperous yeoman and grazier, whose connection with them, though probable, is hazy, migrated south, and the genealogical ground becomes firm. William Rhodes, we know, bought about 280 acres of land in the parish of St. Pancras. This was then open country, and on it Thomas followed William and Samuel Thomas. Living simply, and occasionally adding field to field, they won a modest prosperity. Samuel even acquired a brick and tile works at Dalston, on land which later became the property of the Rhodes Trustees. They were yeomen farmers, doing their duty by their family, their land and their Church. William was Overseer of the Poor for the Parish of St. Pancras and a churchwarden, while his son Samuel, also a churchwarden, was Surveyor for the South Division. He was the great-grandfather of Cecil John Rhodes.

Samuel, like his father, prospered in a quiet way, and while retaining the property in St. Pancras, bought the lease of a small country house near Hoxton. He had three sons, the youngest, William, of Leyton Grange in Essex, being Cecil's grandfather. By William's own account he "prospered to an unusual degree", though in his later years he engaged in a long, expensive and unsuccessful lawsuit; so that when he died in 1842, the fortune he was able to leave his son Francis William Rhodes, though substantial, was diminished. This experience may have given that son his life-long horror of lawyers and litigation.[2]

Francis William Rhodes went to Harrow and Trinity, Cambridge, before being ordained a priest of the Church of England. From 1834 to 1849 he was curate of Brentwood, where by his benefactions he became known as "the good Mr. Rhodes". He even built a small church at his own expense. In 1849 he accepted the living of Bishop's Stortford, where he remained until two years before his death in 1878. The little town remembered him as "a tall, loosely made man, with a fine intellectual head"; also for his sermons which, with an economy his congregation doubt-less valued, lasted exactly ten minutes, were packed with sound doctrine and delivered in a melodious voice. He was charitable, a little eccentric, and held strong opinions. His first wife was a Swiss lady, Elizabeth Manet, who died two years after the mar-riage, leaving him with a daughter. His second wife was Louisa Peacock, who came from South Kyme in Lincolnshire, where her family had a small property. The marriage produced nine sons, two of whom died in infancy, and two daughters, neither of whom married.

Of the sons who survived, the eldest was Herbert, a boy of adventurous spirit, who seems to have done much to inspire his younger brother Cecil with ideas about the world and the Empire, and was his constant companion during the early years at Bishop's Stortford. Herbert was sent to Winchester, where his reputation was rather that of a cricketer than of a scholar, his most note-worthy feat being to take six Eton wickets in the annual match between the two schools. The next son, Frank, was a charming character, who was to fall very much under the shadow of his younger brother. After leaving Eton, he received a commission in the 1st Dragoons, subsequently distinguishing himself at the battle of Tel-el-Kebir and serving creditably in Uganda. In Egypt he won the D.S.O., the Egyptian Medal and the Khedive's Star, being commended by Sir Herbert Stewart as "the best staff officer any commander could ever hope to have". This may have been an overstatement.

Cecil himself described his brother as "a very gallant fellow on the battlefield and also in the ladies' boudoir— perhaps too much of a courtier, but he worked hard and often amused one". The day came when the younger brother involved the elder, by then a colonel, in the disaster of the Jameson Raid, which cost Frank his commission for a time. However, he went as special correspond-ent of *The Times* to the Sudan and, recovering his commission, was in the siege of Ladysmith. He inherited Cecil's estate at New-market, but survived him by only three years, dying of black-water fever at Groote Schuur in 1905. Of all the brothers he was, after Herbert's death, most closely in Cecil's life.

Ernest, the fourth son, also went into the army. Having reached the rank of captain, he retired and tried his fortune in

Australia. Later he joined Cecil in Johannesburg, becoming associated for a time with the Consolidated Goldfields of South Africa. After Frank's death he inherited Dalston Hall, but lived only a few months to enjoy it. The estate then went to his eldest son.

Of Cecil's other three brothers there is little to record. Elmhirst went into the army, staying in it till after the South African War. Arthur was a miner and a farmer in Rhodesia and Natal. Bernard was also a soldier for a while. Cecil was very fond of him, though critical of his "useless life". "Bernard is a charming fellow," he said once. "He rides, shoots and fishes. In fact he is a pleasant loafer." "Loafer" was a term of censure often on Cecil's lips.

His two sisters, Edith and Louisa, led uneventful lives in England, though they paid visits to their brother in South Africa. Edith, energetic and unconventional, was said to be more like Cecil than were any of his brothers except perhaps Herbert. They had frequent disagreements, and once Cecil was driven to the statement that Groote Schuur was not large enough for them both; but they remained good friends and she played a heroic part in salvaging the contents of Groote Schuur from the great fire in December 1896. Elizabeth, Cecil's half-sister, married a Rhodes cousin and played no part in Cecil's life.

As children in the Vicarage at Bishop's Stortford they seem to have been a united family who, however much they bickered among themselves, would always show a solid front to the world. Later, Cecil, hotly though he might criticise his brothers and sisters, would never fail to give them any support they needed. The circumstances in which they were brought up were prosperous and free from worldly cares.

Cecil John, the Vicar's third surviving son, was born in the Vicarage of Bishop's Stortford on 5 July 1853. As one of a large family of children, there was little to single him out from his brothers and sisters, or all of them from those other large families so common in Victorian vicarages. The house, though comfortable and well-furnished, was small. Probably, even before the two elder boys went off to their boarding schools, one or more of the children would be away at Sleaford Manor, the home of Mrs. Rhodes's sister, Mrs. Peacock. Certainly Aunt Sophy and the Lincolnshire countryside bulked as big in Cecil's early memories as the household and Vicarage at Bishop's Stortford. At Sleaford he had many friends, among them in particular the son of the local Vicar, and learnt to ride, though not well, for though he loved to be on a horse, he never had a good seat or hands. Possibly, apart from his mother and his brother Herbert, Cecil's happiest recollections of his childhood were of Sleaford and his Aunt Sophy. Although Frank was her favourite nephew, she took a sympathetic interest in Cecil, who confided some of his earliest dreams to her. Sleaford provided a more spacious background than the Vicarage; and from Sleaford Manor he probably got his life-long regard for the old way of life on a country estate.

At home Mr. Rhodes brought up his large family with firmness, affection and on strict religious principles, laying strong emphasis on the observance of the fifth commandment. The sons, as they grew older, were set to teach in Sunday School, receiving pious books from their father as their reward. Mrs. Rhodes was a gentler and possibly a more sympathetic parent, for however busy she might be with the affairs of house and parish, she always had time to listen to the troubles of her children.

"My mother," Rhodes said,[3] in one of his rare moments of retrospect, "got through an amazing amount of work; she must have had the gift of organisation, for she was never flustered and seemed always to have ample time for all our many and, to us, important affairs. I think now we wore her out."

Of those early days, when Rhodes gave few indications of what he was to become, we have not and could hardly expect to have many memories. "A grubby little boy with ruffled hair," is one description of him that survived. A governess was more complimentary, saying that "he was good-looking, with fair hair, and the nice agreeable way of speaking which runs in the family". Rhodes himself used to tell of a visit he paid, when ten or twelve years old, to a retired admiral who lived nearby. The admiral was eighty and, on Cecil's arrival, was busily planting acorns. The boy wondered why an old man should take so much trouble over trees he could not possibly live to see grow to their full stature, and at last, plucking up his courage, asked him his reason. "My boy," replied the admiral, "I have the imagination, and I already see them as trees with people walking under their shade and when mature providing necessary timbers for many ventures. Today and every day they are growing. I have the pleasure of the conception of their shade and their glory." The thought impressed Rhodes deeply at the time and was one he often recalled.

We have few other memories of the boy. Probably through his love of solitary reflection, his family called him "long-headed Cecil", and in one of the little confessional albums popular in those days he gave as his motto "To do or die". He is also said to have announced his determination never to marry, marriage being already in his view a distraction from the serious business of life. Many boys of thirteen may have made this resolution and later abandoned it. Rhodes made and kept it. Many years afterwards he told a young lady who asked him why he had never married: "When I was a young man and ought to have married—when I was in the mood, so to speak, to get married—I was so poor that I could not afford it, and now, since I have been richer—well, upon my honour, I have not had time to think about it."

Possibly because he was delicate, his father did not send him, as he sent his elder brothers, to a public school. In later years Cecil, while admitting that his health might not have stood the rigours, would regret that he had not had the benefit of the independence and corporate life of Eton or Winchester. Instead of going on to a boarding school, he began and ended his education at the little grammar school of Bishop's Stortford. This establishment, intended chiefly for the sons of local professional men, was founded in 1579. When Mr. Rhodes came as Vicar, it had fallen on rather evil days, but he rebuilt it and sent all his sons there in turn. The classes were mostly held in a room adjoining the old parish church and were presided over by Dr. Goodman, the curate. The school no longer exists, the present grammar school having no connection with it. Cecil, though little of a scholar, was a steady and thorough worker, impressing those who taught him by his dogged determination to master any task set him. History and geography were his favourite subjects, though he appears to have "been strongest in religious knowledge, French and the classics". He even won a small classical scholarship and—more surprising—a silver medal for elocution, an art in which he would not in future display much proficiency.

E. A. Maund, who visited Bishop's Stortford soon after Rhodes's death, found an old gentleman, William Smith by name, who remembered the family, though mainly for their prowess at cricket. "Herbert was the best," he said. "He *could* bowl"—as Eton was later to discover. Both Cecil and Frank appear in a photograph of the school Cricket Eleven of 1869, preserved at

Rhodes House. Herbert seems to have been a lively, attractive boy and was described by one of the masters as "a born actor and a daring climber". Though Cecil was fond of games, he loved still more to wander about the countryside, either alone or in company with Herbert. We can well believe that on these rambles the talk ranged far beyond the affairs of the family or the school. Britain was slowly awakening to the sense of an Imperial destiny and every schoolboy of imagination was becoming as familiar with the names of places in India or South Africa as he was with those in a neighbouring county.

Herbert was the leader, the boy who had ideas and made daring plans, but Cecil was already displaying a remarkable persistence in anything he wanted to do. Frank had a rueful memory of his "long-headed" brother: [4]

"One day Cecil came and asked me to let him have one of my shirts, as he wanted to go to an evening party in London. Well, I wanted that shirt myself that evening, and I told him he couldn't have it. He said nothing, but I knew he didn't like losing a chance, so I watched him. I saw him off to the train. He had neither the shirt on him nor had he bag or baggage with him; but I thought that I'd go to the drawer and just make sure of my shirt. It was gone! Cecil came back that night. 'Well, Cecil,' I said, 'you won over that shirt of mine; but just tell me how you did it, for it wasn't on you when you left here, and you had no parcel with you. What did you do with it?' He chuckled a little, and said drily, 'I put it on under the old one'."

The forbearance of the elder brother is as impressive as the persistence of the younger.

Cecil left the grammar school at the end of 1869, when he was sixteen, the plan being that he should continue his education under his father. He had to begin to think seriously about his future. Mr. Rhodes had made up his mind long ago what he wanted his sons to do. They were all to take Orders and become, he said, "the seven angels of the Seven Churches". In fact not one of them followed his father's calling. "My father," Cecil once remarked, "was anxious that they [his brothers] should enter the Church as a preliminary step to becoming angels: they prefer being angels through the army and I don't blame them."

Among the few early letters preserved at Rhodes House is one to Aunt Sophy, dated 17 July 1868 and marked "Private", which shows the direction of Cecil's thoughts at that time:[5]

"You must have thought it very rude on my part not to have returned your little book before, and also for not having thanked you for the other.

"You may be very sure I was not at all displeased at your very kind letter, and I read it through very carefully three or four times, and still keep it.

"I cannot deny, for it would only be hypocrisy to say otherwise, that I still above everything should like to be a barrister; but I agree with you it is a very precarious profession.

"Next to that, I think a clergyman's life is the nicest and therefore I shall try most earnestly to go to college, because I have fully determined to be one of these two, and a college education is necessary for both . . .

"I am afraid you will not like me for saying this, but it is no use for me to pretend to you that I have since your last letter changed in my course of life, or feelings, or inclinations, for it would not be the truth.

"I think that as a barrister a man may be just as good a Christian as in any other profession.

"But I am sure, whichever of these two I shall be, you will agree with me, it is the best plan to thoroughly make up my mind to get to college.

"How proud you must have been of Frankie's success! I can assure you we were in the highest state of excitement all Friday and Saturday. Miss Hope, who is now staying at Twyford, and who was at the match, told us that she had met a gentleman there who had been a great cricketer in his younger days, and he said he preferred Frank's play to any on the field, because it was not the amount of runs he got, but he said he had never seen anything to equal his defence. . . .

"Remember the first part of the letter up to about Frankie is 'Strictly Private'. I would not shew yours to anybody and respected the word 'Private', written outside.

"I am yrs. C. J. Rhodes."

The letter, though not remarkable as the work of a boy of fifteen, shows a modicum of naïve diplomacy—no doubt obvious to Aunt Sophy—much family feeling, and already a firm determination to go to the University. Reading between the lines, we can imagine that Cecil's inclination towards the law would, he knew, find little favour with that hater of litigation, his father. It was characteristic of him throughout his life to sign letters "C. J. Rhodes", even to intimate friends and relatives.

His programme was to go up to the University first, an expense his father could surely have afforded, and then to become either a barrister or a clergyman. But Providence had other plans for him. Soon after leaving the grammar school, Cecil fell ill. As soon as he was well enough to go out, he was sent to be over-hauled by the family doctor, John Edward Morris, who after-wards recalled that the boy was so nervous and anxious when he came into the consulting room, that he had to be sent off to take a walk in the fields to calm himself down. When he returned, Dr. Morris examined him and realised, but did not openly tell him, that his lungs were affected.[6] As there was a tendency to con-sumption in the family, the Vicar, with the doctor's approval, decided that a long sea voyage would be the best cure. The next thought obviously suggested itself. Herbert was already in Natal. Under an emigration scheme he had obtained a grant of 200 acres in the Unkomaas Valley, where he was trying to grow cotton. Cecil would join him; further than that the planning did not go; the future would depend upon the boy's health.

Cecil was delighted: he would be going to a strange land to join his favourite brother. By his own account he was so excited that he could not sleep the night he heard the news, and at twelve went downstairs to find a map of South Africa. This he studied till morning, "by which time," he added, "Africa possessed my bones". There was much to do before he sailed, people like his Aunt Sophy (who lent him £2,000) to see; and on 21 June 1870, he boarded the wooden barque *Eudora*. That aloof Victorian parent, Mr. Rhodes, for some undisclosed reason, omitted to bid farewell to the son he was unlikely to see for years and might never see again.

A story of Cecil's last days in London was recalled long after-wards by an old lady, Mrs. Bennett of Southampton, who had no more than a single chance contact with him. One night in the summer of 1870 she and her husband went to a concert in the Albert Hall. Next to them was sitting a young man. She did not recall, or at least record, what sort of concert was being per-formed, but the music was evidently very moving, as the young man suddenly buried his face in his hands and burst into tears. So loud were his sobs that they were beginning to attract attention, and Mrs. Bennett bent over and tried to calm him. After the concert he apologised for his behaviour, explaining that next day he was sailing for Africa, the doctors having told him that a sea voyage was his only chance of life. His heart was heavy at leaving England and the music had been too much for him. The Bennetts asked him back to their hotel and asked him his name. It was Cecil Rhodes.[7]

The voyage to Africa was calm, uneventful—even monotonous. Cecil's fellow-passengers were mostly Germans, and agreeable enough. "In the evening we used to collect in the deckhouse and sing songs," he told his mother. He had seen whales, porpoises, flying fish, albatrosses, "we danced about like wild Indians". After a voyage of seventy-two days she anchored in the roadstead off Durban on 1 September.[8]

"The land on first sight looks very grand," he wrote, and going ashore in a boat, he found everything "very rum", including, no doubt, the absence of Herbert, who was not there to meet him, having gone up to the new Diamond Fields, "500 miles in the interior". He had asked a neighbour, Mr. Somerville, to go to Durban to look after his brother and show him round, while another neighbour, a Dr. Sutherland, the Surveyor-General, and his wife, had invited Cecil to stay with them in Pietermaritzburg till Herbert returned. Thither, after three days in a Durban hotel, Cecil went in a "bus and four".[9]

He was in a new world, but the old was still near in his thoughts. From a newspaper he learnt that "the Duke" (the family name for Frank) had made 31 in the Eton and Harrow match. Like any other boy Cecil told his mother about everything except about what she must have wanted most to know—if he was all right in health; and like any other mother, Mrs. Rhodes must have concluded that no news was good news.

The Sutherlands were the kindest of hosts, but Cecil was impatient to reach the farm. While he waited in Pietermaritzburg, he read a lot and saw the sights. He said he was still thinking of taking Holy Orders, and Dr. Sutherland prophesied that he would end his days as a village parson in England.

Sources

Central African Archives: *A Bibliography of Cecil John Rhodes*, Part Two

Notes

1 McDonald, 7–8.
2 Cowan Papers (Rhodes House), ch. 12, p. 16.
3 McDonald, 4.
4 Michell, I, 19.

5 R.H.L. MSS. Afr. s. 115, f. 92.
6 R.H.L. MSS. Afr. t. l, f. 10.
7 R.H.L. MSS. Afr. t. 11, f. 47.
8 R.H.L. MSS. Afr. s. 115, f. 3.
9 R.H.L. MSS. Afr. s. 115, ff. 3, 4 and 5.

AFRICA

IN 1870 Natal was a small and struggling colony, hardly as yet out of its pioneering days. Durban was a jumble of mean buildings, mostly of galvanised iron, with a few roads, covered by blown sand. The majority of the colonists lived in a few small towns, or in farming settlements like the Unkomaas Valley, where Herbert was trying to grow cotton. The Kaffir wars were over, but in the north-east the Zulu power was menacing and as yet unbeaten. To settle in Natal was a hazardous adventure before Ulundi had been fought and Cetewayo's impis had been scattered.

But the country, with its high hills, its deep valleys, its semi-tropical vegetation and its great bare spaces, unpromising though it might appear to an experienced farmer with knowledge of Africa, enchanted Rhodes. "Take the downs at Brighton," he wrote to his mother, [1] "and there is Natal, I believe."

He soon discovered that an even greater danger than the Zulu was threatening the young colony.[2] "People out here do nothing but talk of diamonds," Cecil wrote home. "Everyone is diamond mad." All over Natal the young men, attracted by tales of fabulous finds, were abandoning their farms and hurrying to the Fields. There seemed small point in toiling long hours to drag a precarious livelihood from the soil, when at the Fields a day or two and a little luck might bring a man a fortune. Herbert had already fallen to the temptation, but Cecil had come to South Africa to farm and for the moment farming was good enough for him. All through his life, most of which he spent in offices and mining camps, the blood of his forbears, "the keepers of cows", ran strongly in his veins. To mine might be the way to make money, but to farm was the way to live. He decided to wait for Herbert, not to try and join him at the Fields, and for the present to grow cotton, not to look for diamonds.

The attraction must, nevertheless, have been very strong. About three years earlier some children were playing on a farm by the banks of the Orange River, when a grown-up came along and pocketed what they thought was a marble. It turned out to be a superb diamond; and with it the amazing story of Kimberley began. Until 1870 South Africa had been a poor, neglected land, unsettled save in four regions: the Cape Colony, where a few Boers and British eked out a scanty living; Natal, where an even smaller settlement lived even more poorly; and the two Boer Republics of the Transvaal and the Orange Free State, founded by the *Voortrekkers*, who had gone north to escape the uncongenial rule of the British. In 1870 Cape Colony, the least unprosperous of these communities, had one small railway and an annual deficit, while Natal, with its expensive little wars, was a constant embarrassment to Whitehall. The Transvaal was on the verge of bankruptcy, and the Orange Free State was a small pastoral society of little consequence to anybody.

The discovery of diamonds changed the scene dramatically. A year earlier no one had been much interested in South Africa; then in a few months it became the new El Dorado. The discoveries, which began on the banks of the Orange and Vaal Rivers, attracted some 10,000 prospectors, and presently diamonds, found on the open veld and notably on the Dutoitspan Farm, promised an even richer treasure field.

Problems and troubles started at once. First of all, who owned the Fields? In the past no one had bothered overmuch about frontiers, or needed to bother when land was so plentiful and of so little value. Such frontiers as existed were liable to change from year to year, or rather from one Colonial Secretary at the Cape to his successor. The discoveries made were in Griqualand West, a kind of no man's land ruled at the time by Chief Waterboer. Clearly, unless there was to be anarchy in the new Diamond Fields, someone had to take them over and keep the peace. Everyone began to speak at once. President Pretorius of the Transvaal announced that the river diggings belonged to his republic, President Brand of the Orange Free State claimed the dry diggings, and the diggers themselves formed a republic of their own. But Richard Southey (later Sir Richard), an 1820 settler and a man of vigour and imagination, was Colonial Secretary at the Cape. Apart from a natural desire that his Colony should have the benefit of the new discoveries, he was convinced that neither a bankrupt republic nor a pastoral community was capable of ruling the turbulent mining camps which were springing up. He had another reason for his determination that the Cape should have the Fields. With Griqualand West in the hands of the Transvaal and the Free State, the Cape would be virtually cut off from Central Africa, with all its unknown possibilities. Later Cecil Rhodes, with the same thought, spoke of the disputed territory as "the Suez Canal into the interior". Southey, like Rhodes, was resolved to keep the "Canal" open.

Probably in law the Free State had the better claim, since for some years Waterboer's country had been treated as coming under the Orange River sovereignty. President Brand was the first to move. He sent in magistrates and police, but when a commando arrived and tried to stop a new rush at Bultfontein, it failed, because the miners treated the invasion as a joke and the Boers, however surly they might be feeling, could hardly bring themselves to deal harshly with men who persistently asked them to get off their horses and have a drink.

President Pretorius of the Transvaal was not so prompt, but eventually forbade all prospecting in the river diggings except by three persons to whom he had given the concession. Men who had graduated in the rough school of the Australian gold-fields treated these pretensions with ridicule, and any burgher who tried to enforce them was liable to get a ducking in the river. Southey, meanwhile, had won over Waterboer, the chief to whom the whole territory may be said to have belonged, so far as it belonged to anybody. On Southey's advice the chief formally asked for his country to be incorporated in the British dominions. The Colonial Secretary, Lord Kimberley, readily accepted the application and Griqualand West became a Crown Colony, with Southey as Governor, being handed over some years later to the Cape.

When the Transvaal agreed to arbitration, the award went in favour of Waterboer, whose case, with British support, had been far more skilfully presented. President Brand refused a similar arbitration on the claims of the Free State, but realising that Britain was determined to carry the matter through, withdrew his magistrates. The whole affair was important, not only because it brought the Diamond Fields under the British Flag, but because it gave the two republics a grievance which they were never to forget and deprived them of revenues they could ill afford to lose. Although in 1876 the Home Government implicitly admitted itself in the wrong by paying to the Free State £90,000 as compensation for the loss of Griqualand West, the incident went on rankling.

Meanwhile the squabbling in high places had not checked the inrush of prospectors, miners, speculators, hucksters and younger sons, who poured by the thousand into the new township, first known as New Rush and later named Kimberley after the Colonial Secretary. Stories of marvellous finds, losing nothing in the telling, were a magnet to young farmers like the Rhodes brothers.

Still their immediate care (Cecil's at any rate) was cotton. Herbert's first year was disastrous and the second was not much better. "The cotton crops this year were much hurt by the drought," wrote Cecil, "and Herbert planted his too close, and a kind of worm got into it." With the help of his brother and of Aunt Sophy's £2,000, Herbert hoped to do better in future. He had cleared fifty of his hundred acres at a cost of £9 an acre. Cecil expected to get a grant of fifty acres, and when this had been taken up, cleared and planted with the new cotton seed they were getting from America, results should be more satisfactory.[3]

But Herbert was still trying his luck at the Fields, picking up small diamonds, and Cecil was kicking his heels in the Sutherland home. Once Sutherland took him for a trek, which he greatly enjoyed, despite the sourness of the milk the Kaffirs gave him and the fleas in their huts when he slept in one of them. It was another stage in the process of getting to know Africa. When the party returned, Herbert was back at his farm and the real work began.

The life was hard, but, as Cecil described it to his mother, far from unpleasant. The Rhodes's slept in one hut (furnished with two beds and one table), and lived in another, while for company they had two or three other young men working nearby. One evening, conscious of discomfort, the young men held a council and decided that one of them must marry and so acquire a communal cook. Cecil, as the youngest, was the obvious victim, "but I did not seem to see it"; and he never did see it.[4]

The brothers rose early and spent the day in the fields, supervising the Kaffirs. Of these they had about thirty, and from the start Cecil got on to excellent terms with them. Their name for him was U'Tusai (salt) and he treated them with a kindly firmness they understood and appreciated. "Also this month," he wrote, in a letter hinting at financial shortage,[5]

"I have lent a good deal of money to the Kaffirs, as it is the hut-tax time, and they want money, and if you lend it them, they will come and work it out whenever you want them, besides its getting [you] a very good name amongst them, and Kaffirs are really safer than the Bank of England."

The policy paid. Cecil got a "good name" and Kaffirs would come from long distances to work for him. Neither then nor afterwards did he often stumble in his personal treatment of the African.

The co-operation of the Kaffirs was the more necessary because the farm was having its full ration of Africa's mischances. There was the climate of the valley, very hot at one season and very wet at another. Grasshoppers and boll-worm wreaked havoc among the crops; baboons came down and stole the mealies; the roads by which supplies must come were wretched and might easily be cut by heavy rain.

"We sent last Thursday in for meal to Richmond," Cecil wrote to his mother,[6] "and on Friday the cart was back to Conyngham's. Herbert went down to see the meal and cart safe over. They got the meal over in the boat, as the river was rather high, and then started the oxen and empty cart in at the drifts; neither the fourlouper (*voorlooper*) nor the driver could swim, but the oxen knew the drift, and they thought they would go over all right. When they were about three parts over, one of the front oxen turned and began to go straight downsteam; the other oxen of course followed its example, and cart, oxen and everything began to go rapidly down the river. Herbert, who was on one side of the river, rode across, got a knife, stripped, and jumped in, just as the oxen were in a sort of rapids there at the corner of Conyngham's flat, and were all getting entangled one with another. Herbert swum in amongst them and cut seven loose, the oxen all the time kicking and plunging about him, in a place where the river was just like a whirlpool. It really was a most daring feat, and done quite in cold blood, as he had to cross the river and strip, before making up his mind."

The *Natal Witness* got wind of the story and Herbert became a minor local hero, especially when, three days later, the same accident befell the wagon of a neighbour, and he lost it with six oxen.

Occasionally Herbert (and Cecil too) would take a day off and play cricket at Richmond, the nearest little town; and on Sunday, as befitted sons of the Vicarage, they would don their most respectable clothes and go to church. The respectability must have been merely relative, as Cecil was soon telling his mother that his and Herbert's clothes were worn out.[7]

"I know you would be rather—well, what shall we say?— 'disgusted'—if you saw your two dear boys in shirt and trousers, with more holes than patches, all covered with brickdust, driving the cart up from the river."

In 1871 Herbert and Cecil began to build themselves a brick house. It was to measure 60 × 20 and have a verandah all round. But if it was ever finished, it was never inhabited by the Rhodes brothers.

Cecil went on with his serious reading whenever he could find the time. He had not abandoned the idea of taking Orders, or its corollary of going to the University, and among the neighbours he found a congenial companion in young Henry Hawkins, an old public schoolboy and son of the Resident Magistrate of the Upper Unkomaas. The two boys read the classics together, talked of Oxford, which only one of them was to reach, and made plans for saving enough money to take them there without outside help.

Meanwhile Cecil behaved as though his whole life was to be spent in the Unkomaas Valley growing cotton and, as was always his way, threw himself whole-heartedly into the work of the hour. He was always planning to take up more land, to raise a little more money to clear and plant it, to introduce new and better methods of cultivation. Frank *must* come out and join the brothers: he was "doing nothing at home", in fact in grave danger of becoming a loafer. He must sail by the next ship, try his luck first at the Diamond Fields, and incidentally get some wonderful shooting. Cecil even worked out a budget for his brother's trip, which he reckoned would cost £210 10s., and no more.[8]

The chief worries were bollworm and the dropping price of cotton, which had come down from the neighbourhood of 10d. a pound to that of 6d., a figure which would not cover costs, and the drain of money going out with nothing or very little coming in. But he had the resilience of seventeen and for the moment had every intention of staying in Natal and making good. A time would come when he would change his mind.

Herbert, however, had already changed his. As Cecil wrote later, diamonds were an "awful enticement", and in the middle of March Herbert could resist the enticement no longer. If other men could make fortunes in a few days, why could not he? So off he went, with a wagon, oxen and five Kaffirs, to try his luck once more.[9]

Cecil stayed behind to see to the picking of the cotton, with

the idea of subsequently joining Herbert at Kimberley. The crop
was, on the whole, shaping nicely. Cecil sent some of the cotton
to a show in Pietermaritzburg, and though he failed to win a
prize, his exhibit was highly commended. Diamonds were a
"toss-up", he wrote home:[10]

". . . but the cotton, the more you see of it, the more I am sure
it is a reality. Not a fortune, and not attainable by everyone,
but still, to one who has a good bit of land, money to start it
properly, a fair road, and above all, *a good name* amongst the
Kaffirs, a very handsome income."

So he waited, and in July got in a satisfactory crop, for which
he obtained a poor price. Three months later, in October 1871, he
left the Natal farm, never to return to it. While he was there, his
enthusiasm for what he was doing carried him buoyantly over his
troubles. But when he left he took a more sober view of the
fluctuating price, the pests, the climate, the cattle sickness, the
presence of too much water or the absence of any, and the usual
difficulty which besets anyone in any country who tried to farm
with insufficient capital. "It was an ill-fated valley," he wrote,
"with a capacity to absorb any amount of capital." But cotton-
growing had taught him some valuable lessons—how to make
sixpence do the work of sixpence and a little more, how to fend
for himself and live cheaply, and how to manage Africans. He
had recovered his health and had done what he had set out to do.
"Ah," he used to say in later life, when someone told him something was impossible. "They told me I couldn't grow cotton."

Sources

Central African Archives: *A Bibliography of Cecil John Rhodes*, Part Two.

Notes

[1] R.H.L. MSS. Afr. s. 115, f. 5.   [6] R.H.L. MSS. Afr. s. 115, f. 59.
[2] R.H.L. MSS. Afr. s. 115, ff. 6 and 9.   [7] R.H.L. MSS. Afr. s. 115, f. 54.
[3] R.H.L. MSS. Afr. s. 115, f. 7.   [8] R.H.L. MSS. Afr. s. 115, f. 40.
[4] R.H.L. MSS. Afr. s. 115, f. 47.   [9] R.H.L. MSS. Afr. s. 115, f. 85.
[5] R.H.L. MSS. Afr. s. 115, f. 76.   [10] R.H.L. MSS. Afr. s. 115, f. 77.

CHAPTER THREE

KIMBERLEY AND OXFORD

THE distance from the farm to the Fields being about four hundred miles, the journey had long been the subject of painful calculation. Money was very short and Herbert had taken with him eight out of twenty-four head of cattle, many of those left being unsuitable for transport. He also wanted Cecil to bring up some more Kaffirs to dig—an additional expense. At one time Cecil had thought of travelling very light on horseback and doing the journey in ten days, but in the end he decided to wait until the rains had brought out the new grass and to take a cart drawn by a team of oxen, he himself riding on a pony in front. For luggage he had an unlikely miscellany—biscuits, flour, tea, sugar, "that wonderful box of lozenges my father sent me", a spade and bucket, several volumes of the classics, including Plutarch's *Lives*, and a Greek Lexicon.[1]

The journey, at the pace of the oxen, took a month. The road from Pietermaritzburg crossed the Tugela, climbed up to Van Reenen's Pass over the Drakensberg, and so reached the high *veld*, a vast plain, its expanse broken by the occasional kopje and the rare farm, its solitude by herds of wandering buck. It was a very different South Africa from that left behind in Natal, with a charm which can hardly be realised by the untravelled. As Basil Williams wrote, "the whole country is bathed in a glory of light", and after the steamy heat of the Unkomaas Valley the air was exhilarating. To many boys the loneliness of the long trek would have been its worst trial, but not to Cecil, with his fondness for solitary thought; and we may guess that as he rode, with the country unfolding, map-like, before his eyes, ideas for the future of the land began to form in his mind. He had, however, to keep a sharp lookout. The journey was not without misadventure. One day his pony died, and thereafter he had to tavel on foot. He could not leave the cart for long unwatched because, empty as the country was, bad characters frequented the road to the Fields, looking for what they could pick up from unwary travellers. With all his vigilance, Cecil lost some of his luggage, including, to his especial sorrow, his copy of Plutarch.

At last he reached his destination, Colesberg Kopje. Hardly

had he arrived than Herbert—restless Herbert—handed over his
claims and went back to Natal to have a look at his cotton.
Cecil described the Fields in a long letter home.[2]

"Fancy an immense plain," he wrote, "with right in its
centre a mass of white tents and iron stores, and on one side
of it, all mixed up with the camp, mounds of lime like ant-
hills; the country round is all flat with just thorn trees here
and there."

Near by was Colesberg Kopje or New Rush, soon to be Kimberley, where Herbert had his claims. It was

". . . the richest diamond mine the world ever produced. . . .
Imagine," Cecil went on, "a small, round hill at its very highest part only 30 feet above the level of the surrounding
country, about 180 yards broad and 220 feet long; all round it
a mass of white tents . . . I should like you to have a peep at
the *kopje* from my tent door at the present moment. It is
like an immense number of antheaps covered with black ants,
as thick as can be, the latter represented by human beings."

There were some 600 claims on the *kopje* and about 10,000 people
working on it.

"Take your garden, for instance," he told his mother, with
a memory of the patch of lawn behind the Vicarage, "and peg
the whole off into squares or claims 31 feet by 31 feet, and
then the question is how to take all the earth out and sort
and sieve it. All through the *kopje* roads have been left to
carry the stuff off in carts." Between the claims a strip seven
and a half feet wide was left for a road. ("The carting on the
kopje is done chiefly by mules, as they are so very handy and
have so few diseases. There are constantly mules, carts and
all going head over heels into the mines below.")

Cecil explained for the benefit of the family circle how the
mines were worked.

"To begin with the ground is first picked, then the lumps
mashed up and you put the stuff through a coarse wire
sieving, this lets the fine stuff pass through and keeps all the
stones, which are thrown on one side; it is then hoisted out
of the claim, and either carried or carted to the sorting table,
where it is first put through fine wire sieving, which sieves all

the lime dust away; what remains is put on the sorting table, and then one sorts away with a small scrapper, spreading the stuff out on the table with one scoop and then off with the next. The diamonds are found in all ways; the big ones generally in the hole by the caffre, or else in the sieving; and the small ones on the table. . . . They are only found on these kopjes, and along the river, where they very likely have been carried by water. There are reefs all round these diamond mines, inside which the diamonds are found. The reef is the usual soil of the country round, red sand just at the top and then a black and white stony shale below. Inside the reef is the diamondiferous soil. It works just like Stilton cheese, and is as like the composition of Stilton cheese as anything I can compare it to. . . . They have been able to find no bottom yet, and keep on finding steadily at 70 ft. You will understand how enormously rich it is, when I say that a good claim would certainly average a diamond to every load of stuff that was sorted—a load being about fifty buckets . . ."

"Some day," he remarked with prescience, "I expect to see the kopje one big basin where once there was a large hill."

The letter, written so soon after Cecil's arrival, shows that whatever may be the faults in grammar and construction, he had been using his eyes and sizing up the situation with a shrewdness unusual for one of his years. Three months before his letters home had been full of cotton and its problems. Now he wrote of nothing but diamonds. As always in his life, he was determined to master the work on which he was engaged. He dug, sieved, sorted, and finally sold. The prospects were staggering. "On this *kopje* I should think that nearly every day they find a diamond over 50 carats"; and even if it was slightly tinged with yellow, it would fetch a price. "I found a 17⅝ carat on Saturday, it was slightly off, and I hope to get £100 for it: does it not seem an absurd price?" "I find on an average 30 carats a week." If the price of diamonds kept up, Herbert, who at the moment owned three whole claims, would make a fortune.

After his brother's departure Cecil was by himself. He was only eighteen and he had to hold his own with a crowd of men from every corner of the earth, not to mention "a few thousand natives who have come to work for wages, to steal diamonds, and to lay their earnings out in rifles and powder". It was a rough finishing school and when, a few months later, Herbert returned, bringing with him Frank, who was putting in time before he got his commission in the army, everyone thought Cecil was the older brother; as he was, in everything but years. Frank wrote home:[3]

"We found Cecil in the claim, measuring his ground with his lawyer and in a tremendous rage with another man in the next claim to him, who has encroached on his ground . . . I know the father will be horrified at the idea of Cecil going to law."

Sir Lewis Michell was given a description of him by a young digger, afterwards "a well-known artist" (possibly Seppings Wright).[4] In the little cluster of tents round a gnarled old mimosa tree he saw a Zulu chopping wood and an Indian cook carrying a pile of plates; and then his eye was caught by

". . . a tall fair boy, blue-eyed, and with somewhat aquiline features, wearing flannels of the school playing field, somewhat shrunken with strenuous rather than effectual washings . . . This was my first impression of Cecil John Rhodes."

Another companion of those days, Norman Garstin, also an artist,[5] spoke of

". . . a fair young man frequently sunk in deep thoughts, his hands buried in his trouser pockets, his legs crossed and twisted together, quite oblivious of the talk around him; then without a word he would get up and go out with some set purpose in his mind, which he was at no pains to communicate. He was a compound of moody silence and impulsive action. He was hot and even violent at times, but in working towards his ends he laid his plans with care and circumspection. He was fond of putting the case against himself, and this habit of seeing the other side probably helped him much in his career."

In the raffish company he kept he must have stood out as an unusual character, at one moment a schoolboy and at the next a mature and reflective man. Seated in his shabby flannels on an upturned bucket, he might be sorting diamonds or reading or just thinking, or doing all three by turns. Later, when he was famous, men conjectured that already his thoughts were of empire, or the unknown north, or grand political designs. Those thoughts would come, and remembered conversations with men like J. X. Merriman, his future colleague and later antagonist, suggest that already they were there in embryo; but such was his concentration on the work of today and tomorrow that his mind was more probably full of the problems of diamonds and the course a young man should pursue who was determined, somehow or other, to reach Oxford and had not altogether abandoned the idea of being a parson.

The brothers lived in what was known as the "West End", a mess in which the ruling spirit was a Major Drury, once of the Cape Mounted Rifles and later to be an Indian cavalryman. "After dinner," wrote W. S. Scully, also a member of the mess, of Cecil, "it was his wont to lean forward with both elbows on the table and his mouth slightly open." He had a habit when thinking of rubbing his chin gently with his forefinger. "Very often he would sit in the attitude described for a long time, his thoughts apparently far away, until some interjection showed that he had been closely attending to what was said." His companions would sometimes chaff him on his preoccupation, their banter being always taken in good part. From this period, when he was so much older than his years, doubtless dated the peculiarly formal way of addressing or referring to him as "Mr. Rhodes". To his family, and to no one outside it, he was Cecil: to others, with a few rare exceptions, he was and remained "Mr. Rhodes".

Life was not all work. He acquired a "rusty black pony called Bandersnatch" and a tailless dog which looked like an "exaggerated guinea pig". Aloof, abstracted and sometimes moody though he was, he was making friends, some of whom would be with him all his life. Young Hawkins, with whom Cecil had read the classics at Unkomaas, had preceded him to the Fields. A companion of more note was John Xavier Merriman, son of the fiery Bishop of Grahamstown, a young man of culture, who could talk politics, classical literature and history out of a well-stored mind. Merriman, already member for Aliwal North in the Cape Parliament, recalled that, riding together, he and Rhodes made a compact, which both men kept, to take part in public affairs.

Another young man was to become Rhodes's first partner and share his later enterprises. This was Charles Rudd, scion of an old Northamptonshire family and lately of Harrow and Trinity College, Cambridge, where he had become known as a fine athlete. In 1865, without waiting to take a degree, he left Cambridge on medical advice and, like Cecil, went to South Africa. Despite ill health, for five years he led a roving, adventurous life, before trying his luck at the Diamond Fields. He was a business-like, reliable young man, whose chief drawback as a partner was his inability, owing to the state of his health, to do his share of the drinking which was an unavoidable part of every transaction. This labour, therefore, fell exclusively to Cecil. Rudd told McDonald how for days on end he and Cecil "carried the pay dirt" in bags, boxes or buckets to the sorting tables, and how while so engaged "Rhodes one day broke the little finger of his right hand which, not having been set properly, he was never afterwards able to bend; the result being that it became impossible for him to give a grip in hand-shaking." Another friend recalled how in their financial straits Rhodes and Rudd were once reduced to making and selling ice to the diggers.

Most of the men with whom Rhodes consorted were older than he was, but a close friend of about his own age was Christian Maasdorp. With him Cecil argued hotly, occasionally emerging from the debate with the marks of battle on his face. Warm-hearted and friendly though he was, he had a quick temper. McDonald tells how, rather later, returning to England by sea, he was sitting on deck reading when a slightly older youth, who was a bit of a bully, kicked the book out of his hands. Rhodes flew at him and a battle ensued before an interested crowd of passengers. While the issue was still undecided, the Captain sent two quartermasters to separate the combatants. Rhodes was furious. "Why should you come interfering in my diversions?" he called out. "I protest most strongly. It is a most unwarrant-able interference on your part. I won't have it." The incident exemplified the contrast between the Rhodes who at one moment could brawl like a schoolboy and the other Rhodes who a mo-ment later could protest in terms befitting an elderly gentleman writing to *The Times*. This duality would continue, more decorously but markedly, through Rhodes's life.

In women he took little interest, then as always preferring the company of his own sex. It was noticed that on the few occasions when he was persuaded to attend a local dance, he would always pick out as his partners the plainest girls in the room. In this characteristic conduct he showed both the shyness and kind-heartedness which later, in combination, affected so decisively—and in one instance disastrously—his relations with women.

All the time he was working strenuously and by no means in-effectively, digging Herbert's claims, presently speculating in other claims, always short of money, but although he found no large stones, on the whole prospering. "I average about £100 a week," he told his mother. "Mr. Merriman praises Cecil up to the skies," wrote Frank:

"He says Cecil is such an excellent man of business; that he has managed all the business in Herbert's absence wonderfully well, and that they are all so very fond of him. . . . He says most young fellows when they get up there and do well get so very bumptious, but that Cecil was just the contrary."

Cecil was also making a name for himself as a successful speculator, and "Rhodes's luck" began to be a byword among the diggers. As he had foreseen, the *kopje* became a huge crater, the roadways between the claims being a never-ending source of contention. The "*kopje* walloper", who was a dealer going from sorting table to sorting table and buying what he could, had arrived; and so had those less lawful operators, the diamond thief and the man who dealt in Illicit Diamond Buying (I.D.B.). Cecil had to have all his wits about him to uphold his rights.

In 1872, soon after Herbert returned from England with Frank, Cecil fell ill. He had a slight heart attack, a warning of more of the kind to follow. As the illness seemed to be the result of overwork, Herbert, leaving Frank and Rudd in charge of the claims, borrowed a wagon and a span of oxen and took his brother for a *trek* to the north. While Herbert hoped the journey would bring Cecil back to health, he had another purpose. In the north, far beyond Pretoria, gold had been found in two districts; and that unquiet spirit, whose most constant quality was his affection for his brother, had dreams of discovering a second Kimberley, of gold this time instead of diamonds. His first purpose succeeded; his second failed.

Cecil recovered his health. The northern journey was another turning-point in his life. The brothers trekked slowly along the Missionaries' Road into Bechuanaland as far as Mafeking, where they turned eastward and northward to Marabastad and the Murchison Range, where the finds of gold had been reported. During that long, leisurely *trek* Cecil deepened his knowledge of South Africa, its land, its people and its animals. In the evening the brothers would stop at a small farm and sit on the *stoep* drinking coffee with some old man who, perhaps, as a boy had come north with the *Voortrekkers* many years before; and although a Boer at this time described Cecil as "damnably like an Englishman", his friendliness and unfeigned interest in the people, the life they were leading and the problems they were facing, quickly conquered any prejudice. If the Boers liked him, he in return liked and respected them, as farmers and colonists. The legend that he was "against" the Boers was utterly untrue. He was against Krugerism, but when the day came that he wanted colonists for a new land in the north, he was as ready to take Dutch as British.

So, as he wound his way across South Africa, South Africa wound its way into his heart. He never lost that love for her, for the vast spaces and little farms, the slow, wise old men puffing away at their pipes on the *stoeps*, with the old ladies making coffee in the background; and for the herds of game ranging over a land then largely unoccupied. He even bought a farm of 3,000 acres up in the Transvaal, but he had neither time nor opportunity to look after it. Like the farm at Unkomaas, it was "only sunk money".

During the *trek* ideas which had been revolving vaguely in his head began to take shape. He must make money and make it quickly, to help him to a career; and after that to enable him to transform some of his thoughts into facts. Yet he was still unsure what the career would be. In October 1873 he wrote to his old friend in Natal, Dr. Sutherland: "Whether I become the village parson, which you sometimes imagined me as, remains to be proved." If he did not find the answer at Kimberley, he would surely find it at Oxford. Meanwhile, though he might not be aware of or acknowledge the fact, he had moved away from that country vicarage Dr. Sutherland had once forecast for him.

Certainly, his attachment to Christian doctrine, never very strong, had become even slighter at Kimberley. "One's belief in anything to come," he wrote to Frank, "gets very weak out here when you know nearly every mortal is an atheist, or next door to it." Afterwards he was wont to say that he had decided the odds were fifty-fifty on the existence of God, and that he was prepared to accept it on this basis. But when he had rejected atheism, and on the whole regarded the idea of a world undirected by a Divine Intelligence as unlikely, such other beliefs as he held were extremely vague. If he had become a parson, he would have subscribed without enthusiasm or any attempt at exact definition to the Thirty-Nine Articles, regarding them as the price he would have to pay in order to lead the life of service to his fellow-men for which he had begun to believe he was intended.

Apart from the recovery of Cecil's health, the visit to the gold-

fields of the Northern Transvaal was disappointing, the prospectors finding more quarrels than gold. The brothers returned
to Kimberley. The wagon, which they had bought from Scully,
was a wreck. Although it had cost Scully only thirteen pounds, he
asked thirty for it. Cecil offered him twenty-five, and when he
refused the figure, they agreed to play euchre for the disputed
five pounds. They sat on the ground on either side of a bag of
meal. Cecil won the first and nearly won the second game; then
his luck deserted him, and after two hard games Scully got the
rubber and the five pounds.[6]

Very soon afterwards the little community at Kimberley began
to dissolve. Herbert, that "tall, lean, hatchet-faced man", as
Scully describes him, was on the move again. Perhaps he was
fascinated by travellers' tales of gold in Mashonaland, which
people were beginning to identify with the Biblical land of
Ophir. Or perhaps he was temperamentally incapable of staying
for long in one place. At any rate he handed over his claims and
went off, passing out of his brother's life. During his wanderings
he was arrested by the Portuguese for trying to trade an obsolete
gun for diamonds with Chief Sekukuni and was put in prison.
Later he drifted up to Lake Nyasa, where he met a terrible death.
He was opening a keg of rum in his hut, when the keg burst and
at once he was wrapped in flames. These were put out, but not
before he had been badly burnt. The nearest doctor was at
Blantyre, forty miles away, and hardly had he arrived than
Herbert died. We are not told how Cecil received the news, but
we know that throughout his life his thoughts often went back to
the brother who had always been closest to him and had been his
constant companion at the Vicarage, on the cotton farm and at
Kimberley.

Cecil's heart was still set on Oxford. He had made enough
money to pay his dues and, when at last he could see his way clear,
he went home, leaving his partner Rudd in charge of the claims.
So unequipped was he for a return to civilised life that during the
voyage his only pair of trousers began to disintegrate and had to
be patched with canvas by the ship's sailmaker. He wanted to go
to University College, but its Master, on hearing that he did not
intend to read for an honours degree, refused to accept him.
However, the Master gave him an introduction to the Provost of
Oriel, Dr. Hawkins, a relative of Cecil's young friend at Kimberley, and Oriel was more accommodating. Cecil, by hard
work in unpropitious circumstances, had acquired a sufficient

knowledge of the classics to pass Smalls. He matriculated on 13 October 1873 and kept his first term.

So began a curious double life. Rhodes went into residence when he could, but he had to earn his living. After that first term he did not keep another till 1876, nor his last till 1881, by which time he was a member of the Cape Parliament. Broken though his career at Oxford was, he was ever mindful of his debt to the University.

"Have you ever thought," he said to Bishop Alexander,[7] "how it is that Oxford men figure so largely in all departments of public life? The Oxford system in its most finished form *looks* very unpractical, yet, wherever you turn your eye—except in science—an Oxford man is at the top of the tree."

In the last year of Rhodes's life a visitor quoted the first lines of Matthew Arnold's tribute—"Beautiful city, so venerable, so lovely . . ." "Go on," said Rhodes, "quote the whole passage," and sick and in pain though he was, he listened with absorbed attention.

Oxford was perfectly to his taste, in the opportunities it offered him of serious reading and of sharpening his wits in long disputations, the means by which he cleared his mind on any subject that might be interesting to him. The freedom of life and the discipline of scholarship appealed to him; and he found a society and a way of thought he had never encountered at Bishop's Stortford or at Kimberley.

One of those who influenced him most was John Ruskin, whose lectures were thronged by undergraduates listening to the new gospel of beauty and public service. Ruskin was not content with mere lecturing. He led out a small army of young men equipped with picks and shovels and set them to making a road across the swampy ground near Hinksey. The road was crooked and was never finished. After two months Ruskin abandoned the enterprise, but not before he had vindicated by his example the dignity of manual labour.

" There is a destiny now possible to us," said the prophet, "the highest ever set before a nation to be accepted or refused. We are still undegenerate in race; a race mingled of the best northern blood. We are not yet dissolute in temper, but still have the firmness to govern and the grace to obey. . . .

Will you youths of England make your country again a royal throne of kings, a sceptred isle, for all the world a source of light, a centre of peace; mistress of learning and of the Arts, faithful guardian of time-tried principles, under temptation from fond experiments and licentious desires; and amid the cruel and clamorous jealousies of the nations, worshipped in her strange valour, of goodwill towards men? . . . This is what England must either do or perish: she must found colonies as fast and as far as she is able, formed of her most energetic and worthiest men; seizing every piece of fruitful waste ground she can set her foot on, and there teaching these her colonists that their chief virtue is to be fidelity to their country, and their first aim is to be to advance the power of England by land and sea: and that, though they live on a distant plot of land, they are no more to consider themselves therefore disfranchised from their native land than the sailors of her fleets do, because they float on distant seas. If we can get men, for little pay, to cast themselves against cannon-mouths for love of England, we may find men also who will plough and sow for her, who will behave kindly and righteously for her, and who will bring up their children to love her. . . . You think that an impossible ideal. Be it so; refuse to accept it, if you will: but see that you form your own in its stead. All that I ask of you is to have a fixed purpose of some kind for your country and for yourselves, no matter how restricted, so that it be fixed and unselfish."

The Inaugural Lecture was veritably another turning-point in Rhodes's life. Here, eloquently put, was so much that he had been thinking, a challenge to which the best in him would respond all the days of his life. A rough note, found in his papers, paraphrases Ruskin's thought:[8]

"You have many instincts. Religion, love, money-making, ambition, art and creation, which I think from a human point of view the best, but if you differ from me, think it over and work with all your soul for that instinct you deem the best. C. J. Rhodes."

Outside Oxford the tide was running strongly. Disraeli's administration was in its heyday and a new Imperial creed, at least so far as India was concerned, had begun to touch the imagination of the people. India was all-important and it served to determine policy in Africa as well. The Queen was Empress of India, the shares in the Suez Canal had been bought, the Nile Valley must be guarded. In India, and consequently also in Africa, a strong policy had superseded the vacillations of the past. Whatever Mr. Gladstone might say—and he said a great deal—Rhodes, following events with a keen and critical eye, approved whole-heartedly each forward movement and as whole-heartedly condemned each hesitation.

He was of course older than his Oxford contemporaries and had not, like most of them, been to a public school. His habit of starting a debate on some thought he had picked up may have bored them sometimes, but he was so different, so unusual, and so unconventional that they soon accepted him as a "character", as they accepted the way in which, when he was excited, his voice broke into falsetto. They were doubtless amused by his habit of casually producing a handful of diamonds from his pocket, when he wanted to convince an audience of the shining prospects of South Africa.

He read voraciously, among his favourites being the works of Aristotle, the *Meditations* of Marcus Aurelius, and Gibbon's *Decline and Fall*, some of which he had already studied and learned to value on the cotton farm and at Kimberley. To them he would remain faithful till his death. He was less fond of attending lectures—occasions when he could not choose the subject or argue—and when the Dean of Oriel expostulated with him, he replied, "Now, Mr. Butler, you let me alone and I shall pull through somehow."[9]

Rather incongruously, he joined Vincent's and the Bullingdon, the latter being a sodality of cheerful young gentlemen who were wont to wear grey bowlers and on festive evenings to parade the High with horse-whips and hunting cries. He became a Freemason and got into hot water almost at once because, at the dinner following his initiation, he insisted on revealing to the company the cherished secrets of the craft. During the winter of 1876 he was master of the Drag; he played polo; and once, when the schoolboy momentarily eclipsed the student, he narrowly escaped serious trouble with the authorities. "I was nearly caught going to Epsom," he wrote to Rudd, "but still do not think I shall be sent down." He made many friends, some of whom were later to make their mark. Robert Yerburgh was for many years a Member of Parliament. Dunbar Barton became an Irish judge. Rochfort Maguire was to be a Fellow of All Souls

C. J. R. as a child on a pony (with his sister and a groom)

(a)

(b)

(a) C. J. R. as a boy aged about eight

(b) C. J. R. as a schoolboy aged about sixteen

and a Director of the Chartered Company. Sir Charles Metcalfe was to be Rhodes's companion on many journeys, and to stand by his deathbed.

So interrupted was Rhodes's academic career, that he could hardly have been given rooms in College. Anyhow, he is said to have disliked the food provided by Oriel and to have preferred "digs". Another reason for his preference may have been his health, which continued to trouble him. In his second term he caught a chill rowing and fell seriously ill; in fact, the doctor gave him only six months to live. But he returned at once to Kimberley, where the clear, invigorating air soon put him right.

Even when he was in residence, he never forgot his career and his plans, writing frequent letters of instruction to his partner Rudd, visiting diamond merchants in Hatton Garden, speculating not unsuccessfully in real estate at Hampstead; and in case diamonds failed him and he had to fall back on a profession, he ate dinners at the Inner Temple. The receipt survives at Rhodes House[3] for his payment of the admission fees, £35 6s. 5d. on 16 May 1876.

Hardly was he back from South Africa than the household at Bishop's Stortford began to break up. In November 1873 Mrs. Rhodes had died, to the deep sorrow of her husband and children. Thereafter Rhodes's letters became more scarce, for to her, as to no one else, he had regularly unburdened himself. The Vicar still hoped that his third son, though contaminated by his money-making companions in Kimberley, might end by taking Orders, but Cecil, so far from being moved by Oxford towards a career in the Church, seems gradually to have given up all idea of it. Perhaps it was Kimberley, not Oxford, that turned him from it. "Life on the Diamond Fields," he had written to Dr. Sutherland, "has not strengthened my religious principles." Or it may be that his "religious principles" were shaken not so much by "life on the Diamond Fields" as by Winwood Reade's unsettling book *The Martyrdom of Man*. This was a popular version of Darwinism, reinforced by a rather superficial comparative analysis of Oriental religions, presented with considerable literary skill. "You may imagine the impression it produced on me," Rhodes later commented. At any rate the poor Vicar was not to be the parent of a single angel. Frank had got his commission in a cavalry regiment, and another brother was in the Royal Engineers, "so that we are fast becoming a military family," wrote Cecil. During 1874 and 1875 affairs at Kimberley, which had taken a critical turn, kept

c

him from Oxford, but from 1876 to 1878 he was in residence fairly regularly, returning to South Africa during the Long Vacations. He took his final examinations and got his pass degree in 1881.

In 1878, two years after leaving Bishop's Stortford, his father died. If Cecil's mother's death had been a mournful landmark in his life, that of his father was a minor bereavement. Respect, rather than affection, had marked their relationship; and no letters between father and son have survived, the probability being that they seldom corresponded. The first place in his affections was now shared between a few intimate friends in South Africa and his University.

For him Oxford was not merely a matter of the terms he kept or the friends he made or the books he there found time to read. In Oxford fantasy and fact met, a conjunction which seldom happens in the life of any man. He had dreamed of a city hardly of this world and found it much what he had imagined. He could never understand how Gibbon, one of the authors he most revered, could say that Oxford would as cheerfully renounce him as her son as he would disclaim her for a mother. Gibbon was mistaken, he once told Lady Grey. "No thinker such as he could escape her [Oxford's] compelling influences, her wonderful charm." He certainly had fallen under a spell which bound him more strongly as the years passed, so that, even as he lay dying, his thoughts went back to that city "so venerable, so lovely . . . whispering from her towers the last enchantments of the Middle Age".

Sources

Chilvers, Hedley A: *The Story of De Beers*
Cohen, Louis: *Reminiscences of Kimberley*
Emden, Paul H.: *Randlords*
Phillips, Lionel: *Some Reminiscences*
Rudd, M. A. : *Records of the Rudd Family*
Scully, W. S.: *Reminiscences of a South African Pioneer*

Notes

1 R.H.L. MSS. Afr. s. 115, f. 89.
2 Williams, 26–9.
3 Williams, 30–1.
4 Michell, I, 41–2.
5 McDonald, 21–2.

6 R.H.L. MSS. Afr. s. 115, f. 95.
7 Williams, 42.
8 Williams, 41.
9 R.H.L. MSS. Afr. t. 5, f. 34.
10 Rhodes Papers, C. 26, 19.

CHAPTER FOUR

AFRICA AGAIN

THOSE years at Oxford and Kimberley were among the most formative in Rhodes's life. His decision not to take Orders cannot be pinned to any particular date and was probably the result of long and concentrated thought. While in the rough company at Kimberley, where few men had any religion at all, he had lost the orthodox beliefs of the Vicarage; but he was essentially a religious man, bound to a Power beyond himself and to purposes transcending mere money-making. Since he was convinced that without a philosophy of some kind no man could rightly determine his way of life, a philosophy he must have; and the fundamental point which he had to settle at once was whether or not he could accept the existence of God. While in conversation he might reduce the problem almost to one of the race-course, it is a fair supposition that he could not have reached any other assumption than that there was a God. His mind would have instinctively rejected the idea of a world without a law or a law without a creative and controlling Intelligence. By a paradox, in arriving at this conclusion the men whose works he studied most closely were a pre-Christian philosopher (Aristotle), a pagan Emperor (Marcus Aurelius), an agnostic (Gibbon), and an atheist (Winwood Reade). Such were the unlikely godparents of his philosophy. His basic assumption that there was a God led him on to further reflections. Winwood Reade had been much influenced by Darwin. But evolution, which to Reade was the working of blind forces in a Godless world, was to Rhodes the expression of the Divine purpose. He believed that evolution, besides explaining history, gave the answer to his personal questions. God, he argued, wished to produce the highest type of man, the type, that is, most likely to carry out the Divine Will for the world, to teach all men to live honourably and justly under One Whose service was "perfect freedom". Since Rhodes believed that that type was to be found pre-eminently in the Anglo-Saxon race, God's Will must clearly be that the Anglo-Saxon stock should occupy as much as possible of the earth and that Anglo-Saxon ideas should everywhere prevail in the minds of men.

"It often strikes a man," he said at twenty-four,[1] "to enquire what is the chief good in life. To one the thought comes that it is a happy marriage, to another great wealth, to a third travel, and so on; and as each seizes the idea, he more or less works for its attainment for the rest of his existence. To myself, thinking over the same question, the wish came to render myself useful to my country."

The wish was not ignoble. He went on:

"I contend that we are the first race in the world, and that the more of the world we inhabit, the better it is for the human race. I contend that every acre added to our territory provides for the birth of more of the English race, who otherwise would not be brought into existence. Added to which the absorption of the greater portion of the world under our rule simply means the end of all wars."

A friend of those days, Joseph Orpen, told Ian Colvin that[2]

"About this time [1877] young Rhodes asked him and some other friends to dinner, and at dessert in a curiously shy and solemn manner made a little speech. He thought it right, he said, for every man, at the beginning of his life, to put an aim before him, and for his part he meant to work for the British Empire.'

Although the audience might have felt slightly embarrassed by this confession, Ruskin and, a little later, Kipling, would have seen nothing strange in such a purpose.

What Rhodes's contemporaries must sometimes have found strange and even irksome was his persistence. Not only must he himself hold those ideas: he must also convert to them the company in which he found himself. So he would hammer away at his friends, repeating the same thought and the same phrase again and again, with an insistence which was accentuated rather than modified by that old habit, when he was excited, of breaking into falsetto, or by his incongruous mixture of the language of the lecture room with that of the mining camp. That he managed to persuade at all can only be explained by the personal magnetism which, even in those early days, he seems to have exercised. If the heads of his friends remained unturned by his arguments, their emotions were carried away captive by the sheer force of the strongest personality they had ever encountered.

Philosophers may deride Rhodes's creed as naïve and clumsy, and in the middle of the twentieth century a claim that the British were a divinely appointed people, with a duty rather than a right to override the "lesser breeds", may sound as arrogant as Hitler's doctrine of Aryanism. The point is that Rhodes, having convinced himself of God's purpose for the world, believed that he had also discovered God's purpose for himself. The purpose discovered, Rhodes must carry it out. Education, without action, was sterile; and money, without ideas, was a waste of power. Oxford would equip him intellectually for the work he had set himself to do; Kimberley, and later the Rand, would provide the money.

The idea that a man should use his fortune for some great purpose had long been in Rhodes's mind; and in 1872, when he was trekking north with his brother Herbert, he made his first Will, bequeathing all of which he might die possessed to the Secretary of State for the Colonies, in trust and to be used for the extension of the British Empire. This testament, written on a crumpled piece of paper, was to be replaced five years later by a more formal and circumstantial document.

In September 1877, when he was twenty-four and his fortune was still unrealised, "Cecil John Rhodes of Oriel College, Oxford, but presently of Kimberley in the Province of Griqualand West", made his second Will, the text of which is preserved at Rhodes House. He appointed as his executors Lord Carnarvon, or the Colonial Secretary for the time being, and Sidney Shippard, the Attorney-General of Griqualand West.[3] The whole of his estate was to be handed over to them

". . . to and for the establishment, promotion and development of a Secret Society, the true aim and object whereof shall be the extension of British rule throughout the world, the perfecting of a system of emigration from the United Kingdom and of colonization by British subjects of all lands wherein the means of livelihood are attainable by energy, labour and enterprise, and especially the occupation by British settlers of the entire Continent of Africa, the Holy Land, the valley of the Euphrates, the Islands of Cyprus and Candia, the whole of South America, the islands of the Pacific not heretofore possessed by Great Britain, the whole of the Malay Archipelago, the seaboard of China and Japan, the ultimate recovery of the United States of America as an integral part of the British Empire, the consolidation of the whole Empire, the inauguration of a system of Colonial Representation in the Imperial Parliament which may tend to weld together the disjointed members of the Empire, and finally the foundation of so great a power as to hereafter render wars impossible and promote the best interests of humanity."

The hand of Rhodes the schoolboy, as well as that of Rhodes the dreamer, appears in this document, devoting a non-existent fortune for fantastic purposes to a secret society. Had the Executors ever found themselves in the unhappy position of having to discharge their duties, they would certainly not have known where to begin.

The details should not be taken too seriously. What later became evident was that the making of a Will was Rhodes's way of registering his thoughts at a given moment. As he matured, the thoughts changed and became less childishly improbable. That Will of 1877 was to have many successors. Each marked a stage in Rhodes's thought and development; and as the fortune began to exist and to grow from year to year, the provisions became less bizarre. Yet from one underlying conviction Rhodes never departed. "Homes, more homes," he would exclaim, sweeping his hand across a map of Africa. "I would like," he said, "to see all that red." The homes and the repainting of the map of Africa were essential parts of a grand design.

While Rhodes was keeping his terms at Oxford, the faithful Rudd, with whom he corresponded regularly, looked after the business in Kimberley. The years from 1873 to 1881, when the first fever of discovery had died out, had their ups and downs for the diamond industry. In 1875 a trade depression descended on the world and the price of diamonds dropped to a point at which the mines were scarcely paying their way. Doubts and fears began to appear. One of these was concerned with the gradual exhaustion of the yellow ground, in which the diamonds had been found. Below it was a layer of blue ground, extending to an unknown depth; and many were sure diamonds would not be found in it. Rhodes, on the other hand, by instinct rather than through any geological knowledge, was convinced that they would be found, in even greater quantities; and he was right.

While many abandoned the workings in despair, he and Rudd stayed on, buying up any claims they could get in the De Beers Mine, to which they had moved from the Kimberley Mine, where the claims, being reputed richer, were more expensive. Once the partners could have had the whole of De Beers for £6,000, thereby saving themselves an immense future outlay; but the cash was not available and the chance went by—an opportunity which Rhodes was to lament as lost through lack of courage on his part. In 1880, however, the De Beers Mining Company was formed with a capital of £200,000. Rhodes was the Secretary, and by 1885, when the capital had been increased to £841,550 and he had become Chairman, the Company was the chief owner of the mine.

Another difficulty of those years was the not unnatural tendency of the owners of farms to think they had been cheated over the licences to dig, which they had granted, and to ask for more money—a trouble which continued until in 1875 the Crown bought outright Voruitzicht, the farm which contained the De Beers and Kimberley mines. Rhodes's prediction that one day the *kopje* would become a crater was fulfilled, and until the various claims were absorbed, the owners were always disputing about their boundaries. The roads, undermined by digging, continually fell in, and even when they remained intact, the use of them by several men, all anxious to bring their buckets of dirt and diamonds to the surface as soon as possible, was a fruitful source of quarrels.

Life continued to be primitive and uncomfortable. As yet there was no railway, so that every pound of stores or plant had to be hauled slowly and expensively from the coast by ox-wagon. On the surface water was sometimes so scarce that a man who wanted a bath might have to take it in soda water. Below, however, it was often so plentiful that it would flood the mines and stop the work.

The plain solution for problems like price, boundaries and water was amalgamation. Almost Rhodes's first appearance as a public figure was when for a cut price he secured a contract for pumping out the Kimberley, De Beers and Dutoitspan mines— an experiment in co-operation which, if it succeeded, might prepare men for wider measures of unity. Rhodes and Rudd got the contract; they took into partnership a young man named Alderson, who had some knowledge of engineering; and all they lacked was a pump. This they had to find, and quickly, unless they were to break their contract and justify the suspicions of the owners. Rhodes and Alderson went down to the Colony to try to find the pumps and engines, but Kimberley was 300 miles from the railway, the rains had arrived, and some delay was unavoidable.

The owners had to be persuaded to grant an extension of time, and Hawkins recalled how Rhodes went to a meeting of the Board of De Beers to try to obtain it. "I have never forgotten," Hawkins wrote, "the way in which he, still quite a youth, handled that body of angry men and gained his point."

Eventually the pumps arrived and work began. But Rhodes's difficulties were by no means ended. The plant, being old and in poor condition, often broke down, and there was also a deplorable scarcity of fuel. Early in the morning Rhodes would ride out to meet the heavy wagons in which Boer farmers were bringing in wood to sell in Kimberley, and usually he would get what he wanted while his competitors were still asleep.

One night, however, Rhodes himself wrecked the plant. In the absence of Alderson, he was acting as engineman and, as was his habit, walking absent-mindedly up and down, his thoughts far away. Suddenly there was a tremendous explosion, seriously damaging the engine. He had forgotten to supply the boiler with water and it had burst. Once more the contract, which had just begun to be lucrative, was in danger. But Rhodes had heard that one, Devenish, who was farming in the Karoo, had brought out from England a suitable pumping plant which at the moment he was not using. Rhodes immediately procured a Cape cart and six mules, and by hard driving in eight days reached Devenish's farm. There, however, he met with a rebuff. Devenish would not sell his plant.

"But," Rhodes is reported to have said, "I will pay you a handsome profit and you can order another lot. You are not using this now; it has been lying in your shed for some months."

"That may be," replied Devenish, "but I am not going to sell."

"Think it over," urged Rhodes. "I will come back."

"It's no good," said the farmer, "I will not alter my mind."

As the precious days passed, Rhodes returned again and again. He was most persuasive, but the farmer, stubborn as farmers often are, would not budge. In spite of the deadlock, the two men became quite friendly, and Rhodes was frequently asked in to drink coffee. He turned his attention from the man to his wife and won Mrs. Devenish over to his side. At last the unfortunate farmer, wearied by this war on two fronts, gave way.

"The pair of you are making my life a misery," he said. "Take the plant and be off with you; but I will make you pay me a stiff price for all the worry you have given me over it." The price counted little to Rhodes; the reputation of himself and his partners mattered a great deal. "I may tell you," he said, "that I meant to stay and keep at you till I got your plant."

Even then Rhodes's troubles were not over. He had to get his pump to Kimberley without delay and the wet season was at its worst. The owner of the wagon he hired wanted to wait till the rains were over, as he feared the journey would kill his oxen.

"It will ruin me if you are not there by such a day," said Rhodes.

"It will ruin *me* if I try," retorted the transport man. "My oxen are my only means of livelihood."

Rhodes at once offered to buy them at a good price, and rather to his surprise the Dutchman accepted. "It is right," he said. "As you are a good sort of fellow, I will sell."

Rhodes sat down and, as he had neither pen nor ink with him, wrote out a cheque in pencil. The whole incident illustrated Rhodes's pertinacity, his resourcefulness, and his capacity for getting on to easy terms with people and for turning "no" into "yes". It was perhaps the first time that he had taught himself that "every man has his price".

*　　*　　*

New faces had begun to appear in Kimberley. In 1873, when Rhodes was on his way to Oxford, his ship passed another, carrying among its passengers Barnett Isaacs, the son of a little Jewish shopkeeper in Whitechapel. He was eighteen and on his way to join his brother Harry in South Africa, taking with him as capital sixty boxes of doubtful cigars, which later he would sell at a high price in a place where any cigar, however doubtful, had a buyer. The Isaacs brothers had tried their hands at many occupations— the circus, boxing, conjuring, bar-tending, huckstering, almost anything that came their way. Later Barnett, or Barney Barnato, as, fancying the alliteration, he called himself, used to say of South Africa, "There is nothing this country produces that I have not traded in, from diamonds and gold right away through wool, feathers and mealies to garden vegetables." But while any venture that promised a profit would be taken up, the brothers' main business was that of *kopje*-wallopers.

Barney was soon the brother who counted. He was shrewd, painstaking and tremendously industrious. He had no manners and was almost illiterate. "Rhodes looks down on me," he once said, "because I have no education—not been to college like him."

Taking Barnato at his own words, men were apt to form a low opinion of him. The stories to his discredit floated round Kimberley were fantastic and were mostly either wholly untrue or grossly exaggerated. In his early days Barney thought it bad policy to deny any tale about himself, however derogatory it might be, presumably on the grounds that it was better to be lied about than not to be noticed. The policy may have been sound for a *kopje*-walloper, but later, when he made a position for himself and wished to be considered respectable, he had his regrets; by then the legends were established and could not be destroyed.

Yet he had many good qualities. He was witty, warm-hearted, immensely proud of being an Englishman, generous when he believed the cause was deserving. Above all, when he gave his word he kept it. Like Rhodes, he believed in the diamondiferous quality of the blue soil and, again like Rhodes, when the faint-hearted were panicking and deserting Kimberley, he stayed on. By 1876 he had saved £3,000, with which he bought a claim of his own, so as to become a producer as well as a merchant. With industry and luck his capital grew, and his next step was to turn himself into the Barnato Diamond Mining Company, which he presently converted into the Kimberley Central Diamond Mining Company. He had become someone with whom Kimberley had to reckon. He and Rhodes were too unlike in character and tastes to become intimate. Rhodes, like most people in Kimberley, did not at first take Barnato very seriously, the general view being that he was at worst a rogue and at best a comedian. His qualities of pluck, shrewdness and good-heartedness were only revealed later.

A newcomer of a very different kind was Alfred Beit, who was to figure even more largely in Rhodes's life. When Beit reached Kimberley in 1875 he was twenty-two. The son of a Hamburg Jew, he had been sent to Amsterdam to learn all about diamonds, and subsequently to Kimberley to work for his cousins, D. Lippert & Co. Unlike most of the men with whom he mixed, he thoroughly understood his business.

> "When I reached Kimberley," he related, "I found that very few people knew anything about diamonds; they bought and sold vaguely, and a great many of them really believed that the Cape diamonds were of a very inferior quality. Of course I saw at once that some of the Cape stones were as good as any in the world."

He was introduced to Rhodes by William P. Taylor in 1879. Seymour Fort, author of a biography of Beit, gives an account of a meeting between the two men which may have happened shortly afterwards. One night, when most of the mining fraternity were in bars, Rhodes happened to pass by the little hut which was Beit's office. Through the open door he could see someone working. Rhodes slipped in.

"Hello," he asked, "do you never take a rest, Mr. Beit?"

"Not often," was Beit's reply.

"Well, what's your game?" asked Rhodes.

"I am going to control the whole diamond output before I am much older."

"That's funny," replied Rhodes. "I have made up my mind to do the same. We had better join hands."

Join hands they did, though Beit did not formally become Rhodes's partner and presently fell in with the son of a German general, Julius Wernher, who had come to Kimberley as the agent of Jules Porges & Co., at that time probably the wealthiest diamond merchants in the world. Beit, Wernher and Porges himself went into a partnership which survived as such till 1889, when Porges retired and the famous firm of Wernher, Beit & Co. came into existence.

Beit was soon closer to Rhodes than any partnership could bring him. Between them reigned a complete mutual trust—trust in each other's judgment, integrity and loyalty. Beit was so self-effacing that the world knew little about him and never gave him credit for his shining qualities of mind and character. Unlike Barnato, he was not interested in mere money-making. Rhodes, chaffing him, would say that all he wanted was enough money to buy a carriage and horses for his old mother in Germany. Apart from this ambition, it was the *business* that attracted him; and the day was coming when he would learn from Rhodes of something bigger even than the business.

Beit, with his extraordinary knowledge of and memory for diamonds and his calculating practical mind, would bring Rhodes just what he most wanted. Beit could steady without discouraging; no man knew better what was and what was not possible in the world of diamonds. "Ask little Alfred" became a catch phrase in Rhodes's circle. "There can be no doubt whatever," wrote Sir Percy Fitzpatrick, who knew both men well, "that Beit was Rhodes's financial genius."

Yet another newcomer was a young doctor, who arrived in

Kimberley in 1872. Leander Starr Jameson, who was to become one of Rhodes's closest friends, was a Scot. By some accounts he went to South Africa because he had a patch on a lung and, like Rhodes and so many others, hoped to find health as well as fortune in a new country. According to his biographer, Ian Colvin, Jameson happened to come across an application for a partner by a Dr. Prince of Kimberley. Jameson offered himself, was accepted, and sailed for South Africa. He was then twenty-five, "small of stature, very light and slim of body, keen and confident in look and bearing". He was a highly trained surgeon and diagnostician, already a man of some note in Gower Street; and to his friends his departure from London, where his professional future was assured, must have seemed the act of a madman.

What they may have overlooked was a love of adventure which, all his life, lured him into strange places, and a passion for gambling which inclined him to prefer the dangerous chance to the safe certainty. Of his gambling Kimberley was to tell many stories. In one game of poker he is said to have staked everything—his horse, his carriage, his furniture—lost them all and won them all back again in a single night. Hans Sauer tells how once he played poker with the Doctor, who won from him everything he possessed, but out of kindness returned him his top-boots and surgical instruments. Sometimes Jameson played bridge with Rhodes, the Doctor's wild bidding often leading him into trouble. "Well, Jameson," Rhodes remarked after a rubber, "you went out skirmishing, but the enemy swooped down on you and annihilated you." [4]

After a while Dr. Prince retired, leaving Jameson with the best practice in Kimberley; and soon, with his sure hand and discerning eye, he had no rival. He was an extremely attractive young man, and as he made his rounds in his bowler hat, driving a smart victoria behind two black horses, everyone, well or ill, was glad to see him; while his latest witty saying would go the round of the bars in the evening.

In 1884 Jameson hazarded his professional reputation in what Dr. Hans Sauer has called "The Great Smallpox War". An African on a farm near Kimberley went down with a complaint diagnosed by a group of the leading doctors, headed by Jameson, as a "bulbous disease of the skin allied to pemphigus". Sauer, who gives his version of the incident at some length in *Ex Africa* . . ., disagreed, being sure that the disease was simply smallpox. A tremendous controversy followed. Sauer, a spirited and obstinate young doctor, plunged into it with a horsewhip, and writs for libel flew about, the whole affair eventually going up to the Cape Parliament. The ugly suggestion was made that the doctors, under pressure from the mine-owners, had refused to diagnose the epidemic as smallpox, because they feared that African labour would be scared away from the mines. In the end Sauer won, the disease being pronounced "smallpox pure and simple". Jameson cannot be said to have emerged from the battle with much credit, but evidently his popularity enabled him to survive a setback which might have ruined a lesser man; and Rhodes, who had supported him, cannot escape some of the blame. A more agreeable sequel was the subsequent absence of acrimony on the part of the principals on either side.

There is no record of Jameson's first encounter with Rhodes, though Jameson himself dated it to 1878. In the restricted society of Kimberley the two men must often have met, and Jameson joined the Mess to which Rhodes belonged, named by the ribald the "Twelve Apostles". They were brought into a closer intimacy by Neville Pickering, the dearest of all Rhodes's friends. He has been described as a "frank, sunny-tempered young Englishman". Rhodes took to him at once, appointing him Secretary of De Beers and, leaving the "Twelve Apostles", shared a cottage with him opposite the Club. Better than any other man, except perhaps Herbert, Pickering understood Rhodes, knowing exactly what he wanted at any moment. They rode, shot, did everything together, and such was Rhodes's confidence that when, in October 1882, he made his fourth and shortest Will, it read simply: "I, Cecil John Rhodes, being of sound mind, leaving my worldly wealth to N. E. Pickering." In an accompanying letter Rhodes referred Pickering to the earlier Will, "whose conditions are very curious and can only be carried out by a trustworthy person, and I consider you one". He added in a postscript: [5] "You fully understand you are to use interest of money as you like during your life." Later, when Pickering fell fatally ill, Rhodes nursed him with real devotion. It was over his sickbed that the close friendship with Dr. Jameson began.

* * *

During the Oxford years the Rhodes–Rudd partnership was slowly consolidating its position. When Rhodes first went up to Oxford, he had little more than enough money to pay his expenses at the University: when he came down he was already a moderately rich man, though continually short of cash.

De Beers covered close on fourteen acres. At first no man in Kimberley was allowed to own more than one claim thirty-one feet square; then three claims were allowed; and in 1874 a person or company might have as many as ten. Finally, at the end of 1876, all restrictions were removed and the mines were thrown open. This development, which changed the character of Kimberley, was born of necessity. Roads had continued to crumble away, falls of rock were liable to interrupt work for long periods, disputes about boundaries were innumerable. Attempts were made to deal with the situation through Mining Boards, elected by the diggers themselves; but the job was becoming too big for any system of divided ownership, and gradually the wiser men began to see that a consolidation of interests was the only answer. The process had already started. Originally in the four diamond mines there were 3,600 claims, but by 1885 these had shrunk to 98. The way was becoming clear for the further step which both Rhodes and Beit had been planning.

That, however, was still in the future. Rhodes was growing in wealth and influence, without losing altogether the youthfulness of his years. Even when he returned to Kimberley for the Long Vacation, he did not put aside his books. In 1877 he happened to be travelling in the Kimberley coach with Colonel (afterwards Sir Charles) Warren.

"Rhodes, who sat opposite to me [wrote Warren] was engaged in getting something up by heart, so I offered to hear him. It was the Thirty-Nine Articles of our Christian Faith. We got on very well until we arrived at the Article on Predestination, and there we stuck. He had his views and I had mine, and our fellow-passengers were greatly amused at the topic of our conversation for several hours being on this one subject."

It was the kind of topic that engrossed Rhodes, and one which he would always willingly debate without regard for his surroundings and company.

Sources

Works mentioned under Chapter Three, and additionally:
Colvin, Ian: *The Life of Jameson*
Fitzpatrick, Sir Percy: *South African Memories*

Fort, G. Seymour: *Alfred Beit*
Lewinsohn, Richard: *Barney Barnato*
Sauer, Hans: *Ex Africa* . . .
Warren, Sir Charles: *On the Veldt in the Seventies*

Notes

[1] McDonald, 36–37.
[2] Colvin, *Life of Jameson*, I. 52.
[3] R.H.L. Rhodes Wills, 2.

[4] R.H.L. MSS. Afr. s. 69, vol. 4, f. 5.
[5] R.H.L. Rhodes Wills, 7.

CHAPTER FIVE

POLITICS

HEAVY as were Rhodes's preoccupations with books or business at Oxford or Kimberley, his interest in the wider political scene never flagged. In the background was that grand design to paint large portions of the map red, to settle the earth with Anglo-Saxons, and to federate the British Empire. In the foreground were his plans for South Africa—the union of the Cape Colony and Natal with the two Dutch republics, and the opening up of a road to the north. At Westminster Disraeli's administration seemed at times, though intermittently and without a conscious plan, to be seeking to realise the less unlikely of Rhodes's dreams. But the pace was too slow, and one day in 1876 Rhodes with four of his gay friends sat down in a small room in Kimberley and wrote a letter to the Prime Minister to tell him just where he had gone wrong. Unhappily no copy of this effusion has survived, but Disraeli, if he ever saw it, would have been more than impressed.

Meanwhile there was the political tangle of South Africa. Rhodes knew that if he was to have a hand in unravelling it, he must follow the course on which some years earlier he and Merriman had agreed, which meant—the Cape being the key to the South—entering the Parliament at Cape Town. Merriman was already a member, and in 1880, when Griqualand West was incorporated in the Colony and allotted six Parliamentary seats, Rhodes saw an opening. He would have liked to stand for one of the Kimberley seats, but ran into the bitter opposition of J. B. Robinson, one of the richest men in Kimberley, who, having been among the first arrivals in the Fields, thought that he, and not Rhodes, was the man to represent the Diamond Industry in Parliament. At one time Rhodes had thought of trying to work with him, but soon realised that Robinson, for all his cleverness, was universally distrusted. Robinson never forgave him and was only too ready to thwart him on this and every other occasion. Rhodes then went to Barkly West, a rural constituency where most of the electors were Dutch farmers. "The Dutch are the coming race in South Africa," he declared, "and they must have their share in running the country." So he took his seat, keeping it and the loyalty of his Dutch farmers, despite raid and war, until his death;

and he remembered, no doubt, that his forbears were also "keepers of cattle".

Parliament met in March 1881 under the shadow of grave events. Sir Bartle Frere, the High Commissioner, spurred on by Lord Carnarvon, the impetuous Colonial Secretary, had embarked on an ill-starred policy. Quite correctly, Carnarvon decided that if South Africa were to develop as it should, union was essential. He pursued the right policy at the wrong time and in the wrong way. Neither the Colonies nor the two Dutch republics were as yet ready for the step. Carnarvon could and did suspend the constitution of Natal; probably he would have overcome the hesitations of the Cape Parliament; and in the Orange Free State that wise old man, President Brand, was determined to avoid an armed clash with the suzerain power. The Transvaal was another matter. It was poor, badly governed and on the brink of bankruptcy, but while the small urban population of Pretoria was not unwilling to allow the British Crown to take the strain of the Republic's financial and administrative problems, the farmers, who were the backbone of the country, bitterly resented Beaconsfield's annexation, without any pretence of consulting the people. Forty years earlier they had faced the hazards and hardships of the Great Trek to escape from the British flag; and there it was again, flying over the Government building in Pretoria.

Rhodes, on the threshold of his political career, had watched the blunders of the Imperial Government with dismay. He wanted federation, but not in a form that would arouse the undying enmity of the Dutch. Even as it was, he thought the annexation of the Transvaal might have come to be accepted, but for the mistakes of the Imperial Commissioner, Sir Owen Lanyon, "who conducted the business on the lines of a second-rate line regiment". Finally, after three uneasy years, the Boers rose in revolt. They had been encouraged by the fall of Disraeli's Government in 1880 and the return to office of Mr. Gladstone, that stern critic of his rival's Imperial policies. In December 1880 the Boers wiped out a detachment of British troops in the Transvaal. In the New Year they invaded Natal, repulsed a British attack at Laing's Neck, and inflicted on General Colley the crowning defeat of Majuba.

Such was the situation when Rhodes entered the Cape Parliament, to be a witness, impotent and at a distance, of the humiliating surrender which followed. It left Britain with no more than a rather shadowy paramountcy over the Transvaal and the jubilant commandos with a feeling of superiority over the British Regular

Army. Both the paramountcy and the feeling of superiority were to cause repeated trouble in the years that followed.

The Prime Minister of the Cape at the time was Mr. (afterwards Sir Gordon) Sprigg, a politician of limited intelligence where larger issues were concerned, but of considerable Parliamentary adroitness. A man of expediency rather than of principles, for more than twenty years he dodged in and out of office at Cape Town, indispensable in his own opinion, until in 1902 he fell finally from power, without any of the dire consequences he had presupposed.

In 1881 Sprigg's chief worry was not the Transvaal, where the treatment of the men who had stood by the British was causing distress to many of his colleagues, but Basutoland which Disraeli had annexed and then handed over to the Cape Colony. Sprigg was determined to disarm the Basutos; but they, having in the past fought not without success against Zulus, British and Boers, refused to give up their weapons. Basutoland was the creation of a remarkable chief, Moshesh, who, reigning from the year of Waterloo to that of Sedan, had welded a collection of warring tribes into a nation. Finally, finding the pressure from his neighbours, the Boers, too strong to withstand, Moshesh had appealed for British protection, which was granted. His successor, Letsie, while very ready to accept British help, had observed the inability of the British Government to protect its supporters in the Transvaal. He would not therefore risk the possibility that his people, disarmed, might suffer the same fate; and when the Colony, with such forces as it could command, tried to enforce the order, the Basutos rose and repelled the invaders.

Sprigg, who also had Majuba in his mind, thought he could finish the job without Imperial help, disregarding the fact, of which Rhodes was to remind him, that a population no larger than that of "a third-rate English city" could not aspire to play an Imperial part with success. In fact, all that the Cape Colony looked like getting for its pains was a loss of territory and a large debt. Rhodes, despite his growing distrust of the "Imperial factor", as he called it, had no doubt that the right solution was for the Home Government to take over Basutoland and rule it from Whitehall; and after three troublesome years this was the policy accepted, Basutoland returning to the protection of the Imperial Government.

The new member for Barkly West soon found his feet in his new surroundings. "Watch that man," said Saul Solomon, when

Rhodes took his seat. "He is the future man of South Africa and possibly of the world." He was not and never became a good speaker. His squeaky voice, his occasional boisterous laugh, and his habit of sitting on his hand were the marks of a boy rather than of a serious legislator. One observer remarked that "he is never still from the time he enters the House until he leaves it". In his maiden speech he distressed the Speaker by the persistence with which he alluded to his fellow-members by their names and not by their constituencies; and he refused to wear the usual Parliamentary uniform of a tall hat and a black coat, saying, "I am still in Oxford tweeds and I think I can legislate as well in them as in sable clothing." At least his Dutch constituents appear to have preferred his informal dress.

His maiden speech was on the Basuto question and Sprigg's unhappy attempt to enforce the Colonial Disarmament or Peace Preservation Act of 1877. Rhodes thought disarmament was neither politic nor just. He knew the Basutos, many of whom worked in the mines at Kimberley, and he considered it unfair that, having earned their wages and with them bought themselves guns, they should be forced to hand these over.

Rhodes was rated by one who heard him speak as "a fine broad ruddy Englishman, a jovial looking young squire". Another of his audience, Sir Thomas Fuller, remembered him as

". . . a tall, broad-shouldered man, with face and figure of somewhat loose formation. His hair was auburn, carelessly flung over his forehead, his eyes of bluish grey, dreamy but kindly . . . with deep lines following the curve of his moustache . . . [his mouth] had a determined, masterful, and somewhat scornful expression."

Fuller wrote thus after Rhodes's death: most of the contemporary verdicts seem to have been less favourable. By their accounts Rhodes was ungrammatical, informal, quite unselfconscious, frequently out of order, talking rather than making a speech, and impatient of details of procedure. Yet while a friend prophesied that he would be a Parliamentary failure, what all noticed was that when he spoke, his aim was to persuade his opponents, not to score off them, and something about him suggested that despite appearances, a significant personality had arrived. Behind the repetitions and the clumsy sentences were a forcefulness, a sincerity, a breadth of thought and a statesmanlike foresight, which stood out against the provincial background of the Colony's legislature.

Rhodes, having stated his position on the Basuto question, stuck to it with the tenacity which was to characterise him. The motion on which he spoke was carried by 37 votes to 34. Sprigg, ignoring his defeat, hung on till 4 May, when a direct vote of censure forced him to resign. He went, and Mr. T. C. (afterwards Sir Thomas) Scanlen took his place.

Rhodes meanwhile was making friends both inside and outside the House. Outside it he found in particular the new High Commissioner, Sir Hercules Robinson, who was to become a powerful ally, and Captain Graham Bower, the Imperial Secretary, a very influential man in Cape Town. In order to ensure adequate notice for his speeches, Rhodes bought an interest in the *Cape Argus*, promising that he would not attempt to interfere with its editorial policy. For relaxation he yachted enthusiastically in Table Bay, under the guidance of the Port-captain; and once, later, when he was Prime Minister, he spent a night in rough seas, sailing to the rescue of two lighters which were adrift and in trouble. He delighted in the talk over luncheon at the Club or at Poole's, or at his rooms in Adderley Street, where he could recapture some of the atmosphere of Oxford.

The Cape Parliament might be provincial, but the standard of debate was high. Latin quotations which might even have puzzled some at Westminster were by no means unknown; and at that time Parliament contained a number of men who would have been in place in any legislature. Molteno, the first Prime Minister of the Cape, was still alive. Upington, a witty Irishman, was himself to be Prime Minister in the near future, and later, as Attorney-General, chairman of the Cape Enquiry into the Jameson Raid. There were J. W. Sauer, Secretary for Native Affairs; Saul Solomon, eloquent and deeply sincere; Schreiner, brother of Olive Schreiner the novelist, already known as a brilliant and high-minded young lawyer; and J. X. Merriman, with whom Rhodes had had many an argument at Kimberley.

The most important new friend, however, was Jan Hofmeyr (known to the Dutch as Onze Jan), captor and transformer of the Afrikander Bond. The Bond was an organisation of Dutch farmers, who formed so large a proportion of the electorate. Originally, under the leadership of the Rev. S. J. du Toit, anti-British in sentiment and aim, it was brought by Hofmeyr to a more constructive policy. He was a realist, who had opposed the annexation of the Transvaal, but had been equally opposed to the revolt which triumphed at Majuba. Like Carnarvon and Rhodes, he wanted the Union of South Africa, but differed from them in his private hope that this would not be under the British flag. In the Cape Parliament he worked so quietly and effectively behind the scenes that Merriman nicknamed him "The Mole". While no government could survive for long without the passive support of the Bond, for most of his political life Hofmeyr carefully avoided the responsibilities of office. He would be king-maker, not king, ensuring by the votes he controlled that any government in office followed a policy congenial to the Dutch.

At first sight he and Rhodes were mutually suspicious. Hofmeyr had been warned that Rhodes was "a regular beefsteak, John Bull Englishman"; while Rhodes was inclined to regard Hofmeyr as a dangerous fellow, a potential adversary of the schemes he was turning over in his mind. But when a friend introduced them to each other, their suspicions soon melted away. In fact the two men were nearer to each other than perhaps either supposed. Though for different reasons, each mistrusted the "Imperial factor", Rhodes because he dreaded the frequent changes of policy in Westminster, one of which had lately led to the humiliation of Majuba, and Hofmeyr, because he wanted South Africa to work out its own destiny without the interference of Whitehall. Both men disliked Sprigg's Basuto policy, and both hoped for an eventual federation of South Africa, although they disagreed about the flag which should fly over it. Hofmeyr's immediate purpose was to rescue the Cape Colony from the stranglehold of *laisser-faire* and to protect his farmers from foreign competition, purposes with which Rhodes was in complete sympathy. "I like the Dutch," he said. "I like their homely courtesy and their tenacity of purpose, and we have always got on very well together."

Later Rhodes described very candidly and lucidly the pact he made with Hofmeyr:[1]

"When I first entered Cape politics," he said, "two conspicuous factors weighed with me. One was the constant vacillation of the Home Government, which never knew its mind about us. Many Englishmen cried out at the surrender after Majuba, but the real humiliation was borne by those who, relying on the Imperial pledges, had stood firm in the Transvaal for the old flag. That was one factor, but there was

another. The 'English' party in the Cape Assembly was hope-
lessly divided and individually incapable. And it had no
policy beyond that of serving office. On the other side was a
compact body of nominees of what afterwards came to be
called the Afrikander Bond, who acted all together at the
dictation of Hofmeyr. Hofmeyr was, without doubt, the
most capable politician in South Africa, and if he concealed
in his breast aspirations for a united South Africa in which
Great Britain should have no part at all, the concealment was
very effective. My belief is that he was anxious to maintain
the connection, not out of any love for Great Britain, but because the independence of South Africa was at the mercy of
whatever power had command of the sea. And you must
remember that, though Hofmeyr had no particular affection
for the English, his hatred of the Germans amounted to a
passion. At the time of which I am speaking there was no
danger of British supremacy being threatened by the Transvaal, and still less the Orange Free State. Again, in those
days Hofmeyr was chiefly interested in withstanding Free
Trade and upholding Protection on behalf of the Dutch, who
were agriculturists and wine-growers. I had a policy of my
own, which I never disguised from Hofmeyr. It was to keep
open the road to the north, to secure for British South Africa
room for expansion, and to leave time and circumstances to
bring about an inevitable federation. I therefore struck a
bargain with him, by which I undertook to defend the Pro-
tective system of Cape Colony, and he pledged himself in the
name of the Bond not to throw any obstacles in the way of
northern expansion. He did not like this condition, but I am
bound to say he loyally fulfilled it, thereby incurring the
hatred of the Transvaal Boers, and to some extent losing the
confidence of the extreme members of the Afrikander Bond."

Hofmeyr also gave his version of the friendship:[2]

"I remember," he said, "about the time we were introduced, the Transvaal war broke out, and Mr. Rhodes—perhaps
as it behoved him—was all against the Boers and Transvaal
independence. I was on the other side. But when the war was
over we had a talk with one another, and I said to Mr.
Rhodes, 'It is an awful pity the war broke out.' I was surprised when Mr. Rhodes said, 'No, it is not. I have quite
changed my opinions. It is a good thing. It has made

Englishmen respect Dutchmen and made them respect one another.' Well, when an Englishman could speak like that to a Dutchman, they are not far from making common cause with one another."

Rhodes may have been unduly optimistic, but his words seem to have won him Hofmeyr's confidence. The friendship was important, because, as Rhodes realised, if he was to carry out his plans in the North, he must have the support of the Cape Parliament; and to get that he must somehow secure the sympathy and help of Hofmeyr. Having secured it, Rhodes admitted that Hofmeyr honoured the pact scrupulously, even when it brought him into conflict with his fellow Dutchmen. His loyalty was to be severely tested in March 1890, when Paul Kruger, by then the accepted leader of the Transvaal, was trying to annex Swaziland as the necessary step towards getting an outlet to the sea. Kruger hoped for the support of Hofmeyr and the Bond, but did not get it, and Swaziland came under the protection of the British Crown. "You are a traitor to the Afrikander cause," he thundered at Hofmeyr.

After Majuba, Paul Kruger emerged as the outstanding man in the Transvaal. The British have done him less than justice. For them, with his small eyes, his Newgate fringe, and his rock-like face, he stood for all that was most inimical to the British Empire. But if to his enemies he seemed in body and mind a faithful reproduction of the Neanderthal man, to his admirers he had the quality of an Old Testament prophet. He was a child of the Great Trek who, when he was fourteen, went on Commando with Potgieter against Mzilikazi and shot his first lion. As a young man he went to war again and again. Once, when he was hunting rhino, his rifle burst and blew off most of his thumb. Quite calmly he sat down, pulled out his pocket knife and cut away what was left of his thumb. Gangrene set in and for weeks he was between life and death. With his courage, his stubbornness, his tremendous voice and his ever open Bible, he was to become Rhodes's most formidable antagonist. In his time Rhodes squared a good many people, but he never squared Kruger, and after one or two futile attempts even gave up trying.

For like Rhodes, Kruger had his dream. It was of a united and greater South Africa under Afrikander domination. "Then shall be," he exulted after Majuba, "from Zambesi to Simon's Bay, Africa for the Afrikanders." He must have his outlet to the sea, so that the Transvaal should no longer be dependent on British ports for its supplies. He must secure the wide spaces of Central Africa, to prevent his people being encircled by their enemies and to give them living room for the future. But presently, wherever he turned and whatever he attempted, he was to find Britain barring his path, and in Britain's shadow he could see the burly figure of a man as obstinate as himself and far swifter to move.

That, however, was in the future. For the present the problem was Basutoland, where the new Government of Cape Colony was trying to quell a rising and to compensate those who had suffered loss in the fighting. As these tasks were likely to be far from easy, the Government decided to accept an offer it had received from General Gordon to end the rebellion and subsequently to administer the territory. Gordon, in spite of a brilliant past in China and the Sudan, had been sent off, as he put it, to supervise "the barracks and drains" of Mauritius. Welcoming an escape to more congenial work, he sailed at once for Cape Town, which he reached on 1 May 1882. Having failed to persuade the High Commissioner to visit Basutoland himself, Gordon decided to call a series of *pitsos* or national gatherings. Since another of his stipulations was for the award of compensation to those Basutos who had remained loyal throughout the rebellion, a Losses Commission was appointed, and Rhodes, having been one of the sharpest critics of the policy of the late Government, was invited to serve on it.

So it came about that two remarkable Victorians found themselves for a short time in close association. Widely different in character though they were, they soon found common ground, not least perhaps in the fondness of both men for an unconventional approach to any task they were attempting. Rhodes never forgot the effect of Gordon's appearance unarmed at the *pitsos*, an example he himself was to follow one day in another land. At the same time he was not uncritical, and as usual did not hesitate to speak his mind. Whenever Gordon appeared, he received the biggest ovation, while Sauer, the Secretary for Native Affairs, was practically ignored. "You are doing wrong," Rhodes told Gordon. "You are letting these men make a grave mistake. They take you for the great man and pay no attention to Sauer, whereas you are only in his employment." Gordon made no reply to this plain speaking, but at the next *pitsos* told the Basutos in forcible language that he was only Sauer's servant. Afterwards he took Rhodes aside and whispered to him, "I did it because it was the right thing, but it was hard, very hard."

He then invited Rhodes to "stay with me and we will work to-gether". Rhodes, who was full of his own plans for the future, had to refuse the invitation. "There are very few men in the world," Gordon remarked, "to whom I would make such an offer, but of course you *will* have your way. I never met a man so strong for his opinion; you think your views are always right."

Nevertheless Gordon, the soldier and mystic, with years of service behind him, and Rhodes, the miner and undergraduate of Oxford University, just starting his career, stayed on excellent terms. No doubt each recognised a rare quality in the other. When in October, Gordon, having laid down the lines of a settlement with the Basutos, fell out with the Cape Government and resigned, he and Rhodes parted with regret and mutual esteem. Probably they would not have worked harmoniously together for very long: Rhodes was not the only one who was "strong for his opinion" and, while they may have agreed on much, on many subjects they would always have differed. Once Gordon told Rhodes how he had refused a roomful of gold offered him by the Chinese Government. "I'd have taken it," said Rhodes, "and as many more roomfuls as they offered me: it is no use having big ideas if you have not the cash to carry them out."

Two years later, when Gordon was going to the Sudan, he repeated by cable his old invitation to Rhodes. "Now should I?" Rhodes asked Merriman, fascinated perhaps by the prospect of "squaring" the Mahdi in the company of a man who had attracted him as Gordon had. Merriman thought that as Rhodes was about to enter the Cape Cabinet, the invitation was inopportune; and Rhodes refused it. Gordon went to Khartoum and his death at the hands of the Dervishes. Rhodes was deeply moved when the news arrived. "I am sorry I was not with him," he said again and again.

Sources

Harris, Sir David: *Pioneer, Soldier and Politician*
Hofmeyr, J. H. and Reitz, F. W.: *The Life of Jan Hendrik Hofmeyr*
Kruger, Paul: *Memoirs*
Laurence, Sir Perceval: *The Life of John Xavier Merriman*
Nathan, Manfred: *Paul Kruger, His Life and Times*
"Vindex": *Cecil Rhodes, His Political Life and Speeches*

Notes

[1] Michell, I. 93–5. [2] Williams, 62–3.

CHAPTER SIX

THE ROAD TO THE NORTH

IAN COLVIN recounted, in his *Life of Jameson*, an imaginary conversation between Rhodes and Jameson at Kimberley. The conversation, which is more a monologue by Rhodes, is conjectural: that is to say, it never actually occurred, at least at one time and in the words given; but it gives so faithfully both Rhodes's ideas and his way of expressing them, that it represents brilliantly the sort of conversation between the two men which must have taken place, not once, but many times.[1]

Colvin begins by supposing the two friends either in the sitting-room of their cottage or on a morning ride—"Rhodes sitting with a loose rein, neglectful of his horse, brooding over and reiterating his ideas, as a caveman strikes a flint; Jameson sparing of speech, cynical, but a flint full of fire"; or in the cottage—"Rhodes shouting elemental truths at Jameson from his bath tub" or "rolling in his chair like a whale in deep seas", while Jameson smoked cigarette after cigarette and occasionally threw in a word of comment or disagreement.

"The talk was of the North—the North—the North— Rhodes as he used the word always thrusting an arm upwards and outwards in a northerly direction to convey his idea of the vastness of the unknown—that unclaimed interior. Did Jameson realise that to the north the great plateau of the African Continent continued—up to the Equatorial Lakes, up to the Soudan—cool under the Equator—a country for white men? Could Jameson imagine it, settled, like America, with homesteads, and cities, and railways between them—as big as the United States, as populous, and British from Cape to Cairo? Had Jameson ever thought of the independence of the Thirteen Colonies which became the United States?

"Beyond an occasional mine-manager or two, Jameson had not considered America.

"Well, in the North was something to make up to England for these thirteen lost colonies.

"Still Jameson was unmoved, possibly ribald, so Rhodes fought his way on.

"No, it was not nonsense, but a practical idea. One had worked at it; one had gone some way already. Jameson knew what one had done. It was no laughing matter! It was more important than his pills and pregnancies!

"Let Jameson fairly consider the case in all its bearings and then admit himself cornered. Let him consider it for example *qua* the federation of South Africa. The one question governed the other.

"Jameson could see as far as that? Obvious! He who held the North held 'the balance of the map'—the balance of the map—and here Rhodes kept on repeating for a minute or two, the balance of the map, as one conscious of making a great point. . . .

"There was the secret. The North was the balance, the coveted balance. Kruger wanted it . . . Jameson realised that? Kruger had his hobby. Everyone had his hobby. Kruger wanted a Republic of South Africa under its own flag—a Boer Republic, from the Cape to the Zambesi. But he was landlocked. He had tried to get Bechuanaland. . . .

"Jameson knew that of course: but *here* was the important point. Bechuanaland was the road to the North. Did Jameson follow?—the road to the North, the neck of the bottle, the Suez Canal—Jameson must see that point.

"Of course he saw it—a duffer if he didn't. Well, then, it was not merely the road to the North, but the North itself that Kruger wanted. Why? Because the North was the balance of the map.

"The North was the trump card, the key position, the bulk of the shares. If Kruger got the North, he held a solid block of claims from the Orange River to the Zambesi. He had what the British wanted, which was trade, what the Dutch wanted, which was land—a very strong position. If Kruger had the North, the amalgamation would be on Kruger's terms: he could force all South Africa into his Republic. *Now* was Jameson convinced?

"Here, Jameson, who never missed a point in any argument, would probably observe that the seaports and the railways were still to be in British hands, so that the Republic would still be helpless without an outlet to the sea.

"Yes, Rhodes would reply, a good point, an excellent point; but Kruger had seen to that. Now that he had the gold of the Witwatersrand at his command he could build his Delagoa Bay railway, which would make him independent of the British system. It would beat the British system, for it was the shortest route from the gold mines to the sea. It would govern the trade of South Africa. One had tried to stop it; one had tried to push the Cape railway through the Transvaal to Delagoa Bay; but one could not get the Cape Government to see things in time. If Kruger had the Delagoa Bay line, and if he had the North, he had all the cards, he had all the claims, all the shares, he could force his federation. *Now* did Jameson see the importance of the North? *Now* would he admit himself cornered?

"Here Rhodes's voice went up into his shrill falsetto cock-crow of triumph.

"And Jameson, on his side, considering the matter with half-sheathed eyes, would grudgingly concede that there might be something in it.

"Very good! There were two key positions—the North and Delagoa Bay. One had one's agents in Portugal trying to buy Delagoa Bay; but the Portuguese were obstinate—poor but proud—and the British Government was slack in the matter. No, *there* Kruger looked like winning. But the North remained. For the hundredth time, did Jameson see the importance of the North?

"There was gold in the North. Yes, Jameson had a perfect right to ask what one could possibly want with more gold? A fair point: *qua* gold one had enough; but *qua* power, one must deal with men as one found them. There must be a magnet. Gold had taken one's people into the Transvaal. Gold might take them to the North. . . .

"One had been working at the problem for years—'Rhodes's hobby', one's friends called it. Every man had his hobby—just like Kruger. One had tried the Imperial Government; but one could not count on the Imperial factor. It had failed in the Orange Free State; it had failed in the Transvaal. Let Jameson consider Majuba. Jameson *had* considered it. The Imperial factor feared expense, feared responsibility. . . .

"One had tried the Cape Government . . . lawyers, politicians, merchants. . . . *They* could not see the importance of the North.

"Did not Hofmeyr see it? Yes, Jameson was right. Hofmeyr *did* see it; but Hofmeyr actually wanted Kruger to have it. Imagine it—with Kruger shutting out Cape wine and tobacco. . . . No, the Cape would not help one at all.

"What was there left? One had one's friends and one's money. Did Jameson remember what the East India Company had done? If in India, why not in Africa? In India there had been trade to draw men on, in Africa there was gold. Just suppose, for the sake of argument, the North occupied by a British company. It must then become a British colony. The North would be in British hands, and with the balance of the North in British hands one might federate South Africa on British lines. It put a trump card in one's hands. Now, Jameson had seen that; he had admitted every point as one went along, so he must accept the conclusion."

So Rhodes may have talked and Jameson listened; and if the actual words were not used, the thoughts and the way of expressing them are authentic. Whether Rhodes was digging for diamonds or attending a debate in the Cape Parliament, half his mind at least was in the North. "If we get Mashonaland," he told Shippard, "we shall get the balance of Africa." And to get Mashonaland, the road to the North must be kept open. The imagined conversation would have taken place a few years later, when Bechuanaland had been saved, the Diamond mines amalgamated, the Rand discovered, and Rhodes had become a millionaire. But for long he had been brooding over the ideas he is supposed to have expressed; and certainly they were the impulse that drove him on in his campaign for Bechuanaland and the road to the North.

Basutoland had been an awkward problem for the Cape Parliament and it was interesting to Rhodes, because any problem of South Africa interested him. His next venture into affairs beyond the borders of the Colony was into the vast, vague territory lying to the north-west of Griqualand West, which once was part of it. Most of Bechuanaland is covered by the Kalahari Desert, uninhabited except by a few wandering bushmen. On its eastern borders, however, where it meets the Transvaal, was a No Man's Land of comparatively fertile territory, through which ran the so-called English or Missionaries' Road to the North. Livingstone and Moffat had followed this track on their journeys to Central Africa, and Rhodes himself with his brother Herbert had taken it at the beginning of their *trek* in 1872. Bechuana

tribes lived in villages along the strip of comparatively good land
through which the Road ran. Like the Basutos, they found the
Boers of the Transvaal uneasy neighbours; and although an
award of 1871 barred the Republic from interference in Bechuanaland, the Boers, treating the strip as within their sphere, occasionally raided it and dabbled in the disputes of the tribes.

A few men, like Rhodes, were alive to the potential importance
of the Road, which he described as the "Suez Canal into the
interior". North of Bechuanaland was the country of the Matabele, and north of that again lay Mashonaland. Whatever truth
might lie in the stories of gold which filtered through with returning hunters, traders and missionaries, no one could doubt that
in Central Africa lay a large, sparsely populated tableland with a
climate in which Europeans might live. Rhodes had long looked
on it as a future outlet for British colonisation, but Kruger had
begun to regard it as a likely ground for settling farmers from the
Transvaal, when the Republic's land was no longer sufficient for
them. At the moment no one was ready to make a move. Apart
from distance and bad communications, across the route to
Central Africa lay the savage and warlike Matabele, an offshoot of
the Zulu nation, who undoubtedly would resist any attempt at
penetration. Kruger would have liked to seal the North off from
the outside world until his people were ready to move in and take
it over. This was no new policy: it had been noted much earlier
by Livingstone. "The Boers," he wrote, "resolved to shut up
the interior, I to open it. We shall see who succeeds, they or I."
The Imperial Government, for its part, was averse from incurring
any fresh and expensive liability; while Cape Colony, although
having some trade with Bechuanaland, was not at first interested
in that remote country, still less in the even more remote lands to
the north of it.

Two circumstances, however, combined to end the period of
inactivity. The first was the state of Bechuanaland itself, where the
tribal conflicts worsened and confusion reigned. Some of the
chiefs regarded themselves as the friends of the English, others of
the Boers; while both parties imported adventurers, under
promises of land, to help in their wars with each other. Cattle
and horse-thieving were rife all along the border and sometimes
over it. Everybody agreed that something ought to be done and
no one was anxious to do it. Meanwhile some of the Boer
raiders, whose tribal friends, with their help, had had the best of
the fighting, having decided to settle down, proclaimed two small

independent republics on the territory they had occupied. One was Stellaland, with its capital at Vryburg, where a farmer from the Transvaal, van Niekerk by name, was chosen or chose himself as administrator. The other republic, in what was known as the Land of Goshen, was ruled from Rooigrond by another Boer, Gey van Pittius.

These republics lay athwart Rhodes's road to the North and therefore held the key to the interior. Rhodes quickly scented the potential danger. "Is this House," he asked the Cape Parliament, "to allow these petty republics to form a wall across our trade route?" His "Suez Canal" had been blocked; the future of the Colony was imperilled; and, as a lesser but immediate inconvenience, the native mine-workers from Kimberley were being stopped and robbed as they passed through Stellaland and Goshen on their way to and from their homes in the North. Either the anarchy and disorder would continue and communications be virtually cut, or the republics, establishing some sort of order, would become satellites of the Transvaal (if they were not annexed to it) and might well end or at least impede trade with the South by a thirty per cent tariff, such as the Transvaal had already imposed on goods from the Cape. Yet while the Imperial Government was unwilling to allow the Transvaal to intervene, it would not itself move.

In 1882 Rhodes, after warning the Cape Parliament of the danger of drift, secured for himself a place on a commission which was investigating a dispute about the boundaries of Griqualand West. Exceeding the terms of his appointment, he went on to Vryburg, where he met van Niekerk. He found that already the Transvaal had a design to annex Stellaland, but he believed that the settlers, although opposed to being taken over by the Imperial Government, had no objection to joining Cape Colony. Mankoroane, one of the chiefs who had been dispossessed of his land, gave him a long list of all his grievances and offered to cede what was left of his country.

With this information Rhodes returned to Cape Town, where he tried without success to prod the Prime Minister, Scanlen, into action. "Part with the interior road," he said, "and you are driven into the desert." On the strength of Mankoroane's request and in accordance with the alleged wishes of the settlers, he wanted Scanlen to annex Stellaland at once. "For goodness' sake," Rhodes begged him, "meet Parliament with *some* policy. . . . I put it to you, if you have to go out, is it not better to go out on what is a real policy?" But, as he remarked bitterly, "the mists of Table Mountain covered all". Scanlen would do nothing to jeopardise further his shaky position. He depended on the votes of the Bond, and Hofmeyr thought that if the Imperial Government did not want Stellaland, the Transvaal, which did want it, should be allowed to have it.

In fact Rhodes found few to support him in the Cape Parliament. Even Merriman, who was in general agreement with him, flitted from one impracticable idea to another. "I do not agree with you as to your plan of a chartered company for this district," Rhodes wrote in October 1885. "It is a poor country and no company could cope with the intrigues of the Transvaal. It must either remain under the Imperial Protectorate or else be annexed to the Cape Colony. Any other plan will simply hand the interior over to the Transvaal." Fortunately, outside Parliament, he had an ally of weight in the High Commissioner, then in the prime of his powers. Sir Hercules Robinson never allowed the "mists of Table Mountain" to obscure his vision. Seeing and realising both the danger and the possibilities, he began to rely more and more on Rhodes.

The second circumstance, however, was what decided the question. Germany, for long indifferent to schemes for expansion overseas, suddenly turned her attention to Africa. For years a colonial party had been vainly striving to awaken the interest of the German Government. After 1870 missionaries, explorers and merchants began to add their efforts; the popular imagination was stirred by suggestions that Germany might win an African empire of her own; and in 1882 Bismarck decided that the time was ripe to change his policy. If there was to be a scramble for Africa—and one looked like beginning—Germany should be in it. The British were busy in the East and South, the French in the North, but some unclaimed territory still remained. To the West of Bechuanaland, itself a No Man's Land, lay Damaraland and Namaqualand, stretching from the Orange River to Portuguese Angola, still unexplored and unappropriated. There, in a climate suitable for white settlement, could be the beginning of a colonial empire. The moment seemed propitious, with Gladstone, his face set against more annexations or protectorates, in power in London. Earlier Sir Hercules Robinson and the Cape Government had urged annexation on Whitehall, and in 1878 Lord Carnarvon had reluctantly taken over Walfisch Bay, which contained the only good harbour on the West coast. That was as

(b) C. J. R. in his forties

(a) C. J. R. as an undergraduate aged about twenty-four

C. J. R. having "a chop on the *veld*" (with Grimmer and his servant, Tony)

far as Whitehall would go until, on 1 May 1883, official circles in London were thrown into consternation by the news that the German flag had been hoisted at Angra Pequena on the coast of Namaqualand.

This action changed everything. Not long before Bismarck had been so far from thoughts of annexation that he had asked whether, in the event of a German merchant setting up a factory in Namaqualand, the British would protect it. He had added an assurance that he "had not the least design to establish any footing in South Africa". For some months he got no answer, and when at last it came, it was so vague and unsatisfactory that Her Majesty's Government had to admit the Germans must protect themselves. Subsequently the Cape formally claimed the country, but it was too late. Once the German flag was flying, prestige was involved. Bismarck would suffer no interference, and a ship from the Cape was warned off the new port by a German gunboat.

In London the German intervention ended the period of insouciance. The Government had changed again and Lord Derby, now at the Colonial Office, sent urgent messages to the Cape, seeking arguments to rebut the new German claim that no other country had shown any interest in South-west Africa. This time it was the Cape which was careless. Scanlen was too busy with his own precarious Parliamentary position to produce, as he might have done, the evidence that in the days of Sir Bartle Frere some sort of administration of Namaqualand had been attempted. Even Rhodes allowed himself to be silenced; he had just become Treasurer-General in the Ministry, a post which he held for only a few weeks, not even long enough to produce a budget, before Scanlen was forced to resign. Rhodes and Merriman used to say to each other, "We must have Damaraland," . . . but the rest of the Cabinet were uninterested.

On 24 April 1884 Bismarck proclaimed a German protectorate over Damaraland and Namaqualand and Upington, who had succeeded Scanlen, made a belated protest. The flag was flying, the deed was done: a land which Britain had never professed to want was not worth the risk of endangering Anglo-German friendship. Two months later the Foreign Secretary, Lord Granville, recognised the German Protectorate. Walfisch Bay, for what it was worth, remained in British hands, but the rest of the coast and potentially the whole of the interior had passed to the Germans.

Would they stop there? Namaqualand and Damaraland might

D

have little value; but to the east of them lay Bechuanaland, as yet the property of nobody but the tribes and two republics of doubtful stability and friendship; and to their north was the unknown interior. Rhodes soon found his tongue again.[2]

"Do you think," he asked, "that if the Transvaal had Bechuanaland, it would be allowed to keep it? Would not Bismarck have some quarrel with the Transvaal, and without resources, without men, what could they do? Germany would come across from her settlement at Angra Pequena. There would be some excuse to pick a quarrel—some question of brandy or guns or something—and then Germany would stretch from Angra Pequena to Delagoa Bay. I was never more satisfied with my own views than when I saw the recent development of the policy of Germany."

The fêting in Berlin of a Transvaal delegation then visiting Europe added force to Rhodes's words. "Don't part with an inch of territory to the Transvaal," he adjured Upington. But it was not so much of the Transvaal that he was thinking: it was of Germany.

So the future of Bechuanaland, and in particular of the two little republics of Stellaland and Goshen, had taken on a new importance. If the Germans were to be kept out of Central Africa and the Cape's road to the North was to remain open, Bechuanaland must be secured. When the delegation from the Transvaal reached London with a request for a rectification of the border which would bring Stellaland and Goshen under the control of the Republic, they found a new atmosphere. Gladstone had gone, and his successor, though not a Beaconsfield, took a different view of Africa. The missionaries had also been at work, denouncing the Boer treatment of the natives in their territories and winning the support of bodies like the Aborigines Protection Society and of a number of influential people. Prominent among the missionaries was the Rev. John Mackenzie, a tactless enthusiast, who had worked with zeal and sympathy for twenty years among the natives of South Africa, had won their confidence and, by speaking fearlessly in their defence, had brought on himself the hatred of the entire Dutch population.

Sir Hercules Robinson, who had come home to advise the Colonial Office, argued strongly against conceding the request of the Transvaal. The High Commissioner, the missionaries, the Aborigines Protection Society, and Rhodes and Merriman made an incongruous but formidable combination, which the Government could scarcely ignore. At last it made up its mind, with a decision to put Stellaland, Goshen and the Missionaries' Road outside the frontiers of the Transvaal; while at the same time, with a promise from the Cape to contribute to the expense, it accepted in principle the idea of declaring a protectorate over Bechuanaland.

So far so good, but Whitehall moved with agonising deliberation. Before making a formal declaration, it wanted more information. Graham Bower was sent up to Stellaland, and returned with a favourable report on the conduct of the settlers. The Government's next step was to appoint the Rev. John Mackenzie as Deputy Commissioner—in a country not yet under its protection. The choice was unfortunate, for Mackenzie had made up his mind before he started. The Boer settlers, being in his eyes robbers of the land and oppressors of the African, must be driven out with a strong hand. With so many Dutch in its borders, Cape Colony could not be trusted to administer the country properly, and Westminster must take charge. His feelings towards Rhodes are indicated by his description of him as "an inexperienced store-keeper at Kimberley".

Mackenzie began his mission by quarrelling with the settlers in both republics, and went on, without any authority, to hoist the British flag, thereby practically proclaiming annexation. He then demanded a force of police to support his action and, while he was waiting for them, consorted with some of the worst of Mankoroane's trouble-makers. He seemed, Rhodes declared, to be working for "a split upon race lines"—a development to be avoided at all costs.

Rhodes had his chance when the Cape Parliament having refused to make the contribution required by the Imperial Government, Upington introduced a Bill to annex Bechuanaland to the Cape. Hofmeyr, who was supporting the claims of the Transvaal, disliked it. To him and his followers Rhodes pointed out that the two republics blocked the way to the interior, which would have a vast importance to the future of South Africa. But would it not be folly, he asked, to hand over the road and the North to a State which had lately imposed a high tariff against the Cape? As to Mackenzie, he had shown only too well that, while he loved the natives, he had no sympathy with the white settlers. The Bill was the right solution. "If the Cape do not act, the Imperial Government would interfere," and a second Majuba might be the result. "We must not," he concluded, "have the Imperial factor in Bechuanaland." He must have realised that his solution was favoured by none of the parties directly concerned. The settlers would probably have preferred joining the Transvaal, from which most of them had come. Mackenzie and the natives themselves, disliking the Transvaal, wanted Whitehall to take over. There was, however, or seemed to be, a good prospect that both parties would accept annexation by the Cape, because each preferred this to the plan favoured by the other.

While Rhodes's denunciation of the "Imperial factor" pleased Hofmeyr and his followers and softened their opposition to the Bill, it annoyed the press at home. In the light of later events it seems odd that Rhodes should have made his first appearance before the British public under a suspicion of disloyalty to the Mother Country. Rhodes was anxious to refute the imputation. "Do not", he wrote to Lord Harris, "be led away by the assumption that I am pro-Dutch in my sympathies. I had to consider the best mode of checking the expansion of the Boer Republic— the interior. The only method I can [do] so is to enclose them by the Cape Colony."

Something had to be done quickly about Bechuanaland, where Mackenzie was causing such a commotion. Both the Transvaal and the Cape Government declared him a danger to peace, and finally Sir Hercules Robinson recalled him, appointing in his place as Deputy Commissioner Rhodes himself.

Later in an election speech, Rhodes gave his version of the interview which ended in his appointment.[3]

"The Governor said: 'Oh, you can go up, but I can give you no force to back you up. You must use your own judgment.'

"I replied, 'Will you allow me to do what I like?'

" 'Yes,' said the Governor, 'but if you make a mess of it, I shan't back you.'

"I said, 'That is good enough for me.' "

Some of Rhodes's friends reproached him with rashness, because although the country swarmed with lawless and homicidal characters, he went there practically unattended, having with him one servant only, a coloured man. His first visit was to Stellaland, where he called upon van Niekerk and his lieutenant, Groot Afrian de la Rey, a giant noted for his violence. Rhodes described the meeting thus:

"When I spoke to de la Rey, his answer was, 'Blood must flow', to which I remember making the retort: 'No, give me my breakfast, and then we can talk about blood.' Well, I stayed with him a week. I became godfather to his grandchild and we made a settlement."

The farmers agreed to recognise a British protectorate, provided van Niekerk was left as administrator, the land titles were confirmed, and Mackenzie's recent proceedings were cancelled. In due course the agreement was accepted by the High Commissioner and confirmed by the Home Government.

The Land of Goshen, to which Rhodes went next, was less organised and orderly. Van Pittius was sulky and rude. He had brought in more filibusters from the Transvaal and in Rhodes's presence launched an attack on Montsioa, in Mafeking, where Bethell, a Briton who was fighting against the invaders, was killed in cold blood. Rhodes was powerless to intervene. With a warning to the filibusters that they were making war on the British Government he returned to Stellaland. There he learnt that van Pittius had forced Montsioa to cede most of his land and that General Joubert, the Transvaal border commissioner, had confirmed the treaty; while a few weeks later Kruger broke the London Convention by proclaiming a protectorate over Montsioa's territory "in the interests of humanity".

This was too much for the "Imperial factor", which Rhodes had hoped, vainly as he now saw, to eliminate from Bechuanaland. Lord Derby, the Colonial Secretary, told Sir Hercules that Kruger must withdraw the proclamation, which he did. As Upington was still haggling with the Bond and the Home Government over the terms of annexation, Rhodes feared that unless immediate and resolute action were taken, Bechuanaland would be lost. On his advice troops were sent out from England and Sir Charles Warren was given the command. Meanwhile, however, Upington, probably with the object of asserting the claims of Cape Colony, himself went to Goshen with his Treasurer, Sprigg, to try to make an agreement with van Pittius. He got his agreement, but on terms so unfavourable and humiliating that Robinson at once repudiated it, with the enthusiastic support of the people of Cape Town, some of whom burnt their too-complacent ministers in effigy.

In January 1885, Warren, as Special Commissioner, arrived with 4,000 troops. He confirmed Rhodes's agreement with van

Niekerk (although afterwards he tried to repudiate it) and went
up to Bechuanaland. There Rhodes joined him in "a big slouch
hat, the shabbiest and most ragged of coats, and a very dirty pair
of white flannel trousers, with old tennis shoes as his footgear".
He was very grumpy and, when asked his name and business,
merely grunted, "Rhodes!" Warren, who was an irascible
officer, can hardly have been pleased by his dress and demeanour.

Nor was Rhodes for his part favourably impressed by the
arrival of Mackenzie, whom the High Commissioner, aware of
the dislike felt by the Dutch for the missionary, had warned
Warren on no account to have with him. A meeting had been
arranged with Kruger at Fourteen Streams on the Vaal. Warren
sent an advance party of 200 dragoons. Since Kruger had as
escort a handful of artillerymen, the contrast did not sweeten
the proceedings. At Fourteen Streams two men, who were to
cross each other's paths so frequently and fatally, had their first
meeting. Kruger was then sixty. "I have learnt one thing,"
he once observed grimly, "to distinguish friends from foes."
He certainly seems to have discerned in Rhodes a potentially
dangerous adversary. "That young man will cause me trouble,"
he is said to have remarked, "if he does not leave politics
alone and turn to something else. Well, the race-horse is swifter
than the ox, but the ox can draw the greater loads. We shall
see."

Actually, with Warren present and dominating the discussion
on the British side, Rhodes did little beyond listen and talk about
cattle-raids and land-titles and complain of Joubert's conduct at
Rooigrond. According to John Mackenzie, as Joubert was a
rival for the Presidency of the Republic, Kruger was not displeased by Rhodes's criticisms. Impressed as much perhaps by
the evidence of Britain's determination as by the penniless state
of his treasury, Kruger gave way.

One of the claimants to Bechuanaland having retired, the real
division was then between Warren and Mackenzie on one side
and Rhodes and the Cape Government on the other. Rhodes
wanted to placate the settlers in Stellaland and Goshen, so that
with their assent, and with the Transvaal not competing, the
Bond would agree to the annexation of the republics by the Cape,
leaving the Imperial Government to exercise some sort of protectorate over the northern part of Bechuanaland. But the
Imperial factor, once summoned, was not to be dismissed so
cursorily. Warren, with Mackenzie at his elbow, did not want

the Cape Colony in at all and thought the whole country should be annexed. He ignored Rhodes's advice and even his presence, disowned the settlement Rhodes had made with Kruger's Attorney-General about compensation for cattle-thefts, and repudiated the agreement with van Niekerk about Stellaland and the land titles there. He next arrested van Niekerk on a charge of murder, of which he was later acquitted. This was too much for Rhodes, who resigned his office as Deputy Commissioner and left the country.

Warren, after cabling to the High Commissioner that Rhodes's presence was "prejudicial to peace", proclaimed martial law throughout Bechuanaland and descended upon the Land of Goshen, from which van Pittius and his volunteers had fled. Then, still accompanied by Mackenzie, and inflated with a sense of the importance of his Imperial mission, he made a martial progress through the country, in the course of which he managed to embroil Khama, chief of the powerful Bamangwato tribe, with his nearest neighbour, Lobengula, King of the Matabele, by accepting from the former a concession of land which belonged to the latter. Finally he rounded off his blunders by ordaining, to the fury of the Dutch throughout South Africa, that only settlers of pure British origin were to be allowed to enter Bechuanaland. By this time he seems to have alarmed and offended nearly everybody, including the High Commissioner and the Cape Ministry; and the Home Government, at last alive to the consequences of his arbitrary conduct and scared by his grandiose schemes for establishing a Crown Colony in Central Africa, recalled him, albeit with kind words.

But the harm was done. The Road was safe, but only at the price of admitting the Imperial factor. To that extent Rhodes had failed for the moment. The Dutch refused to have anything to do with Warren's arrangement, which appeared to confirm all their suspicions of British perfidy, and the Bond would not hear of the Cape Colony making any contribution towards the Imperial Government's expenses. Yet Warren, despite his mistakes, had made a settlement of a kind. Both Germany and the Transvaal had been warned off the country: a Crown Colony had been established in the south to cover both the freebooting republics and the adjacent tribal territory; and North Bechuanaland had become a British Protectorate.

In the Cape Parliament that June Rhodes tried to sum up Warren's performance.[4]

"I remember," he said, "when a youngster reading in my English history of the supremacy of my country and its annexations and that there were two cardinal axioms—that the word of the nation, when once pledged, was never broken, and that when a man accepted the citizenship of the British Empire, there was no distinction between races. It has been my misfortune in one year to meet with the breach of the one and the proposed breach of the other."

Yet there is rather more to be said for Warren's handling of the affair than Rhodes and later his biographers have been ready to allow. Admittedly he was a "political" soldier, who stood for Parliament as a Liberal as soon as he got home. While Rhodes was always inclined to make the best arrangement he could for the future without troubling himself too much about irregularities in the past, Warren approached his task with a soldier's unreadiness to compromise with what he regarded as very nearly a rebellion. The two men differed about Bechuanaland, as they had differed about Predestination: their perspectives and values were too widely apart.

Rhodes carried the argument into the columns of *The Times*. His letter, which covered four pages of small type, was surely one of the longest that any newspaper can ever have accepted for publication. He wrote it in the bedroom of the hotel in Chester where he was staying with Ralph Williams. The latter describes how, when he had finished dictating, Rhodes, leaning against the mantelpiece, with his hair ruffled and his coat flung on the floor, asked Williams to read the letter through to him. "Now I am going to be Warren," he said, "and am going to cut your arguments to pieces"; as he did. Afterwards Williams put the case for Rhodes in his book *The British Lion in Bechuanaland*; while Warren has been defended by his biographer, Watkin Williams. Out of much conflicting evidence and many contradictory statements judgment on balance supports the claims of Rhodes.

But despite his forebodings, the solution did not work badly. The settlers accepted the decision and Sir Sidney Shippard, the first Resident Commissioner of the Protectorate, was a jealous guardian of the tribes in his charge. Ten years later, on Rhodes's initiative, the Crown handed over the Colony to the Cape—a consummation only possible through Rhodes's influence with the Bond, which had not forgotten his earlier resistance to Warren. By then his interest had shifted farther north, where a situation was developing not entirely different from that in Bechuanaland.

Sources

Works mentioned under Chapter Five and additionally:
Agar-Hamilton, J. A. L.: *The Road to the North*
Colvin, Ian: *The Life of Jameson*
Mackenzie, John: *Austral Africa*
Williams, Ralph: *The British Lion in Bechuanaland*
Williams, Watkin: *The Life of Charles Warren*

Notes

[1] Colvin, I. 83–8 (Quoted by permission of Edward Arnold (Publishers) Ltd.)

[2] "Vindex", 114–15.

[3] "Vindex", 98–9.

[4] "Vindex", 126.

CHAPTER SEVEN

AMALGAMATION

BASUTOLAND and Bechuanaland went far to convince Rhodes that he could not rely either on the Imperial Factor or on the Cape Government. The first was remote, subject to the vicissitudes of politics, over-sensitive to the fitful breezes of public opinion. The second was too small and parochial to take large views or to pursue adventurous policies successfully. Nevertheless Rhodes recognised that both Westminster and Cape Town, properly directed, would be indispensable to the great purposes he had in mind: Westminster because behind it were the might and prestige of the British Empire, and Cape Town because, being nearer, it was as a rule better informed.

Rhodes and Merriman once discussed half-seriously a plan for giving up their seats in the Cape Parliament, entering the House of Commons at Westminster, and forming a "Colonial Party", which, they thought, would provide a knowledge and direction so far lacking in London. Momentarily they may have been attracted by the idea. They were both young men, often exasperated by the slowness and obtuseness of their elders, and in open rebellion against the futilities of Sprigg and Upington. Of another Cape Minister, Rhodes wrote to Merriman in 1883 that he was "sick of that old woman".[1] In the same year he lamented, "Politics to me are perfectly hopeless. I shall stand again and believe I shall be returned, but I have not much heart in the matter."[2] In Westminster at any rate they would be sharpening their wits against some of the best brains in the British Empire. However, they soon rejected a thought which they had never entertained seriously. Both men knew that their future was in South Africa, where Rhodes had still to make the fortune needed for his plans, and Merriman the brilliant career he would never quite achieve. But it was clear to Rhodes that in future he must rely mainly on himself. He must make a great deal of money, and make it quickly, for recurring heart attacks were warning him that his time would probably be short. Never a patient man, his impatience increased as he realised how much there was to do and how short was the span of life he was likely to be allowed. "The great fault in life is its shortness," he was remembered as saying. "Just as one is beginning to know the game, one has to stop." It was a thought on which Marcus Aurelius, too, had often brooded.

This acute sense of the vastness of his task and the probable shortness of his life explains, if it does not always justify, Rhodes's readiness to take short cuts, the ruthlessness with which he overrode obstructions, human or otherwise, and his occasional carelessness of the means he employed to win the ends he judged essential and urgent. In those years grew up the legend of a hard, unscrupulous man, who would make money by any means and crush opposition with a high hand. The legend was a half-truth, more deadly than a downright falsehood. Rhodes could be and often was hard, unscrupulous and overbearing, when he believed that for his purposes he had to be; but for every just grievance his critics may cite, there are twenty tales of kindness and generosity. Money meant little to him apart from the capacity it gave him to carry out his schemes. What he had he gave away recklessly, sometimes, it is true, to someone whose services he wanted to enlist, but much more often just to anyone who was hard up. When he lent, he never expected to be repaid. "You occupy almost a unique position," he wrote to someone to whom he had advanced some money.[3] "I have lent in my life many sums amounting to a great deal to my friends. You are one of the few who have ever returned a loan." "Look what's happened!" he once exclaimed in surprise:[4] "This bloody fool's paid me back!"

In spite of the rough, cynical way in which he spoke, he was probably quite touched, not by the return of a sum of money he did not need, but by the honesty of the sender. Possessions in themselves counted for little with him—neither his own nor other people's. If someone required something, and he or a friend had it and had no immediate need of it, the obvious course was to make the transfer; and later in life he would embarrass a succession of secretaries by the readiness with which he would present their shirts to stray shiftless callers.

* * *

Bechuanaland had been a necessary but tiresome interlude, necessary because the road to the North had to be kept open, tiresome because it distracted Rhodes from what he was trying to do at Kimberley, where the day of the small digger was passing fast. Even by 1878 more than a quarter of the surface claims had been covered by fallen reef. The Mining Board, which had replaced the Diggers' Committee in 1874, was at the end of its resources and practically bankrupt. By 1885, in the four chief mines—Kimberley, De Beers, Dutoitspan and Bultfontein—only 56 private holdings survived. The remaining claims were held by 42 companies, like De Beers or Barnato's Kimberley Central Diamond Mining Company. Even so, the operations of 98 independent proprietors over an area of no more than 70 acres became more and more difficult. Millions of tons of reef fell; shafts had to be sunk to the buried claims; pumping was a perpetual necessity. As the claim-holders encroached upon and burrowed under the territory of their rivals, disputes about boundaries multiplied and in the circumstances were almost insoluble. The cost of mining grew, while the supply of diamonds, being totally unregulated, fluctuated wildly; and with it the price.

As Rhodes saw clearly, the only solution was an amalgamation, which would at the same time enable diamonds to be mined more economically and control supply and price. This was no new idea. In 1880, after the fall of Scanlen's government, Merriman had gone up to Kimberley to explore the possibilities of amalgamation, but the resources at his command were inadequate for the project. The De Beers Mining Company, of which Rhodes was first Secretary and then Chairman, was in a slightly stronger position, though always short of money. Rhodes's aim was to make his company the sole proprietor of what he called that "nice little mine", and from that starting-point to attempt amalgamation. The greatest stumbling-block would obviously be the Kimberley Central Mine, where Barney Barnato had been building up a commanding position for himself. Kimberley Central was better than De Beers (although Rhodes would never admit as much), and Barnato was a richer man than his rival. By 1885, when Rhodes told a friend he was making about £50,000 a year, Barnato's income was nearer £200,000. Yet somehow, if amalgamation was to come about, Barnato must be "squared" or squeezed out. Barnato had no intention of being squeezed out and no desire to be "squared". He was perfectly confident of the capacity of Kimberley Central, with its larger output, to meet any competition from De Beers; and he was equally sure that in an amalgamation he would be swallowed up and Rhodes would do the swallowing.

By 1887 Rhodes had reached his first objective: his company had become the sole owner of the De Beers mine. But although

De Beers was able to halve the cost of production per carat and to pay bigger dividends on the enlarged capital, Barnato met every move with one of his own; and as his was the richer mine, neither the competition nor the over-production greatly troubled him. In his view he was bound to win. Either Kimberley would undercut De Beers out of the diamond market altogether, or he would compel Rhodes to come to a working agreement to limit costs.

Rhodes once estimated the demand for diamonds at four million pounds a year. Every engaged young man, he assumed, would want diamonds for the lady he was going to marry. If the stones were cheap he would buy more, if expensive, fewer, but the total expenditure would always be in the neighbourhood of four million pounds. This was a very rough reckoning, but implied, as was probably true, that however cheap diamonds might become, the amount spent on them would not vary greatly from year to year. Obviously, therefore, over-production and a cut-throat competition might be welcomed by the young men, but would be far from helpful to the producers.

Rhodes, as was his habit, began by trying to persuade Barnato to join him in amalgamating the Diamond Mines, and during the years that followed renewed his proposals from time to time. Barnato would not listen to them. Why should he? It was better to be the biggest man in Kimberley Central than second in command to Rhodes in some huge corporation. As it was, his position was immensely strong and he was his own master. He would be a fool to imperil what he had won for the sake of an advantage which he was sure would be his anyhow if he waited.

Whatever the outcome might be, in May 1887 the two chief antagonists, Rhodes and Barnato, were facing each other on a stage set for battle. Kimberley, which watched the preliminary moves in the contest with a fascinated interest, at first favoured Barnato's chances of victory. But certainly Rhodes was the more impressive figure.

His interests already ranged far beyond Kimberley. He had had an education in the humanities at Oxford; he sat in the Cape Parliament; he had been in the public eye over the Bechuanaland business; the British Conservatives had even asked him to be their candidate for one of the Bristol seats; he was a member of the Kimberley Club, which had shut its doors on Barnato; and probably, from years of study, Rhodes had a better technical knowledge of diamonds than had the other. If his moodiness or

moroseness in any company he did not fancy, his bursts of
boisterous falsetto laughter over something that was not really
funny, his inability to mix freely with people had made him
enemies, he had many firm friends; and even his foes respected
him. They knew him to be straight in his dealings and to have
ideas beyond mere money-making. They liked his boyish enthusiasm and occasional acts of uncalculating generosity. In
1887, when he was in London, W. T. Stead had just been tried
and sentenced for his courageous book on a social scandal, *The
Maiden Tribute to Modern Babylon.* "Here is the man I want," exclaimed Rhodes. He tried to visit Stead in Holloway Gaol and,
when refused admission, went on to Exeter Hall to join in a
public protest against the sentence. Stead never forgot what he
had done, and men in remote Kimberley, who may have had no
great fondness either for Stead or for Exeter Hall, gave Rhodes
credit for his gesture.

As for Barnato, he was so gay and good-humoured that people
could hardly help liking him; but no one respected him. He was
a mountebank, round whom clung a number of probably false
but distinctly unsavoury stories of I.D.B. and double dealing.
While his mind worked with extraordinary speed, he lacked
stability; he was quicksilver where Rhodes was solid rock. While
Rhodes read and pondered, Barnato trusted to his flair and
gambled.

In the competition over production, which was the first round,
Rhodes was clearly getting the worst of it. In the second round,
which began in May 1887, he attacked Barnato's only vulnerable
spot, the ownership of the Kimberley Mine. While Barnato's
Company held a preponderance of the claims in it, two substantial blocks were outside his control. These belonged to
W. A. Hall & Company and the much larger *Compagnie française
des diamonds du Cap*, colloquially known as the French Company.
Rhodes first tried to buy W. A. Hall's shares, but was outbid by
Sir Donald Currie, the shipowner, who also had thoughts of
amalgamation and secured the shares for £110,000. Rhodes
then told two of his friends to join the ship in which Sir Donald
was travelling to England and to try to persuade him to part with
the shares. Sir Donald was tempted by the offer, but when the
ship called at Lisbon and he discovered the quoted market price
of his shares, he found this was higher than Rhodes's offer.
"You young thieves," he exclaimed irascibly to the two gentlemen, "had I listened to you, I should have sold at a loss." The

"young thieves", however, cabled Currie's decision to Kimberley, where Rhodes promptly beared the market to such effect that by the time the ship reached Plymouth, the shares were not even worth what Rhodes had offered for them. Currie threw in his hand, though he refused to have any further dealings with Rhodes.

Frustrated over W. A. Hall's claims, Rhodes turned his attention to the more important French Company. By now he had realised that if he was to bring about amalgamation, he would need staunch allies and plenty of money. Of his allies the most dependable was Alfred Beit, "little Alfred", who had fallen under the spell and had begun to share Rhodes's political opinions. Beit's financial genius was invaluable to Rhodes. He knew, better than Rhodes, the market value of anything. He had not only a flair for figures, but a knowledge of diamonds unrivalled in Kimberley. When once he had handled a stone, he never forgot it. On one occasion, when a man tried to sell him some stolen diamonds, Beit recognised them at once as having passed through his hands some seven years earlier. Lionel Phillips, who was to be closely associated with both men, declared that "Rhodes could never have achieved what he did at Kimberley nor in Rhodesia without Beit". Of the two men Beit was a much more patient negotiator. He used afterwards to say that he could have carried through the amalgamation for about half the amount it cost Rhodes.

Beit was a man of irreproachable probity. Barnato told Rothschild that if he, Barnato, had had Beit's reputation for honesty, he could have made "millions". Beit walked through Kimberley so modestly and unobtrusively that except for a few intimates like Rhodes, no one really knew him. He was extraordinarily generous and, sensitive himself, in making a gift to a man was absurdly careful not to wound his self-esteem. The world was unaware of his true character and, while he lived, did him a good deal less than justice. When he died in 1906, Sir Percy Fitzpatrick, who had known him well in South Africa, went to his funeral at Tewin Water, where he found himself walking beside W. T. Stead.

"Fitzpatrick," said Stead, "you knew him well. There was something Christ-like about Alfred Beit."

Fitzpatrick replied that he had often thought as much, but had flinched from saying it for fear of exciting the derision of those who did not know him.

Stead answered: "Why be afraid to say it? *You* knew him, *they* did not."

Beit brought to Rhodes more than his friendship and his brains. By his association with the powerful firm of Jules Porges & Co. of Paris, he controlled a great deal of capital, which in the cause of Amalgamation he was prepared to place at Rhodes's disposal.

Another ally of a very different kind was F. S. Philipson Stow, a rather mysterious figure, whose part has hardly been touched upon by Rhodes's biographers, although the largeness of it cannot be in doubt. Many years later, when he was back in England, Philipson Stow wrote an account of the Amalgamation. He never finished or published it, but the manuscript of it, which he left to his son, gave what is probably the best contemporary record of the early stages of the battle and was freely drawn upon by Chilvers in his *Story of De Beers*.

Philipson Stow was a lawyer, whose intimacy with Rhodes began in 1881. He was keenly interested in Amalgamation, and as he was a close friend of Francis Baring-Gould, the Chairman of Kimberley Central, he may be said to have provided a listening post in the other camp. Rhodes brought him an elaborate scheme for amalgamation—"folio after folio of intricate figures"— which the lawyer considered added up to something quite impracticable. His task was then to supply something better.

A third man, whose share in the battle for Amalgamation should not be ignored, was not an ally but a bitter enemy. He was J. B. Robinson, "the Buccaneer", as he came to be called, who in 1880 had managed to filch one of the Kimberley seats from Rhodes. He hated Rhodes for his success (which rivalled his own, he thought), for his influence, and for daring to have ideas beyond the mere making of money. From the start to the finish of Rhodes's career, the moment Robinson discovered that Rhodes wanted to do something, he made it his business to try and thwart him. Although a mean and miserly man, who would never, if he could help it, part with a penny to a deserving cause, he would spend money like water in pursuing his vendetta.

In a sense the enmity of a man like J. B. Robinson was a compliment. He had come to the Diamond Fields in the early days. Kimberley's stomach was far from squeamish, but the business methods of "the Buccaneer" were too much for it. Men might distrust Barnato, but at least they laughed at him and drank with him. Men distrusted Robinson, but neither laughed at nor drank

with him. Quarrelsome, vindictive, litigious and insanely ambitious, so far as is known no generous word or act is recorded
to his credit.

When he was an old man and a baronet, Lloyd George was
induced to suggest that a peerage should be bestowed on him.
Such was Robinson's inflated opinion of himself that he thought
the honour entirely appropriate; but the uproar when the news
reached South Africa was reflected in a more discreet hubbub in
London. It transpired that not very long before the Courts had
condemned Robinson to pay more than half a million pounds
because in the purchase and re-sale of his Randfontein interests he
had made "large and illicit profits for himself". The House of
Lords, already scandalised by this revelation, protested even more
vehemently when Lord Selborne, a former High Commissioner
in South Africa and a highly respected peer, disclosed that
Robinson's "sympathies had never been with this country"; in
other words, as everyone in South Africa knew, that he had been
an active supporter of Krugerism.

Such was the reaction of their lordships that Robinson could
only ask the Prime Minister for leave to refuse the offer of a
peerage. Characteristically, he then let it be known that "the
title did not cost me a single penny". As he never got the title,
the statement was probably true. Obituary notices are normally
kind and a little blind to defects, but when Robinson died in
1929, the *Cape Times*, under the heading of *Nil Nisi Malum*, spoke
of "the almost incredible malignity of his nature". "The loath-
someness of the thing that is the memory of Sir Joseph Robinson," the paper concluded, would "live in the records of South
Africa for all time".

Since Rhodes was for Amalgamation, Robinson naturally
worked hard against it. In the process he practically bankrupted
himself, being rescued from ruin by Alfred Beit, who hated to see
anyone, however hostile and unpleasant, go under. Probably
Robinson, being the man he was, resented Beit's generosity; and
when later it suited him to work as Beit's partner on the Rand,
where he found the fortune he had missed at Kimberley, he conceived a fresh grudge when Beit was proved right and he himself
wrong over an assessment of the comparative merits of the East
and West Rands.

Money being the sinews of war, Rhodes had to have it. The
obvious place in which to find it was the City of London, which
hitherto had held itself aloof from South African speculations.

While Barnato had contacts with the City, Rhodes as yet had none; but he had to make them. He consulted Beit, who had influential connections on the Continent. Beit managed to interest some French and German financiers, who formed a syndicate and offered £750,000 in exchange for a block of De Beers's shares. This was something, but not enough, the amount which Rhodes considered he would want being £1,400,000. There remained the City. Beit suggested a few names, which Rhodes rejected as being those of firms of insufficient standing. "I'd much sooner deal with the Rothschilds myself," remarked Beit, and Rhodes pounced on the name. The Rothschilds had the biggest financial house in Europe. In 1875 Lionel Rothschild had advanced four million pounds to enable Disraeli to buy the Khedive's shares in the Suez Canal. Some years later, when Nathaniel had succeeded Lionel, the firm had lent eight million pounds to the Egyptian Government. In all the world of finance no name stood higher than that of the Rothschilds, and Rhodes felt that if he could enlist their help, victory over Barnato was practically assured.

He made his first approach through an American engineer, who was working for him, Gardner Williams, a friend of another engineer, E. C. De Crano, who advised the Rothschilds on South African affairs. On Rhodes's instructions, Williams drew up a comprehensive report on the diamond industry and its prospects if Amalgamation went through, indicating that Rhodes would need financial help; and this report Gardner Williams sent to De Crano. The weeks went by and no answer came, till at last Rhodes, fuming with impatience, himself left for London, taking with him Gardner Williams, whom meanwhile he had made General Manager of De Beers.

Gardner Williams has left an account of the mission to London. The scheme for Amalgamation had reached Rothschild, and he was favourably impressed with it, as presently he was with Rhodes. At the close of the interview, Rothschild said: "Well, Mr. Rhodes, you go to Paris and see what you can do in reference to the purchase of the French Company's property, and in the meantime I shall see if I can raise the million pounds which you desire."

As Rhodes was leaving, Rothschild stopped De Crano. "You may tell Mr. Rhodes," he said, "that if he can buy the French Company, I think I can raise the million pounds sterling." These favourable replies, guarded though they were, from so exalted a financial power, were all that Rhodes wanted.

With a million behind him, he could now approach the French Company. A price was named and accepted, of £1,400,000, Rhodes intending to borrow £750,000 from Rothschild and to find the balance by issuing 50,000 De Beers shares to Beit's continental syndicate at a rate of £15 a share. So far all had gone well, but Rhodes had reckoned without Barnato, who, owning one-fifth of the shares in the French Company, had been kept informed of what Rhodes was doing and was well aware why he was doing it. When the proposal was put to the shareholders, Barnato countered with an offer of £1,700,000, which the directors of the French Company could not disregard. All that Rhodes could do was to hurry back to Kimberley, see Barnato, and try to persuade him to withdraw his offer. Barnato of course refused. Rhodes's proposal, he declared, was not fair. "It might be good enough for me," he said gravely, with his tongue no doubt wedged firmly in his cheek, "but what about all the other shareholders who are looking to me to get them a good price for their shares?"

Although Rhodes appeared to have been checkmated, one of his favourite axioms was, "If you cannot manage a thing one way, try another". He tried another. He told Barnato it would be a pity to waste any more money in cutting each other's throats. If Barnato wanted the French Company, he could have it. Rhodes would buy it at Barnato's price and then hand it over to him. He would not even ask for cash in payment, only for the equivalent of the price paid in Kimberley Central's recently issued new shares. Strangely enough, Barnato did not see the trap and walked straight into it. After all, he may have reckoned, he would still retain control of the mine, as the shares he was handing over amounted to only a fifth of the increased capital. But what Rhodes wanted was not the French Company, but a firm foothold in Kimberley Central, and this he would now get.

The second round, therefore, although it ended apparently in Barnato's favour, was really Rhodes's. After the business of the French Company had been completed, there was a lull, almost a deadlock. Barnato was ready for the next move and Rhodes was mustering his forces for a further attack. He was back at Kimberley, having left his power of attorney with Philipson Stow in London. The competition in production having started afresh, Rhodes's engineers reported to him that the Kimberley Mine was getting better and better and would soon be in an impregnable position.

Rhodes made one more attempt to "square" Barnato, but the latter, whose company was still in control of the Kimberley Mine and therefore able to produce diamonds more cheaply than ever, was obdurate. He could afford to be so because he was winning, or so he thought; and he was quite unmoved when Rhodes threatened to flood the market with diamonds. As he had more and better diamonds, and could sell them at a lower price without loss, he could ignore Rhodes's threats as he had ignored his blandishments. The only course remaining was to go on with the war.

At the end of February 1888 Rhodes summoned his allies to a meeting at Poole's Hotel, Cape Town, to plan the next step. This was to be a bid in the open market to buy sufficient shares in Kimberley Central to gain control of the company. The process would require a lot more money, probably two million pounds. From where was it to come? Once more Rhodes had recourse to Beit's counsel. "Oh," answered Beit airily, "we will get the money if only we can buy the shares." And get it somehow he did.

So began the strangest and most nerve-racking game of beggar-my-neighbour. Rhodes bought recklessly; Barnato followed suit; and at a time when the price of diamonds barely covered the cost of production, the shares of Kimberley Central soared to fantastic heights, rising in a few months from £14 to £49. The game was becoming ruinous, and the only question was whose nerve or resources would crack first. One circumstance, however, began to swing the advantage over to Rhodes. Beit and his friends, who were doing the buying for him, were staunch. What they got they held; though there is a story that once, when Beit went to his partner Wernher, a cautious man, to confess a wild bout of buying, Wernher replied: "Oh, that's all right. I found the firm was getting more Kimberley shares than I liked, so I have sold a lot at excellent prices." That was exceptional. Despite Wernher's misgivings, Beit and his associates bought between 22,000 and 23,000 shares, keeping all but a handful of them. Barnato's friends, on the other hand, were not so reliable. When the price rocketed to dizzy heights, they could not always resist the temptation to unload and take their profit, even although they knew they were selling to the enemy.

Meanwhile Rhodes and Barnato were still meeting and discussing their duel, Rhodes renewing his offers and Barnato refusing them. But the odds had begun to run strongly in favour of

De Beers. "I'll tell you what you will find out presently," said Rhodes half-seriously, "and that is that you'll be left alone in the Central Company." Sure enough a day came when Rhodes, having started with one fifth of the shares, could claim to have increased his holding to three-fifths. Barnato saw that he was beaten. In March 1888 he surrendered, accepting terms which gave Rhodes the control he wanted. He had no ill feeling, and Rhodes, to celebrate the occasion, invited him to luncheon behind those sacred doors of the Kimberley Club which he had never before been allowed to pass. "Well, you've had your whim," said Rhodes with consummate tact; "I should like to have mine, which you alone in Kimberley can satisfy. I have always wanted to see a bucketful of diamonds; will you produce one?" Barnato, delighted, poured all the loose diamonds he had into a bucket. Rhodes lifted them out by handfuls, letting the glittering stream flow back through his fingers. That was the naïve end to what had not been in all its phases a very pretty story.

* * *

For Rhodes, of course, amalgamation was by no means the end: it was only the beginning. First, he had to clear up the position in Kimberley, where a natural reaction set in after the excitements of the battle. As soon as Barnato had agreed to come to terms, Rhodes took Beit for a walk. For a while they were silent, Beit trotting along to keep up with the longer strides of his companion. Then Rhodes turned to him. "Tonight," he said, "they will talk it all over with their wives, and tomorrow they will sell like hell." He was right: they did; and in a few weeks the price of De Beers dropped from £45 to £34. The fall in the shares was of little consequence. What mattered more was the feeling that arose when it was realised that the "rationalisation" of the diamond industry and the resulting economies in production would throw many people out of work. When this truth dawned on Kimberley, Rhodes became for a time so unpopular that he had to have police protection. He and De Beers did what they could to help the victims, and for many of them later he would find employment and opportunities on the Rand or in the North. While some hardship was inevitable, its scale was much exaggerated; but although the actual decrease in the number of employees in Kimberley was not quite 200, Rhodes did not escape the resentment of the sufferers and their families.

In addition to the personal grievance, there was a vague, but

justifiable, feeling that Kimberley would never be the same again.
That sprawling ant-heap, in which thousands of men once
scrambled for diamonds, had nearly disappeared before Amalgamation. It went altogether when one vast corporation took control and everyone became its employee. No longer could a man
look forward to the adventure of finding a great diamond and
making his fortune. Most of the fun and colour of life left Kimberley, and with them went the "characters" of the early days, the
survivors of the soldiers, sailors, Fenians, Australian diggers,
younger sons and Jews who had thronged to the Fields in the
'seventies. Never again would the community be enlivened by
men like Champagne Charlie or Stafford Parker, the President of
the River Diggings, who performed his duties in a grey top hat
and frock coat. They were going anyhow; most of them had
already gone; but Amalgamation drew the dividing line between
the old and the new Kimberley. The new Kimberley soon became little more than an uninteresting mining town like fifty
others of its kind.

What was certain was that monopoly had arrived, with its
vices as well as its advantages. The new corporation went on to
acquire the two smaller, independent mines, Dutoitspan and
Bultfontein. With Barnato no longer in the field, they surrendered without much compunction, being encouraged to be
amenable by a big fall of reef. Subsequently, as other mines
appeared, like the Wesselton and Premier, they too were absorbed, so that at one time De Beers controlled ninety per cent
of the world's supply of diamonds. In this way, besides being able
to produce diamonds systematically and economically, De Beers
could adjust supply to demand and avoid the occasional over-
production which had been the bane of the industry in the past.

After Amalgamation a new Corporation had still to be formed,
and this presented fresh difficulties. Some of them came from
Barnato himself. One of his objections to Amalgamation had
always been that, although he might be an original director, he
could and very likely would be removed by the shareholders
when he stood for re-election. He now suggested and Rhodes
accepted the idea of constituting life governors, of whom Barnato
would be one; while the capital of the new De Beers Consolidated
Mines, as the Corporation was called, was fixed at the modest
figure of £100,000 in £5 shares, all of which, except twenty-five,
would be held by the life governors. These would be Rhodes,
Beit, Barnato and Philipson-Stow. (There could have been a fifth,

but none was appointed.) The City did not like the plan, but in the end reluctantly accepted it.

More serious trouble came from Philipson Stow, who could not abide Barnato. "The day that man comes on the Board," he wrote to Rhodes, "I go off; and there will be others with me." Rhodes had to exercise all his powers of persuasion before Philipson Stow would agree to be a colleague of Barnato's. ("Yes," Barnato remarked drily, when he heard that the hitch had been overcome, "I thought I must have been holding things up.") Philipson Stow had another grievance. He believed Rhodes had promised him that his friend Baring-Gould, who had been Chairman of Kimberley Central, would be a life governor. Rhodes for some reason refused to sanction the appointment and Philipson Stow never quite forgave him.

Gravest of all was Barnato's objection to the Trust Deed of the new Corporation. Rhodes intended—and made no secret of his intention—to use the resources of De Beers Consolidated to enter and open the North. Indeed this had been the motive behind all he had done. While Barnato had been thinking only of diamonds, Rhodes had never swerved from his grand design of bringing the British flag into Central Africa, of building a railway which would be the spinal cord of a continent, and of creating a great new Dominion. Barnato was not interested in high-falutin schemes of this sort. His business was business, not politics or Empire-building; and at luncheon after luncheon he argued obstinately against the enormous powers with which Rhodes wished to invest the new De Beers. In fact, some of the members of the Kimberley Club took exception to the frequent and flamboyant presence of Barnato and unearthed a rule which limited to once a month the number of times a member might bring in the same guest to luncheon. Rhodes riposted by proposing Barnato for membership, and no one dared to blackball him.

Rhodes went further. He meant to build Barnato up into a serious citizen. Not only must he be a member of the Kimberley Club: he must also be a member of the Cape Parliament. There was a vacancy for one of the Kimberley seats. With Rhodes's support, Barnato should have it. Merriman was furious at the contempt of the Cape Parliament which he thought the candidature implied, but Rhodes stood firm. "If he is good enough to be a co-director with me," he told the employees of De Beers, "he is good enough to represent us in Parliament."

The final meeting over the Trust Deed took place in Dr.

Jameson's cottage. Rhodes brought Beit, and Barnato his
nephew, Woolf Joel. After Barnato had put his view that the
Corporation's job was simply to dig for and market diamonds,
Rhodes appealed to him as a man of imagination not to limit the
future scope of the company. In the unknown North might lie
treasures far exceeding those of Kimberley, and the Company
would be committing a tragic error if it debarred itself from
touching them.

"Aren't those just dreams of the future?" put in Woolf Joel.
"Dreams don't pay dividends."

"No, my friend," replied Rhodes, "they're not dreams, they're
plans. There's a difference."

He produced the maps he had brought, and step by step took
his audience through territory after territory, through Bechuanaland, Matabeleland, Mashonaland, along the Zambesi, till he
reached the great lakes. He appeared to know all about these
lands which to the others were little more than names, who ruled
them and how, who would be friendly and who hostile, and what
wealth might be awaiting the prospector and miner. As was his
way, he blended skilfully and persuasively the ideal with the
material, making his appeal first to the one and then to the other.
To whom, he asked, should this vast area, with all its possibilities,
belong? To Germany, which was already stretching across
Africa to link her new settlements in Namaqualand with her other
new settlement in Tanganyika? To the Transvaal, an impover-
ished republic of backward farmers? Or to the British Empire?

Beit seems to have been much moved by the harangue, but
Barnato felt that he was being taken right out of his depth. The
argument went on and on as the hours slipped by. In the end
what moved Barnato was probably less what Rhodes had said
than the conviction and sincerity with which he said it; also
perhaps a thought of the genuine friendliness Rhodes had been
showing him. At 4 a.m., after the meeting had lasted eighteen
hours, Barnato, struggling with sleep, capitulated. "Some people
have a fancy for one thing, and some for another," he said. "You
have a fancy for making an empire. Well, I suppose I must give
it to you."

The Trust Deed certainly endowed the new Corporation with
the widest powers. It could carry on mining of every sort, build
railways, establish water supplies, act as bankers, annex and
govern a territory, raise an army and fight a war. Nothing like it
had been seen since the days of the East India Company. Kim-

berley Central had to call a meeting of shareholders to endorse the
Amalgamation. The great majority were of course in favour of
it, but an objecting minority carried their case to Court on the
grounds that under Kimberley Central's deed of association, it
could only unite with "a similar company"; and whatever the new
Corporation was, it was clearly to be something vastly different
from Kimberley Central. So the Court found; whereupon
Rhodes and Barnato promptly put Kimberley Central into volun-
tary liquidation. "If you cannot manage a thing one way, try
another," as Rhodes used to say.

It can hardly be denied that everyone except the stubborn in-
dividualists benefited from the Amalgamation: the shareholders
because with working expenses down to ten shillings a carat and
the price maintained at thirty shillings, the new Company was
able to declare large dividends for many years; the miners because they were well paid and cheaply housed in more attractive
surroundings; and the Government because it drew a steady
revenue from a single large company.

Rhodes, at the age of thirty-six, may be forgiven the triumphant
tone in which he addressed, on 31 March 1888 a special meeting
of De Beers shareholders.[5] He described the severe opposition
that he had had to overcome. The choice lay "between the ruin
of the diamond industry or the control of the Kimberley Mine".
Had he failed, "they (the shares in De Beers) would have been
below par". Then had come his tussle with Barnato, who
"fought me tooth and nail". Rhodes had won because his shareholders were staunch, whereas Barnato's were "selling out round
the corner". After going at some length into the reasons why
Dutoitspan and Bultfontein, in their own interests, should now
join De Beers, and giving a rosy forecast of the future of the
Corporation, he concluded by declaring that the Board's ambition
was "to make it the richest, the greatest and the most powerful
company the world has ever seen".

It was a long speech, of nine thousand words, delivered without
a note, and it so enraptured the shareholders that, after passing a
vote of thanks to the Board, Mr. Robinson proposed payment of
a gratuity of ten thousand guineas to the Chairman and of five
thousand to each of the Directors. Rhodes refused this handsome
offer. "I don't care for any of these bonuses," he said, "and I
don't think my co-directors do. . . . My pleasure has been in
beating them all round." He went on to pay a special tribute to
Beit, who had advanced £250,000 out of his own pocket, without

asking either commission or interest. It is to be observed that although Rhodes gave all the appearance of speaking with the utmost candour, he evidently thought the time had not arrived for him to mention publicly his plans for the penetration and development of the North.

To pass from high finance to harlequinade—there was still the question of Barnato's candidature for the parliamentary seat of Beaconsfield. With sturdy support from Rhodes, he fought his election with characteristic boisterousness, parading the division in a silver-grey frock-coat with coloured lapels, and a pale grey top hat, while in his button-hole flamed an enormous red carnation. He drove about in a coach drawn by four grey horses and was escorted by postilions in gay uniforms and jockey caps. Indefatigably, he went from meeting to meeting, and when he could not convert by argument, he would take an objector into the nearest bar. Every speech he made was a *coup de théâtre*, and while he might sometimes be at a loss for a fact, he never failed to raise a laugh. His opponents raged over his vanity and showmanship, but although the fastidious Merriman made the most scathing comments, Barney, with his cockney humour, was unassailable; and when some of the rougher elements at his meetings tried to beat him up, he enlisted a bodyguard of toughs, who gave them a good drubbing. "If a man is going to hit you," he used to say, "hit him first." The election was in November. Barnato romped in by a handsome majority; and it is said that that night "Kimberley was swimming in whisky". But no one—not even Barney himself—could say why he wanted to be a member of Parliament.

Sources

Chilvers, Hedley, A.: *The Story of De Beers*
Emden, Paul H.: *Randlords*
Fitzpatrick, Sir Percy: *South African Memories*
Lewinsohn, Richard: *Barney Barnato*
Williams, Gardner: *The Diamond Mines of South Africa*

Notes

[1] R. H.L.MSS. Afr. t. 5, f. 40.
[2] R.H.L. MSS. Afr. t. 5, f. 43.
[3] R.H.L. MSS. Afr. t. 5, f. 244.

[4] R.H.L. MSS. Afr. s. 69, vol. 4, f. 6.
[5] "Vindex", 747–81.

CHAPTER EIGHT

THE RAND

"WORK never did anyone any harm," Rhodes used to say with more vehemence than accuracy. Certainly he honoured this profession of faith, for seldom can a man have crowded more work into five years than he himself contrived to accomplish between 1886 and 1891. In 1886 the presence of gold on the Witwatersrand was definitely established, and during the next two years the battle for the Amalgamation of the Diamond Mines was joined and won. In 1888 Charles Rudd was sent on his fateful mission to Matabeleland. The Charter followed in 1889, and in 1890 Rhodes became Prime Minister of Cape Colony, itself a position which might have been expected to exact the whole of a man's time.

Rhodes's work was his life. He was unmarried, his father and mother were dead and, except for an occasional brother or an even rarer sister, he saw nothing or very little of his family, his companions being the men with whom he worked. Yet one agonising preoccupation he had during these years in the illness of Neville Pickering whom, setting all else on one side, he nursed with devotion through a long and fatal illness.

With his Life Governorship of De Beers and whatever else he had made out of diamonds, Rhodes was already a rich man when the Rand brought him a second fortune. Many have laid claim to the discovery of what was to become the richest gold-field in the world. There had been false starts, one of which took Herbert and Cecil to the Northern Transvaal in 1872; and just before gold was found on the Rand, there was a rush to Barberton. The glints of gold on the Murchison Range, in the Marabastad District and in the De Kaap Valley all ended in disappointment and were responsible for the scepticism with which the first reports from the Witwatersrand were received. There the men with the best claim to be the pioneers were the Struben brothers, Fred and Willie, who were convinced that gold would be found somewhere under the black undulating *veld* south of Pretoria known as the Witwatersrand; and early in the spring of 1886, one of their men, George Walker, working on the Langlaagte farm, struck the layer of gold which was to become the Main Reef.

The news of the strike found Kimberley incredulous. The Strubens had talked so much about the gold on the Witwatersrand that, when it was actually found, few believed in it. Two men, however, took the chance and went north. One was J. B. Robinson, ever on the watch for opportunities of re-making his fortune; and as he had only just escaped bankruptcy, he was financed for his expedition by Beit. The other man was Hans Sauer, the doctor who had fallen out so badly with Jameson. Each having tried to conceal his destination and purpose from the other, when they left the coach at Potchefstroom to continue their journey to the Witwatersrand by country cart, they were disconcerted to discover that both were bound for the same place. Robinson, on reaching the Rand, promptly bought Langlaagte farm for £1,500, a purchase on which he was to found his claim to be the true pioneer of the new gold-field. Sauer, who was still a poor doctor, bought no land, but took a few samples, which convinced him of the genuineness of the discovery.

To obtain the necessary financial support, he hurried back to Kimberley, where he was advised to see Rhodes, whom he barely knew. He went to Rhodes's cottage and found him in bed. Rhodes did not appear to be deeply interested in Sauer's tale or in his samples. Diamonds he understood perfectly, but of gold he was suspicious. However, he asked Sauer to come back the next day, and Sauer when he arrived found Rudd and two Australian miners in the cottage with Rhodes. The miners had brought pestle, mortar and gold panning dish with them and in a few minutes were able to assure Rhodes of the presence of gold in the samples.

Rhodes then asked Sauer to leave for Pretoria without delay and buy claims for him. Sauer demurred. He was a doctor, he reminded Rhodes, not a gold miner. Who would look after his patients during what might be a long absence? But Rhodes, probably forseeing this difficulty, had already arranged for a *locum tenens*. Sauer asked for twenty per cent as his share of any properties he might acquire, but accepted Rhodes's offer of fifteen per cent. He was also to have £200 for his expenses. These matters having been settled to his satisfaction, he agreed to start for the Witwatersrand the next morning. Secrecy about the journey was obviously desirable. While Sauer was a mere doctor, whose comings and goings would normally excite little interest, he had just seen Rhodes, whose movements were closely watched by the mining community. If, immediately after the interview, Sauer started for the Rand, people would draw the obvious conclusion that something important was happening up there and Sauer might find that he had company on his journey. He therefore decided that, instead of starting from Kimberley, he would make his own way to the first stopping-point on the road to Pretoria and join the coach there. Being a vigorous active young man, he got up early in the morning and walked the distance. In due course the coach arrived, and sitting in it, to his surprise and annoyance, were Rhodes and Rudd, who thereby made nonsense of Sauer's careful little plan.

On arrival at Pretoria, they made their way to the Witwatersrand, where they put up in a small hotel, before moving into a farm which they bought. The rush to the gold-fields had begun, with J. B. Robinson, who was still being financed by Beit, well in front. He and Rhodes both inspected the De Plessis property. They were shown some samples, but Rudd was convinced that the mine had been salted and persuaded Rhodes to refuse to buy. Robinson bought the property and a neighbouring farm, and with them founded the Robinson Mine, valued five years later at fifteen million pounds. In fact at this stage the "Buccaneer" was picking most of the plums. In the other camp Sauer, by his own account, was the optimist, buying options wherever he could get them, while Rudd, economical and cautious, was the sceptic, supported by most of the geological experts, who still discounted the new discoveries. Prominent among the unbelievers was Rhodes's own expert, Gardner Williams. "Dr. Sauer," he said, "if I were to ride over these reefs in America, I would not get off my horse to look at them. In my opinion they are not worth bell room." After this one perfunctory look at the Rand he dismissed it contemptuously, a blunder for which he had to endure the chaff for years.

In spite of the experts the rush went on. "Newcomers hurried up every day," wrote Sauer, "by ox-wagon, by horse-wagon, by mule-wagon, by every sort of imaginable vehicle."

Rhodes knew nothing about gold and, to Sauer's dismay, let some golden opportunities slip by him. Sauer had acquired a few options of particular promise. One of them, for which he paid only £250, covered some of the ground on which Johannesburg would be built, and two years later the municipal valuation of it amounted to more than three million pounds. But serious news had come to Rhodes from Kimberley. Neville Pickering was dying. Rhodes at once left the Rand, promising to wire his decisions about the options from Kimberley. This he failed to do, his thought being all for his friend. Jameson was looking after him, and the two men sat at Pickering's bedside. Just before he died he looked at Rhodes. "You have been father, mother, brother and sister to me," Jameson heard him whisper.

He was buried in Kimberley cemetery. Rhodes went to the funeral in his old clothes. He had not known such sorrow since the death of his mother and, passing from hysterical laughter to tears, kept plunging his face into his handkerchief. Barnato, good-hearted little man, "sniffed and blubbered" beside him. "Ah, Barney," said Rhodes in his falsetto voice, "he will never sell you another parcel of diamonds." Rhodes gave up the cottage he had shared with Pickering, going to live with Jameson in his little bungalow with its corrugated iron roof and verandah. Those who knew him best believed that he took years to recover from his grief at Pickering's death.

He still had his works and his plans. Sauer's options had lapsed and perhaps Rhodes did not altogether regret them. Gold was so different from diamonds. "It is all very well," he said to Sauer, "but I cannot see or calculate the power in your claims." He went on to explain what he meant. "When I am in Kimberley," he said, "I often go and sit on the edge of the De Beers Mine, and I look at the blue diamondiferous ground, reaching from the surface a thousand feet down the open workings of the mine, and I reckon up the value of diamonds in the 'blue' and the power conferred by them. In fact, every foot of blue ground means so much power. This I cannot do with your gold reefs."

But even if he could not reckon up the power in gold, the power was there and presently he returned to the Rand where, although others were ahead of him now, he contrived to pick up some promising properties. "The opinion is steadily growing," he admitted, "that the Rand is the biggest thing the world has seen," and he sent Rudd home to raise capital in the City. Beit had come up with all the other men from Kimberley and was operating with that mixture of boldness and caution which had served so well at the diamond mines. At one time Rhodes, the "great amalgamator" as men were now calling him, was hopeful of amalgamating gold as he had amalgamated diamonds; but Robinson, the biggest power on the Rand, was a very different customer from Barney. He was a lone wolf, who besides had an ingrained dislike for Rhodes. So the idea was abandoned and the two men settled down to compete instead of to co-operate.

Robinson on the trail was formidable. He understood the

Boers whose farms he had to buy and was ready to pay the prices they had begun to demand, stiff though these were, knowing full well that they were only a fraction of the real value of the land. He was aware of the lure of ready money to simple people and always carried a box containing about five thousand sovereigns about with him. Once, while Rhodes was bargaining with a farmer in the orchard, Robinson took his box of gold into the kitchen and bought the land from the farmer's wife. Sometimes, however, Robinson made mistakes, for at this stage he knew little about gold. He formed a poor opinion of the East Rand where Beit was concentrating, and lost the chance of a fortune there.

Rhodes's methods of acquiring claims were delightfully haphazard, a mixture of hard business and relaxation. Once he coached Sauer on the right way in which to conduct a negotiation, turning himself into a Boer farmer and constructing the conversation that would take place. The line of argument subsequently pursued by the real farmer ran very close to Rhodes's anticipation of it. On another occasion Rhodes and Sauer went off claim-hunting with their shot-guns. On the way to the farm they were to visit, they flushed some plover and between them bagged a brace. They then had a look at the farm. On their return they were riding down a little valley when a *swart-ringhals*, the black spitting cobra of South Africa, reared under the nose of Rhodes's mare. She shied violently, stumbled and fell, throwing Rhodes over her head, but fortunately out of the snake's striking distance. He got up, angry and flustered, abusing his companions and the mare. This mischance may have decided him against taking up his option on the farm he had been inspecting. He had a deep dislike for snakes and would never, if he could avoid doing so, go out of doors after dark. As his habit in those days on the Rand was to sleep in his wagon, twenty yards or so from the house where he had dined, he would be escorted to his bed by men with lanterns.

The farmers' prices were going up steadily. Rhodes paid £70,000 to van Wyk for Botha's Reef. He thought that some big poplar poles he saw lying about might be useful as pit props, but van Wyk would not hear of including them in the sale. Beit was busily going round too, troubled less by the stubbornness of the farmers than by the quantities of indifferent coffee he had to drink with them. Once, before he could clinch a bargain, he had to take seven pots of it at a sitting. He and Lippert operated independently from Rhodes, not competing with him, but working for their own company, Wernher, Beit and Co., which was to become one of the richest on the Rand. (Wernher once remarked that everybody thought he was just Beit's first name.) Barney Barnato was very late in the field, having been scared by the adverse reports of the mining engineers. When he arrived, he bought recklessly and at too high a price; so that when a setback occurred in 1889, he lost heavily.

The setback frightened everyone. The Reef had reached a pyritic zone in which the early primitive methods of extracting the gold no longer served. People began to say that after all the Reef was only an old river bed, while to add to the miners' troubles a drought paralysed the ox transport, which was still the only means of communication between Johannesburg and the outside world. However, the drought passed, a new cyanide process was introduced, and confidence was slowly restored.

Other new men had arrived—the Ecksteins; Lionel Phillips, who began by working for J. B. Robinson, and went on to become adviser to H. Eckstein & Co. and to be President of the Chamber of Mines; James D. Taylor, who could talk to the farmers in their own tongues; and, rather later, a brilliant young Irishman, Percy Fitzpatrick, the future statesman and author.

In 1887 Rhodes formed the Goldfields of South Africa, afterwards transformed into the Consolidated Goldfields of South Africa, with a capital of £125,000. He gave it a Trust Deed similar to that of De Beers, so that he could use the revenues in the development of the North. The original arrangement allowed him to draw one third of the profits, a privilege which he later exchanged for a block of Ordinary shares valued between £1,300,000 and £1,400,000. He was now immensely rich, how rich no one—not even he himself—rightly knew. Probably he was getting between £300,000 and £400,000 a year from the Rand alone, as well as about £200,000 from De Beers. Once he tossed a pile of papers over to Beit and asked him to work out how much he was worth; but such were the ramifications of his estate that an answer would have been difficult. He kept several running accounts, was always overdrawn on them, and seldom had any ready money on him. On a visit to London he was so short of cash that he had to borrow in order to pay his hotel bill.

*   *   *

Even more important than the addition the gold of the Rand made to Rhodes's fortune was its effect on the Transvaal. In 1888 Rhodes could tell the Cape Parliament that the Colony was "the dominant state in South Africa".[1] So it then was; but with the opening of the Rand the Transvaal, passing from penury to affluence, began to outstrip it. Gold was creating the modern city of Johannesburg in what had been nearly a desert and had saved a republic on the verge of bankruptcy. But it had also brought in a new and unstable population of miners, soon outnumbering the burghers, of whom there were perhaps 25,000, spread over the country. They, and particularly their President, Paul Kruger, viewed the transformation with mixed feelings. Naturally they were pleased with their new prosperity, even though the extruded farmers began to suspect that they had parted with their land for much lower prices than it was worth. They intensely disliked the flood of new people, the *Uitlanders*, as they were called, who poured into the country. In their view— and not in their view only—Johannesburg was a sink of iniquity, alien, grasping and godless.

Kruger's problem was how to deal with these people, so many of whom were mere adventurers, and his mistake was his inability to distinguish between those who were good and those who were bad citizens, between those who would stay and work and those who would go as soon as they had made their fortunes. To him they were all *Uitlanders*, necessary, perhaps, for the money they brought to an empty Treasury, but an evil none the less. He felt that, unless he was careful, he would wake up one morning to find the hated British flag flying again over Pretoria and the republic being ruled by the riff-raff of Europe. When in his predicament he consulted President Brand of the Free State, that wise old man advised him to "make friends with his *Uitlanders*". But the counsel was hardly to Kruger's taste. He would tolerate them, but never would he allow them equal political rights with his burghers. "Their rights!" he exclaimed. "Yes, they'll get them—over my dead body!" This point of view was emphasised in the Franchise Law of 1890, opposition to which became the rallying point for the *Uitlanders*. Kruger never swerved an inch from his opinion, which ultimately was to bring to his people war and annexation, and to himself a death in exile.

Actually many of the *Uitlanders* would have agreed that it was hardly reasonable to expect him to grant political rights through which the burghers would be outnumbered in their own country. Political rights were a good slogan, but the majority of the *Uitlanders* would probably have been quite content to do without them if they could have had a sensible, reasonably efficient and honest government. Instead they had to put up with monopolies, corruption and injustice. Johannesburg did not even get a railway until 1894, and that, when it arrived, produced fresh grievances. All this, more than any denial of the vote, was what irked them; and whenever there was a slump in the gold-fields, the miners blamed the malice and incompetence of the Government.

Kruger's own attitude was far from conciliatory. He did his best to sow dissension among the *Uitlanders*, supporting for instance one mining organisation, the Association of Mines, against its rival, the Chamber of Mines. In 1890 he visited Johannesburg and made a tactless speech, which infuriated the whole community; but he showed his feelings most clearly in another speech he made there five years later, when he addressed his audience, in language more of the Old Testament than of the nineteenth century, as "People of the Lord, you old people of the country, you foreigners, you newcomers, yea, even you thieves and murderers". The mining community, who were left in no doubt which were their categories, were not in the least appeased by Kruger's subsequent explanation—that if there happened to be any thieves and murderers among his audience, he intended his words for them too.

Rhodes, who had had his first contact with Kruger over Bechuanaland, had two unfruitful meetings with him in the early days of the Rand. At the first of them the President, pointing his pipe in the direction of Rhodes, said, "Tell him I have heard all these stories (of maladministration) before. I am here to protect my burghers as well as the Rand people. I know what I have to do and I will do what I consider is right." On the second occasion Rhodes proposed Kruger's health at a luncheon in Johannesburg. The President in his speech explained his position. He understood the grievances of the miners and promised some reforms, but refused to yield an iota on political rights.

> "Wealth cannot break laws," he pronounced. "Is it a good man who wants to be master of the country, when others have been suffering for twenty years to conduct its affairs? It is the unthankful people to whom I have given protection that are always dissatisfied, and, what is more, they would actually want me to alter my laws to suit them."

Kruger's attitude, as Rhodes recognised, was not entirely unreasonable. If he had redressed the genuine grievances of the *Uitlanders* and perhaps allowed Johannesburg a measure of municipal self-government, he would have put himself without question in the right. But he allowed his dislike of the British to govern his actions, and would neither let the *Uitlanders* manage their own affairs nor himself manage them properly.

Rhodes had little sympathy with the *Uitlanders*; but he had welcomed the opening of the gold-fields as being likely to bring into South Africa more people of British stock, and he found Kruger's stubborn attitude intolerable. Here was a man whom he would never be able to "square"; very soon he gave up even trying, having concluded that the Union of South Africa under the British flag, on which he had set his heart, would never happen while Kruger was President of the Transvaal. There was no common ground on which the two minds might meet.

"I regard him," Rhodes told the Cape Parliament on July 23rd, 1888, "as one of the most remarkable men in South Africa, who has been singularly unfortunate. When I remember that Paul Kruger had not a sixpence in his Treasury when his object was to extend his country over the whole northern interior, when I see him sitting in Pretoria with Bechuanaland gone, and other lands around him gone from his grasp, and, last of all, when he, with his whole idea of a pastoral Republic, finds that idea vanishing, and that he is likely to have to deal with a hundred thousand diggers, who must be entirely out of sympathy and touch with him, I pity the man."[2]

Kruger neither wanted nor needed Rhodes's pity. He had his purpose, and to it he would adhere with a tenacity rivalling that of his adversary. The irresistible force was meeting the immovable mass, and from the collision would come the greatest tragedy in South African history.

Sources

Chilvers, Hedley A.: *Out of the Crucible*
Colvin, Ian: *Life of Jameson*
Emden, Paul H.: *Randlords*
Jacobson, D.: *Fifty Golden Years of the Rand*
Sauer, Hans: *Ex Africa . . .*
Weinthal, Leo (ed.): *Memories, Mines and Millions*

Notes

[1] "Vindex", 225.   [2] "Vindex", 204.

CHAPTER NINE

THE CONCESSION

HOWEVER compelling the calls of Kimberley or the Rand, Rhodes always kept one eye on that great territory stretching north from Bechuanaland across the Zambesi and east to Portuguese Mozambique. From hunters, travellers and missionaries, men were beginning to learn about this northern land. Fact and legend mingled together. It was Sheba. It was Ophir, whence gold had been brought to Solomon. It was Monomotapa, which may have been the fabulous realm of Prester John. Less fancifully, it was a new Kimberley or a new Rand, only waiting to be developed by the white man. And much of it—the point which weighed most heavily with Rhodes—was a high plateau where white men might live and rear their families.

Over all this conjecture loomed the inescapable fact that beyond Bechuanaland, and running north and north-east to a shadowy frontier, lay the kingdom of Matabele, the most formidable fighting race in South or Central Africa, barring the way to adventurers, or indeed to anyone who had failed, despite bribery or royal favour, to be given "the road".

The Matabele themselves were newcomers. Their first king, Mzilikazi, had been the commander-in-chief of Chaka, king of the Zulus. In 1817, having aroused the envy and suspicion of his lord, Mzilikazi, taking with him the *impis* under his immediate command, had moved off into the country which was to become the Transvaal. Thither too came the Boers, rather later, on their "Great Trek" to new lands, where they would be plagued neither by the hated British flag nor by the British tax-collector. Between the two bodies of migrants clashes were frequent and bloody. The Amandabele or Matabele, as Mzilikazi's people were called, retained the ideas and habits of the Zulus. All cattle were their property of right; all peoples were their lawful victims, to be slain, plundered or enslaved at their pleasure; war and hunting were the only proper occupations for men, beef and beer their only diet; and every young man was a soldier, under the same iron discipline as had built up the army of Chaka. Between such people and Boer and Basuto no peace was possible; and after some years of fighting and raiding,

Mzilikazi and his horde drifted north, as destructive as a crowd of locusts.

Leaving the wastes of Bechuanaland behind them, they crossed the Limpopo and penetrated the granite hills of the Matopos. Beyond them they found the land they were seeking, a land of broad pastures occupied mainly by the unwarlike Mashone and Barotse, who could be raided with impunity. Here till 1868 Mzilikazi ruled, a despot whose amusement was war and whose only punishment was death. Once, from the east, a party of Boers under Potgieter tried unsuccessfully to drive him out, and thereafter the Transvaal wisely left him alone. Pretorius had declared the country the property of the Transvaal, but when the British Government protested, he allowed the matter to rest. After Majuba, Joubert had written a friendly letter to one of Mzilikazi's sons, warning him against the British, but this again he failed to follow up. In the south the Bechuana, who had managed to acquire some rifles, were generally able to keep Matabele raiding parties at bay. In the north the unwarlike Mashona suffered the attentions of their neighbour as best they might.

The presence of a few missionaries, like John Smith Moffat, the brother-in-law of Livingstone, of a few hunters, and of a handful of traders was tolerated. Apart from them, and from the young men who came back from the mines at Kimberley, the Matabele knew nothing of the outside world. They were savages, assured of their invincibility, scornful and intolerant of strangers. It is true that in 1867, the year before Mzilikazi's death, miners were given permission to dig for gold at Tati, on the edge of the disputed No Man's Land between Bechuana and Matabele; but there they had to stay. Occasionally hunters were given "the road", but at the first hint that they were prospecting and not merely hunting, they had to leave in haste.

Mzilikazi, having carefully removed any of his family who might threaten his throne, left no indisputable heir. A son, Nkulumane, was said to be in Zululand, or alternatively to have been murdered by his father's orders thirty years earlier. There was his brother, Ubuhlelo, but no one was sure what had happened to him and probably he too had been murdered. There was yet another son, Lobengula, who had been taken from the royal *kraal* as a child and brought up, it was said, by the witch-doctors who lived in the caverns of the Matopos. Umnombate, the *induna* who stood highest with Mzilikazi, and after his death had appointed himself regent, decided to make Lobengula king, a prospect which so alarmed the young man that he fled from his *kraal* and took refuge with the missionaries. But when it was clear that no serious rivals were coming forward, he was persuaded to return. On 17 March 1870 he was installed as king of the Matabele and, after a little trouble with a pretender, established his authority beyond question.

Although not a warrior like his father, Lobengula was a much more intelligent man, with some awareness of the outside world he had never seen. He was determined not to allow the white men into his country if he could keep them out. He knew that, while his *impis* could kill a few intruders without difficulty, they would be no match for the white armies which would subsequently come against him. Much of Lobengula's anxiety to keep white men out of his country sprang simply from his dread of some murderous incident which would bring trouble and reprisals. He was not interested in gold or diamonds, although he amassed a treasure from the presents of visitors and from the contributions of the boys returned from Kimberley. He wanted only to be left in peace with his sixty-eight wives, his cattle and his beer. His chief worry was his army of some 15,000 fighters—perhaps more—restless, arrogant, and eager to wash their spears in the blood of strangers.

He was intensely superstitious, being surrounded by witch-doctors, whose business it was to produce the results they knew he wanted; and, perhaps from his upbringing in the Matopos, he dabbled in magic himself. While in theory a complete despot, before coming to any important decision, he always sought, and often followed, the advice of his *indunas*. He was capable of acts of revolting cruelty, but probably these were committed more from policy than from inclination. Understanding his subjects, he was sure that he could only rule them by the most savage punishments. A white trader once witnessed the punishment of a man who had been caught stealing the royal beer. On the king's orders, his lips, which had tasted it, were first cut off; then his nose, which had smelt it; then the skin of his forehead was peeled down to cover his eyes, which had seen the beer; and finally the mutilated wretch was taken off and hurled to the crocodiles in the river. He was full of suspicion and even, at the prompting of the witch-doctors, had his favourite sister killed. But if he trusted none of his own people, he had a regard for the white missionaries, as he thought they would give him disinterested advice; and although he demanded slavish submission from his subjects, he respected men of other races who showed by their bearing that they did not fear him.

Many of the Europeans who saw him left descriptions of him; and as for superstitious reasons he did not like to be photographed, their stories are almost all we have. One white visitor spoke of "the intense blackness of his colour" and of his "benignant smile". E. A. Maund, who had been on Warren's staff in Bechuanaland and been sent on a mission to Bulawayo, described him as a "gross fat man, with a cruel restless eye". On the other hand Shippard said that in spite of his obesity, he had "a most majestic appearance", while a French explorer declared him "the most imposing monarch he had ever seen, except the Tsar Alexander". J. Cooper Chadwick, who saw him almost daily between 1887 and 1890, gives a good portrait of him:

> "Lobengula stands over six feet in height, but is so enormously fat that it makes him look smaller, though his proud bearing and stately walk give him all the appearance of a savage king. His features are coarse, and exhibit great cunning and cruelty; but when he smiles the expression completely changes, and makes his face appear pleasant and good-tempered."

Usually he was naked, except for a kilt of monkey-skins. His chief *kraal* was in Bulawayo ("the place of the man who was killed"), where grew the *indaba* tree, still to be seen, under which he dispensed justice. Although he had two brick houses, built for him by an English sailor, he preferred living in an ox-wagon.

Such was Lobengula, who was to enter so fatefully into Rhodes's life. Cruel and crafty though he was, he was not an ignoble figure. Most of those who dealt with him agree that he had intelligence unusual among the Matabele, and a personal conception of good faith, so that when he had given a promise, he tried to honour it—which was more than could be said for some white men with whom he had dealings. His fall and that of his kingdom were inevitable. If the Matabele had been merely primitive, they might eventually have adapted themselves to the laws and customs of civilisation. But they were impossible neighbours. Their only occupation was war, their approach to life was homicidal, and they were so well satisfied with themselves that they would never have changed their habits without a struggle. They had to be broken, if Central Africa was ever to enjoy, by European standards, peace and a chance of prosperity. But although it would be idle to sentimentalise over their passing, it must be admitted that the treatment of Lobengula does not form a chapter in the history of Africa of which white men should feel proud.

*   *   *

Sir Hercules Robinson was spending the Christmas of 1887 at Grahamstown, when suddenly Sir Sidney Shippard, the Administrator of Bechuanaland, arrived, closely followed by Rhodes, with a tale to interrupt the pony-racing and seasonal junketing which the High Commissioner was enjoying. Rhodes had had a report of three officers who had been in Bulawayo, and what they had to say was confirmed by a message from the Government agent in Pretoria. It seemed that Kruger had made or was about to make an agreement of some sort with Lobengula. He had sent one Pieter Grobler to the king to negotiate a treaty of protection; and Grobler, it appeared, had succeeded in getting a document signed by him. Ostensibly it amounted to no more than an exchange of friendly messages and promises of protection, a grant of jurisdiction to the South African Republic over its citizens in Matabeleland, and the right to establish a consul there; but on the strength of it Boers were said to be already claiming the right to take up concessions in Lobengula's country.

The king, dreading the Boers, who were looking for land, more than he dreaded the British, who appeared to be more interested in minerals, subsequently denied that he had ever agreed to the treaty. Certainly no one had heard of the place where it was supposed to have been signed; the only white signatories were Grobler and his brother; and the *indunas* who were mentioned as having witnessed Lobengula's mark could not be identified. Grobler was a rascal, who had scarcely been appointed the first consul of the Transvaal in Matabeleland when he was overtaken by his past. Some years before he had sold to Khama, Chief of the Bamangwato tribe of Bechuanaland, some horses which he guaranteed as "salted", and therefore immune from the prevalent horse-sickness. After Khama had paid for them, Grobler went off, while the horses fell sick and died. Now, on Grobler's way back to the Transvaal, he and his party were intercepted by a detachment of Bamangwato, and in the scuffle that ensued he was mortally wounded, in Shippard's opinion by one of his own men.

Naturally, on the principle that the guilty party in any crime is most likely to be the man who profits by it, people suggested that Rhodes, or at least the British, had contrived the death of Grobler. Kruger was convinced of it, and even a recent biographer of Rhodes, Felix Gross, has hinted at this conclusion. There is not a scrap of evidence to support the charge and it is difficult to believe that Shippard, who held a searching enquiry . into the affray, strongly as he supported Rhodes, would have deliberately falsified the official report he sent in.

Rhodes had not even heard of this event when he visited the High Commissioner. He was alarmed by what seemed to him to be a new attempt by Kruger to gain a foothold in his own Promised Land. Grobler was only one danger. Other people, including a German Count, were visiting Bulawayo and dropping honeyed words into the royal ears. A little earlier the Portuguese had issued a map on which they showed Lobengula's territory as Portuguese possession; and while they had withdrawn this in the face of a protest from Lord Salisbury, their ambitions too could not be discounted. There was no time to lose, and Rhodes besought Sir Hercules to take immediate action.

He was in his most persistent and persuasive mood. As he afterwards told a Cape audience, "I have found out one thing, and that is, if you have an idea, and it is a good idea, if you will only stick to it you will come out all right." Now with all his tenacity he stuck to his "good idea" that the Transvaal should not be allowed to have Matabeleland. It may have been on this occasion that, by his own later account, he invited the High Commissioner to go with him and look at the old blockhouse on Table Mountain.[1] "Those good old people, two hundred years ago," he said, "thought that blockhouse on Table Mountain was the limit of their ideas, but now let us face it today. Where are we? We are considerably beyond the Vaal River, and supposing that those good people were to come to life again today, what would they think of it and their blockhouse?"

Sir Hercules said: "But where will you stop?"

"I will stop," replied Rhodes, "where the country has not been claimed."

Out came the map and, somewhat to the Governor's dismay, Rhodes pointed to the southern boundary of Tanganyika. The Great Powers at home had marked the map, but had done nothing. "Let us try to mark the map," he added, "and we know that we shall do something."

"Well," said Sir Hercules, "I think you should be satisfied with the Zambesi as a boundary." He was weakening and Rhodes was relentless. He took a piece of notepaper and measured first what the Dutch had done, then what had been done in the lifetime of Sir Hercules, and finally what he himself wanted to do. Sir Hercules gave in. "I will leave you alone," he said. As Barnato once ruefully observed, "He ties you up and you cannot resist him."

Nevertheless the High Commissioner would not be pushed too far. Rhodes wanted the model of Bechuanaland to be followed and a protectorate declared over Matabeleland and Mashonaland, but Sir Hercules knew quite well that the Colonial Office, remote from Rhodes's persuasive oratory, would not go so far just yet. He agreed, however, that Shippard should write a despatch to his assistant, John Moffat, son of the old missionary, who was with Lobengula at the time, bidding him ascertain the truth about Grobler's agreement and try to induce the king to sign a treaty acknowledging the exclusive influence of Britain in Matabeleland. This was not all Rhodes had wanted, but for the moment it sufficed. After returning to Kimberley, he sent off a messenger to Bulawayo, who covered the 700 intervening miles so rapidly that the despatch reached Moffat before the end of January.

John Moffat was a worthy member of a family outstanding in the history of Central Africa. Courageous and tactful, he had long known Lobengula well. The king, who called him "Joni", liked him; after all, he was the son of the man whom Mzilikazi had trusted so far as he had trusted anyone. Rhodes could have had no better ally or agent. Moffat came in at exactly the right moment, when Lobengula was becoming worried by the wooing of white men and in particular by the unwelcome interest the Transvaal was beginning to take in his country. He gave Moffat a cordial welcome and, after a review of 12,000 savage warriors and a ceremonial slaying of bullocks, Moffat broached his subject, with the missionary Helm acting as interpreter.

"I want no Boers," Lobengula is reported to have said. "They stole my father's country and they would like to come here and steal mine." The British were different, he told Moffat, but the Queen must not send in too many of her people. When Moffat enlarged on the dangers of foreign encroachment and on the power and benevolence of the Great White Queen, Lobengula was so impressed that, after very little argument, he signed a treaty which not only promised perpetual friendship with her, but pledged him not to cede any of his country to a foreign power or to sign a treaty without the approval of the High Commissioner.

"The Chief Lobengula," ran the treaty, "Ruler of the tribe known as the Amandebele, together with the Mashona and Makalaka tributaries of the same, hereby agrees to the following articles and conditions. . . .

"That peace and amity shall continue for ever between Her Britannic Majesty, her subjects and the Amandebele people; and the contracting Chief, Lobengula, engages to use his utmost endeavours to prevent any rupture of the same, to cause the strict observance of his treaty, and so to carry out the treaty of friendship which was entered into by his late father, the Chief Umsiligaas, with the then Governor of the Cape of Good Hope, in the year of Our Lord 1836.

"It is hereby further agreed by Lobengula, Chief in and over the Amandebele country, with the dependencies as aforesaid, on behalf of himself and people, that he will refrain from entering into any correspondence or treaty with any Foreign State or Power to sell, alienate or cede or permit or countenance any sale, alienation or cession of the whole or any part of the said Amandebele country under his chieftainship, or upon any other subject without the previous knowledge and sanction of Her Majesty's High Commissioner for South Africa.

"In faith of which I, Lobengula, on my part have hereto set my hand at Gubulawayo, Amandebeleland, this 11th day of February, and of Her Majesty's reign the 51st.

Lobengula, his X mark.

Witnesses: W. Graham.

G. B. Van Wyk.

Before me, J. S. Moffat,

Assistant Commissioner."

Once again, as over Bechuanaland, "Grandmama", as Rhodes sometimes irreverently styled the British Government, had saved him, though without much idea of what she was doing or why she was doing it. The favour shown to Rhodes by officials like Robinson, Shippard and Moffat has often been criticised, but it is unnecessary to hunt for traces of corrupt bargains. It is much more likely that, recalling what had happened in Swaziland, where the chief had drunk himself to death with champagne while rivals quarrelled over concessions, the Matabele *indunas* thought it better to deal with one powerful body, represented by a man they knew, than to throw Matabeleland into the scramble for Africa.

Actually the terms and language of the treaty bear a close resemblance to those of a score of treaties which men like Johnston and Lugard were making in different parts of Africa. They were not so sinister in intention as they have since been represented, their purpose being quite as much to close a door to other European nations as to open it for the British. Recent research in official papers has shown, moreover, that Rhodes's policy of surrounding the Transvaal in order to cut off Kruger from the north and the sea coincided at this time with the policy of the British Government at Westminster, even if Rhodes quite misunderstood Salisbury's motives, which were set in a much wider context than that of Southern Africa.

Lobengula, who was unfamiliar with the language of treaties or the ways of the white man, probably understood little of the verbiage to which he had scrawled his mark, thinking that by merely making a few friendly promises he had won the protection of a powerful and well-disposed monarch against the aggressions of Boers and Portuguese. But he had always been warned that whatever verbal undertakings he might give, he should never sign anything. Until then he had followed this prudent advice: now he disregarded it, and in so doing had taken the first step on a road which would lead him to the loss of his kingdom and his life.

* * *

When the news of Moffat's treaty reached London with the commendation of Sir Hercules Robinson, various considerations predisposed Lord Salisbury's Government to endorse it; but respect for Rhodes's judgment was not among them. Lord Knutsford, Salisbury's Colonial Secretary, did not even know who Rhodes was, and confused him with Graham Bower. Salisbury himself scoffed at the idea of an "all-red" route from the Cape to Cairo, but he was already becoming nervous of penetration into Africa by other European powers, both the French in the north and the Germans in the south. He therefore brushed aside the protests of Portugal and the Transvaal, the weakest of Britain's rivals, who could not make their protests effective without the support of stronger powers, and accepted the treaty.

Rhodes had secured a negative option of a sort in Matabeleland.

At least it was an option which excluded the Germans and Boers. Two disquieting possibilities, however, remained. The first was that Lobengula might change his mind and repudiate the treaty he had accepted. The second was that representatives of other British enterprises might move in before Rhodes was ready. His intelligence service was good and he had many friends among the officials. Probably he had already had news of forthcoming visitors to Bulawayo. It was therefore essential that without loss of time he should make his own approach to Lobengula; and before he left Grahamstown, anticipating the success of Moffat's mission, he sent up one of his own men, Fry, to act as his agent in Bulawayo. Unknown to Rhodes, Fry was a sick man, suffering from cancer. He had hardly reached Bulawayo before he fell seriously ill. He had to leave and a few weeks later, when he was back at Kimberley, he died. So, as Rhodes put it, the vacuum which Nature abhors had still to be filled; and as he could not go north himself, he chose three men whom he thought he could trust: Rudd, Thompson and Maguire.

Tall, bearded and melancholy, Charles Rudd had been his partner from the earliest days in Kimberley. Although neither adventurous nor imaginative, he was a sound man of business; above all else, he was completely loyal and reliable. The second member of the party was a young South African, F. R. Thompson, known as 'Matabele' Thompson, who had acted as Rhodes's secretary in Bechuanaland. Later Rhodes had put him into De Beers's to organise a system of compounds for native labour, in a successful attempt to check illicit diamond-buying. Besides having acquired some knowledge of native languages and the native mind, Thompson had been in Bulawayo before and it was believed that Lobengula had taken a fancy to him. He seemed a suitable envoy, but had one unfortunate weakness. Some years before he had seen natives murder his father by driving a ramrod down his throat and out at his back. No boy could ever forget such a horror, and in a tricky situation Thompson was apt to lose his nerve. This weakness was later to have consequences nearly fatal to Rhodes's plans. When told he should go to Bulawayo, Thompson replied, "I must ask my wife." "I knew you would say that," replied Rhodes, and pulled out of his pocket her written consent.

The third man in the party was an odd choice. He was Rochfort Maguire, a trained lawyer who had been up at Oxford with Rhodes, gaining there a double first and a Fellowship of All

Souls. A cultured, learned, dapper little Irishman, a College common-room would have seemed the most appropriate background for him, and a Central African *kraal* the least. In practical affairs he was so hopeless that he could not even open a tin of salmon. That Rhodes should have enlisted for his purposes three men so different and incongruous is a proof as much of his insight as of his extraordinary power of persuasion. Rudd would look after the business side, Thompson could deal with the Africans, and Maguire would put any agreement into good legal English. Rhodes also had the peculiar idea that on the journey Maguire would coach Thompson in the classics to comfort him for a failure to pass into Oxford.

As Rhodes's plans took shape, ambiguity developed between what he wanted and his delegates said he wanted on one side, and on the other what Lobengula thought he was being asked to give. Rhodes was not primarily interested in the gold or diamonds he might find in the north, though naturally they entered into his calculations. Behind him he had Kimberley and the Rand, and although the demand for gold might be almost unlimited, that for diamonds was so artificial that the discovery of a new Field could be less of an asset than of an embarrassment. Rhodes's real purpose, from which he never departed, was the extension of Cape Colony into Central Africa and the creation there of settlements, where men and women of the British race might work out a new destiny for themselves and their country. To present his plan in that particular form would be, he judged, imprudent, if not fatal. "Pure philanthropy," he said, "is all very well in its way, but philanthropy plus five per cent is a good deal better." If he was to get the money needed to occupy and develop the new territory, he must be able to offer that five per cent, without which he thought neither the Government nor the investors of the United Kingdom could be persuaded. Of this naturally Lobengula knew and was to know nothing; and had he known, he would have understood little beyond the unpalatable fact that someone was after his land, in which he would have been right. Gold was only the bait: Rhodes's real purpose was to win the country.

He seems to have arrived very quickly at the conclusion that the right way to present his plans to the British Government and public was by putting forward the old expedient of a Chartered Company. The most famous example of this was the East India Company which, starting as a purely trading body, had become possessed of a vast empire. In Africa, too, there were the Niger

Company, The Imperial East Africa Company and the African Lakes Company—all trading bodies which, often unwittingly and against the wishes of their shareholders, had painted portions of the map red. A Chartered Company held the promise, which in the past it had not always fulfilled, of empire-building on the cheap. There would be no charge on the Treasury of the United Kingdom, and the shareholders, lured by the hope of gain, would become, like the East India Company, the founders of an empire.

First, however, Rhodes must have something to offer the investor, and his "philanthropy" could not promise his "five per cent" unless he could secure the grant of mineral rights over the land he wanted. In fact, he must get a concession of these from Lobengula, and the obtaining of this was the purpose of the journey which Rudd, Thompson and Maguire were undertaking. Put baldly in this way, Rhodes's designs have the appearance of cynical duplicity. One side of him was cynical and deliberately deceptive, but the gold of the North meant more to him than just a bait for the British investor or a means of blinding an unlettered savage king to the real objective. Enormous sums would be needed to occupy and develop the great territory he coveted. If the British Treasury was not to be asked for these, the Chartered Company would have to find a lot of money; and this, without the minerals, it would not have.

The three men left Kimberley at the end of August, carrying with them a letter to Lobengula from Sir Hercules Robinson, introducing Rudd and Thompson as "two highly respectable gentlemen who are visiting your country", without a word of the purpose of their visit. Rudd, who took with him his son Frank, and Denny, a friend of his son, kept a diary of the journey in a notebook of 120 pages.[2] The party reached Bulawayo on 20 September 1888. Here they found Moffat and were quickly given an audience by Lobengula. They took off their hats, shook hands with him, and presented him with a greeting gift of 100 sovereigns. "The king is just what I expected to find him," wrote Rudd—"a very fine man, only very fat, but with a beautiful skin and well-proportioned." "A curious face," he added: "he was partly worried, partly good-natured and partly cruel; he has a very pleasant smile." So the negotiations began, with the Rev. C. D. Helm of the London Missionary Society interpreting. The talks were continually interrupted by the king's pre-occupation with making medicine, usually for the purpose of bringing rain. The visitors were fed like "lions at the Zoo", with masses of partly cooked meat, which they had to tear to pieces with the aid of a kind of stick; and they were of course expected to drink quantities of tepid beer.

Unfortunately for Rudd and his party, they were not the only visitors. Others had arrived at Bulawayo with the same purpose as Rhodes's. There was E. R. Renny-Tailyour, representing Edward A. Lippert and a group of German banks. Lippert, although a cousin of Beit, disliked him and was only too ready to thwart him. Another serious rival was Lieutenant E. A. Maund of the Bechuanaland Field Force, who had called on Rhodes and argued with him during Warren's expedition. Subsequently, on Warren's orders, Maund had gone to Bulawayo, where he had ingratiated himself with Lobengula. He was now representing the Exploring Company, in which the ruling spirits were Lord Gifford and Mr. George Cawston. They too, like Rhodes, were hoping to get a concession of the mineral rights and in fact got one of doubtful validity over part of the country. Later Maund wrote a great deal, which is preserved at Rhodes House but mostly unpublished, about his negotiations and his relations with Rhodes.

There was another competitor in the Bechuanaland Exploration Company; and besides the serious rivals was what Thompson called the "Foreign Legion"—a band of needy adventurers who prowled about the *kraal* like human jackals. A visitor of a very different sort was the Anglican Bishop of Bloemfontein, Dr. Knight-Bruce, whose blameless object was to open a mission in Mashonaland. Lobengula, although gratified by the presents he was receiving, began to get worried by the importunacy of the visitors, all of whom, except the Bishop, were promising him advantages, denigrating their rivals, and asking for the right to dig for gold. Meanwhile his warriors were anxiously awaiting his orders to rise up and slaughter the whole crowd.

Unaware that Helm had become one of Rhodes's men, Lobengula listened sympathetically to his argument that the king's wisest plan was to make friends with one group—the strongest— and send everyone else away. Lotje, one of his most trusted *indunas*, having been promised gifts by Thompson, was giving the same advice, and there could be no doubt that the strongest group was the one which had behind it the wealth of Kimberley and the Rand. The trio soon discovered that the Matabele were uninterested in promises of payment by sovereigns, which were of little use to them, and that the bargaining point which appealed to

Dr. Jameson lecturing at the
Imperial Institute in 1894

Telegram From Board	No. 1	Date 3 Aug 95	Translation recd 5/8/95
Code Word	**Cypher**	**Translation**	
Unvrauschen		Earl Grey	
Unvrundet		to Rutherford Harris	
		saw	
Heldenthum		Secretary State for Colonies	
		he	
Emporhelen		considers	
		Crown Colony	
Vormaus 20194		having been transferred	
Schirbing		to	
tafelrund		Cape Colony	
baumkieper		at	
Kuppelband		moment	
		entering	
tienlaufen (		office	
Nerancadao 94400	x	if he has	
		shown	
practical		practical	
muthigkeit		most	
		sympathy	
Unbegangen		"Mr Rhodes'	
mickerig		policy	
Keutradem		but	
		although	
haussinne		he is friendly	
		very	
emporulen (emporulen)		considers	
		cession	
nachruhm		Protectorate	
baumkieper		at	

Telegram From Board	No. 2	Cyphered	Date 3 Aug 95
Code Word	**Cypher**	**Translation**	
Castgebühr		near	
Feldkriese		date	
		utterly	
tropfmeister		impossible	
		his attitude	
Letzlein		on	
		this	
mineuride (minerkunde)		point	
einkommand		without compromise	
		decisive	
		state	
		presence	
Unbegangen		Mr Rhodes	
tafelbaum		England	
aufgeld		will not alter	
		his mind,	
Schneehuhn		that	
Unbegangen		Mr Rhodes	
Kinderbier (Kinderbier)		must leave	
		him alone	
modehut		for the present.	
Lochtron		in his opinion	
tirilande 19030r		he agrees to	
ochütteln		transfer	
		Crown Colony	
luftbauch		in order to	
		avoid	
hoffgeld		immediate	
husigine (hausgine)		further	

Telegram from Board   No. 3   Date 3 Aug 95

Continued

Code Word.	Cypher.	Translation.
augenwinke		Construction
langkieper (landkiper)		are
		much
		upset
schnehuhu		that
trafalre	191800	It was not
		they (?thy) ✗
dannerstott		case
beytracht		because
metscheo		sale
hudelaga		the Bechuanaland Railway Co
schnbeny		to
tafelgund		Cape Colony
vantages		had not
vansteines		taken
		place
unmundet		to Rutherfoord Harris
kaarungel (kharunge)		explain
mashinti		Parliament
milchaft		potion
		cause
palastdame		remark
schnbeng		to
extenstlee (vikurshte)		convince
hildenham		Secretary of State
literabee		no
lanafnide (kanafride)		breach of faith
mashul		on our part
hintekum		but
		he

Telegram from Board   No. 4   Date 3 Aug 95

Cento

Code Word.	Cypher.	Translation.
emporheben		Still
stumpfkopf		considers
buchchen		B.S.A. Company
bankrott		if
bandroll		finance
bordeuen		favorable
		is
		obligated
		to
schubang		proud
muftchen		at one
rotundelli		with
phatbel		railway
mulitat.		towards
		Palapye
uebertrach		..

The earliest of the "Missing Telegrams" (sheets 1–2)

The earliest of the "Missing Telegrams" (sheets 3–4)

See Appendix A, pp. 485–6

Telegram from Harris to Rhodes of 4 November 1895
(as received in Cape Town)

See Appendix A, p. 486

Lobengula was an offer of rifles and ammunition. This they made, but still the king temporised. On his way to Bulawayo, nominally to enquire into the killing of Grobler, was no less a man than Sir Sidney Shippard himself, the representative in Bechuanaland of the Great White Queen. Surely it would be unwise as well as discourteous to come to any decision before seeing and hearing this powerful man? So Lobengula kept Rudd and his companions waiting. They shot and bathed, played whist, backgammon or chess, and made so little progress that Rudd, losing heart, began to ask Lobengula for the road. This, however, the king was unwilling to give—fortunately for Rudd.

Shippard arrived on 16 October after a dreadful journey. Spies reported having seen him taking a bath and were sure that he was a magician. At first Lobengula was doubtful about giving the road to someone who might bewitch him, but in the end Moffat persuaded him of the imprudence of refusing. Shippard had brought with him an escort of sixteen troopers—another objection to the visit in Lobengula's eyes—and while they waited for permission to go on, Matabele warriors swarmed round with insulting and provocative remarks which the troopers, fortunately failing to understand, received with unshakable good humour. On his arrival Shippard, who was accompanied by his A.D.C., Major Goold-Adams, afterwards Sir Kenneth Goold-Adams, Governor of Queensland, took some pains to impress Lobengula.

A bald, pot-bellied little fellow with Dundreary whiskers, Shippard nevertheless achieved an unlikely appearance of dignity. Although it was the hottest season of the year, he wore a tightly buttoned black frock-coat (on which he pinned the Star of the Order of St. Michael and St. George), grey kid gloves and patent-leather boots. On his head he had a large white solar *topi* and he carried a malacca cane with a silver knob. As he walked into the king's *kraal*, which was filled with nearly naked savages, he may have looked a little over-dressed for his surroundings; but evidently Lobengula was pleased, as after the usual greetings and gifts had been exchanged, he ordered chairs to be brought under the *indaba* tree and asked his visitors to be seated. With Shippard were Moffat, Helm and Dr. Knight-Bruce.

Of the conversation no record has survived, but Shippard appears to have tendered advice to the king, and in doing so can hardly have failed to commend the claims of his friend Rhodes, in whom Lobengula, who always referred to him as "Ulodzi", showed a particular interest, even referring to him as "big

brother". At any rate, when Shippard left a few days later, the
situation had changed in favour of Rudd, Maguire and Thompson. Several more meetings were held. At one of them the
indunas suggested a concession of the mineral rights in part of the
country only. According to Thompson, Rudd would have
accepted this offer, but was prevented from doing so by his colleagues, who threatened that, if this was all they were to get, they
would leave the country at once. Their departure was not at all
what Lobengula wanted and, on 30 October, he suddenly sent
word that he was ready to give the concession.

The delegates found him sitting on a brandy-cask in a corner
of the buck *kraal*, "hustled and anxious", but in a good temper.
The *indaba* that followed lasted for two days. Rudd pushed home
his point that unless Lobengula could get the friends and the
arms the concession would give him, sooner or later he would be
attacked by a bad neighbour and driven out of his country. Helm
and Lotje, the friendly *induna*, told the same tale, and at last
Lobengula suddenly said he would sign the document. He
scrawled his mark on it, the elephant seal was added, and the deed
was duly witnessed.

By it Lobengula was to receive £100 sterling "on the first
day of every lunar month", while 1,000 Martini-Henry rifles,
with 100,000 rounds, were to be delivered with "reasonable
despatch". A steamboat "with guns suitable for defensive purposes" on the River Zambesi was also to be delivered or, failing
that, the sum of £500. The steamboat, which was Rhodes's idea,
never materialised. In return Lobengula assigned to the grantees
"the complete and exclusive charge over all metals and minerals
situated and contained in my kingdom . . . together with full
power to do all things that they may deem necessary to win and
procure the same". Since he had been much molested by persons
seeking concessions, the grantees were authorised to exclude all
such people from the king's territory. Finally Lobengula undertook "to grant no concessions of land or mining rights from and
after this date" without the consent of the trio or their assigns.
(The Tati Concession was expressly excluded.) The document
carried Lobengula's mark and the signatures of Rudd, Maguire
and Thompson, the witnesses being Charles D. Helm and J. J.
Dryer.

How much of all this Lobengula grasped is doubtful. Probably
he thought that presently "Ulodzi" would arrive and dig a big
hole like the one at Kimberley, and that the new concession

would be just another Tati, which had given him no trouble. How imperfectly he understood the reality of what he had done appears from his oral stipulation that not more than ten white men should come in to dig. The great advantages he foresaw were that he would get rid of the people who were pestering him and would be able to arm his *impis* with rifles, which would be more effective than assegais in repelling Portuguese or Boer intruders and dealing with the Bechuana.

The Concession was signed at midday, and by four o'clock, before Lobengula had time to change his mind, Rudd was on the road to Kimberley, leaving Maguire and Thompson to fill the gap left by his departure. The story of the Concession nearly had a grim ending during his journey through Bechuanaland. Having separated from his son Frank, and Denny, he lost his way in the desert. The temperature was 112 degrees in the shade, and water was very scarce, although he carried a supply of such inappropriate beverages as champagne, brandy and stout. At last, overcome with heat, thirst and weariness, he just had the strength to bury the gold he was carrying and (it is believed) the precious Concession in an ant-bear hole, writing what he had done on a piece of paper which he fastened to a tree. He then remounted a horse as weary and thirsty as its rider and rode on. The horse fell and Rudd was hurt. It seemed to be the end of the adventure. But as he lay delirious, some Bushmen found him, restored him with water, and took him to the nearest village, whence, after recovering the Concession and the gold, he made his way on to Kimberley.

* * *

Needless to say, Rhodes was delighted with the news of the Concession, a copy of which was at once sent to the Colonial Office with the commendation of the High Commissioner. "The Governor," Rudd wrote to Thompson, "was very pleased to hear the result of our mission and raised no difficulty as to the guns." Actually both Sir Hercules and later Lord Knutsford grumbled over the clause promising a supply of rifles and ammunition to a savage monarch, this being contrary to the General Act of the Brussels Conference, to which Great Britain was a party. For the moment the clause was kept quiet and Rhodes comforted the High Commissioner by assuring him that the Matabele always pushed up their sights, thinking that by so doing their bullets would go farther and hit harder; and with Robinson on his side he knew he had little to fear from the Colonial Office.

The Concession having been secured, a lot had to be done quickly. He must found his Company and get a Charter for it. He must establish his rights by sending a party up to Mashonaland. The first delivery of the promised rifles must be made; and he must eliminate, by purchase or with a high hand, the various people who were claiming to have acquired rival concessions from the king.

Before he had got far with any of these tasks, affairs at Bulawayo began to go ill. Thompson and Maguire were at first successful in holding off the competitors who still lingered in the royal *kraal*. The Fellow of All Souls was actually sent off with an *impi* of savage warriors to turn back from the borders of Matabeleland Alfred Haggard, brother of the novelist. But the Portuguese were said to be moving down from the Zambesi and eastern Mashonaland, while a Boer mission, which arrived, was busy unsettling the king's head, telling him he had in fact sold his country, a statement which, though repeatedly contradicted by Thompson, was uncomfortably near the truth. Most troublesome of all was Maund, who managed to re-establish himself in the royal favour.

Before long Thompson and Maguire found they were regarded almost as hostages. If anything went wrong, or if they were unable much longer to comply with Lobengula's demand for the production of the Concession, their lives would be forfeit, and they had only to glance at the expectant warriors to realise how welcome an order for their liquidation would be and how quickly it would be carried out. The horrible fate of Thompson senior was very much in the mind of his son, who was further disconcerted by his faithful servant's habit of whispering to him every night, "Ou, Master, we never come out of this country alive." Nor was Thompson much comforted by a cheerful letter from Rhodes, begging him to stay and offering him £2,000 a year, a proper house, the despatch of Mrs. Thompson to relieve his loneliness, as well as a share in the Concession which would make him a millionaire.

Maguire was not frightened but bored—bored with the company he had to keep, with the unchanging diet of beef and beer, which gave him indigestion, with the filth, the smell and the garbage of the *kraal*, and with the tedium and hardship of a life for which he was quite unsuited. Finally he was seen by the Matabele brushing his teeth with pink powder in the royal fountain, an action which was interpreted as an attempt to poison the water and led to the confiscation of all his toilet kit, including a

precious bottle of eau-de-Cologne. This may have been the deciding event. At any rate he became so uncomfortable that, as
soon as an opportunity offered, he slipped away from Bulawayo,
leaving Thompson alone there to represent Rhodes.

As serious as the fall from favour of Thompson and Maguire
were the activities of Maund who, working for the Exploring
Company, got out of Lobengula a concession of the mineral rights
in the Mazoe Valley. This directly contravened the Rudd concession, whose validity he consequently sought to disprove. He
and Rhodes's other rivals gave the old king no peace. They
assured him that he had granted Rudd far more than permission
just to dig a big hole in the ground and that the British Government was not behind Rhodes. A little inconsistently, they suggested a doubt of whether the Great White Queen, on whose
friendship Lobengula now relied, even existed. Maund then had
an idea which was to give many people a lot of trouble.[3] Why, he
suggested to Lobengula, should he not send two trusted *indunas* to
London, to act as his "eyes and ears", to establish the existence of
Queen Victoria beyond a doubt, and to carry her a message from
the king? Lobengula was delighted with the suggestion. With
some help he composed a suitable letter, and from among his
indunas chose two trusted men, Mshete and Babayan, who would
act as his emissaries. Probably he told them more than he put in
his letter, which in fact was merely a request for protection against
the Portuguese, who had encroached on his territory.

With the letter and the two *indunas* Maund started off, travelling
to Kimberley through the Transvaal and not through Bechuanaland, where Rhodes might have arranged to have the party
stopped. While he was at Kimberley, he visited the Club, where
he saw Dr. Jameson. The doctor, realising that the journey
might embarrass Rhodes, persuaded Maund to go across to the
cottage where he and Rhodes were living. Rhodes, who was
lying on his bed, bombarded Maund with questions. Why had he
come through the Transvaal? Did he not realise that the Rudd
Concession was impregnable? Would he show Rhodes the letter
to the Queen? Maund's answers were friendly but evasive.
When he refused to show the letter, Rhodes became heated and
dictatorial. The journey must be abandoned. Maund must join
forces with him. The Exploring Company would let him down,
whereas he, Rhodes, could offer many inducements. "See what I
did" for so-and-so and so-and-so, he exclaimed, naming some of
his beneficiaries.[4] He saw nothing wrong in trying to bribe a

man from his duty to his employers. But Maund, by his own account, resisted every blandishment. Later Rhodes told him that he had asked the High Commissioner to "quad" him;[5] but before Maund left Cape Town, the situation had changed. Rhodes and Beit had hurried off to London to "square" the Exploring Company. Fortunately, one of their agents was a railway engineer, Charles Metcalfe, an old Oxford friend of Rhodes, and with his help Rhodes and Beit had little difficulty in buying a big block of the Exploring Company's shares, while Gifford and Cawston consented to become directors of the new Corporation which Rhodes was trying to form.

This settlement did not end Rhodes's troubles, as other claimants to concessions turned up with the most fantastic claims, of most of which he disposed by generous payments; while in the offing an old adversary, the missionary Mackenzie, was busy trying to mobilise public opinion against the Rudd Concession. But at any rate Rhodes and Maund were no longer on opposing sides: they were allies, and at Cape Town Maund showed Rhodes Lobengula's letter, which after all could not be read as an attack on the Rudd Concession. In fact Rhodes commented that it was "the very stick I wanted".[6]

Eventually Maund and his *indunas*, with the approval of the High Commissioner, continued their journey to London. Before delivering their letter to Queen Victoria, the *indunas* saw Lord Knutsford, to whom they seem to have conveyed a general complaint from Lobengula about the people who were plaguing him for concessions. They then saw the Queen, delivered their letter, and received presents to take back with them to the king. Afterwards they enjoyed a carefully prepared tour, which included, for their special benefit, a display of the effect on targets of machine-gun fire. The display would have been more impressive if the guns had not shown an inconvenient tendency to jam. Society, having a growing interest in Central Africa, lionised the *indunas* and gave them a very flattering reception.

Rhodes was in London, busy with the affairs of the Charter and the Exploring Company. He and Maund were now on the friendliest terms.[7] "You go back to him (Lobengula)," said Rhodes, "with your *indunas* and presents from the Queen and keep the old buster in good humour." Maund's task, however, was not to be so simple. A reply from the Queen to Lobengula's letter had been drafted by Knutsford for the *indunas* to take back with them. Unfortunately it was not a reply to the king's letter, but to the complaints voiced personally by the *indunas* to the Secretary of State. Lobengula was advised not to grant concessions of land hastily and not to part with all his property to any one man. "A king gives a stranger an ox, not his whole herd of cattle," the letter concluded.

Although the Rudd Concession dealt only with minerals, the letter might be read as a warning more against Rhodes than against the Portuguese and the other concession-hunters. Maund declares that he saw the danger at once and rushed off to Rhodes's hotel with the letter. Rhodes was dismayed and sent Maund back to Knutsford to get him to alter the letter, but Knutsford either could not or would not comply, his excuse for refusing being that the Queen, who had approved of what he had written, had gone abroad and that on his own responsibility he could not tamper with royal correspondence. Rhodes's next idea was that Maund had better drop the Queen's letter by accident into the sea on the voyage back, a drastic course which Maund says he rejected at once.

Less dangerous, but even more hostile, was a letter from the Aborigines Protection Society, which had entertained the *indunas* to breakfast and sent Lobengula a general warning against signing away his property. One of the *indunas* had caught a cold and kept silent. The other merely thanked "the elderly gentleman for a good breakfast". Even though Maund was now in a sense Rhodes's employee, he felt an obligation to deliver both letters. He says he thought Rhodes reluctantly accepted the situation. But no one knew better than Rhodes that the *indunas*, instead of being "the very stick I wanted", might turn out to be a stick for his own back. His comment on the whole affair scarcely supports the portrait of a man not unduly worried. Maund, he wrote to Cawston, the Chairman of the Exploring Company, was a liar.[8] "If it was not so serious it would be laughable to think that our own servant should be devoting his brains at our expense to destroy all our plans."

Maund, while determined to deliver the Queen's letter, had brought his conscience to the point of agreeing to hold up the letter from the Aborigines Protection Society; but those astute philanthropists, no doubt anticipating some accident to their message in transit, took the precaution of sending a copy to a Mafeking paper, which printed it. In these circumstances Maund delivered both letters to Lobengula, increasing his misgivings over what he had done. The whole incident of the *indunas* was subsequently the subject of a long and rather acrimonious controversy between Maund and Marshall Hole, later the Civil Commissioner at Bulawayo and a historian of the Matabele.

*   *   *

The unfortunate king was getting more and more uneasy. Maguire had gone and Thompson had deceived him, while the other white men in the *kraal* kept warning him that he had given his country away. In his perplexity he consulted the missionaries, in whom he retained a touching confidence. What did the Concession mean? he asked them. That the white men could dig anywhere in his country, in his *kraal* or in his garden? The replies were not reassuring, and the two letters brought back by the *indunas* greatly increased his dismay. To have granted a concession which was a monopoly was surely to have given away "his whole herd of cattle", the very mistake the Queen had warned him not to make.

At last he took action. He had long been suspicious of Lotje, the *induna* who had advised him to put his mark and seal to the Rudd Concession. The man had betrayed him and anyhow for a mere subject was unsuitably rich in cattle. Lobengula called a meeting of the *indunas*, at which he bitterly reproached Helm and Lotje for misleading him. For Lotje his words were a sentence of death. The old man was led outside; according to Marshall Hole he was strangled; according to Maund he was beaten to death with knobkerries. What is certain is that he was murdered and that afterwards, on Lobengula's orders, his wives and household—over three hundred men, women and children—were barbarously put to death.

Early the next morning Thompson drove out to the mission station to consult Helm. As he was starting, an African on a grey horse rode up behind him. "Tomoson," he called in a low voice, "the king says the killing of yesterday is not over." Thompson was sure this was a friendly warning, probably from the king himself, giving him a hint to save his life. At that moment a crowd of young Matabele in war dress appeared. Thompson's nerves, already overstrained, snapped. "They will wipe us all out," he told Maund. Cutting his fastest horse from its traces, he jumped on its back and rode hard for the south. He had neither hat nor saddle, food nor water, and by sundown he was in the Kalahari Desert. After spending the night in a tree (for fear of lions) he rode on next day till his horse foundered. Then, walking or running, he covered thirty or forty miles until, parched with thirst, towards evening he found a waterhole.

Next day he fortunately came on a trader with a small mule-wagon, who gave him a lift to Shoshong, Khama's capital; and from there he made his way to Mafeking. In his own account he emphasises that he had never meant to stay in Bulawayo after he had had by cable the code word "Runnymede", which would mean that the Charter was through; and as, a few days earlier, the cable had come, he regarded himself as released from his under-taking to stay in Bulawayo. His whole story, however, is one of panic.[9] He bolted to safety, without apparently giving a thought to what might happen to the white men remaining in the king's *kraal*. Nor—more naturally—did he have much consideration for the feelings of Rhodes, confronted once more with that vacuum he rightly dreaded.

* * *

When Thompson's cable, giving a lurid account of what was happening and what he believed was about to happen in Bulawayo reached Rhodes, he had just got back from England, and was planning expeditions to Katanga, Gazaland, Nyasaland and other territories he was hoping to bring within the orbit of the new Chartered Company he had founded. Thompson's bulletin dismayed him. Lobengula was the key to all his enterprises. If he now repudiated the Concession, all would have to start again.

Eight months earlier, when Maguire and Thompson were sup-posed to be keeping Lobengula friendly, a notice had appeared in a Mafeking newspaper. It purported to come from the king and announced that he was suspending the Rudd Concession pending an enquiry into its terms. The genuineness of the notice was doubtful, for the author might as easily have been one of the rival concessionaires as Lobengula. But it was an indication to Rhodes that all was not going smoothly at Bulawayo. There were also the rifles and ammunition promised under the Concession and not yet delivered. If Lobengula accepted them, he could hardly repudiate the agreement afterwards. They were ready to go, but someone reliable should see that they reached their destination. Rhodes would have liked to travel north himself, but with so much happening at once, he could not spare the time. He thought of sending Rudd, but that most trustworthy of partners was ill. There was only one other man of the necessary calibre—Dr.

Jameson—and having come to this conclusion, Rhodes opened
on his friend with all his batteries of persuasion.

The Doctor did not want to go. He had his patients and his
practice to consider. He could not afford to leave them for some
months on a journey which was not his business. According to
Colvin, Rhodes used every argument. He was in a difficulty and
Jameson, as a friend, would surely wish to help him out of it.
Jameson needed a holiday (although a less likely holiday resort
than Matabeleland could hardly be imagined). The shooting was
excellent (but Jameson did not much care for shooting). The
future was in the North, and the man who got in quickly, with an
allotment of shares, would make his fortune. It was a choice
between the humdrum of an assured medical practice and the
glorious gamble of a new country; and Jameson could not deny
his liking for a gamble. So the argument went on, with Jameson
contesting every point and Rhodes returning undiscouraged to
the attack.

"No," wrote Colvin, "Jameson would not make an ass of
himself. There were other arguments, many others. Now
qua fun, *qua* excitement, *qua* seeing life, *qua* the really big
thing, *qua* all that duty business too! But they could go over
it again tomorrow morning."

The idea of the gamble, or his friendship with Rhodes, or the
appeal to his sense of duty, or perhaps a combination of arguments may have decided Jameson. Despite the air of cynicism he
liked to wear, he was a romantic at heart, and the thought of personal advantage weighed little with him. He agreed to leave as
soon as possible, with 500 rifles and 500,000 rounds of ammunition, in the company of the contractor who had undertaken to
convey them to Bulawayo, and of a young doctor, Rutherfoord
Harris, who now enters Rhodes's circle to the latter's immediate
advantage and ultimate undoing.

They made their slow journey north, through Mafeking to
Shoshong, across the No Man's Land between Bechuana and
Matabele, to Tati, and on to Manyami's *kraal*, where they ran
into Lobengula's guards in all their savage panoply. There they
were halted by the king's orders, and Jameson, ignoring the
scowls of the warriors, rode on by himself to Bulawayo to ask for
the road. He was given an audience and is said to have been the
first man, white or black—though Shippard must surely have been
another—to approach Lobengula without crawling or to speak

to him without squatting on the ground. Perhaps because of his small stature the breach in protocol was overlooked. At any rate in a very short time he had charmed the king into friendship. He stayed for ten days in Bulawayo, delivered the rifles and ammunition, spoke to the king of Rhodes, and then returned to Kimberley. He was reticent about his journey. "Matabeleland was a little rough," he wrote to his brother, "but I am glad I went, though I don't think financially I shall be any the better."

Six months later, Rhodes, striding in his perplexity about the verandah of his cottage, turned again to Jameson. According to Seymour Fort, he handed Thompson's telegram to his friend in silence. After asking one or two questions, Jameson said, "I will go."

"But when can you start?" asked Rhodes.

"By the post-cart tomorrow morning at four," replied Jameson, "and take Thompson back with me."

He was to have two companions, Denis Doyle and Major Maxwell, men with experience of natives, the former being described as "a skilled interpreter" and the latter as a "good-natured guffy". At Mafeking Jameson found Thompson, whom he persuaded with some difficulty to go back with him to Bulawayo.

The circumstances of this second visit to Bulawayo were much less favourable than they had been on the earlier occasion. With Thompson's flight, which apparently had greatly angered the king, the Concession was in real danger. The friendly Lotje was dead and discredited. The *indunas* had returned with their disturbing letters. Lobengula, who had been indulging unwisely in the brandy and champagne provided by the would-be concessionaires in his *kraal*, was enduring a bad attack of gout, as well as sore eyes. He was in great pain and a very bad temper. When Jameson arrived in the *kraal* and was presented, the king grumbled, "What use is it telling me any more lies? I will not be satisfied unless I can see Ulodzi himself." When he caught sight of Thompson, he said angrily that the man was a liar and a coward and he did not want to talk to him.

Jameson's task was not only to restore friendly feelings and have the Concession confirmed, but somehow to get from the king a permission, which Lobengula was bound to be most reluctant to give, for a party of pioneers to come north and start digging. Rhodes could not have picked a better man to do the work. Jameson began by treating Lobengula as a patient, relieving his pain by morphia injections, and prescribing a course of treatment for his gout. Lobengula, grateful for the ease afforded him, was captivated by Jameson, by his gaiety, good humour and charm. He was the only man who had ever dared to chaff him and was quite unafraid of the warriors. Lobengula made him an *induna*, dressing him in a cloak of ostrich feathers and in oxtail garters, and taking him to a grand review of the *impis*. On 10 December, Jameson got the king's permission for the digging to start; and a few days later for the pioneers to enter Mashonaland, the only condition being that the new honorary *induna* should accompany the white *impi*.

While Jameson was in Bulawayo, an incongruous party arrived —two officers, a corporal-major and a trooper in the Royal Horse Guards, in their red coats, breast-plates, helmets and top-boots. A more unsuitable attire for the hot weather in Central Africa could hardly be imagined, but this was Her Majesty Queen Victoria's way of returning the visit of the *indunas*, and the appearance of the four suffering soldiers undoubtedly impressed the population. The Guardsmen brought with them a letter which fortunately they showed to Jameson before delivering it to the king. It was quite inappropriate, couched in the jargon of Whitehall. Jameson tore it up and composed another letter, commending the Charter and Rhodes in terms which greatly pleased Lobengula.

"A funny life," commented Jameson on his visit, "living in a wagon in the bush with the pure unadulterated savage . . ." Although he had got what he wanted, there was "a great probability of ructions in the future". He had come up, as he thought, for a week and had stayed for months. Though he did not say as much, he had saved the Concession and with it the Charter which Rhodes had just obtained.

Thompson went back with Jameson and did not see Bulawayo again till 1904, when the Matabele kingdom had passed into history. At the railway station one of Lobengula's *indunas*, whom he had known in the old days, accosted him. "Ou, Tomoson," he said, "how have you treated us, after all your promises, which we believed!" Thompson could give him no answer.

Sources

Colvin, Ian: *The Life of Jameson*
Hiller, V. W. (ed.): *Gold and the Gospel in Mashonaland*
Hole, H. M.: *Lobengula*
         The Passing of the Black Kings

Mason, Philip: *The Birth of a Dilemma*
Moffat, R. U.: *John Smith Moffat—A Memoir*
Thompson, F. R.: *Matabele Thompson—An Autobiography*

Notes

[1] "Vindex", 337–8.
[2] Published in Hiller, *op. cit.*
[3] Maund Papers (Rhodes House), 29, p. 9.
[4] Maund Papers, 17, p. 11.

[5] Maund Papers, 18, p. 12.
[6] Maund Papers, 20, p. 2.
[7] Maund Papers, 25, p. 9.
[8] R.H.L. MSS. Afr. s. 73, f. 190.
[9] Maund Papers, 23, p. 2.

CHAPTER TEN

THE CHARTER

FROM the first Rhodes had had little doubt that whatever was done in the African interior would have to be done by him, using for the purpose the formidable strength he was building up at Kimberley and on the Rand. As the business in Basutoland had shown, Cape Colony was too poor, too weak in manpower, and too provincial in outlook as yet to take on the burden of an empire. Whitehall, on the other hand, was remote, bound with red tape, and uncertain in purpose. It might change its policy with its Government, and even if in the end the right policy prevailed, the Civil Service mind would never tolerate the short cuts and high-handed acts which Rhodes often deemed necessary. Whitehall might accept a *fait accompli*, but the onus of accomplishment would rest with Rhodes himself.

"My plan," he wrote in August 1888, just before Rudd started for Bulawayo, "is to give the chief whatever he desires and also offer H.M. Government whole expense of good government. If we get Matabeleland we shall get the balance of Africa."[1] He had given Lobengula what he wanted, or at least what that bewildered monarch supposed he wanted, and the balance of Africa was Rhodes's—on paper; although the nine words which would impress H.M. Government, and public opinion in Britain, had still to be made good.

Rhodes's first object was to eliminate the competition of rival concessionaires, who had secured, or thought and claimed they had secured, grants of some sort to mineral rights in the territory covered by the Rudd Concession; for then, and only then, would he have a clear title for the Charter he hoped to obtain. With his most formidable rivals, the Bechuanaland Exploration Company and the Exploring Company, he had little difficulty. Gifford and Cawston were themselves suggesting incorporation under a Charter empowering them to work the minerals in the countries of Khama and Lobengula and to build a railway to the Zambesi. Rhodes had only to compare the prospects of success of a company with a capital of £50,000 with those of one supported by the thirteen millions of the Goldfields and De Beers, to convince the Colonial Office, and presently Gifford and Cawston, that there

was really no choice. They realised that if they refused to come to
terms, they would assuredly find themselves in a fierce battle with
the strongest financial power in South Africa, on the top of the
war with the Matabele, into which they were likely to be drawn.
Sensibly, they compromised. They agreed to an amalgamation,
with themselves on the board of any new company which might
be formed; and so they found themselves directors first of a Central Search Association and then of the United Concessions
Company, successively the precursors of the greater organisation
which Rhodes hoped to found.

A later claim put Rhodes to a lot of worry and expense. Among
the prowlers in the royal *kraal* at Bulawayo was E. R. Renny-
Tailyour, who was acting on behalf of Edward Lippert, a German
banker who had settled in the Transvaal. In November 1891,
nearly three years after the Rudd Concession was obtained,
Lobengula granted Lippert the land and settlement rights over
the territory covered by what had then become the British South
Africa Company. This new Concession, in addition to carrying
Lobengula's great Elephant Seal with the signatures of four witnesses and two interpreters, was certified by J. S. Moffat, the
Assistant Commissioner in Bechuanaland. Lippert was a cousin
of Beit, with whom he had quarrelled—"little Alfred" never
quarrelled with anybody, but people sometimes quarrelled with
him. Probably Lippert had not the slightest intention of trying
himself to settle Mashonaland; but having detected a flaw in the
Rudd Concession, which dealt only with mineral rights, undoubtedly he intended to profit by his discovery and incidentally
to annoy his cousin. He and Renny-Tailyour accordingly worked
on Lobengula's feelings and fears until he agreed to part with his
land rights to someone who was an antagonist of Rhodes. It may
be that the king did not understand what he was doing; or it may
be that he thought he was being very clever.

Rhodes had an inkling that some mischief was brewing and,
with the help of the High Commissioner, tried to prevent Renny-
Tailyour and Lippert entering Matabeleland. He was, however,
too late. Lobengula made the grant, which was of doubtful
value, as it might be construed as contravening the terms of the
Rudd Concession. Rhodes, who believed that German bankers
and the Transvaal Government were at the back of the business,
began by questioning the validity of Lippert's grant. He asked
the advice of Chamberlain, who said: "Well, you have got the
gold of the whole country, so I should say that even if you have

it not in theory, you have it in practice. But I should like you to
get some territorial acknowledgement from Lobengula, further
strengthening your claim as a whole." Rhodes then decided to
try and buy Lippert out, but Lippert was not an easy seller. He
felt he had the whip hand and was determined to embarrass the
cousin he so disliked.

He may have been brought into a better frame of mind by an
incident recorded by Sir Percy Fitzpatrick. In 1891, a few months
after Lippert had got his Concession, Beit himself visited
Mashonaland. Rhodes was anxious to get a report from a reliable man on how his Pioneers were faring, or whether gold in
any quantity had been discovered, and on what was happening
about the land and Lippert's Concession. Beit made what was,
for a city-bred man, a hazardous and uncomfortable journey
through a country of flood, lion, *tsetse* fly and Matabele. One day
he and his companions were camping by the Shashi River, when
a Cape cart drove up. In it were Mr. and Mrs. Lippert. They can
hardly have been pleased to find that they had stumbled on the
camp of the detested cousin, but were almost at the end of their
tether, having exhausted their provisions and been warned not to
attempt to reach Bulawayo.

Beit rose to the occasion magnificently. He asked them to
luncheon and they stayed for three days as his guests. "I cannot
recall," wrote Fitzpatrick, "a more cheery or delightful picnic."
No doubt delicate questions were avoided by host and guests, but
Lippert may have been mollified by Beit's kindness, as presently
he agreed to accept a sum, which was nevertheless still exorbitant,
for his Concession. Many years later, the courts decided against
its legality, so that Rhodes had not really bought anything of
value. He had, however, got rid of a tiresome competitor at a
critical time, and the judgment was anyhow much too late to
affect the settlement of Rhodesia by the British South Africa
Company.

Having won over his most dangerous competitors, Rhodes
turned his attention to the smaller fry, some of whom put forward
the most outrageous claims. They were, he said, "like locusts".
There were the assigns of one Thomas Baines, hunter, explorer
and artist, who in 1870 had acquired mining rights between the
Gwelo and Hunyani Rivers. The claim had laid dormant for
nearly twenty years and been repudiated by Lobengula, but
Rhodes paid £10,000 for it. As "Matabele" Thompson once said
of him, "He generally paid four times as much as anyone else

would think of paying." Another insistent claimant was the
Wood-Francis-Chapman Concessions Company, which dubiously
owned rights in a disputed territory between the Shashi and
Macloutsie Rivers, the Company's agents being among those
who had made life difficult for Thompson and Maguire in the
king's *kraal*. Yet another claimant was the famous hunter Selous,
who tore up his concession when Rhodes gave him £2,000 to
compensate him for his time and trouble. The business of getting
rid of about a dozen rivals was tedious and expensive, Rhodes declaring later that it had been the most difficult part in founding a
new dominion; but by patience, persistence and the weight of his
purse he cleared his title. Some of the men he paid off out of hand
with lump sums; to others he gave pensions; and a few, like the
optimistic gentleman who wanted to be compensated because the
Rudd Concession had prevented him from applying for a mining
license in Matabeleland, he could afford to send empty away.

Rhodes had other adversaries. Arriving in London in the
spring of 1889, he discovered that he could not avoid entangle-
ment in British politics, and that his opponents would not only be
the disappointed financiers and prospectors. On the warpath
against him was his old enemy of Bechuanaland days, the Rev.
John Mackenzie, the self-constituted champion of the African,
who was supported by the Aborigines Protection Society and—
for less obvious reasons—by the London Chamber of Commerce.
None of them was prepared, without strong protest, to see
Rhodes installed as the dictator of a Chartered Company which
might exploit the people of Central Africa. More serious still was
the attitude of influential members of both Houses of Parliament,
who formed a committee containing such men as the Duke of
Fife, Joseph Chamberlain, Earl Grey and Sir T. Fowell-Buxton.
Disliking the Rudd Concession, they threatened to resist any grant
of a Charter; while behind them was the implacable Labouchere,
a critic of every Imperialist enterprise and of Rhodes himself,
whom he regarded and treated as the arch-offender. Since
Labouchere was as sincere as he was able, the House of Commons
listened to him, and the chances of "squaring" him in the usual
way were negligible.

Rhodes, however, also had his friends, prominent among
them Lord Rothschild, who, as the father-in-law of Lord Rosebery, shortly to be Prime Minister, was a power to reckon with.
The faithful Sir Hercules Robinson, too, had come to England
and was busying himself converting to Rhodes's cause the

F

Colonial Office, from Lord Knutsford downwards. Robinson could be caustic and, in castigating the opposition he found in England, gave some offence by his reference to "the amateur meddling of irresponsible and ill-advised persons"—an obvious thrust at Mackenzie and the Aborigines Protection Society.

A new ally was W. T. Stead, the editor of the *Pall Mall Gazette*, who had gone cheerfully to prison for his convictions and in his columns expounded a practical and benevolent Imperialism, as distinct from Jingoism. Although for some years Rhodes had been an appreciative reader of the *Pall Mall Gazette*, he had never met Stead, who had taken Mackenzie's side in the Bechuanaland business and was inclined to share his view of the Rudd Concession. A mutual friend, Sir Charles Mills (then Agent-General for Cape Colony in London), brought them together. Stead was at first reluctant to meet Rhodes, but eventually cancelled a previous engagement so as to accept an invitation to luncheon. In the afternoon Stead stayed on, he and Rhodes talking together for three hours. Immediately afterwards Stead wrote to his wife: "Rhodes is my man." Rhodes had poured out his plans for the world. "His ideas are federation, expansion and consolidation of the Empire," Stead wrote; and to further these he intended to devote the millions he was making. "It seems all like a fairy dream."

The admiration, though not the agreement, was to survive the strain of Raid and war. Rhodes talked to Stead as he talked to few others—to Neville Pickering once in Kimberley and to Jameson sometimes perhaps, though Jameson's surface cynicism was liable to shut him up "like an oyster", and later to Albert Grey. "He is not religious in the ordinary sense," concluded Stead, "but has a deeply religious sense of his duty to the world." If from that day in April 1889 Rhodes was Stead's man, Stead was equally Rhodes's. He consented to become a trustee of the Will of March 1891, and in the *Pall Mall Gazette* and later in the *Review of Reviews* gave disinterested and valuable support to Rhodes and his ideas.

It was natural that Rhodes should meet almost everybody in London interested in Africa at this time, particularly as the far-reaching and almost unlimited implications of his projected Charter led others to hope that it might become the vehicle of their own unrealised aspirations. Among those whose acquaintance he first made in 1889 were two who were to hold very different opinions about Rhodes, though they later became man and wife: Frederick Lugard, then a junior officer in the army, and Flora Shaw, who already had a considerable reputation as the Colonial expert on *The Times*. Lugard was employed by the African Lakes Company, which had been founded by Scottish business-men and missionaries to develop what is now Nyasaland; but it had run into acute financial difficulties and its directors welcomed Rhodes's suggestion in the summer of 1889 that his proposed Chartered Company should take over its business. Lugard also welcomed Rhodes's intervention, and went to see him in London to discuss how he might take charge in Nyasaland as a servant of the Chartered Company. But to his intense resentment Rhodes dropped the scheme and left England without seeing him again, or even telling him that he was leaving.

Lugard never forgave Rhodes for this treatment, which led to his own career being diverted from Nyasaland to Uganda. Their paths were to cross again in 1895, when both were engaged in plans for developing parts of the Bechuanaland Protectorate with European settlers; but Lugard refused to take employment under the British South Africa Company in any circumstances. Flora Shaw, on the other hand, who also met Rhodes for the first time in 1889, very quickly fell under his spell, and when she became friendly with Lugard as well (which was not until 1893), she did her best to persuade him that he was mistaken about Rhodes. She assured Lugard in November 1895 that Rhodes was com-pletely unselfish and unsordid: "He cares neither for money, nor place, nor power, except in so far as they are a necessity for the accomplishment of the national idea for which he lives." When she wrote those words she was already embroiled with Rhodes in the conspiracy which led to the Jameson Raid—a fact which might have made Lugard still more sceptical had he known it. He was always glad to have steered his course clear of Rhodes's, and deeply regretted that his future wife had not.

The man who was successful, where Lugard failed, in enlisting Rhodes's support for his schemes of developing Nyasaland in 1889 was Harry Johnston, who fell under Rhodes's spell as com-pletely as Flora Shaw, but not for so long. Johnston was an artist, zoologist, naturalist, explorer and empire-builder, who had been a friend of Stanley; and in 1889 was appointed Consul-General in Portuguese East Africa. In the spring of that year Johnston, still in London, was invited to dinner by the assistant editor of the *Fortnightly Review* to meet "an extraordinary fellow over from South Africa, Cecil Rhodes". The other guests at a slightly incongruous party were Walter Pater and Frank Harris. Johnston, like Stead, fell at once under the spell. He and Rhodes talked till midnight and then, as the dinner-party broke up, went on to Rhodes's hotel. There, still in evening dress, but without the daunting presence of the other guests, they went on talking till it was time for breakfast.

Johnston, who was noted for his habit of marching through darkest Africa with a white umbrella, also had his ideas about the future of the Continent, and these in many respects ran parallel to Rhodes's. His immediate concern was to save Nyasaland from the slave traders, and ultimately from the Germans or Portuguese. His ultimate ambition, like Rhodes's, was to build a railway through Africa from south to north, and already he had coined the expression, borrowed by Sir Edwin Arnold and eagerly adopted by Rhodes, of the Cape-to-Cairo Railway. Rhodes was of course enchanted to find such a kinship of minds. He wrote out at once a cheque for £2,000 to help Johnston, who was being stinted of money by the Foreign Office, to carry out his plans in Nyasaland, and told him of his own scheme to found a Chartered Company. The two men then settled the future of Africa between them. Rhodes was to give Johnston practically a free hand between the Zambesi and the White Nile, while he himself extended the future Charter Government up to Lake Tanganyika and possibly farther north.

Johnston, as a consul, was under the Foreign Office, and therefore served as a link with Lord Salisbury, the Prime Minister and Foreign Secretary. He too was an empire-builder in his own way, which was not Rhodes's, nor quite Johnston's. "Who is Mr. Rhodes?" Salisbury asked Johnston, when the latter told him of the schemes he and Rhodes were hatching: "Rather a pro-Boer M.P. in South Africa, I fancy." Salisbury was wise and shrewd, "a great master of flouts and gibes", his old leader Disraeli had called him. With a strong sense of history and of political realities, he had to consider the map not of Africa only, but of the world. Rhodes, with his eye fixed on Central Africa, never quite understood the give and take of international affairs, how the Home Government might deem it desirable to beat a retreat in East Africa in order to make an advance in the Pacific, or to appease the French fishermen off Newfoundland, so as to secure a more sympathetic attitude from France towards a British expansion in Nigeria. Horse-trading of this kind (and there was plenty of it in the scramble for Africa) was all right to Rhodes when it resulted in a gain in his own part of Africa, but all wrong if it involved a concession there.

Salisbury had a further difficulty which Rhodes did not always appreciate. The Prime Minister genuinely wanted to bring all South and Central Africa under British control, but was hampered by the parsimony of Her Majesty's Treasury and in particular by the housewifery of his unyielding Chancellor of the Exchequer, Goschen. To those who thought of the Prime Minister as the unquestioned master of his Cabinet, Salisbury's inability to produce quite small sums of money to support the activities of Johnston were inexplicable, but one of his Chancellors (Lord Randolph Churchill) had already resigned and he could not risk, by flouting the opinions of Lord Randolph's successor, to lose him too.

On occasion Salisbury could speak with no uncertain voice, but none knew better than he that for much of the time he was bluffing. In 1889 an adventurous Portuguese soldier, Major Serpa Pinto, to further his country's vague claims to interior empire, marched into the Shiré highlands with 700 armed Arabs and killed a number of Makololo tribesmen, who were under British protection. An ultimatum, backed by movements of the Royal Navy, was sent to Lisbon and led to Pinto's withdrawal. The shakiness of the Portuguese royal house was another of Salisbury's preoccupations, which Rhodes once described contemptuously as a "monarchial myth". The Braganzas survived the crisis, although a mob broke the windows of the British Embassy in Lisbon. Pinto withdrew, and next year a Convention gave the British the right to extend their settlements round Lake Nyasa and in the Shiré highlands. Portugal in return was allowed to push her trade in the country to the west of these. The Portuguese Cortes refused to ratify the Convention; Rhodes began to move in the north; and Salisbury was beset with fresh appeals to do nothing that would embarrass a precarious monarchy. Nevertheless he stood firm, and in 1891 a new Convention, which practically embodied its predecessor's conditions, was accepted by both countries.

Salisbury was ready to deal firmly with the Portuguese, and even with the more redoubtable Germans, while his humanity, derived from his strong religious feelings, was shocked by the horror of the slave trade, which so far only the British had been active in suppressing. He had, however, a profound regard for the sanctity of international contracts and an anxiety to observe the proprieties of diplomatic intercourse. These sentiments were later to bring him, and still more Johnston, into conflict with Rhodes, whose approach to international problems was more light-hearted. Salisbury was, as Johnston presently became, distrustful of empire-building by private enterprise. So long as Rhodes was able, from his own fortune, to ease the Prime Minister's relations with his Chancellor of the Exchequer, Salisbury was sympathetic and even encouraging; but when the empire-builder began to make complications for the Foreign Office with foreign governments, the sympathy and encouragement faded away. Nor was Salisbury much impressed by the more grandiose of Rhodes's ambitions. He described the projected Cape-to-Cairo Railway, Rhodes's "fish's backbone", as "a curious idea which had lately become prevalent". It would mean a long British strip flanked by German and Belgian territories. "I cannot imagine a more inconvenient possession," he said; or, he might have added, one more likely to arouse the suspicions of foreign powers.

Justice has only long afterwards been accorded to Salisbury's diplomatic work, during his two administrations, in expanding the Empire. He checked the activities of the French in Egypt and Uganda by acknowledging the Republic's rights to the hinterland of Algeria. With Germany he exchanged Heligoland, then deemed a useless and provocative possession, for Zanzibar, thus acquiring for Britain not merely the island which had been the *entrepôt* of the slave trade, but also rights over the coast of what later became Kenya. He made an agreement with the Italians which settled the dispute over the Red Sea *littoral*: and in West Africa, against the opposition of French and Germans, he helped to establish the great British colony of Nigeria. The feelings and language of Rhodes, when he learned of some diplomatic retreat which appeared to affect his African plans unfavourably, were mild, compared with those of Dr. Karl Peters, the German pioneer, when he found that his Government had allowed Zanzibar, Uganda and Nyasaland to pass under the control of his British rivals.

* * *

For the moment Johnston was an enthusiastic ally of Rhodes; and Salisbury, primed and prodded by him, was disposed to be accommodating. The politicians proper presented a tougher problem. Rosebery, under the persuasions of his father-in-law Rothschild, was friendly; the Conservatives would usually follow their leader; but there was a minority which presently, in Westminster's way, might be a majority.

By an action later called in question, Rhodes had secured support in an unlikely quarter, the Irish Parliamentary Party, which was devoted to the cause of winning Home Rule for Ireland and was disinclined to encourage imperialistic designs elsewhere on the part of the Government of the United Kingdom. In the autumn of 1887, when Rhodes was travelling back to the Cape, a fellow-passenger was Swift MacNeill, a prominent Irish Nationalist Member of Parliament, who was as close as anyone could be to the counsels of its remarkable and secretive leader, Parnell. Rhodes, whose interest in Party politics was coloured by his plans for the British Empire, had disliked the Home Rule Bill of 1886, because under it the Irish Members would leave Westminster. In his view, by this simple exclusion what might have been the beginning of an Imperial Federation had been transformed into an act of separation. If in a future Bill this particular blemish could be removed and Irish members (probably in reduced numbers) were to continue to sit in the British House of Commons, a precedent would have been created for the future representation of Britain's colonies.

Rhodes declared his readiness, if these circumstances were realised, not merely to support a Home Rule Bill, but to pay £10,000 into the funds of the Nationalist Party. So he assured MacNeill, who on his side told Rhodes that he thought Parnell would make no objection to the stipulation. Later, when he had returned to England, MacNeill wrote to Rhodes that this assumption was correct, and in 1888, when Rhodes too was back in London, MacNeill arranged for Parnell to meet him at the Westminster Palace Hotel, where Rhodes was staying. The interview was not very easy. Afterwards Rhodes said that Parnell was "the hardest man but one to convince whom I ever met. . . . He trusted no one." The one exception was perhaps Kruger, or perhaps Sir Michael Hicks-Beach, though in both those cases Rhodes failed.

Parnell did not give Rhodes all he wanted, but in the exchange of letters which followed the meeting, he wrote, "My own feeling upon the matter is, that if Mr. Gladstone includes in his next Home Rule measure provisions for such retention [of Irish members at Westminster], we should cheerfully concur in them, and accept them with good will and good faith, with the intention of taking our share in the Imperial partnership." As to the subsequent representation of the colonies, on which Rhodes was insistent, all that Parnell would say was that if any of them should, in sharing "the cost of Imperial matters", express a wish to be represented at Westminster, "I quite think it should be accorded to them". Rhodes replied with a cheque for £5,000 as a first instalment, believing that a Home Rule Bill in the form suggested would lead "not to disintegration, but really to a closer union of the Empire".

Later, when the news of Rhodes's gift became known, people were not slow to say that as usual he was giving bribes to get his way. The suggestion was hardly fair. In 1887, when the gift was first proposed, the Charter was still remote. Rhodes may well have thought that it was worth his while to secure the sympathy of the Irish Party, but his reason was perfectly genuine. He wanted Imperial Federation and believed that a Home Rule Bill, instead of being a measure of disruption, could prepare the way for colonial representation in the Parliament of Westminster. The custom by which wealthy men pay large sums of money into the Party coffers may be reprehensible, but is quite common, and there is seldom any suggestion of impropriety. Tactically, Rhodes's gift was not very prudent, but the affair was an example less of unscrupulous conduct than of political naïveté. However, Parnell kept his pledge, even after political catastrophe had overwhelmed him, and in the abortive Second Home Rule Bill of 1892 Irish representation at Westminster was retained.

Rhodes's second intervention in party politics was also criticised, but whereas his gift to the Irish Party came too soon to be associated with the Charter, his gift to the Liberal Party came too late. In 1890 Schnadhorst, the brilliant party organiser, who had once secured and held Birmingham for Joseph Chamberlain, visited the Cape for reasons of health. He saw Rhodes at Kimberley and discussed with him the prospects of what was then known as Liberal Imperialism, a creed favoured by Rosebery and some of the more promising members of the Liberal Parliamentary Party. Rhodes, while sympathetic with much of the Liberal policy, feared that the Liberals, if returned to power, would evacuate Egypt, the terminus of his projected railway. Schnadhorst, whose purpose was frankly financial, tried to reassure him, and later, when both were back in London, suggested that, with a General Election in the offing, a subscription to the funds of the Liberal Party would be timely and welcome. Rhodes made two conditions—the first that his contribution should be kept secret, and the second that if a future Home Rule Bill excluded Irish Members from Westminster, his cheque should be returned to him. While Egypt was not mentioned, it was, as he wrote later, "the paramount thought in my mind", and in a postscript to the letter which accompanied his cheque, he deplored a recent speech by John Morley in favour of the abandonment of Egypt, adding, "If you think your party hopeless, keep the money, but give it to some charity you approve of. It would be an awful thing to give my money to breaking up the Empire." The money was kept and presumably spent; Egypt was not abandoned; and when the whole affair came to light in 1901, it was clear that there had been no corrupt bargain and that Schnadhorst had not divulged Rhodes's gift to the leaders of the Party.

* * *

Having cleared his title to the Rudd Concession, eliminated the competition of rivals, and won some popular support for his plans, Rhodes's next task was to get his Charter. He was anxious to visit his new kingdom as soon as possible. "I am awfully restless," he told Newton, the Assistant Imperial Commissioner in Bechuanaland, in August 1888, "that I cannot get away to run my hobby in Matabeleland." "I am coming as soon as possible," he wrote in the same month; "You may rely on me as I come being prepared to stop and work for our big objects even if it is a matter of years: I shall bring what you much need in a great undertaking, the 'sinews of war', both in my private fortune and my trust deed with twenty millions behind it."[2] But this was to anticipate events. Until he had that "trust deed", that is the Charter, he could do little about his "hobby". With the help of Sir Hercules Robinson, he had brought over on to his side Lord Knutsford, the Colonial Secretary, and with that of Harry Johnston he was assured of the sympathy, or at least the complaisance, of Lord Salisbury.

On 30 April 1889 Gifford, Rhodes, Rudd and Beit, applied for a Charter which would empower them to extend the railway and telegraph northwards, to encourage emigration and colonisation, to promote trade and commerce, and to develop minerals. It will be observed that although the Rudd Concession dealt only with the last purpose—"to develop minerals"—Rhodes assumed that the other objects of the new Chartered Company were or would be covered; and that by a myopia we must regard as astonishing, the discrepancy between what the Concession gave

and what the Charter would authorise did not at first occur to
anybody of consequence. Knutsford, forwarding the proposal to
the Prime Minister, pointed out that a Chartered Company
would save the Treasury the kind of heavy expenditure it had
incurred most unwillingly over Bechuanaland; that the operations
of such a body would be subject to the control of the Government; and that if the Charter were refused, Rhodes could in fact
obtain much the same result, without the control, by proceeding
under the Joint Stock Companies Act. Salisbury, conscious of
the difficulty he had in extracting money from the Treasury or the
House of Commons for his schemes in Central Africa, gave his
approval to the application, even though his private feeling was
that most of the objects of the new Company would be more
properly pursued by the Government.

He authorised Rhodes and his allies to go ahead and draft the
Charter they wanted, but warned them that they would be wise to
include among their directors men of "social and political standing". The quartet who made the application might be well known
in South Africa and even in the City of London, but a wider fame
was desirable on the Board of a Chartered Company. Rhodes
consulted his friend, Colonel Euan Smith, to discover who were
the right people to ask. Their first idea was to invite Lord Balfour of Burleigh to be Chairman; but as he held a minor office in
the Government, he was unlikely to be attracted. The next suggestion was the Duke of Abercorn, who, besides his title, had
great estates, especially in Northern Ireland, and had sat for
twenty years in the House of Commons. He had the right social
and political qualifications and, on being invited, agreed to serve.

For the other directors the Duke of Fife, son-in-law of the
Prince of Wales, was an obvious trump card; and he too accepted
the invitation. The third man was perhaps the most important of
all. Prominent among the members of the South African Committee, which had been so critical of the Rudd Concession, was
Albert Grey, the grandson of the Prime Minister of the Reform
Bill, whom Rhodes now, following his old policy of conciliating
the opposition, invited to join the Board. Grey, who hardly knew
Rhodes, was at first at a loss to know what answer to give. He
consulted Salisbury, who told him that if Rhodes was prevented
from carrying out his plans in Central Africa, the Government
was most unlikely to take action and no one else could step in
with any hope of success. Undecided by this oracular answer,
Grey then went to Joseph Chamberlain and asked his advice.

"Well," said Chamberlain, "I know only three things about Rhodes and they all put me against him: (1) he has made an enormous fortune very rapidly, (2) he is an Afrikander [meaning that he was not an Imperialist], (3) he gave £10,000 to Parnell." Grey replied that he understood Rhodes to be nevertheless "a single-minded patriot". "Well, I have given you my advice," retorted Chamberlain, "you must decide for yourself."

After some heart-searching, Grey decided to accept the invitation and to join the Board. He was a priceless asset to it. Lord Milner once said of him, "He has a record of public service of which any man might be proud," while Leonard (afterwards Lord) Courtney, an honoured public figure, called him "the Paladin of his generation". His integrity was or seemed to be a guarantee of the respectability of any cause he made his own. He was an ardent Imperialist, on the noblest grounds. "The Empire is my country," he would write in autograph books: "England is my home." Himself a man of innumerable friends, he fell at once under the spell of Rhodes. Later Harold Begbie once asked him who of all the men he had known impressed him most. "Cecil Rhodes," he replied at once, adding: "for the bigness of his mind and the tenderness of his heart." He believed that Rhodes's occasional uncouthness was but an armour for his shyness. "Under a rough exterior and behind an uningratiating manner, he had the heart of a child." This was a partial picture. When Albert Grey made a friend, he would hear no ill of him, and while he had penetrated behind the "rough exterior" and "uningratiating" manner, there was a side of Rhodes which Grey neither saw nor probably allowed himself to see. The conquest of Grey was a most important achievement: Rhodes had turned an adversary into an ally, and had secured the name and friendship of one of the most respected men in public life.

The Charter had then to be drafted to the satisfaction of the Colonial and Foreign Offices and the Privy Council, before submission for the Queen's signature. Rhodes, having finished his work on the drafting, began to be impatient of waiting in London, particularly since, as the news of what he was doing began to get around, society was showing a disposition to lionise him. Mere social functions were never to his taste. "I see," he said, "no reason to make my interior a dustbin for anyone." As the hostesses of London appeared to think otherwise, he determined to return to South Africa, where so much work was waiting for him.

Before he left, and before the Letters Patent granting a Royal

Charter of Incorporation to the British South Africa Company
had received the royal signature, he declared a wish to pay the
Government at once the £30,000 he was undertaking to find for a
telegraph line from Mafeking, as well as the £4,000 a year offered
by the Charter for the establishment of a British Resident in Bulawayo to advise Lobengula. Very deliberately the Colonial Office
accepted both offers in principle; whereupon Rhodes by return
of post asked to whom the cheque should be made payable. The
Colonial Office, which did not like being hustled in this way,
answered after a week's delay, "Not so fast; you must wait till the
Charter is granted." Rhodes could never wait and, as soon as he
got back to South Africa, cabled to the Colonial Office for 250
miles of telegraph wire, with the poles to carry it. The Colonial
Office was as cautious as Rhodes was impatient: it would neither
accept the cheque nor send off the equipment until the Charter
had been signed.

Her Majesty gave her signature (which Rhodes had been treating as the merest formality) on 29 October 1889. The date might
be described as the birthday of a new Colony. The powers
granted to the British South Africa Company were enormous. It
could operate throughout the whole of South Africa north of the
Colony of Bechuanaland, north and west of the Transvaal, and
west of Portuguese East Africa. On Rhodes's insistence, against
some opposition, no northern limit was fixed. Within this vast
and vaguely defined area, the Company could:

> "make treaties, promulgate laws, preserve the peace, main-
> tain a police force, and acquire new concessions. It could
> make roads, railways, harbours, or undertake other public
> works, own or charter ships, engage in mining or any other
> industry, establish banks, make land grants, and carry on any
> lawful commerce, trade, pursuit or business."

All the panoply of a modern state was extracted from the concession of mineral rights which was all Lobengula thought he had
given away.

Certain safeguards were included. Clauses protected native
rights, freedom of worship, and any other concessions which
might still, despite Rhodes, be in existence. The Secretary of
State had a limited right of supervision, and after twenty-five
years, or sooner if the company abused its privileges, the Charter
could be revoked. Rhodes in fact was given all he wanted.

The capital of the new Company was fixed at a million pounds in £1 shares, of which the promoters took 90,000 in exchange for the rights and concessions they were handing over, and the United Concessions Company, the precursor of B.S.A., was given a half share in any future profits. Notwithstanding these considerable reservations, subscribers poured in. De Beers took 200,000 shares, while, to Rhodes's satisfaction, 150,000 were applied for by Dutch and British colonists. In London the wildest tales were circulating, of a land, *The Times* remarked in a leading article, "three times the size of the United Kingdom"—a land of milk and honey, gold and diamonds. Here was Rhodes's philanthropy plus five per cent about to be quoted on the London Stock Exchange, in a combination irresistible to the large and small investor, even to those who applied for a single share so that they might have a minute part in so great an enterprise.

Rhodes at the time was still in South Africa, but everyone, even, to his special gratification, the London bus-drivers (whom he regarded as public opinion *par excellence*), were talking of him and his plans. He was only thirty-six and already had done great things. As for opposition, it wilted away amid the storm of approval. Labouchere asked a few questions in the House of Commons and the Aborigines Protection Society made a few gloomy prognostications, but in almost every other quarter the satisfaction was complete.

Sources

Works mentioned under Chapter Nine, and additionally:
   Begbie, Harold: *Albert, Fourth Earl Grey*
   Cecil, Lady Gwendolin: *The Life of Robert, Marquis of Salisbury*
   Fitzpatrick, Percy: *South African Memories*
   Oliver, Roland: *Sir Harry Johnston and the Scramble for Africa*
   Perham, Margery: *Lugard*
   Stead, W. T.: *The Last Will and Testament of Cecil J. Rhodes*

Notes

[1] Central African Archives RH/1/3/1.   [3] Williams, 137-8.
[2] Central African Archives RH/1/3/1.

CHAPTER ELEVEN

THE PIONEERS

WHEN Rhodes returned to South Africa in August 1889, he could afford to lose and, as usual, lost no time. Even while the Charter was awaiting the royal signature, he was pushing the railway up from Kimberley and scanning more closely than ever the map of Central Africa. Beyond Matabeleland and Mashonaland was that absence of frontier he had been so careful to ensure, that broad tract bordered on the west by Portuguese Angola, on the north-west by the Belgian Congo, on the north by the No Man's Land round Lake Nyasa, and on the east by Portuguese East Africa. Others besides Rhodes were casting jealous eyes on the interior. The Transvaal Boers were reported to be organising a *trek*, the Portuguese had not given up hope of reasserting their claims and were rumoured to be preparing an expedition, while the Germans, though temporarily quiescent, were by no means disinterested and had not relinquished their ambitions of driving a wedge across Africa from Damaraland. Even the Belgians in the north were stirring. In Nyasaland the African Lakes Company was fighting a losing battle against the Arab slave raiders, the Portuguese and bankruptcy. The interior was as full of problems as it was of promise. Besides that vacuum in Bulawayo which Rhodes had dreaded was a vacuum in Central Africa, which was even more dangerous. The Charter made bold claims, but the real test was still to come. Rhodes must break through the Matabele crust into the vast almost empty interior. A lot of people might claim it, but the first occupier would have it.

Meanwhile in Bulawayo Lobengula, whose suspicions Jameson had momentarily lulled, was having renewed misgivings. He did not deny the Concession. There it was, in Moffat's keeping, and Queen Victoria had recommended the Charter in the letter brought by the party of Royal Horse Guards and edited by Jameson. But his understanding of what he had given away differed widely from Rhodes's understanding of what he had got. Lobengula insisted that he had granted only the right to dig "one hole". With his approval Jameson had sent out a few prospectors to Ramaquebana, above Tati. They had dug and found nothing. "Well," said the King to Jameson, "you had better look for another place." Could he go east? asked Jameson. "Yes," replied the king; and that one unguarded word was sufficient. Jameson traced on the map a route which, avoiding Matabeleland, would penetrate into Mashonaland. Lobengula not only assented to this new plan, but gave permission for some of his people to be enrolled to help cut the road. Jameson returned to Kimberley, having got what he wanted, while Lobengula at last took delivery of the rifles, which had been lying at Mvatjwa, and by so doing implicitly endorsed the validity of the Concession.

The truth is that his mood was always changing. When Dakatela (Jameson) was there, with his hypodermic needle, his gaiety and his charm, the king was compliant; but when Dakatela was gone the king began to listen to the voices of his *indunas*, who kept telling him he had given away his country. He would then slip back into suspicion and hostility, until rumours that the Portuguese or the Boers were on the march inclined him once more to Rhodes and the Charter as the lesser evils. So at one moment he wanted Rhodes to move quickly; at the next he did not want him to move at all.

Rhodes was untroubled by the question of what Lobengula's kingdom comprised or by repetitions of the "one hole" argument. On one view the kingdom was Matabeleland proper; but Lobengula claimed that any country his raiding parties could reach were in his empire. Thus this would include Mashonaland and possibly Barotseland and Manicaland. (In 1888 Queen Victoria officially recognised Lobengula as sovereign of both the Matabele and Mashona peoples.) Rhodes's plan was to obtain Lobengula's permission to send a party through, so that he could throw his tentacles into these more distant lands, where he would stake claims and make treaties with the ruling chiefs.

In May 1890 he summoned to a council of war at Kimberley some of the young men who had begun to work for him. A photograph of those days shows them in a group. Rhodes is sitting in the middle, genial and calm of countenance. On his right is Harry Johnston, wearing a peculiar little cap. On his left is Colquhoun, already known for his adventurous journeys of exploration in western China and on the frontier of Burma. Also in the group are Rochfort Maguire, clad once more as a Fellow of All Souls might be expected to be; John Moir, the founder of the African Lakes Company; Grant, son of the man who with Speke had discovered the source of the White Nile; and Joseph Thomson, who had already won fame by his journeys in Masailand,

Nigeria and the Sudan. Seldom can the Kimberley Club have sheltered so unusual a gathering. They met, got their instructions from Rhodes, and went off to the north on their various missions, with what success will presently appear. Essential to that success was the despatch of the expedition to occupy the land.

*   *   *

Rhodes now began to grapple seriously with problems of recruiting, organising, equipping and routeing. He found no lack of recruits. In fact, as had become usual with his enterprises of another sort in those days, the issue was heavily over-subscribed and many men had to be turned away. He wanted his pioneers young, fit and preferably unmarried: men who were first-class shots and if possible had experience of or an aptitude for some trade: in fact they were to be a community in embryo. He also wanted them to come from every district in South Africa, including the Republics, so that the sentiment behind the pioneers would be spread widely. The new country would then not be just another British colony. It would belong to the Cape, and therefore ultimately to the future Union of South Africa. The terms he offered were generous—pay of seven-and-sixpence a day, 3,000 acres of farm land, and fifteen gold claims.

He recognised that to guard the column on the march, he must also have a small force of disciplined men. These gave him more trouble than the pioneers. He began by approaching Colonel Sir Frederick Carrington of the Bechuanaland Police, who had very expensive ideas. He wanted 2,500 men and for himself the local rank of major-general. The cost of such an escort would have been prohibitive. The Chartered Company had a wide purse, but if it was to start off with a military expedition on the scale proposed by Carrington, its funds were likely to be exhausted before the actual settlement and development of the country had begun. Besides, a military expedition was just what Rhodes wanted to avoid, as it would certainly clash with Lobengula's *impis* and would be fighting in thick bush, where the Europeans would lose much of the advantage of their superior weapons.

Rhodes had reached a deadlock when one day, shortly before Christmas 1889, he was breakfasting at the Kimberley Club. There, seeing someone he vaguely recognised as a "man from the Interior", he went and sat by him. The man was Frank Johnson, aged twenty-three, who, while serving with the Bechuanaland Border Police, had visited Matabeleland, subsequently becoming General Manager of the Bechuanaland Exploration Company.

"Typically," he wrote,[1]

"without saying good morning or asking where I had come from, Rhodes plunged straight into his troubles. 'Carrington wants to be made a major-general at my expense,' he almost screamed. 'Now you know the interior. How many men do you think are wanted?'"

Johnson had snorted with contempt on hearing Carrington's estimate and replied light-heartedly, "2,500 men? Nonsense! Why, with 250 men I would go anywhere in Africa."

"I can see the picture now," Johnson recalled:

"Rhodes, without comment, going on with his eggs and bacon for a minute. Then, looking up, the practical financier spoke. What would a force of 250 men cost? I replied that I had not the remotest idea, but as the Cape train did not leave till next morning, if he would give me the use of a room in his house opposite the Club, with plenty of foolscap, I could tell him by lunch-time."

Having been a quartermaster-sergeant, Johnson had no difficulty in working out the cost and returned to Rhodes with a figure of £94,100.

"That's splendid," said Rhodes. "You are quite right. I will not make Carrington a major-general. I appoint you to command the expedition. When will you start?"

This was going much too fast; and to Rhodes's astonishment and anger the young man replied that nothing would induce him to serve in the Chartered Company so long as Gifford and Cawston, who had greatly offended him when he was with the Bechuanaland Exploration Company, were on the Board. After a stormy discussion, Johnson left to catch his train to Cape Town, while Rhodes went round Kimberley showing the plans and estimates to his friends, who all assured him that Johnson was a "stupid or reckless young man" and that Carrington was right.

Nevertheless Carrington wanted a million and Johnson less than a hundred thousand to do the same job. Also Rhodes, having formed a poor opinion of most of the soldiers with whom he had had dealings, preferred to trust his own judgment of a man and liked the look of Johnson. On 26 December he sent him a wire, bidding him meet the train from Kimberley next morning.

Rhodes, on arriving, simply said, "Take me where we can talk."
Climbing into a hansom, they drove to the top of Adderley Street,
where they got out. (As usual Rhodes had no small change on
him and Johnson had to pay the driver.) They turned into
Government Avenue and for nearly three hours walked up and
down it under van Riebeeck's great oaks. "I was alternately jeered
at, threatened and bribed," wrote Johnson. "I was ultimately
to be made a director of De Beers, to be given a seat in the Cape
House of Assembly, given a big bonus—in a word, I was to be a
made man if I but carried the thing through successfully on my
own estimates."

In the end, Johnson, who although a very obstinate young
man was hungry and wanted his breakfast, had an idea. "Look
here," he said, "you give me a cheque for £94,000 and I will hand
your country over to you fit for civil government. I shall thus
be a contractor and not a servant of your Company."

Rhodes, without a sign that he had heard what Johnson had
said, walked on for at least a hundred yards, with his hands behind his back, weighing his intuition against what his friends at
Kimberley had told him. At last he said, "I'll give you that
cheque. Now let's go to Poole's and have breakfast."

Over the eggs and bacon Johnson suggested that the necessary
contract should be drawn up by a lawyer.

"We'll go to no lawyers," snapped Rhodes. "If you are capable
of organising this expedition, you are capable of drawing up the
agreement." When it was ready, it was to go to Sivewright, who,
as a personal friend, would pronounce upon it. That point being
settled, a cheque for £20,000 on account changed hands.

According to Frank Johnson's story, the total agreed was
£94,000, but the report of the Directors of the British South
African Company for the eighteen months from October 1889 to
March 1891 concludes: "The cost to the Company of this expedition was £89,285. 10. 0. apart from the obligation to grant land
and mineral rights." The explanation may be that in the process of
organising the pioneers, their numbers were reduced from 250 to
200, 100 armed and mounted Bamangwatos, for the purpose of
cutting the road, being substituted for 50 settlers. At any rate
Johnson was to prove even better than his word.

*   *   *

Meanwhile Rhodes had also been busy over the question of the
route the column should take. It might follow the Missionaries'

Road to Mafeking, continue north-east roughly along the line of the Crocodile River, and then push across the Macloutsie River by the 'Royal Road' to Bulawayo. That, as the direct and easiest route, was the one which Rhodes at first favoured. He depended much for advice, however, on the most noted hunter of his time, Frederick Courtenay Selous, then a man of forty, with an unequalled knowledge of Central Africa. Selous was convinced that the sight of a long straggling column of wagons and marching men would be a challenge too tempting for the Matabele warriors to ignore. The column would never get through without heavy fighting under every disadvantage.

Rhodes eventually yielded to Selous's arguments. The alternative was, as far as possible avoiding Matabeleland altogether, to send the column into Mashonaland, which was doubtfully part of Lobengula's empire and was anyhow a good way from his capital and his *impis*. The trouble about this route was that the pioneers would have to traverse 460 miles of trackless wilderness, cutting a road the whole way. On one flank would be Lobengula, on the other the Boers, and much of the ground was bushveld and swamp, which would be ideal for ambushes. Several rivers too had to be crossed, and unless the pioneers could get through before the rains broke in November, they were unlikely to get through at all. In spite of these disadvantages, however, Selous was sure that at all costs the column must avoid the Matabele *kraals* and capital on the more direct road.

Having won Rhodes's consent to the longer route, Selous went up to Bulawayo to try to get Lobengula's, and also to make sure that the men the king had promised Jameson for cutting the road would be forthcoming. Lobengula knew Selous, and had not quite forgiven him because once he had shot a hippopotamus without the royal permission. Lobengula would not hear of the proposed route. "There is only one road to Mashonaland," he told Selous, "and that goes through my country and past Bulawayo." He reverted to his old grievance, the failure of Rhodes to visit him. "I want to see the big white chief himself," he grumbled.

As Selous could get nothing out of the king, he went back to Kimberley. Rhodes was anxious to accept Lobengula's invitation, but Selous begged him not to venture his person in Bulawayo. He believed that Lobengula would certainly seize him as a hostage, and even if he did not kill him, would keep him out of action at a time when his direction was essential to the success of the expedition. Since Rhodes could not be spared and Doyle, being little more than an interpreter, was quite inadequate to fill the vacuum, Jameson, now known to the Matabele as "Rhodes's Mouth", must return to Bulawayo and keep Lobengula quiet during the critical months when the pioneers were preparing for their march. Selous seems to have intended accompanying Jameson to Bulawayo, but the latter, who must have known of the king's grudge against the great hunter, managed to shake him off at Tati and went on alone.

The preparations now began to go forward apace. In addition to the pioneers, men had to be recruited in a hurry to form the five troops of British South Africa Company's Police who, the High Commissioner insisted, were required to protect the expedition on the line of march. The command of these was given to Lt.-Colonel E. G. Pennefather of the Inniskilling Dragoons, who had seen service in the Zulu and Boer campaigns. Johnson would head the pioneers, with three assistants as his squadron commanders. Colquhoun, who had had wide administrative experience in India, was to be the chief magistrate and first Administrator, while Selous of course was the guide. Since Jameson would also join the expedition as Rhodes's representative, holding his power of attorney, the command was a good deal divided and it would not always be easy to determine the responsibility for a particular decision.

Young army officers and recruits began to arrive at Mafeking, the first point of assembly, and by April, after some sifting, a likely lot of pioneers had been enrolled. They included farmers, artisans, miners, doctors, lawyers, engineers, builders, bakers, soldiers, sailors, cadets of good family and no special occupation, cricketers, three parsons and a Jesuit. Marshall Hole could claim with justification that "no finer *corps d'élite* than the British South Africa's Company Police and the Mashonaland Pioneers had ever been raised". Back at Kimberley, Rutherfoord Harris, who was now local secretary of the Chartered Company, was acting as Adjutant and Quartermaster General, and often rather more. When the muster was fairly complete, the whole expedition moved by a twenty days' march to Macloutsie, on the edge of the territory in dispute between Lobengula and Khama.

Rhodes himself was most anxious to join the pioneers, but was prevented by a political crisis. As the crisis ended in his becoming Prime Minister of Cape Colony, he obviously could not possibly leave Cape Town and plunge for an indefinite period into the wilderness. Meanwhile, in two quarters the preparations had not escaped unfavourable attention.

As early as September 1889, Rhodes had been perturbed by rumours, later confirmed by Selous, of an impending Boer *trek* into Mashonaland. "You cannot allow a single Boer to settle across the Limpopo," he told the Imperial Secretary, "until our position in the north is secure." Sir Henry Loch, who had succeeded Sir Hercules Robinson as Governor and High Commissioner, after protesting to Kruger, met him at Blignaut's Pont in March 1890, Rhodes being present at the interview. Kruger knew all about the projected *trek*, which was being organised by would-be pioneers in the Waterberg district of the Transvaal, under the leadership of one Adendorff. When Loch pointed out that the *trek* would contravene both the London Convention of 1884 and the Pretoria Convention of 1890, Kruger could hardly gainsay him. At any rate, for the moment he was more concerned with Swaziland and the possibility of securing access for the Transvaal to a port on the east coast.

In return for some rather vague assurances from Loch on the subject, he promised to discourage the *trek* and refrain from interfering with the Charter. He may have yielded so easily through disappointment over his failure to win the support of Hofmeyr and the Bond, whom Rhodes had won over to his view that the settlement of Mashonaland could only be made under the Charter and that Dutch as well as English would be welcome to share in the enterprise. Kruger, having given his word, kept it, and the proposed *trek* never materialised. As an additional precaution, Loch had ordered parties of the Bechuanaland Police down to the Transvaal border, with instructions to turn back any intruders.

Another, less serious and quite unconnected, *trek* was being organised by one van Reenen, who had obtained a promise of farms in Manicaland from the Portuguese Consul-General at Cape Town. With these men, as with a recalcitrant rump of Adendorff's trek, Jameson, who was slipping about like quicksilver, dealt promptly and adroitly. Independent *treks*, he warned the Boers, could not be countenanced; but any of them might enter Mashonaland as settlers under the Charter and would be allotted farms.

Meanwhile, in Bulawayo, Lobengula, whose spies were telling him all about the preparations on the Macloutsie, was becoming more and more restive. His warriors were clamouring for permission to attack the gathering pioneers and he had lost any confidence he had ever had in Doyle, who, he declared, had "given my words falsely to Rhodes".

In April Jameson, at Bulawayo, had found Lobengula in a most difficult mood. When told of the plans for the pioneer column, he objected strongly. What was the need for police and soldiers? he asked. Jameson answered that they were simply to protect the column from attacks by Boers or Portuguese or anyone else who might molest them. Why did not the column take the obvious road through Matabeleland? Because, said Jameson, the Queen had given an order that there was to be no interference with the Matabele. He had an answer to every objection. Before leaving he had a final interview with the king, whom he described as an "unwieldy mass of dark copper-coloured flesh", stirring restlessly in the darkness of his hut. His account was given later to a friend, Howard Pim:[2]

"The old man was asleep," he said, "wrapped in his karosses. Presently he woke, bounced to his feet and, stark naked, raged about the hut. 'Who told Selous he could make that road?' he shouted, and would not listen to a word I said. Still snorting defiance, he suddenly plunged through the door. We tried to follow, but he bolted into his women's quarters, and we could not follow.

"Returning to our waggon, we awaited developments, as messengers were going to and fro. Later in the day the King's oxen were driven up and inspanned, and the old man climbed into the waggon and drove away. After some trouble I found out he had gone to his sacred goat *kraal* some 10 miles away. We were not interfered with, so after dark I inspanned also and followed him.

"Again we arrived before dawn, and I waited until I saw smoke rising from the *kraal*, which was surrounded by a palisade. Doyle and I walked over and entered. In the centre the King was sacrificing; his back was to us; the victim on a small altar in front of him, and beyond in a semi-circle his doctors.

"The floor of the *kraal* was thick with dung, so he could not hear our footsteps, but we were in full view of the doctors, and he quickly saw they were looking at something behind him, and turned round.

"I never saw astonishment so plainly written on any face. He stood motionless, his jaw dropped, and with wide open mouth he gaped at us. We walked right up to him; as we did so the doctors, with murmurs of rage and horror at our sacrilege, closed round us. I stopped, he was still motionless, and then I said—'The King told me *I* might make the the road. Did the King lie?'

"How long the silence lasted I do not know, but at last he raised himself to his full height, looked me straight in the eyes—'The King never lies,' he said; waved his doctors back to their places, turned his back on me and continued his sacrificing. 'I thank the King,' I said. We left the *kraal*, returned to Palapye, and, as you know, the expedition went through unmolested."

With that grain of assent Jameson had to content himself. He went off and never saw Lobengula again.

After Jameson's departure, the position once more deteriorated. Lobengula began to summon his *impis* to Bulawayo and sent the High Commissioner a formal protest at the preparations on his borders. Maxwell, now in charge for the Charter, took on himself to warn the missionaries and any other white people still in the capital that they had better leave. This threatened exodus further angered the king and the warriors, who saw some of their prospective victims about to escape. Yet, grumble as he did, Lobengula kept his men under control.

By the middle of June 1890, all was ready at Macloutsie and the High Commissioner gave his consent to the entry of the column into Mashonaland by the route agreed upon, as soon as Major-General (later Lord) Methuen was satisfied with its general efficiency. The High Commissioner did more than consent. He authorised the posting of a strong force of the Bechuanaland Police on the Matabele border; and these, Selous believed, were chiefly responsible for Lobengula's later inactivity. Had he loosed his *impis* on Jameson's column, he would have exposed an almost undefended capital to attack.

Neither Methuen's inspection nor his address to the officers seems to have been very serious.

"Gentlemen, have you got maps?"

"Yes, Sir."

"And pencils?"

"Yes, Sir."

"Well, gentlemen, your destination is Mount Hampden. You go to a place called Siboutsi. I do not know whether Siboutsi is a man or a mountain. Mr. Selous, I understand, is of the opinion that it is a man; but we will pass that by. Then you get to Mount Hampden. Mr. Selous is of opinion that Mount Hampden is placed ten miles too far to the west. You had better correct that; but perhaps, on second thoughts, better not. Because you might possibly be placing it ten miles too far to the east. Now good morning, gentlemen."

Seldom can a serious expedition have been sped on its way with so light-hearted a valediction. But the die was cast. On 27 June the march began and the advance guard of pioneers crossed the Macloutsie River, the main body of police following, while the remainder, under a young officer, Sir John Willoughby, of whom more will be heard, formed the rearguard. There were 200 pioneers, 500 mounted police, and a large contingent of native porters. The total force numbered about 1,000. Selous had gone ahead with the natives, who were laboriously cutting the road.

At Tuli trouble began. The natives, alarmed by the appearance of twenty Matabele, deserted in a panic, and only the arrival of 200 armed Bechuanas, under the command of Khama's brother, enabled the work to continue. Also to Tuli came a message from Lobengula:

"Has the King killed any white men that an *impi* is collecting on his border? Or have the white men lost anything that they are looking for?"

To which Jameson, ignoring the sarcasm, replied:

"Rhodes has no complaint against the King. These men are a working party, protected by some soldiers, and are going to Mashonaland along the road already arranged with the King."

Just then Doyle, who had been to Cape Town and was proposing to return to Bulawayo, overtook the column and, warned of Lobengula's anger against him, joined it. As the pioneers advanced, Lobengula sent one more message, carried by Colenbrander and Chadwick, who reached the column just after it had crossed the Sabi River. The message was addressed to Pennefather and complained that the king had never given permission to dig in Mashonaland. Colenbrander explained the king's predicament with his warriors; but Chadwick believed that he intended the message to arrive too late to halt the column and had really sent it to save Chadwick's and Colenbrander's lives. Much as he might wish to avoid a break with Rhodes and Jameson, he was uncertain whether and for how long he could control the mounting excitement. Both men reported that he had mobilised his army and that it was clamorously demanding the order to march."Wait for my word," he told his *impis*, but he never gave the word.

Selous may have been right in thinking he was deterred from giving it by the presence on his borders of the Bechuanaland Police. More probably he realised that to attack the column would be not merely to break with Rhodes, his defence against Boers and Portuguese, but to defy a power of whose might he had become conscious. Since ninety wagons and a sawmill were being conveyed along roads every yard of which had to be cut, an ambush and attack on the line of march could hardly have failed, and would probably have ended in a massacre. Whatever may have been the reason for Lobengula's restraint, some credit must be allowed to a savage monarch, who may have been feeling with some cause that he had been tricked.

Pennefather replied to his last message with military terseness: "In obedience to the Queen's orders, I must go on, but I will remain on the high *veld*, and then, if the Queen orders me back, I will go."

The column was struggling along through swampy bush. Johnson speaks of "the impenetrable dense and heavy bush through which we had to cut our way, and the seemingly endless number of big rivers over which a possible bridge had to be found—often at the cost of a big detour". Horse sickness had broken out. Where the bush was thickest, two parallel roads had to be cut, so that two columns might march alongside each other and, in case of attack, the head and tail of each could be turned inwards to form a *laager*. At night, when a proper *laager* was formed, under the protection of a 10,000-candle-power naval searchlight, sleep was murdered by the roaring of lions and the howling of hyenas; but not, fortunately, by the yells of the Matabele warriors.

Contrary to the opinion of most of the officers, Jameson was confident Lobengula would not attack them. Anyhow, if he did, he would be beaten. Like the gambler he was, the Doctor had decided, he said, to "go nap on the Charter", and all the savages in Central Africa were not going to stop him. His only anxiety was for the weather. His letters to Rutherfoord Harris at Kimberley bristled with his impatience to push on. "It will be as much as we can do to get in before the rains commence." He had been rubbing in this truth so persistently that he thought he had made himself "rather objectionable" to Pennefather. All the same, at the rate they were going they would be at Mount Hampden before 30 September, "and we will be there", he wrote.[3]

In the middle of August the column reached the mountain barrier beyond which was the plateau of the Mashona country. Once on it, they were safe, for the country was open and with every mile they put between them and Bulawayo, the likelihood of attack lessened. Selous, who had guided the column so skilfully through the bushveld, now found a gap in the barrier up which it could climb. He named it "Providential Pass", and on 17 August the pioneers stood overlooking their Land of Promise—league upon league of rolling country, as far as the eye could could reach, of grassy plain dotted with clumps of trees and bush, empty except for a few wretched Mashona settlements.

On the 19th, after building a small fort and leaving a garrison in it, the column resumed its march, moving north towards Mount Hampden which, as Methuen had warned the officers, was several miles off its mapped position. Presently they were in country well beyond the range of Matabele raiders, and Jameson and Colquhoun went off to make friends with the local chiefs. On 11 September the pioneers were in sight of Mount Hampden, and two days later the entire force paraded, a salute of guns was fired, and the flag was run up. The chaplain, Canon Balfour, said a prayer and possession of a sort was taken of Mashonaland in the name of the Queen. The final fort, built on the spot, was named Salisbury after the Prime Minister.

The pioneers, after the weary miles they had trudged, were delighted with the land they saw round them. "The country is magnificent," wrote Frank Johnson ecstatically. Moreover he had already found gold and extensive traces of ancient workings.[4] Naturally no time was lost in sending the good news of safe arrival to Rhodes. "When at last I found that they were through to Fort Salisbury," he said, "I do not think there was a happier man in the country than myself."

Sources

Colvin, Ian: *The Life of Jameson*
De Waal, D. C.: *With Rhodes in Mashonaland*

Fort, G. Seymour: *Dr. Jameson*
Hole, H. M.: *The Making of Rhodesia*
Selous, F. C.: *Travel and Adventure in South-East Africa*

Notes

[1] Article by Frank Johnson in the Pioneer number of the *Rhodesia Herald*, 12 September 1930.

[2] R.H.L. MSS. Afr. s. 8, f. 4.
[3] Rhodes Papers, C. 3.8.
[4] Rhodes Papers, C. 3.48.

CHAPTER TWELVE

PARLIAMENT AND OFFICE

DURING the years when, simultaneously rather than consecutively, Rhodes was amalgamating the Diamond Mines, acquiring his interests on the Rand, getting his Concession from Lobengula and his Charter from Whitehall, and preparing the party of pioneers, he had little time to spare for the Cape Parliament. He remained the Member for Barkly West, although, after his brief experience of office in Sprigg's Government (which ended, as he put it, "nominally on a bug", in other words as the consequence of an adverse motion on phylloxera), he treated his Parliamentary duties a little casually. He had other and more serious work to do and was never one of those who would attend Parliament day after day, whatever the business might be, content to listen to dull speeches on unimportant subjects.

The South African scene was changing. In March 1889 Brand, the wise and friendly President of the Orange Free State, died. His successor, Reitz, was an ardent nationalist, who looked to Pretoria rather than to Cape Town for guidance and lost little time in giving Kruger an agreement which in the future was to become little other than a blank cheque. In May of the same year Sir Hercules Robinson, the High Commissioner and Governor who more than once had come to Rhodes's help, retired and was succeeded by Sir Henry Loch, whose confidence Rhodes had to set about winning.

In May 1890 the Prime Minister, the ever-green and ever-ready Sprigg, brought in a bill of grandiose railway construction, which the critics regarded as a flagrant piece of vote-catching. Some of the new lines included in the scheme were demonstrably uneconomic, though they would be useful to isolated farmers, who naturally welcomed the bill. The cost was to be more than seven and a half million pounds. Rhodes, who had not been near Parliament House since his re-election in 1888, hurried to Cape Town to take the oath and his seat, without even waiting, he said, to pack his portmanteau. More railways he wanted, but in the right places and at a reasonable price; and he was not disposed to suffer Sprigg's jobbery in silence. When Sauer and Merriman joined him in pulling the bill to pieces, Sprigg was defeated and resigned.

A new Premier had to be found. The ruling force in the Cape Parliament was the Bond, under Hofmeyr, which held thirty-three out of seventy-four seats, not enough to command a majority, but quite enough to make life difficult for a Government uncongenial to the Dutch. There were no other organised parties, most of the remaining forty-odd members being in small groups, attached to some particular leader like Sprigg or Sauer or Merriman. Hofmeyr having declined to form a Ministry himself, and having refused the Bond's support to Sauer, the Governor sent for Rhodes.

The crisis broke when the pioneers were on the point of starting for Mashonaland. Rhodes, who anyhow was not ambitious of adding the Premiership to his other work, wanted to accompany them. However, at so crucial a moment a friendly administration at the Cape was essential to his plans, and since no one else seemed available, he accepted the Governor's invitation. At first he had some qualms about the compatibility of the office of Premier with his other commitments; but "I thought," he said, "of the positions occupied in De Beers and the Chartered Company, and I concluded that one position could be worked with the other, and each to the benefit of all." He was fortified in his decision by the Bond's promise to give him "a fair chance in carrying on the administration".

His "Cabinet of all the Talents", as it was dubbed, included some of the best brains and most influential personalities in the Cape Parliament. Merriman, an old but occasionally captious friend, who had recently described the Mashonaland enterprise as "an open filibustering expedition", accepted the Treasurership. Sauer, "the Bumbler", a brother of Rhodes's friend Hans, was another Minister who carried weight in the House and the Colony. Sivewright, the new Commissioner of Public Works, was a successful speculator, an expert on electricity, and a personal friend of Rhodes. Faure, the Secretary for Native Affairs, was a shrewd Dutch lawyer, who was always turning up to fill some office in a new Ministry. As he and Sivewright were both members of the Bond, their adhesion was important. Sir James Rose Innes, the Attorney-General, was a much respected lawyer of British descent. Rhodes had certainly got the talent—indeed, as events soon showed, rather too much of it, since his Cabinet comprised three members of the former Opposition and two of the Bond.

They seldom saw eye to eye with each other, as they held strong
and often conflicting views on the native question and on the
relations with the republics.

Sir Hercules Robinson, who had watched many governments
come and go, did not think that Rhodes's Cabinet, with Hofmeyr
outside it, could long survive. It is a proof of Rhodes's gift for
reconciling incompatibles that his first Ministry lasted for as long
as three years. Its eventual downfall was brought about by Sivewright, to whom, as a friend and one of the ablest of his colleagues, he left many of the details of administration. Sivewright,
as Commissioner of Works, gave away to a personal friend, without calling for tenders, the contract for supplying refreshments
on the Cape Railways. Merriman, Sauer and Innes, who all had
keen noses for improper practices of which for some time they
had suspected their colleague, were up in arms at once; but
Rhodes, who was in England, while repudiating the contract,
could not bring himself to ask Sivewright for his resignation.

In his perplexity Rhodes consulted Hofmeyr, who advised
him to resign and reconstruct his Cabinet. At first he was reluctant to go on, but having tried without success to induce
Hofmeyr to take his place, and having elbowed the Chief Justice,
Sir Henry de Villiers, out of a Premiership which he thought had
been offered to him, Rhodes took Hofmeyr's advice. Sauer,
Merriman and Rose Innes refused to serve, even though Sivewright
was no longer to be a Minister; so Sprigg, letting bygones be bygones in the amiable way of the Cape politician, consented to come
in as Treasurer. W. P. Schreiner, the young lawyer, was the new
Attorney-General, and Laing took Sivewright's place. The new
Ministry may have had less talent, but certainly had more co-
hesion. At any rate it easily won the election of 1894, when it
secured nearly fifty out of seventy-six seats.

*   *   *

In 1890, soon after taking office, Rhodes declared that his
would be a "South African policy". He meant what he said, and
in his two administrations he set himself, in a determined business-like way, to resolve some of the outstanding problems which
for long had claimed his thoughts. Territorially, his policy, he
declared, was "the expansion of the Cape Colony to the Zambesi". In the north his young men were busy pushing a very
movable frontier up to the back doors of the Portuguese and the
Belgians.

Farther north still, Rhodes had his eye on Uganda as a link in the chain of his "all-red route". In 1892, first Salisbury's government and then Gladstone's which succeeded it in August, were on the brink of abandoning the British stake in Uganda, but Rhodes indignantly brought pressure to bear on both, including the financial inducement of meeting part of the cost himself. Salisbury was unimpressed, but Gladstone's principal ministers, Rosebery and Harcourt, gave serious consideration to Rhodes's proposition. He probably exaggerated his influence, however; and although the decision to abandon Uganda was postponed, it was not Rhodes's doing. His anxieties were not finally removed until Rosebery succeeded Gladstone and proclaimed the British protectorate over Uganda in 1894.

To the north-west of the Cape Colony, Bechuanaland was an old field of controversy. Its southern parts were under the Colonial Office, but in 1895, with the consent of the Home Government, the Cape annexed the Colony. The Protectorate of Bechuanaland, through which Rhodes's railway would have to pass, was a different problem. Two Liberal Colonial Secretaries, Knutsford and Ripon, had promised to hand it over to the Chartered Company at an undetermined date, but in 1895 Rosebery and the Liberals went out of office and Salisbury and the Conservatives came in, with a new Colonial Secretary, Joseph Chamberlain, blowing like a strong wind down the dusty corridors of the Colonial Office. Khama and the other principal Bechuana chiefs were much opposed to the suggested change, and Chamberlain would eventually only part with a strip of the Protectorate on the western border of the Transvaal. The strip gave Rhodes access from the north to Mafeking, a concession which was soon to have grave consequences.

In the east, Rhodes enlarged the borders of the Colony by bringing in Pondoland. This was a native territory, east of Cape Colony and south-west of Natal, which had been giving some trouble, the people being persistent cattle-raiders and much addicted to witchcraft. In 1893 Sir Henry Loch, visiting Pondoland, was treated with studied insolence by Sigcau, one of the most important chiefs, who kept His Excellency waiting for three days before seeing him. Since Natal, which had just been given responsible government, was talking of taking the country over, Rhodes, after "a scamper through the Transkei", as Merriman called it, resolved to see what he could do. In the Transkei, through which he travelled in great state with eight cream-

coloured horses, he made a provocative speech attacking Natal
and its Premier, Harry Escombe, for presuming to have designs
on Pondoland. He also had an amusing and characteristic encounter with a child. "My boy," he said expansively, "I'll send
you to Oxford." "No, you won't," retorted the boy, and Rhodes,
who liked the young to stand up to him, was delighted.

The subsequent excursion to Pondoland was more serious, being
undertaken against advice and with an armed escort. On arrival,
Rhodes sent for the truculent Sigcau and, mindful of the chief's
insult to Sir Henry Loch, kept him waiting for three days before
he would see him, the aptness of the reprisal greatly pleasing the
natives. With his escort and their maxim gun, Rhodes took the
chief to a field of mealies. The gun was fired and the mealies
were mown down. "That is what will happen to you and your
tribe," Rhodes told Sigcau, "if you give us any further trouble."
The moral of the demonstration was doubtless taken, for when
Rhodes went on to announce that Pondoland had been annexed
by the Cape Colony, no trouble followed; and thereafter a few
police were adequate to keep the peace.

*   *   *

Having in recent years turned out three Ministries which had
earned its displeasure, the Bond had formed the habit of using
premiers for its own purposes: Rhodes now used the Bond for
his. Its members liked and supported him, approving of his
ambitions for the Colony, his regard for its interests, and, with
reservations, his vision of a future united South Africa. Many—
perhaps most—of them may have thought of a Union under a
flag of its own. Rhodes was frank with them about his position.
"If I have to forfeit my flag, what have I left?" he said. "If you
take away my flag, you take away everything"; and Hofmeyr,
with his dread of Germany, was content to accept, for the time
being at any rate, Rhodes's slogan of "the government of South
Africa by the people of South Africa with the Imperial flag for
defence".

The march to Union, as Rhodes then saw it, would be sure but
slow, through a Customs Union, a Railway Union, a common
native policy, and common educational institutions, with political
Union as the logical climax. This must come not by violence, but
by patient conversion. Rhodes recalled from the days of his boy-
hood the old Admiral, who had planted trees he could not hope
to see fully grown, but "had the pleasure of the conception of the

shade and the glory". In those days, at least, Rhodes was still content to be patient and to let the trees grow.

While waiting for Union, he was determined to assert the position of the Cape Colony as the dominant state in South Africa. In July 1890, one of his first acts on becoming Premier was to move a resolution condemning the Home Government for making an agreement with Germany affecting territory south of the Zambesi, without having consulted the Cape Colony. He constantly pressed the advantages of Colonial Preference on a Westminster Parliament still wedded to Free Trade; and in November 1892, in the speech he made at the second Annual Meeting of the British South African Company, he turned from the Company's business to foreshadow, in effect, the whole policy of Imperial Preference which Joseph Chamberlain was to adopt some thirteen years later.[1]

He also wrote formally to President McKinley to protest (without avail) against the McKinley tariff. He used Cape balances to relieve a financial depression in Australia and entered into direct relations with the governments of Canada and New South Wales. The Colony was the Colony's business and he would suffer no interference from Whitehall in its domestic concerns; but the Empire was the business of all who belonged to it. In 1891 he even tried to buy from Portugal the province of Lourenço Marques, by which he would have secured a valuable outlet to the sea for his new territories. Unhappily he failed, because Portugal, though in financial straits, was proud of its Imperial past and the Government dared not sell one of its remaining possessions. Rhodes never ceased to deplore a failure which he put down to "monarchial myth" and to "old-womanish shortsighted statesmanship".[2]

The Railway and Customs Union for which Rhodes was working was shipwrecked on the intransigence of President Kruger. The whole question was linked up with that of the ports. Rhodes had little difficulty in making an agreement with the Orange Free State for the extension of the railway from Kimberley to Vryburg on the Transvaal border. The next stage, which would carry the line on to the Rand, was not so easy. The two republics, being inland countries, had to take all their imports through the Cape Colony and Natal and had a just grievance because the Colonies were pocketing all the Customs duties that came their way. Rhodes's plan was for a Customs Union on terms which would correct this inequitable situation, but Kruger's was to connect the

G

Transvaal by a railway to Delagoa Bay and divert the traffic from the Cape. Eventually he agreed that the Cape line might cross the Vaal and be extended to Johannesburg, but only because he needed a subsidy from the Cape for his own railway to Delagoa Bay; and as soon as this was working, he raised the rates on the section of the Cape railway on Transvaal territory and imposed heavy duties on Cape produce.

In 1894 Rhodes went to see Kruger at Pretoria to protest against his unfriendly attitude. "If you do not take care," he warned Kruger, "you will have the whole of South Africa against you." Probably this was the occasion, mentioned by Rose Innes, when the two men parted, "shaking their fists at one another". Kruger, who had just been re-elected President, was unmoved. He would not lower rates and eventually forced the Cape traders to abandon the railway and carry their goods through Transvaal territory by ox-wagon. Thereupon Kruger closed the border drifts which the wagons had to cross. This time, however, he had gone too far. Schreiner, the Attorney-General, declared his action a breach of the London Convention. Chamberlain supported him and the Cape Government and privately agreed to bear half the cost of a military operation against the Transvaal, should this be necessary. Rhodes's prophecy was being fulfilled, and Kruger, not yet ready to challenge the joint opposition of Britain and the Cape Dutch, climbed down.

In the field of education Rhodes was able to carry out a scheme to establish in Kimberley a School of Mines which would serve the whole of South Africa. He was less successful with his proposal for a Central Teaching University at Cape Town, drawing its students from both races and from republics as well as colonies.

"The young men who will attend it," he said, "will make the Union of South Africa in the future. Nothing will overcome the Associations and aspirations they will form under the shadow of Table Mountain."

He gave and collected large sums of money, but in the end the scheme was killed by racial feeling and the antagonism of academic vested interests.

Most important of all for the future was Rhodes's native policy. He had begun by saying, "I have no native policy. I could not afford to say I have. I am a beginner at these things. . . . Still, give me a trial, as I hope to do it well." But if he had as yet no policy, he had strong convictions. One of these was of the need for a common native policy throughout South Africa. He always deplored the fact that the British and the Boers fundamentally disagreed on native policy, which meant, in his significant phrase, mixing up "the native question with the race question". In the two republics no African had a vote, in Natal he was practically excluded, but in the Cape, since 1853, the franchise qualification for black and white was a £25 yearly occupation. These different arrangements would be a barrier to Union; and with Rhodes Union mattered most of all.

At the same time he had his own views about how the native should be treated. "Mr. Rhodes is a very reasonable man," Sir William Harcourt once gibed. "He only wants two things. Give him Protection and give him Slavery and he will be perfectly satisfied." This was to do Rhodes a good deal less than justice. He was genuinely fond of the African, whose affections he had his brother Herbert's gift of winning. His servants were devoted to him. "He was a good Baas to work for," one of them once said. "He never swore or spoke strongly to me."[3] In the early days at Unkomaas he had learnt to treat the natives as people and never to trample on their feelings. He always knew their names and faces, recognised them again after a lapse of years, and chaffed them when he saw them in a way which delighted them. "The natives are children," he told Parliament, "and we ought to do something for the minds and brains that the Almighty has given them. I do not believe that they are different from ourselves."

But though they had the same potentialities as white people, mentally they were still in their childhood, and to admit them in that state to equal political rights would be madness. "It is just as if," he said, "the Lord Mayor and his Corporation were to suddenly proceed to Stonehenge and finding the Druids there discuss with them municipal legislation." Eventually Rhodes arrived at his famous declaration of "equal rights for all civilised men, irrespective of race, south of the Zambesi". But it was not until much later that he explained what he meant by "civilised" man: "a man whether white or black who has sufficient education to write his name, has some property, or works, in fact is not a loafer." Civilisation, not colour, was what counted; and in his view the white man's duty was not to part with the control of his country to men whose fathers had been naked savages, but to civilise the savage and turn him into a citizen.

The African's brain and hand must first be trained. He must learn the responsibilities of ownership. He must be protected against the ravages of drink, a point on which many of the Dutch differed with Rhodes. Above all, he must be prevented from becoming a loafer, that type of man for whom, black or white, Rhodes had so searing a contempt. To accomplish much of this, segregation would be necessary. In a reserve of his own the African would be less exposed to the vices of the European. He could have his own plot of land. He could manage his own local government and so acquire the rudiments of political education. Nowadays the word "segregation" sounds harshly in our ears; but there is a vast difference between the kind of segregation Rhodes favoured and the *apartheid* of the modern nationalist. The underlying philosophy is different; and so are the end and the purpose.

Rhodes was aware of the disagreement on native policy among his colleagues in the Cabinet and Parliament. Hofmeyr and the Bond were, generally speaking, in sympathy with their compatriots in the republics, while Sauer, Merriman, Rose Innes and Schreiner were liberals, who objected to any whittling away of the political rights of Africans in the Cape Colony. Even they, however, could not blind themselves to the changes which had come and were still coming over the Colony. In 1853, when the franchise was fixed, the proportion of black to white was only about two to one; but by 1891 the proportion had so grown that in general constituencies the African vote could be decisive. The development of the Transkei and the impending annexation of Pondoland would accentuate the problem which, when eventually the vast new territories of the North were added, might become unmanageable. Meanwhile no one had any coherent policy for dealing with it.

In 1891, though Hofmeyr was hesitant, many members of the Bond pressed for the passage of what was known as the Strop Bill, which provided, in certain circumstances, for the flogging of disobedient native labourers. As Merriman and Sauer strongly opposed the Bill, it was dropped. Rhodes himself was in favour of it, which was the cause of Olive Schreiner's disillusionment with him. Regarding the African as a child, he could see little wrong in a measure which gave him the same treatment as, in civilised countries, was dealt out to children. If he was wrong, at least he was logical.

The Franchise and Ballot Bill of 1892 was an even more serious business. The franchise is important not only for the right it conveys, but as an indication of the way in which a man or a class or a race is regarded. The vote makes the law, and the franchise bill is the expression of men's opinion on the suitability or otherwise of their as yet unenfranchised fellow-countrymen to assume the duties of citizenship. The part of Rhodes's Franchise Bill which pleased the Bond was that which raised the occupier's qualification to £75 and would have the effect of diminishing the number of African electors, while the owner's qualification, which chiefly affected the European, was left unchanged at £25. The Bill also imposed a stricter educational test. The liberals in the Cabinet reluctantly accepted these provisions for the sake of the Ballot, which they wanted; whereas the Bond, for the sake of the higher voting qualification for Africans, swallowed the Ballot.

Rhodes himself, who knew that he had to compromise between the two forces in his Cabinet, did not like the Ballot. "I object to the ballot *in toto*," he declared. "I like to know how a person votes—not, I hasten to say, for any ulterior purpose," but, he explained (a little inconsistently), so that he could keep an eye on loafers and I.D.B. men, who might vote for "free liquor and robbery". Presumably his interest was academic, because he added, "I would never discharge a person for his vote." The change in the franchise he was ready to accept as part of a compromise, though he said, "I could never accept the position that we should disqualify a man on account of his colour."

Rhodes did not conceal his sense that the great advantage of the Bill was that it lessened a gap between the Cape Colony and her neighbours. The Bill was a move in the direction of the republics, but in an even more important piece of legislation the Colony was the pioneer. The Glen Grey Act of 1894 has been sharply criticised as illiberal and a forerunner of *apartheid*, but the criticisms were often unfair. Rhodes explained the objects of it in an important speech moving the second reading of the Bill.[4]

"If you are really one who loves the natives," said Rhodes, "you must make them worthy of the country they live in, or else they are certain, by an inexorable law, to lose their country. You will certainly not make them worthy if you allow them to sit in idleness and if you do not train them in the arts of civilisation."

Rhodes firmly believed that the native, in his existing stage of development and in his own interests, should be given every stimulus to work and should be protected by segregation against the vices of Europe. The Glen Grey Act therefore imposed a fine or tax of ten shillings on any African who had not worked outside his district during the previous twelve months. This, Rhodes insisted, was not a form of slavery.

"I was much more of a slave," he remarked, "than any of those natives . . . for nine mortal years of my life; and it was compulsory slavery too . . . six years at school I had to work five hours during the day and prepare work for the next day for three hours in the evening, while at College I was compounded in the evenings and not allowed out after nine o'clock."

Parliament was unimpressed by this picture of schoolboy and undergraduate slavery and Rose Innes was unkind enough to interject, "And you never went out, I suppose?" Actually the clause, which Europeans as well as natives disliked, never worked and was repealed eleven years later.

The other provisions of the Bill were more durable. New native reserves were created; the Africans were allotted, took up, and worked their plots of land; education was much improved; and the native councils, which were put in charge of local government, flourished. In 1903 a select committee of the Cape House reported that "the operations of the Act have been, as they were intended to be, most beneficial to the natives concerned".

The Bill, which Rhodes described as "a Bill for Africa", did not have an easy Parliamentary passage. Rhodes forced it through the House and even had recourse to an all-night sitting, an expedient without precedent in the annals of the Cape Parliament. Then and later the purpose of the Act was misunderstood by many. Its importance was perhaps less in anything it did than in its influence upon future native policy in South Africa.

"We are prepared to stand or fall by it," said Rhodes: "it is worth fighting and worth falling by. . . . If the Glen Grey policy is a success, we shall see neighbouring states adopting it. . . . I hope we shall have one native policy in South Africa."

*   *   *

In 1890, when Rhodes became Premier, the Cape was facing a serious financial crisis, caused by over-speculation on the Rand. Several banks failed, but Merriman and Rhodes, with the confidence of the City of London behind them, restored the credit of the Colony. Four years later Sprigg, then the Treasurer, was able to claim that it had never stood so high.

Four million pounds of the Colony's exports of six million were diamonds, but while Rhodes watched over the interests of Kimberley, he never forgot the importance of farming in the economy or the preponderating presence of farmers in Parliament and the constituencies. One of the most useful of his measures was the Scab Act of 1894, which provided for the compulsory isolation of flocks infected by scab, and practically saved the wool industry of the Colony from extinction. The Dutch farmer, being a stern individualist, did not like compulsion; the Bill had to be forced through in the face of the Bond's qualms: but the compulsory powers remained almost intact. The Colony's orange-groves were being destroyed by insect pests, and by introducing the American ladybird and more scientific methods of growing and packing fruit, Rhodes did much to build up the industry.

Vines had also to be protected, if only because about a third of the members of the House sat for vine-growing districts. The vine-yards, which were being ruined by the phylloxera, were saved by the introduction of American vines reputed to be immune; but every attempt to secure a preference for Colonial wines in the British market failed before Whitehall's obstinate affection for Free Trade.

In numerous other ways Rhodes strengthened the farming industry. He imported Arab stallions to improve the breed of Cape horses and, through the Sultan of Turkey, much-prized Angora goats to cross with the Cape stock. No previous Prime Minister had been so solicitous of the country's interests; and to the greater satisfaction of the Bond he was economical as well as progressive. Sprigg's ill-starred scheme of railway development would have cost the Colony seven and a half million pounds; whereas Rhodes put through more careful and sensible plans at a cost of only £700,000.

In 1895 Rhodes, with five years of successful administration behind him, stood on a height he would never reach again. Not Parliament only, but the people of the Colony, Dutch and British, had grown to be proud of their Premier, of the wide views he expressed, and of his influence on the world beyond Table Mountain. They never knew where he would be or what he might be doing next. He might be visiting farms in the back areas, or bringing off big business at Kimberley or on the Rand, or dining

with Queen Victoria at Windsor, or annexing territory in the
North, or charming fresh capital out of the British investor. The
world was going well with him, and despite occasional setbacks,
his record of success was remarkable. He had almost a Midas
touch, turning everything to gold, or diamonds, or a new
dominion. No difficulty was too formidable for him to surmount, or at least to challenge. He was pushing the telegraph,
and after it the railway, north through Central Africa into
Uganda, and beyond it to Wady Halfa. When asked what he
would do about the Dervishes, who still ruled savagely from the
borders of Uganda to those of Egypt, he replied, "I do not propose to fight the Mahdi, but to deal with him. I have never met
anyone in my life whom it was not as easy to deal with as to
fight." People might laugh at his sanguine expectations, but they
would repeat his words, half believing that the man who had
dealt with Lobengula and turned Barney Barnato from an enemy
into an ally would continue his victorious career and even anticipate the expedition which Lord Kitchener was already preparing
for the conquest of Khartoum.

In Parliament Rhodes was supreme. There seemed no reason
why his Government, reconstructed perhaps from time to time,
as the older men fell out and the younger men arrived, should not
go on for ten years or longer. His authority was founded largely
on his friendship with Hofmeyr and the support of the Bond.
In 1891, when he attended the Congress of the Bond, he told the
assemblage, "Your ideas are the same as mine"; for the Bond,
like Rhodes, wanted to "remove difficulties and obstructions
from the way of Union". He and Hofmeyr would often ride
together in the early morning and discuss the questions which
would figure in the business of the House that day; and the
ground was always well prepared in the lobbies. A few sticklers
like Merriman took exception to these dealings outside the
Chamber, but Rhodes was unrepentant. When some of his
British supporters in Kimberley grumbled that he was consulting
the Dutch overmuch, he replied: "I think if more pains were
taken to explain matters to the Bond party, many of the cobwebs
would be swept away and a much better understanding would
exist between the different parties."

Less defensible, but in his view equally proper, was his habit of
giving priority to members of the Bond when jobs were to be
filled or shares in one of his undertakings to be allotted. In
England, where opinion on the subject was stricter, such trans-

actions were criticised as approaching bribery; but Rhodes was thinking less of the lobbies than of the future, of interesting the Dutch in Northern expansion and of associating them more closely with the administration of the Colony. At one time he had the idea of forming a local board of the British South Africa Company and offered the post of chairman successively to Hofmeyr and the Lord Chief Justice, Sir Henry de Villiers. When both men refused the invitation, the scheme for a local board was dropped.

In 1895, when Hofmeyr retired from Parliament, Rhodes lost his most valued supporter and most shrewd adviser. During the critical months that followed he sorely missed his friend's wise counsel. It is a fair conjecture that if Hofmeyr had still been at his elbow, the disaster of the Jameson Raid would never have befallen.

Even without Hofmeyr, Rhodes was in a unique position in Parliament. From time to time—especially in the early days of his Premiership—someone would question the compatibility of his position in the Chartered Company and his office under the Crown. Rhodes always had the same answer. "Should the interests of the Cape Colony," he said in 1891, "and those of the Chartered Company be considered to clash, I shall at once place my resignation as Prime Minister in the hands of His Excellency the Governor." As in that event the Cape would lose its Premier, the point was never pressed.

Parliament in those days was a quiet, gentlemanly body, which frowned on personal acerbities. Rhodes's conversational and unconventional style of debate was now much to its taste. On one occasion, when the Government was under fire, he disarmed the Opposition by simply remarking that it was his birthday. Although he would wander far off the subject of the debate, what he said was never dull and, even if irrelevant, was often important. He did not use notes, was always persuasive, and avoided wounding remarks.

Once Dr. Jameson reproached him for his repetitiveness. "Leave me alone," Rhodes replied: "I know what I'm about. It's only by repeating yourself that you can get an idea into people's heads." So he would hammer away at some point, until by sheer persistence he had convinced or at least silenced his hearers. He was incorrigibly informal in manner and dress, and continued to shock his Dutch supporters, who wore a formal black, by appearing in a brown tweed suit.[5]

Even when they did not agree with him, the members did not forget their good fortune in having a man of Rhodes's calibre as their Premier. At times he was too much of an Englishman for the backveld Boer, and at others times too much of an Afrikander for the ardent Imperialist. He could be impatient, ruthless, domineering, irregular in his methods; but all, British or Boer, respected his brain, his gift for getting things done, his devotion to the Colony, and his complete personal integrity in money matters. A day would come when many of them would change their minds, but in 1895 he was still their chosen and revered leader. As Merriman, critical though he became of his erstwhile colleague, put it: "The country is never likely to have another Prime Minister in exactly the same position as Rhodes, for there is not a man in the Government who takes less out of the pockets of the country and is more modest in his demands."

Sources

Hofmeyr, J. H., and Reitz, F. W.: *The Life of Jan Hendrik Hofmeyr*
Innes, James Rose: *An Autobiography*
Kruger, Paul: *Memoirs*
Laurence, Sir Perceval: *The Life of John Xavier Merriman*
MacQuarrie, J. W. (ed.): *The Reminiscences of Sir Walter Stanford.*
Walker, E. A.: *W. P. Schreiner—A South African*

Notes

1 "Vindex", 298–320.
2 Maund Papers (Rhodes House), 7, p. 10.

3 R.H.L. MSS. Afr. s. 69, I, f. 38.
4 "Vindex", 371–90.
5 R.H.L. MSS. Afr. s. 69, IV, f. 11.

CHAPTER THIRTEEN

THE UNKNOWN COLOSSUS

AFTER leaving the Vicarage at Bishop's Stortford, Rhodes had for many years no real home. In Kimberley he lived in rooms or messes or shared a cottage with Pickering or later with Jameson. In Cape Town he went into lodgings or a hotel, usually taking his meals at the club. In London he stayed at the Westminster Palace Hotel in Victoria Street and afterwards at the Burlington, where a suite of rooms was reserved for him. So he lived, often expensively and not always very comfortably.

In 1888, when his kinsman, William Rhodes, the owner of the family property at Dalston, in Hackney, came out to Kimberley, Rhodes had the idea of buying the estate, although London had swallowed it up and no house went with it, its only attraction being its connection with the family. William Rhodes, who had married Cecil's half-sister Elizabeth, was not very anxious to sell, and the negotiations hung fire, being only completed on board ship at Cape Town—on a sheet of writing paper. Having acquired the property, Rhodes presented enough land from it to make a public square for Hackney, and later, when he was about to buy a place in the country and wanted money quickly, mortgaged the rest of Dalston for £70,000.

He was still homeless in 1891 when, as Prime Minister, he needed more dignified and convenient accommodation. To obtain it he first rented, and two years later bought a house at Rondebosch, outside Cape Town. This was Groote Schuur, the Great Granary, an old building dating back to the days of the Dutch East India Company. It had passed from owner to owner, and finally to a Mrs. van der Byl, who sold it to Rhodes. By degrees he bought up adjoining farms on the lower slopes and in the little valleys of Table Mountain, so that in the end he had an estate of some 1,500 acres.

The house had suffered from the indifferent taste of its previous occupiers and from a fire in 1866 that destroyed the thatch, which had been replaced by an unsightly roof of slate. In the task of restoring and adding to Groote Schuur, Rhodes had the good fortune to discover a young British architect, Herbert Baker, with an enthusiastic interest in the Dutch colonial style. In South

Africa architecture and interior decoration had fallen on evil days. The old Dutch houses, which had beauty and dignity, were no longer being built; the craftsmen, who had given grace to them, no longer existed; and the lovely old furniture, fashioned in South African woods, was no more being made. Corrugated iron, "Brummagem", the shoddy mass-produced furniture and fittings of Europe in the late nineteenth century, filled the land. It was Baker who restored the past and showed the beauty a modern functional building could wear. South Africa has made insufficient acknowledgement of its debt to his genius; or to Rhodes, who gave him not only his opportunity, but an inspiration which lived on when Rhodes was dead, to be expressed in many noble buildings in South Africa and other lands.

Baker wrote an account of his relations with Rhodes, showing a side of him the world hardly realised. Rhodes wanted much more than convenient quarters to occupy when the Cape House of Assembly was sitting. He wanted something which would both recall the past of the Cape Colony and suggest its greater future; and Baker, who liked to build to an idea, a thought, or maybe a striking phrase, entered on the work with understanding and enthusiasm.

Groote Schuur was to be no mere affair of bricks and mortar. As a start, the house had, as it were, to blend with its background, the towering height of Table Mountain, that majestic landmark for mariners, from those who rounded the Cape of Storms with Vasco da Gama to the crews of the latest liner outward bound from Southampton. To Rhodes, as later to another great South African, Field-Marshal Smuts, it was more than a mountain to be climbed or viewed from a distance. Rhodes, who had never grown out of his habit of brooding thought, would seat himself on its slopes, often at a point from which he could see both the Atlantic and Indian Oceans—the spot where Watts's statue, "Physical Energy", now stands. He would watch the changing light and colour on sea and mountain, and from them and from himself draw out the idea he would presently give to the world.

Rosebery once called him a "practical visionary". This withdrawal into meditation was a habit he practised everywhere and all his life, beginning in the days when he leaned over a garden gate, with the smell of the maltings in his nostrils, and looked across meadows to the River Stort. He could not understand how others could be unmindful of the fascination of solitary thought. His brother Frank was once telling him of a *safari* he had been on.[1] The shooting, he said, had been excellent, but the evenings in camp had been long and boring. "Boring?" exclaimed Cecil. "Couldn't you *think*?" Above all other places Table Mountain was the spot where he could think, in a communing which was almost a form of religious worship.

Since leaving the Vicarage, Rhodes had not been a churchgoer, but if religion is a consciousness of God and a resolution to try to lead a life in conformity with God's will, Rhodes was a religious man. This was recognised by the Archbishop of Cape Town in a moving address at his funeral, in which he quoted Rhodes as having once said: "There is a better thing for South Africa than materialism, and that is religion." As always, what Rhodes meant by "better" was to be measured in practical terms of human happiness.

"You don't seem to care for money," his banker and friend, Lewis Michell, once said to him.

"For its own sake, no," replied Rhodes; "but it is a power and I like power." But it was not power "for its own sake" that he liked, but power to carry out the work he believed God had put him into the world to perform. It was as pointless to have money without ideas, as to have ideas without money; and it was on Table Mountain that so many of the ideas came to him.

"The fact is," he told a gathering of chapel-goers when he was laying the foundation stone of a new chapel, "I don't care to go to a particular church even on one day in the year, when I use my own chapel at all other times. I find that up the Mountain one gets thoughts, what you might term religious thoughts, because they are thoughts for the betterment of humanity, and I believe that is the best description of religion, to work for the betterment of the human beings who surround us."

When he was riding or just sitting on Table Mountain, he told Baker, "I am really saying my prayers." For, loosely as he sat to doctrine, he had a firm belief in the efficacy of prayer. "Prayer is good," he once said to General Booth, the founder of the Salvation Army. "It brings before you the duties of the day, pulling one up to face the obligations for their discharge." His conceptions of God and of prayer may have been unorthodox, or at least too limited, but their reality and his sincerity can hardly be disputed.

He himself was not unconscious of the indefiniteness of his religious beliefs. He once met General Booth on a visit to a Salvation Army settlement. On the journey back Rhodes shared a compartment with the General's son, Bramwell, who suddenly asked him if he was happy. "Happy?" replied Rhodes. "I, happy? Good God, no! . . . I would give all I possess to believe what that old man in the next carriage [the General] believes." To Bramwell Booth Rhodes seemed "a man of profound melancholy . . . a great soul dwelling in the shadows".

The Mountain was Rhodes's chapel, and one to which he wanted other people to come, so that they might share with him its beauty and perhaps the thoughts that flowed from it. He planted trees and shrubs to delight their eyes—hydrangea, bougainvillea, plumbago—and cut paths and roads for the people to tread. "I love to think that human beings will walk that road long after I am gone," he once said. The human beings came, walked his paths, admired his shrubs, even picnicked in full view of his windows. Trespassers were not prosecuted, but encouraged. Provided they left no litter about—for he hated litter nearly as much as he hated loafers—Rhodes welcomed them. One Sunday afternoon, when crowds were filling the gardens, Rhodes remarked to an invited guest, "Some people like to have cows in their grounds, I like to have people." Groote Schuur was less a private property than a public trust. He tried to add to its attractions by importing the rooks and singing birds of England, but they refused to be acclimatised, except the starlings, which flourished excessively and became a pest. He enclosed a great space within which the wild animals of Africa—buck, zebras and ostriches—lived and throve. He even kept some lions in a cage, with the intention of one day housing them in a colonnaded house of classical style. But for him better than gardens or birds or animals was the back *stoep* with its view of Table Mountain and, in the foreground, of clumps of stone pines and masses of hydrangeas.

The estate, however, was to be no mere pleasure-ground. Close by was a model fruit-farm, which was to be a pioneer of better fruit-growing in the Colony. Rhodes found a young Englishman with Californian experience, Pickstone by name, who was told, to his astonishment and alarm, to buy "the whole Drakenstein Valley". Although Pickstone did not buy the whole valley, which would, he objected, have cost a million, he bought several farms and became the first manager of the Rhodes Fruit Farm

Company. Some years later Rhodes wrote to Lord Milner, then High Commissioner:[2]

"In a small way I have tried to encourage fruit cultivation in the Cape Colony and possess some twenty or thirty farms in the Paarl and Stellenbosch districts. Owing to their special knowledge the men in charge of these farms are almost entirely English, who have studied fruit-cultivation in California; and for the first time we have a number of English on the land in these districts. At first they were looked upon with suspicion and distrust by their neighbours. This feeling has now totally altered. They mix socially with the neighbouring farmers; they are inter-marrying with the Dutch and the whole tone of these districts is changing."

While Rhodes had the secondary purpose of bringing British emigrants on to the land, he was determined that the farms should pay their way. "A scheme," he said, "founded on philanthropic lines is of no benefit to the community, but a business scheme, which can pay a dividend, is of undoubted assistance to any country."

Besides fruit-growing, Rhodes experimented in stock-breeding and the improvement of pasture grasses; he also, with Baker's help, started a tile and brick works, with the products of which he built a model village for Hottentots and coloured labourers on the estate. Williams gives the story of a coloured woman resident there:

"Let me tell you," she said, "that I was living with all my family in a little one-roomed *pondokice* [mud hut], as most of us coloured labourers are obliged to live, and the 'Big Master' came to see me and he looked at me and my hovel and said, 'Now if I give you a nice cottage, all beautifully clean and pretty for the same rent you pay for this hovel [10*s.* a month], will you promise me to ever keep it as you find it, clean and bright?' 'Yes,' I replied, and the 'Big Master' smiled and did as he said, and now I and all who live here keep our cottages as you see them today, always *skoon en blink* [clean and shining], for you see at any moment the 'Big Master' may come and we must keep our promises. Don't come and tell us any lies about him, for we know what he has done and we love him."

The village had a church, a school and a house for the pastor; and no alcoholic drink was allowed.

*   *   *

Groote Schuur itself, Rhodes told Baker, had to be restored to its original appearance, with a high-pitched roof of thatch and the gables which had gone. "I want the big and simple, barbaric if you like," he said. The deal planks and cheap fittings were ruthlessly eliminated, the former being replaced by teak and the latter by craftsmen's work. The house was to be a blend of the classical and the old South African, the beginning of a new era in the architecture of the country and the first of many buildings which in time would make Cape Town the worthy capital of a great country. One of the first of these buildings was to be the University he never lived to see. The building, which was to look like Oriel, was to be paid for out of the profits of the Kaffir compounds at Kimberley, "out of the Kaffir stomach", as he crudely put it; but the opposition was too strong and Cape Town had to wait twenty years for the University of Rhodes's vision.

Meanwhile he busied himself reclaiming and rebuilding the old Dutch homesteads of the Peninsula. He also sent Baker round the countryside to find and buy old furniture, and with it the rooms at Groote Schuur were sparsely but handsomely furnished. Unlike Beit and some of his brother millionaires from Kimberley and the Rand, Rhodes did not collect pictures, but he had one portrait, "my lady" as he called her, attributed to Reynolds. He also had some good examples of old Dutch glass and Oriental china, in the slightly incongruous company of a soapstone bird found in the Zimbabwe ruins of Southern Rhodesia. Sauer adds that he also kept a large collection of phalli.

No part of the house was stamped more clearly with his individual taste than was the library. He was not a bibliophile, first editions and rare bindings making no appeal to him. He collected the books he wanted to read or consult—books about Africa, its early history, its exploration, its peoples, its antiquities, its minerals—treatises on politics and mining, old maps and books of travel. These he frequently consulted; and even at the height of a crisis, as in 1895, his interest in exploring African antiquities occupied much of his time. His old love of Gibbon led him into an extravagant and unrewarding experiment. His own knowledge of Latin and Greek being too sketchy for him to read the authorities Gibbon quoted in *The Decline and Fall of the Roman Empire*, he conceived the idea of having them translated, typed and indexed. Hatchard, the London bookseller, was commissioned to carry out this extravagant task. According to Williams, the complete works of the Fathers of the Church, flooding into his library, were too much for him and he called off the operation after it had cost him about £8,000.

Rhodes had little leisure while he was in residence at Groote Schuur, for there were always people to see or work to be done; but on his voyages to and from England he read voraciously— novels perhaps, but more often a book of travel or one on the borderline between religion and philosophy. One book much pondered over and recommended to his friends was Dean Farrar's *Seekers after God*. Rhodes continually returned to his old favourite, *The Meditations of Marcus Aurelius*, a copy of which, heavily marked by himself, he carried about with him everywhere. Much of it he knew by heart, and he would quote with appreciation such passages as, "Can any man think he exists for pleasure and not for action and exertion?" At this, and perhaps at any time in his life, his reading was less for the purpose of discovering new ideas than for that of finding support for the ideas he already had.[3]

Pagan philosophers, like Seneca and Epictetus, particularly those who seemed to be groping after Christianity, appealed strongly to him, perhaps because he too was always groping; and he would often quote from Aristotle: "The utmost good of man is the virtuous activity of the soul and pursuit of the highest virtue throughout life." Such a philosophy was congenial because it was closely akin to his own thinking. The speculative or the factual, not the dogmatic, appealed to him. "Let a man be a Buddhist," he said in the course of an argument about religion, "let him be a Mahommedan, let him be a Christian or what you will; let him call himself what he likes, but if he does not believe in a Supreme Being he is no man—he is no better than a dog." But while in one mood his conviction of the existence of God seemed unshakable, in another he would lapse into the scepticism which rated the chances of God's existence as probably no higher than fifty per cent. At any rate he judged a religion by its good works rather than by its faith; so that among religious organisations the Jesuits, the Salvation Army and the Nuns of the House of Nazareth won his warmest regard and most generous support. Of the saintly contemplative he would have had little understanding.

He frequently read Plutarch's *Lives* and Plato's *Dialogues*, but
was most at home perhaps in the life and thought of the Augustan
age. People noted, and he himself rather fancied, a supposed
resemblance to a Roman emperor—Hadrian or Titus—and he
arranged for Herbert Baker to travel to Italy to make a special
study of the architectural remains of the Caesars.

*   *   *

In Groote Schuur Rhodes dispensed a lavish, rather undis-
criminating hospitality. Members of the Cape Parliament,
pioneers from the north, farmers, visitors from Europe were all
made welcome. He loved to talk his own "shop"—about the
Empire and the north, or gold and diamonds—and enjoyed
listening to the "shop" of other men, provided it was intelligent.

The young of both sexes were always welcome, not only
because he liked them, but because he saw the future as theirs.
Sometimes they tried him. "The young in South Africa," he
told Baker, "want locking up"—that is more discipline. But the
young South Africans carried their country's fate in their hands.
"Of course, of course," he said, "they must soon take up our
work; we must teach them what to do and what to avoid." He
seized every chance of injecting into them his ideas, often to the
point of revolutionising their lives. Albert Grey said that he
knew "men whose characters had been entirely changed by Cecil
Rhodes". The acknowledged debt of Grogan and Hubert
Hervey, and other young men to his inspiration has already been
recorded. Another, Colonel Weston Jarvis, declared that Rhodes
"always made me feel such a devilish fellow".

Life at Groote Schuur was pleasantly informal. In the early
morning Rhodes would go for a ride over the Cape Flats or up
the Mountain with a guest or friend like Merriman, a ride of long
silences broken by a flood of talk—of Cape politics, of the latest
news from the north, or just of his ideas. Bishop Alexander,
who arrived to stay before the marriage of his daughter to a
pioneer, and to see Rhodes give away the bride with tears rolling
down his cheeks, wrote an account of his visit:

"It has been my lot during a long life to converse with
some of the most distinguished talkers of the day. I must
say that, in my opinion, Cecil Rhodes would have been hard
to beat when he was quite at home with his company, and
sure of understanding and sympathy. There was power of

thought, originality of expression, and more humour than those who knew him slightly were ready to credit him."

On one point all are agreed—that he had a horror of loose talk and bawdy stories.

In the afternoon he would be attending to his Parliamentary duties in the House of Assembly, and in the evening would entertain his guests and himself with more talk (always diverting) and parlour games (not always). He would ask some question such as, "Who is the cleverest man you have met?", his own answer, which he was waiting to give, being Albert Edward Prince of Wales. Once at breakfast he started a game of capping quotations, at which he astonished the company by his proficiency—until Bishop Alexander caught him with a *Book of Familiar Quotations* on his knees. One wet afternoon in an English country house he beguiled the time by forming a circle and asking questions out of *Whitaker's Almanac*, until a growing restiveness induced him to put an end to the ordeal with the words, "I think we've learned something from our game."

A lady who knew him well spoke of his "great grey eyes and a smile of singular and persuasive charm, like the sun on a granite hill". Eyes are deceptive things, however: one of his secretaries wrote of his "piercing light steel-blue eyes". It was at his eyes rather than at the heavy frame that men looked when they met him. His weight was fourteen or fifteen stone, but few remarked on his bulk, nor is it apparent in photographs or portraits.

Rumour repeated the most false and fantastic stories about his alleged intemperance. Edmund Garrett, however, the brilliant young editor of the *Cape Times*, who would burst in on him without ceremony and once woke him up with a shower of pebbles on his bedroom window, insisted that "it would be hard for a man of the active world to plan out a more strenuous, temperate, almost abstemious life than that of Cecil Rhodes in his prime", and Hans Sauer, another close friend, said that "he lived a most abstemious and regular life". Such evidence, far worthier of credence than idle gossip, cannot be ignored. Actually, with his diseased heart, Rhodes could not have lived and worked as he did in any other way. He was not a teetotaller. Although he gave up spirits, he enjoyed a glass of white wine, such as Rudesheimer 1833, which was his favourite, and, like Bismarck, often drank with his dinner a mixture of stout and champagne, but always in moderation; and Kümmel was a favourite liqueur. The stories of habitual drunkenness, repeated by one of his later biographers, were complete fabrications, perhaps due to his habit of sipping many drinks one after another and leaving them all unfinished.

Another legend, equally unfounded, was that he hated women. "Women!" he told one of his secretaries, "of course I don't hate women. I like them, but I don't want them always fussing about." Most of his friends agree that he had no wish to marry. "I have never yet seen the women whom I could get on in the same house with," and that was particularly true of his sisters. Yet Le Sueur maintains without corroboration, that he proposed marriage "several times" to "a very charming daughter of a Cape family" who later married a soldier. There is also the famous story of his courtier-like reply to Queen Victoria when she accused him of disliking women: "How could I possibly hate a sex to which your Majesty belongs!" "I can't believe he is a woman-hater," was the Queen's conclusion. "I think he is a charming man and so easy to get on with." He detested the Victorian blue-stocking, the hostesses who gushed and tried to lionise him, and the women who fussed over him and attempted to order his life for him. He was very fond of his sister Edith, but she was a masterful lady and when she arrived to stay with him, he handed over Groote Schuur to her and went to live elsewhere, on the grounds that the house was not big enough to hold them both. Another lady, who was a neighbour, came to dinner and, sitting next to him, tried too obviously to charm him. But all she got out of him was a grunted complaint—"I wish you'd drain your fishponds, they breed mosquitoes," adding, "You know it is only the *female* that makes that horrid noise and bites people." The truth is that he liked intelligent women, such as Lady Lugard (Flora Shaw), Mrs. van der Byl, Mrs. Colenbrander and (for a time) Olive Schreiner, just as he liked intelligent men, those, that is, who were doers and not merely talkers; and of these many were among the visitors to Groote Schuur.

Perhaps the most remarkable and perplexing woman of his acquaintance was Olive Schreiner, who was already famous as the author of *The Story of an African Farm* when she first came into his life, probably in 1890. She did so of her own accord, and the earliest and only surviving letter between them, unfortunately bearing no date, shows her characteristically taking the initiative in inviting him to visit her. "You are the only man in South Africa I would ask to come and see me," she wrote, "because I think you are large enough to take me impersonally." She continued to think the same even when her admiration for him later waned; and even when she was bitterly attacking him after the Jameson Raid, she still acknowledged his greatness. The emotions which his personality stirred had the unhappy effect of dividing her talented family: her mother and one brother, Theo, remained his devoted admirers, but her other brother, William, joined her in turning against him. She was undoubtedly the ablest of them all, and perhaps the only South African of either sex who was truly a match for Rhodes.[5]

No one was in a position to know him better than his secretaries, though not all were dependable witnesses. Some of them recorded the most affectionate memories of a master who could be very irritable and exacting, but was never inconsiderate. "I am so sorry for all your trouble," he would often say and, even if he went on to give more trouble, he meant the words. There was Henry Currey, who left when he married, to Rhodes's distress; Charles van der Byl; Gordon Le Sueur, who was with him for only a short time at the end of his life; Bob Coryndon, who did not want the job and soon left; Jack Grimmer, a good-natured, simple young fellow, who hardly pretended to be a secretary and was more a companion; and Philip Jourdan, the first real secretary after Currey and, by Rhodes's account, the best he ever had.

Probably Rhodes was fondest of Grimmer, who always, to his annoyance, addressed him as "Mr. Rhodes", but talked to him with a bluntness even Rhodes's contemporaries would hardly have used. Perhaps for this reason the friendly relationship was often interrupted by flaming rows, which usually ended with an apology from Rhodes for something he had said. Grimmer had an unfortunate weakness for drink, and when he was overcome by it Rhodes always pretended it was a touch of "fever".[6]

Philip Jourdan was a young official in the Cape House of Assembly. Having admired Rhodes from a distance, one day, to his delight, Rhodes asked him to come and work for him. "I thought he was the most generous man I ever met," said Jourdan, generous, not only to his secretaries, but to anyone who came to Groote Schuur in search of help. Rhodes claimed, not very correctly, that he could tell at once if a man was a deserving case. "I like him," he would say of some visitor, "he has clear blue eyes which look one straight in the face." But whatever might be the colour of the visitor's eyes, he was seldom sent away empty-

handed. Rhodes was no doubt too inclined to suppose that
money was the answer to every trouble and to assume wrongly
that that was all people wanted from him. Once one of his
brothers arrived. "Well, what do *you* want?" asked Rhodes, and
was surprised when his brother replied, "None of your damned
money anyway." But Rhodes had the last word: "Well, it's the
first time in your life that you didn't." No man was an easier
prey to the out-of-elbows adventurer, or dispensed his largesse
more bountifully and with less discrimination or hope of return.

A man is seldom a hero to his secretary, but Rhodes's young
men loved and venerated him, perhaps because he treated them as
friends rather than as employees. His casual ways must often
have irked them sorely—his habit of stuffing the pockets of his
old coats with valuable documents, the invariable absence of
small change, the engaging but sometimes embarrassing readiness with which he would give away his secretaries' clothes to
any wanderer, and his haphazard treatment of his correspondence.
"He receives letters and loses them sometimes, answers them
never," wrote Stead. After Rhodes's death a drawer in the curio
room at Groote Schuur was found full of unopened letters.[7]
Once he flung a great pile of securities and other papers at Beit,
with a request to be told what he was worth, because he seldom
had the faintest idea of his financial position at the moment.

Irritable, casual and exacting he might be, but if his secretary
was in a difficulty or needed a holiday, out would come the cheque
book and the young man would go off with a cheque for some
staggering amount in his pocket. Nor did his kindness end with
gifts of money. When Groote Schuur was burnt down in 1896,
he gave up his bedroom to his secretary and himself slept in a
blanket in the corridor. Small acts of kindness of this sort made
up for many irritable outbursts, especially as these were usually
followed by an apology to the offending secretary. "Every day I
try to become humbler, but it is hard," he once confessed. It was
hard, and many were the failures, but he went on trying.

No man was less inclined to stand on his dignity. In 1895, he
was travelling from Constantinople to Brindisi in a grain ship,
which ran into a storm after leaving Athens. Rhodes went to his
cabin, but finding that his secretary had nowhere to sleep,
brought him in. Then, learning from him that the other passengers were huddled on deck trying to find some shelter, he
made them come in too—"the most evil-looking human beings I
have ever seen," drenched and bringing with them "the most

THE UNKNOWN COLOSSUS 215

vile-smelling food," said his secretary ruefully. Rhodes's only comment afterwards was that the night had not been as bad as the one he had spent in a tug with Captain Penfold from Simon's Town, trying to bring in to safety a barge which had broken away from its moorings.[8]

Rhodes's servants, like his secretaries, loved him, much as they stood in awe of him. He treated them with extravagant generosity and always made sure that he paid a man enough wages for him to qualify for a Parliamentary vote. Most faithful of all was his personal servant, valet, cook, courier, nurse, friend and paragon, Tony de la Cruz, a coloured man from Mozambique. Tony went everywhere with him, watching and fussing over his health, and even buying his clothes.

"Tony," Rhodes would call out as he rode into camp after a day of working or shooting, "have you got grilled chops and a mealy potato for dinner?"

"Yes, Sir," replied Tony.

"That's clever, Tony; how did you think of that?"

"Because I know what the Baas likes."

"And did you remember the onions, Tony?"

"I forget nothing the Baas cares for," was the smiling reply.

An Englishman is judged personally not only by his relations with his servants and employees, but by his attitude to sport and animals. Rhodes was no sentimentalist. He was fond of animals which served a purpose—the horse he could ride and the dog he could take out shooting. For the dog which was merely a house pet—a canine loafer, as it were—he had no liking. "I invited you to dinner, but not your infernal dog," he grumbled to a guest who had brought with him a dog which barked. But for the working dog, which would put up birds for him, he could have a great affection, and he was deeply distressed when Con, J. G. McDonald's dog, who had won him many of those half-crown bets he loved to lay on shooting matches, jumped into the jaws of a crocodile.

Although the best was not too good for his guests, even when they were farmers from the backveld who presumably would not distinguish between a good and an indifferent wine, Rhodes himself enjoyed the simple life. "Come, Metcalfe," he would say, "let's go and have a chop on the *veld*"; and off they would go, as gleeful as schoolboys, to lead the simple life for a few days. Simple though it was, he had certain rules he expected his companions to observe. After the ride or walk with which the morning began, he expected everyone to appear bathed and shaved. He must always have a "clean camp".

He was not, however, insistent on what he regarded as a correct appearance, when anyone's feelings might be hurt. A young man, E. W. Smith, visiting Kimberley on his way to the north, was invited to dinner.

> "I was dismayed," he wrote, "to find quite a company. Dr. Jameson was there, Sir Charles Metcalfe, Hans Sauer and others, and they were all dressed for dinner." Mr. Smith was not. Having just come off the train, he was wearing an old blue suit, travel-stained. "You may imagine my embarrassment. Mr. Rhodes was a long time coming to join us. We waited and waited, and when at last he appeared, he was wearing an old blue suit as shabby as my own." Later Mr. Smith discovered what had happened. Rhodes was already dressed for dinner, when he was told that his young guest was not; "and he had gone back and hunted up this shabby suit to keep me in countenance." He then seated Mr. Smith beside him at dinner "and talked to me like a father".

The simple gesture won him an ardent adherent.[9]

When Rhodes visited London, life was more formal and less congenial, though on his morning rides in the Row he surprised and probably shocked the sticklers for correct dress by appearing in the white flannel trousers and old brown bowler hat he wore when he was riding about the Cape peninsula. Prominent people, like Moberly Bell of *The Times* and W. T. Stead, would make their way to his suite at the Burlington to discuss with him the affairs of Africa and the world. He also cultivated the politicians, especially Liberal Imperialists like Lord Rosebery, Lord Ripon and Sydney Buxton. With that doughty warrior, Sir William Harcourt, he never reached friendly terms. Harcourt was alarmed by the magnitude of his schemes and the occasional irregularity of his methods. "Rhodes is an astonishing rogue and liar," he told Wilfrid Blunt; but with Harcourt a man was black or white and, if not understood, was black. Chamberlain—at first at any rate—was another sceptic. His first meeting with Rhodes at a dinner-party was disastrous, but in time the antipathy lessened, though relations were never cordial and a thoughtless gibe (repeated by a reputed friend) about Chamberlain's hobby of orchid-growing was not forgotten or forgiven.

The Queen and the Prince of Wales, on the other hand, were

more appreciative of him. He dined at Windsor on 24 February 1891 and again on 4 December 1894. Rhodes, Sir Henry Loch told Her Majesty, was "a very remarkable, honest, loyal man, and entirely anti-republican . . . a tremendously strong man". "I had a long conversation with Mr. Rhodes," the Queen recorded in her diary in December 1894. "He said he had had great difficulties, but that since I had seen him last, he had added 12,000 miles of territory to my Dominions." As gratifying to Her Majesty was Rhodes's belief that the Transvaal, "which we ought never to have given up", would ultimately return to the Empire.

Rhodes had in turn warm admiration for the Prince of Wales, whom he first met at a dinner-party given by the Duke of Fife, his son-in-law and one of the Directors of the Chartered Company. The Prince thought Rhodes "a wonderful character and so lucid in his explanations". Subsequently Rhodes stayed at Sandringham, and used to write to the Prince about his doings and plans.

During these years of achievement, Rhodes's health, which had troubled him so often when he was young, held up fairly well. Had it been otherwise, he might have taken better care of himself and curbed his activities. "Work never did anybody any harm," he was fond of saying, but in the decade 1887 to 1897 too much hard work harmed him fatally. He must have been aware of the threat from his heart, even while he ignored it. "I have only one thing to complain of," he told Baker, "that the Almighty won't give me ten more years to live." In 1891, while out riding with Merriman, he fell heavily from his horse, many thought to the lasting damage of his health. On another occasion, when touring the south-western districts in the Colony with Sivewright, they were snowed up, their cart was overturned and Rhodes was thrown out and badly bruised.

In 1895, after a bad bout of influenza and malaria, his heart trouble recurred; and he had another bad attack in 1897, when he was unconscious for several hours. By then he could no longer be blind to the precariousness of his life. "The great fault of life is its shortness," he is recorded as saying. "Just as one is beginning to know the game, one has to stop." Or, as he said to McDonald, "Everything in the world is too short, life and fame and achievement." Once he showed Edmund Garrett his pulse, "standing out as it were in a knot, and, as the artery pumped and laboured, one could count the throbs by the eye". "You never saw a man with a pulse like that," Rhodes said with pride.

In the past he had been patient, up to a point and against his nature, but now he was beginning to realise how short his time would be. He could not hope to live to see his dreams become facts. In 1895 his friends were conscious of the change—of a growing readiness to take short cuts, of a new irritability and violence in language, an intolerance of anybody or anything making unnecessary demands on his precious and dwindling time. During the few years that remained to him, "Time's winged chariot" thundered ever more loudly in his ears. His impatience, his sense of the shortness of life and of the mass of work he still had to do began to affect his judgment; and he was ill-served by some of the friends he had gathered round him.

Sources

Baker, Herbert: *Cecil Rhodes by his Architect*
Booth, Bramwell: *Echoes and Memories*
Buckle, G. E.: *Letters of Queen Victoria*
Cook, E. T.: *Edmund Garrett*
Emden, Paul H.: *Randlords*
Hobman, D. L.: *Oliver Schreiner, her Friends and Times*
Sauer, Hans: *Ex Africa . . .*
Stead, W. T.: *The Last Will and Testament of Cecil J. Rhodes*

Notes

[1] R.H.L. MSS. Afr. t. 10, f. 200.
[2] Williams, 301-2.
[3] Maund Papers (Rhodes House), I, f. 4 and 5.
[4] R.H.L. MSS. Afr. t. 11, f. 25.
[5] Rhodes Papers, C. 27, 142/12.
[6] R.H.L. MSS. Afr. s. 69, I, f. 17.
[7] Maund Papers (Rhodes House), 19, f. 3.
[8] R.H.L. MSS. Afr. t. 5, f. 189.
[9] R.H.L. MSS. Afr. t. 11, f. 168.

CHAPTER FOURTEEN

AN EXPANDING EMPIRE

"I WALKED between earth and sky," Rhodes once said to Flora Shaw, later Lady Lugard and then *The Times* correspondent in South Africa; "and when I looked down I said—'This earth shall be English', and when I looked up, I said—'The English should rule this earth.'" Flamboyantly as these words may fall on ears today, they revealed the force which drove Rhodes forward. He answered less than most men to the spur of fame, or at least his answer was different from theirs. Fame to him was little, if it was not the recognition of a special achievement, for to him what a man was mattered much less than what he did; provided that what he did was linked to some ruling purpose. A book was to be judged by its practical effect on the reader, a work of art by the lesson it taught; effect and lesson being the same for both—

"To make the world a better place
And life a worthier thing."

A world dominated by the British would be a better place, and the kind of life the British brought with them, representing the distilled wisdom of the ages, the best that was in Greece and Rome and the Christian ethic, was worthier than any other kind. So in all simplicity to read God's purpose for himself, his country and the world. When he placed his hand on the map of Africa and murmured, "All red, that's my dream", he saw himself as no more and no less than the instrument of a destiny shaped by God. This was not Jingoism, but faith, a faith which, with all its limitations, he was resolute to follow.

*   *   *

When the pioneers had broken through the Matabele crust into Central Africa, they would have taken a big step, but only the first. So Rhodes had held that meeting at Kimberley in May 1890, when he had sent out a handful of young men to push through lands as yet unclaimed towards frontiers as yet undefined. In the south-west were the Germans, north of them the Portuguese in Angola, and north of them the future Congo State of the Belgian king, Leopold. On the east were the Portuguese again, and beyond them the Germans, occupying, a little tentatively at first, the territory which is now Tanganyika. In the centre was a vast country, much of it a plateau on which Europeans might settle, a jumble of warring tribes, distracted from their quarrels by the sporadic appearance of Arab slave-raiders from the coast and from Zanzibar.

With the eastern seaboard, low-lying, malarial and sparsely occupied by the Portuguese, Rhodes was concerned only from the point of view of his new Dominion's need of a port. The interior, higher, healthier, mineralised, and suitable for settlement, was his first objective. So, even while the pioneers were gathering at Tuli, and later making their long march into Mashonaland, his young men started off with the intention, on the pattern of the Rudd Concession, of trying to persuade the chiefs of the interior to come under the shelter of the Charter and Cecil Rhodes.

There was no time to lose. The Portuguese were beginning to think seriously about their hinterland. In the years of their greatness they had sent out an occasional expedition and had made some kind of vague agreement with the shadowy empire of Monomotapa; but in their decline they had been content to leave the interior alone. One day they would cut a swathe across Africa and join Mozambique to Angola; for the moment they would merely cherish old claims which they were too proud to abandon and too feeble to exploit. With such an attitude Rhodes had no patience, especially since, if the Portuguese ever linked up their colonies, they would build a barrier to a British dominion, which he saw as designed by "manifest destiny" to stretch ultimately from the Cape of Good Hope to the shores of the Mediterranean.

The Rudd Concession, followed by the Charter, stirred the Portuguese from their long sleep. Rhodes, *homem horrivel*, as Lisbon began to style him, was trying to filch *their* interior, with reputed mineral resources which might one day fill an empty treasury. Already they were having trouble with the British over the country later to be known as Nyasaland, where that irrepressible consul, Harry Johnston, with a tiny contingent from the Indian Army, a handful of Zanzibari police, and three small cannon, was putting down the slave trade and in the process dealing roughly with some of Portugal's friends.

One trouble was that all the frontiers were uncertain, liable to shift in a week when one chief overcame another, so that it was hard to say exactly what territory was comprised in any treaty or agreement. Both London and Lisbon, reluctant to quarrel, were aware of the need to define more exactly their respective spheres of influence, London with occasional apprehensions supporting Rhodes and Johnston, and Lisbon reiterating its dubious historical claims. The Anglo-Portuguese Convention of 1890, that "wretched treaty", as Rhodes called it, which the Portuguese foolishly refused to ratify, gave most of Manica and all Gazaland to Portugal. Rhodes blamed Johnston for the treaty, but his bitter reproaches were unjust. Johnston was not responsible, although he urged Rhodes to accept it on the curious grounds that if he did not, "that old schemer, the King of the Belgians", would come in and snatch parts of the company's estate.[1]

Rhodes was delighted with the hitch, urging his young men to take as much territory as they could, so as to present the governments in Europe with *faits accomplis* that could not be ignored when negotiations were reopened. The pioneers were already on their way to Mashonaland when the Convention was rejected by the Cortes. Beyond Mashonaland lay Manica, almost out of range of Matabele raiders and ruled over by Umtasa, a slippery gentleman much addicted to alcohol. He claimed to be, and probably was, independent both of Lobengula and of his other neighbour Gungunyana, who dominated the coastal territory of Gazaland with a tribe which, like the Matabele, were an offshoot of the Zulus.

The Portuguese of course claimed not only Gazaland and Manica, but also Mashonaland, the last two on an alleged deed of cession of 1630 and on the evidence of a few ruined forts and abandoned plantations, which might be held to imply occupation. Neither Rhodes nor the Foreign Office regarded the claims as of any substance. The Charter, they maintained, covered all Lobengula's country up to the River Sabi, which the Foreign Office (but not Rhodes) was prepared to recognise as the Charter boundary. Such a frontier left most of Manica to the Portuguese; and whatever the legal position (if any legal position was ascertainable), Rhodes took the rough and ready view that the Portuguese had had their day and their opportunity, and that their day had passed and their opportunity had been neglected. "They are a bad race," he wrote of them, "and have had three hundred years on the coast, and all they have done is to be a curse to any place they have occupied." It was now his turn to try to make something of the land they had so patently abused; and whatever the legal rights may have been, there can be little doubt that, in the interests of the inhabitants, the Chartered Company was the better occupier.

Naturally the Portuguese did not accept this opinion. When the first rumours of British expansion reached them, they made belated efforts to assert themselves. A new Corporation—the Mozambique Company—undertook the commercial exploitation of a large part of Umtasa's country. One of their most competent officers, Colonel d'Andrade, was active in trying to spread Portuguese influence about the southern tributaries of the Zambesi, his operations alarming Lobengula and being one of the factors influencing his decision to sign the Rudd Concession. A much less respectable agent was the Goanese, Manuel Antonio de Sousa (or Gouveia, as he was more often styled), a thoroughgoing scoundrel who was appointed Capitão Mor (Military Governor) in the province immediately north-east of Manica, where he raided and plundered without any hindrance from Mozambique. To some extent d'Andrade and Gouveia cancelled each other out, since while the former went round the *kraals* distributing guns and flags and expatiating on the benevolence of Portugal, the latter was busy robbing the inmates of their possessions and their freedom for his enrichment and of their daughters for his harem.

Neither man went through the formality of annexing the districts they visited, regarding Umtasa as a feudatory of Gungunyana (the status which Umtasa repudiated), Gungunyana himself being by their reckoning a vassal of the Portuguese Crown. This association depended on a treaty of 1861 and an act of vassalage of 1885, instruments of extreme dubiety. Both Gungunyana and Umtasa in fact stoutly denied that they had ever been the feudatories of the king of Portugal.

Rhodes, on the strength of these denials and of Umtasa's claim to be a paramount chief independent of Gungunyana, asked Colquhoun to go with what speed was possible to Umtasa's *kraal*; Jameson to reconnoitre the coast; and Aurel Schultz, a doctor in the Colonial Service already known as an intrepid explorer, to visit Gungunyana.

Schultz, in the guise of a prospector, arrived at his destination at a critical moment. Gungunyana, who had fuddled away what wits he had with "trade rum and inferior wine" supplied by the Portuguese, had just launched an expedition to crush a rebellious tribe and, being beset by concession-hunters and Portuguese plotters, was very ready to accept the protection of the British.

The Portuguese were giving him great trouble and his prayer was that the Queen of England "should take him by the hand and not let him go". After several *indabas*, at which Schultz assured the chief, with doubtful authority, that an agreement with the Chartered Company was equivalent to one with the British Government, Gungunyana declared his readiness to concede full mineral and commercial rights in return for defence, an annual subsidy, and a supply of rifles and ammunition. Having in his sober moments some astuteness and, despite his protestations to the contrary, a considerable fear of the Portuguese, he refused to ratify this concession until the rifles, ammunition and a first instalment of the subsidy had reached him at his *kraal*. This condition, as probably he was aware, was likely to present formidable difficulties. The easiest route from the Cape was by sea and up the Limpopo, but it was generally believed that a bar at the mouth of the river made passage impossible. Further, even if this obstacle could be negotiated, and although Gungunyana declared that "the whole coast is mine", the Portuguese gunboats and posts were most unlikely to allow a consignment of arms for an obviously undesirable purpose to go through. The overland journey was even more forbidding. Gungunyana's *kraal* was 400 miles from Umtali, the nearest station of the Chartered Company, and Umtali was more than 500 miles from the Company's base at Tuli. No road of any kind had been cut from Umtali to the Chief's *kraal*, and any transport had to pass through a wide belt of *tsetse* country, which would certainly be fatal to oxen.

A fresh complication was the arrival at the *kraal* of a small Portuguese force under the command of Almeida, the Superintendent-in-chief of Native Affairs. Gungunyana, elated by his potations and by the return of his victorious warriors from their punitive expedition, was in no mood to be bullied by anyone. "That man," he said, pointing to Schultz, "is now my friend, but if his people treat me as the Portuguese have, I will kill him!" He explained that he allowed the Portuguese flag to fly at his *kraal* merely out of courtesy and that, if he chose, he would pull it down and hoist the Union Jack in its place. When Almeida argued that the dispute must be settled between the two Governments concerned, Gungunyana cried: "Not without consulting me shall you settle this question!" Meanwhile he importuned Schultz for further signs of his good faith and the Company's bounty. Where were the rifles and ammunition promised? He had heard that the Company had presented Lobengula with two valuable bulls—as it had, though they soon died of neglect—and he wanted a similar gift. He would also like a horse and two mastiffs. His greed was insatiable, the more irritating to Schultz because he suspected that simultaneously, when he was absent, the chief was making fervent protestations of loyalty to the Portuguese.

Everything in fact depended on the delivery of the rifles and ammunition, which would quiet Gungunyana's fears and easily outweigh any Portuguese promises. Schultz sent a message to that effect to Rutherfoord Harris who, despite the obvious risk, decided to lose no time in trying to run a cargo up the Limpopo. Within a few days of getting Schultz's message, Harris had bought the *Countess of Carnarvon* of 100 tons, and found a captain who knew the East African rivers. Quickly loaded with rifles, ammunition and a detachment of the Company's Police, she was off up the coast, and by 17 February was in the mouth of the Limpopo. She negotiated the bar, which was not so formidable an obstacle as had been supposed, and started upstream. That evening, when she had drawn in to the bank and anchored, some Portuguese came aboard and were cordially entertained. Next day she passed a customs-house, from which the guests of the previous night, having run up the Portuguese flag, came out and shouted after them. The Captain, disregarding their signals, steamed on for two or three hours, dropping anchor near a village which, the local chief told him, was the spot where the arms for Gungunyana should be unloaded.

The Captain at once discharged his cargo and messages were sent to the Chief's *kraal* to ask for carriers, the rifles and ammunition being meanwhile stored in a hut. One of the Company's officers, Stevens, riding a mule sent down by Schultz, started for the royal *kraal* with the money, leaving the arms behind in the charge of another officer, Pawley. Hardly had Stevens gone than a detachment of about 150 African soldiers, led by Portuguese officers, arrived at the village, occupied the landing stage, and took possession of the rifles and ammunition. The *Countess of Carnarvon*, having played her part, hove anchor and left for Durban, with orders to return in a week's time to pick up Schultz and Stevens. Pawley then became engaged in a wrangle with the Portuguese, who demanded the payment of £2,000 as customs duty before releasing the arms. After vehement protests, he agreed to give a personal bond for the amount; whereupon, with surprising complacency, the Portuguese released the cargo, which was promptly conveyed to Gungunyana's *kraal* by the carriers.

Jameson, meanwhile, who had been told by Rhodes to make for the coast, had been having misadventures. He had left the pioneer column with Colquhoun, meaning to accompany him as far as Umtasa's *kraal*. Unfortunately, while lightheartedly trying for a bet to jump over a fallen tree, he was thrown from his horse, breaking two ribs, and had to return to the column in a litter. He was not the man to allow a little mishap to stop him and was soon preparing to resume his journey. Probably he was not sorry to part company with Colquhoun, with whom his relations had become very strained. As an old Indian Civil Servant, the latter had his own ideas of official procedure and disliked Jameson's rather happy-go-lucky ways.

Colquhoun had been appointed Administrator and considered that Jameson, who was merely Rhodes's personal representative, should take orders from him; whereas Jameson, corresponding directly with Rhodes, occasionally produced instructions which countermanded something Colquhoun had arranged. A dyarchy of this kind was bound to produce complications, even between two men of congenial disposition, and Colquhoun and Jameson were too different in temper and background to be congenial. For some reason Colquhoun did not approve of Jameson's projected journey to the coast and had forbidden it. Jameson was neither deterred nor disturbed. As soon as he was sufficiently recovered from his accident, he prepared to leave, taking with him Johnson and a collapsible boat for use on the rivers. Before they had gone far, a trooper overtook them with a message to tell them that they were both under arrest and must return at once. "Damn the fellow!" was Jameson's light-hearted reply. "I got him his job."

Jameson's ribs were still in plaster and riding must have been a torture to him, but they went on. They reached Fort Maçequeçe, where they met the Portuguese Intendente of Native Affairs, Baron de Rezende, who received them coolly and did not ask them, as they had hoped he would, to spend the night in the relative comfort of the fort. Going on, they met General Machado himself, the Governor-General of Portuguese East Africa, who was as friendly as de Rezende had been cold. With him they left their horses, which were most unlikely to survive in the *tsetse* country through which they must pass, and for three days they marched through bamboo forest till they reached the banks of the

H

Pungwe, where they launched the Berthon boat. Still in pain from his ribs, Jameson, who had never rowed, insisted on pulling an oar. At a friendly village they were given a grass hut for the night, which they lit with a candle stuck in a bottle. Johnson accidentally knocked the bottle over, the hut caught fire, and in a few minutes not only it, but the whole village, had been burned down, an accident for which the inhabitants had to be liberally placated and compensated.

Jameson's position was serious. The three men had lost all their clothes, except the singlets they were wearing, one pair of boots, and a single dancing shoe, the property of Jameson. They had also lost nearly all their stores, a 7 lb. tin of icing sugar being the only food that survived; and most of the paper money they had brought with them had vanished. The appearance Jameson now presented, as the emissary of the Chartered Company, was neither dignified nor even decent, yet it is recorded that he left the village with "roars of laughter". The party went on downstream, protected from the tropical sun only by their singlets, plagued by mosquitoes and often nearly capsized by hippo or buffaloes. At night, when they made a camp ashore, they were pestered by lions, which were much more venturesome than their brothers in the interior. More than once the tidal bore nearly swamped the boat and their only bailer was the icing tin. But their one chance was to press on to the mouth of the Pungwe, where Johnson had arranged, rather casually, for a ship, the *Lady Wood*, to meet them and pick them up. As they approached the sea, the boat was nearly sunk by the waves, but when they had almost lost all hope of making their rendezvous with the steamer, or indeed of escaping with their lives, they suddenly saw two sticks like masts. They rowed towards them. The ship actually was the *Lady Wood*, which was about to give them up and return to Cape Town.

Night fell and at first the voyagers were cheered by seeing the riding lights of the steamer. When presently the light went out, extinguished by an over-careful captain, they drove the boat blindly on through the darkness in what they trusted was the right direction. By great good fortune it was, and just as they were beginning to feel desperate—for the sea was rising, the boat was half swamped, and a strong tide ruled out any possibility of a return to the shore—the dark mass of the steamer towered above them.

They were safe, after a series of disasters and almost miraculous escapes. After being revived with brandy, they resumed their odyssey in comparative comfort, and before long Jameson was reporting on his reconnaissance to Rhodes at Kimberley. Fleeting as had been Jameson's glimpse of the mouth of the Pungwe, he had seen enough to be assured that there was the perfect port of the future, with no bar to block it and an ample anchorage for big ships. Johnson was so impressed with the possibilities of the future port of Beira that he at once began to make plans for a coach service from there to Mashonaland, ignoring alike the Portuguese and the *tsetse* fly.

"I am in splendid condition," Jameson had written to his brother from Cape Town, "and have had a capital trip."

* * *

Colquhoun meanwhile, with Selous, had reached the *kraal* of Umtasa, by his own reckoning the Paramount Chief of Manica. He gave the visitors a royal welcome, as Colquhoun himself described it,

". . . attired in a naval cocked hat, a tunic . . . a leopard skin slung over his back, the whole toilet being completed by a pair of trousers that had passed through many hands, or, rather, covered many legs."

Before him danced the court jester, crying his praises in the most extravagantly fulsome terms, and behind him came girls, carrying calabashes of Kaffir beer, and *indunas* and others.

Umtasa was a poor creature. His dominion had been much diminished by the defection of some of his under-chiefs and the Portuguese treated him with contempt, having bestowed on him the honorary rank of Sergeant-Major, whereas Gungunyana was a Colonel. Umtasa, for his part, much as he disliked the Portuguese, was in great fear of their agent and his neighbour, Gouveia. Having heard exaggerated accounts of the pioneers, he was anxious to make friends with them. He swore to Colquhoun that he had signed no treaty with Portugal, had given away nothing to anybody, and was entirely independent of Gungunyana. With suspicious alacrity he signed a document granting exclusive commercial and mineral rights to the Chartered Company and binding himself to make no concession of his land to anyone else.

So far all had gone well, but as prospectors, with alleged concessions, were reported to be at work already in Umtasa's alleged kingdom, Colquhoun went off to see some of them and warn

them off the Company's new ground. He also sent Selous to the
Portuguese fort of Maçequeçe, where Baron Joso de Rezende
gave him a chilly reception and accused him of trespassing on
Portuguese territory. The Baron also sent Colquhoun a protest,
carried by two Portuguese gentlemen and two of Umtasa's men,
whom that shifty monarch had despatched to make his peace with
the Portuguese. Selous returned to the *kraal*, where he confronted Umtasa with the evidence of his double dealing. In no
way abashed, he merely implored Colquhoun not to abandon
him.

Colquhoun, however, had to return to Mashonaland and the
pioneers, who by then had reached the neighbourhood of Mount
Hampden and founded Fort Salisbury. He left behind one of his
escort who could speak the language, and promised to send a
detachment of police with the balance of the subsidy promised in
the Concession. He then returned to Fort Salisbury, making *en
route* treaties with the chiefs through whose territory he passed.
From Salisbury he sent Captain Patrick Forbes with a small force
and instructions to occupy as much ground as he could, particularly to the east towards Pungwe Bay, and if necessary to
seize Maçequeçe. Prospectors and settlers would follow.

When Forbes reached Umtasa's *kraal*, he found the Chief in a
state of terror. D'Andrade was at Maçequeçe with two or three
hundred men, threatening punishment. Forbes, although his
entire force consisted of only eleven men, sent him a message demanding his withdrawal, and to Salisbury an urgent request for
reinforcements. D'Andrade, who had been joined by de Rezende
and Gouveia with over two hundred natives, did not even deign
to answer Forbes's message, but pointed out to the officer who
bore it that Umtasa was Gungunyana's vassal, that the country
was occupied, that a railway was about to be built from the coast,
and that Lobengula, Gungunyana and Gouveia would all join in
ejecting the intruders.

Next day Gouveia, with about seventy black soldiers, entered
the *kraal*, hauled down the Union Jack, and hoisted the Portuguese flag outside the Chief's hut. The situation was critical,
but news arrived that Lieutenant (afterwards Sir Eustace)
Fiennes was on his way from Salisbury with twenty-five men.
D'Andrade now appeared at the *kraal* and invited all the Europeans there to meet him the next day to hear Umtasa's formal
recognition of Portuguese sovereignty.

Just before the meeting started, Fiennes arrived with the reinforcements. The Portuguese, confident in their superior strength, were taken completely by surprise when Forbes and his police appeared at the *indaba* and, after hauling down the Portuguese flag, arrested d'Andrade, de Rezende and Gouveia for "insult to the English flag". D'Andrade was dignified and icily aloof, but Gouveia, grovelling, could only beg the British to spare his life; while his African soldiers, who easily outnumbered the police, without the slightest hesitation flung down their rifles and bolted. Their comrades in Maçequeçe also fled, leaving ungarrisoned the fort with all its stores.

Daring and impudence had won. The collapse of the Portuguese, and particularly of Gouveia, who had terrorised the neighbourhood for so long, deeply impressed the natives with the superior strength of the Company. Forbes proceeded to send d'Andrade and Gouveia to Colquhoun, who passed them on to Tuli, where Jameson set them free on condition that they continued their journey to Cape Town. De Rezende, who was released by Jameson, returned to Portugal, where his account of the indignities he had suffered aroused the greatest indignation. Feeling in Lisbon ran high; public meetings were held; and students and other young volunteers came forward to form an expeditionary force for the vindication of Portugal's ancient rights in East and Central Africa.

Forbes, having established the Company's position in Manica, began to press eastward towards the coast, making treaties with all the petty chiefs he met on his way. Although many of his men were down with fever, he was within two days' march of the sea when he received peremptory orders from Colquhoun to retire at once to Maçequeçe. The advance had been made in the convenient hiatus created by the refusal of the Portuguese Cortes to ratify the Anglo-Portuguese Convention of August. Now, realising that they were threatened with the loss of their East African colonies and possibly with a war against Britain, the Portuguese saw sense and on 14 November 1890, accepted a provisional agreement establishing the *status quo* for six months and allowing the Company a right of way to Mashonaland through Beira. How far the Company's acquisitions between August and November could be regarded as falling within the *status quo* might be disputed, but clearly no new territory could be taken after 14 November, and Rhodes, smarting under a stern rebuke from Whitehall, had to call off his young men. Forbes retired from the Pungwe district, but left Captain (later

Sir Melville) Heyman with a detachment of police to protect Umtasa's *kraal*.

Undiscouraged, Jameson determined to return to the coast, hoping no doubt to pit one Latin phrase against another, *beati possidentes* against *status quo*. Who knew what might happen? The agreement of 14 November was only provisional. The Portuguese might change their minds again and repudiate it. Or they might break it, as later in fact they did, and so justify reprisals. At any rate he went, accompanied by Denis Doyle, who could talk to the tribes in their own tongues and Dunbar Moodie, a prospector. The journey—another heroic performance— belongs less to the story of Rhodes than to that of Jameson. For fifteen months he, a city doctor, had been almost continuously on the move; he had hardly recovered from a nasty accident; and now, to add to his discomfort, the rains had come, turning much of the country into a quagmire and every river to be crossed into a roaring torrent. All three men got malaria, and at one time Doyle was so ill that Jameson almost despaired of his life, remembering gloomily that on behalf of the Company he had promised Mrs. Doyle £10,000 if her husband died, a pledge he himself might have to honour.

Still they struggled on, through forest and mangrove swamp, reaching Gungunyana's *kraal* at last after a journey of seven weeks and nearly 800 miles, at the very moment that the arms and ammunition were being delivered. Their horses had foundered, they had practically waded over flooded country for the last fifty miles, they had lost most of their stores in a stream, and were an unimpressive delegation, even by Jameson's minimising account "pretty ragged and famished". But their presence put fresh heart into Gungunyana who, despite the daunting presence in his *kraal* of Almeida, a Portuguese officer of high rank, called together his councillors and with little hesitation signed a document confirming the Concession to Colquhoun of 4 October. He then picked out two of his *indunas* to speak for him to Queen Victoria, taking with them an elephant tusk as a token of submission.

Jameson and his companions then resumed their journey, Doyle being still so ill that he had to be carried on a stretcher. At last they reached the Limpopo and the *Countess of Carnarvon*, but beside her lay an unwelcome sight, a Portuguese gunboat. The *Countess of Carnarvon* was arrested, all her passengers except Jameson and Doyle being moved into the gunboat, and continued her voyage in charge of a boarding party. Three days of the greatest discomfort followed, for the weather was stormy and the passengers in the gunboat were herded into a filthy hold. Fortunately, Jameson, suspecting trouble on the coast, had sent a man with the precious concession by land to Delagoa Bay, so that when the Portuguese searched the three travellers, they failed to find what they were seeking. At Delagoa Bay the prisoners were set free, the *Countess of Carnarvon* being detained until intervention from London secured her release.

In due course Gungunyana's *indunas* reached London, where they saw Queen Victoria and the Prime Minister, to whom they delivered the king's message begging for protection from the Portuguese. Unfortunately they were too late. By a final agreement of 11 June 1891, Gazaland was conceded to Portugal. The document which had cost Jameson so much trouble and suffering became valueless, and Gungunyana was severely punished for his temerity.

There were, however, moments still to come when another result seemed possible. Contrary to the terms of the provisional agreement, the Portuguese began to stop ships going up the Pungwe. Rhodes, learning of their action, decided to send Sir John Willoughby to break the blockade. When someone objected that he might be killed, Rhodes replied in an excited falsetto, "Not a bit, not a bit, they'll only hit him in the leg, only hit him in the leg." The Portuguese did not hit Willoughby in the leg, but Willoughby did not himself reopen the Pungwe. In April 1891 he started to steam up it with a small flotilla, but Portuguese gunboats at once appeared, with their guns trained on the intruders, who gave way under protest. Willoughby returned to Durban, where his complaints brought British warships to the coast; and it was the turn of the Portuguese to give way.

*   *   *

Heyman, it will be recalled, had been left with a small force to keep an eye on Maçequeçe with its abandoned stores, as well as on Umtasa. On 3 May reports were received of an advance on the fort by a Portuguese force. With it were some of the young Portuguese who, in a moment of patriotic enthusiasm, had volunteered to go to Africa. They were raw, mostly untrained, and quite unfitted to fight in a tropical country. During the long march from the coast many went down with fever and others fell out for one reason or another; but on 6 May the survivors reached and occupied Maçequeçe. Though their numbers had been reduced to about 500, Heyman had less than fifty men under his command and no hope of reinforcements, since most of the Company's police were busy dealing with a threatened incursion of Boers into Mashonaland. However, he had a stout heart, and having also a 7-pounder gun, he took up a position on a hill commanding the approaches to Umtasa's *kraal*. When Colonel Ferreira, the new "Governor of Manica", announced that he had come to drive out the English, Heyman returned a defiant answer. Next day, after some Portuguese officers had made a reconnaisance, an extraordinary battle in an undeclared war followed. The Portuguese advanced in two columns, which deployed and opened a heavy fire at a range of 600 yards. Heyman pulled in his picket and returned the fire. The Portuguese marksmanship was execrable: in two hours they did not hit a single man in Heyman's force, even by accident. While the officers led with courage, the men had no stomach for a fight. With their superior numbers, they could easily have outflanked and surrounded Heyman's detachment; but he, foreseeing that they might attempt to do this, made signals, which would easily be read by the Portuguese, to imaginary reinforcements in his rear.

After the officers had made many attempts to get to close quarters, suffering in the course of them several casualties from the well-directed British rifle fire, the Portuguese retired to the cover of the fort. The 7-pounder was brought forward, but Heyman had only sixty rounds, and just as these were exhausted, a lucky shot from the Portuguese artillery put the gun out of action. The last of the 7-pounder's shells had been even luckier, for it fell in the middle of the fort, and the Portuguese, supposing that the British had found the range, and having seen their best officer fall severely wounded, fled in panic. Next day, the enemy having vanished, Heyman entered the fort, dispersed the natives who were looting it, carried off the guns and ammunition the Portuguese had left behind, and blew up the derelict building.

The Portuguese had gone, and pursuit should have followed panic. Heyman had no carriers; his men had no boots and their clothes were in rags; but he had had his orders from Rhodes. "Take all you can get," Rhodes had told him, "and ask me afterwards." He knew that the Portuguese, realising their blunder of the previous year, were trying desperately to turn the *modus vivendi* of November into a proper treaty; and before they could do this, Rhodes wanted his port on the east coast, a side door which would save the overland journey of 1,600 miles from Cape Town to Mashonaland. The Portuguese, aware of his hope, of his insouciance towards frontiers and treaties, and of his habit of staging a *fait accompli*, were ready to agree to almost any terms. Even before the fall of Fort Maçequeçe, the heads of a new convention had been initialled by Lord Salisbury and the Portuguese Minister for Foreign Affairs. This Heyman was not to know, and a few days after the occupation of the fort, he mounted a patrol under Fiennes to pursue what was left of the Portuguese force on its flight to the coast. For it was a flight undisguised: there was no fighting. When Fiennes with his handful of men appeared, the Portuguese either surrendered or fled again. The advance, it seemed, would stop only at the sea.

Unfortunately for Rhodes's plans, two gentlemen were hurrying up from Beira to meet Fiennes. While he was waiting for two days at the Revue River for reinforcements, no less a person than the Anglican Bishop, Knight-Bruce, arrived in his camp, with the news that Major Sapte, Military Secretary to the High Commissioner, was close behind him with orders to withdraw immediately to Maçequeçe. It was a bitter disappointment, for in a few days Fiennes would have had Beira. But an official order, backed by weighty episcopal warnings, was more than Fiennes could withstand; and he turned back. Rhodes never forgave either the Bishop or the Military Secretary. "Why didn't you put Sapte in irons?" he complained, "and say he was drunk." Jameson would have done it, but Fiennes was not Jameson: he was a professional soldier.

So he and the Company lost the glittering prize of Beira and the outlet to the sea, while the harried remnant of the Portuguese expeditionary force escaped. On 11 June 1891 the Portuguese House of Peers formally assented to the new Convention, which extended the Company's sphere in Manica, but gave Maçequeçe, Gazaland and the coast to the Portuguese. At the same time transit by land or river from the coast to the interior was to be allowed. The eastern boundary, which Rhodes had hoped to keep open, was finally settled.

*   *   *

In the north-east was the country later to be known as Nyasaland, important less for potential minerals than for its geographical position. Like Bechuanaland, it was a "Suez Canal" to the north. The Germans were coming in from the east, the Belgians from the west; and once they had met and made a common frontier, an all-British Cape-to-Cairo railway line could not go through. In 1894 Lord Kimberley, the Foreign Secretary, did his best to secure a connection of a sort between Nyasaland and British East Africa by entering into an agreement with the Congo Free State for the lease of a port at the north end of Lake Tanganyika and of a strip of land between that lake and Lake Albert Edward. The Germans, however, who were much more alive to their African interests than the Portuguese had been, at once protested. The strip which would connect the domain of the Chartered Company with British East Africa would also separate German East Africa from the Congo and be a hindrance to mutual trade. After some argument Her Majesty's Government gave way, and another of Rhodes's dreams was dissipated.

Nyasaland, with its crumbling kingdoms, its Arab slave-raiders, its Scots missionaries and its insolvent Company, remained an uncertain territory till 1889. Johnston, now "Her Majesty's Commissioner and Consul-General for the territories under British influence north of the Zambesi", was fighting a desperate battle with Arabs, Portuguese and a Foreign Office which demanded results for which the Treasury was too parsimonious to pay. The African Lakes Company, founded by the Moir brothers, was brought almost to bankruptcy, and since in 1886 the Portuguese had closed the port of Quilimani, Johnston had no line of communication to the coast. They had followed up this unfriendly action with the military expedition under Major Serpa Pinto which, advancing by the Shiré River, proposed to take over the country on behalf of his Most Faithful Majesty the King of Portugal. Johnston, however, was indomitable, and when Pinto attacked the friendly tribe of Makololo, he persuaded Lord Salisbury to declare a British Protectorate of what was to be Nyasaland, Rhodes having promised the necessary financial support; and in 1889, when the Zambesi was declared an international waterway, Johnston could again receive his supplies up it and the Shiré River.

Pinto, after giving the Makololo another beating, had gone back to Mozambique, but his successor advanced and threatened Blantyre, calling on the British missionaries and traders to put themselves under the protection of Portugal. Now it was Britain's turn to be angry. The Portuguese were impudently molesting a British Protectorate and Lord Salisbury replied with an ultimatum; whereupon Lisbon sent orders for the evacuation of the

Shiré highlands and the Makololo country. So what had begun as a combination of missions and trading stations became a British protectorate. The Anglo-Portuguese Convention of 1891 settled the future of Nyasaland and established its communications by the rivers to the sea. In January 1896, Johnston could report to Lord Salisbury that "there does not exist a single independent avowedly slave-trading chief within the British Central African Protectorate, nor anyone who is known to be inimical to British rule".

When Rhodes and Johnston had met in London in 1889 and later in Africa, they had worked out a programme, or at least a pattern, for Central African expansion. The Chartered Company, making treaties and winning concessions, would press on to the north, while Johnston held his own among the Lakes. The African Lakes Company would eventually be swallowed up by the Chartered Company and meanwhile eke out a precarious existence with the help of Rhodes's subsidy of £10,000 a year, the sum which induced Salisbury to declare a British Protectorate. The northward advance could then be resumed.

Up to a point the plan worked. It was finally frustrated by two circumstances. The first was the clash of two strong personalities between Rhodes and Johnston. Each had his own ideas of how the advance should be made; each had his own responsibilities, Rhodes to his shareholders, Johnston to Her Majesty's Government. Johnston was determined that the country he had done so much to free should not be subjected to a new exploitation, Rhodes was afraid that Johnston would bring in that "Imperial factor" whose interventions he had learnt to distrust. Johnston made little allowance for the serious financial position of the Chartered Company, and Rhodes made none for Johnston's obligations to his other master, the Foreign Office. Indeed, Rhodes had always intended to use Johnston as an instrument for manipulating the Foreign Office, as he manipulated the Colonial Office by means of the High Commissioner.

Johnston loathed the Lakes Company, which he described as "a miserly, fanatical, uncultured set of Glasgow merchants". But he gradually arrived at the conviction that the Chartered Company, though different, was little better. The serious trouble was his dual responsibility. In February 1891 by agreement with Rhodes, he had become Commissioner for the Charter lands west of Nyasaland, known as the Company's sphere of influence, receiving from the Company an annual subsidy of £10,000, to be spent at his discretion either in the Protectorate or in the sphere of influence. Actually Johnston found that he needed the whole subsidy for the Protectorate, and in January 1893, he had to ask Rhodes for a further annual sum of £5,000. A new agreement was necessary, and for this Rhodes demanded the reversionary land and mineral rights in the Protectorate.

Johnston went down to the Cape and stayed at Groote Schuur to discuss the details; but the visit was not happy.

"Rhodes's manner," wrote Johnston, "had become much more sombre; he had long fits of sulky silence, alternating with rapid conversation, so full of great propositions backed by monetary proposals, that one almost felt obliged to ask him to pause while a notebook and pencil could be fetched."

"I enjoyed my stay at the Cape immensely," Johnston wrote afterwards, "except when you used to get cross of an evening and abuse me like anything over the drawing-room fire when we dined alone."

He was forced to accept Rhodes's terms, hard though he thought them. The money had to be found, and without that grant-in-aid which as yet the Treasury showed no signs of giving, the Chartered Company was his only hope. If that failed, all his work would be ruined and Nyasaland would fall back into the hands of the slave-raiders. So the two men agreed that the subsidy should be increased to £17,500 for five years, in return for the transfer to the Company of all Crown lands and the mineral rights.

Although Johnston sometimes overstated his case and never properly understood Rhodes's difficulties, his purpose and integrity were unchallengeable. Beyond a relatively small consular salary he got nothing for his immense labours and even had to pledge his small private fortune to cover the debts he had incurred in the public service. Yet he had a *folie de grandeur*, which was very evident in his long rhetorical letters. They delighted Salisbury, who had a genuine regard for his abilities, but often caused consternation in the Foreign Office and annoyed Rhodes. "When you next write," he once replied pathetically to one of Johnston's screeds, "please grumble less." But Johnston was bound to grumble. He did not know where to turn for money, and Rhodes had only, *more suo*, to take his cheque book out of his pocket.

The terms arranged at Groote Schuur went to the Foreign

Office and the Colonial Office, which in transforming them into a formal agreement introduced two changes. They extended the period of the subsidy to ten years and insisted that the whole of it should be spent in the Protectorate. Rhodes was furious, believing, apparently wrongly, that Johnston was responsible for the alterations. Rutherfoord Harris, as South African Secretary of the Company, described the draft agreement as "a pure mockery", and Rhodes wrote to him, "I am not going to create with my funds an independent King Johnston over the Zambesi." Harris did nothing to allay the ruffled feelings on both sides. The Company, while continuing the subsidy of £10,000 a year, much of which Johnston had anticipated, turned the financial screw so hard that the poor man, at his wits' end for money, had to make a final attempt to get it from the Treasury. To his surprise he got it. Rosebery was now Prime Minister, and seeing Johnston's straits, agreed to defray the deficit and pay a grant-in-aid. So the Company lost Nyasaland.

Johnston never forgave Rhodes for his charge of treachery. In February 1892 Rhodes sent a letter which was almost an apology. "All writing does harm," he wrote, "when two friends have differed. You had better as soon as possible come and see me on your road home." But Johnston was by then implacable. He had had enough of Rhodes and the Chartered Company. Towards the end of the year there was a final settlement and a formal reconciliation, arranged by that persistent peacemaker, Albert Grey. "But," wrote Johnston, "even at that meeting he [Rhodes] said he never wished to see me again and he never did."

The other circumstance which thwarted Rhodes was the rapidity with which the Belgians in the Congo and the Germans in German East Africa moved to a common frontier. King Leopold had started his operations in the Congo Basin in 1876 and had since pushed an undefined and movable frontier steadily to the east. In 1885 Germany had annexed a large territory claimed by the Sultan of Zanzibar, subsequently extending her rule southward to the Portuguese border and west to Lakes Tanganyika and Nyasa. The two frontiers at last met, the only gaps being one between Lake Albert Edward and Lake Tanganyika in the north, which Kimberley tried and failed to keep open, and another in the south-east between Lake Tanganyika and Lake Nyasa, across which the Lakes Company had made what was known as the Stevenson Road.

In 1890, when Britain was settling with Bismarck the frontier between German East Africa and British Central Africa, the first draft of the treaty conceded the Stevenson Road to the Germans. Rhodes, who still hoped to keep open his road to the north, at once gave orders for two forts, Fort Abercorn and Fort Fife, to be built on the road; and in its final form the Treaty left it and them to the British. "Oh," said Rhodes, chuckling and rubbing his hands together, "I knew they could not give up a fort named after a member of the Royal Family." The victory was relatively unimportant, since for the time the British northward advance was blocked. A world war had to be fought before Tanganyika finally passed out of German control and Rhodes's old aim of a continuous strip of British territory from North to South was realised after a fashion.

*   *   *

North of Matabeleland and south of the Congo lay Barotse-land, a large domain, visited at rather rare intervals by Loben-gula's raiders, and ruled in 1890 by Lewanika, an enlightened, far-sighted paramount chief of a quality not unlike that of Khama, Chief of the Bamangwato. His subjects were a mixed race, until recently dominated by Basuto immigrants. "Witchcraft flour-ishes among them," wrote a young pioneer. "Manners they have none and their customs are beastly." Lewanika had been watch-ing apprehensively events among his neighbours. Having him-self become Chief by a revolution, his internal position was not very secure; and beyond his borders Portuguese, Belgians, Ger-mans, Matabele and now the British were approaching. In 1887 he was warned that Lobengula's *impis* were about to make a foray into his country, and was feeling so uneasy that he sent a message to his friend Khama, asking him how he had managed to obtain British protection, which would suit Barotscland too, if the terms were satisfactory.

At about this time a French Protestant missionary, Coillard, arriving in the royal *kraal* with his Scots wife, sought and ob-tained permission to stay. When Lewanika expatiated on his difficulties, Coillard supported the Chief's idea that his best policy would be to put himself under the protection of Queen Victoria. His first approach to the British Government having been tepidly received, he began, like Lobengula, to be plagued by concession-hunters; and although suspicious of their intentions, he eventually parted with the mineral rights in Barotseland for twenty years to one Ware, a hunter and trader from Kimberley, who subsequently sold them to the Chartered Company for £9,000 in cash and 100,000 Chartered shares.

In October 1889 Rhodes, learning of Lewanika's troubles from Sir Sidney Shippard, through whom the Chief's request for British protection had passed, sent Frank Lochner, a former officer of the Bechuanaland Police, to Lewanika's *kraal*, with instructions to try to obtain a comprehensive concession. Lochner's start was much delayed by the heavy rains that year, but finally, though weakened by fever, he reached Lealui with two companions in March 1890. Although welcomed and entertained by Coillard, they found Lewanika in a highly suspicious frame of mind. He wanted British protection, but was determined not to part with any land or to admit a crowd of prospectors. Lochner did his best to persuade him that the protection of the Chartered Company was the same as the protection of the Queen—that rather large assumption on which Rhodes's opponents at home later fastened with some eagerness. Lewanika, apparently convinced, celebrated the Queen's birthday on 24 May with a display of fireworks organised by Lochner, and a *pitso* or council was summoned for 26 June to go into the whole question of the concession.

The *pitso*, when it met, was much divided, European rivals of the Chartered Company having been busy disseminating doubts of Lochner's integrity and intentions. At the critical moment, however, an emissary arrived with a letter from Khama, strongly advising the Chief to make terms with the Chartered Company, which was composed of the "Queen's men". So impressed was the *pitso* by this advice that it unanimously decided in favour of the principle of a treaty with the Company. Lewanika then showed himself an unexpectedly hard bargainer. He would accept a subsidy of not less than £2,000 a year; in return for which he conceded full mining and commercial rights over the whole of his territory. He undertook to try to suppress witchcraft and slavery; and while recognising the protectorate of Queen Victoria, he kept his own constitutional authority and the towns, lands and cattle of his people. The Company for its part promised protection from his enemies and the presence of a British Resident, and further to refrain from mining in the part of Barotseland inhabited by the Barotses proper. On the signing of the agreement, he presented Lochner with two large ivory tusks as a token of his allegiance to the Queen.

"See how things grow," said Rhodes gleefully, when the news

of the treaty was brought to him: at a stroke of the pen he had added 250,000 square miles to his new territory. But his troubles in Barotseland were not quite over. He made the same mistake of leaving a vacuum which had been nearly fatal to him at Bulawayo. Lochner, sick and tired after his efforts, returned to the Cape; Johnston, who was to have taken his place, could not leave Nyasaland; and the promised British Resident never appeared. In his continued absence Lewanika's misgivings returned, while the rival traders kept warning him that he had been deceived, that he had given away his country, and had not even got the desired protection of the British Crown. One of these rivals, at his request, even wrote to Lord Salisbury to tell him that the Chief repudiated the Concession, which had been given under false pretences, and that Lochner, who had pretended to be an emissary of Her Majesty, was in fact only an agent of the Chartered Company. Salisbury may not have relished having his hand again forced by Rhodes, but he came to the Company's help. Loch, as High Commissioner, was instructed to send Lewanika an assurance that he was under British protection and that the Queen fully recognised the Chartered Company. Presently, he added, Consul Johnston would come to Barotseland as her Commissioner.

When neither Johnston nor any other Resident arrived, the king's misgivings returned. He had many opponents and feared another revolution. He still did not understand the relationship between the Crown, which he revered, and the Company, which he mistrusted. Rhodes's adversaries in the London press picked up his complaints and embroidered them. The ivory tusks had been a gift to Queen Victoria. Why then were they decorating the board-room of the Chartered Company's offices in the City? The *Daily Chronicle* went so far as to describe this alleged misappropriation as "the meanest form of embezzlement". Lewanika's doubts died slowly and were not really dispelled till 1897, when at last a Resident Commissioner arrived. R. T. A. (afterwards Sir Robert) Coryndon, the man appointed, quickly won the confidence of the king, and a new era of peaceful and progressive administration began.

Four days after the signing of the Barotseland treaty, an Anglo-German agreement was made, giving Germany what became known as the Caprivi Strip, a narrow belt of territory from a point in northern Namaqualand to the Zambesi. The Strip was an anomaly and a nuisance, if only because it indicated that the

Germans were still looking across Africa with an eye to joining east and west; but it had little practical importance, except that it confirmed Rhodes in his distrust of the "Imperial factor". With the Portuguese the Company was more fortunate. The rejected draft treaty of 1890 would have handed over to them all the land west of the Zambesi as far as the Katima-Molilo rapids, but the revised version accorded Lewanika his rights up to twenty degrees east, thus restoring to him the south-western corner of his kingdom.

*   *   *

North of Barotseland lay the independent territory of Katanga or Garenganze, ruled over by Mushidi or Msiri, an able savage who with 500 wives (including a Portuguese lady whom he had bought for a parcel of ivory) lived in a palace of wattle and daub and decorated his stockade with the heads of his decapitated victims. Katanga was still a No Man's Land which, as early as 1875, had been reported highly mineralised by the missionary and traveller, D. Crawford. It was known to have copper and believed to have gold, enough at any rate of both to tempt that realistic monarch—Satan, as Rhodes later called him— Leopold, king of the Belgians. While the sovereign rights of the International Congo Association (later the Congo Free State) had been recognised, and probably covered Katanga, there had been no effective occupation and no concession; so that in 1889 the way still seemed open for Rhodes and the Chartered Company to move in.

Early in that year Johnston, after dealing with Serpa Pinto, returned to Blantyre, where he met Alfred (afterwards Sir Alfred) Sharpe, a private traveller who had come to Nyasaland to hunt and trade. Since Sharpe had been crossing country as yet unvisited by Rhodes's men, Johnston suggested to him that on the further expeditions he was contemplating he should make treaties and secure concessions for the Company which was being formed. When Sharpe agreed, Johnston appointed him Vice-Consul and Deputy Commissioner.

Sharpe planned to make three expeditions. The first was to the land of the chiefs at the south end of Lake Nyasa. The second was in the general direction of the Luangwa River. The third and most ambitious was to Katanga, which he hoped to reach by way of Lake Mweru.

At the same time Rhodes had decided to send another man on

the same mission. In the little group which met at Kimberley in May 1890 and was later nicknamed 'Rhodes's Apostles', was Joseph Thomson, who was described by Marshall Hole as "without question the most intrepid African explorer since Livingstone". The same writer stated that Rhodes was unaware that Sharpe had also been commissioned to go to Katanga. But both Johnston and Thomson were at Kimberley for that May meeting and appear in the photograph of the "Apostles". It is hard to believe that when Thomson was given his instructions, Johnston should not have mentioned that he had just sent Sharpe on the same errand. It is more likely that Rhodes knew of Sharpe's intended journey and, as the object of it was so important, thought that if two men were given the same destination, at least one of them would reach it.

Sharpe's first two missions were successful. He found traces of gold workings and made several treaties on the now familiar pattern. Returning to Blantyre in July 1890 to prepare for the more formidable expedition to Katanga, he encountered Thomson, who had come in through Quilimani, eluding with some difficulty the Portuguese, who had fired on him. Sharpe was proposing to enter Katanga from the north by Lake Mweru, Thomson from the south by Lake Bangweolo. They decided to adhere to their separate plans, hoping to meet at Bunkeya, where Mushidi lived.

Sharpe started and was soon in trouble with his carriers, who did not like long journeys which took them far from their homes. He reached Kazembe, a little to the south of Lake Mweru, but the chief there had an old feud with Mushidi and put every obstacle in the way of Sharpe's further progress, so that at one time he was reduced to a single carrier and one piece of trading-cloth. Forced to go back to more friendly country and find carriers, Sharpe made a second and successful attempt. Avoiding Kazembe, he reached Mushidi's *kraal* early in November, "a plenipotentiary with scarcely a shirt to his back". Perhaps through the unimpressive appearance he presented, he then ran into fresh trouble.

King Leopold had sent three small expeditions to try to bring Mushidi to terms. Between the concession-hunters, who importuned him and decried their rivals, and the missionaries, who gave him more disinterested advice, Mushidi scarcely knew in which direction to turn. Among the missionaries was one Arnot, on whose counsel the chief particularly relied. Arnot had warned him against signing any document which might give away his country. Possibly Arnot would have distinguished between Sharpe, who represented the Chartered Company, and the men of straw, who represented no one but themselves and would sell anything they could get to the highest bidder. But Arnot was not there, having left on a journey to Angola; and when a ragged Briton appeared with a request for a concession and talk about the protection of the Queen and the evils of the slave trade, Mushidi suspected the worst. Such was his resentment that Sharpe began to fear for his safety. In Arnot's absence the missionaries would not speak for him; Joseph Thomson, who would have confirmed his story, had not appeared; and after spending some anxious days, Sharpe was escorted out of the country, being lucky to escape from it alive.

He had failed. There is, however, a fascinating tale, which came from an old explorer and hunter and is confirmed by Crawford, the missionary. By their account, after Sharpe had left, Mushidi had second thoughts, stimulated maybe by a strange dream he had about London, which of course he had never seen, and even more by a report that the Belgians were on their way and would find friends in Bunkeya. If Sharpe were telling the truth—and he appeared to be an honest man despite his rags—the great Queen would protect him against all intruders. "Sons of the dust, we know the English to be the true people," he roared to his *indunas*, and got Crawford to write an urgent letter to Sharpe, bidding him return and promising to comply with his requests. Unfortunately Sharpe never got the message. It was intercepted by a Captain W. G. Stairs, a Nova Scotian in the employment of the Belgian Katanga Company, who destroyed it.

Thomson meanwhile, approaching from Lake Bangweolo, had had even worse luck than Sharpe. Smallpox attacked his porters and he lost most of them by illness or flight. He obtained a number of concessions *en route*, including two from chiefs who also bore the name of Mushidi, thereby causing much confusion. Himself sick, Thomson with his diminished party at last reached the wilderness bounded by the Watwa swamp, south of Lake Bangweolo. There his long-suffering porters mutinied and the rains set in. In great pain and still dogged by smallpox, Thomson had to turn back without having even crossed the borders of Katanga.

Where both Rhodes's ventures had failed, the Belgians succeeded. The expedition commanded by Captain Stairs, who was accompanied by several other Britons and Belgians, reached

Bunkeya. By representing himself as British and an officer—
he had in fact served in the Royal Artillery—Stairs got a favourable reception from the king, but later, elated by his success, he
hoisted the Congo flag, and Mushidi fled. He was pursued to the
kraal where he had taken refuge, and in the brawl that followed,
was shot dead.

In this fashion the Belgians got Katanga, with its great deposits
of copper which make it geologically as well as geographically
part of the Copper Belt of Northern Rhodesia. Stretching eastward, Katanga almost cuts the present Federation in two, giving
it a kind of wasp-waist between Portuguese East Africa and the
Belgian Congo. This anomaly came about through a series of
mischances—the absence of Arnot, an intercepted letter, the
heavy rains, and a Nova Scotian who forgot the claims of his
flag.

*   *   *

The northward expansion had had its triumphs and its setbacks.
The Chartered Company got Mashonaland, Barotseland, most of
Manica and the territory, once the hunting ground of slave traders
and the *tsetse* fly, which was now covered by Sharpe's and Thomson's treaties. It failed to get Gazaland, part of Manica, Nyasaland (for a time), Katanga and the Caprivi Strip. Such a balance
sheet scarcely does justice to the heroic labours of the young
men whom Rhodes sent out to make a dominion. For relatively
small rewards they endured hardships and faced dangers which
would daunt most men. For months, in the hackneyed phrase,
they carried their lives in their hands; some of them died; many
of them were broken in health from their journeys. They—more
than any statesmen—were the founders of the Federation to be.
They knew what they were doing and why they were doing it.
They were of a kind now vanished, Imperialists not for what they
could get but for what they could give.

The driving force behind such men was Rhodes, whose leadership inspired them to effort and sacrifice. His brain and will
power were behind them and his pertinacity was extraordinary.
He would never yield a position until quite clearly it was untenable or untakeable. "The story of the importunate widow," he
liked to say, "is the best in the Bible."

If a man had once served him, Rhodes never forgot him—or let
him go. When he was in London in 1893, he found that Hans
Sauer, the young doctor who had helped him to secure his pro-

perties on the Rand, was there reading for the Bar. On several days they met for breakfast at Rhodes's hotel, and Sauer became more and more infected by Rhodes's enthusiasm for his new country. Eventually Rhodes took a used envelope out of his pocket and scrawled on a corner of it a message to Beit: "Dear Beit, please form a syndicate for Sauer and Williams to act in Rhodesia." Beit laughed at Rhodes's unconventional business habits, but the syndicate was formed and Sauer, relinquishing his forensic ambitions, went back to Africa. The incident shows Rhodes's impact on young men, who would cheerfully discard all their plans in order to work for him.

Soon naturally, if not inevitably, the new territory got its name. This was once said to have originated in 1892 with two young men who were working on the *Cape Argus*, but a year earlier (on 14 August, 1891) Rhodes had written to Stead: "They are calling the new country Rhodesia, that is from the Transvaal to the south end of Tanganyika. The other name is Zambesia."[2] In November of that year Rhodes, in his speech to the shareholders of the Chartered Company, spoke of Zambesia and Jameson more than two years later of Charterland. But the better idea seems to have occurred independently to a lot of people and by 1895 to pioneers, to the press of Cape Colony, and to the Company itself the land was Rhodesia. Imperial sanction lagged behind and was not forthcoming till 1897. Rhodes, who at first objected to the name, soon relented. "Well, you know," he said, "to have a bit of country named after one is one of the things a man might be proud of."

He himself paid his first visit to his territory in October 1891; just over a year after the arrival of the pioneers. Plenty of troubles were waiting for him. The rains of 1890 had almost washed the pioneers away. The rains were the worst in memory. Every river had overflowed its banks and the whole land was under water. The settlers were cut off from each other and from their supplies, the road from the south having become a quagmire. Many actually died of starvation or fever; and the survivors, being without cattle or crops, were reduced to living on pumpkins and millet bought from the nearest *kraal*. Many were so discouraged that they returned to the south, though these were mostly those who had swarmed into the country in the wake of the pioneers, hoping for easy gold.

The land was infested by lions, but almost more troublesome were the rats, which descended on the settlements, devouring any stores they could reach and even nibbling the fingers and toes of sleepers; one audacious rat even made off with Jameson's false teeth, which were lying in a tumbler of water by his bedside. After the rats, like another plague of Egypt, came the snakes, some of them extremely poisonous. Even to a settled community that winter would have been a sore trial; to the pioneers it was a disaster, and in their extremity they were inclined to lay the blame for their misfortunes on the Chartered Company, and particularly its South African Secretary, Rutherfoord Harris.

They had some real grievances. Johnson had promised every pioneer 3,000 acres of land freehold, but until later, when Rhodes bought the Lippert Concession, the land was not the Company's to give away. The minerals were an even greater grievance and disappointment. The main gold reef, which was expected to rival the Rand, was never discovered. Here and there gold was found, but not in any quantity; and the man who had come north hoping for a gold-mine, and expecting at any rate a farm, began to believe that he would get neither. Even the gold that was found produced a grievance through the regulation by which the Company retained a half interest in any claim that might be pegged.

Worst of all was the complete lack of proper communications. Even when the rains ended and the road was open again, haulage from railhead cost from £60 to £70 a ton; and the settlers were still having to import everything they needed. Rhodes did what he could to hasten the extension of the railway and telegraph from the south, and Johnson was trying to open up communications with Beira; but the work was slow and the need was desperate.

Beit was the first of the directors to visit the territory. He arrived during the rainy season of 1890 to have a look round, to examine the mining possibilities, and to enquire into the settlers' grievances. It is another sign of Rhodes's compelling influence that a city-bred man like Beit, who even went shooting in Scotland in a London lounge suit, should cheerfully have braved the discomforts and dangers of a howling wilderness. Simultaneously arrived Lord Randolph Churchill, in search of health and a fortune. He found neither, and was so depressed by his failure and by the adversities of the journey that the articles which he wrote for the British press were distinctly pessimistic and further lowered the price of Chartered shares on the London Stock Exchange.

In fact the financial situation was one of Rhodes's most pressing anxieties. The Company had started with a capital of a million, about half of which had gone on the pioneers, the extension of roads and telegraph, the innumerable concessions, each of which involved a payment, and the police, who were the heaviest of the Company's burdens. While so much money was going out, very little, if any, was coming in, and quite clearly, without drastic retrenchment, the Company would be insolvent in the near future.

This was the position confronting Rhodes when he arrived for a lightning first visit of seven days. "I am off to Mashonaland after a very trying session," he wrote to Stead, "so I feel like a schoolboy about to enjoy his holidays. . . . I quite appreciate the enormous difficulties of opening up a new country, but still, if Providence will furnish a few paying gold reefs, I think it will be all right. Please understand it is no personal avarice which desires this, but, as you know, gold hastens the development of a country more than anything. . . . I wonder if the Supreme Power will help me to this object, for it is certainly a disinterested one, or whether out of pure mischief he dooms it to failure. . . .

"The matter that troubles me is that there are over 2,000 people in Mashonaland, and as soon as the rain falls, they will be shut in for four months, that is from December until May, and the question is will the food last?"

He went on to complain of Portuguese unco-operativeness: they would do nothing themselves, and out of pride would not allow him to do anything; whereas 100 miles of light railway would save the situation. Lord Salisbury had ignored the need for a clause in the recent treaty authorising the Company to build such a railway; all that the Foreign Office cared about was getting the Portuguese trouble settled. Meanwhile men were threatened with starvation. He concluded:[3]

"If I am worn out, please remember never abandon Mashonaland: it is the key to Central Africa . . . it is worth more than all your other African possessions."

Rhodes came through Beira, risking the temptation which the person of the *"homem horrivel"* would offer to the Portuguese. Travelling first by river and then by road, he went to Salisbury. On the way he fell in with Bowden, a cricketer, who was taking up goods for the store he had opened at Umtali. When he fell sick, Rhodes gave him one of his few and precious bottles of whisky; and when one of the party protested, he gave Bowden the protester's pony.

At Umtali he met Jameson. Afterwards he described the meeting to his shareholders:

"I found the position at the time as follows: a discontented population of about 1500 people and an expenditure of about £250,000 a year upon police. Things looked rather bad, because it was not only the large number of police, but also the feeding of them, which had to be done by carting the food for 1700 miles from the coast. Dr Jameson and myself talked matters over, and he said, 'If you will give me £3000 a month I can pull through.'"

At Salisbury Rhodes was met by a "Vigilance Committee" armed with a formidable list of grievances. The pioneers had been promised gold claims, which they had not received, and farms, but had been told these could not yet be allotted. Native labour was scarce and food was ruinously expensive. There was also the hated 50/50 regulation, which was discouraging mineral development. In fact the discontent was general.

Rhodes in his reply won the "Committee" over by his sympathy and readiness to help. He would not withdraw the 50/50 regulation—though much later a system of royalties was substituted for it—but he was able to meet many of the settlers' complaints. Johnson's promise of fifteen gold claims to every pioneer would be honoured. The farms would be given. Stores of food were being accumulated. Everything possible was being done rapidly to improve communications.

Having allayed the discontent at Salisbury, Rhodes and Jameson made a quick tour of the country, riding, shooting and visiting gold workings, all to the accompaniment of a storm of chaff between the two friends. Wherever they went, they met and talked with the settlers, hearing their complaints and, when possible, helping them. They spoke plainly, without respect of persons, a little impatient sometimes when Rhodes talked to hungry and disappointed men of the Imperial enterprise on which they were engaged.

"I would have ye know, Mr. Rhodes," said the Scots spokesman of the delegation, "that we didna come here for posterity." Another aggrieved settler, when asked what he thought of the country, had replied, "Well, if you want my opinion, it's a bloody fyasco." And thereafter "bloody fyasco" became a catchword between Rhodes and Jameson.

"Well, how much do you want?" was Rhodes's stock question.

And when he was told, ten, fifty or a hundred pounds, the amount was at once forthcoming, usually from his own pocket. When his arguments failed to convince, his generosity often succeeded; and he left the settlers a good deal happier than he had found them. In the few years of life that remained to him, he never lost his regard for the pioneers and first settlers. "Your young men," he tactfully called them when speaking to the Bond. "*My* young men," was his more usual description. He was immensely proud of them and of what they had done; and his doors and purse were never closed to them.

In seven days and six nights Rhodes and his party travelled 625 miles. When someone remarked that never before had anyone covered so great a distance in so short a time with only draft animals, De Waal, a member of the Bond who had been taken on the trip, retorted with some truth that no one else would ever want to.

In August 1891 Colquhoun resigned his post as Resident Commissioner. Although he had continual disagreements with Jameson and was hardly fitted by his Indian experience to cope with the teething troubles of a new colony, he had done some good work, establishing a rough and ready administration throughout the country, to which the laws of Cape Colony were applied. His departure enabled Rhodes to appoint Jameson to succeed him, and the Doctor, with his common sense and courage, his blarney and banter, was a man after the settlers' hearts. "Rhodes may have the big ideas, but it is the Doctor who carries them out," wrote one of the young men. At first Jameson had the help of the unpopular Rutherfoord Harris, whose energy was always greater than his tact. Harris, however, had an unfortunate accident, being attacked and mauled by a crocodile while he was bathing in a river. The settlers, unsympathetic, repeated with glee the story that next day the crocodile was seen floating dead on the waters of the Shangani.

The need for retrenchment was urgent. Of about 3,000 settlers some 650 were police, and the annual cost of maintaining them was at least £150,000 (Rhodes said £250,000). Jameson rapidly reduced their numbers to 150 and the expense to under £8,000. At poker or politics he was always ready for a gamble, and many thought the risk he was running was indefensible. The country was still unsettled and at Bulawayo Lobengula's *impis* were truculent and unbroken. (Actually the king had accepted the settlement with as near an approach to good grace as was possible to him, and had even applied for and taken up some gold claims.)

Since forty policemen were obviously inadequate to do more than deal with such lawlessness as might arise among the settlers themselves or their African servants, Jameson, using the colonial burgher system, created a Volunteer Corps, the Mashonaland Horse. Every able-bodied man was given a rifle and ammunition and was liable to be called up to defend his country.

The new colony was settling down. With the ending of the rains, a steady stream of immigrants began to trickle in, mining machinery arrived, and everywhere the prospectors and farmers were hard at work. Zambesia, Charterland or Rhodesia had not yet found its feet, but at least it had taken on a semblance to the land of promise Rhodes had foreshadowed. ". . . And when I looked down, I said, This earth shall be English." And so it was.

Sources

Colquhoun, A. R.: *Dan to Beersheba*
Colvin, Ian: *The Life of Jameson*
Crawford, Robert: *Thinking Black*
De Waal, D. C.: *With Rhodes in Mashonaland*
Gale, W. D.: *Zambezi Sunrise*
Grey, Albert: *Memoir of Hubert Hervey*
Hole, H. M.: *The Making of Rhodesia*
Oliver, Roland: *Sir Harry Johnston and the Scramble for Africa*
Sauer, Hans: *Ex Africa . . .*
Warhurst, Philip: *Anglo-Portuguese Relations in South Central Africa, 1890—1900*

Notes

[1] Rhodes Papers, C. 3. 63.
[2] R.H.L. Rhodes Wills, 19.

[3] R.H.L. Rhodes Wills, 19.

CHAPTER FIFTEEN

THE MATABELE WAR

ON 29 November 1892, at the second Annual Meeting of the British South Africa Company, Rhodes told the shareholders that:[1]

"We are on the most friendly terms with Lobengula. The latter receives a globular sum of £100 a month in sovereigns, and he looks forward with great satisfaction to the day of the month when he will receive them. I have not the least fear of any trouble in the future with Lobengula."

Although the picture of Lobengula's satisfaction on receiving his sovereigns may have been fanciful, the terms were friendly enough and Rhodes was not expecting any trouble in the near future. The point is important in view of what was to follow and the charge, often brought, that for financial reasons Rhodes was determined to pick a quarrel with Lobengula.

It is true that the financial situation of the Chartered Company was far from happy. The "second Rand" had been a mirage. The settlement of Mashonaland, though remarkably cheap, had almost exhausted the Company's capital; so far hardly any revenue was coming in; and in March 1892 the Company's bankers refused to honour any more Chartered cheques without a guarantee. The settlers were getting their farms, but no substantial return in trade or taxes could be expected for some years; and meanwhile unusually heavy rains had disorganised communications, held up the extension of the railway, and kept the cost of carriage at a forbidding figure. In these adverse circumstances the price of Chartered shares drooped, and then dropped. Afterwards Rhodes's critics declared that his obvious remedy was to create a new expectation of profit. If Mashonaland was not El Dorado, Matabeleland might be. Since Tati on its borders had gold, other places in Matabeleland might have it too. Yet so long as Lobengula and his *impis* were in Bulawayo, the whole country was insecure and no one could hope to develop it. Therefore Lobengula and his *impis* must be eliminated.

So, roughly, the indictment against Rhodes ran, strengthened by the fact that, when the trouble started, Chartered shares went up and not down, but supported by no proper evidence. In fact, the charge that the war was a conspiracy on the part of Rhodes is rebutted by the facts, as well as by all that he said and did at the time. Jameson had just been allowed to reduce the police to forty, an action he would hardly have taken if trouble was in prospect. Among soldiers, mindful of the Zulu War, the opinion was that a force of at least 7,000 men would be needed to break the Matabele power, involving an expense which would bankrupt the Company. Finally, war was certain to bring in the "Imperial factor", which Rhodes distrusted so whole-heartedly; and among the Liberals, who returned to power in 1892, were many who disliked the Chartered Company and its African enterprises.

Rhodes—and his critics—may have been slow in realising that a black king at Bulawayo and a white settlement in Mashonaland could not co-exist peacefully for very long. The European and Matabele ways of life were too widely apart. Lobengula could no more understand British ideas of law and property than the white settlers could understand the workings of the Matabele mind. Lobengula had accepted the Charter with misgivings and the presence of the pioneers with suspicion. But the country, he understood, was still his. He must not interfere with the white men, when they were digging for gold under the concession he had granted them; but the Mashonas were his subjects and he would deal with them as he had always dealt with them. The white men could have their law for themselves, but he would have his law for those whom he regarded as his property, his "dogs" as he called them. Such a dyarchy was impossible, and sooner or later two systems so opposed were bound to conflict.

At first, as Rhodes had told his shareholders, Lobengula gave no real trouble, though soon he was indulging mildly in his old practice of trying to sell over again something with which he had already parted. Innes wrote to Rhodes in August 1890 about the German threat to "Zambesia". Colenbrander, Rhodes's agent in the royal *kraal*, reported the presence and intrigues of Germans and others. Their activities did not amount to much, and obviously any concession they might get out of the king would be worthless; but none the less his attitude was a little disquieting. Other informants were also disturbing Rhodes during 1891 with other more or less well-founded rumours: for instance, Moffat told him that "agitators" were at work trying to rouse the *indunas* against the Charter; Lady Brand reported from the Orange Free State the prevalent feeling that Mashonaland ought to belong to the

Boers; du Toit warned him of an imminent Boer *trek* to the North, backed by General Joubert. General Joubert himself wrote to Lobengula early in 1892, proposing a pact of friendship. [2]

Even more disquieting was Lobengula's practice of sending his *impis* into Mashonaland to punish anyone who had incurred his displeasure. Although he ordered them not to touch the white men, and they obeyed him, the same immunity was not always enjoyed by the white men's cattle, the Matabele probably arguing that since Mashonaland was the king's, by Matabele custom all the cattle in it were his too—a point of view unlikely to commend itself to the white farmers. The appearance of Lobengula's *impis* had a further disturbing effect on the Mashonas. They had been promised, or thought they had been promised, the protection of the white men; yet here were the Matabele back again at their old games, while the white men just stood by and wrote protests to Bulawayo. Clearly they acted in this way because they were weak and frightened, and not unnaturally the immediate reaction of the Mashonas, on the appearance of an *impi*, was to leave their work on farm or mine and fly to shelter at a distance; and equally naturally the farmers and miners objected.

The Mashonas were being troublesome in other ways. The first awe they had felt on the arrival of the pioneers was wearing off. These after all were people like themselves and no more of a match for the Matabele than they were. The white men, too, had some incomprehensible rules about property, whereas if a Mashona liked an object, he just took it. They had queer ideas about regular work, to which the Mashonas objected, holding that work was an evil to which a man submitted when he was hungry and left as soon as he was full. But the worst trouble was the Matabele raiders.

The settlers had also had disappointments—the paucity of gold, the excessive rains and the high prices. But more terrible than any of these were the savages, who suddenly appeared and speared their servants to death or frightened them away. Protests to Lobengula had little effect, and in fact were a fresh grievance to him. "I thought you came to dig for gold," he retorted, "but it seems you have come to rob me of my people as well." The Mashonas *were* his people; and when Jameson talked of troublesome natives as "rebels", the Colonial Office corrected him. Lobengula was not going to abandon his rights, and the one effective way he had of asserting them was to order out occasional *impis* to harry the Mashonas.

Incidents began to occur. Lobengula sent in a party of warriors to punish a chief, who had unwisely assumed that the coming of the white men had relieved him of his obligation to give tribute to Bulawayo and paid for his contumacy with his life. In January 1892 a French prospector was murdered by a local chief, and when the police arrived, they were fired on. In April a farmer was assaulted and robbed, and in the fighting that ensued, a chief and twenty-one men were killed. The Colonial Office was distressed and Labouchere thundered, but the firm action taken undoubtedly impressed the Mashonas.

Next year the trouble came to a head. Copper wire presented an irresistible temptation to the natives in the neighbourhood of Rhodes's telegraph line. In May 1893 about 800 yards of wire between Tuli and Victoria were cut and taken away. Investigation implicated a petty chief named Gomalla; and when the police arrived to collect a fine, with suspicious alacrity he handed over some cattle. In fact they were not his cattle: they belonged to Lobengula, who had sent them to Gomalla for herding. Any tampering with the royal cattle was a crime akin to treason, and Lobengula, when he discovered what had happened, sent Jameson an angry expostulation. Jameson at once returned the cattle with an explanation, but Lobengula, regarding Gomalla's offence as serious, determined to make an example for cattle-stealers.

He got Colenbrander, who was still at Bulawayo, to send a message to Jameson that an *impi* was on its way to Mashonaland to punish the offenders, but had strict orders not to molest the Europeans. Actually the message only arrived with the *impi*, on a July morning when the settlers round Victoria woke up to find the country swarming with Matabele, wearing their war-plumes, and burning, butchering and hunting down the Mashonas like animals. The raiders, in their excitement, even forgot the king's orders. They entered the settlers' farms, slaughtered their servants and carried off their cattle.

The magistrate at Victoria was Captain C. F. Lendy, who had already written to Lobengula warning him of the trouble his *impis* might cause. He now telegraphed the news of this latest incursion to Jameson, who, although not as yet seriously worried, decided to go to Victoria himself without delay. Meanwhile he told Lendy to demand the return of the cattle stolen from the settlers and to order the raiders back over the border. If it was necessary to expel them, tact and as little force as possible should be used. "The Victoria people," he telegraphed to Rutherfoord Harris, "have naturally got the jumps." His was hardly the language of a man who was determined to force a war.

In a few hours the situation had become serious. All the Mashonas in the neighbourhood who had escaped the Matabele *assegais* had either fled to their *kraals* or taken refuge in the fort at Victoria, where the able-bodied inhabitants were enrolling as volunteers, mounting machine-guns on the walls and throwing out pickets. On 14 July Manyao, an elderly *induna*, arrived in Victoria with Lobengula's letter and a brusque demand for the Mashona fugitives sheltering in the fort to be handed over to him. He offered one insolent concession: he would not kill them near the river, where they might pollute the water, but would despatch them in the bush. Lendy of course refused to comply, but said that if Manyao cared to bring a charge against the Mashonas, he would try it as a magistrate. Nothing could have shown more clearly than this exchange the unbridgeable gulf between the European and the Matabele points of view.

Three days later Jameson, arriving, quickly decided that the business was more serious than he had supposed, for the roads round Victoria were strewn with the corpses of slaughtered Mashonas. He had already replied to Lobengula's letter with a polite, but firm, insistence that the *impis* should withdraw. Neither he nor Lobengula wanted a war, but the tempers of the settlers were rising. They had had to put up with a lot during the past few days, had had to look on helplessly while their servants were slain and their cattle stolen; and they were anxious to deal with the Matabele "now and for ever", as they put it. Jameson, after talking with them, cabled to Harris that he intended to treat the marauding *indunas* "like dogs". He was still sure that Lobengula did not mean to fight and would even "be pleased at some of his young bloods being thrashed".

On 18 July Jameson had a meeting with Manyao, who was attended by between two and three hundred armed men, including a young, truculent *induna*, Umgandan, whom Sauer, also present, described as "the handsomest African native I have ever seen". Jameson wanted the Matabele to go and the Matabele did not want to leave until the Mashonas sheltering in the fort had been handed over. Jameson spoke sternly. Manyao followed, and then Umgandan, making a strong case for the king. Jameson replied that he had heard what they had to say and that if any Matabele were on the Victoria side of the Tokwe River at

sundown, they would be fired on. When Umgandan broke in with
an insolent remark, Jameson asked Manyao if it was true that he
had no control over the younger men. Manyao having replied that
it was, the Doctor told him to take the older men off to the other
side of the river and that he himself would deal with the younger
men. "Now go," he ended up, "or I will drive you across."
Manyao went, but Umgandan merely replied, "Very well, we will
be driven across."

Jameson told Lendy to send out a strong patrol in two hours'
time. If the Matabele resisted, the patrol was to attack them. He
was taking a fearful risk in pitting thirty-eight men, all he could
mount at the moment, against a force of more than 3,000, but
being Jameson he took it. The patrol found that, instead of going,
the Matabele were rounding up more of the Company's cattle and
attacking a *kraal*. They were so employed when the patrol arrived
and opened fire. The mounted tactics and good marksmanship of
the white men were too much for the warriors, and they fled
headlong to the Tokwe River, having lost fifty or sixty men. One
of the first victims was Umgandan himself, but most of the others
were *maholis* or slaves.

The Matabele were unlikely to accept the humiliation of a defeat by so small a force, and that evening Jameson saw Sauer and
asked him to find out from some of the Boers in Victoria how
many men would be needed to fight the Matabele. Presently
Sauer returned to report a unanimous opinion that "a mounted
force of from 800 to 1,000 men would suffice".

Jameson spent the rest of the evening at the telegraph office.
When he cabled the news to Rhodes, the only reply he got was:
"Read Luke xiv 31". Jameson read: "Or what king, going to
make war against another king, sitteth not down first, and con-
sulteth whether he be able with 10,000 to meet him that cometh
against him with 20,000?" Jameson telegraphed back that he had
read the passage in St. Luke and that it was all right.

But Rhodes was far from feeling all right. The Company's
Treasury was empty and he himself had spent all his ready money
on the telegraph. He did not know where to turn for the cash he
would require to carry on a war. To his objections Jameson
would only reply, "You have got to get the money." Rhodes got
it by selling 40,000 of his own holding of Chartered shares at the
low market price prevailing, most of the proceeds going to the
purchase of horses.

The High Commissioner was a more awkward proposition.

Whatever Loch's private opinion might be, his duty was to pass on the instructions of his masters at Whitehall; and Lord Ripon, now the Colonial Secretary, had no affection for the Chartered Company. Apart from his sensitiveness to the attacks of Labouchere and his friends on the back benches, he suffered more acutely than most Liberals from the nightmare of an expensive colonial war. Jameson had sent to Bulawayo a claim for compensation, and Loch told him the claim must be dropped. At the same time Loch wrote sternly to Lobengula, bidding him punish his unruly warriors and respect the property of the white men; and while he warned Rhodes and Jameson that there must be no offensive action against the Matabele, he admitted that the Company should be ready to meet an attack, and even sanctioned an increase in the numbers of Bechuanaland Police at Macloutsie.

Actually Lobengula began by taking the news of the rebuff to his army very well. Jameson had sent him a message of explanation, in which he emphasised the heinousness of cattle-stealing. With this opinion Lobengula heartily concurred. He hoped the stolen cattle had been recovered and even admitted the possibility that he had been unwise to allow an *impi* to go so close to Victoria. Presently, however, Manyao and his *indunas* arrived at Bulawayo with their tale of discomfiture. Many Matabele had been shot and others had been hustled over the River Tokwe. Never had an army, reputed invincible, suffered so dire a humiliation, and the returned warriors, who had fought so feebly, had to face the jeers and taunts of their comrades who had stayed at home.

In his indignation Lobengula now sent a defiant answer to Loch's warning but friendly message. No compensation would be paid for the missing cattle and the settlers must at once hand over the Mashonas they were sheltering. The king's only regret was that his men had not captured more beasts. To underline his displeasure, he refused to accept the monthly payment due under the Rudd Concession and recalled a force of 6,000 men he had sent on a raid into Barotseland. So high was feeling running at Bulawayo that Colenbrander, his high-spirited wife and most of the Europeans there deemed it prudent to leave for the comparative safety of Tati.

Lobengula, fiercely as he might speak, still did not want war. Nor as yet did Rhodes and Jameson. But events and people were too much for them. Lobengula had his furious *impis* to control. Rhodes and Jameson had their settlers, who were smarting under their losses, confident after Lendy's easy victory, and anxious now

I

to have a reckoning with Lobengula. Most of them had come round to the view that the moment of decision had arrived. Either they must break the Matabele or they must give up the idea of a white settlement in Central Africa.

If they were to tackle the Matabele, they had little time to lose. In a few weeks the rains would start and practically immobilise mounted troops. The settlers would be cut off from the south, and the Matabele, in their own good time, could sweep down on the settlements and destroy them piecemeal. The wilder men began to say that if Rhodes, Jameson and the Home Government would not give them the word, they would take the matter into their own hands and march. They had the men and the arms and no lack of trained officers.

At any rate all were agreed that preparations should be made. Lendy started enlisting men for what became known as the Victoria Column, while Jameson hurried back to Salisbury to recruit a second column there. Since pay was beyond the resources of the Chartered Company, every volunteer was to be rewarded, when the war was over, with a farm of 6,000 acres, 20 gold claims, and a share of any loot that might be won. Afterwards this agreement, loosely and hurriedly drawn up, came in for sharp criticism; but given the imminence of a Matabele attack, Jameson had to have the men and could offer them no other reward. The command in the field was given to Major Patrick Forbes, the officer who had behaved with such coolness and daring at Umtasa's *kraal*. After placing the column at Fort Victoria under the command of Captain Allan Wilson, a promising young officer who had served in the Cape Mounted Rifles and the Basuto Mounted Police, Jameson hurried down to Tuli, where he arranged for more volunteers to be enrolled and led by Captain (or Commandant) Pieter Raaf, a Dutch Colonial who had served with distinction in the Zulu War and, being magistrate at Tuli, promptly offered his services. This third column was joined by the Bechuanaland Police under Goold-Adams, sent to Tuli by the High Commissioner with orders to act only in defence, and by a force of fighting Bechuanas lent by Khama.

Lobengula meanwhile was not being idle. He too was mobilising his army, his wizards were "doctoring" the roads into Mashonaland and Bechuanaland, and his pickets were out keeping an eye on the enemy. Still dreading a war with the whites, he decided to try the effect of an appeal to the Queen. This he entrusted to Moshete, one of the *indunas* who had been to England with Maund. The High Commissioner too, mindful of Lord Ripon's instructions, was doing his best to avoid hostilities and, in view of the approaching rains, was advising the Company to disband its troops and try to reach a peaceful settlement. But both sides had gone too far, and at the end of September fighting broke out, when a patrol from Victoria was fired on by about fifty Matabele on the Mashonaland side of the border. A few days later Goold-Adams's Police were also fired on. These incidents at last made up the High Commissioner's mind. He told Goold-Adams to occupy Tati and authorised Jameson to drive the Matabele a safe distance from Victoria.

A few days before, in a last bid for peace, he had written to the king inviting him to call in his *impis* and to send a party of *indunas* to Cape Town to "talk matters over so that there may be peace". By then most of the white people had left Bulawayo, but a trader, James Dawson, after reading the letter, agreed to accompany the king's half-brother and two *indunas* to Tati, on the first stage of their journey to the south.

It was an ill-fated mission. The party reached Tati, where Goold-Adams had arrived with a strong detachment of the Bechuanaland Police. Dawson, instead of at once reporting the purpose of the journey, went off to have a drink and then dinner, leaving the three Matabele in the care of a mine foreman. Goold-Adams, hearing of Dawson's arrival, assumed that he had escaped from Bulawayo and that the Matabele were his escort. Since skirmishing had already started and shots had been exchanged, he treated them as prisoners of war and had them arrested. The *indunas* took fright, resisted violently, and were killed by the troopers. The king's half-brother, who had stood quietly by, was not harmed, and presently, when Dawson had explained the misunderstanding, was allowed to return to Bulawayo with his woeful tale.

Lobengula was furious at what he regarded as an act of treachery. He had sent his *indunas* on an errand of peace and they had been slain. "The white men are fathers of liars," he exclaimed. He ordered his army to assemble and came out of the royal enclosure, daubed with paint in the old Zulu way and carrying an *assegai*. This, in the sight of the army, he drove into the earth before him. It was the traditional declaration of war; and in the excitement, few noticed that the shaft of the *assegai* snapped. That night the *impis* went out to meet the enemy.

* * *

Rhodes, who had been busy buying horses and sending them up-country to Jameson, was also in the middle of the tiresome crisis over Sivewright's misdemeanours and the reconstruction of his Cabinet. As soon as he could get away from Cape Town, he hurried to Beira, to enter Rhodesia by the route he had followed before. With him were Metcalfe, Le Sueur and the faithful Tony; and on the road between Beira and Maçequeçe, he met Sauer, whom Jameson had sent up to escort him to Salisbury.

By this time Rhodes had no illusions about the possibility of peace and, in view of the warlike mood of his "young men", was reconciled to the need of having a final settlement with Lobengula. His first thought had been to send Jameson all the help he could, and his second to keep the "Imperial factor" out of the business. He wanted no assistance from that quarter, if assistance meant the interference of Westminster and Whitehall in the settlement that would follow the war; and at the same time he could not conceal his impatience with Sir Henry Loch who, except for sending the Bechuanaland Police to Tati, was not going to help him, or be asked to help him, but at the same time was trying to prevent the Chartered Company taking action on its own account.

Sauer has told how Rhodes, having arrived at Umtali with every sign of haste, pushed on till he was half way between Marandellas and Salisbury. The haste then vanished and the party camped for some days three or four miles off the road on pleasant, well-wooded ground, where they had good sport shooting partridges. Sauer was puzzled by Rhodes's high spirits and sudden change of mood, but one morning a policeman rode in with letters from Salisbury. Having read them, Rhodes ordered camp to be struck at once, and in a very short time the party was hurrying on again. The letters brought the news for which Rhodes had been waiting—that the Victoria and Salisbury Columns had joined and started for Matabeleland. It was now too late to stop them, but for days Rhodes had been expecting a cable from the Colonial Office forbidding the invasion. He had therefore hidden himself in the bush, where no cable could reach him.

The war was short and sharp. Forbes had under his command rather under 700 men, with five Maxims, three other machine-guns, and two 7-pounder field guns. At Tati Goold-Adams and Raaf had 220 policemen, 200 volunteers, and 1,000 of Khama's men, with two field guns and four Maxims. The size of Loben-gula's army is uncertain, but with the return of his *impis* from

Barotseland, he cannot have had fewer than 12,000 warriors and may have had as many as 18,000. He had the rifles delivered by the Chartered Company, but would probably have been wiser to have left them in their wrappings. His men were untrained in their use and, as Rhodes had foreseen, believed that the higher the sights were raised, the straighter the bullets would fly, so that most of the fire went well over the target. The Matabele would have been more formidable if they had fought like their fathers with *assegais*, making full use of cover and attacking by night or at dawn. However, Lobengula himself was no soldier, and his warriors were too confident that they could eat up the white men at a meal to bother overmuch about tactics.

Jameson had planned a converging movement on Bulawayo, carried out with the utmost possible speed, the Victoria and Salisbury columns coming in from the east and the Tuli column from the south. The former met with no serious resistance until they reached the Shangani River, although they had an anxious passage through the Somabula forest, where the dense bush and a thick fog would have made an attack very dangerous to them. Actually the Matabele had laid an ambush, but missed their quarry in the fog. After crossing the Shangani on 24 October, the columns formed *laager* on the far side; and there at dawn the next morning the Matabele attacked. They surprised the native camp and slaughtered many of the wretched camp-followers; but on turning to the *laager*, were checked by the fire of Maxims and rifles. As visibility improved, they drew back; but at 5.30 a.m. renewed their attacks. Twice they came on with fury and desperate courage, only to be repelled by the fire of the white men; and with daylight the 7-pounder guns completed their discomfiture. By 9.30 the battle was over. The Matabele removed most of their dead and wounded, but it was reckoned that they had had between five and six hundred casualties out of a force of about 5,000 men. Such was the discouragement that the commander of one of their regiments committed suicide by hanging himself from a tree. The Company's forces had two dead and six wounded, though a number of friendly natives, with their wives and children, had been speared in the opening attack.

For seven days the columns pushed on, meeting with very little opposition, till they reached some high ground near the source of the Imbembesi River. In the early afternoon of 1 November they were watering their horses, when some 7,000 Matabele began to advance on them through the bush. A disaster was narrowly

avoided, as the horses stampeded, and dismounted the column
would have been almost helpless. The Matabele tried hard to cut
the horses off, but some of the Company's men, under heavy
fire, headed them and brought them back to the *laager*. The
Matabele continued to attack fiercely, at one point getting to
within 150 yards of the wagons; but as at the Shangani the steady
fire of Maxims and rifles drove them back and the 7-pounders
turned a defeat into a rout.

The Imbembesi battle was decisive. About 7,000 Matabele, the
flower of Lobengula's army, were engaged; and only the wreck
of an army drifted back to Bulawayo, about twenty miles distant.
As later the Company's columns approached it, they heard a
rumble, like a roll of thunder, and saw a dense cloud of smoke
rising. Lobengula had set fire to his *kraal*, blown up his store of
cartridges and abandoned his capital.

On 4 November the Mashonaland columns, headed by a pipe-
major of the Royal Scots, marched in and hoisted the Company's
flag in the middle of the ruins, among which, to their surprise,
they found two white traders sitting on a roof, Lobengula having
personally intervened to save their lives. The third column, under
Goold-Adams and Raaf, arrived in Bulawayo some days later.
It had had very little serious fighting, but had been delayed by the
desertion of Khama and his men.

The war being almost over, peace had to be made. Just before
the battle of the Shangani, the High Commissioner had passed on
to Rhodes the gist of a cable he had had from Ripon. "The
Secretary of State has directed," Loch reported, "that all negotiations with Lobengula are to be conducted by me as High Commissioner and under my complete control." Rhodes was furious.
Ripon may have been justified under the terms of the Charter, but
the Company, which had fought and won the war with very little
help from Whitehall, surely should have some say in the peace.
But feeling at home was high, and all Rhodes's old enemies were
after him. *Truth* joined in the hunt with ever-increasing scurrility
and incoherence:

> "Mr. Rhodes . . . the head of a gang of shady financiers
> who forced on a war with the man through whose kindness
> they have pocketed millions, conducted it on the principle
> that 'godless heathen' ought to be mowed down with maxim
> guns if they happen to inhabit a country where there may be
> gold, and their envoys murdered in order that a rotten Com-

pany might be saved from immediate bankruptcy, and the financing gang might be in a position to transfer more money from the pockets of British investors into their own."³

On 9 November Labouchere moved the adjournment of the House of Commons in an abusive speech, to which Rochfort Maguire, now a Member of Parliament, made an effective reply; but the Government, while refusing to associate itself with Labby's wilder accusations, would not withdraw its instructions to Loch, and an awkward quarrel with the Chartered Company was in the making.

That a clash was avoided was due not to Gladstone, Ripon and Loch, or to Rhodes, but to Lobengula. While the great ones were arguing about who was to make peace, the man with whom it would have to be made had disappeared into the bush, with his wives, his baggage and the remnant of his army. It looked as though the winner of the war between Rhodes and Whitehall would be the party who got possession of the king's person. Where he had gone, or was going, no one was certain, but the rains were now imminent, and unless he could be found before they broke, he might vanish in the north and the war drag on for months.

Jameson began by sending him a letter, in which he urged the king to come at once to Bulawayo, promising him safety and friendly treatment. If he refused, he would be pursued. Lobengula had with him a rascally, semi-literate half-caste named John Jacobs, who read Jameson's letter and wrote a reply at the king's dictation, or so he afterwards stated. Lobengula said he would come, but asked what had happened to the *indunas* he had sent on a peace mission. He was also worried to know where he could live in Bulawayo, his houses having been burnt down; and he ended up with a request to "please be so kind and send me ink and pens and paper".

The poor man was at his wits' end. He could trust no one, least of all the white men, who had taken his country, destroyed his army and killed his messengers. Jacobs was an unreliable witness, who abandoned the king soon afterwards; but by his account the letter to Jameson had hardly gone when Lobengula inspanned his oxen and started to *trek* in the opposite direction to Bulawayo. No white man ever saw him again.

Jameson, after waiting for some days for Lobengula to arrive, decided that the king would have to be followed and brought in.

All organised fighting had ceased, but a large body of Matabele was known to be at Inyati and believed to be covering the king's retreat. After a call had been made for volunteers from all the three columns, Major Forbes left Bulawayo with a mixed force and three days' rations. They reached Inyati, which had been a station of the London Missionary Society, and found it wrecked and looted. The king had gone on, and Forbes, after receiving reinforcements and supplies from Bulawayo, took up the spoor again. The rains had now started and every track was becoming waterlogged; so after a while Forbes divided his force. He went on himself with a flying column of 160 picked men, and sent the rest back with the wagons to Inyati to await his return.

Just ahead of Forbes, making for the Shangani, was Lobengula with his worn-out oxen. Sick and discouraged, he resolved to make one more attempt to appease the white men. They had come and taken his country for gold, and he still had the bags of sovereigns which Rhodes had described him as receiving every month with such satisfaction. Perhaps, he naïvely argued, if he gave the white men this gold, they would stop pursuing him. He put the sovereigns—perhaps a thousand of them—into a bag and gave it to an *induna* with the oral message: "White men, I am conquered. Take this and go back."

The *induna* passed on the bag and the message to two men, who went back to find the column. Perhaps through fear, the messengers went round it and came in from the rear. They saw two troopers—batmen with pack-horses—handed over the bag of gold, repeated Lobengula's message, and were thankful to slip back into the bush. As for the troopers, nobody having seen the encounter, they decided to divide the sovereigns and forget the message. Lobengula's ill luck with his mail persisted to the end. Forbes never knew that the king had made this overture and continued his pursuit. Afterwards the story leaked out, the two troopers were brought to trial, and were given heavy sentences; though two years later these were quashed on the ground that the evidence was insufficient, and that anyhow the magistrate had exceeded his jurisdiction.

The message, if delivered, might not have saved Lobengula, who was probably a dying man; but it might have saved Allan Wilson and his famous patrol. Forbes, uncertain whether Lobengula had crossed the Shangani, asked Wilson to pick out a few men, with the freshest horses, to ride ahead and to try to discover where the king had gone, but to return before nightfall. Wilson started off with twenty-one men, many of whom were officers, and at nine and eleven that night, two parties of two and three men respectively returned. Wilson, they reported, had reached Lobengula's camp, but as he was in danger of being cut off by the Matabele guarding the king, had taken up a position in the bush, where he would wait until the main body joined him.

Forbes was now in a dilemma. Wilson had disregarded his order to return. In the heavy rain, the Shangani was rising fast; and if he took his whole force across, they might be unable to come back. He could, and no doubt should, have again ordered Wilson back to the *laager*, but he seems to have doubted that Wilson would have come; and there was also the possibility that if he did obey he would lose an opportunity, which might not recur, of catching the king. The course Forbes actually took was barely defensible: he sent a further twenty-one men across the Shangani to reinforce Wilson, who would then have more men than he would need for a patrol, but not enough to fight an action. Knowing Wilson, Forbes must have guessed that the reinforcement would tempt him to try to brush aside the opposition and capture the king.

The twenty men went off at midnight, and soon Forbes heard heavy firing on the further bank of the river, which was still rising. He moved the main column forward, but in the morning was himself attacked by a large force of Matabele; and by the time he had extricated his men, the river was hardly fordable. Having lost several men and horses, he returned to the *laager* of the previous night, where he could only await events.

He got one last piece of news from Wilson. It was brought by three scouts, who had swum the river with great difficulty. Before daybreak that morning, they reported, the patrol, reinforced by twenty men, had made a bold attempt to rush the royal wagons, but had come under such heavy fire that they had had to fall back. Wilson had then sent off the three scouts. When they left, the patrol was retreating, hard-pressed, into the bush and the rest of the story was pieced together afterwards from the accounts of the Matabele and by the discovery, two months later, of the bleached bones of a number of white men and several horses. The patrol had evidently put up a desperate resistance in a small clearing, until they had fired away all their ammunition. They had risen, sung, it was believed, a verse of God Save the Queen, shaken hands and been shot or speared to death.

Forbes of course as yet knew nothing of their fate. His own predicament was bad enough, as he had several wounded men and his provisions were nearly exhausted. He could not cross the river, which was now a raging torrent; and with Matabele swarming round his diminished force, he would be hard put to it to reach the stores and the rest of the column at Inyati, eighty or ninety miles away. He decided to make the attempt and for some days struggled on, with his men starving and in rags, his horses worn out, and the Matabele hanging persistently on to his flanks. More than once they nearly caught him in the bush, and finally he escaped only through a ruse of Raaf's. When at last the column reached open country, it was able to defend itself more effectively, and eventually was met by a relief force under Major Heany, who was accompanied by Rhodes and Jameson. By then Forbes's men, in the words of one who saw them arrive, were in "a terrible plight", but the worst of their trials were over and three days later they reached Bulawayo.

The sacrifice of Wilson and his men was needless, for Lobengula was dead. After calling back his men from the pursuit of Forbes, he, his three sons and some loyal followers resumed their retreat towards the Zambesi. To reach it they had to cross a *tsetse* belt, fatal to their horses and oxen. It has been recorded that Lobengula, knowing the end had come, called his surviving *indunas* to him and bade them to look in future to Rhodes for protection. "He will be your chief and friend," the king told them. Then he died—by one account of smallpox, by another of poison, and by a third of a broken heart. His people wrapped his body in the hides of two newly flayed oxen and buried it in a cave.

Cruel, savage and stained with the guilt of thousands of murders though he was, he had redeeming qualities. He had kept faith, to the best of his ability, with Jameson, and had held back his *impis* from attacking the pioneers. To the end he had protected the white men in his *kraal*. He had never wanted war and had tried without avail to make peace. The Matabele Empire was as out of date as a prehistoric monster and had to disappear before peace or any sort of civilising influence could come to Central Africa. Yet the manner of its passing leaves an evil taste in the mouth. The Rudd Concession was obtained nearly by false pretences, and the men who warned Lobengula that he had sold his country were right. If he had realised that Rhodes's purpose was not only or chiefly to dig for gold, but to found a settlement, he would have refused to set his seal to the concession. Once he had done so, the rest followed inexorably. He had taken the first step from his royalty to a miserable death.

In his dealings with the white men Lobengula never really understood what he was doing. Rhodes, who knew very well what he was doing, cannot be altogether exonerated. He justified it by his old argument that the savage must give way to civilisation. The Matabele, he said were "the last ruthless power of barbarism that existed in South Africa. I knew . . . that that power must pass away; but I also felt that it was a question of subsequent years." He had faced "an appalling situation". He had tried to postpone the war and had only accepted it as inevitable when he realised that his settlers, if restrained from fighting, would abandon the country. "You found," he told the conquerors of Matabeleland in Bulawayo, "you had no choice other than to fight or to leave the country of your adoption."[4]

Nevertheless Rhodes was touched by the fate of the "naked old savage", as he called him, and perhaps as a measure of amends took charge of three of his sons, and of their sons. He did not want them to stay in Rhodesia, where they might have become a rallying-point of rebellion, but took them to Groote Schuur, where he treated them with kindness and had them educated, one of the grandsons being given the name of Rhodes. Yet with that insensitiveness which was also typical of him, he would sometimes refer callously in their presence to the circumstances of Lobengula's death.

*   *   *

The fighting having ended, deputations began to arrive in Bulawayo to make peace. Jameson told them that men who handed over their weapons would be allowed to return to their *kraals*. Some complied, but the great majority, uncertain of the fate of their king, buried their weapons. The outcries in Parliament were undiminished and the Colonial Secretary cabled to the High Commissioner that considerable uneasiness was being caused by reports that townships were being marked out, that the Matabele cattle were being seized, and that the men were being prevented from sowing until they had given up their weapons. Loch therefore, although recognising the desirability of disarmament, insisted that it should be "construed in a very liberal spirit".

Rhodes, meanwhile, who had returned to Cape Town, was fighting for a free hand in the settlement of the country the Company had conquered. In his negotiations with the High

Commissioner he had two advantages. One was the Company's readiness to rule the country without help from Her Majesty's Treasury. The other advantage was the death of Lobengula and the absence of any obvious successor. Rhodes told Jameson to push on with the settlement of Matabeleland without waiting for Imperial approval. The men who had fought must have the farms and the mining claims they had been promised. "It is your right," he told them, "for you have conquered the country." Two large reserves of land were set apart for the natives. The king's vast herd of cattle, most of which were farmed out, presented a more difficult problem. A certain number of head were handed over to *indunas* as their private property, while the balance —about 70,000—were vested in the Company, but left in the charge of the natives who had been looking after them, to form a pool from which distribution could later be made to the tribes. A new township was laid down in Bulawayo and, as soon as the rains ended, prospectors and farmers, engineers and traders began to come in. Administratively the country was joined to Mashonaland, where the machinery of government was already working.

All this was done only in the teeth of official opposition at the Cape, and also of the Aborigines Protection Society in London, which is vividly reflected in Rhodes's correspondence. Never was his distrust of the "Imperial factor" more marked. During October and November 1893 he bombarded Rutherfoord Harris, the Company's secretary, with instructions to prevent the intrusion of Imperial officials or police. For the same purpose, he ordered Jameson not to leave Bulawayo. He also sought the support of his political allies at the Cape: Schreiner, for instance, whom he assured in a letter of 26 October that Rhodesia contained gold and was a white man's country; and the dependable Sprigg. His appeal to Sprigg is not extant, but Sprigg's reply (undated) shows how things were going: [5]

"... I have had great difficulties with the High Commissioner. He takes up the ground that we have no right to give him advice upon matters outside the Colony. This is of course untenable—you will remember the long fight that we had in eighty-four with Sir H. Robinson upon this very question. I feel quite at home in the business. We requested that our minute recommending a free hand to the Company should be sent by cable to the Secretary of State. This was not done at once but yesterday afternoon on a pressing request the H.C. sent it through. I intend putting some other machinery in operation in England to effect our object. I hope you will fully understand that I consider the interests of the Company and of the Colony identical in regard to the settlement to be made so there is no occasion for you to hurry down here . . ."

To Rutherfoord Harris, early in November, Rhodes wrote in forthright terms, characteristic both in their bluntness and their torrential incoherence.[6] The letter is interesting because it also contains Rhodes's first appreciation of the campaign itself:

"As to your telegram of yesterday afternoon, stating that you had received reply from Governor in answer to yours saying we did not want Imperial Police to remain at Bulawayo as we should have our own, and Governor saying he wishes to maintain his line of communication and that he proposes to have Goold-Adams for that purpose, you should certainly now let correspondence drop as we have made our position quite clear. I shall probably get the use of the Imperial Police during the rains without pay, and we have the Governor's clear assurance about administration. If His Excellency sticks to his statements to you our difficulty will be the English people who thinking that Matabeleland is a fat thing and knowing that the Bechuanaland is of small value would like to rob us of Matabeleland and add it to the Protectorate. They dislike Charters and will not recognise their being English, we must watch them closely for we know the predatory instincts of our race, their present position is entirely due to plunder and when not plundering a foreigner sooner than do nothing they plunder each other. I agree with His Excellency that I had better wait here a few days awaiting developments and then come at once and see him. I send you by telegram Forbes' official report on the battle of Shangani —the crux is they only fired 4,000 shots, the shooting must have been excellent—Willoughby's report concurs. I think you should publish the report, it would please the sentiment of Glory, you will notice one in eight shots found its billet, the average in European warfare being I think about one in nine thousand—I had a long talk with Hurrell who took my despatch to Jameson and who is back here. He left them on 28th about 30 miles from Bulawayo. He says all the men are in most excellent spirits and they have a fight nearly every day, they have plenty of food, both cattle and sheep—my only source of alarm is that horses may knock up, it is the one thing that prevents men from patrolling enough."

Eventually, perhaps partly because Rhodes had the advantage of possession and partly because Loch was increasingly preoccupied in 1894 by troubles with Kruger and the Boers, Rhodes gained the greater part of what he wanted in Rhodesia. Her Majesty's Government finally approved the substance of his settlement, and on 18 July 1894 an Order in Council gave effect to it. As Rhodes put it in a speech in Cape Town on the northern situation in January of that year:[7]

"I thought it would be a good thing to have an idea in connexion with one's politics, and try steadily to carry it out. . . . If you have an idea, and it is a good idea, if you will only stick to it, you will come out all right."

The compliance of the Government at Westminster was undoubtedly accelerated by a change in public opinion in Britain. Labouchere had overstated his case against Rhodes and the Company's men, whom he had accused groundlessly of atrocities, and when Selous and others of those who had fought in the war came home and told their stories, sentiment swung round in favour of Rhodes. People began to feel that the conquest of a great territory by a handful of men, most of whom were not professional soldiers, was a feat of which they should be proud and not ashamed. Men who knew something of recent South African history contrasted the long and expensive campaign against the Zulus with the defeat of the Matabele, which besides being so much quicker, had not cost the British taxpayer a penny; and all were thrilled by the story of the last fight and gallant end of Wilson and his men.

Rhodes too had been deeply moved by the one disaster which had marred his victory. At first he was inclined to blame Forbes for it and, when he met the column returning from the Shangani, it was noticed that he would not speak to its commander. Later he may have realised that he had been a little harsh in his judgment and that Forbes, if guilty of an error of judgment, had been so placed that almost any action he had taken might have been proved wrong. By Rhodes's order the remains of the whole party were removed to consecrated ground near the Zimbabwe ruins, and later re-interred at the spot in the Matopo Hills where his own grave was to be. There they lie under Tweed's granite monument, having passed into the history of the land they had fought to win.

Sources

Cloete, Stuart: *African Portraits*
Colvin, Ian: *The Life of Jameson*
Crale, W. D.: *One Man's Vision*
Harris, Sir David: *Pioneer, Soldier and Politician*
Hole, H. M.: *The Making of Rhodesia*
Mason, Philip: *The Birth of a Dilemma*
Sauer, Hans: *Ex Africa . . .*

Notes

[1] "Vindex", 303.
[2] Rhodes Papers, C. 2. 2. (Innes); C. 3. 122 (Colenbrander *via* Harris); C. 3. 185 (Moffat); C. 3. 163 (Lady Brand); C. 2. 20 (Du Toit).
[3] *Truth*, 30 Nov. 1893.
[4] "Vindex", 333.
[5] Rhodes Papers, B. 41 (to Harris); B. 43 (to Harris); B. 49 (to Jameson); B. 37 (to Schreiner); B. 58 (Sprigg to Rhodes).
[6] Rhodes Papers, B. 48 (to Harris).
[7] "Vindex", 332.

CHAPTER SIXTEEN

AT THE SUMMIT

IN 1894 and 1895 Rhodes stood at the summit of achievement. So far his success had been almost unbroken. He had amalgamated the diamond mines. He had won a second fortune from the gold of the Rand. He had saved the road to the North and obtained his concession from Lobengula. With the diamonds of Kimberley and the gold of the Rand behind him, he had founded the Chartered Company. He had sent his first settlers into the North. He had secured a great province for the Empire. He had won his war against the Matabele. Against such a background of success, his failures and frustrations seemed minor or only temporary setbacks. He had not gained from the Portuguese an outlet on the east coast. The Germans and Belgians between them had blocked any farther northward advance. His Cape-to-Cairo railway and telegraph had advanced marvellously, but had still a long way to go. He had failed to federate South Africa.

In 1894 his personal position at the Cape seemed supreme, almost impregnable. He was Prime Minister, with an unparalleled record of accomplishment, and faced an Opposition which had dwindled to eighteen out of a House of seventy-six. He had settled the prickly franchise question, forced the Scab Act upon a reluctant but hypnotised Bond, brought the railway to the borders of the Transvaal, annexed Pondoland, and in the Glen Grey Act had laid the foundations of a native policy. He had still to place the coping stone on the fabric he had built up so patiently. "I have a greater and bigger idea," he said at Queenstown in 1894, ". . . and that is the union of South Africa."

The most serious obstacle to his policy was of course the Transvaal, but it was not the only one. To isolate the Transvaal, in order to bring Kruger eventually to terms, it was necessary for Rhodes to control all the surrounding territory. To the north and the south of the Boer Republic he either had, or was well on the way to winning, all the control that he wanted. To the east and the west it was not so easy. Kruger craved an outlet to the sea, which he might obtain either at Kosi Bay, in the only part of the South African coastline that had not yet been annexed, or at Delagoa Bay, in Portuguese territory. The former was eventually closed to him by British annexation in 1895, but Delagoa Bay was always the more valuable target. Successive British governments had repeatedly tried to acquire Delagoa Bay from the Portuguese, for fear that both the port and the Transvaal might fall under foreign domination, particularly that of the Germans. Rhodes began to take a hand in the operation in the early 1890's.

A letter to him from Merriman, his ministerial colleague, on a visit to London in February 1892, reported that he had enlisted the support of Balfour, Goschen, Lord Knutsford and Lord Rothschild for the project of buying Delagoa Bay from the Portuguese. But unfortunately the Portuguese were indifferent to the proposition, partly, according to Merriman, because Lord Randolph Churchill had told their Ambassador in Paris that the Chartered Company was about to go bankrupt. Merriman counselled secrecy and patience, and nothing more is heard of the project until a year later. Then in February 1893 Maguire telegraphed from London to ask for Rhodes's authority to offer £700,000 to the Portuguese, and Rhodes immediately agreed.

The offer was prompted by the activities of a Bavarian nobleman, settled in Lisbon, by name Baron Carl de Merck, who had been introduced to Rhodes by the Colonial Office—perhaps even by Loch, the High Commissioner, himself. He was reputed to have great influence with the Portuguese government, but it became increasingly clear during 1893 that the Portuguese would decide nothing before the settlement of an arbitration case concerning an earlier concession for the Delagoa Bay railway. Since this settlement, known as the Berne Award, was not reached until 1900, it is not surprising that Rhodes was unable to make progress. He gradually became disillusioned with Baron Merck, and tried other courses. He tried, for instance, to mobilise support from Rosebery, whose curt reply survives, dated 23 May 1895:

"Thanks for telegram but it would not be possible for this government to do anything of that sort."

What Rhodes's proposition was is not known, but it was evidently something "on the personal", as he would have called it. The whole attempt fizzled out, as did more than one other later attempt, and an unseemly wrangle developed between Rhodes and Merck about the terms of the latter's commission. In 1895 Merck threatened legal action, but he seems not to have proceeded beyond the issue of a writ.[1]

To the west of the Transvaal, the crucial area in which Rhodes was still far from attaining all that he wanted, was Bechuanaland, the key to the North. Bechuanaland was divided by the River Molopo into the Crown Colony to the south, where Rhodes had fought out his struggle with Mackenzie and Warren a decade earlier, and the Protectorate to the north, a much vaster area which was technically within the domain of the Charter. Rhodes considered that the Crown Colony should go naturally with the Cape Colony for geographical reasons; and eventually this settlement was achieved in the middle of 1895, when the annexation of the Colony by the Cape was proclaimed with the assent of the Imperial Government at Westminster. But he found it much harder to get his own way over the Protectorate, which he wished to annex formally to the Chartered territories on the same basis as Mashonaland and the rest. The opposition to his plan came from the local chiefs, particularly Chief Khama of the Bamangwato tribe, who had won the respect of the missionaries by his determined efforts to suppress the evil of drink. With the missionaries' support, the chiefs implored the Imperial Government to maintain the Protectorate.

Rhodes conducted a prolonged campaign while he was Prime Minister to overcome the scruples felt at Westminster over his claim to the Protectorate. There is no doubt that on paper his claim was well-founded. Early in 1895 he put together a dossier of papers on the subject, from which the following quotations are taken.[2] It traced the claim back to the first application for a Charter in 1889 and showed that it had always been the intention of the Chartered Company, acknowledged and accepted by the Imperial Government, to take over eventually the administration of the Protectorate. When the Charter was granted, Knutsford had written to Loch, the High Commissioner, that it did not "supersede or affect the protectorate of Her Majesty over the country north of British Bechuanaland (i.e. the Crown Colony) and south of the 22nd parallel of south latitude". This proviso was made necessary by the fact that the Protectorate lay geographically within the area of the Charter: otherwise Knutsford's words would have had no point. Rhodes always understood that eventually the protectorate would lapse in favour of the Company, and by 1892 the Imperial Government was beginning to feel the expense of the Protectorate so severely that the question of a take-over date was seriously considered.

Loch at any rate had no doubt that the solution lay along these lines. He wrote to the Duke of Abercorn, as Chairman of the

Chartered Company, on 19 August 1892, a long letter about the problems of the new territories. He stressed, for instance, the impossibility of demarcating a frontier between Lobengula and Khama, and the reckless habit of all the chiefs of giving away incompatible concessions. He then went on to summarise the present position in words which completely concede the principle of what Rhodes sought, leaving open only the question of timing:

". . . The country to which I am referring is within the area of your Company's Charter and I will tell you exactly how I regard the position. An enormous area was included in the Charter and if all had to be taken up and worked at once, the Company would have required a capital of nearer five millions than one, but the position, as I understand it, is this—the British South Africa Company was to establish themselves first in Mashonaland and develop the wealth of that country before embarking in further liabilities.

"The Imperial Government in the meanwhile administering the remainder of the country under the High Commissioner with as much economy as the necessities of the position permitted, so that the Company might have breathing time to gradually feel their way and fairly establish themselves in Lobengula's country, before undertaking further liabilities. The land and rights under the High Commissioner's administrative control being in the meanwhile conserved for the Company. The Imperial Government to acquire if possible, some revenue from the country in reduction of heavy expenditure. Years may however pass before the British South Africa Company are in a position to take over the administration of this great area either in part or altogether, but I think as the Company gradually acquire and work concessions in the Protectorate and expand their operations in Mashonaland they should contribute towards the cost of the High Commissioner's administration and thus reduce the burden on the English taxpayer. Of course political considerations would have to be considered as to the manner, the time and conditions on which the transfer of the Administration was carried out."

No doubt as a result of Loch's pressure, Ripon, the Liberal Colonial Secretary of the day, agreed in December 1892 to the construction of a railway through the Protectorate by a British Company, to be subsidised partly by the Imperial Government and partly by the Chartered Company. He promised, too, that British officials would encourage the Bechuana chiefs to grant concessions to the Chartered Company of "minerals, agricultural lands and town-sites, over areas not already made the subject of valid concessions to others", and would refuse to recognise any other concessions granted in the Protectorate subsequent to the date of the Charter, that is, 28 October 1889.

Ripon's instructions were far from conceding all that Rhodes wanted, even in principle, but he ever afterwards attached great importance to them. The matter was next reopened actively in 1894, when Loch approached Rhodes with a proposal for the annexation of the Protectorate to the Crown Colony of Bechuanaland, apparently without prejudice to its ultimate administration by the Chartered Company. In putting forward this extraordinary solution, in a letter to Rhodes on 17 July 1894, Loch wrote that he had "no knowledge what the views of Her Majesty's Government might be on the subject—probably strongly adverse to any proposal of the kind". Such were the proconsular methods of the 1890's in South Africa. The value of the letter to Rhodes, however, was that it clearly implied acceptance of his claim to the Protectorate for the Chartered Company and made the timing of it conditional only on "circumstances", particularly the financial ability of the Company to "secure the proper administration of a country almost double in extent that is at present under the administration of the Company in which as yet no minerals have been discovered, and within which native land rights, etc., will have to be protected".

Rhodes's reply to Loch, dated the same day, rejected the proposal and re-asserted the Company's claims in the most positive way:

"I have thought a good deal over your suggestion that the Bechuanaland Protectorate should be annexed to the Crown Colony of British Bechuanaland, and I feel it my duty to submit to you my views on the proposition.

"It will be extremely difficult, once it has been annexed, for it ever to become part of the Chartered Territories. When the Charter was granted, its sphere of operation was defined as commencing from the boundaries of the Crown Colony of British Bechuanaland, and the understanding was that, as soon as we showed ourselves able to undertake the responsibility of the Protectorate, it should become a portion of the

Chartered Territories. It was on account of this understanding that we undertook the extension of the railway from Kimberley to Vryburg and subsequently to Mafeking which is on the point of completion—and we are now arranging for the extension to Gaberones, with the ultimate object of reaching Palapye and all this has been undertaken by our Company on the understanding that the British Protectorate should ultimately become a portion of the Chartered Territories. Meantime the system of administration of the Chartered Territories has gradually changed, under your direction, from direct control by a Board to a Nominee Council, which, as the Territories develop, will ultimately change into government by the people. A glance at the map will show that the Territory North of Mafeking, including Mashonaland and Matabeleland, will naturally form one state, and my desire is that nothing should mar this conception.

"The original policy with this object in connection with the Charter has been confirmed by Lord Ripon's letter of the 22nd December 1892 and by your own letter to the Duke of Abercorn, and I feel sure that the satisfactory reports of the development of Matabeleland and Mashonaland warrant my belief that it will not be long before we shall be able to offer Her Majesty's Government to take the responsibility of the Protectorate, and thus relieve Her from her present heavy expenditure."

It should be noted that Ripon's letter of instructions to Loch (which was in fact dated 20 December 1892) does not bear so strong an interpretation as Rhodes puts upon it, though Loch's letter to the Duke of Abercorn certainly does.

This was one of the most important matters which he wanted to see settled during his visit to London at the end of 1894. It has been alleged, though there is no proof, that his desire to settle the future of the Protectorate was already linked in his mind with the need for a "jumping-off place" for possible action against the Transvaal—in other words, with the plot that precipitated the Jameson Raid. Rhodes always had many ideas in his mind at the same time, and they were often linked together. But it is certain in any case that he would have pressed for a settlement of the Protectorate at this time even without any ulterior motive, if only because it had been hanging fire for so long.

While he was in London in November 1894, he discussed the

matter with Ripon, and sent him a memorandum summarising their conversation. He declared that:

"When the Charter was granted . . . it was thoroughly understood that the Chartered Company would relieve Her Majesty's Government of the expense and responsibility of the Protectorate so soon as the Company had satisfied Her Majesty's Government that it was in a position to do so."

In support of this claim, he quoted a letter from Knutsford to the Duke of Abercorn dated 21 June 1892, stating that:

"Lord Knutsford approved this course up to a certain point, for he had not abandoned the hope which he was led to entertain when the Charter was applied for, that the British South Africa Company would itself undertake the development of the Bechuanaland Protectorate as mentioned by Lord Gifford in his letter of April 30th, 1889, when applying on behalf of the promoters of the British South Africa Company for a Charter."

Ripon replied to Rhodes's memorandum on 30 November, saying that:

"Speaking generally, I regard your letter as setting forth the situation correctly, and when the proper time arrives, Her Majesty's Government will be prepared to entertain favourably any reasonable proposals, such as those sketched in your letter, if put forward officially by the British South Africa Company."

He added that "on coming into office we adopted the policy of our predecessors towards your Company, and it is plain . . . that they contemplated the ultimate acquisition by the Company of administrative authority in the Protectorate". Rhodes thus had a clear admission that his claim was well-founded.

But he was still no nearer to getting the Protectorate. In the early part of 1895, after he had returned to Africa, Lord Grey continued the pressure on his behalf. In February he was able to report that Ripon approved Rhodes's proposals, but Loch was strongly against them. Consequently it was untimely to approach the opposition (which meant essentially Chamberlain) to secure their acquiescence, because Loch would formally protest and his protest would "have to be submitted to Parliament". A month later Sydney Buxton wrote to Rhodes from the Colonial Office to say that the time was still unripe, particularly since the opposition were incensed by the announcement of the name of Sir Henry Loch's successor as High Commissioner, who was none other than Sir Hercules Robinson, in fact his own predecessor. In April Grey reported that, despite Ripon's advice, he had nevertheless sounded Chamberlain, who replied: "If the Government bring forward this proposal I will not look for arguments against it." But he emphasised that Chamberlain could not speak for the whole of his party, whose main object naturally was to bring the government down. In June Ripon actually circulated a memorandum to the Cabinet supporting Rhodes's plan; but in the same month the government duly fell, without the "proper time" for Rhodes to get his own way having arrived. Nor was it ever to arrive.[3]

*   *   *

Nevertheless his visit to London at the turn of the year 1894-95 was an undoubted success in every other respect. He had become much more than a big figure in Cape Town and Kimberley and Bulawayo. In the City of London, of course, his name had a magical power, the general belief being that anything he touched would turn to gold or diamonds. Actually his biggest venture, the British South Africa Company, had not as yet answered these expectations. Many years were to pass before it even declared a dividend, and its financial position was more precarious than Rhodes's cheerful orations indicated. Nevertheless his appearances at the Annual Meeting provoked scenes of wild enthusiasm. Such was the anxiety to hear him that the largest hall obtainable in the City could not hold all the shareholders who wanted to be present; and even Le Sueur, his private secretary, arriving once a little late, could not get in. In his speeches Rhodes was careful to make no promise of immediate benefit. "When your shareholders came into our Company," he said in January 1895, "you came into a speculative concern, certainly not into Consols or French *Rentes.*"

What was the Company's estate? It was, he told them, a country about twelve hundred miles long by two hundred miles wide, most of it suitable for white settlement and highly mineralised, as a recent report by John Hays Hammond, the American consulting engineer, had demonstrated. The present might be a little bleak, but the future was golden. The rest of his speech he gave to wider issues. At the centre of the Empire was Britain, a great manufacturing and trading community, dependent for her life upon her markets. Foreign countries were taking these from her by the erection of high tariff walls; but the Company had just established a new market, already profitable and of vast potential value to the Home country. In fact he was offering not in his old phrase, philanthropy plus five per cent, but imperialism with a future possible fifty per cent; and the shareholders, enchanted by the distant prospect, were content to overlook the absence of a present dividend.[4]

In 1894 Rhodes was the biggest lion in London. "I met Rhodes at dinner last night," Sir Hercules Robinson wrote to Sir Lewis Michell. "He is in great form and being made much of all round. He dined and slept at Windsor on Tuesday last, and next Sunday is to stay with Lord Rosebery at Mentmore." The visit to Windsor must have been the occasion when the Queen asked Rhodes what he had been doing since she had last seen him. "I have added two provinces to Your Majesty's dominions," he replied. "Ah," said the Queen, "I wish some of my Ministers, who take away my provinces, would do as much." Even Sir William Harcourt, the most redoubtable of his critics, relaxed so far as to invite him to "pay us a visit in our Forest, almost as savage as your Matabeleland", and offered jocularly to sell him timber for his telegraph poles.

The Liberals went out of office again in 1895, after failing to pass an Irish Home Rule Bill which Rhodes greatly preferred to its predecessors. He was disappointed over the defeat of the Liberals, since, apart from a few back-benchers like Labouchere, he had found them sympathetic with his designs. Lord Salisbury, on the other hand, was an enigma. It is true that in 1891 he had publicly described Rhodes as "a very considerable man, a man of very many remarkable powers, and remarkable resolution and will"; but some of his private observations were less flattering. Also he had that disconcerting addiction to international "swapping", that is to giving away something Rhodes valued in exchange for something he regarded as comparatively worthless. Lord Rosebery, by contrast, against the clamours of some of his back-benchers, had refused to evacuate Egypt and had declared a protectorate over Uganda. Also he was the son-in-law of Rothschild, who had stood behind Rhodes more than once.

Beyond Royalty and Cabinet Ministers and Members of Parliament was the proverbial man in the street, who was beginning to accept Rhodes as something like a national institution. Lon-

doners had learnt to recognise that burly, untidy figure, as he
came out of the Burlington Hotel to drive to the City or to ride,
unconventionally clad, in Rotten Row. To them he was the man
who had added two provinces to the Queen's dominions and
soundly whipped Lobengula. He particularly appreciated the
appreciation of the London bus-drivers and cabbies.

But he was hardly conscious of his new standing in society in
the conventional sense. "Jameson and I," he complained, "came
home after giving a new dominion to the Empire, and we found
that nobody took any notice of us, but that all your people were
full of excitement because a Mrs. Somebody hadn't been elected to
the School Board." This was an exaggeration: quite a lot of
people were "taking notice". *The Times*, which had once been
tepid, had turned in his favour; its correspondent in South Africa,
Flora Shaw (afterwards Lady Lugard) was a friend and confidante; while the formidable Manager, Moberly Bell, was a frequent visitor at the Burlington. The Travellers' Club blackballed
Rhodes, through the efforts, it was believed, of Wilfrid Scawen
Blunt, an old enemy, but the Athenaeum promptly elected him.
On 1 January 1895 he became a Privy Councillor, but since he
was in the Mediterranean at the time, he was not formally sworn
until February.[5]

His fame had over-stepped the boundaries of Britain and
South Africa. Early in 1895 he went to Turkey to try to persuade
the Sultan to part with some prized Angora goats, the export of
which was forbidden. His friends were sure he would fail, but at
Constantinople the Ambassador had no difficulty in arranging an
audience. Rhodes, careless as ever about his clothes, turned up
at the Palace in a flannel suit, and the Ambassador, greatly
shocked, told him to go off and get his frock coat. "That's impossible," replied Rhodes, "for I don't possess one." Casting a
predatory eye on the Ambassador's dark overcoat, he insisted
on annexing it. It was much too small, but by taking off his
flannel jacket, he could just squeeze into it. The Sultan took an
immediate liking to him and let him have the goats he wanted,
much to the future advantage of South Africa.

Returning, he travelled from Constantinople to Brindisi in a
grain ship. From Athens he wrote affectionately to his friend and
colleague, Schreiner. Leaving Athens, the ship ran into very
stormy weather. Rhodes retired to his cabin, but presently finding
that his personal servant, John Norris, had no berth, invited him
in; and soon afterwards he had most of the other passengers with

him as well. The incident was an example not only of his kindness and thought for others, but of the absence of any inclination to stand on his dignity or to claim special privileges. Many a man of his distinction, though he might have invited his valet in to share his cabin, would have jibbed at the idea of filling it with an assortment of grubby Levantine peasants.

Rhodes was already having to pay the price of his great labours. In 1894 he was described by Michell as "thin, grey and haggard"; and J. G. McDonald, when he saw him at Salisbury, said that he was "more worn out than I had seen him on any previous occasion, and was somewhat exacting and petulant at first, but this soon wore off after a few days on the *veld*". Indeed he was never better or happier than when he was having "a chop on the *veld*" with Metcalfe or some other congenial companion, living simply and shooting for the pot. He was a very fair shot, but inclined to be wild. He would alarm his companions who, to his annoyance, would throw themselves on the ground when he raised his gun. He took an especial delight in shooting matches, at which the standing wager was half-a-crown.

His petulance and impatience were becoming very noticeable, particularly to his secretaries, who were, however, familiar with the moods of "the Old Man", as they called him, and knew that he would atone for occasional outbursts of anger by acts of great kindness. When they were ill, he nursed and prescribed for them himself; and when he thought they needed a holiday, he would pack them off with a handsome contribution towards their expenses. But when he thought they were exploiting his generosity, he could be stern and even niggardly.

The impatience and petulance grew, the more he realised the deterioration in his health and the shortness of the time he would be allowed for the work he had still to do. The obstructiveness of men and governments was intolerable, when the realisation of his dreams was endangered.

"It is a fearful thought," he wrote to Stead, who was at this time perhaps his closest confidant, "to feel that you possess a patent and to doubt whether your life will last you through the circumlocution of the forms of the patent office. I have that inner conviction that if I can live, I have thought out something that is worthy of being registered at the patent office. My fear is, shall I have the time and opportunity and I believe, with all the enthusiasm bred in the soul of an inventor, it is not self-glorification I desire, but the wish to register my patent for the benefit of those who I think are the greatest people the world has ever seen, but whose fault is that they do not know their strength, their greatness and their destiny."

Secure in his own knowledge that gold and diamonds were no more than the means to his end, he did not mind the charges of Labby and his brood that his motive was money—and more money. What he did mind was the obstruction of people in authority, who should know better. He did not mind the Aborigines Protection Society describing him as "an unscrupulous trader": in return, he called them "the negrophilists of Exeter Hall". But he did mind Lord Ripon and the High Commissioner trying to take the future of Matabeleland out of the hands of the Chartered Company. Indeed, his relations with Loch, who in the past had been far from unhelpful, were fatally prejudiced by the attitude he had taken, on instruction from Downing Street, over the Matabele War. As Colonel Bigge wrote to the Queen in 1895, "The position between him [Rhodes] and Sir H. Loch is now greatly strained." But Ripon's and Loch's time was up. Ripon disappeared with the Liberals in 1895, and in the same year Loch, going home on leave, decided not to return to South Africa.

The new Secretary of State for the Colonies was none other than Joseph Chamberlain. He had never quite overcome his first distrust and dislike of Rhodes, aroused partly, perhaps, by the gift of £10,000 to the funds of the Irish Nationalist Party and by that injudicious *bon mot* about orchids, which had of course been repeated to Chamberlain. In their views about the Empire the two men were very close to each other. They both hoped and worked for its closer union. Rhodes was obsessed with the danger that foreign countries, and particularly the United States, by sheltering their industries behind high tariff walls, would shut Britain out of their markets; and a day would come when Chamberlain, with the same thought, would try to convert and commit his Party to the policy of Imperial Preference.

Rhodes went further. With his Will in mind he wanted finally to bring the United States into the Imperial circle again.

"Deeper than the Labour question," he wrote, "is the question of the market for the products of labour, and that, as the local consumption of England can support only about six millions, the balance depends on the trade of the world.

. . . I believe, until the world comes to its senses, you should declare war—I mean a commercial war—with those who are trying to boycott your manufactures. That is my programme. You might finish the war by union with America and universal peace—I mean after a hundred years and a secret society organised like Loyola."

Rhodes and Chamberlain were both strong, opinionated men, and even when their object was the same, each wanted to pursue it in his own way. At the outset, however, Rhodes's dissatisfaction was with Salisbury rather than with Chamberlain. "Mr. Rhodes is rather difficult to keep in order," Salisbury had complained to the Queen in 1891, and difficult no doubt Mr. Rhodes continued to be.

"Is it not awful?" Rhodes wrote bitterly to Stead in 1894. "But of course Lord Salisbury has made a diplomatic success. He has got a troublesome question off his hands, and the practical question of how these people [the pioneers] shall be fed is not now a matter of consideration. . . . The Portuguese Treaty stops everything. . . . One clause in the Treaty insisting on the immediate construction from the East Coast of a light train would have saved the situation. But for the sake of European politics, and in order to settle the question, this was not done and we shall have to face great misery through this.
"Even now, if Lord Salisbury would face the situation, there is just time, but there is no use asking it; he will not, and I am tired of cabling and stating the position; it merely leads to an exchange of diplomatic notes and nothing is done."

Rhodes was not *en rapport* with either Salisbury or Chamberlain. He was not the kind of man who would be a comfortable guest at either Hatfield or Highbury. He could not refrain from preaching his cause or airing his grievances; and neither the aloof, philosophical Prime Minister nor the forceful Colonial Secretary relished the treatment. They had to be polite when they met him, because he was an important man, the most important of all the Colonial Premiers, and they could not afford an open breach. So when they could not escape his lectures, they had to suffer them with such patience as they could muster.

Loch went, unregretted by Rhodes, the more so since his successor was Rhodes's old ally, Sir Hercules Robinson, who in his retirement had become a Director of De Beers. He had delighted Rhodes by his scathing description of the Labbyites as men who wanted to play the part of the Good Samaritan without the oil and twopence. Many people had qualms over the reappointment of a man who, they feared, was in Rhodes's pocket, though Bigge told the Queen he thought that Robinson "would quite hold his own with Mr. Rhodes". It is clear that Rhodes intervened vigorously to secure the reappointment of Sir Hercules, though he felt it necessary to deny, in a speech at Queenstown on 3 April 1895, that there had been any such intrigue. The letters of Queen Victoria show both the fact of his pressure and her own reluctance, which was reinforced by the publicly expressed doubts of eminent South African figures such as Rose Innes and J. W. Sauer. There survives a letter from Sir Hercules to Rhodes on the possibility of his return dated as early as July 1894. Grey wrote to Rhodes in April 1895 that the appointment had almost been frustrated. There was evidently a rival intrigue, in which Edmund Garrett (soon to become editor of the *Cape Times*) played a part, aiming to appoint Alfred Milner instead. Robinson was impossible, it was said, on grounds of "guinea-pigging, age and infirmity", according to Garrett. But Rhodes prevailed, and Milner had to wait another two years for his turn.[6]

The appointment was welcomed by imperialists as well as by Rhodes, because relations with the Transvaal threatened to be critical and no Briton knew the South African scene as well as the old High Commissioner. Sir Hercules returned to the Cape at the end of May 1895. He may have been less confident than Bigge of his capacity to hold his own with Rhodes. He could not have been unaware that Rhodes had suggested and pressed for his return, and when Rhodes wrote to congratulate him on it, he replied (with a trace of sarcasm): "I file that letter. If we come to disagree on anything, I promise to take that as indicating that I am wrong."

Despite disappointments and troubles, the worsening of his health, the occasional recalcitrance of Her Majesty's Government, and the financial stresses of the Chartered Company, Rhodes could count many blessings. In the infant townships and farms he could see, rising from the wilderness, his great plan taking shape. If only he could live to see it in full form! "You must never hurry anything," he told the people who were giving him a banquet in Cape Town after his return from Matabeleland.[7] "Do not think for one moment," he concluded, "that I do not recognise all the fences that I have to take. It may be in the future that a fence will meet me that I cannot get over, but it is satisfactory to think that in the past, in connection with this conception of mine, I have been as yet able to surmount the fences in front of me."

He knew that to surmount them he must have patience as well as daring, but he also knew how brief was the span likely to be allotted him and, like Napoleon, he would have said that men might ask anything of him but time. Moreover, he knew two things about the future of South Africa of which others were as yet only dimly aware. One was that the gold-bearing prospects of the deep levels on the Rand were incomparably richer than had been suspected even a year earlier, so that Kruger's position was likely to grow stronger rather than weaker. The other was that the mineral wealth of Rhodesia was nothing like so great as the Chartered Company's shareholders had been led to expect: there was no second Rand. It was the conjunction of these considerations with the deterioration of his health in 1895 that led him to the fatal impatience of the Jameson Raid.

Sources

Brett, M. V.: *Journals and Letters of Reginald, Viscount Esher*
Cook, E. T.: *Edmund Garrett*
Crewe, Marquess of: *Lord Rosebery*
Gardiner, A. G.: *The Life of Sir William Harcourt*
Garvin, J. L.: *The Life of Joseph Chamberlain*
James, R. V. R.: *Rosebery.*
Robinson, R. & Gallagher, J.: *Africa and the Victorians*
Walker, E. A.: *W. P. Schreiner—A South African*
        Lord de Villiers and his Times
Warhurst, Philip: *Anglo-Portuguese Relations in South Central Africa, 1890–1900.*
Wolf, Lucian: *Life of the First Marquess of Ripon*
Stead, W. T.: *The Last Will & Testament of Cecil J. Rhodes*

Notes

[1] Rhodes Papers, C. 25. 1 to 35 (Delagoa Bay file).
[2] Rhodes Papers, C. 3B. 232.
[3] Rhodes Papers, C. 3B. 236 (Grey); C. 3B. 242, enclosure (Buxton); C. 3B. 242, 245, 249 (Grey).
[4] "Vindex", 417–42.
[5] Rhodes Papers, C. 27. 46.

[6] Rhodes Papers, C. 27. 39 (Robinson to Rhodes); C. 3. 242 (Grey); C. 16. 41 enclosure (Garrett to Harris); C. 16. 42 (speech by Rhodes); Royal Archives, Windsor (Queen Victoria's correspondence).
[7] "Vindex", 360.

CHAPTER SEVENTEEN

CONSPIRACY

THE most formidable fence had still to be surmounted. In all that
Rhodes had done or tried to do, one obstacle had confronted him.
In Bechuanaland, in Lobengula's *kraal*, over the projected Customs Union, over his greater scheme for a union of South Africa,
he was aware of the presence of one man, stubborn and strong-
willed as he himself was, opposed to him on every point. When
Kruger first met Rhodes over the Bechuanaland dispute, he had
prophesied that the young man would cause him trouble if he
went on meddling in politics. Subsequently Kruger had seen no
reason to change his opinion.

When Rhodes was returning south in 1891 after his first abortive attempt to reach his new territory, he called on Kruger in
Pretoria. It was at the time when Rhodes was trying to buy Delagoa Bay from the Portuguese, and of course he knew that it was
also an important target for the Transvaal. It is therefore curious
that Rhodes, with his own eyes on Delagoa Bay, should have
broached the subject to Kruger when he met him at Pretoria. "I
know the Republic wants a seaport," he said. "You must have
Delagoa Bay." Possibly he merely wished to see what Kruger's
reaction to the idea would be. Actually the old man merely
pointed out that the Bay belonged to the Portuguese and that
stolen goods were accursed. "This young man I like not," Kruger
told Joubert afterwards; "he goes too fast for me. He has robbed
me of the North. I cannot understand how he manages it, but he
never sleeps and he will not smoke."

No one could have criticised Kruger on the second count, the
fumes of strong tobacco from his pipe being a sore trial to other
visitors besides Rhodes. Colquhoun describes the President as
sitting in "a leather-covered armchair, in dirty-looking clothes,
his hair and beard long, a big Dutch pipe in his mouth, and a huge
red bandanna handkerchief hanging out of the side pocket of his
loose jacket." Close to his chair was a spittoon, in constant use,
although it is recorded that Kruger's marksmanship was indifferent. Such was the unheroic, slightly unsavoury figure whom
Rhodes had begun to recognise as his chief antagonist. Rhodes
might say publicly and unwisely that he pitied Kruger, who was a

disappointed man, but he knew that Kruger was an implacable enemy of the British, and particularly of Rhodes himself, who, in his view, was shutting the Transvaal in a *kraal*, having stopped the expansion of the Republic westwards into Bechuanaland and north into Mashonaland. Finally, when Kruger had acquired Swaziland and was close to the East coast, the British Government (Kruger believed at Rhodes's instigation) annexed Amatongaland and again cut him off.

Nevertheless Kruger behaved reasonably over the plan for a Boer incursion into Mashonaland, known as the Adendorff *trek*, partly because he found that at the Cape the Bond was backing Rhodes. Sir John Willoughby was first sent to see Kruger on the subject, but could get nothing out of him. Jameson then tried, with more satisfactory results, for Kruger agreed to give no encouragement to the trekkers. "Damn you fellows!" said Jameson after the meeting. "You have all been telling us he has not another year to live, but he will see us all under—like an old elephant." Jameson then went off and dealt with the trekkers, with Adendorff, with the Banyailand men who, to the number of over 100, tried to cross the Limpopo and had to be turned back, and finally with van Reenen.

In 1893 Kruger was elected for a third time as President, with a narrow majority (believed by many to have been faked) over Joubert. He was then sixty-eight, with the mental rigidity of his years, but the physical strength of a much younger man. For some time he had had trouble with the problem of the *Uitlanders*, those cosmopolitan "squatters" in Johannesburg. They were asking for votes, but as they outnumbered the Boers by about three to one, if Kruger gave way, in a very short time they would be ruling the country. "You see that flag," Kruger said when urged to make some concession. "If I grant the franchise, I may as well pull it down." Possibly he was right. The enfranchisement of the *Uitlanders* on equal terms with the burghers might have ended the Republic: it would certainly have ended Kruger.

He had some justification for refusing to give votes to a lot of people who had come to the Rand to make money, and most of whom would probably leave when they had got all they wanted. To him they were an ungodly rabble who were trying to take away his country. So far some sympathy must be felt with his point of view; and many of the *Uitlanders* would have seen it, but for two important circumstances. The first was that, while Kruger disliked the *Uitlanders*, he needed the money they brought, because without it the Republic would be bankrupt. Although they had no say in the government, they were paying a very high proportion of the taxes. In 1886, when the Rand was proclaimed, the revenue of the Transvaal was £196,000; ten years later it had risen to nearly four million. The other circumstance is that a wiser man than Kruger, while determined to keep the country in the hands of its burghers, would have conceded something—a wide measure of self-government on the Rand, for example—and would at least have given the Republic a reasonably good and honest administration. Had he done so, the majority of the *Uitlanders* would probably have been satisfied. Most of them were not seriously worried about the vote. Lionel Phillips, a leading figure in the mining industry, wrote to Beit in June 1894 that he "did not think many people cared a fig for the franchise". What they did care about was to be allowed to pursue their lawful business without undue interference.

As Rhodes himself said, "If I were President Kruger, I might not have given the *Uitlanders* the franchise, because that might have ended my own power. But I would have made my new population comfortable and given them justice." Kruger would give neither comfort nor justice; yet if he had not muzzled the ox which was treading out his corn, he might have ended his days as President of the Republic. There was the railway to Delagoa Bay, built at extravagant cost by a group of Dutch and German financiers, along which he tried to force the gold of the Rand to travel. His Hollanders were a venal gang. Corruption was widespread and notorious. There were also the monopolies, and especially the Dynamite Concession, which amounted to an extra tax of £600,000 on the mining industry. The Republic's regulations about education, language, the police and a dozen other matters provided additional grievances, and the mine-owners, after protesting and expostulating in vain, not unreasonably concluded that until they had votes, they would get no redress. These facts should be recalled, if only because in retrospect there has been an attempt to idealise the Republic, which was in fact rotten to the core, an unpleasant blend of primitive pastoralism and urban racketeering.

At first the possession of land or one year's residence qualified a man to have a vote. In 1882 the period of residence was extended to five years; a further law in effect deferred enfranchisement until a man had lived in the Republic for fourteen years, and insisted on his being a member of the Protestant Church, a

K

landowner and a naturalised subject for two years, while in 1894 the franchise was virtually limited to persons born in the Republic.

So long as the mining industry flourished and fortunes were being made, the *Uitlanders* were prepared to put up with a great deal, but in 1894, when a serious depression fell on the Rand and the share-market collapsed, the manifest incapacity of the Government to devise any remedial measures, to lower taxes or the cost of living, or to provide the promised railway, brought the discontent to a head. With a view to allaying the unrest, Kruger paid Johannesburg one of his rare visits. It was a disaster. A noisy and disorderly crowd surrounded the house where he was staying and tore down and trampled underfoot the Transvaal flag. The President was furious. The incident confirmed his dislike of Johannesburg, and he vowed he would never visit it again—a promise which he kept for five years, sometimes making considerable detours to avoid entering a place which he now looked on as a City of the Plain.

Meanwhile the *Uitlanders* persisted in trying to secure redress of their grievances, but in 1893 a petition for the extension of the franchise, signed by 13,000 *Uitlanders*, was received by the *Volks-raad* with mockery. In 1892 they formed the National Union to work for their rights, choosing as their Chairman Charles Leonard, an eloquent young lawyer. Its renewed protests met with the same blank refusal, and in August 1895, when a petition carrying 38,000 signatures was rejected in the Rand by 16 votes to 8, one of the members invited the *Uitlanders*, if they wanted political rights, to come and fight for them.

No one likes to be treated as a second-class citizen; to be compared, as Kruger compared the *Uitlanders*, to the baboon in his yard; or to be addressed, as he addressed them, as "thieves and murderers". It was becoming clearer every month that constitutional agitation would make not the slightest headway against the unyielding attitude of a stubborn old man. Kruger himself said so. "Tell your people I shall never give them anything. I shall never change my policy," he assured them.

The burghers were not all so intransigent, and possibly, if people had had patience, a change for the better would have come. Kruger would have died or been superseded by a more moderate man, like Lukas Meyer, leader of the so-called Progressive Party in the *Raad*. Graham Bower, the Imperial Secretary at Cape Town, was convinced that the contrast between the kind of government that Kruger was giving the Republic and the kind that colonialism was giving the Cape and Natal was so glaring that soon Krugerism would be utterly discredited. But the *Uitlanders* were not patient people, and as insult was added to injury, feeling began to run very high

So far the Imperial factor had taken no special cognisance of the woes of the *Uitlanders*, but it was called upon to act in 1894 when the Republic commandeered British subjects resident on the Rand to serve in a war against a petty native chief. Five of the commandeered men, who refused to obey the order, were arrested. At once an appeal was sent to the High Commissioner, who, on instruction from the Imperial Government, went up to Pretoria in June. Kruger yielded with a bad grace, but Loch's visit gave rise to an absurd incident, which was interpreted as a studied insult. The President had gone in his carriage to Pretoria station to meet the High Commissioner. When they were both in the carriage, an enthusiastic crowd of Britons, elbowing the escort out of the way, took the horses from the carriage and dragged it to the hotel. That would not have mattered very much, but a man climbed on to the box-seat with a Union Jack fastened to a stick; and during the drive to the hotel the folds of the flag fell over the President. He rose angrily and struck at it with his stick, but the standard-bearer, unconscious of what was happening behind him, continued to allow the flag to droop negligently over the Presidential form. On arrival at the hotel, where the High Commissioner got out, Kruger intended to drive back to his house. But there were no horses and their human substitutes had joined the cheering throng in front of the hotel; so that the poor President was stranded until some burghers arrived to rescue him.

This mishap left Kruger angrier than ever. He had had to give way over the commandeering, since "suzerainty", which he professed to believe had been ended by the London Convention, was involved; but to be insulted in his own capital was more than he could stomach. Nevertheless in 1895 he was persuaded to forget his vow and to revisit Johannesburg to open an agricultural show. The *Uitlanders*, on their best behaviour, were respectful, but unenthusiastic, and the President was so far unappeased as to refer to them privately as "lickspittles".

The *Uitlanders* were not appeased either. The National Union continued to recruit new members and talk began to turn from constitutional agitation to the possibility of something more

forcible. There were perhaps 80,000 *Uitlanders* and 15,000 Boers
of fighting age in the Republic. With numerical odds of more
than three to one in their favour, people began to hint that they
had better go to Pretoria with arms in their hands to get their
rights. How they were to get the arms and set about a rebellion,
and what they were to do when they had won, if they did win,
they had not as yet considered in any detail.

The possibility of a rising of the *Uitlanders* had been seriously
discussed—though it was not a very serious possibility—at the
time of Loch's visit to the Transvaal in June 1894. Loch had
written to Lord Ripon, the Colonial Secretary, proposing that he
should make preparations for armed support of such a rising, if
it came, by means of an increased force stationed close to the
frontier. Ripon rejected the proposal, and it lapsed. But the idea
survived, and Loch's plan was later alleged to have been the
pattern and precedent of the Jameson Raid. It is fair to point out,
however, that Loch never contemplated deliberately provoking a
revolution in Johannesburg (which was Rhodes's plan a year
later); still less did he plan intervention by military force from
outside the Transvaal before any such revolution in Johannesburg had ever occurred, as Jameson did at the turn of the year
1895–96.

*   *   *

Meanwhile in September 1894, Rhodes visited Mashonaland
and Matabeleland, taking with him Jameson and John Hays
Hammond, the American mining engineer, who had just been
in Johannesburg. The purpose of the journey was to obtain a
detached assessment of the minerals in Rhodesia. Hammond's
report was in some respects disappointing, but Rhodes was determined to have and publish the facts. According to Hammond,
he made "not the slightest attempt to influence my opinion", although on it might depend the Chartered Company's chances of
raising fresh capital.

We are told that during the long rides and the evenings round
the camp-fire, the conversation was less about minerals than
about the troubles of the *Uitlanders*. "Unless a radical change is
made," Hammond assured his hearers, "there will be a rising of
the people of Johannesburg." Rhodes was impressed and many,
like Hans Sauer, believed that in that journey and those talks with
Hammond lies the origin of Jameson's disastrous adventure.

What Hammond had said bore out the opinion that Rhodes

himself, as head of one of the leading mining companies on the
Rand, was beginning to form. His logical and in some ways
rather naïve mind probably reasoned as follows. There was going to be a rising. His sympathies were naturally with the rebels,
because Kruger, besides being a nuisance to the mining interests,
was an obstacle to all his plans for the union of South Africa.
The rising must succeed, because failure would leave Kruger
stronger than ever and the *Uitlanders* a great deal weaker. The
Johannesburg people might be able to do the job by themselves,
but they might meet with stiff resistance, and if they did, in the
confusion and disorder which would follow, the lives and property of the *Uitlanders* would be in peril, not so much from the
Boers as from the 80,000 natives employed in the mines; and the
presence of a small force on the border would therefore be a wise
precaution.

So far no serious exception can be taken to the designs which
were beginning to take shape in Rhodes's mind. He had done
nothing to foment the discontent, neither his firm nor Alfred
Beit's having even joined the National Union. Also in his mind
was the possibility of a German intervention, which the Imperial
factor would certainly not tolerate. Cape Town, where British
troops were stationed, was a long way off; but a comparatively
small force coming in quickly from the north or north-west might
be decisive.

When Rhodes and Jameson went to London at the end of
1894, this was as far as the scheme had got. Neither man was
aware of the slippery slope at the top of which they were standing,
or how swift would be the transition from the lawful to the questionable, and thence to the indefensible. Jameson, with the
laurels of the Matabele War fresh on his brow, was fêted like a
hero. He was given the C.B., and during his visit addressed a
meeting at the Imperial Institute. With Rhodes sitting beside
him, he spoke of the shining future of South Africa as a federation. There was of course an obstacle—a handful of Boer ob-
structionists; but presently, Jameson suggested, even they would
"see reason".

During this visit Rhodes saw Rosebery, the Prime Minister of
a falling Ministry, and confided some of his thoughts to him.
Although he certainly pressed for the transfer to the Chartered
Company of the Bechuanaland Protectorate, it does not follow
necessarily that he disclosed the intention to use it as a base for
military operations against the Transvaal, or even for the support

of a rising in Johannesburg if a rising came. On the face of things, however, Rosebery and Ripon were sympathetic and disposed to fall in with Rhodes's proposals, though they were in no particular hurry.

Rhodes was perhaps inclined to exaggerate the extent of his influence over Rosebery. He cherished the mistaken belief that it was his persuasion which had induced Rosebery to accept responsibility for Uganda in 1892. Correspondence between the two men was at this time fitful, and on Rosebery's side comparatively indifferent: for instance, one of the few letters from him in the Rhodes Papers, dated 27 March 1894, is merely a courteous and diffuse apology in reply to a complaint from Rhodes at getting no answer to his previous letters. Another, written on 26 August 1895, at a crucial moment in the negotiations over the Bechuanaland Protectorate which were by then in the hands of Chamberlain, amounted simply to a refusal to intervene with Chamberlain on Rhodes's behalf.

Since it has sometimes been alleged (and Rhodes himself even confirmed it to both Sauer and Bower) that Rosebery was privy to the plans which culminated in the Jameson Raid, it is worth placing on record that neither the Rhodes Papers nor the Rosebery Papers seem to contain any documentary evidence which would support the allegation. Rhodes was sometimes apt to imagine—as is shown by his earlier misunderstanding with Schnadhorst over the conditions of his contribution to the Liberal Party funds—that he had made his meaning clearer than it appeared to the recipient of his confidences. It may well have been so in the case of Rosebery and Rhodes's plans for the Bechuanaland Protectorate. But Rosebery later vigorously denied that there had been any such confidence, and the documents, so far as documents can prove a negative, bear him out. The only significant letter between the two men during the critical period is that from Rosebery on 26 August, the terms of which suggest quite the opposite of a guilty secret. Rosebery wrote as follows, after consulting Ripon, in answer to a letter from Rhodes which does not survive:[1]

"Many thanks for your letter.

"I can't very well approach Chamberlain in the way you wish on any subject. But with regard to the Bechuanaland Protectorate there is, as I understand, this particular difficulty: that it was agreed that Sir H. Robinson should look into the matter on his arrival and report. Now I have not seen this report, (if indeed it has been sent in) nor has Ripon. So that I cannot well pass over Robinson and his report and give assurances in ignorance of what the Governor has to recommend. I do not think however that my not making this communication to Chamberlain matters much one way or the other. I hope you are getting on well with him and with Robinson . . . "

It would be hard to imagine anything more disappointing to Rhodes at that date, or less suggestive that Rosebery was familiar with any sinister significance in Rhodes's anxiety to acquire the Bechuanaland Protectorate for the Charter.

Meanwhile, earlier in 1895, two other events occurred which had considerable influence on the situation. The first of these was a *rapprochement* between Kruger and the Germans. The German Emperor was distinctly interested in South Africa. He had already allowed guns and ammunition to be sold to the Republic, and with the opening of the new railway from Delagoa Bay, the supply became easier and less conspicuous. When he thought that Rhodes might seize the port by a *coup de main*, he sent the warships there, a challenge which impressed everybody except the British Government. This incident was followed by a banquet at Pretoria on the Kaiser's birthday. Kruger celebrated the occasion with a speech which could hardly go unnoticed. After referring to the welcome he had been given when he visited Berlin, he went on to say:

"I know I may count on the Germans in future, and I hope Transvaalers will do their best to foster the friendship that exists between them. . . . I feel certain that when the time comes for the Republic to wear larger clothes, you [the Germans] will have done much to bring it about . . ."

Kruger had here probed a sensitive spot. Rhodes was not afraid of the Portuguese, who were just an encumbrance; but he was very much afraid of the Germans, who had by no means wholly relinquished their South African ambitions or their plan ultimately to link their settlements in German South-West Africa with their other settlements in Tanganyika. This new German threat was a powerful additional argument for clearing up the position in the Transvaal.

Later in the year Kruger took another disturbing step. In

order to encourage his new railway from Delagoa Bay, he first
raised the rates on the Cape line from the Vaal River to Johannesburg, and then, when Rhodes retaliated by organising supply by
ox-wagon, closed the drifts, or fording-places. This time he had
gone too far. Not only had he roused against him the Bond in
the Cape Parliament, but he had come up against the new Colonial
Secretary, Joseph Chamberlain, who was not a man to submit to
bullying tactics. Chamberlain sent Kruger an ultimatum, with the
support not only of Britain, but of the Cape Government, which
agreed to bear half the cost of an expedition, if this were necessary. Troops were ordered to South Africa, and for some weeks
war seemed not only possible, but probable. In these circumstances no one was surprised when Jameson announced the
formation of a new volunteer corps, under Willoughby's command, and a few young British Regular officers arrived in Salisbury.

Although the crisis over the Drifts, lasting from August to
October, provided the opportunity and the cover for movements
of armed forces and an unsuspicious concentration of troops near
the frontiers of the Transvaal, the preliminaries had already been
in train some time before. On 17 June Colonel Frank Rhodes had
telegraphed to his brother asking whether a firm decision had
been taken to "withdraw police from Macloutsie or at least not
to increase present forces there". Two days later, evidently in
response to that enquiry, Bower (the Imperial Secretary in Cape
Town) telegraphed to Milton (the Chief Secretary in Salisbury)
that "the detachment at Macloutsie is to be reduced to fifty all
told, and will probably be further reduced later on". Macloutsie
was the station in the Bechuanaland Protectorate nearest to
Rhodesia, and the policemen stationed there were in fact destined
to be embodied in Jameson's force. It is thus clear that Bower
at least knew what was happening as early as June, though what he
imagined to be the purpose of it at that date cannot be guessed.[2]

The situation had therefore fundamentally changed since
Rhodes's talks with Hammond in Rhodesia in 1894. The Germans had shown signs of interference and the Home Government, with the support of the Cape Dutch, was threatening war
over the closing of the drifts; while the National Union was reinforced by the accession of the Consolidated Goldfields of South
Africa and the Wernher/Beit companies. Till then they had held
aloof; but Rhodes had come to the conclusion that the next worst
outcome to an unsuccessful rising would be a successful one which

established an *Uitlanders'* Republic, controlled possibly by Rhodes's old enemy, J. B. Robinson. This result could, he thought, be avoided if he, despite his position as Prime Minister of Cape Colony, took a more active part in the plot. Before, his plan had merely been to provide a force which could intervene if a rebellion took place. Now he began to assume responsibility for the rebellion itself. As he later said, "the only justification for revolution is success"; and there is little doubt that the more he thought about it, the more determined he became to ensure, firstly, that there should be a revolution in Johannesburg, secondly, that it should succeed, and thirdly, that he should be the master of events.

How much of all this was as yet known to the High Commissioner and to the British Government has never been fully disclosed. The earliest accounts of the Raid were written without access to the papers of Sir Graham Bower, the Imperial Secretary. Bower, after his retirement, wrote his version of the whole affair and a copy of his record is in the Library at Rhodes House, as well as in the municipal archives at Cape Town. His account carries so much authority that no apology is offered for drawing freely upon it. While holding strong opinions and writing as a man with a just grievance, he is a careful and honest witness of the facts, although the inferences he draws from them should often be accepted with reserve.

In 1895 Bower had been Imperial Secretary for eleven years, and was probably the best-informed British official in South Africa. During the whole period that Sir Hercules Robinson was High Commissioner, Bower was his right-hand man. He had a great but not uncritical respect for his chief, with whose views he was generally in complete accord. Both Robinson and Bower, like Rhodes himself, were "colonialists"; that is, they disliked both the Krugerism of the Transvaal and undue interference from Whitehall. The model for the future, they considered, was the responsible government under which the Cape and Natal had prospered. In 1889, when Sir Henry Loch succeeded Sir Hercules, Bower continued as Imperial Secretary.

"Sir Hercules," he wrote, "was cold and calculating, very cautious and without any personal ties or personal friendships or hatreds. His first instinct was to secure his safety. Sir Henry Loch was hot-headed, vain, impulsive, and with strong likes and dislikes. In the case of Sir Hercules my

difficulty generally was to get him to move at all. I spent my
time with Sir Henry Loch in figuratively holding on to his
coat-tails."

Sir Henry was the more likeable of the two, despite the numerous warm disputes he had with his Imperial Secretary. As an
ex-cavalryman, with a dash of Rupert in his composition, the
High Commissioner was inclined to charge first and argue afterwards. In 1894, when Loch went up to Pretoria to discuss the
Swaziland Convention and the commandeering of *Uitlanders*,
Rupert was in the ascendant and was rather carried away by the
demonstration that so angered Kruger. Indeed, Loch told Bower
that "he had only to lift up his hand to make the Transvaal a British
province". He intended, he said, to go on to Johannesburg to
talk to the *Uitlanders*. Bower thought this design so injudicious
that he tendered his resignation; whereupon Loch, who had taken
time to think and to consult others, agreed to give up the idea.

Neither Loch nor Bower can have been unaware of the schemes
of the *Uitlanders*. But Loch was on his way out. He resigned—
Bower maintained in a moment of pique, not expecting his resignation to be accepted and much annoyed when it was. Before
he left, he told Bower that he was to be recommended for the
post of Governor of Newfoundland; and in due course Bower
was told the appointment would be offered him. He never got it.
When Robinson was asked to return to South Africa as High
Commissioner, he stipulated on the grounds of his age and ill
health that Bower should stay on as Imperial Secretary. Bower
did not particularly want to stay; but he had himself urged on the
Colonial Office the reappointment of Sir Hercules, preferring his
"cold-blooded calculating nature" to Loch's impulsiveness. As
he wrote to Sir Montagu Ommanney on 11 May 1906:

"Sir Hercules was a man who, in his prime, had the clear-
est head, the best judgment and most balanced mind of any
man I ever knew. As he grew older and his health failed him
his energy and decision failed too."

Between the two extremes of Imperialism or Chamberlainism
and Hollanderism or Krugerism, as Bower called them, Robinson
would steer the wise middle course of Colonialism or Consti-
tutionalism. If trouble was coming, a man with an established
reputation and long experience would be better than some newcomer who had everything to learn. Robinson was respected and

trusted by British and Dutch alike, and if an arbiter should be needed, he would be the best man. At the time Bower did not know that Rhodes had urged the appointment. Nor did he realise that Robinson, at seventy-two, with dropsy and a weak heart, was a very sick man. Some surprise was felt that Robinson, in these circumstances, was so ready to return to his old office. He told Bower that "he wanted to do something for his family, which I understood to mean, save money, to get a peerage, and to provide for his son-in-law, in some post". When Robinson insisted that Bower must go back too, "loyalty and duty left no choice open to me", and he agreed to forget Newfoundland and to return to South Africa.

Sir Hercules had one other anxiety. He was the nominee of Lord Ripon and a tottering Government. He had quarrelled with Chamberlain, who, when the appointment was announced, attacked it in the House of Commons. If the Unionists won the impending Election, his posting might be cancelled. When the Election was followed by the surprising news that Chamberlain was to be the new Colonial Secretary and therefore the master of High Commissioners, Robinson's apprehensions grew. They were, however, proved groundless, as Chamberlain at once sent him a friendly message. Robinson was so distrustful that for some time he could not bring himself to reply, quoting to Bower, "Dangerous as an enemy, untrustworthy as a friend, but fatal as a colleague." It is significant that in the time of trouble which lay before South Africa, the Colonial Secretary should have disliked the High Commissioner, and the High Commissioner should have had a deep distrust of the Colonial Secretary.

At any rate, by mid-1895 Robinson was already in South Africa, where he paid an early visit to Pretoria. There he conceived the rather odd notion that a G.C.M.G. might be offered to Kruger. The Colonial Office, on being asked, not unnaturally hesitated and told him to consult Rhodes, who replied, "As a Minister I am in favour of it; as a man I am against it." The offer was never made.

In October Bower had an important and highly confidential talk with Rhodes.

> "He then told me that the capitalists of Johannesburg had joined forces with the National Union and that a revolt would take place. My distinct idea is that he told me that the rising would not take place for two years, but his friends deny this,

and although I am firm in my recollection, I do not feel
sufficiently confident to swear to it. He also told me that he
was going to move the Police from Matabeleland to Mafeking to be available for use if required. As he said, 'You fellows are infernally slow. If you don't act, I will.' He then
said, 'Am I to tell the Governor?' At first I hesitated and,
turning my back on him, looked out of the window to think."

That Bower should imagine a revolution could be kept in cold
storage for two years shows his naïvety. That he should have had
even a momentary hesitation is surprising and even shocking, so
obvious is it that the Governor should have been told. Bower
explains that he was anxious to keep Robinson out of the business,
so that, when the trouble came, he would be uncommitted and
impartial.

"But on reflection I felt that the High Commissioner
ought to know and said, 'You must tell the Governor.' He
said, 'All right,' and told me that both Lord Rosebery and
Chamberlain knew."

Rhodes then went into the Governor's room, where he stayed
for about half an hour. On his departure Bower waylaid him.
"He has taken it rather badly," said Rhodes, "and does not
wish the subject mentioned to him." Later Rhodes assured his
brother Frank that he had told the Governor everything.

Next day Bower went in to see the Governor and began to
speak about Johannesburg. Robinson stopped him, saying: "The
less you and I have to do with these damned conspiracies of
Rhodes and Chamberlain the better." Bower, who had little
affection for the *Uitlanders*, or capitalists, as he called them, and
none for Chamberlain, fervently agreed. The Governor added,
"I know nothing about it," and "was very angry and impatient
at my mentioning the subject".

So, if we are to credit Bower, whose evidence tallies pretty
closely with what we know from other sources, Robinson knew
all about the "damned conspiracy", but was determined not to
know. In 1900 Jameson told Lady Milner that "the High Commissioner knew every detail of the arrangements, and as the time
approached his train was kept in readiness for him to start at a
moment's notice". Whatever may be thought of Jameson's conduct, he was not a liar. He further added that, as Robinson's
doctor, "private interviews were very easy to arrange on the

score of his health". "The whole scheme," Robinson told Bower in November, "is I believe, sheer piracy, but I know nothing about it and have nothing to do with it."

Chamberlain had already received a fairly clear indication that something was going to happen in the Transvaal. If a force was to be able to intervene swiftly in Johannesburg, its obvious starting-point would be somewhere in the Bechuanaland Protectorate, a few miles from the Transvaal border. The Protectorate was still under the Colonial Office, but Rhodes was continuing to press for the Chartered Company to take it over, partly in the hope that minerals might be found there, and partly because his railway to the North must run through it. On 9 July 1895 he wrote to Chamberlain that he was "anxious to take over the Bechuanaland Protectorate at once". He added, reminding Chamberlain of the earlier bargain: "You will find if you look at correspondence that Protectorate is promised to Charter; it is merely a question when you will hand over." He undertook to extend the railway from Mafeking to Bulawayo within four years and offered to accept any conditions Chamberlain wanted for the protection of the natives. He also hoped for a Customs Clause to ensure that "the duty on *British* goods shall not exceed the present Cape tariff".

Chamberlain, who wanted a railway, but not the Chartered Company, in Bechuanaland, sent a non-committal reply. At this point the egregious Dr. Harris, having recovered from his crocodile bite, re-enters the story. Rhodes sent him to London to try to hasten the transfer of the Protectorate, and on 1 August 1895 Harris, accompanied by Earl Grey, who was to make the necessary introduction, went to see the Colonial Secretary. Chamberlain, unimpressed by Harris, declared that he favoured the railway, but would hand over only a strip of land sufficient for its passage. Even over the strip he refused to be rushed. This was not all Rhodes wanted, and Harris decided that the moment had come to be more communicative. When, however, he volunteered some confidential information about the unrest in Johannesburg, Chamberlain stopped him. "I am here in an official capacity," he said. "I can only hear information of which I can make official use. . . . I have Sir Hercules Robinson in South Africa; I have entire confidence in him, and I am convinced that he will keep me informed of everything that I ought to know." The inference is that Chamberlain already knew enough not to want any further information.

Harris having retired with a rebuff, Grey returned to try to persuade Chamberlain to listen. According to Chamberlain's own account, he still refused to be told, but Grey, a man of reputed integrity, afterwards recorded that he had told Chamberlain an *Uitlander* rising was inevitable and the stationing of a force on the Transvaal border a wise precaution. The only contemporary account of the interview of 1 August is given in one of the so-called "missing telegrams" drafted immediately afterwards by Rutherfoord Harris.[3] The full version of it is to be found in the Rhodes Papers, which contain both the text as deciphered at Cape Town (truncated of the last few sentences) and a confirmatory letter giving the complete text. It shows that Harris was as clumsy at drafting as he was at diplomacy. But the substance is clear. Chamberlain, like Sir Hercules, knew a little and did not wish to know more. At least both men knew that the *Uitlanders*, with the encouragement of the Prime Minister of Cape Colony, were plotting a rebellion and that Rhodes wanted to place a force on the border, ready, if required, to intervene.

Rhodes's reputation was to be so disastrously damaged by the conspiracy that nothing was too bad for his enemies to believe of him. But at least two myths deserve to be dissipated. One was that he engineered the conspiracy for purposes of financial gain. The shares of the Chartered Company were falling, and people talked of its approaching bankruptcy as they did on many other occasions. The idea was that a successful take-over of the Transvaal would send the Company's shares soaring. Hostile biographers have always hoped that Rhodes's business papers would eventually reveal evidence of financial manipulations consistent with this theory, but they have so far failed to do so. Indeed, his correspondence shows, for what it is worth, that in August 1895 he was selling shares in the Chartered Company, which is understandable in the state of the market and his need for money, but does not suggest that he was expecting a spectacular rise. No evidence has ever emerged to refute his own claim that there was "no sordid motive" for the conspiracy.[1]

It must not be supposed, in the second place, that because the territory of the Protectorate was to be used for Jameson's jumping-off point, therefore this was the only interest Rhodes had in it. He was perfectly sincere in wanting to develop the Protectorate, and particularly to settle Europeans in it on a permanent basis. The area which he particularly wanted to settle was the north-west corner, near Lake Ngami and Ghanzi, chiefly in order to shut out German infiltration from South-West Africa. A party of trekkers, mostly Boer in origin, was held ready in mid-1895, to cross from the Crown Colony into the Protectorate to take up a concession given by the Bechuana chief, Segkoma; but he made difficulties, about which Rhodes indignantly protested to the Imperial Secretary, Sir Graham Bower, in August. This particular *trek* was frustrated by events later in the year, and only a handful of Europeans ultimately entered the Protectorate to settle. Rhodes tried again, however, with a second Ngami Trek in 1897, again without success. At least he cannot be accused of insincerity in this respect, nor of being solely preoccupied with the destruction of the Transvaal Republic in 1895. Indeed, the fact that many of his trekkers came from the Transvaal confirms his own argument that his quarrel was not with the Boers but solely with Kruger.

Nor does it follow that, because the main immediate need for the border-strip adjoining the Transvaal was connected with the conspiracy, therefore the ostensible purpose, that of building a railway and developing the territory, was a cynical deception. Railway-construction was Rhodes's passion, and the surviving correspondence of the middle of 1895 leaves no doubt that both he and his subordinates, particularly Metcalfe, Beit and Harris, were working energetically for the extension of the Bechuanaland Railway, not treating it as a bluff. A very long letter from Harris to Rhodes, written at sea on the way to England in July 1895, deals exhaustively with the technical and financial problems of the railway, and with nothing else whatever. Similarly, Beit's correspondence with Rhodes in the later part of the year is clearly concerned genuinely with the financing of the railway, whatever else he may also have had in mind. The railway-strip, in fact, served a dual purpose, but its ostensible purpose was not less real than the concealed one.[5]

The negotiations for the transfer of the Bechuanaland strip dragged on through the summer. Harris had three more interviews with Chamberlain—on 10 August, 5 September and 6 November. It is therefore reasonable to accept the opinion of most students of the Raid, that if what was called the "Jameson Plan" was not known to Chamberlain before, he learnt quite a lot about it during the summer. Fairfield, the official in charge of South African affairs at the Colonial Office, must also have known, although, as he was very deaf, he may not have taken in all that he was told. Harris himself insisted that he had told him

and on 4 November cabled to Rhodes, that he had spoken to
Fairfield. How much Harris told Fairfield is obscure, and was
later made obscurer by a clerical error which introduced the word
"open" after the word "spoken" in the version of the telegram
shown to the Select Committee of the House of Commons in
1897. It has generally been supposed—and Harris so insinuated,
after Fairfield was dead—that the word "open" implied a full and
frank avowal by Harris. The Select Committee assumed it, and
Fairfield was not there to deny it, having died of a stroke soon
after the Enquiry began. Bower considered that he was made a
scapegoat to protect his master, and that knowledge of the intention to sacrifice him hastened his end. But whatever Harris
did or did not tell Fairfield, it is certain that the sinister word
"open" was not in the telegram which he sent to Rhodes, the
text of which, as deciphered at Cape Town, survives in the Rhodes
Papers.[6]

Probably Harris babbled to quite a lot of people. One of his
confidantes was Flora Shaw, now in charge of Colonial affairs on
The Times and a strong adherent of Rhodes. Harris told her
something, and in a very short time she got the whole story out
of him. Eventually she became a prominent participant in the
plot herself. The telegrams relating to the Raid, which eventually
became public before the Select Committee in a manner most
embarrassing to herself and *The Times*, contain an interesting indication that she came late into the conspiracy. Unlike the names
of all the other principals, the code-book used for the telegrams
contains no coding for her name, so that it was always transmitted
en clair as "Flora"—a typical example of the reckless insecurity of
the whole operation.[7]

*   *   *

Meanwhile the strip had still to be handed over, and Chamberlain refused to be stampeded. Khama, who was afraid that his
people would lose their land and that liquor would find its way
into the country, was very unhappy about the transfer and eventually came to England himself with two of his fellow chiefs.
Chamberlain would give no final answer till he had seen and
heard them. "Is the Great Queen not able to protect us against
the Chartered Company?" Khama asked Chamberlain. The
Colonial Secretary wanted the railway to go through, but was
determined to save the Bechuanas from maltreatment or exploitation. In the end, although conceding the strip, he insisted on

reserves in it being set aside for the natives. Rhodes was furious that so much land should be allocated in perpetuity to 60,000 of "the laziest rascals in the world", as he wrote to the Duke of Fife.[8] He told Harris the settlement he had made was "a scandal". But he had to have his jumping-off place, and so he agreed with an ill grace to Chamberlain's terms. The cable announcing the cession reached the High Commissioner on 7 November, and promptly Jameson began to muster his force at Pitsani Botlugo, twenty-six miles north of Mafeking.

The excuse given for assembling over 500 men at a small and unimportant village was the need to protect the building of the railway line. The pretext was too flimsy to deceive any but those who were determined not to know. As the first of the "missing telegrams" shows, the line did not even exist in August, and Chamberlain knew it. But he would not have been the man he was if, with the crisis on the drifts breaking and an ultimatum to Kruger in the offing, he was not altogether sorry for the presence of a body of armed and disciplined men on the Transvaal border. On the excuse of the Ashanti War, he was getting troops to South Africa—a battalion from India and another from Barbados. But long before they could reach Cape Town, war might have been declared, with the loyalists in Cape Colony almost defenceless. More than that he still neither knew nor wished to know.

At the beginning of October, when he was enjoying a holiday in Spain, Chamberlain wrote a letter to Robinson, asking for his views on the situation in South Africa. Sir Hercules replied at length on 4 November. He considered that the *Uitlanders*, who were suffering under genuine grievances, had given up hope of constitutional redress. "It seems almost certain, therefore, that a revolt will take place sooner or later." What would happen next? In Sir Hercules's opinion, neither party in the Transvaal wanted it to become a British colony. They would prefer to remain independent in an "Anglicised and liberalised republic". He thought that directly news arrived of a rising, he, as High Commissioner, should go to Pretoria and order a constituent assembly to be elected by the votes of all white male adults in the country, thereby forestalling the Hollanders in Kruger's entourage, who might appeal to Germany for support. What the decision of the constituent assembly would be was uncertain.

During the summer of 1895, however, any fighting spirit the *Uitlanders* might have had was becoming blunted. In 1890, when times were bad, they were anxious to rise, but not ready. In 1895, when the National Union had been joined by most of the big men on the Rand—though not by J. B. Robinson or Barney Barnato—when rifle associations had been formed, and the Imperial Government was threatening the Republic with war, they were not so unprepared. But with the gold industry prospering once more, they were much less anxious to fight.

As Sir Hercules had told the Colonial Secretary, most of them had no wish to see the country a British colony, subject to the control of Whitehall and the interference of missionaries. Although as yet the question of the flag had not become an issue, probably all that most of the *Uitlanders* really wanted was to get rid of Kruger and his corrupt foreigners and to see a more reasonable and honest administration installed in Pretoria; and in this aim quite a few burghers were with them. Indeed, there are grounds for believing that for many of the *Uitlanders* the rising was no more than a gigantic bluff. They believed that there would be no rising, but that the threat of it would bring Kruger to his senses and perhaps to his downfall.

How little prepared the *Uitlanders* were for revolution is well shown in a letter to Rhodes, dated 25 October 1895, from his brother, Colonel Frank Rhodes, who was intended to be the military director of the operation. The letter begins with a general account of dissatisfaction with the Transvaal Government, and goes on: [9]

"The big increase during the past year in the water consumption indicates as well as anything the tremendous increase that has taken place in the population of this town. Mr. Difford, the Cape Government Railway Agent, informs me that people are coming into the place at the rate of 250 per day. The trains often contain as many as 400 and rarely less than 200, or on an average about 250; in other words the population is being added to at the present time at the rate of 75,000 per annum. The effect of this influx is plainly discernible, the hotels are crammed full, and it is most difficult to find a house, while owing to the demand for masons, carpenters, etc.: for building purposes, mechanics' wages are advancing rapidly. This influx is no doubt partly due to the effects of the boom, but looking at the extensive work which will have to be undertaken at the new deeper level concerns alone, there is every probability of the population continuing to increase at a rapid rate for some time to come. The

Government do not appear to realise the importance of this increase of population on the Rand, and are making no provision for it, but on the other hand are courting dissatisfaction in every quarter by their action over the Drifts question and the manner in which they cramp the industries of the country by imposing heavy import dues on raw and manufactured goods."

After giving some examples of the grievances against the Government (for instance, over the price of mealies or maize), Colonel Rhodes concludes:

". . . The block on the Netherlands line has caused considerable inconvenience, but so long as people are making money individually in Johannesburg they will endure a great many political wrongs. The Jewish element is also a damper on any political agitation, and nothing is being done beyond a few desultory telegrams and deputations, which are treated with disdain, being sent to Pretoria. As long as people here continue to make money there is little to fear, but should a serious drought set in and a number of the mines have to suspend work, with the result that a large body of men may be thrown out of work, there are many of the factors present to cause serious trouble."

Rhodes must have thought this an odd letter to receive from a soldier whose function, in his eyes, was precisely to create and organise trouble.

It is clear that very different ideas were afoot in Johannesburg from those of Rhodes and Jameson. In fact, in the early autumn of 1895, three distinct plans may be said to have been in progress. The first was that of a small group of *Uitlanders* for a rising, or rather the threat of a rising, which would transform the Transvaal into a liberalised republic under the Presidency, probably of Lukas Meyer, leader of the Progressive Party in the *Volksraad*. The second—more a hope than a plan—was that of Chamberlain. It was that trouble would break out in Johannesburg, that the High Commissioner should go up to arbitrate, and the result, perhaps distant, certainly doubtful, but most desirable, would be that the Transvaal, becoming once more a British Colony, would be ready in the near future to join a South African Federation.

The third design was of course the "Jameson Plan". Rhodes, suspicious of the *Uitlander* scheme for a liberalised republic, also mistrusted the Colonial Office. His idea was that a rising must take place and must succeed. Certainly the High Commissioner should go up to Pretoria as the nominal arbiter, but Jameson would be there too with a sizeable force, and the vital decisions for the future would be taken not by the *Uitlanders*, nor by Chamberlain, but by Rhodes himself. As he said afterwards: "You might be sure that I was not going to risk my position to change President Kruger for President J. B. Robinson." He might have added: "Or for President Chamberlain."

During November, Charles Leonard, the Chairman of the National Union and of the new Reform Committee, and Lionel Phillips, representative in Johannesburg of Wernher, Beit & Company and President of the Chamber of Mines, went to Cape Town to see Rhodes and to ascertain, if possible, his precise intentions. Neither Leonard nor Phillips was a warlike figure, Phillips in particular being a cautious man of business with a peaceful disposition. With Rhodes were his brother Frank and J. H. Hammond. "We read to him," said Leonard afterwards, "the draft of our declaration of rights," and when he reached a reference to Free Trade in South African products, Rhodes, who had been leaning against the mantelpiece smoking a cigarette, suddenly turned round. "That is what I want," he said. "That is all I ask of you. The rest will come in time. We must have a beginning, and that will be the beginning. If you people get your rights, the Customs Union, Railway Convention and other things will all come in time."

At that stage at any rate Rhodes was ready temporarily to forego the Union Jack. In the long term his attitude was stiffer. "I of course would not risk everything as I am doing," he cabled to Rutherfoord Harris, "excepting for British flag." But for the moment he was satisfied that if the *Uitlanders* got the vote, a Railway and Customs Union would follow, and after them political union. Perhaps his judgment was right: at any rate the delegation went away satisfied; but events were out of control.

By this time Rhodes was up to his neck in the plot. Jameson was to have a force of 1,500 mounted men, with Maxims and guns, and to take with him 1,500 spare rifles and some spare ammunition. Meanwhile some 5,000 rifles and a million rounds were to be smuggled into Johannesburg. So, when Jameson marched in, he would be able to dispose of about 9,000 armed men, with machine guns and artillery. The plot included the seizure of the fort and magazine at Pretoria, where 10,000 rifles, ten or twelve field guns, and twelve million rounds of small-arms ammunition were stored. Having taken away what they wanted, the raiders would destroy the rest. As the fort was a flimsy structure, with one wall uncompleted, and was guarded by only 100 men, most of whom would be asleep, its capture did not seem to suggest a very difficult operation.

Dr. Harris was to buy munitions and see to the smuggling of them into Johannesburg. This he began to do, mostly through De Beers (of which Rhodes was still Managing Director) and through the Chartered Company's agents at Cape Town and Port Elizabeth. Harris plunged into the enterprise with the zest of a schoolboy playing an exciting game. The arms were packed in oil drums, or under coal; but all Harris's energy failed to get more than 3,000 rifles, without any Maxims, into the hands of the *Uitlanders* by the end of the year. For communication Harris devised a ridiculous code, which was as likely to deceive the recipients of his messages as anyone else. The rising was "the Races" or "the polo tournament" or more often "the flotation". The High Commissioner was "the Chairman", Jameson "the contractor", and the conspirators themselves were "the subscribers".

More serious than these childish exuberances of Harris was an undated letter which Jameson procured from the leaders of the newly established Reform Committee, when he visited Johannesburg towards the end of November. In order to strengthen his position, he induced five of the leading men to sign an undated letter, setting out the grievances of the city, forecasting a conflict involving peril to "thousands of unarmed men, women and children of our race", and inviting Jameson to come to their aid if the need arose. The five men—Leonard, Lionel Phillips, Frank Rhodes, Hammond and George Farrar, whose signature was added later at Cape Town—were in fact giving Jameson a blank cheque which he could use when he pleased.

Possibly the letter, disingenuous though it was, would not have mattered so much if the principals had been in agreement about Jameson's force and when it should move in. The Reformers thought he would have 1,500 men, whereas Jameson believed he was committed to no more than 800, and in fact mustered only 500. The Reformers thought that Jameson would not stir until he was summoned by them, and Jameson thought that in the last resort he was to be the judge. Rhodes of course understood that it was for himself to give the marching orders.

There was an equivalent muddle over dates. The day originally
fixed for the rising fell during the Christmas Races; but presently
the discovery was made that the Races coincided with the Dutch
nagmaal, when large numbers of armed burghers would be in
Pretoria. Worst of all was a continuing misunderstanding over
the flag. Dr. Harris was determined to hoist the Union Jack;
most of the Reformers wanted a republic under the Transvaal's
own *Vierkleur;* while Rhodes's attitude was still uncertain.

The command was another weak point. The force at Pitsani
was to be led by Sir John Willoughby, a young regular soldier
who had not as yet shown any signs of military genius, but had
been Jameson's staff officer in the Matabele War. The volunteers
in Johannesburg were to be commanded by Colonel Frank
Rhodes, sportsman and lady-killer, also a regular soldier and a
very gallant man, who might have conducted with success a
minor military operation carried out in strict accordance with
Field Service Regulations, but was quite unfitted to be in charge of a
complicated conspiracy. He took the whole business very
lightly. When Jameson went to Johannesburg in November, he
naturally wanted to confer with Frank Rhodes. He made an
appointment, but when he reached the house, all he found was a
note: "Dear Jimjams, sorry I can't see you this afternoon, have an
appointment to teach Mrs. X. the bike." The incident was
absurd, but revealing. Sir Frederic Hamilton, then editor of the
Johannesburg *Star,* who tells the story, suggests that the choice
of Frank as a conspirator and of Harris as a diplomat was a sign in
Rhodes of illness and failing powers.[10]

Sir Frederic also records a conversation with Jameson. Hamilton had expressed some doubts about the whole enterprise.
"You do not know the Maxim gun," Jameson replied. "I shall
draw a zone of lead a mile each side of my column and no Boer
will be able to live in it." In fact, as Belloc wrote,

> *"Whatever happens we have got*
> *The Maxim Gun, and they have not."*

Jameson knew little of war and its logistics—nothing save what
he had learnt in the fight against Lobengula's half-armed savages.
But the Boers were not savages. If they were deficient in Maxim
guns, they had rifles and knew how to use them—better, certainly,
than the miners and clerks of Johannesburg. Five years later the
Boers stood for three years against the might of the British
Empire; and Jameson was expecting to overthrow them in three

days. So overweening was his confidence and so abysmal his ignorance of what he was undertaking that he told Howard Pim that "anyone could take the Transvaal with half-a-dozen revolvers", and Sauer that with 500 troopers armed with *sjamboks* (whips) he would drive the Boers into the sea.

It is difficult not to conclude that Jameson was suffering from *tête montée*. His victories in the Matabele War, and perhaps the C.B. awarded to him, had intoxicated him. It is said that he had been reading Macaulay's *Essays* and saw himself as a second Clive. He had no patience with the hesitations and fears of the *Uitlanders*, who might be good talkers and businessmen, but were not men of action. Neither had he much confidence in fellow-conspirators like Frank, who abandoned an important conference in order to give a lady a bicycle lesson; or Harris, whom he once described, not without some justice, as "a muddling ass". He had faith in himself and in Rhodes, who so often had brought success out of failure. He believed that he knew Rhodes's mind and could interpret his orders in their spirit, even if he ignored the letter.

It is still a puzzle that so many able men could have been drawn into so muddled a plot. But in 1895 Rhodes had won an immense influence over the minds of his contemporaries. If he was behind the conspiracy, they argued, success was a certainty. What they did not realise was that they were committing themselves, their lives and their fortunes, to a sick and impatient man. During that year Rhodes's health deteriorated further. He had a bad attack of influenza in August. He was beginning to say that he would not live beyond forty-five and must finish his work in the time allowed him. But although failing health drove him ruthlessly forward, he had his qualms. "Though the little Doctor has a good headpiece," he said, "he can also be a damned fool, and as stubborn as a mule."[11]

As for Paul Kruger, the prospective victim of the plot, he naturally knew all about it. The nods and winks and whispers of Harris alone would have turned speculation into certainty; and in Johannesburg itself the coming rising was the talk of the town. James Bryce, later a Liberal Minister and Ambassador to the U.S.A., who was there at the time, said that "never before was there except on the stage so open a conspiracy". Everybody was talking about it. Kruger was content to wait and watch, to go on importing arms and ammunition from Europe, and to plan a fort which would dominate the City of the Plain. "Take a tortoise," he told his burghers before the end of the year; "if you want to kill it you must wait until it puts out its head, and then you cut it off." Undoubtedly he was thinking more of the Reformers in Johannesburg than of Jameson in Pitsani. He scented trouble, but that Jameson might march in on his own initiative and start it probably occurred to him no more than it occurred to Rhodes, or Chamberlain, or the High Commissioner.

Sources

Bower, Sir Graham: Manuscripts at Rhodes House (MSS Afr. s. 26 and s. 63)

Colquhoun, A. R.: *Dan to Beersheba*

Colvin, Ian: *The Life of Jameson*

Fitzpatrick, Sir Percy: *The Transvaal from Within*

Garvin, J. L.: *The Life of Joseph Chamberlain*

Hofmeyr, J. H., & Reitz, F. W.: *The Life of Jan Hendrik Hofmeyr*

Hole, H. M.: *The Jamson Raid*

Kruger, Paul: *Memoirs*

Marais, J. S.: *The Fall of Kruger's Republic*

Pakenham, Elizabeth (Lady Longford): *Jameson's Raid*

Sauer, Hans: *Ex Africa . . .*

Van der Poel, Dr. Jean: *The Jameson Raid*

Notes

[1] Rhodes Papers, C. 27. 58.
[2] Rhodes Papers, C. 3B. 247.
[3] Rhodes Papers, C. 3B, 255. See also App. A, p. 485.
[4] Rhodes Papers, C. 9. 45, 46; C. 24, 45.
[5] Rhodes Papers, C. 3B. 257 (Ngami trek); C. 3B. 256 (Harris); C. 24. 44 (Beit).
[6] Rhodes Papers, C. 3B. 266. See App. A, p. 486
[7] Rhodes Papers, C. 3B. 266. See App. A, p 487.
[8] Rhodes Papers, C. 3B. 274.
[9] Rhodes Papers, C. 10. 103.
[10] English Historical Review, vol. LXXI No. 283 (April 1957).
[11] Maund Papers (Rhodes House).

CHAPTER EIGHTEEN

THE RAID

THE story of the Jameson Raid has been told many times, notably by Hugh Marshall Hole, Dr. Jean van der Poel, Lady Longford (Elizabeth Pakenham), and the biographers of Rhodes and Jameson. Here and there the various accounts may disagree on this fact or on that, and in the degree of blame to be assigned to the different principals; but about what actually happened they show few discrepancies. This is surprising, not only because the Raid is still a controversial subject, but also because it is certain that, as Graham Bower repeatedly asserts, at the subsequent Enquiry some important telegrams were withheld altogether and others were edited. Nor did the Enquiry pursue the truth very assiduously: it even came to be known derisively as "The Lying in State at Westminster".

In the middle of December the leading actors in the coming drama were viewing the projected rising or the "Jameson Plan" rather differently. Chamberlain, after winning his point over the Drifts, was watching the doings of the *Uitlanders* with interest, but apparently paying little attention to the Doctor at Pitsani. Probably he thought the rising would succeed and was only anxious about what would follow. On 11 December and again on the 24th he cabled to the High Commissioner. In the first message he approved of Robinson's proposal that, as soon as the trouble began, he should go up to Pretoria to arbitrate. The second cable told of the impending arrival of troops in South Africa and, reverting to the rising, warned Robinson that, before he went up as arbiter, he must consult the Secretary of State and also the Cape Ministry, which of course meant Rhodes.

Chamberlain, however, had a troublesome new preoccupation in the dispute with the United States over the Venezuela boundary which at one time threatened to lead to war. This new crisis coloured his views on the projected rising in South Africa. "It seems to me," he wrote to his Permanent Under-secretary of State, Sir Robert Meade, "that either it [the rising] should come at once or be postponed for a year or two." What he did not want was that the rising should be postponed for six months, when the dispute with the United States might be coming to a head.

Inspired, so Graham Bower thought, by Chamberlain's impatience, Lord Grey and Maguire cabled to Rhodes urging him to hurry up the preparations. Robinson and Bower, convinced that Chamberlain meant to force the pace, complained to each other that he was "over-riding the hounds". Probably this view was less than fair to Chamberlain who was thinking more of Venezuela than of South Africa.

On 26 December Chamberlain wrote to his chief, Lord Salisbury, to tell him that a rising on the Rand would take place "in the course of the next few days". Apart from the troop movements arranged by the War Office and his own instructions to the High Commissioner, there was nothing to be done. He concluded: "If the rising is successful it ought to turn to our advantage." Chamberlain's part may be judged by what he later told Flora Shaw.

> "The fact is," he said, "I can hardly say what I knew or what I did not. I did not want to know too much. Of course I knew of the precautions, the preparations, if you like, in view of the expected trouble in Johannesburg, but I never could have imagined that Jameson would take the bit between his teeth."

What Chamberlain knew was that a rising was being prepared, that Jameson was on the border ready to intervene if and when he was summoned, and that Rhodes was implicated. This degree of complicity is confirmed by Bower's story that when Beit arrived in Cape Town in December, he brought with him a message from Chamberlain to Rhodes, bidding him postpone his "fireworks" till at least a fortnight after the transfer of "the Crown Colony of Bechuanaland" to the Cape Colony. Later the Colonial Office denied the authenticity of this message, but neither Beit nor Bower is likely to have invented it to deceive Rhodes.

The High Commissioner was still playing the ostrich. When he had to discuss that most uncongenial of topics with Bower, he talked of "sheer piracy": and undoubtedly be believed that Chamberlain knew a lot more than Chamberlain in fact did. Robinson's legs were swollen with dropsy and he had a bad heart. He would not even see Newton, the Resident Commissioner for Bechuanaland, when he arrived in Cape Town on 18 December and asked for an interview, as he had been perturbed by warlike talk among Jameson's officers. "The whole thing is a piratical conspiracy," grumbled the old man; "I won't see him."

In Johannesburg the ardour of the Reformers cooled rapidly
during December. A revolution was something to talk about, and
the threat of it might force Kruger to make concessions; but
they were profitably busy in the new gold boom, and anyhow
most of them were not the kind who mount barricades. They
were not cowards or traitors, as people were soon ready to say
they were. Of the leaders—Frank Rhodes, Charles Leonard,
Lionel Phillips, J. H. Hammond and George Farrar—Hans
Sauer, who knew them well, wrote: "I had known all these five
men for years and I can state in the most emphatic manner that
not one of them was capable of playing the traitor to anybody or
anything."

They can hardly be blamed for being the most reluctant of
rebels. They knew the temper of their followers, and that it was
not the temper of revolutionaries. People have generally assumed
that the plot foundered on a difference of opinion over the flag,
that Rhodes insisted on the Union Jack and that the bulk of the
Uitlanders wanted to keep the *Vierkleur* and a Republic. But
Rhodes made it clear to successive deputations that he was not
demanding the Union Jack at once. Of course he wanted it, but
eventually, not immediately, believing that when Kruger and his
Hollanders had been swept away, South Africa would gradually
unite and only one flag would then be conceivable. "You have
been worrying about the flag," he told one of the deputations
which came to him for reassurance, "I never have." The question
would settle itself, in ten, twenty or fifty years.

The flag, therefore, was little more than a pretext for delay, a
straw clutched by desperate hands. It is true that on the Reform
Committee opinions differed. Phillips, Leonard, most of the
Afrikanders and all the Americans wanted a liberalised Republic,
Hammond going so far as to say he would shoot anyone who
raised any flag but the *Vierkleur*. Undoubtedly they were per-
plexed by rumours and by Harris's insistence that Rhodes would
hoist the Union Jack; and although Rhodes reassured them, their
doubts persisted. The fact that the question was regarded as still
unsettled is a symptom of the utter unreadiness of the rebels.
They had received guns and ammunition—not so much as they
had been promised, but perhaps 3,000 rifles—and did not even
bother to unpack half of them. They had not begun to muster
their men properly. When Hamilton asked Frank Rhodes on
Christmas Eve, two or three days before the rising was due
to start, if he would have enough men to seize the arsenal at

Pretoria, Frank replied airily, "Lots, my dear fellow. I don't exactly know how many, but I should say from the lists that have been handed me, quite four hundred, perhaps more."

Yet the plan was there, arranged with Jameson when he visited Johannesburg in November. A public meeting of the National Union was to be announced for 27 December, to distract the attention of the Boers. Just before it was held, the arsenal at Pretoria would be seized, and just after, a provisional government would be set up. The High Commissioner would then be asked to come north, bringing Rhodes with him. Such was the plan, and the more the Reformers thought about it, the less they liked it. With some realisation of the morass of muddle and misunderstanding in which they were struggling, they persuaded Frank Rhodes to cable to Jameson to postpone the "polo tournament" for a week. Jameson replied, protesting against delay, as the longer the rising was put off, the greater was the likelihood that the Boers would get wind of it; and eventually the Reform Committee agreed to a postponement of only two days. Saturday, 28 December, then became the appointed date.

On 22 December the Committee persuaded *The Times*' correspondent in South Africa, Colonel (afterwards Sir Francis) Younghusband, to go and see Rhodes, and try to clarify the position about the flag. By this time Rhodes had begun to realise the truth that the flag, about which he had already given an assurance, was only an excuse for doing nothing. "All right," he told Younghusband, "if they won't go into it they won't, and I shall wire to Jameson to keep quiet." As Younghusband was leaving, Harris ran after him and said: "Oh, Rhodes says that when any rising takes place it must be under the British flag." So far as we know, Rhodes had said nothing of the sort, and we can only concur with Flora Shaw's statement that "Harris was the mischief maker of the whole affair". He had misrepresented Chamberlain, hinting that he not only knew all about the plot, but would support it; and he misrepresented Rhodes, whose mouthpiece he claimed to be. In a sense he was: he sent the cables and signed the cheques. It is a mark of Rhodes's failing grip that he was ready to entrust his fortunes and his future to a man like Harris, to give so little supervision, to spend and allow Beit to spend large sums of money on a conspiracy of the details of which neither of them knew very much.

On Christmas morning the Reformers followed up the mission of Younghusband by sending Leonard and Hamilton to Cape

Town to convince Rhodes that the rising must be further postponed to 6 January. They were becoming uncomfortably conscious of the extent to which they had committed themselves. They were sure that the postponement was necessary. But would Jameson, with his force at Pitsani and that undated letter of invitation in his pocket, be equally sure? Their doubts were well founded. Jameson was becoming more and more restless. He had his own men of the Mashonaland Mounted Police at Pitsani, and at Mafeking 300 men of the Bechuanaland Border Police were awaiting discharge—or enlistment with the Company. So far only about 100 had accepted Jameson's invitation, and presently the others, unless they changed their minds, would go. Whereas the Mashonaland men were mostly young recruits, the Bechuanaland policemen were veterans, and Jameson did not want to lose them. He was also still worried by the thought that, with delay, the Boers would suspect his intentions. Surprise was essential; he hoped to be in Johannesburg almost before the Boers knew that he had crossed the border; and the Reformers, with their hesitations, were threatening to wreck the whole plan.

Above all, he chafed for action, supremely confident that he would get through. The flag question did not disturb him. Of course he and his men would fight under the Union Jack: what flag the Reformers fought under was their business; and what happened afterwards hardly concerned him. He could see no reason for delay, being ignorant of the confusion in Johannesburg. The plans were in black and white, the rifles had been sent, Chamberlain and the High Commissioner, he believed, were in the plot, and bases with rations and remounts had been surreptitiously organised along the route he would follow. Doubtless he was less heedful of the objections of the *Uitlanders* because he remembered how often Rhodes had told his young men not to treat the injunctions of authority too seriously, but, like Nelson, to put the telescope to the blind eye.

What was his exasperation when on Boxing Day he received two cables. One was from his brother Sam in Johannesburg:

"It is absolutely necessary to postpone flotation through unforeseen circumstances here altogether unexpected, and until we have C. J. Rhodes's absolute pledge that authority of Imperial Government will not be insisted on. Charles Leonard left last night to interview Rhodes. We will endeavour to meet your wishes as regards December, but you must not move until you have received instructions to."

The other telegram, needless to say, was from Harris:

"C. Leonard will . . . arrive Capetown Saturday morning. You must not move till you hear from us again. Too awful! Very sorry."

The telegrams were definite enough, but neither was from the one man to whom Jameson would have listened. All that he had from Rhodes was a telegraphic reminder of the Company's right to have a force at Pitsani. But Jameson was concerned not with what lawyers might think, but with what the Boers might do. He sent several telegrams in succession to Harris urging immediate action as planned. He had, he said, already sent out the men to cut the telegraph wires, which were red-hot with messages during the Friday and Saturday—Hammond to Harris, Phillips to Beit, Jameson to Harris. On Saturday Harris himself sent a telegram to Jameson:

"Goold Adams arrives Mafeking Monday, and Heany, I think, tonight. After seeing him you and we must judge regarding flotation, but all our foreign friends are now dead against it and say public will not subscribe one penny towards it even with you as director. Ichabod."

Having spoken, as he supposed with the authority of Rhodes behind him, Harris retired to his house two miles beyond Rondebosch, without making any arrangement for the delivery of messages during the weekend. Presumably he was satisfied that Jameson would not move without further instructions. So were Leonard and Hamilton who, after seeing Rhodes, telegraphed to the Committee that they had received "a perfectly satisfactory assurance on the flag question". But, they added, there still seemed to be some misunderstanding. The Reformers should continue their preparations "without any sort of hurry . . . Jameson has been advised accordingly".

Johannesburg was less confident than Cape Town. The Reformers were beginning to know the Doctor and feared that mere telegrams would not stop him. On Boxing Day, therefore, they tried a last expedient. Two of Jameson's officers, Major Heany and Captain Holden, were in Johannesburg for the purpose of liaison. The Committee decided to send them both off to

Pitsani, one by road and one by rail. One or both should reach Jameson before the 28th. But when Heany was asked what he thought Jameson would do when he got the message, the Committee drew little comfort from his reply—"He'll come in as sure as fate."

In Cape Town, meanwhile, Rhodes had given up hope of anything happening quickly. For some time he had not been on speaking terms with Bower. The Imperial Secretary had been steadily administering what he called "shower-baths", in other words throwing buckets of cold water on the whole plan. At last Rhodes, annoyed by the repeated discouragement, told Bower he was being a traitor to his master, the Colonial Secretary, who approved of the conspiracy. When Bower in dudgeon rose to go, Rhodes told him not to speak to him again.

Bower was therefore rather surprised when on 28 December Rhodes sent for him. He went to Groote Schuur, where he found Rhodes on the old tennis court overlooking the glen. Rhodes said: "You will be glad to hear that the revolution has fizzled out like a damp squib. You can tell the Governor: he will be glad to hear it." Jameson, Rhodes went on, would gradually reduce his force, though staying at Pitsani. Rhodes remarked that he and Beit "had contributed largely to the funds of the Revolutionists". He was nevertheless still a rich man and "would spend the rest of his money in developing the North". Bower added: "He also told me that Younghusband had told the conspirators that Chamberlain insisted on the English flag. He and Beit were in favour of this, but others were not. This was the ostensible cause of the collapse, but the real reason was that they did not want to risk a fight."

Bower passed on this information to the High Commissioner, who promptly cabled it to Chamberlain. But they were all reckoning without Jameson, who on Saturday morning telegraphed to Harris:

"Received your telegram Ichabod re Captain Maurice Heany. Have no further news I require to know. Unless I hear definitely to the contrary shall leave tomorrow evening and carry into effect my second telegram of yesterday to you, and it will be all right."

Harris, away from his office during the weekend, did not get the message till Monday. Jameson telegraphed even more explicitly to his brother Sam: "I shall start without fail tomorrow night."

He had made up his mind, or perhaps, as Marshall Hole argued, it had been made up for him by a Reuter telegram from Johannesburg, which reported that the situation there was acute, that men were being secretly armed, and that women and children were leaving the Rand. Jameson interpreted the news as meaning that the plot was no longer a secret and that the Reformers were at last acting. The two emissaries, Heany and Holden, both arrived, Holden on Saturday evening and Heany on Sunday morning. Heany was an old friend and, when he had delivered his message, Jameson got up, left his tent, and walked up and down for twenty minutes alone. As he walked, he may have thought, as later he was to exclaim: "You may say what you like, but Clive would have done it!" What else passed through his head we cannot know, but by then his frame of mind was such that only a categorical order from Rhodes would have stopped him. He went back to the tent. "I am going in," he told Heany, "and you, what will you do?"

"Go in with you," replied Heany without a moment's hesitation.

Jameson conceived that he had one further duty, to report his decision to Harris. The telegram reached Cape Town at 10.30 on Sunday morning, when no one with authority to deal with it was likely to be about. That afternoon the wires to Mafeking were cut and all communication with the Cape was suspended. The wires to the Transvaal should have been cut too, but the work was bungled. There is a story that the trooper, detailed for the duty, got drunk and, instead of dealing with the telegraph wires, cut down and buried long strands of wire from a farmer's fence. The result in any case was that no one in Cape Town could communicate with Jameson, whereas news of his departure could be telegraphed to Pretoria.

At three o'clock in the afternoon Jameson paraded his force of 356 men. He read them the undated letter of invitation and told them that the ugly situation foreshadowed in it faced them. Everything had been prepared and troops would come out from Johannesburg to meet them. There was no compulsion, but he believed all would wish to follow him. The speech was received with wild enthusiasm; the troops cheered and sang "God Save the Queen"; and not a man fell out.

The officers had been told of their destination a day or two earlier. Some of them, feeling anxious about their commissions, went to their commanding officer, Sir John Willoughby, who

Groote Schuur as rebuilt after the fire of December 1896

C. J. R. during the Matabele Rebellion in 1896

seems to have assured them that their commissions would be perfectly safe and that no one would bother them. Afterwards Willoughby explained he had been informed by Jameson that the expedition was being undertaken with "the knowledge and assent of the Imperial authorities". The truth of this statement is questionable. What Jameson did believe and probably said was that if the Raid succeeded, all would be forgiven and no one would be punished; and that the British Government knew all about it.

Shortly after sunset the column, accompanied by a 12½-pounder field gun and six Maxims, moved off along the road leading over the Transvaal border to Malmani, the appointed rendezvous with the Police from Mafeking. A hundred and ten of these had joined the service of the Company, about fifty preferring to await discharge. Their officers, Major Raleigh Grey and Captain the Hon. Charles Coventry, both addressed the troops, and about a dozen more of the time-expired men agreed to join the expedition. At about ten p.m. the column of 122 men, with two 7-pounder guns and two Maxims, took the road to Malmani. The two columns met, joined and started off on their ill-starred ride.

*   *   *

Chamberlain had one more word for Rhodes. Fairfield had written to the Secretary of State, who was spending Christmas at his home at Highbury, outside Birmingham. Evidently there had been talk and chaff in the City about the pending collapse of the revolution in Johannesburg, word of which had somehow got about. Bourchier Hawksley, Rhodes's solicitor, had suggested that Rhodes might order Jameson to go in and make the revolution by himself. The story hardly rings true of that most reticent of lawyers, but so Fairfield reported. He pointed out that if Rhodes did send such an order, he would be infringing the terms of the Charter. Apparently the idea had never occurred to Chamberlain who, improbable though he may have thought it, took the precaution of cabling to the High Commissioner, telling him to warn Rhodes that if anything of the kind happened, "I should have to take action under Articles 22 and 8 of the Charter." The warning would have been more effective if it had been sent a few days earlier. Even if it is taken as clearing Chamberlain from complicity in the Raid, it was too late.

At eleven o'clock on Sunday night Bower got a message from

L

Groote Schuur, asking him to go round there at once. Late as was the hour, Bower went. Rhodes was in his bedroom, very excited.

"He told me that Jameson had entered the Transvaal with all his men, but he had sent to stop him and things might yet come right. . . .

"I was staggered by the news. Every telegraph office was shut, and the Governor was ill and could do nothing even if he had been well. . . .

"Rhodes said: 'There must be no recrimination. I will take the blame, but I am ruined.'

"I said: 'You won't stand alone.'

"He then said, 'I will resign tomorrow.' "

Next day the High Commissioner would need all his strength, and Bower decided to leave him in peace that night. But at five o'clock next morning he sent round a note with the news. When the High Commissioner arrived, he exclaimed involuntarily, "Good God! He has not gone in without a rising! If so, you never told me." Both the terms of Bower's note and the nature of Sir Hercules's reaction are inconsistent with the later myth of the High Commissioner's total innocence.

Bower explained that he too had not dreamed that Jameson would do any such thing. He suggested a telegram at once to Newton, the Commissioner of Bechuanaland, ordering Jameson to return. Sir Hercules hesitated.

"Perhaps Chamberlain has sent him in," he suggested. "He is such an extraordinary fellow it is possible he may support Jameson."

However, in the end he telegraphed to Newton at Mafeking and wrote to Rhodes, who had also telegraphed to Jameson: "On no account whatever must you move." But the line was cut, the telegram was not sent, and Jameson never got the order from the only man who could have stopped him. Having done what he could, Rhodes had to turn his attention to the entertainment of Lord Hawke's visiting cricket XI for luncheon at Groote Schuur, without giving the guests an inkling that anything untoward had happened.

On Monday the 30th Schreiner, his personal friend and most faithful of ministers, went to Groote Schuur. The previous day, alarmed by the talk he had heard, Schreiner had been to see Rhodes to warn him to keep clear of the rumoured rising in Johannesburg. Rhodes, still hoping that his telegram to Jameson might get through, had merely shrugged his shoulders and said, "Oh, that's all right." Now Schreiner had had telegrams from the magistrate and police inspector at Mafeking, sent by despatch riders to the nearest station beyond the cut wires. It was dark before Schreiner could find Rhodes and show him the telegrams.

"The moment I saw him," he said, "I saw a man I have never seen before. His appearance was utterly dejected and different. Before I could say a word he said, 'Yes, yes, it is true. Old Jameson has upset my apple-cart.'

" 'What do you mean, what can you mean?' replied Schreiner. 'Why did you not say anything to me yesterday when I was here?'

" 'I thought I had stopped him,' Rhodes explained. 'I sent messages to stop him and did not want to say anything about it if I stopped him.'

" 'Why do you not stop him now?' asked Schreiner.

" 'Poor old Jameson,' Rhodes answered. 'Twenty years we have been friends, and now he goes in and ruins me. I cannot hinder him. I cannot go in and destroy him.' "

The magnitude of the calamity was becoming apparent to him. At one stroke Jameson had destroyed the work of years. Rhodes would lose his ministers, the trust of his friends, the support of the Bond, and had put his precious Charter in peril. But there was still a chance that Jameson would get through and the rising succeed. He would do nothing to jeopardise this—or his old friend.

But presently another old friend, Hofmeyr, left no doubt of the Bond's reaction. "If Rhodes is behind this, he is no more a friend of mine," he exclaimed, and sent Kruger a telegram wishing him success against "Jameson's filibusters". He went to see Bower to demand a proclamation against the Raiders. He drafted one himself and the High Commissioner accepted it; but Rhodes hurried round to plead for delay. In Hofmeyr's presence he told Bower he had offered to resign.

"Mere resignation is not enough," Hofmeyr retorted. "You must issue a manifesto repudiating Jameson, suspending him as Administrator of Rhodesia, and declaring that the law will be set in force against him."

"Well, you see," said Rhodes, "Jameson has been such an old friend, of course I cannot do it."

"I quite understand," rejoined Hofmeyr, "that is quite enough, you need say no more."

Hofmeyr departed, and never forgave Rhodes; nor did Rhodes ever forgive him, and when a cousin, the Reverend Adriaan Hofmeyr, later tried to bring them together again, it was Rhodes who refused the more stubbornly. Hofmeyr's reaction was one more of sorrow than of anger. He used to declare that he felt "as though the wife of his bosom had been torn from his side", a simile which particularly exasperated the bachelor Rhodes. In Rhodes's later years, Hofmeyr spoke more sympathetically of his former friend, but Rhodes never reciprocated.

Other Boer friends of Rhodes were sharply divided in their reactions towards him after the Raid. Most followed Hofmeyr, including the grand old lady of Cape Town, Mrs. Koopmans de Wet, who broke off all relations with Rhodes. Others found the break harder, and many sent him messages of sympathy. Among the most touching messages was one from old Mrs. Schreiner, who was English, though her children thought of themselves as Afrikanders or Boers. Whichever way their sympathies carried them, there is no doubt that the Raid was a Great Divide for the Dutch and British colonials alike.

Meanwhile the High Commissioner was convinced that Hofmeyr was right in insisting that a proclamation must be issued denouncing Jameson. Hofmeyr's draft was accepted as the basis of it, over Rhodes's protests. But last minute alterations were made, and there was some delay in clearing it with Schreiner, as Attorney-General, for which Hofmeyr and others unjustly blamed Bower. Actually Rhodes and Garrett, the editor of the *Cape Times*, were responsible for the delay; and the latter also contrived to send a despatch to a friendly newspaper in Johannesburg deliberately undermining the force of the proclamation.

Rhodes, still determined to do what he could for Jameson, next cabled to *The Times* a copy of the "letter of invitation", Harris having thoughtfully inserted the fictitious date, 28 December. Many were deceived by this spurious appeal for "helpless women and children", and to stimulate the popular enthusiasm the new poet laureate, Alfred Austin, published an atrocious poem, *Jameson's Ride*, which it would be kinder to forget. But what cannot be forgotten is the deceit practised, or condoned, by Rhodes in the immediate aftermath of the Raid. The mistake of allowing it to happen at all was relatively venial compared to the disastrous follies committed afterwards; and for some of these

Rhodes was even more to blame than he was for Jameson's adventure.

*   *   *

Meanwhile Jameson and his men, unconscious of the stir in London and Cape Town, were riding towards Johannesburg. They crossed some flat open country, hurrying to reach a defile which the Boers might block. Riding through Monday night, they arrived at Doornport, where they picked up rations and forage, but found that most of the remounts collected there for them were a poor lot of unbroken coach-horses. They were overtaken by a message of protest from Joubert and by the High Commissioner's order to go back. As by then they were more than half way to Johannesburg and had exhausted the food supplies in the dumps, Jameson could hardly have complied, even if he had been ready to do so. The same reply was sent to a further order from Sir Jacobus de Wet, the British Government's Agent in Pretoria.

By now, in rocky, hilly country, they were aware of being dogged by a party of Boers. There was a little firing and one of the Mashonaland men was wounded. The Raiders were heading for Krugersdorp, where they hoped to meet a force coming out from Johannesburg. Instead they encountered two bicyclists with letters from the Reform Committee. One letter was from Frank Rhodes and Lionel Phillips, but as it was torn up at once its exact contents are uncertain. Some of the fragments, however, were picked up on the *veld* months later and pieced together. Rhodes and Phillips seem to have declared that all was quiet in the city, that they would send men to meet the column, that Jameson was a fine fellow, and they would "all drink a glass along [with] you". The bicyclists brought another letter from Dr. Wolff, the man who had organised the dumps, giving the route Jameson was recommended to follow.

Willoughby, nominally commander of the force, wanted to avoid Krugersdorp, which he was sure would be defended; but Jameson overruled him, saying that their friends from Johannesburg would be waiting for them there. When one of the bicyclists asked Jameson if he needed any help, he either said or concurred in the suggestion that if a force were sent out from Johannesburg, "more for show than anything else", they would be of assistance. The whole story has been bedevilled by a conflict of evidence; but what is likely enough is that Jameson sent some message back

to Frank Rhodes, welcoming an offer to send 200 men to Krugersdorp. His own men, he said, were "in great heart although a bit
tired".

The Raiders now advanced on Krugersdorp. As they drew
near, they found that the Boers were holding a strong line of
defences in front of it. After shelling the position, Willoughby
gave orders for a frontal attack. The Boers lay low till the range
shortened, and then opened a heavy fire, which brought the
attack to a standstill. Another force of Boers was hanging on to
the Raiders' rear, so that they were almost surrounded. Willoughby then ordered a flank march to the south, the only route still
open. They had not gone very far, when they heard firing on
their left and in the failing light saw a large body of men moving
towards some mine buildings. Willoughby was sure they were
Frank Rhodes's men from Johannesburg. "To leave our supposed friends in the lurch," he wrote in his despatch, "was out of
the question. I determined at once to move to their support."

The new arrivals were not from Johannesburg; they were Boer
reinforcements, whose appearance was being greeted by a *feu de
joie*. By the time Willoughby had discovered his mistake, the
last outlet to the south was closed. The Raiders were tired and
hungry; they had been marching and fighting for three days and
nights without proper rest; they had suffered several casualties;
and they were beginning to be dispirited. When they bivouacked
for the night, continual sniping allowed them little sleep, and
next morning the patrols sent out to reconnoitre came at once
under a well-directed fire. Nevertheless, and despite several
casualties, the column pushed on, and in the running fight that
followed got within ten or twelve miles of Johannesburg. Their
position was desperate, but in the message Jameson sent to the
city by a bugler, all he could bring himself to say was, "I am
getting on all right, but you must send out some men to meet
me."

Between the column and Johannesburg lay the long ridge of
Doornkop, which had to be carried. But by now the attackers
themselves were under attack, for the Boers were closing in.
The Raiders' field guns ran out of shells; the Maxims, for want of
water, began to jam; and the small-arms ammunition was nearly
exhausted. Though they put up a gallant fight, they could not go
forward or back or stay where they were. In fact, their position
was hopeless. At nine-fifteen on 2 January 1896 someone—it was
uncertain who—hoisted a white cloth and the "cease fire" was

sounded. It is recorded that Jameson, seeing the sign of surrender, fell over as if shot.

*   *   *

The first intimations the Reformers received that Jameson had actually marched were two characteristic telegrams from the incredible Harris. In the first, addressed to Abe Bailey, he styled himself "Godolphin" a new *nom de guerre*. The telegram ran:

"The veterinary surgeon has left for Johannesburg with some good horseflesh and backs himself for seven hundred."

Any doubts this slightly cryptic message may have left in the minds of the recipients was dispelled by a second telegram to Arthur Lawley (afterwards Lord Wenlock):

"The contractor has started on the earthworks with 700 boys; hopes to reach terminus on Wednesday."

Why these messages should have been addressed to Abe Bailey and Lawley, rather than to Frank Rhodes, was a mystery Harris never explained. The Reformers had scarcely recovered from the shock of these unwelcome tidings, when a Government official in Pretoria informed them that "the news had been known there for some hours", and that the burghers who had gathered for *nagmaal* were forming commandos.

The first effect on the Reformers was tonic. For weeks they had havered. Now they cast off vacillation for a brief moment. They formed an executive committee under the chairmanship of Phillips, Leonard being still in Cape Town, and considered what they should do. It was too late to carry out the original plan of seizing the arsenal at Pretoria, as the Boers would be on the alert. About 1,200 of the rifles which had been smuggled in being still unpacked and in their hiding-places, the Committee, led by Lionel Phillips, started at once to get them out and remove the grease. Since the Government had prudently confined its police to barracks, an ex-dragoon from Northern Ireland, Andrew Trimble, was appointed to keep order in the city. This task he performed with admirable efficiency; in fact, he soon showed himself the best revolutionary of the lot. Volunteers were enrolled, earthworks were started, and the few machine-guns available were sited. But although hundreds of men were outside the headquarters at the Goldfields office, clamouring for rifles, the only armed body to be formed was a small force under the command of Colonel Bettington.

The Reformers had in fact set up—under pressure—the provisional government envisaged in the original plan; and having done this, their energy oozed away. As usual there were two parties on the Committee. One—the smaller—was in favour of carrying through the revolution, the other—the larger—of negotiating, from strength as they hoped, with Kruger. Either policy was plausible: what was neither plausible nor possible was to try to carry out both policies simultaneously; but that is exactly what the Committee did. They were confident that with 700 men—Harris's figure was badly out—Jameson would break through. But if they supported him, the Boers in Pretoria whose numbers were reported to be 5,000, might attack them before he arrived. They therefore issued a non-committal notice, which neither repudiated Jameson nor associated themselves with him; they unpacked and began to distribute what arms they had; and they hoisted the *Vierkleur*, deliberately upside down, over the Goldfields building. Then they telegraphed to the High Commissioner imploring him "to intervene to protect the lives of citizens who for years had agitated constitutionally for their rights". Several inflammatory speeches having been made outside headquarters, the crowd sang "Rule Britannia" and "God Save the Queen".

If the Reformers were nervous about what Kruger might do, he was equally nervous about what the Reformers might do. They had been filled with exaggerated stories of armed Boers marching to attack Johannesburg, and Kruger with even more exaggerated stories of the number of weapons in the city, believing these to include at least 20,000 rifles and some field guns. Kruger, who also was uncertain if Jameson would break through and whether he would be supported by the British Government, decided to play for time. He began by sending two respected and moderate men to invite a deputation from the Reformers to meet a Government commission in Pretoria. The Reformers were delighted with the invitation, for here were signs that the second plan of frightening Kruger into submission was coming off. A deputation of four, led by Phillips, went at once to Pretoria, where it met a commission, of which the principal member was Chief Justice Kotzé, who had been coquetting with the Reformers and might be supposed sympathetic. How far Kruger's overture was genuine may be doubted.

Bower believed that it was, but it is more likely, in view of subsequent events, that Kruger never meant to keep the promises given by the Commissioner to "consider" grievances when presented in a "proper" manner and to redress them. Phillips, however, thought that the Government was scared. He offered a guarantee that if Jameson were allowed to enter the city unmolested, he and his men would leave the country at once. When the Commission expressed a doubt about the representative character of the Reform Committee, Phillips telegraphed to Johannesburg for a list of members and, when it arrived, handed it over. Seldom can hard-headed businessmen have placed their necks more neatly in a noose. The Commission then produced the proclamation ordering Jameson to withdraw and suggested that, as the High Commissioner was coming up, pending his arrival there should be an armistice. The deputation agreed.

Having secured exactly nothing and presented a list of the leaders to the Transvaal Government, the deputation returned to Johannesburg well pleased with themselves. Phillips, addressing a noisy crowd, told them as much of the news as he thought they should hear. Unmindful of the armistice, he assured them that Jameson, who should be in the city within a few hours, would not be abandoned. But Kruger and Joubert, having immobilised Johannesburg, sent off to the commandos facing Jameson the field guns they had been keeping back at Pretoria to protect it against the *Uitlanders*.

So much for the peace party. During the absence of the deputation in Pretoria, the Committee had been exchanging messages with Jameson, telling him what a fine fellow he was, that they were waiting to have a drink with him, and also apparently offering to send out men to meet him. Now, at the request of de Wet, they sent a less encouraging message, with the High Commissioner's proclamation, hoping that on the strength of it Jameson would turn back, but not explaining their situation to him. Jameson's second and less optimistic message then arrived, and Frank Rhodes, guessing something of the truth and feeling honour demanded that something should be done, ordered Bettington with his 120 men to ride off at once to Jameson's support. But when Bettington had gone two or three miles he was recalled, the other members of the Committee having pointed out that his intervention would be a breach of the armistice.

Soon afterwards Hans Sauer, Rhodes's Afrikander friend who had recently joined the Reform Committee and was acting as its

liaison with the Boer authorities, brought them the news of the
surrender at Doornkop. Jameson and his men had been promised
their lives by the victorious Commandant, Cronje, a pledge
which was subsequently repudiated. In the fighting the Raiders
had had 16 men killed and 56 wounded. Some 35 men were
missing and may have slipped away. By nightfall the unwounded
prisoners, to the number of about 400, were lodged in Pretoria
gaol.

Meanwhile the High Commissioner, after some telegrams had
been exchanged, had decided that his moment had come and
boarded his train for Pretoria. He received formal notice of
Rhodes's resignation on the way. On arrival he found Kruger in
a very unyielding mood. The President now held a winning card
in the shape of Jameson and his men. Unless Johannesburg disarmed at once, he said, the Raiders would be shot and the commandos would attack Johannesburg. His own people, he told the
High Commissioner, were very angry and he could not easily
hold them in. That was almost certainly true.

Sir Hercules, faced with what was virtually an ultimatum,
rather lost his head, and disregarded his instructions from
Chamberlain to insist on redress of grievances. De Wet told him,
wrongly, that Jameson's surrender had been unconditional, and
neither man troubled to check the facts. The High Commissioner
forgot the *Uitlanders'* grievances or the possibility that Kruger
was bluffing, and telegraphed the terms to the Reform Committee, urging acceptance. He went further, and assured the
Committee that if they laid down their arms they would be
"acting loyally and honourably", but that if they refused, they
would "forfeit all claim to sympathy from Her Majesty's Government". Some of the Committee were for fighting it out, but the
majority realised that they would have to give way; particularly
when de Wet, amid frequent interruptions, asserted that "not a
hair of the head of any man in Johannesburg will be touched".

Finally, with further noisy protests, the crowd yielded. Kruger
had won. On 9 January he proclaimed a pardon for those who surrendered their weapons, and almost simultaneously ordered the
arrest of all the members of the Reform Committee, whose names
had been given him so conveniently by Lionel Phillips. Among
those arrested was even Hans Sauer who, having heard of the
possibility of trouble, had come up to Johannesburg only at the
end of December and, without knowing much about the Raid or
being in sympathy with it, allowed his name to be added to the

Committee. He expressed deep indignation at finding himself, an Afrikander, in gaol with the others; though he and some others were later let out on parole. The arrested Reformers in fact included many anti-Kruger Boers, as well as Americans and many other nationalities—even a Turk—besides the British.

Kruger, having got what he wanted, agreed that Jameson and his men, as British subjects, should go to England for trial. He had his own victims, the Reformers, and was the more determined not to let them off lightly because they had given him a bad fright. He had been told that there were 20,000, 30,000 or 40,000 rifles, with field guns, in the city, and the meagre total of arms handed in angered him. Either he had been deceived before or he was being deceived now.

*   *   *

In England the news of the Raid caused the greatest excitement. The first reaction was one of shocked surprise, but with the publication of the bogus letter of invitation and with *The Times* strongly supporting the Reformers, opinion began to swing in their favour. It swung even more strongly on 3 January, when the German Emperor, having learnt of Jameson's surrender, cabled to Kruger to

". . . express my sincere congratulation that, supported by your people, and without appealing for the help of friendly powers, you have succeeded by your own energetic action against armed bands which invaded your country as disturbers of the peace, and have thus been enabled to restore peace and safeguard the independence of the country against attack from outside."

This was too much even for those who were denouncing the Raid. The telegram implied that British suzerainty no longer existed and that, if Kruger had needed help, Germany would have given it. Arriving at almost the same moment as the news of Jameson's surrender, it aroused intense feeling in London and Cape Town—even from Hofmeyr, whose old suspicions of Germany were at once reawakened. In Britain people began to say that what had happened was not Germany's business anyhow, and that maybe more had been behind Jameson's unfortunate action than they had supposed. Three years later, when Rhodes himself saw the Kaiser, he explained in his naïve way that the telegram had helped him:

"You see," he said, "I was a naughty boy and you tried to whip me. Now my people were quite ready to whip me for being a naughty boy, but directly *you* did it, they said, 'No, if this is anybody's business, it is *ours.*' The result was that Your Majesty got yourself very much disliked by the English people, and I never got whipped at all."

At the time this consolation must have been slight indeed. The first days of January were among the most agonising of Rhodes's life. He could not and would not repudiate Jameson. All he would acknowledge, even to his colleagues on the Board of the Chartered Company was that "Jameson had started without his knowledge or consent". But *he* had sent Jameson to Pitsani, *he* had provided the Reformers with arms and money, and the world would hold *him* responsible. Partly in distress of mind and partly to avoid visitors with awkward questions, he absented himself during most of the daytime, rambling about Table Mountain, among the hydrangeas, which were then out in all their glory. One of the few women who knew him well, Dr. Jane Waterston, found him one day looking at the mountain and at a great bank of blossom. As she came up, he waved his hand at the prospect. "Do you know what this means?" he asked, and before she could answer, said: "Peace."

But just then he had little peace in his own mind, even on the mountain. His work was in ruins. He and his Cabinet had resigned. The Charter was in jeopardy through the implication of its officials in the plot; while De Beers and the Goldfields had been grossly misused by their Managing Director. The union of South Africa was farther off than it had ever been, for what he had hoped would be a short cut turned out to be the longest way round, if not a dead end. Presently, with the news of Jameson's surrender and of the arrest of the Reformers, he had other anxieties, as tormenting and more personal. Jameson was to go to England to stand his trial, while his brother Frank, to whom he was devoted, and others of his closest friends were to be tried for their lives in Pretoria.

He could spend the days on the mountain, but at night he had to go home—with his thoughts and fears and anxieties. It is possible that he suffered a heart attack. Jourdan, his private secretary, recalled of those days:

"I do not think he slept a wink for five nights. Tony, his personal servant, told me, 'The Baas walks up and down his bedroom, which is locked, at all times of the night.' "

Some of his friends, unlike Dr. Waterston, were careful to avoid him, like a leper. He kept saying, "Now that I am down, I shall see who are my real friends." They were few enough, but the thought seemed to comfort him. On 15 January he sailed to England—to face the music, he explained, but still more to try to save the Charter.

Sources

Works mentioned under Chapter Seventeen and additionally:

Brett, M. V.: *Journals and Letters of Reginald Viscount Esher*
Bryce, James (Viscount): *Impressions of South Africa*
Drus, Ethel: Bulletin of the Institute of Historical Research, vol. xxv (1952), pp. 33–61
        English Historical Review, vol. LXVIII, No. 269 (October 1953,) pp. 583–93
Garrett, F. E: *The Story of an African Crisis*
Innes, James Rose: *Autobiography*
Stead, W. T.: *The History of the Mystery*
Walker, E. A.: *Lord De Villiers and his Times*
Report of the Select Committee on the Jameson Raid (Cape Town, 1896)
Second Report from the Select Committee on British South Africa (H.M.S.O. 311, 1897)

CHAPTER NINETEEN

THE AFTERMATH

WHILE Rhodes was at sea, Chamberlain had three weeks to make up his mind how to receive him. The situation was changing almost daily, and it was difficult to see how it would settle down. Public opinion in England was bewildered. It had been worked up on the side of the jingoes by the publication of the "letter of invitation" in *The Times*, by the Kaiser's telegram, and even by Alfred Austin's execrable poem. But soberer heads appreciated that something must be wrong under the surface. Otherwise, why had Rhodes had to resign, why were Jameson and his officers being sent home under arrest to stand trial in London, why had the High Commissioner been obliged to return from Pretoria with nothing achieved, except to make the Reformers at Johannesburg surrender to Kruger? James Bryce (later Viscount Bryce), who had visited the Transvaal shortly before the Raid, wrote to Rhodes on 10 January that public opinion in England was still "not committed" on the Raid.[1] Rhodes was at sea, nearing England, when Bryce's letter reached the Cape. But although thus out of touch with the changing situation, he did his best to influence it in his own direction even while he was at sea. A message from him to Chamberlain through the Chartered Company on 31 January served warning that Britain was in danger of losing the loyalty of British settlers not only in the Transvaal but throughout South Africa.

Chamberlain was also using the interval to do what he could to improve the situation from his own point of view, which was not the same as that of Rhodes, except in the one particular that he too regarded the continuation of the Chartered Company as desirable, or at any rate necessary. He had taken advantage of the flow of public opinion to re-establish his personal popularity: the keynote was set in a speech on 21 January in which he spoke of "sensational occurrences" that sometimes pass away without a trace. His view of the situation was that it was ripe for an "act of vigour", no matter at whom directed. "It does not much matter which of our numerous foes we defy," he told Salisbury, "but we ought to defy someone." The target might be the Germans, with their impertinent interest in Delagoa Bay, to

which a British naval squadron had already been despatched.
Consistently with that gambit, Chamberlain's personal suggestion
for Rhodes's defence was that he should find evidence of a
German–Dutch plot in the Transvaal. Or the target might be
the French, whose interests both in West Africa and in the Nile
Valley were increasingly obnoxious to Chamberlain. Or it
might be Kruger himself.

Chamberlain was indignant with the High Commissioner for
having decided, on his visit to Pretoria, that the time was not
ripe for pressing the Government's demands. He believed that
he could easily impose his will on Kruger if they once met face
to face. A visit to London by the Transvaal President would solve
many problems and show that the Imperial Government had not
lost the initiative. The same idea was put forward from South
Africa. Contacts with Kruger at second hand enabled Chamberlain to assure the Prime Minister on 27 January (quite mis-
takenly, as it turned out) that Kruger would certainly accept an
invitation to London. He was drafting a despatch on proposals
for municipal reform at Johannesburg, such as Kruger had promised in the aftermath of the Raid, and he had no doubt that everyone could be satisfied. Little did he then understand the mentality of Kruger, or the damage that had been done to Anglo-Boer
relations and the balance of power in South Africa by the Raid.

Rhodes arrived in England on 4 February. He saw Chamberlain two days later, but in the meantime several intermediaries
passed to and fro. Chamberlain used Rhodes's friends, Lord
Rothschild and Reginald Brett (later Viscount Esher), to sound his
mind and intentions. Brett was developing into a professional
homme de confiance between the great, and he enjoyed the task.
W. T. Stead, the brilliant but erratic journalist who shared the
secrets of Rhodes's current Will, also saw him and reported on his
interview; but Stead's reports were apt to be coloured by his own
enthusiasms. In the opposite direction, B. F. Hawksley, who was
solicitor both to Rhodes personally and to the Chartered Company, went to the Colonial Office to drop hints of which much
more was to be heard in the next twelve months. Chamberlain's
friends characterised them as blackmail, and were not far wrong.

Rhodes told Brett that he intended to be "perfectly frank" in
his interview with Chamberlain. Perfect frankness, as Brett
readily understood, meant that he would admit his complicity in
the plan for a rising at Johannesburg and for Jameson's force to
support it, but not in the Raid as it actually took place. What

Brett could not know was that such an admission would be no news to Chamberlain, and that furthermore Chamberlain was in exactly the same boat. He innocently conveyed Rhodes's intention to Chamberlain, who replied that he would rather not receive confidences which might oblige him to take legal action against Rhodes. The allusion was no doubt to the Foreign Enlistment Act, under which it was an offence even to prepare an expedition on British soil against a friendly state, an action of which Rhodes would have stood guilty even if Jameson had never started. Chamberlain was advised that a prosecution would not succeed, but he had not yet decided that it could be avoided. The subject being embarrassing, his message to Rhodes was therefore that he preferred not to discuss "recent events" but rather "the present condition of affairs in the Transvaal and the future of the Chartered Company". He gave no indication of his own views on the latter point, which to Rhodes was all-important. But perhaps Rhodes already sensed that Chamberlain preferred to allow the Chartered Company to continue its operations because he could think of no alternative. At any rate, Rhodes agreed through Brett to fall in with Chamberlain's wishes.

At the same time Hawksley was engaged in strengthening the ground on which his master was to tread. Undoubtedly he did so on instructions, but the instructions were, if anything, not strong enough to suit Hawksley's vigorous temperament. He was a lawyer, not a politician; and he had, or was shortly to have, in his possession, evidence which appeared to suggest that Chamberlain had been involved in Rhodes's conspiracy "up to the neck", in Rhodes's own words. The evidence consisted of a dossier of telegrams exchanged between London and the Cape in the latter part of 1895, none of them initiated by Chamberlain but many of them implying his complicity in unmistakable terms. The fifty-four telegrams in Hawksley's dossier, some of which were suppressed at the time and have ever since remained "missing", have been the subject of far-ranging controversy. It need not be pursued further after the researches of modern historians, which have sufficiently shown that Garvin's *Life of Joseph Chamberlain* was too kind to him by half. Although the telegrams alone could not have convicted him of complicity, they should certainly have led to pertinacious investigation of his conduct, which could hardly have ended except in his resignation.

Hawksley sincerely and consistently wanted to reveal the incriminating telegrams to public view. Rhodes, on the other hand, thought them more valuable held in reserve. His policy gradually took the shape of bartering the telegrams against the Charter. He would refrain from publishing the telegrams, which would so severely damage Chamberlain, if Chamberlain would save the Charter from abrogation, for which his enemies were clamouring both at the Cape and in London. There was perhaps never a clear-cut bargain on this exchange because nothing was clear-cut in Rhodes's relation with Chamberlain in 1896. For one thing, Chamberlain did not really suffer from the guilty conscience which the researches of later historians have indicated that he ought to have felt. For another, he did not really want to abolish the Charter himself. And a third consideration was that Rhodes, who seldom read or wrote the communications which bore his name, had no very precise idea how damning (and therefore how useful to him) the telegrams in Hawksley's dossier really were.

Hawksley, however, saw things in black and white. He believed that his dossier could destroy Chamberlain and save not only Rhodes and the Charter but also Jameson, for whose defence he was made responsible. When he went to the Colonial Office on the day of Rhodes's arrival in England, he did not yet have the telegrams in his possession: they were still with Rutherfoord Harris; and Harris may have given him an exaggerated idea of their contents. But he knew enough about them to make a threat on their possible use to Fairfield, who conveyed it to Meade, and together with Meade to Chamberlain. Chamberlain did not appear to be worried, but he asked to see the dossier. Hawksley ignored the request, until it was renewed more pressingly in the summer.

When Chamberlain saw Rhodes on 6 February, neither Hawksley's threats nor the Jameson Raid were mentioned at all. Brett had done his work well. Lord Selborne, the Under-Secretary, who was present at the interview, reported that "it had been most satisfactory and that Rhodes had shown a great amount of common sense". Rhodes and Chamberlain seem to have been equally satisfied. They talked only about the future of Rhodesia and the Charter; and they talked realistically, which meant not as if recent events had never taken place but only as if they had done no more than create a new situation which needed to be confronted with reason and without emotion. Rhodes offered to put the Company's police under the Imperial Government's control, but to continue to pay them. He asked, and Chamberlain agreed, that the Company should continue to appoint magistrates, judges and civil officials. He opposed the creation of a new post of British Resident in Rhodesia. Perhaps the appointment of Grey to succeed Jameson as Administrator was mooted. It was all cool and forward-looking; and that was all.

Rhodes did not stay long in London after the interview at the Colonial Office. He had little business there. He had already seen the Board of Directors of the Chartered Company on 5 February, and probably offered them his resignation; but after his talk with Chamberlain had passed off so well, they did not think fit to accept it. Only one other noteworthy event occurred during his stay in London. He dined with Moberly Bell, the Assistant Manager of *The Times*, and at the dinner-table he met a remarkable lady who was to play a disastrous part in the closing years of his life, the Princess Radziwill. Born in the Polish nobility, she was the divorced wife of a prominent Russian aristocrat, who had lived for some time at the imperial court of Berlin, where she had met Salisbury during the conference of 1878. The facts of her life are not easy to disentangle from the falsifications of her romantic imagination; but she was certainly not, as she was later represented, a mere social climber. She was witty, cultivated, intelligent, a superlative linguist, and a forger and fabricator of genius. But at the time she made no impression on Rhodes, who could not remember her at all when she next re-entered his life. He left London a few days after his interview with Chamberlain, and returned to South Africa by way of Egypt, Beira and Rhodesia.

The bright outlook with which Rhodes and Chamberlain parted was soon overclouded for both of them. Chamberlain's contacts with Kruger proved abortive, partly because of his own clumsiness, and partly because Kruger's assessment of the situation which they were to discuss differed greatly from his own. The despatch on municipal government for Johannesburg, on which Chamberlain had been working when Rhodes arrived, was published prematurely on 7 February, nearly three weeks before Kruger could receive it. The decision to publish it in London was apparently taken to placate Rhodes, since Hawksley had told Fairfield that knowledge of it would do "much good" among the *Uitlanders*. But the natural result was to annoy Kruger, who retaliated, when he at last received the despatch, by publishing his reply to it before delivery. The correspondence between Chamberlain and Kruger continued until April, becoming colder and colder. It was clear that, so far from discussing concessions to the *Uitlanders*, what Kruger wanted to discuss in London was a list of such subjects as the abrogation of the Charter, the punishment of Rhodes, compensation for the Raid, and the supersession of the London Convention of 1884. On these terms the visit was impossible, and the invitation was finally withdrawn.

Chamberlain was reminded of another of his difficulties in the House of Commons on 13 February, when the debate on the Queen's Speech was used as an opportunity to attack Rhodes and to demand an enquiry into the Raid. In the state of public ignorance at the time, it was not difficult to defend Rhodes without actually lying, in words which deserve to be quoted because they could equally be applied to Chamberlain's own position:[2]

> "I say to the best of my knowledge and belief that everybody, that Mr. Rhodes, that the Chartered Company, that the Reform Committee of Johannesburg, and the High Commissioner, were all equally ignorant of the intention or action of Dr. Jameson."

In other words, because nobody knew or could have known that Jameson would do what he did—not even Jameson himself, probably, until twenty-four hours beforehand—therefore all were equally innocent. Of course, what they were innocent of was not what they would have been accused of, had Parliament really known the facts; but at that time no one outside the circle of complicity was able to draw such a distinction.

It was not so easy to answer the clamour for an enquiry. Chamberlain had himself made a promise to Hofmeyr by telegram early in January that there should be an enquiry. It was not only demanded in the House of Commons, but was soon to be demanded in the Cape Assembly, where a Select Committee was appointed at the end of May as a milder expedient in substitution for a more ferocious proposal that the Charter should be revoked. An enquiry was also held in the Transvaal, which published a selection of documents found in the captured trunk of one of Jameson's officers, Major the Hon. Robert White.[3] The papers in *de trommel van Bobby White*, as it was popularly called by the Boers, first gave the public a glimpse of the extent of Rhodes's personal complicity in the conspiracy, but they need not have worried Chamberlain except with the fear that Rhodes, in his desperation, might reveal more. The conviction of the Reformers in Pretoria at the end of April, and the approach of Jameson's trial in London in July, must have aggravated Chamberlain's anxiety about the prospects of an enquiry such as the House of Commons desired.

Once it was clear to Chamberlain that Kruger could not be enticed to London on acceptable terms, he turned to other devices to distract public attention from the morbid preoccupation with disinterring the past. He and Salisbury—though there is not much doubt that Chamberlain and not Salisbury was the driving force of the government—were still meditating their "act of vigour". The possibility of a further approach to Portugal to acquire possession of Delagoa Bay was considered, with the support of a vigorous memorandum by Selborne, who was Salisbury's son-in-law as well as Chamberlain's Under-Secretary. Probably fear of Germany's reaction, not necessarily in South Africa but in other areas where the Imperial Government needed support, precluded the pursuit of this course. Simultaneously the first steps were being taken towards the reoccupation of the Sudan, which had been abandoned after Gordon's catastrophe at Khartoum in 1885. Chamberlain even contemplated, quite cold-bloodedly, precipitating a war with the Transvaal in order to forestall the pressure for an enquiry into the Raid. He was deterred partly by Salisbury and partly by Bower, the High Commissioner's Imperial Secretary, who quixotically offered himself as a scapegoat at the proposed enquiry in order to avert a war.

Meanwhile, enquiry or no enquiry, Hawksley was still threatening to reveal the Colonial Office's guilty secrets. He urged Bower to tell the truth in order to help Jameson at his trial; but Bower refused, putting patriotism above personal justice. Again in Jameson's interest, Hawksley renewed his threats at the Colonial Office, probably going further than Rhodes would have wished. By the middle of May Chamberlain was beginning to be nervous. The publication of the documents in *de trommel van Bobby White*, immediately followed by the savage sentences passed on the Johannesburg Reformers (six of whom were condemned to death, though none was to be executed), had been followed by a storm of publicity. On 1 May *Le Temps* in Paris published a story that the Transvaal Government had "proofs that in 1894 Sir Henry Loch . . . proposed to the Reform Committee the invasion of the Transvaal". The story was a grotesque perversion of the truth—for one thing, the Reform Committee had not existed in 1894; but the truth itself had an unedifying flavour in the circumstances, and the denials of Lord Loch (as he now was) in the House of Lords must have made many readers meditate that there could be no smoke without fire.

The revelations from Pretoria led to a fresh debate in the House of Commons, during which Chamberlain again defended Rhodes on 8 May. But on the previous day he had demanded the resignation of Rhodes and Beit from the Board of the Chartered Company. The demand was communicated to Rhodes, who was now otherwise engaged in Matabeleland, by Hawksley. His reply was peremptory: "Let resignations wait—we fight Matabele tomorrow." Chamberlain was therefore denied the sop which he had hoped to offer the House of Commons. The debate was acrimonious, Sir William Harcourt in particular vehemently attacking Rhodes and demanding the revocation of the Charter. The same demand was made by J. X. Merriman in the Cape Assembly a few days later, but Rhodes's other former friend and subordinate, W. P. Schreiner, opposed so extreme a step. It was Schreiner also who moved, in friendly terms, a motion to grant Rhodes leave of absence from the current session of the Cape Assembly. He and Harcourt were each the recipient of characteristically touching letters from Rhodes in Matabeleland a few weeks later.[4]

To Harcourt Rhodes wrote on 13/14 May, while on campaign in Matabeleland, to unburden himself because, as he said, "I do not know what will happen during the week." He recognised that Harcourt's strictures on himself had been made from a sense of public duty, but he did not want to meet his own fate without trying to avoid misunderstanding. "I have tried to unite South Africa, and no sordid motive has influenced me." The rebuttal of a "sordid motive" occurs three times in the letter. For the rest, he did not care how bitterly he was blamed. The sincerity of the letter is as unmistakable as its naïvety in expression. It ends with the words: "good bye".

To Schreiner he wrote at greater length on 3 July, before the end of the campaign to which his letter to Harcourt referred. Rather unusually, he numbered the paragraphs, in order to isolate and emphasize his points. He urged Schreiner to stay in politics for the sake of South Africa, and declared that "I am not going to run away from Africa and I will remain here unofficially and carry out the big idea". He expressed no regrets for what had happened, except that it had divided Schreiner's own family. He explained his reasons for haste: Kruger was only temporary, but what he feared was "a huge English speaking republic in Transvaal which will absorb the North and leave the Cape out at the shank end of the Continent". Against this he set his own aim of "union under the English flag under responsible government", and "to keep the north with the Cape whatever happens". His letter began with a heartfelt expression of thanks, and ended with "the golden rule which advice you gave me Possess your soul in patience". This was a chastened and perhaps downcast but also a resilient Rhodes, determined to make what he called "a new beginning".

Hawksley was also in touch with Rhodes, though intermittently, but he did not much like his instructions. Being Jameson's legal adviser as well as Rhodes's, he believed that Rhodes's tactics were prejudicial to Jameson's defence. To protect the Charter, Rhodes would not allow Chamberlain's complicity to be revealed. But Jameson had given his subordinates to understand that the Imperial Government was behind their adventure. Hawksley would have liked to produce evidence to justify their belief in court. There was, or was thought to be, some ground for believing that Hawksley did not much like Rhodes: such was Fairfield's view, for instance, as expressed to Chamberlain in December 1895. At any rate, he clearly chafed at his instructions not to incriminate the Colonial Office or its servants. These instructions were reluctantly conveyed to Jameson's counsel, Sir Edward Clarke. Even so, the conviction of Jameson and his officers was not a foregone conclusion: the jury tried to evade a categorical verdict of Guilty, but the Lord Chief Justice firmly directed them to return it.

Jameson's trial lasted from 20 to 29 July. In the weeks preceding and during the trial, Chamberlain had been wrestling with the problem of the proposed enquiry into the Raid, and Hawksley had been making things as difficult as possible for him without actually contravening Rhodes's instructions. He again reminded the officials of the Colonial Office of his dossier of incriminating telegrams. Chamberlain again asked to see them. They were sent to the Colonial Office early in June and seen by Chamberlain and Selborne, both of whom wrote memoranda on their contents, dated 6 June. The dossier was returned to Hawksley with their comments on 17 June. Chamberlain's memorandum, the essential parts of which have since been published, does not suggest that his conscience was any more troubled than before.[5] But he realised that, at best, his position would look bad, especially as Rutherfoord Harris was a crude reporter of delicate interviews. He offered Salisbury his resignation at once, but it was refused. So great was the Government's confidence in him, in fact, that he was even urged to take the chair himself at the Enquiry when it came.

But Chamberlain's troubles were still only beginning. Harcourt had written to him on 21 May demanding the removal of Rhodes from the Board of the Chartered Company. It was impossible to continue taking No for an answer, and by 26 June the resignations of both Rhodes and Beit had been obtained. But that was not enough to appease Rhodes's enemies. Kruger renewed his demands for the trial of Rhodes, which Chamberlain described to the Transvaal Consul in London as "unfriendly and threatening". The Report of the Select Committee of the Cape Assembly on the Raid was published on 17 July, with a strong condemnation of Rhodes. It was becoming increasingly difficult to evade an enquiry at Westminster, especially since many of the most important witnesses (including Rhodes himself) had not been available to the Cape Committee. Hawksley himself took it for granted that an enquiry must be held, and visited the Colonial Office to discuss its composition. Finally Chamberlain gave way. On 30 July he moved in the House of Commons for a Select Committee. Although the end of the session a few days later nullified its appointment, there could be no withdrawal from the principle that had been conceded.

The inevitable postponement of the Select Committee of the House of Commons was by no means the end of the matter, nor even a respite for Chamberlain. Hawksley was conscious of holding an advantage over Chamberlain, even without the publication of the telegrams. It was at his suggestion, on Rhodes's behalf, that George Wyndham was appointed a member of the Select Committee; and Chamberlain, making the best of a bad job, at once arranged for Wyndham to go to South Africa to make a more explicit bargain with Rhodes, to the effect that the telegrams should be suppressed and the Charter safeguarded. On the same ship with Wyndham were Bower and the High Commissioner, who had visited London during the summer, no doubt partly at least in order to avoid being called before the Cape Town Enquiry. Jameson had seen these two in London shortly before his own trial began, and reported them to be in "a mortal funk", which he himself had the pleasure of increasing by assuring them that the telegrams would be published in the next few days. But Jameson, like Hawksley, was over-optimistic about obtaining Rhodes's permission to publish. Wyndham's mission was eventually successful, no doubt chiefly because Rhodes was already determined against publication in any case.

Hawksley, who did not know his master's determination,

renewed the pressure on Chamberlain in August. He now had Lord Grey to help him independently. On 20 August Hawksley reminded Chamberlain through Fairfield that "reasons other than the ostensible ones were intimated to him why the acquisition by the Chartered Company of the Bechuanaland Protectorate was urgently necessary". On the same day Grey told Chamberlain that Rhodes "knows that the publication of these miserable cables will do him good, not harm". To Grey Chamberlain replied with the threat that if the telegrams were published the Company might lose its Charter. But to Fairfield he admitted, in commenting on Hawksley's communication, that "charges of the kind indicated in his letter, although they might be discredited and laughed at in this country, would do much harm in South Africa and on the Continent".

Hawksley gave the screw a further turn in September. Sir John Willoughby, who was sentenced to a term of imprisonment with Jameson in July, wrote a letter to the War Office, on learning that he and his fellow-officers were to lose their commissions, in which he claimed to have had an assurance from Jameson of the "knowledge and assent of the Imperial authorities" in their adventure. The letter was accompanied by a covering letter from Jameson referring to "the telegrams now in the possession of Hawksley". There is little doubt that Hawksley organised this new move, and it may be presumed that Chamberlain played a part in organising the riposte, which was a peremptory snub from the War Office to Willoughby on 15 September. For the time being Hawksley had exhausted his ingenuity, though not his determination. Meanwhile Wyndham was nearing his objective, which was to find Rhodes and seal his bargain with Chamberlain.

Sources

Works mentioned under Chapters Seventeen and Eighteen

Notes

[1] Rhodes Papers, C. 26. 6.
[2] H. C. Debates, 4th series, vol. XXXVII.
[3] Transvaal Green Book No. 2, included as Appendix A to the Report of the Select Committee at the Cape.
[4] Gardiner, *Life of Sir William Harcourt*, II, p. 392; Walker, *W. P. Schreiner*, p. 81.

[5] In part by Garvin, III, 110–11; more extensively by Ethel Drus, *Bulletin of the Institute of Historical Research*, XXV, 41 seq. The earliest of the "missing telegrams", which is given incompletely in Chamberlain's memorandum, appears in full in App. A, pp. 485–6.

CHAPTER TWENTY

RHODESIA IN PERIL

RHODES's difficulties at this time were of a very different kind from Chamberlain's. He cared little whether there was an enquiry at Westminster or not, so long as the Charter was safeguarded. He was content to acquiesce in the unflattering verdict of the Cape Committee, on which his friends Schreiner and Upington and Fuller had sat, as well as his enemies (as he now saw them), Merriman and Innes. The conclusions of the Cape Committee, within their narrow limits—and all conclusions were limited beside Rhodes's visions—were accurate and adequate. They had concluded that "the part taken by him in the organisation which led to the inroad headed by Dr. Jameson was not consistent with his duty as Prime Minister of the Colony". Well, he had resigned from being Prime Minister. They also concluded that "the principal officials" of the Chartered Company in Cape Town (naming Beit, Rhodes and Rutherfoord Harris) were involved in the plot and were "active as promoters and moving spirits throughout". Well, all of them had resigned their posts in the Company. No useful purpose could be served by further enquiry, except to endanger the Charter itself. But at the present moment what was in danger was not simply the Charter but the very territory to which it applied.

The first signs of impending trouble in Matabeleland had begun to appear as early as February 1896. Many circumstances contributed to them. The Matabele had never regarded themselves as completely defeated in 1893. If they were beaten, they reasoned, why had they been allowed to keep their weapons? The administration to which they were subjected was suited neither to a conquered people nor to a proud people that thought itself unconquered. Jameson was no administrator, except in matters which excited his interest, of which the welfare of black Africans was not one. He had formed an exaggerated idea of his own abilities, which Rhodes shared, from the easy defeat of Lobengula. His subordinates were typical of a pioneering phase in their attitude to the Africans. (Olive Schreiner's *Trooper Peter Halket of Mashonaland* gives a harsh but not unfounded picture of them.) There were many standing grievances, to which was added early in 1896 an outbreak of the cattle disease known as *rinderpest*. Many cattle died of it; many others were slaughtered on the orders of the High Commissioner as a precaution. The Matabele were seething with bitterness, worked upon by their witch-doctors.

Jameson provided the opportunity for rebellion by withdrawing the Company's white police to raid the Transvaal. The native police, who remained, were looked upon by the Matabele with hatred untempered even with respect. The news that the white men were fighting each other, and that Jameson had been beaten and captured, was itself an incitement to the Matabele. Supported by an eclipse of the moon in February, the witch-doctors assured them that the hour to destroy the white man had come. The rising began in the middle of March, every white man within reach being brutally murdered, not excepting the women and children. Rhodes had reached Beira when the bloodshed began, and was already on his way to Salisbury when he first heard of the murders. He had another bout of malaria on his way inland, but nothing would stop him from intervening personally to avert the final disaster.

It is easy to guess why he had already decided to make for Rhodesia, and why he had chosen the route *via* East Africa. His future lay, if anywhere, in what he called the North: a leading article in *The Times* had told him so as he was leaving London in February, but he knew it already. Not only did he not want to return to the Cape for the time being; he did not even wish to pass through it on the way to his North. Many of his friends urged him to come to Cape Town for the opening of parliament at the end of April. Grey, Harris, Maguire and others all telegraphed to him in this sense, and some of them perhaps attributed his refusal to cowardice.[1] But if he came to the Cape, he would not only have to attend Parliament but also to attend the Select Committee, whose Report duly censured him for not doing so. All this would further endanger the Charter. His friends did not seem to realise how much more serious still was the danger in the North.

Rhodes had other reasons for the route he chose. When he left London, he was without any official occupation, and his time was his own. The natural task for the rest of his life was to consolidate the North by pushing ahead the transcontinental communications of which he had dreamed so long: the "all-red" route from the Cape to Cairo for his railway and telegraph. Egypt was the other terminus of the route, and he wished to see it. As it happened, the fateful preparations for re-entering the Sudan from Egypt were in progress at the same time, and the troops began to move on 12 March; but there is no reason to suppose that Rhodes had any interest in the operation. It was not until Kitchener took charge of the Sudanese operation, building a railway as fast as he advanced, that Rhodes began to take the same intensely personal interest in the advance from the north as in his own from the south. But that turning-point was still nearly a year away. If he had been asked in 1896 why he went to Egypt, he would probably have replied that it was for the practical purpose of buying donkeys to use in Rhodesia, or seeing what lessons could be learned there of agricultural value.

Having reached Salisbury *via* Beira just after the storm broke, Rhodes threw himself energetically into the task of organising the relief of threatened areas and counter-attacks against the Matabele. The authorities at Cape Town quickly realised that the rebellion was serious, perhaps more serious than Rhodes himself estimated. Regular officers were sent to organise counter-measures: Colonel Sir Richard Martin (later Deputy Commissioner of Rhodesia) to command the settlers' hurriedly raised territorial force; Lt. Colonel Herbert Plumer (later a Field-Marshal and a Viscount) to raise a Matabeleland Relief Force, starting from Mafeking; and finally General Sir Frederick Carrington in early June to take general command of the operation, with Colonel Baden-Powell (later the hero of Mafeking and founder of the Boy Scouts) as his Chief of Staff. For once Rhodes got on well with the senior officers, and took to military life. He even assumed the personal rank of Colonel without benefit of the Queen's commission, in order to impose his authority on two officers of equal rank who would serve under him but not under each other. Grey, who was now Administrator in Jameson's place, justified the irregularity in a letter to the High Commissioner, who apparently feared unfavourable comment in England. A medal struck by the British South Africa Company, which survives in the National Museum of Southern Rhodesia, bears the inscription: "Colonel the Right Hon. C. J. Rhodes, R.H.V." It would have amused him as a Privy Councillor, to know that he might be suspected of pretensions to military rank above his proper station in life.

Everyone who has written about Rhodes is agreed that this was his finest hour. The courage, tenacity, patience and wisdom which he displayed between April and October 1896 were not foreign to his nature, but they had never before been seen in effective combination. Courage, in the physical sense, did not in fact come naturally to him, as many who knew him bore witness. He could be brave on impulse, as when he set out one night to the rescue of a yacht caught by a storm in Table Bay. But he had not the cold-blooded indifference to danger which characterised, for instance, his friend Chinese Gordon. In the campaign against the Matabele, however, he became noted, almost with surprise, for his courage. McDonald, his estate manager and later his biographer, remarked on his "extreme coolness under the hottest fire", and recorded that he still insisted on wearing his customary white trousers, although they made him an easy mark. All who were with him in 1896 had similar comments and anecdotes. Fuller supposed that he was seeking atonement for the past, "careless of what became of him"; and whether he was right or wrong, the comment shows that Rhodes had taken his friends by surprise.

Another surprise was his ferocity towards the Matabele in the campaign. Contemporaries regarded Rhodes as exceptionally enlightened in his attitude towards natives, though they were judging him by their own standards and the standards of the time, which have long ceased to be acceptable. Many of them, particularly those of Boer descent, betray in their own writings attitudes towards native Africans which show how faint an enlightenment would have struck them as startling. One may quote, for instance, the odious account by Rhodes's secretary, Le Sueur, of his own treatment of Lobengula's sons, and of "a young reigning Sultan" on a visit to Groote Schuur, whom he regarded as just another nigger; or the bald assumption by two other Afrikaners in Rhodes's retinue, Hans Sauer and De Waal, that the Zimbabwe ruins could not have been built by Africans because the natives were congenitally incapable of creative activity. By their standards Rhodes was practically what he himself called disparagingly a 'negrophilist'. But Olive Schreiner and the missionaries saw him in a less favourable light. The best that could be said of him in this matter—and he often said it himself —was that he regarded the natives as children, who might one day attain the adult level of the white man but were still far from it. Even that was only true of him in theory. In practice it would be truer to say that he regarded them as domestic animals: which is not to imply cruelty, for Englishmen are usually kind to domestic animals. But unlike children, dogs are not expected to grow up into human adults; and unlike children, dogs may be shot when they get out of hand. That was certainly Rhodes's attitude to the Matabele in the early weeks of the rebellion.

He entered into the killing with gusto between April and July. Eye-witnesses describe how he would return to a scene of action after it was over, to count the African corpses again in order to settle an argument. He is reported to have advised a police officer in Rhodesia not to spare the natives when they threw down their arms and begged for mercy. "You should kill all you can," are the words attributed to him; "it serves as a lesson to them when they talk things over at night. They count up the killed, and say So-and-so is dead, and So-and-so is no longer here, and they begin to fear you." Such stories quickly gained circulation, because they fitted the mood of the Europeans of Rhodesia in the terror they were living through. The most bitter picture of their reaction to danger, and of Rhodes's in particular, is to be found in Olive Schreiner's contemporary novel, *Trooper Peter Halket of Mashonaland*. Rhodes is the undisguised villain of this story of the rising, the original edition of which contained a frontispiece photograph of a row of Africans hanging from trees, with armed and smiling Europeans posed beside them. It was suggested to Rhodes that he should issue a writ for libel against his former admirer in 1897, but he took no action.

Extreme severity in retaliation by the Europeans was probably the only alternative to surrender in the first stages of the rebellion; and at first it worked well enough. The main centres of population were soon safe from further threat. When Bulawayo was relieved early in June, Rhodes delivered a kind of victory speech there in which he looked optimistically to the future. They would become a self-governing body, he told the settlers; a "new state" in South Africa and a component in the "South African federation"; and the Charter would eventually lapse. But meanwhile it would continue to promote the development of the country, and his own ideas on that development "would begin and end with railways". He was anxious, however, not to be guilty of over-optimism, as he had been in the past about the prospects of gold-mining and the pacification of the Matabele. Of gold he said nothing; of the Matabele he warned his hearers that they were not like the Cape Kaffirs. "You meet them, and they suffer defeat one day, but the next day they reappear as if nothing had happened."[2]

Events were already beginning to convince Rhodes that repression was not the answer to the native problem. The Matabele had been repeatedly beaten in the field, but they had simply retired into the impenetrable Matopo hills, where a final victory over them was virtually impossible. Moreover, their neighbours and former subjects, the Mashona, supposedly a less warlike race, had also risen in revolt during June, and more than a year was to pass before they were beaten. In the course of July 1896 General Sir Frederick Carrington became pessimistic about the prospect of the operations. He wanted to retire into winter quarters and wait until the following year to resume the attack. Such a decision, though militarily sound, would have been extremely expensive; and a very large proportion of the expense was falling on the Chartered Company, which could not afford it. Rhodes had to find an alternative plan.

He was in a strangely exalted mood in the middle of 1896, as he often was in face of the challenge of adversity. It is apparent in the surviving fragments of his correspondence, such as the letter to Harcourt in the middle of May, repudiating "the idea of a sordid motive" for his part in the Raid; or the movingly frank letter to Schreiner of 3 July, in which he explained his motives more illuminatingly than at any other time; or even the quaint effusion to an unnamed Duchess, in which he told her that "you always make me feel that you are my exact idea of an Englishwoman". What is common to all these outpourings of his soul is that each is heavy with foreboding, explicit or tacit, with an awareness that in a few days he might be killed in action, leaving his life's work unfulfilled and even ruined by himself. Yet there is also a sense of exhilaration in them, a sense of meeting a great challenge to which he knew himself to be equal if he was spared from the *assegais* of the Matabele. It is to be found, too, in the anecdote of this period about his conversation with Grey, whom he woke up in the middle of the night in Bulawayo to share his suddenly realised delight at being alive, and in good health, and an Englishman.

He was living in a world of his own during those weeks, as it were among dreams that were more real than reality. The blows of reality glanced off him, and it was as well they did, for there were many of them. He heard of the condemnation of the Reformers in Pretoria, including his brother Frank, at the end of April; of the bitter debate in the Cape Assembly preceding the appointment of the Select Committee in May, and his own condemnation by that Enquiry in July; of the conviction of Jameson and his officers and the appointment of the House of Commons Select Committee at the end of July. On Jameson's conviction he commented that it was "a tribute to the upright rectitude of my countrymen who have jumped the whole world". Such words also belong to the unreal world in which Rhodes was now living, above good and evil; for he was commenting upon a reckless and ignoble crime, about which even his supporter Garrett had now admitted in the *Cape Times* that "of the theory of chivalrous audacity not a rag remains". Defiantly, and with perfect indifference, he transmitted through Hawksley his readiness to come home to stand trial whenever the British government might desire. That was at the end of July. A week later, in the only world that was immediately real to him, he had begun to turn a new dream into substance.

The Matabele were beaten in the field but not crushed. Rhodes had seen that they never would be crushed by military methods, and he sensed that they were willing to come to terms. He decided to try negotiation instead of force, even at the risk of his life. There are several first-hand accounts of the series of peace conferences (*indabas*) which took place from August to October, written either by participants or on the basis of first-hand accounts.[3] They differ, naturally, on details. In particular, how exactly the first contacts with the Matabele chiefs came about is uncertain: it is likely that many possible lines were simultaneously explored, and more than one bore results. It is also uncertain to what extent the military commanders were aware of the exploratory contacts before the conference began: probably there was a deliberate concealment at first, and a blind eye was turned when concealment was no longer possible. At any rate, there is no disagreement in any of the accounts that the initiative and imagination which gave substance to the elusive possibilities of peacemaking belong wholly to the credit of Rhodes. No other man could have retrieved the disastrous situation which the folly of his over-trusted subordinates had created.

The belief began to grow among the Europeans at quite an early stage that the Matabele were as anxious as themselves to end the bloodshed. Nevertheless the first contacts were abortive. Hans Sauer, the brother of Rhodes's former ministerial colleague and once Jameson's antagonist in Kimberley, claims in his memoirs, *Ex Africa . . .*, to have made the first approach to Lobengula's surviving brother, Likuni, who was living just

outside Bulawayo; but Likuni refused to help. Next he approached
Johan Colenbrander, who had once enjoyed the confidence of
both Lobengula and of Rhodes, but was now on bad terms with
the Rhodesian administration. Colenbrander, having no personal
quarrel with Rhodes, agreed to help, and sent two natives out to
carry a message to Sechombo, one of the rebel leaders in the
Matopos; but they too failed to produce any results, and never
returned. Colenbrander tried again, by using his influence on
two prisoners who had been captured from Sechombo's forces, to
convince them of the white men's good faith. In this he was
finally successful, but before he could use them as intermediaries,
a better opportunity occurred to use the services of John
Grootboom, a native scout of Tembu origin who could speak
both English and Matabele.

The first-hand accounts of Sauer and McDonald differ about
the circumstances in which Grootboom first became available.
Sauer says that he, Rhodes and Grimmer came across Grootboom
by chance on a chicken-hunting expedition, in the neighbourhood
of a *kraal* which turned out to be inhabited by several relatives of
Lobengula, including a widow of Lobengula's father, Mzilikazi.
The old woman was carried off to Rhodes's camp, and Grootboom pursued his contacts with the Matabele rebels on daily expeditions into the hills. At last he succeeded in meeting their
leaders. McDonald, on the other hand, says that Grootboom was
introduced into Rhodes's camp by an official of the Native De-
partment, and that Rhodes sent him out with two other natives
on an expedition into the Matopos, which lasted six days. They
learned of the possibilities of negotiation with the rebel leaders
through the fortunate chance of overhearing two old women
gossiping by a stream. After making contact with the chiefs, and
waiting several days to overcome their suspicions, Grootboom
was finally visited by "a very old woman" through whom he
finally met the chiefs and arranged a parley between them and
Rhodes. McDonald does not identify the old woman, but it may
well be that she was again the widow of Lobengula's father. Her
portrait, at any rate, hung in Groote Schuur to the end of Rhodes's
life, though it is uncertain how much she really contributed to the
events which led up to the negotiations. Grootboom's role,
however, was clearly crucial in all accounts.

Once Grootboom had reported that the rebel chiefs were
ready to meet Rhodes, the preparations for his entry into the
Matopos began; and so did General Carrington's objections,

Sketch of C. J. R. by General (later Lord) Baden-Powell in 1897

C. J. R. at "the View of the World" in the Matopo Hills (later the site of his grave)

which Rhodes overcame with difficulty. At first it was intended that an armed force should accompany Rhodes's party, or at least a group of officers, but Grootboom and Colenbrander insisted that their presence would be fatal. The Matabele were expecting only four or five men, unarmed; and the party was finally made up of Rhodes, Colenbrander, Sauer, Grootboom, James Makunga (a native interpreter who had accompanied Grootboom in the earlier contacts) and Vere Stent, a journalist who wrote a first-hand account of the adventure in the *Pretoria News*. Stent's account is much the best that survives, being almost contemporaneous, unlike Sauer's, and being also written by an eye-witness, unlike McDonald's. In later years the number of people who claimed to describe the famous *indaba* in the Matopos at first hand became ridiculous, and virtually nothing new has been added to the story by later hands except romantic fictions. Stent, Sauer and Colenbrander are reliable witnesses, and their accounts are usefully supplemented by that of McDonald who, with Grimmer, accompanied Rhodes's party on the first stage of its ride out of camp.

The meeting-place with the Matabele was four or five miles from the camp, in a small clearing among the hills approached by a narrow and precipitous track. On arrival the party halted by the remains of an ant-heap, where Rhodes ordered them to dismount as a gesture of confidence. Rhodes refused to show a white flag: that was for the Matabele to do, he said, and after a short interval they did so. Some twenty or thirty warriors—more, according to Sauer—then emerged from the surrounding scenery and gathered in a semi-circle round Rhodes. It was, as he said now or later, "one of those moments in life that make it worth living". Colenbrander was already sure that they were in no danger, the Matabele were resolved on peace. At his prompting, Rhodes opened the discussion with a Zulu phrase: "The eyes are white." The chiefs confirmed that the eyes were white, that peace was to be made, but first they wanted to speak to Rhodes as to their father. With Colenbrander as interpreter, the *indaba* then began. "We heard," says Stent, "a wonderful oration," by two chiefs in succession, Somabulane and Sechombo. It lasted, says Sauer, two and a half hours.

They began with a history of the Matabele people: their quarrel with Dingaan's Zulus, their battles with the Dutch and with the contemptible Mashona, their settlement in new lands and their struggles with the neighbouring Barotse, and the coming of

M

Rhodes's pioneers. They had been content to live as subjects under the conquering white men, but not to be treated as dogs. They complained of the insults and injuries of the Native Commissioners and Magistrates, and the oppression of the tax-collectors and native police. Rhodes told them that all these things would be rectified, but reproached them with murdering white women and children. Somabulane retorted that the Europeans had killed Matabele women and children first, and Colenbrander told Rhodes that this was unfortunately true. Rhodes promised redress of all their grievances, and the chiefs confirmed that there would be no more fighting. At nightfall the *indaba* broke up. Rhodes and his party rode back to camp, and Stent and Sauer went on to Bulawayo to telegraph the news to the world. Stent admits that they took the opportunity to buy Chartered Company shares before releasing their story, but he expressly denies that Rhodes made any such deal or had any opportunity to do so.

The first *indaba* was not the end of the matter. A second followed, because the chiefs wanted to see Sir Richard Martin as the Queen's representative. But Martin wanted to have an armed escort with him, and dropped out when Rhodes said this was impossible. Even without him, and without Sauer who had gone about his own business, the European party was larger on the second occasion. Stent was present again, and McDonald and Grimmer joined them, together with Colenbrander's wife and her sister. The Matabele gathering to meet them was less friendly on this occasion, because there was a party among the chiefs who wanted to continue the fight. The warriors came armed, and Rhodes's party found themselves surrounded at first by hostile and menacing faces. Rhodes rode in among them alone, and argued imperiously with the bellicose younger chiefs. Most of the elder chiefs supported Rhodes, delighted to see him stand up to their juniors in a way that they had not dared to do themselves. The meeting ended in another successful assertion of his personality over the hostile element, but the danger was not yet over, for the most truculent of the dissident chiefs were not present.

After the second *indaba*, Rhodes moved his camp in the direction of the area where Holi, the most recalcitrant of the diehards, had his hide-out. It took weeks of patient waiting before he joined in the general surrender, no doubt reduced by starvation rather than by any desire for peace. Meanwhile a succession of chiefs, including Babayan, who had been sent by Lobengula to see Queen Victoria years before, gathered at Rhodes's camp to pay homage and talk to the great white man, whom they now called "the Separator of the Fighting Bulls". McDonald's description of his patience and gentleness and even humility at this time makes without doubt the most attractive chapter in his biography. His indignation at the desecration of Mzilikazi's tomb by British soldiers, and the restitution which he made for it, were also characteristic of his better nature. Another side of his nature, not necessarily a lower one, was shown when he took the opportunity to have Mzilikazi's skull examined to see if he had a brain capacity commensurate with his great achievements; but it turned out to be disappointingly small.

The rebellion was over, and finished for good. No further conflict took place between Europeans and Africans in Rhodesia south of the Zambesi during Rhodes's lifetime, or for many years after. The last *indaba* took place in the neighbourhood of Bulawayo on 13 October. Nothing remained to settle except the details of restoring a tolerable existence to the Matabele, to whom Rhodes, as a beginning, gave 4,500 bags of mealies at his own expense. Civilian officials and more ladies were present at the later meetings: Grey, as Administrator, and Lady Grey; and Sir Richard Martin, whom the Matabele chiefs specially revered as the representative of the Queen. George Wyndham had also arrived, and it was with him and Grey that Rhodes accidentally found the spot in the hills which he called the "View of the World", and where he chose to be buried.

Rhodes's mind then turned confidently to thoughts of peace and reconstruction. It was at this time that he chose the site of his farm at Inyanga, and commissioned McDonald to buy 100,000 acres for him and to construct a dam to irrigate them. The moment when the tension eased after a time of great anxiety and danger, was, as so often in Rhodes's life, the moment when he turned to the land for relief. Nothing would have pleased him more, according to his intimate friends, than to give up the struggle of public life and empire-building in favour of leisure on his vast agricultural estates. But he was cursed with the conviction that he was cast for the role of Cincinnatus, just as Jameson believed that he was cast for that of Clive. He still believed that his political career was not ended but just beginning.

Sources

Baden-Powell, Sir R.: *The Matabele Campaign*
Gardiner, A. G.: *The Life of Sir William Harcourt*
Innes, James Rose: *Autobiography*
Sauer, Hans: *Ex Africa* . . .
Schreiner, Olive: *Trooper Peter Halket of Mashonaland*
Stent, Vere: *A Personal Record of some Incidents in the Life of Cecil Rhodes*
Tredgold, Sir Robert: *The Matopos*
Walker, E. A.: *W. P. Schreiner—A South African*

Notes

[1] Michell, II. 152; Rhodes Papers, C. 2. 140; C. 3B. 277; C. 27. 63.
[2] "Vindex", 483–8.

[3] Stent, 27–62; Sauer, 309–24; Mc-Donald 247–72. Colenbrander also published his own account in *South Africa*, vol. 33, 1897.

CHAPTER TWENTY-ONE

PRELIMINARIES TO THE ENQUIRY

THE arrival of Wyndham at Rhodes's camp was a reminder of another subject which could not be put out of mind much longer. There was no longer any possibility of evading the Enquiry by the Select Committee of the House of Commons into the Raid, even though it had been put temporarily in abeyance at the end of the last parliamentary session. It is not known what passed between Wyndham and Rhodes, but it may be assumed that Rhodes was now finally convinced that the Charter could be saved by shielding Chamberlain and the Colonial Office from censure. He made his plans accordingly. It was necessary for him to attend the Enquiry himself, not only because he had given his word to submit himself to judgment, but also to make sure that his more obstinate supporters, such as Hawksley and Harris, did not disobey his instructions and reveal their evidence of Chamberlain's role. On the other hand, Grey must at all costs be prevented from attending the Enquiry, since his well-known honesty would hardly be proof against thorough questioning. Rhodes telegraphed Hawksley accordingly:[1]

"Grey's presence is indispensable here. I do not know who can take his place. It is true we are through the war but it will require great tact during next six months to administer and carry out new native policy. Surely some consideration should be given to this country as well as to the London Committee. If his evidence is essential it can be given later on. It would be better to take it here."

In the event Grey was never summoned. His absence was one of the many elements in the story of the Enquiry which made it appear to hostile critics to be a calculated fraud.

Rhodes could not be satisfied, however, merely to safeguard the Charter and its territory. There was also the unsettled status of the Bechuanaland Protectorate, which the Raid had left in the air. Rhodes still argued that it had been promised to the Chartered Company both by Chamberlain and by Ripon, and that the episode of the Raid did not affect those promises in the slightest degree. Moreover, without the Protectorate he would have no control

357

over communications between the Cape Colony and Rhodesia; and communications—meaning the railway and the telegraph— were now the passion of his life since he was out of active party politics. The Bechuana chiefs were less content with the *status quo ante*, into which they had been rushed by Chamberlain in November 1895. Khama, the most important of them, tried to abrogate the agreement. Rhodes, who had been indignant enough at the terms on which he was to have had the Protectorate a year before, was not prepared to let it slip altogether on account of a blunder which, in his view, had nothing to do with the case.

His argument was set out in a long telegram sent on his behalf to the Chartered Company in Cape Town on 27 November by Metcalfe:[2]

"Have seen Mr. Rhodes, he maintains his position about Khama's agreement and Protectorate and it is his duty to shareholders to see that their interests are not sacrificed whatever may be the cost to himself but he is quite willing that correspondence should go home by letter not by cable but he wishes the Imperial Secretary and His Excellency to understand he does not consider that anything should be changed as to the Protectorate merely on account of the Jameson Raid, and if such a policy is intended he should like to have early intimation as he would have to consider his position as regards the shareholders, apart from which his own opinion is that proper policy for the future is the constitution of a self-governing state working with the Cape stretching from Mafeking to Tanganyika. However he agrees that nothing can be done until he reaches London and after the enquiry in the House of Commons, he however hopes that meantime no steps will be taken which would embarrass this solution. Mr. Rhodes would be glad if you would show this telegram to the Imperial Secretary for the information of His Excellency. Further as to a settlement between the Charter and the people he sees no difficulty when they are ripe for self-government but he would point out that the Charter are the only body that can do it as they possess everything in the country excepting the air."

Though the sender was Metcalfe, the style is the jaunty style of Rhodes at the height of his confidence. The prospect of the Enquiry now worried him little, but his supporters were none the less worried on his behalf. W. T. Stead and F. E. Garrett devised between them the extraordinary notion of concocting a semi-fictional version of the Raid, to be released simultaneously in London and Cape Town at Christmas, as a means of mitigating Rhodes's offence by setting the story in a wider context. Stead wrote the story under the title of *The History of the Mystery* with no attempt at concealment of the principal characters: Rhodes, Chamberlain, Jameson, Kruger, Robinson, Bower, Rutherfoord Harris, and even Flora Shaw, all appear under easily penetrable pseudonyms. (Chamberlain, for instance, was disguised as Blastus, King Herod's chamberlain in the Acts of the Apostles.) Stead clearly had access to confidential information about the Raid, and he knew about the incriminating telegrams. There is no doubt that the energetic Hawksley was his source, and it is in his letters to Hawksley that Stead's intention in publishing *The History of the Mystery* is most clearly seen.[3]

There was a considerable correspondence between the two men during and after the preparation and publication of the *History*. When recriminations were in full flood between the various parties at the beginning of 1897, Stead wrote a letter to Hawksley on 27 January which clearly sets out his own motives and intentions. It clarifies a number of points which have been disputed. Firstly, it asserts that the idea of the publication was Stead's alone: no one put him up to it, and he would have done it in any case even if Hawksley had refused to help him. "Your share in it," he told Hawksley, "was limited almost entirely to eliminating or modifying statements or expressions, which you considered might possibly be detrimental to the interests of Mr. Rhodes." Secondly, he had not actually seen the telegrams in Hawksley's famous dossier. He reproaches Hawksley on this point: he would have been greatly helped by a glimpse of them; "but as you know I have never seen them even to this day." Thirdly, he repudiates as "monstrous" the current complaint that "but for the publication of my story, the Select Committee would never have been held". On the contrary, he wrote the *History* only after being privately assured, in the most categorical terms, by the Leader of the House of Commons, Arthur Balfour, that the Enquiry could not be avoided.

He had then written the *History* on the justifiable assumption that the telegrams were bound to be published and were bound to do harm. But he made certain miscalculations: he did not foresee that some of the most damaging telegrams would be suppressed, and he was wrong in taking Chamberlain's downfall for granted. Nor did he assess correctly the effect which his own publication would have on the course of events, particularly as it was accompanied by blunders which almost reproduced, on a minor scale, the fiasco of the Raid.

What Stead was up to had become common gossip several weeks before the date of publication. A proof copy was in Garrett's hands in Cape Town in November. It was obvious to him, and to many others who heard more or less detailed accounts of what it contained, that Stead's work, with its open hint at Hawksley's dossier of telegrams, would make it inevitable for the Select Committee to demand all such documents to be produced. In other words, Chamberlain's complicity would probably be revealed. To Garrett this could only be a matter of suspicion, but to others, such as Fairfield and Hawksley, it was an inescapable fact. Fairfield and Hawksley, as it happened, would have welcomed publication of the telegrams, but Hawksley knew that Rhodes would not. At this point Rhodes intervened himself, with a telegram through Milton (his former secretary, now Chief Secretary and later Administrator at Salisbury) dated 28 November: [4]

"Send following cable from me to Harris and also to Maguire: Begins, I am strongly against any attack on Chamberlain or Colonial Office inform Hawksley of this. The book sent to me had no attack on Chamberlain or Colonial Office. If any additions have been made making such an attack they must be removed before publication. Ends."

It is not clear what version Rhodes had seen, but it would be surprising if he interpreted Stead's original version as containing no attacks on Chamberlain or the Colonial Office. His intervention, at any rate, caused Harris to approach Stead, who agreed to black out all references to the incriminating telegrams. It was too late to re-set all the type, so that the booklet as published in London had a sinister and suspicious appearance. It was also too late to stop Garrett at Cape Town from publishing an extensive review in the *Cape Times* on 8 December, in which he quoted some of the very passages that Stead had blacked out. The attempt to help Rhodes had thus ended in a fiasco so far as Rhodes's own tactics were concerned. There was at best a certain melancholy satisfaction for Hawksley, who was conniving at Rhodes's tactics with extreme repugnance. He telegraphed to Cape Town on 5 January: [5]

"Received your telegram and Maguire's of 3 January. Of course every step must be taken in order to prevent production of telegrams but whether or not produced evidence must be given to effect that communications with Colonial Office in 1895 by Rt. Hon. Earl Grey, Mr. Beit, Mr. Maguire, Dr. Harris (passage torn) as already stated in our letter to E. Fairfield of 20 August and that those in Africa in acting relied on these communications. Happily Mr. Rhodes and Dr Jameson being then in Africa are not involved by merely acting on advices received. Gratefully admit you have absolutely followed advice given and confident all (it) will be right."

A few weeks later he wrote personally to Rhodes savagely attacking Chamberlain (whom he accused of making insinuations about himself amounting to "a charge of professional misconduct") and adding: [6]

". . . Ever since the Government promised the House of Commons that an enquiry should be made I have never wavered in my opinion that the whole truth must come out and each person take the responsibility properly attaching to him. Any other course must lead to disaster.

"I believe the tactics now proposed are wrong and will do much harm. . . ."

Rhodes was already in London by this date and the Select Committee was formally re-appointed by the House of Commons on 29 January.

* * *

Rhodes had travelled to England by way of Salisbury, where he spent most of December; thence to Beira, where he wished to make arrangements for the completion of the railway inland to Mashonaland; thence to Port Elizabeth and Cape Town, where he was not yet sure of his reception, despite encouraging telegrams and invitations from his supporters in advance. The last weeks of 1896 were still dogged for him by bad news. The settlers of Rhodesia were full of grievances, which Rhodes paid out more than £10,000 on the spot from his own pocket to appease. There was a stormy Extraordinary General Meeting of the Chartered Company in London in November over the underwriting of an issue of new shares; there was even discord among the Directors and eventually the Duke of Fife resigned from the Board, though he took another fifteen months to do so. Another blow was that Rhodes's beloved house outside Cape Town, Groote Schuur, was burned to the ground on the night of 15 December. Finally, Jameson underwent a serious operation, for which he was released from imprisonment. Only this last news moved Rhodes at all. The story is well known (though his graceless secretary, Le Sueur, cast doubt upon it), that when Grey was in the process of breaking the news to him about Groote Schuur, Rhodes went white with agony at the thought that he was about to say Jameson was dead.

Better news began to greet him as he approached the Cape. Stevens, the Company secretary, telegraphed from the Company office on 14 December promising him a "great reception", with corroboration from his devoted Bondsman, De Waal.[7] He had a foretaste at Port Elizabeth, where he made an exuberant speech on 23 December. "I was told that my public life was at an end," he declared, "but the first thing I told them was that it was only beginning." He assured his hearers that there would be no recurrence of the Matabele rebellion (though the Mashonas were still not yet beaten); the creation of a new state in the North was a step towards the union of South Africa; and in that union "the question of race" never occurred to his mind (by which, as always, he meant that there should be no conflict between British and Boers). It was also in this speech that he first referred to the "unctuous rectitude" of his countrymen, which he was going to face.[8] Alarmed friends tried to persuade him to modify the phrase—to substitute "anxious" for "unctuous". But he would not do so; he liked the phrase, and repeated it. The population of Port Elizabeth, predominantly British, received him rapturously. To them, as Lord Loch wrote from England to De Villiers a few days later, it was like the return of a prodigal son, because they had always regarded Rhodes as too much of an "Afrikander"— that is to say, pro-Boer.

At Cape Town on 27 December his reception was even more enthusiastic. It took him less by surprise, partly because of what had already happened at Port Elizabeth and partly because he had already received, and accepted by telegram, an invitation to a public meeting, though he had stressed that he would have preferred to avoid it.[9] At the public reception, his friend Fuller saw him in tears, and heard him say: "Such appreciation as this generally comes after a man is dead." Fuller entertained him to dinner that night with thirty parliamentary colleagues, to whom he spoke frankly afterwards of "his great mistake". At Fuller's urgent entreaty, he agreed to make the same admission in public on the following day, and did so. Then he left for Kimberley, where he made a typically hard-headed and practical speech to the Annual General Meeting of De Beers.[10] The immediate prelude to his departure for England could hardly have been more satisfactory.

When he sailed from Cape Town early in January, he shared the *Dunvegan Castle* with an odd assortment of fellow-passengers. There was his sister Edith accompanying him, and also his faithful henchmen, Hans Sauer and Johnny Grimmer. There was Colonel Baden-Powell on his way home from the Matabele war and R. T. Coryndon, one of the pioneers of Mashonaland and later British Resident in North-Western Rhodesia. There was Olive Schreiner, carrying with her the manuscript of *Trooper Peter Halket of Mashonaland* for publication in England—a bitter and in some respects unjust attack upon Rhodes personally, with whom she was no longer on speaking terms. And there was F. E. Garrett of the *Cape Times*, with whom Rhodes discussed how he would occupy his time if he were sent to prison, as he still seriously thought possible. They evidently agreed also to make a final effort to avert the Enquiry, and each of them visited Chamberlain for this purpose shortly after reaching London, Garrett on 25 January and Rhodes the following day.

Chamberlain would undoubtedly have liked to oblige them, but he could not do so in the face of critics in the House of Commons. Nor could he tell those critics, who were chiefly out for Rhodes's blood rather than his own, that it was to protect himself rather than Rhodes that he would have liked to avoid the Enquiry. Sir William Harcourt, for instance, who was continually pressing for the Enquiry from the Liberal front bench, was nevertheless convinced of Chamberlain's innocence. He even joined in urging Chamberlain to be chairman of the Select Committee himself. No evidence has ever been produced for the story that he deliberately let Chamberlain down lightly because he knew the truth and knew also that Rosebery, the Liberal leader until his resignation in October 1896, had himself been a party to the plot. The story was widely canvassed in later years, among others by some who claimed to have heard it from Rhodes himself. In the absence of reliable proof, it is difficult to believe. It is certain in any case that Harcourt never wavered in his insistence on an Enquiry, though he was prepared to be co-operative in the selection of its members.

The rest of the Select Committee were chosen, in accordance with custom, to reproduce the balance of the parties in the House of Commons. Given that the principal target of the Enquiry was Rhodes, its composition presented no particular danger to Chamberlain. Sir Henry Campbell-Bannerman, the principal Liberal member besides Harcourt, was equally convinced of Chamberlain's innocence. Henry Labouchere, the Radical, was much more suspicious of Chamberlain, but no less determined than the others to make Rhodes his principal victim. George Wyndham, the imperialist Conservative, was a friend of both Chamberlain and Rhodes. The other members of the Select Committee had no *parti pris* in the matter of the Raid, though Edward Blake, an Irish Nationalist, may be supposed to have been hostile to Chamberlain without being predisposed towards Rhodes. (No doubt he knew, however, that Rhodes had once given financial support to Parnell.) The Attorney-General, Sir Richard Webster, and the Chancellor of the Exchequer, Sir Michael Hicks-Beach, should have been solely concerned to elicit the truth; but neither suspected Chamberlain and both disapproved of Rhodes. The same may be fairly assumed of the others, none of whom played a forceful role: W. L. Jackson, the chairman (later Lord Allerton), Sir William Hart-Dyke, C. A. Cripps (later Lord Parmoor), J. C. Bigham (later Viscount Mersey) and J. L. Wharton on the Conservative side; John Ellis and Sydney Buxton on the Liberal side. But for all their good intentions, the conspiracy to conceal the truth from them already rested on secure foundations.

Chamberlain had laid his plans early. Wyndham had been sent to Rhodes in August 1896. Bower had been bullied into writing his confession in November, incriminating himself but not the High Commissioner or Colonial Secretary. Grey was safely out of the way in Rhodesia and Chamberlain had written to him giving reasons for not producing the notorious telegrams, which were well calculated to satisfy Grey's conscience; he told him that their disclosure might "be used by the enemies of England, both on the Continent and in the Transvaal, and would seriously embarrass future action". Selborne was completely loyal, and indeed hardly less implicated than Chamberlain himself. Rhodes seemed to have accepted the proffered bargain. His solicitor, Bourchier Hawksley, was difficult: hence the attempt to discredit him in Rhodes's eyes to which Hawksley's letter of 28 January refers. Some of Chamberlain's own subordinates were also difficult. One of them, Lambert, actually pointed out to the Colonial Secretary that he was using contradictory arguments, when he claimed firstly that he did not know about the concentration of Jameson's force at Pitsani, and secondly that it was justified. To Meade he admitted what was undeniable, that "I knew all about the revolution; I knew nothing of anything so mad as Jameson's raid."

Of Chamberlain's subordinates, Fairfield and Bower were the most difficult, because they had been chosen as his scapegoats. Bower was a retired naval officer: upright, loyal and patriotic as the best of his kind, and unaccustomed to being ordered to lie for Queen and Country. But he was also naïve. He believed that by agreeing to lie he had averted a war. He believed that such a war would otherwise have been launched either by Chamberlain, to forestall the Enquiry, or by Kruger, as soon as he learned that the High Commissioner, whom he warmly respected, had also been implicated in the plot. He even believed that he would be let down lightly at the Enquiry, and later rehabilitated and rewarded after a token punishment. With these simple ideas, Bower was a hopeless witness. He made a perfect hash of his "confession", which he wrote early in November 1896 and tried to withdraw two months later, on the ground that he had thought of a better defence. It might have been foreseen that he would break down under interrogation, as he did. Fairfield, on the other hand, an experienced Civil Servant with no illusions, would have put up a better front, however much he disliked it. But his premature death in April 1897 silenced him for ever before the Select Committee could call him. It has been suggested that his end was hastened by the knowledge that he was to be sacrificed to shield his master, the Colonial Secretary, just as Bower was sacrificed to shield his, the High Commissioner.

The High Commissioner himself, now Lord Rosmead, presented Chamberlain with one of his most awkward problems. He had been prevented from attending the Cape Enquiry in 1896 by being called to London for consultation. Could he now be prevented from attending the Westminster Enquiry by being detained at the Cape? It might seem intolerable and even disrespectful to the House of Commons, but there was one circumstance which could make it acceptable. Lord Rosmead's age and deteriorating health made him obviously ripe for retirement; but his successor had still to be appointed, and it would not do to leave the post untenanted for too long an interval. Chamberlain decided in January to appoint Sir Alfred Milner to be the new High Commissioner. The post was offered to Milner on 18

January and announced early in February. Discussion of the terms of his appointment, together with farewell dinners, occupied the whole of March and extended into April. Milner sailed for South Africa on 17 April and arrived at the Cape on 5 May. Since the Select Committee began its sittings on 5 February it was certain that Lord Rosmead could not be available for it, however prematurely he left Cape Town; he sailed, in fact, on 21 April. His contributions were therefore limited to telegraphic protestations on reports of the evidence which displeased him. On these he could not be examined. When he returned to England, it was already too late; he was a dying man, and survived only until October 1897.

One by one the dangers were thus removed. It was a matter of relief not only to Chamberlain but to Rhodes also, since the preservation of the Charter was now firmly linked to the protection of Chamberlain's secret.

When the Enquiry opened, Rhodes and Chamberlain were already virtually accomplices. A by-product of the Raid, on which they saw perfectly eye to eye, came up to be dealt with at this time and to seal their accord. President Kruger had claimed compensation for the Raid on an extravagant scale, which Chamberlain had no intention of meeting. The conduct of the Transvaal Government at the turn of the year 1896–97 was in any case not such as to incline the British Government to be conciliatory. They had suppressed a prominent English newspaper, *The Critic*, in December, and passed the Aliens Expulsion Law and the Immigration Law, both directed against the *Uitlanders* and both, in Chamberlain's view, contrary to the Convention of 1884. In January 1897 a dispute had broken out between the Transvaal Government and its Chief Justice, on the right of the courts to test legislation by reference to the Constitution (*Grondwet*), which Kruger proposed to solve by simply passing a new law repudiating the existence of any such right. In despair of dealing with the Transvaal Government as reasonable men, Chamberlain was meditating a strong *démarche* (which was in fact presented in April) and had been restrained only with great reluctance from sending military and naval reinforcements to South Africa at the end of 1896.

It was in this climate of hostility that Kruger's formal claim for compensation was received. Chamberlain consulted Rhodes, who consulted Michell and Beit. Beit replied on 29 January that he agreed with Rhodes that "practically the Transvaal has on balance no claim against us", but he undertook to see Chamberlain and Selborne on Rhodes's behalf. Michell went further: in a reply dated 1 February, he argued that both the Raid and the abortive rising in Johannesburg cost the Transvaal Government very little, and that if anything they made a profit on both, thanks to the equipment captured from Jameson and the fines paid for the release of the Reformers. The actual cost of the whole fiasco can probably never be assessed, but there exists an account prepared on Beit's instructions in November 1897 showing that Wernher, Beit & Co. paid out "in connection with Johannesburg Rising and Jameson Raid" a total of over £300,000, a figure which Rhodes himself later raised to £400,000. Most of this was repaid by Rhodes personally and it was certainly not the whole of his outlay. He had no inclination to pay any more to soothe Kruger's ruffled feelings, nor was Chamberlain inclined to press him. No settlement of Kruger's claim was ever reached. It was still outstanding when the Boer War swallowed it up with so much else of South African history.[11]

* * *

While waiting for the Enquiry to begin, Rhodes was still busy with other interests. Shortly after his arrival in London, he received a telegram from Kitchener, now the Sirdar (Commander-in-Chief) in Cairo, asking if he could spare the "three locomotives Gordon asked you for", evidently to assist his advance into the Sudan. Rhodes at once agreed. This was the beginning of an intermittent but constant telegraphic correspondence between the two men, almost always concerned with their respective advances into the interior of Africa; though their railway lines were never to meet, as Rhodes hoped they would, and it was never seriously the intention of any government at Westminster that they should.

Another of Rhodes's favourite projects at the time was the purchase of land in South Africa for British settlers on a large scale. His banker and biographer, Sir Lewis Michell, records that Rhodes bombarded him with cablegrams urging expedition in this matter while he was in London. It was another of the dreams which never caught the imagination of British Ministers in time, but which they perhaps mildly welcomed as helping to keep Rhodes out of mischief. It also served another purpose—to remind him painfully that there was now bad blood between British and Boers. A Boer friend, T. J. Louw, wrote to tell him of the hostility of Dutch farmers in the Cape Colony towards him;

and his agent, Syfret, reported that many Boers were reluctant to sell farms to British buyers.[12]

His heart and imagination were still in Africa while the "unctuous rectitude" of his countrymen kept him physically in London. Although he had no official position at this time, everything in southern Africa still revolved about him, and everything that was going on was reflected in his correspondence, whether it was officially his business or not: the affairs of De Beers, which still was his business, and of the Chartered Company, which was not; the construction of the railway and the telegraph; the pacification of the territories which now inalienably bore his name, and the settlement of the Bechuanaland Protectorate, whose future was in the melting pot.

De Beers presented no problems: the diamond industry was "becoming a matter of course and uninteresting", as he had told the shareholders in Kimberley in December. It went "like clockwork". That did not prevent some awkward disagreements between Rhodes and the London Board, though these had not yet come to a head.

The Chartered Company and the North were another matter. Nominally Rhodes had no *locus standi*, but in practice his former subordinates were so accustomed to writing to him that they continued regularly to do so: Grey and Milton from Bulawayo and Salisbury; Stevens, the Company Secretary, from Cape Town. Thus Rhodes was kept privately, no doubt irregularly, in touch with the things that touched him most nearly: the state of the Mashona rebellion, which was expected to flare up again in January 1897, and was not finally crushed until October; the plans for a new *trek* of European settlers into the Bechuanaland Protectorate; the criticisms which Sir Richard Martin had passed on the administration of Rhodesia, which filled Rhodes with indignation; the question of Rhodesia joining a customs union with the Colonies, on which Rhodes advised delay; the advance of the railway from Mafeking towards Bulawayo, and of the telegraph still farther northwards. It was impossible for anyone who had once had dealings with Rhodes to treat him as if he were merely a private citizen with no legitimate concern in such official matters. His advice was law to his devotees, even when other men were nominally their masters.[13]

He saw much of Jameson during the time of waiting. They had not met since the Raid. Jameson had been released from prison in failing health; he was depressed and doubtful how Rhodes would regard him. But Rhodes sought him out of his own accord, and Jameson's brief records of their first meetings show that his doubts were quickly set at rest. "C. J. Rhodes is here in capital form, and is going to come out all right," he wrote to a friend on 5 February: "Commission a nuisance, but can't be helped." They met "very often", but Jameson avoided visiting Rhodes at the Burlington Hotel, where he was staying. The friendship was renewed as if nothing had happened, or rather as if it had been purified and strengthened in the fire. For the rest of his life Rhodes continued to claim Jameson as his constant companion, and the only doctor whose advice he could really trust. Friendship, loyalty and the sharing of a great vision meant infinitely more to Rhodes than the mere questions of right and wrong which were about to be scrutinised by the unimaginative men at Westminster.

Sources

Works mentioned under Chapters Seventeen and Eighteen and additionally:

Hicks-Beach, Lady V.: *The Life of Sir Michael Hicks-Beach*
James, R. V. Rhodes: *Rosebery*
Mackail, J. W. & Wyndham, Guy: *The Life and Letters of George Wyndham*
Spender, J. A.: *The Life of the Rt. Hon. Sir Henry Campbell-Bannerman*
Stead, W. T.: *Joseph Chamberlain: Conspirator or Statesman?*
Thorold, Algar: *The Life of Henry Labouchere*

Notes

1 Rhodes Papers, B. 141 (undated, probably Dec. 1896).
2 Rhodes Papers, B. 97.
3 Rhodes Papers, C. 11. 1 (enclosures).
4 Rhodes Papers, B. 98.
5 Rhodes Papers, C. 4. 1 (addressee unnamed).
6 Rhodes Papers, C. 11. 1 (enclosure).
7 Rhodes Papers, C. 3. 290.
8 "Vindex", 495–506.
9 Rhodes Papers, B. 142.
10 "Vindex", 808–17.
11 Rhodes Papers, C. 24. 63 (Beit); C. 15. 5 (Michell); C. 24. 50 (cost of Raid).
12 Rhodes Papers, C. 2. 157 (Louw); C. 21. 2 (Syfret).
13 Rhodes Papers, C. 1. 1 (Grey to Rhodes); C. 17. 1. seq. (Ngani Trek); B. 315 (Rhodes to Stevens on Charter administration); B. 267 (Rhodes to Grey on Customs Union).

CHAPTER TWENTY-TWO

THE SELECT COMMITTEE

On 16 February Rhodes had to come back to earth at last, when he was called before the Select Committee for the first time. The Committee was charged with two functions:

"... to inquire into the origin and circumstances of the Incursion into the South African Republic by an Armed Force, and into the Administration of the British South Africa Company, and to Report thereon. . . ."

It sat normally twice a week so that the six sittings over which Rhodes's examination was spread occupied three weeks, beginning on 16 February and ending on 5 March. The long period of time accounts for the very different impression created by Rhodes at the beginning and the end of his examination. In spite of his contemptuous indifference to the Enquiry, he was involuntarily overawed by the august surroundings at first. Brett described him after the second sitting on 19 February as "pitiful", and all accounts agreed that he was nervous and ill at ease. After his last appearance before the Committee, however, it was no less generally agreed that he had "got the better of them".

His method of turning the tables was to enlarge the scope of the Enquiry to the scale of his own vision of Africa. From the first he insisted that the Raid was only a detail in a much larger canvas. In his opening statement he made the crucial admissions which were, from his point of view, all that needed to be said on the side-issue of the Raid, namely that "Dr. Jameson went in without my authority" and that "I am willing generally to accept the finding as to facts contained in the Report of the Committee of the Cape Parliament". But that was only the beginning of the matter. What he wanted to make the Select Committee understand was the broader picture: the intolerable grievances of the *Uitlanders*; the danger of Germany intruding in a British sphere of influence; the importance of developing practically virgin territories (including the Bechuanaland Protectorate as well as Rhodesia, South and North) through the only practicable medium, that of the Chartered Company; the goal of union for South Africa under the British flag. Most of this was contained, in essence, in his opening statement. All of it had become explicit and taken on clear and firm substance before he withdrew three weeks later.

But the first day went badly for him. Some eye-witnesses—and there were two future biographers among them—thought him nervous, others thought him haughty and condescending; all agreed that he made an unfavourable impression. At first he answered in abrupt monosyllables. The impression he no doubt wanted to create was that of a blunt, practical Colonial unused to the finesses of Westminster politicians; a plain man who had erred and admitted it and had nothing to conceal. Unfortunately he had much to conceal by virtue of his understanding with Chamberlain, and when Harcourt—his principal interrogator for the first two sessions—began to put his finger on the sensitive spot, Rhodes's answers ceased to be simple and straightforward and became rambling and incoherent. His equivocation began at the 94th question, when Harcourt drew his attention to the claim in his statement that he had been acting within his rights in placing a force on the borders of the Transvaal. If so, asked Sir William, was there any reason why he should not have informed the High Commissioner that he was so doing? "You want an answer?" replied Rhodes in a lame attempt to gain time; and on being pressed, he told his interrogator to ask the High Commissioner himself.

The question was not pressed further: Rhodes had thus established the right to refuse to answer any question which would incriminate another person. Nor was he seriously pressed later in the day, when he refused to say whether the "Chairman", who had been urged by his brother Frank to come to Johannesburg for the "flotation", was or was not the High Commissioner—though at the second session he admitted the identification. The reason why Rhodes was not further pressed was no doubt simply that the majority of the Select Committee had tacitly agreed to protect the Queen's representatives, both at Cape Town and in London, in the national interest. Among the leaders of the Government and Opposition on the Committee this was due partly to politic expediency which needed no discussion, and partly to a genuine conviction of the innocence of Chamberlain and Robinson. The minorities on the Committee, represented at opposite extremes by Labouchere and Wyndham, concurred for different reasons: Labouchere because he wanted only to destroy Rhodes, and Wyndham because he was privy to the understanding with Chamberlain. Rhodes began to sense, probably by the end of the first sitting and certainly at the second, which followed three days later, that he had the Select Committee at his mercy. Their conflicting interests cancelled each other out and coincided only in opposing the revelation of the truth about the role of Her Majesty's representatives.

At the second session, in the intervals between giving offhand answers to questions of detail about the conspiracy, Rhodes began to lecture the Committee about the broader picture. He explained his motives for promoting the revolution at Johannesburg, which were not to destroy the Republic but to bring it into a South African federation under the English flag. "You might be sure, sir," he told Harcourt, "that I was not going to risk my position to change President Kruger for President J. B. Robinson." The well-chosen phrase helped to raise the level of the whole enterprise from a squalid adventure to a patriotic act of statesmanship. A man of vision, with such goals in mind, could not be expected to pay too much attention to trivial details. "I knew the broad thing that was going to happen," he admitted, but he could not be expected to have read every telegram that went out in his name. This legitimate contention paved the way for his first refusal, near the end of the day, to produce the cables that had passed between London and Cape Town before the Raid. As to written instructions, for which he might be held more directly responsible, he declared loftily that "I never write letters". It was nearly true, and it contributed neatly to the self-portrait of the Colossus.

At his third appearance before the Committee, on 23 February, Rhodes treated his interrogators to a still wider view of the international scene. He compared the situation in the Transvaal to that in Crete, where Greek troops had landed a few days before to try to liberate the island from Turkish rule. In both cases, he implied, the use of force by the oppressed and the intervention of their compatriots were perfectly natural. That did not mean, however, that he had ordered or sanctioned Dr. Jameson's action. The force at Pitsani, as he saw it, might have been used only after a rising at Johannesburg, or it might never have been used at all, on the assumption of a successful and bloodless rising. He agreed that Jameson had no precise instructions, but merely knew his "general views". When he was confronted with Bobby White's quotation of his saying that "you cannot expect a Prime Minister to write down that you are to seize ports, etc., but when he gives you orders to the contrary, disobey them", Rhodes replied with dignity: "You often speak more freely at your dining-table than you would in public, because you do not expect what you say to be reported." It was a well-calculated appeal to the instinctive ethics of the honourable gentlemen who confronted him, and it sufficed.

When he appeared for the fourth time on 26 February, Rhodes was fully master of the situation. He successfully resisted again the attempt to compel him to produce the cables exchanged between himself and Harris before the Raid, with the enigmatic excuse that he was not in possession of his communications. (The clue to the enigma is that the telegrams lay at that very moment in his Counsel's bag; so at least Rhodes told Rosebery, who recorded it in his betting-book, in May of the following year.) He demanded that his actions should be judged by the objects which he had in view, meaning the unification of South Africa. When Labouchere began questioning him for the first time, he admitted, though not without some initial evasion, that the foreign power whose intervention in South Africa he dreaded was Germany; and the recollection of the Kaiser's telegram would have been enough to restore public opinion to his side. Labouchere was by far the most pertinacious of his interrogators, but by this time Rhodes was confident enough of himself to counter-attack pugnaciously. He rebutted Labouchere's argument that the Cape Colony was following a protectionist policy; he dismissed the question of the flag as unimportant; he even surmounted without difficulty the awkward introduction of Flora Shaw's name for the first time. As for Labouchere's attempts to force him to incriminate Chamberlain, he lightly side-stepped them again and again by invoking his self-adopted rule about not "getting into third parties". He finished the day with a flourish by gratuitously telling the Committee that he had not read Stead's *History of the Mystery*, which was almost certainly an untruth.

By the following session, on 2 March, Rhodes clearly had nothing more to worry about. Public opinion, at any rate in London, was now strong on his side. People admired the impudence of his answers, the force of his personality, the breadth of his vision, and the simplicity with which he sat taking his frugal meal of sandwiches in the committee-room between sessions. Even Labouchere felt the attraction of his antagonist, as he later admitted. "I like Rhodes," was Labby's verdict: "I like his porter and sandwiches—an entirely honest, heavy person." His last questions were perfunctory and largely beside the point.

He tried to disprove Rhodes's contention that "anything that is worth having in the way of concessions [in the Transvaal] is held by the Germans", but Rhodes retorted with references to the dynamite monopoly and the electrification of Pretoria. He tried to prove that if the Raid had succeeded, Rhodes would have profited from the increased value of the Chartered Company's shares, but the argument was unconvincing. After a few more brushes, Labouchere handed the questioning over to Bigham and Wyndham, who treated the great man gently and skilfully. A clear and reasoned picture of the *Uitlanders'* grievances emerged for the first time. When Chamberlain took over on the sixth and final day of his interrogation, 5 March, Rhodes had nothing more to worry about. Nevertheless, in the light of subsequent knowledge about the relations of the two men, their exchanges have an ironic interest.

J. A. Spender, the eminent journalist, who witnessed the Enquiry, described it afterwards with brilliant perception, as "a stubborn but extremely obscure duel" between Chamberlain and Rhodes. Circumstances had made them allies, and each was obliged in his own interest to protect the other; but there was no love lost between them. Rhodes blamed Chamberlain for failing to support his plans—not for the Transvaal, over which Rhodes recognised that he had no one to blame but himself, but over the North and particularly the Bechuanaland Protectorate. Chamberlain could not forgive Rhodes for the outrageous irresponsibility with which his agents, particularly Harris, had treated their confidential conversations in the Colonial Office; and the testimony of those agents—Harris, Beit, Maguire and Hawksley— was a nightmare still to be endured by the Colonial Secretary. Knowing these facts, which were unknown to the public and to the rest of the Select Committee alike in 1897, one need not wonder at the puzzling character of the interchanges between Rhodes and Chamberlain on 5 March.

On the surface Chamberlain appeared to be helping Rhodes to make his own case, which was perplexing to an audience who wrongly supposed that their relationship was that of prosecutor and defendant. In fact he was safeguarding himself against the still unpredictable revelations of Rhodes's subordinates. Careful listeners could detect a hidden tension between them, without possessing the clue to its real nature. The most that they could learn for certain, with Chamberlain's help, was that the *Uitlanders'* grievances were real, and not created simply by Rhodes's money; that there had been nothing that was not wholly straightforward about the transfer of Bechuanaland to the Cape Colony and of the strip in the Protectorate to the Chartered Company; that the Transvaal situation was a menace to peace which affected the Imperial Government as well as the Cape Colony; that the plan for the High Commissioner to go to Johannesburg as soon as disturbances broke out was no more than Loch had intended to do eighteen months earlier, without prompting from Rhodes; that Rhodes was the one British South African statesman, prior to the Raid, who had enjoyed the support of the Dutch. With that, and a few more desultory questions from other members of the Committee, Rhodes was allowed to stand down, and there was no indication that he might be recalled.

On the day that Rhodes finished his evidence, he was immediately followed by two unexpected witnesses who might have been sent by providence to underline his triumph. They were two Boer members of the Cape Legislative Assembly, T. A. Louw and M. M. Venter, who happened to be in London. They expressed a wish to give evidence in support of Rhodes's contention that the development of Rhodesia must continue to be carried out by the Chartered Company. Theirs was virtually the only evidence the Select Committee ever heard on the second item of its terms of reference, the administration of the British South Africa Company, and it was entirely unsolicited. Nothing could have been more satisfactory from Rhodes's point of view. The two Boers were naturally subjected to hostile examination by Labouchere at the next sitting, on 9 March, but they would not be shaken in their conviction. By this time Rhodes was sufficiently sure of his triumph to pay no further attention to the Enquiry, beyond reading an occasional commentary sent to him by Hawksley. No intimation had been made that he might be wanted for further examination, so within a few days of completing his evidence, he left the country.

He made a short tour of France, Spain and Italy, looking among other things for olive-trees suitable for transplanting to Rhodesia. By the end of March he was back in England again, but only for a few days. He sailed for the Cape on 3 April, a fortnight before Milner, the new High Commissioner, whom he had evidently made no attempt to see. The one person he was looking out for was W. P. Schreiner, who had also come to give evidence to the Select Committee; and he contrived to catch the same boat as Schreiner back to the Cape. Until this time the political breach between them after the Raid had not injured their personal friendship, but Schreiner had gradually become persuaded (partly, no doubt, by his sister Olive) that Rhodes had in fact been actuated by the sordid financial motive which he personally had refused to accept during the debates in the Cape Assembly. What passed between the two men during the voyage is unknown, but they parted bitter enemies for life when the ship arrived at Cape Town.

On the day of his arrival, 20 April, Rhodes made a speech to a large audience in which he used for the first time a phrase that later became celebrated: "equal rights for every white man south of the Zambesi". On a later occasion, but not on this one, he was persuaded to alter the word "white" to "civilised", in order not to alienate the Coloured vote in the Cape Colony. But probably the modification meant little to Rhodes in his own mind, because he regarded the civilisation of the African native as a goal so remote as to be merely theoretical. "White" and "civilised" would mean the same thing for as far as the imagination could stretch, so there was nothing to be lost by substituting the less offensive epithet. The purpose of his declaration of policy was in any case the same: to resume and complete the reconciliation of the two white races, British and Dutch. Many of both races had assured him that he was still the only man who could do so. He believed it, and still did not appreciate how bitterly the folly of the Jameson Raid had divided them. Still less did he realise that the cynical farce of the Enquiry was to do more damage still.

On the day after his arrival, 21 April, he attended the Legislative Assembly for the first time since the Raid. There was practically no demonstration of hostility, but the sitting was in any case cut short by an adjournment to take leave of the retiring High Commissioner, Lord Rosmead, who sailed for England that afternoon. Rhodes did not yet intend in any case to resume an active role in Cape politics, much to the relief of the new High Commissioner, Sir Alfred Milner, who arrived on 5 May. The two men had still not yet met when Rhodes left Cape Town for the North early in June. While he was on his way to Bulawayo by train, he learned of the suicide of his old associate, Barney Barnato. The news deeply shocked him; it was about this time that he began to think again about his own Will, which had lain untouched since 1893. "It would be very ridiculous," he wrote to Michell, "to lose one's ideas by death." He spent the rest of the year in Rhodesia, as much of it as possible travelling and camping on the *veld* with his favourite companions and secretaries.

His correspondence was dealt with spasmodically, in rough and ready fashion, during these pleasant days on the *veld*. The two secretaries who generally accompanied him, Jourdan and Le Sueur, have left descriptions of his haphazard methods. But it cannot be said that his correspondence was neglected, although on Rhodes's part it consisted mainly of telegrams. The incoming letters were voluminous, and most of them were dealt with in Rhodes's name by one of his secretaries. Those that he dealt with himself were rather arbitrarily determined: the business of De Beers or the Chartered Company, the politics of Rhodesia or the Cape, the personal messages of Grey or Hawksley or Beit, the Select Committee and the aftermath of the Raid. He would telegraph personally, for instance, to a business associate to find a job for a man who lost a leg in the Raid; or to seek some mark of distinction for the leaders of the Afrikander Corps in Matabeleland; or to report to Grey that the Enquiry was drawing to a close, and to felicitate him on not having been called; and he telegraphed "almost daily" to Michell.[1] But it was almost true, as he had told the Select Committee, that he "never wrote a letter". In particular he tried to avoid replying to the innumerable *billets doux* from women admirers.

There was one, unfortunately, which he failed entirely to ignore. Princess Radziwill, who had met him at the beginning of 1896, wrote to him on the day he left England to return to the Cape, and the letter caught up with him on the *veld*.[2] Her letter begins:

"You will be very much surprised to read these lines, but I have so often wished you at Jericho and heaped upon your head, things that were the reverse of blessings, that now that we have become acquainted, and that I must confess to it, my prejudices against you have disappeared, I feel I cannot let you sail for 'the dark Continent' without wishing you God speed with all my heart. I had imagined you quite different from what you really are and fancied your only craving was money. I am sure now that I was mistaken, and that you only care for power in the good and true sense of the word. . . ."

Her letter enclosed a coin which she said was once carried by "the great general Skobeleff" and it ended by asking Rhodes to write to her when he had time at her "town house, St. Petersburg, Dmitrowsky No. 3". Rhodes could not remember having made her acquaintance, and it may be taken as certain that he did not accept her invitation to a correspondence. (His earliest known letter to her is dated April 1899.) But he was to rue bitterly her re-entry into his life.

*   *   *

Meanwhile the Enquiry was moving clumsily along to its futile conclusion, and several correspondents were keeping Rhodes in touch with its progress. During March two sessions were devoted to Bower, whose performance was pitiable and disastrous to himself; and four sessions to Schreiner, who made an excellent impression of dignity, intelligence and honesty, with the undoubted advantage of not knowing the dreadful truth. There followed Jameson, Lambert (of the Colonial Office), Newton (the Resident Commissioner in the Bechuanaland Protectorate) and Rhodes's brother Frank. In April the witnesses began to move more rapidly across the scene: after Colonel Rhodes came Sir John Willoughby, Major Heany, Dr. Wolff, Rutherfoord Harris, Lionel Phillips, and so on through the familiar list of names. By the time the Select Committee had seen Harris, it was becoming obvious that a good deal of the truth was being concealed from them. The existence of the undisclosed telegrams had been established at an early session, but it was not until 4 May that Hawksley was compelled to hand over the Company's cipher, so that the texts held in cipher by the Telegraph Company, and reluctantly surrendered by them, could be deciphered. Even so it was not possible to obtain all the incriminating texts, because the Telegraph Company had already destroyed those prior to November 1895. Harris could be examined, however, on most of those dated from 2 November onwards, and Hawksley was repeatedly but vainly ordered to produce the rest. They totalled eight in number, and have gone down to history as the "missing telegrams", though parts of most of them are now known, and the full text of the earliest has turned up in the Rhodes Papers.

The story of the telegrams is complex and outrageous, but it need not be pursued in detail further than is necessary to establish Rhodes's role. What the Select Committee was told was an affront to its credulity, but its credulity seems to have been almost unlimited. It is certain, for instance, that even the published versions of some of the telegrams were edited. It is certain, too, that the explanation of the disappearance of some of the missing eight was not true, since three of them were dated later than 2 November and cannot therefore have been destroyed by the

Telegraph Company, as was said, at the end of October. A faint light on what happened is shed by a passage in Rosebery's betting-book, recording a conversation with Rhodes in May 1898. Rhodes told him, among other curiosities, that W. L. Jackson, the Chairman of the Select Committee, had himself "severely edited" one or more of the telegrams. It is a remarkable accusation against the Chairman, but it cannot be considered impossible or even improbable, judged by what is known of his performance at the Enquiry. Moreover, circumstantial evidence suggests that it could only have been with some such august connivance that the three "missing telegrams" dated after 2 November disappeared. The story of the Enquiry is still a tissue of unsolved mysteries.

It seems particularly extraordinary in retrospect that the Committee should not have deduced from Harris's evidence, so far as it went, that Rhodes would have gained far more than Chamberlain if the whole dossier had been published. But such is the case. The Report's verdict on the telegrams was as follows:[3]

> "The fact that Mr. Rhodes (after having authorised that they should be shown to Mr. Chamberlain) has refused to allow them to be produced before the Committee leads to the conclusion that he is aware that any statements purporting to implicate the Colonial Office in them were unfounded, and the use made of them in support of his action in South Africa was not justified. . . .
>
> "It cannot reasonably be doubted, having regard to the use already made of these telegrams, that they would have been produced to your Committee if their contents could in any way have relieved Mr. Rhodes or his subordinates from the responsibility now attaching to them."

In a way all these words were true, though Chamberlain, who signed them himself, knew that they were not true in the way that the public would understand them. It can easily be appreciated how angry Hawksley was at the false position in which he was put by Rhodes's insistence on keeping his bargain with Chamberlain.

After refusing for the third time to produce the still "missing telegrams" to the Select Committee, Hawksley wrote to Rhodes on 5 June:[4]

> "I do not bother you by sending copies of the cables we have lately exchanged but I have just this morning received your

cable sent off at 1.40 yesterday Friday saying that you adhered
to your original opinion that the cables should not be produced. Of course I shall act accordingly. . . . The Committee
has now adjourned over Whitsuntide and the Jubilee and
does not meet until the 25th instant when the sittings will be
private for the consideration of the interim report which will
contain a statement that we have refused the cables, but I
gather nothing will come of it so far as the House of Commons is concerned though I am uneasy as to the view the
public will take. I think Mr. Chamberlain has behaved very
unfairly and of course both he and Selborne have lied out-
rageously. . . ."

The reason why no further action was taken against Hawksley
was the Committee's desire to complete the Report in time for
debate in the House of Commons before the end of the session.
The Enquiry's progress was delayed by the celebrations of Queen
Victoria's Diamond Jubilee in June, in consequence of which
there were no sittings between the 4th and 29th (four days longer
even than Hawksley expected). Not only was the House of Commons impatient: Innes, who was in London for the Jubilee, told
Harcourt that any further delay would make a disastrous impression in South Africa. Hence Hawksley was allowed to get
away with his contumacy (much to his own regret, as one member
of the Select Committee rightly suspected) and Flora Shaw, the
last witness, successfully blandished the Committee with her cool
charm and brilliant impudence. The Report was written, mainly
by Harcourt, at great speed in the first week of July. Hawksley
learned that it would be hostile to Rhodes several days before it
was published. He telegraphed Rhodes accordingly, and received
a brief reply on 8 July:[5]

"Your cable received—Regret learn report hostile but maintain my position that in public interest matter should rest."

The Report was published on 13 July, and it was indeed hostile
to Rhodes and his associates. Lord Rosmead, the Secretary of
State, his Under-Secretary and officials were all exonerated;
Bower and Newton were declared to have failed in their duty.
There was no justification for Rhodes, who had deceived the
High Commissioner, his fellow-Ministers and fellow-directors of
the Chartered Company; Beit and Maguire were also guilty
parties; and an "absolute and unqualified condemnation" was

expressed of the Raid. The only relieving features of the Report
were that the existence of genuine grievances on the part of the
Uitlanders was admitted, and the allegation that some of the conspirators took part for "stock-jobbing purposes" was rebutted.
On this last point, and also on the exoneration of Chamberlain,
Labouchere dissented, and wrote a minority report of his own.
Like him, but for totally different reasons, Wyndham and Blake
also refused to sign the majority Report. They were not the only
people to be dissatisfied. The comments of the press were
scathing. But Rhodes was content, because the Charter was saved.

He had had good reason to be anxious for it up to the last.
The Select Committee had as the second task assigned to it that
of scrutinising the conduct of the Chartered Company's administration in Rhodesia, and of making recommendations for its revision if necessary. The scrutiny might well have been disastrous
for the Charter if the Select Committee had ever addressed itself
to the task. In fact it failed to do so, in its haste to produce a report
on the Raid before Parliament rose; and there never was a second
part to its Report. But Rhodes could not be sure that no busybody
would insist on continuing the work of the Enquiry into its
second task. There was some danger in the summer of 1897 that
he would be recalled to England precisely for this purpose. Sir
Richard Martin had been making sharp criticisms of the administration on the spot, which Rhodes instructed the Chartered Company's officers firmly to rebut.[6] Chamberlain sent a message to
Rhodes in May asking him whether he wished to give evidence
on the second part of the Enquiry.

He replied through Stevens and the new High Commissioner
on 20 May, evading the suggestion.[7] He was about to go to the
Chartered territory, he said, in order to "unofficially assist Lord
Grey with many pressing matters"; to visit all the Matabele
chiefs as he had promised; and to go on to Mashonaland, which
was "still in a disturbed state". He had read a Reuter report that
the Select Committee intended to send a commission to Rhodesia,
which he thought "a most excellent suggestion", because they
would see "the great work the Charter had done". Nothing more
was heard of the proposal to continue the Enquiry. But Rhodes
could still not feel easy in his mind. As soon as the Report on the
first part of the Select Committee's terms of reference was published, the attack began again. There was a motion in the House
of Commons for a debate on 15 July, and a further attack on
Rhodes and the conduct of the Enquiry on 19 July, when Balfour,

the Leader of the House, agreed to a full-dress debate. Rhodes's friends had not yet given up the idea of betraying Chamberlain in order to rehabilitate Rhodes, and he had difficulty in restraining them. Two telegrams to London from Rhodesia, both dated 22 July, show how strongly Rhodes was being pressed.[8]

Both were addressed jointly to Beit, Maguire and Hawksley. The first was from Rhodes himself:

"Cable 19th July received. My refusal of production of cables was on public grounds. As you know personally they would have improved my position with the public. I still maintain this position. If necessary you can publish this after consultation with Rothschild, leaving to your discretion time and form."

The second was from Jameson, who had rejoined Rhodes only in the last few days, after visiting Milner at Cape Town on the way:

"Have seen cable to Rhodes re deceiving subordinates. You should publish denial of this from me and say that I was sole agent and responsible for everything connected with subordinates. Refer to my second day's evidence for explanation of any apparent deception of subordinates."

With these final refusals to incriminate Chamberlain, the three agitated addressees in London had to rest content. Rhodes had his reward in the debate in the House of Commons four days later.

The debate lasted two days, 26–27 July. In winding up on the second day, Chamberlain declared that "the Government do not intend to abolish the Charter". He went even further so far as Rhodes personally was concerned, by not only refusing either to prosecute him or to deprive him of his privy councillorship, but declaring that he had done nothing reflecting on his "personal position as a man of honour". The defence of Rhodes by one of his judges astounded the House; but coming at the end of the debate it left no possibility of reply, though one member tried to follow Chamberlain from the Government back benches, and was shouted down by his own side. The story was widely believed, and later published by Labouchere, that Chamberlain was speaking under duress. A Radical M.P., it was said, was sitting opposite him with the "missing telegrams" and other fatal documents in his pocket, awaiting a signal from a friend of Rhodes in the gallery (no doubt Hawksley himself) to produce them if Chamberlain failed to give Rhodes what Hawksley later called a "certificate of honour". The story was not denied by Hawksley in later years, but there is no explicit trace of it in his correspondence; and it would mean, if it were true, that he was prepared to disobey Rhodes's categorical instructions, which is unlikely. What he and Beit and Maguire had failed to appreciate was that to destroy Chamberlain's political career, if that had been the outcome of a complete disclosure, would not have helped Rhodes in the least. It would also have destroyed the Charter, which Chamberlain was pledged to safeguard, as probably no other Colonial Secretary would have done.

That Hawksley still maintained his position, and still failed to understand Rhodes's policy, is shown by the last letter he wrote on the subject at this time, on 28 August. After referring to an earlier letter which is not extant, he goes on:[1]

". . . Since Grey has come home I have had several talks with him but he has no new light as he does not appear to have been in communication with Mr. Chamberlain since the end of 1896.

"As I have heard nothing further from you I assume you prefer to leave matters alone and to ignore the damning paragraphs in the Report of the Select Committee.

"From something Grey said it occurs to me you may be under the impression that some disclosures were made to the Committee other than those that appeared in public, but I have no reason to believe that this is so. You will have seen what cables the Committee did see. So far as I am aware they have seen no others and of course I did not produce my correspondence with Mr. Chamberlain in 1896."

The letter continues in pessimistic vein: Grey had only just begun to appreciate the strength of public feeling against the Company (implying that Rhodes had not); Chamberlain was away and the Colonial Office would give no indication of its intentions towards the Company; and Hawksley felt that it was time for him to resign his position as the Company's legal representative. His reason was that his advice had been persistently disregarded, with disastrous results. The letter continues:

". . . I do not think you appreciate the disastrous effect upon the Chartered Company and all those connected with it that has been brought about by the policy governing us in connection with the enquiry of the Select Committee or the effect

upon both the Government and the Opposition—and indeed
England generally. There is nothing to be gained by enlarging upon this but it is right to bring the facts before you. I
bitterly regret that I did not retire altogether when it was
determined not to play the game with the cards upon the
table, letting all the facts be brought out and each man bear
the responsibility properly attaching to him. I urged this,
you will remember, as long ago as February 1896 when you
were here and again in May 1896 when Sir Hercules Robinson
and Sir Graham Bower came home. . . ."

Hawksley never departed from this view, which he reiterated
in a letter to Michell when the story of the "missing telegrams"
was revived and re-embellished early in 1900. But both then, and
again a year later when another opportunity arose, he acted faithfully in accordance with Rhodes's instructions that they were not
to be published. The copies which he held were finally destroyed
after Rhodes's death, either by his trustees or by Hawksley's son.
His correspondence strongly suggests that, like the good lawyer
he was, he never contemplated disobeying his instructions, however misguided he may have thought them and however much
he may have misunderstood Rhodes's motives.

Hawksley was Rhodes's man. Neither he nor Chamberlain
seems to have spared a thought for the principal victims of the
policy of concealment, who were Bower and Newton. Both were
dismissed from the Colonial service, on a private understanding
that they would be re-employed after a decent interval. Newton
accepted an unattractive post early in 1898, but Bower waited in
vain for the rehabilitation which never came. The one redeeming
feature in his tragic story is that no bitterness ever arose between
himself and Rhodes. Rhodes offered him the post of Administrator of the Chartered territory north of the Zambesi, which was
the least he could do in the circumstances; but Bower thought it
unwise to become an employee of the Company, perhaps remembering that Sir Hercules Robinson had accepted positions in
Rhodes's enterprises between his two tenures of the post of High
Commissioner.

The Colonial Office at last appointed Bower Colonial Secretary
of Mauritius in August 1898, a step downwards which could only
be acceptable if it led to adequate promotion later on. He called
on Rhodes at the Cape on his way out in October 1898, and urged
him to re-forge his alliance with the Bond. There were no re-

criminations. Three years later, in July 1901, Bower wrote to Rhodes from Mauritius on his return to prominence in Cape politics:[10]

"A Natal paper just come in says that you are preparing a scheme of conciliation and federation.

"I always said that you would again come to the front as the great amalgamator and I need hardly say how pleased I am to see that you are again showing yourself in your old role.

"I know nothing of South African politics nowadays but I know the men and that is enough. *Geduld en moed alles sal regt komen.* Meanwhile I wish you to know that your friends do not forget you but wish you all success in the New Year."

Once more, there were no recriminations on Bower's side. But no rehabilitation, nor even promotion, ever came to him. He wrote in vain self-justification to the Colonial Office, and put on record his account of the events leading up to the Raid more than once;[11] but since he would not allow them to be published until fifty years after the Raid, his loyal and quixotic character has only been justly recognised since his death.

Sources

Works mentioned under Chapters Seventeen, Eighteen, and Twenty-one

Notes

[1] Rhodes Papers, B. 334 (to Gardner Williams); B. 307 (to Chartered Company); B. 289 (to Grey); Michell, II, 206.

[2] Radziwill Papers (Rhodes House); Le Sueur, 302.

[3] Select Committee Report (H.M.S.O., 311), p. xv.

[4] Rhodes Papers, C. 11. 2.

[5] Rhodes Papers, B. 352.

[6] Rhodes Papers, B. 315.

[7] Rhodes Papers, B. 257.

[8] Rhodes Papers, B. 380 and 381.

[9] Rhodes Papers, C. 11. 3.

[10] Rhodes Papers, C. 16. 76.

[11] R.H.L. MSS. Afr. s. 26 and s. 63; and papers in the Public Library, Cape Town, quoted by Dr. Jean Van Der Poel, *The Jameson Raid.*

N

CHAPTER TWENTY-THREE

A NEW BEGINNING

FOR Rhodes the Raid now belonged to history. Not that he ever tried to forget it, or to excuse it. But it had become a historical watershed by which he, like others, would date events as before or since the Raid. There were still, of course, constant reminders of it: victims to be compensated, broken lives to be repaired, bills to be paid, bitter taunts to be endured from former friends. Those whom the Raid ruined were Rhodes's first concern. Jameson was put in charge of the extension of the transcontinental telegraph northwards from Salisbury; he was even invited to stand for election to Parliament towards the end of 1897, and Rhodes declined to discourage his candidature, despite the remonstrances of his political friends.[1] Bower was offered employment as Administrator in North-Western Rhodesia and Rhodes told Grey he could "think of no one else but Bower"; but he refused. Willoughby, Heany and others were settled in Rhodesia; another Raider who had lost a leg was sent to Gardner Williams for a job. Still the bills kept coming in.

Stevens was instructed to pay three months' wages and a bonus to all the police who went in with Jameson. Eckstein & Co. produced a new account as late as November 1897. Nor was that the last. In May 1898 Rhodes told Rosebery in a private conversation, which Rosebery recorded in his betting book, that the Raid had cost Beit and himself close on £400,000 each, which was nearly £100,000 higher than the assessment of the previous November. Not that Rhodes was particularly worried by the figure; it was in the same conversation that he also told Rosebery that he expected to leave an income of £500,000 a year to support the scheme of scholarships which he had in mind in his Will, though this was a considerable over-estimate. But he was becoming a little impatient as the costs continued to mount up even in 1898. "I am inundated with claims for damages" he telegraphed to the Chartered Company on 23 August. "I protest against Hawksley being blackmailed. You must fight any further case." But there is no record of any case being fought.[2]

Nor could he expect ever to be forgiven. The Raid had divided South Africa on the very line of cleavage which he had always sought to avoid. His motive had not been "English versus Dutch", he protested to Harcourt in his letter from the *veld* during the Matabele rising. But that had been its consequence. Hofmeyr said that after the Raid he no longer felt divided in his loyalties: Rhodes had thrown back the cause of civilisation in South Africa for twenty-five years. All the Cape political leaders of Dutch descent, not to mention those in the Transvaal and the Orange Free State, reacted on the same lines as Hofmeyr. The ordinary Dutch colonial did not necessarily feel so strongly, and many wrote to Rhodes and went to his meetings to assure him that they still regarded him as the one man who could unite white South Africa. He took pride in this; but they were swimming against the tide, which was expressed more truthfully and with vindictive satisfaction by Olive Schreiner, when she wrote to her brother in 1899 from the north of the Cape Colony: "The hatred of Rhodes is so intense, so fierce, that even I am astonished." She hardly troubled to conceal that she was also delighted.

Among the political leaders, it was not only those of Dutch descent who turned whole-heartedly against Rhodes. His breach with the Bond was virtually final, and the Bond included Merriman and other English-speaking South Africans as well. The Schreiners, too, were not Boers, being half-English and half-German: W. P. Schreiner now went over to his sister's view of Rhodes, though his mother and his brother Theo remained loyal. The catastrophe dissolved many political alliances in Cape politics, and the individuals re-grouped themselves on personal bases, in which one of the most important factors was that of being for or against Rhodes. Some of those who turned against him were willing in later years to be reconciled, provided that he were sufficiently contrite; but that was precisely what infuriated him most. The attempt at a reconciliation with the Bond in 1900, for instance, was initiated by Hofmeyr, but rebuffed by Rhodes. It was Rhodes who considered that Hofmeyr had done him a personal injury, not *vice versa*, after the first shock of horror in January 1896. As his critics saw, his sense of divine mission convinced him that he could not be in the wrong.

Rhodes often expressed himself bitterly in later years against Merriman, Hofmeyr and other former friends for their attitude. It has been denied by some of his chroniclers, but the evidence of his intimate friend Fuller is decisive. Fuller once remonstrated with him over the vindictiveness with which he spoke of his ex-allies. His treatment of them was "not that of a gentleman", said

Fuller—a reproach to which Rhodes was peculiarly sensitive. Fuller believed that Rhodes never quite forgave him for that criticism, but he records that at other times Rhodes spoke in conciliatory terms of the same people. The difference between Rhodes and the other politicians at the Cape was that for him, but not for them, the past was over and done with; he had, according to his lights, accepted responsibility and paid the penalty; it was time to let bygones be bygones and look to the future. That was what he meant when he said that his political career was only just beginning. It was also what he had in mind when he said that his "great mistake" had enabled him to see who were his true friends. But in the judgment of the best of his contemporaries—Schreiner, Innes, Merriman, for instance—it was only the most undesirable of his colleagues who were what he called "true friends".

What was the future to be? As always, he had innumerable projects in his mind, both private and public. He also had certain overriding principles which served as touchstones by which he tested the value of his projects. The guiding principles merged successively into each other: the reconciliation of the white races in South Africa, growing into a union under the British flag, which should expand from end to end of the African continent and form the working model of an independent unit in a world-wide English-speaking Empire of similar units, including Canada, Australia, New Zealand, and not excluding the U.S.A. As he once put it to W. T. Stead, who perhaps understood the mystical side of Rhodes better than any of his contemporaries, however much they might quarrel on methods, "if there be a God, I think that what He would like me to do is to paint as much of Africa British-red as possible, and to do what I can elsewhere to promote the unity and extend the influence of the English-speaking race."[3] It is essential to realise that even the most mundane and superficially trivial of Rhodes's activities were not, in his own mind, unrelated to these Olympian principles.

He bought and developed farms in Rhodesia to prove that it was a white man's country. He bought farms in the Dutch-inhabited areas of the Cape Colony in order to settle Englishmen on the land so that the two white races might gradually intermingle and grow into one people. (With a curious but characteristic blind-spot, however, he did not pursue the converse policy of trying to bring Boers into his industrial enterprises at Kimberley and Johannesburg: Americans and Germans served his commercial purposes better.) He developed communications to knit his territories together, coal mines and dynamite factories to render them economically independent, fruit farms and irrigation projects so that they could export agricultural products as a reserve against the day when their minerals would be exhausted or no longer in demand. His agricultural innovations were numerous: new strains of cattle, donkeys, goats and sheep; new kinds of grass, lucerne, vines, olives, maize; even a new insect, the ladybird, to protect orange trees against the aphis. Always there was an immediate practical aim in view as well as the long-term development of the South African union: rubber was to be grown in Barotseland, for instance, because of the coming of the bicycle,[4] just as the output of diamonds from Kimberley was once related in Rhodes's mind to the demand for engagement rings.

All his projects were undertaken at this time, and indeed for the rest of his life, by Rhodes as a private individual. Although he was restored to the Board of the Chartered Company in April 1898, its powers were by then sharply restricted; and although he never ceased to be a member of the Legislative Assembly, he held no further political office. In a sense, it is impossible nevertheless to regard any activity of Rhodes as purely private. But it is possible to distinguish those which fall, as it were, into his public and private sectors respectively, using distinctions that would be applicable to a more ordinary figure. Developing his farms, rebuilding Groote Schuur, entertaining writers and artists and sportsmen and social figures, collecting books and maps and curiosities of African history, all belong to the private sector, though all of them were also related to the political purposes of his whole life. In the public sector, in the latter half of 1897 and throughout 1898, his preoccupations fall under three heads. There was firstly the consolidation and development of what he still regarded as "his" territories: Rhodesia both south and north of the Zambesi, and the Bechuanaland Protectorate. There was secondly the extension of the means of communication across Africa—the railway line and the telegraph. There was thirdly the prospect of re-entering the political arena at the Cape in order to mould and revitalise the policy of union. In all these projects Rhodes knew that his success or failure would depend on a common unknown quantity: the nature of his relations with the new High Commissioner, Sir Alfred Milner.

Rhodes did not seek out Milner during his first six months in the country. Both men were wary of each other, and Rhodes

preferred to form his first impressions at second hand: through
Jameson, who called on Milner in July on his way to the North;
or Grey, who saw Milner later in the same month on his way back
to England, and reported on their interview by letter.[5] Milner,
of course, had had many warnings about Rhodes, which was like
warning a mountaineer about Everest. Chamberlain told him in
a letter dated 5 July 1897 (three weeks before defending Rhodes
as a man of honour in the House of Commons) that Rhodes
"certainly does not come out well in connection with the South
African Inquiry". Milner discovered for himself that the Dutch
at the Cape were far less disposed to forgive Rhodes than some
of his English-speaking supporters believed. On the other hand,
he quickly realised that Rhodes was still incontestably the most
important man in South Africa. "They are all dwarfs, except
Rhodes, who is a really big man," he wrote to Goschen on 28
September. Rhodes's policy was broadly right, he wrote to Selborne even earlier, and Rhodes was the only man big enough to
carry it out.

That letter to Selborne, dated 2 June 1897, is cardinal for
Milner's early impressions of Rhodes, before they had met on
South African soil. The admiration is unstinted, but the criticism
is also penetrating. Rhodes, he found, was "too self-willed, too
violent, too sanguine, and in too great a hurry". Rhodes was still
"just the same man as he always was, undaunted and unbroken
by his former failure, but also untaught by it". In two succinct
sentences, Milner summarised Rhodes's character as he now saw it.
"Rhodes is a great developer, but he is not a good administrator."
That was exact; but better still was this: "Men are ruled by their
foibles, and Rhodes's foible is size." The tone of Milner's comments became less judicial as more and more questions of practical
detail came up between them for settlement, and he appreciated
that correspondence was no way to settle things with Rhodes.
He was "just as hectoring and grasping with me as with either of
my predecessors," wrote Milner in November; and the only way
to convince him of anything was face to face. But it seemed that
Rhodes was deliberately evading him.

Even when the Bulawayo–Mafeking Railway was opened by
the High Commissioner on 4 November, with a speech in which
he gave Rhodes full credit for his initiative, Rhodes was not
present. Le Sueur says that Rhodes made a "plausible excuse" for
absenting himself. Milner complained of the difficulties created
for him by "the fact that Rhodes is ill, or sulking". Both men's

insinuations were unjustified. Rhodes had in fact been seriously ill, first with malaria and then with heart trouble. Jameson reported him as suffering from a fever in October; Rhodes wrote to Fuller on the day of the ceremony at Bulawayo that he had to keep quiet, and on the following day that his heart was better. He planned a sea-voyage to recuperate, and instructed Stevens to buy a yacht, but cancelled it in mid-November when he felt unexpectedly better.[6] Finally he met Milner, twice on successive days (23 and 24 November 1897) at Salisbury and Umtali. Their conversation is not on record, but the meeting seems to have made a beginning in the removal of grounds for suspicion between them. Milner, writing to Chamberlain a week later, expressed great surprise at the co-operative attitude which Rhodes had shown over several of the matters outstanding between them. Rhodes never uttered a word of criticism against Milner, though he was far from always getting his own way in matters over which he required the High Commissioner's support.

The earliest such case concerned the Bechuanaland Protectorate. The strip of territory across which the railway advanced from Mafeking to Bulawayo, conceded in haste for well-known reasons in 1895, was only the beginning of the settlement of the Protectorate's future. Rhodes reiterated his claim that the whole Protectorate had been virtually promised to the Chartered Company first by Ripon under the Liberal Government and then by Chamberlain. He ridiculed the idea that the Raid should make any difference to the agreement. Milner, on the whole, agreed with him, but thought that a little delay would do no harm. He suggested to Selborne that it might be possible to control Rhodes "by means of the Protectorate". "Let him wait for it and let him deserve it," was Milner's policy. But his account of the way Rhodes intended to develop the Protectorate, as part of a new northern Colony ("which I may remark in passing, though nominally self-governed, will be virtually an absolute monarchy with Rhodes as monarch") horrified Chamberlain, who wrote back for the first time to put a restraining hand on his High Commissioner. At the same time an old antagonist of Rhodes, the Rev. John Mackenzie, re-emerged with a letter to Milner urging the Bechuanaland Protectorate should "again come into direct Imperial control".

Rhodes did not intend to allow the question to be evaded by postponement. He was already promoting a new *trek* of intending settlers in the area of Lake Ngami. Before they could set out, the question of their land-titles had to be regulated, and the decision would necessarily create a precedent for the future. Who was to grant them land, the Chartered Company or the Crown? Rhodes insisted that the Crown must not do so, since that would entail a claim to ownership; but someone had to do so, and that without delay. One of Rhodes's agents in the matter of the Ngami Trek was the Rev. Adriaan Hofmeyr, a cousin of the leader of the Bond. He saw the High Commissioner in mid-July, and reported to Rhodes that Milner thought the whole of the Protectorate should eventually pass under the Charter; but that was on 15 July, before Milner had received Chamberlain's restraining letter of 5 July. Grey undertook to discuss this problem, among others, with Chamberlain in London; but meanwhile it was left in the air, and Milner gave Grey "a pretty direct hint" not to bother Chamberlain too much.[7]

Adriaan Hofmeyr continued to press Rhodes, and Rhodes continued to press the High Commissioner through Stevens in the Chartered Company office at Cape Town. Adriaan Hofmeyr reported on 24 August that thirty-seven trekkers were waiting to start, and on 17 December that they must be on their way by March. (He was rewarded for his persistence, in Rhodes's characteristic way, with 1,000 shares in the Capetown Tramway Company, allotted by Wernher, Beit & Co. on 30 October.) Rhodes asked the Chartered Company on 25 October to tell the High Commissioner that "no land in Protectorate can be granted without consent of Charter", under the agreements which he had made with Knutsford and Ripon; but he agreed that there were also objections to the Company granting land-titles.[8] In January 1898 he came down to Cape Town in person to talk to Milner about it. "He bothers my life out over it," Milner wrote to Selborne on 26 January, but he intended to stand firm. He argued that it would be wrong to allow the Chartered Company to claim ownership over these lands, but equally wrong to grant it to anyone else. In the end, the Imperial Government allowed the trekkers to proceed in mid-1898, and thirty-seven farms were allotted to them in the Ghanzi district; but they received their land-titles from the High Commissioner, and the British South Africa Company passed out of the story with Rhodes's claim unsatisfied.

The Bechuanaland Protectorate thus remained under the protection of the Crown. Rhodes still continued for several years to insist that his claim was well founded, if not to the whole territory, then at least to the railway-strip. In August 1898 he wrote to the Secretary of the Company that "any repudiation of our claims to future administration of the Protectorate and right to the land seems to me nothing short of robbery", resting his argument on his correspondence with Lord Ripon in November 1894. He proposed in the same month to go to England after the coming session of Parliament to re-open the matter with Chamberlain. But when the time came for his next visit to England, there were even more important and more controversial matters on his mind. The status of the Company had also been greatly changed by that time. Although Rhodes finally saw that he was fighting a losing battle for the Protectorate, he clung tenaciously to his claim on the historic strip along the border of the Transvaal, from which Jameson had ridden forth and along which—more important for the future—his Bechuanaland Railway was built.

It was not, however, until late in 1900, when the settlement in anticipation of the end of the Boer War was already under discussion, that Rhodes was finally able to assure the Company that its title to the railway-strip was to be granted.[9] Final confirmation of the title of the Chartered Company to the lands ceded by the Bechuana chiefs in the east of the Protectorate came only after Rhodes's death. Apart from the Ghanzi area in the west, they were the only areas of the Protectorate in which European settlement was to be developed. It took place, for natural reasons, chiefly along the line of the railway; and the same pattern of development was later repeated in Northern Rhodesia.

So Rhodes's tenacity won a limited victory in the end, if only posthumously. But the main issue had already been decided against him when the new High Commissioner, reinforced by the Secretary of State, stood firm in the last few months of 1897. Milner came well out of this first encounter with Rhodes, and was also able to assure Selborne that they were "not at loggerheads". He added cheerfully: "We have got on capitally so far."

The future of the Protectorate was a subordinate part of a much bigger problem, namely the future status and function of the Chartered Company in the northern territories. Here Milner expected much more difficulty with Rhodes and was surprised at his readiness to accept a radical revision. In essence, Milner saw that the Chartered Company had done a good job in economic development but a poor one in administration. Rhodes stoutly defended the Company's administrative record, but was quite prepared to give up that side of the task. He often declared that the future administration of the settlers must be self-government and that the Company should henceforth confine itself to exploiting the natural resources of Rhodesia. Milner feared that self-government would still mean government by Rhodes, but there was already a sufficiently strong feeling against the Company among the settlers to make that outcome less likely.[10] Rhodes was perfectly ready in any case to make self-government work, as he had more than once declared, and even to welcome the "Imperial factor" in Rhodesia. He saw that such changes would relieve him of innumerable petty problems and responsibilities and perhaps that it would facilitate his restoration to the Board of the Company, once it had ceased to be virtually a sovereign power.

This was not at all what Milner expected in advance. Early in his tenure of office, he wrote to Selborne that "generally speaking, the Rhodes game is to get rid of Imperial control in the B.S.A. Company's territory". A representative Council, he argued, "will simply be Rhodes, even more completely than the Company is". The new constitution for Rhodesia which Milner and Chamberlain were debating by correspondence in the latter half of 1897 was therefore drafted with a view to keeping Rhodes in his place. But Rhodes had no conflicting ambitions so far as running the administration of Rhodesia was concerned. His correspondence with Milton, the acting Administrator at Salisbury in Grey's place, shows him disposed to refer to the Government for decisions which once he would have taken himself without a second thought: for instance, the allotment of land to a friendly missionary from Nyasaland, or to loyal supporters such as the Moodies at Melsetter, or the recruitment of native labour from outside Rhodesia.[11] Milner did not become aware of Rhodes's real thoughts on the future of Rhodesia until they met in the last week of November, and then he was surprised how readily his suggestions, including an "Imperial representative", were accepted.

The one point on which Rhodes had an *idée fixe* was his favourite "customs clause", by which Rhodesia would be debarred from ever putting a tariff on British goods higher than the existing tariff in the Cape Colony. Curiously enough, Rhodes forgot to raise this point at his first two meetings with Milner, and had to send a telegram after they had parted, on 11 December, asking Milner to accept[12]

". . . what is termed my customs clause, namely, that the duty imposed on imported British goods in the territories called

Rhodesia should never exceed the present Cape tariff which, as you are aware, is one for revenue purposes and not for protection. The last Liberal government was favourable to it provided I agreed to the word British being struck out, but I declined and so the matter dropped."

To this Milner agreed and so did Chamberlain. It was the almost unconscious starting-point of their own dedication to the idea of an Imperial tariff system.

The better part of a year was spent in hammering out the details of a new constitution for Rhodesia. Hawksley kept in touch with the discussions in the Colonial Office on Rhodes's behalf,[13] and Milner kept Sprigg informed at the Cape, both as Prime Minister and as a friend and mouthpiece of Rhodes; for Sprigg and Rhodes were looked upon by Milner as respectively the nominal and the real head of the Government in 1898. But Rhodes made no difficulties, apart from his insistence on the customs clause. An undated letter from him to Milner argued the precise phraseology of the clause: the British Colonies should not automatically be included with the United Kingdom, since "many of them have most unfair tariffs to the Mother Country"; and the Cape tariff should be extended to include "such increases as have been agreed upon in proposed Natal, Free State and Cape Customs Union", which came into being in May 1898. Rhodes had his way over the second point, but not the first.

Rhodes's determination on the "customs clause" was so strong that in March 1898 he went to England to make sure of it. During his stay he was re-elected to the Board of the Chartered Company and addressed the Annual General Meeting on 21 April, at which he had an enthusiastic reception.[14] He explained that the Government had raised no objection to his re-election "as we have become a commercial company". He set out the future of the territories, reminding the shareholders that they were responsible "for the northern part of Rhodesia as well as the southern". Semi-responsible government had come, but the majority on the elected Council would remain in the hands of the shareholders, and the economic development of Rhodesia would still be their responsibility.

His imagination then soared away from the banalities of an Annual General Meeting. He told them that "the conquest of Africa by the English nation is a practical question now", and that public opinion in England had changed, so that it was at last generally recognised "that England by itself is a hopeless proposition". It was therefore a necessity to expand; but it was also a moral obligation. "I hold the theory that England's duty in the world is the administration of new countries." But he gave them not only great thoughts but hard, immediate realities. He outlined the sequence of development as he had seen it, from the days of the lonely prospector to those of the corporate capitalists. He hinted that there would be help from the Government in raising a cheap loan for the extension of the railway from Bulawayo to Tanganyika—over-optimistically, as it turned out. He assured them that he was getting his own way over the "customs clause". He ended by referring to himself and his downfall. "I have had two years of trial, but it has made me a better man." The shareholders rapturously agreed.

The "customs clause" was not to be secured quite so easily as Rhodes believed when he was in London. On his return to Rhodesia in June he found that the Salisbury Chamber of Commerce was opposed to entering a customs union, which they saw as the ultimate goal of Rhodes's efforts. Chamberlain refused to agree to the proposed differentiation between the United Kingdom and the Colonies.[15] The clause finally read:

"No Customs duties levied on any articles produced or manufactured in any part of Her Majesty's Dominions or in any British Protectorate and imported into Southern Rhodesia shall exceed in amount the duties levied on such articles according to the tariff in force in the South African Customs Union at the commencement of this Order, or the tariff contained in the Customs Union Convention concluded between the Colony, the Orange Free State, and Natal, in May 1898, whichever are the higher."

It was good enough to satisfy Rhodes that he had won his point. It is also enough to claim for him the place of a pioneer in the policy of Imperial preference.

The constitution containing the "customs clause" was promulgated by Order in Council on 20 October 1898. It provided for a Resident Commissioner appointed by the Colonial Secretary to represent the Crown, and Executive and Legislative Councils to represent the settlers. But the "general administration of affairs" was still to rest with the Company, who would appoint and pay one or more Administrators, subject to the approval of the Secretary of State. It was not a bad compromise, and Rhodes was content with it, perhaps chiefly because he was content with Milner, whose work it largely was. "The constitution for the South is all right and will work," he wrote to Grey on 8 February 1898. It was at this time that Rhodes put in writing to the Company his view that "our best friend is the Imperial Government". Before long he was urging everyone to "trust Milner".[16]

The constitutional settlement of the territories north of the Zambesi, though it took longer, was not intrinsically more difficult than that of Southern Rhodesia. Rhodes was less personally involved north of the Zambesi, for he never crossed the river himself. Knowing Northern Rhodesia only at second hand, his ideas for its development were less clearly formulated than in Southern Rhodesia. It figures relatively little in his correspondence, but a letter to the Secretary of the Chartered Company on 24 August 1898 gives a glimpse of his mind and his method:[17]

"Captain Lawley has obtained a very good concession from Lewanika, King of Barotseland, which I hope the Board of Directors will do their utmost to get ratified by the Foreign Office.

"In my opinion the territory north of the Zambesi should be left to the Foreign Office. Coryndon can get same powers as Codrington. When the Railway gets north of the Zambesi the territory will practically become part of Southern Rhodesia. Matabeleland and the country under Coryndon's jurisdiction can be administered by the Administrator for Matabeleland, and Mashonaland and Mpseni's country can be administered by the Administrator for Mashonaland."

He was faithful to his earlier method of indicating his personal choice of the right man for the job, and leaving the rest to the man on the spot. He had men such as Coillard, the French Protestant missionary, and later Coryndon in Barotseland, where a protectorate was proclaimed in October 1897; and Turner, whom he chose to suppress a rising of the Angoni tribe in January 1898; and Codrington, whom he sent as Milton's deputy a few months later; and Arthur Lawley, now the Administrator of Matabeleland, later Lord Wenlock and a Governor in Australia and the Transvaal. These were Rhodes's men, some of them known as the "Apostles". But he was also full of ideas himself on matters great and small.

The railway and the telegraph were paramount, of course. But there was also the importance of driving a hard bargain with the

Portuguese in Angola about the boundary of Barotseland, on account of the future importance of rubber. There was, too, the puzzle of an area in the north where "in a forest on the hill side there is a patch where the trees are brown and not green", which Rhodes sent a young man to investigate, thus touching on the first possibilities of the Copper Belt. There was even the matter of protecting elephants, about which he was moved to telegraph Codrington from Madeira on his way to England in 1899. And there was the question of employing white or black police: Rhodes urged that only African police should be employed north of the Zambesi, because white men would die of fever, and so would their horses. Moreover, as he wrote to Grey on 8 February 1898:

> "Their day's work would be—eating 3 meat meals, lying on their backs on stretchers for the balance, reading Tit Bits and devoting their conversation to cursing the country and the Chartered Company."

This is one of the perceptions which justify the view that Rhodes had no inherent prejudice in favour of whites over blacks. At least his contempt was allocated impartially.[11]

For the rest, he was content to leave Northern Rhodesia in good hands. The Order in Council settling the constitution of North-Western Rhodesia, which was promulgated on 28 November 1899, gave the Company a decidedly subordinate status in comparison with Southern Rhodesia, but satisfied Rhodes by containing an identical "customs clause". Two months later, on 29 January 1900, the settlement of the north was rounded off by a further Order in Council confirming the status of North-Eastern Rhodesia under the Commissioner for Nyasaland—in other words, outside the domain of the Chartered Company altogether. Still Rhodes had no objection; though being by that time besieged by Boers in Kimberley, he would have been in no position to make an effective protest in any case.

*   *   *

His mind was not on the legalistic details of constitution-making: it was on the grand design. The overriding principle was that whatever might be done, in whatever context, it should be so contrived as to facilitate and not impede the ultimate goal of unification. The common "customs clause" was one step in that direction. Another was the creation of a single network of com-

munications. The railway and the telegraph, spreading from end
to end of Africa, not only north to south but east to west also,
were Rhodes's major pre-occupations between the Raid and the
Boer War. As he had written to the Company Secretary in support of Captain Lawley's new concession, he believed that the
extension of the railway north of the Zambesi would make the
union of Northern and Southern Rhodesia practically inevitable.
With Kitchener advancing southwards into the Sudan, the old
dream of uniting Africa in a network of communications became
what Rhodes called "a practical question", and he burned with
competitive ardour to reach Uganda first. But there were great
difficulties in his way, not the least of which was that the Imperial
Government had twice failed (under Salisbury in the Anglo-
German Convention of 1891 and under Rosebery when the
Anglo-Congolese Treaty of 1894 collapsed) to gain for him a
connecting strip of all-British territory on the way.

The advance of the telegraph was the easier of the two problems.
The occasional obstacles were technical and not insuperable. The
route northwards from Salisbury had to be altered, on Jameson's
advice, because natives cut the wires, elephants destroyed the
poles, and maintenance seemed impossible. Then permission had
to be sought from the Portuguese to take it through their territory to Blantyre in Nyasaland, and also of course to maintain and
protect it there. It reached Blantyre in April 1898 and advanced
thence to Fort Johnston and Fort Abercorn, arriving about the
end of 1899. Meanwhile Rhodes had to face the problem of taking the telegraph (like the railway in due course) across either
German territory or the Congo. Early in 1899, having armed
himself with calculations based on the Australian telegraph-
system in order to deal with questions of costs, he set out to
solve the problem involved. First he went to Cairo with Jameson, to arrange the terms on which his telegraph would be connected with the Egyptian telegraph. In Cairo he corresponded
with Cromer about the rates to be charged, and found him un-
accommodating. This did not alter the high opinion which he
expressed of Cromer: perhaps rather he admired the High Commissioner all the more for his business acumen. Then he went on
to Europe, to see the Kaiser and King Leopold.[19]

He had no difficulty in reaching a satisfactory arrangement
quickly with the Kaiser. An agreement was signed by Rhodes
and the German Government for a telegraph-route through German East Africa, or Tanganyika, on 15 March 1899. The terms

were that the African Trans-Continental Telegraph Company should erect the telegraph-line at its own expense, but the owner-ship should eventually pass to the German colonial government, which would be responsible for maintenance. Rhodes was highly pleased with the result, though it is difficult to see why, unless it was that he was more pleased with the Kaiser's personality. It was on the occasion of this visit that Rhodes had a famous and fateful conversation with the Kaiser in which they joked about the consequences of the Kaiser's telegram to Kruger in January 1896, so helpful as it had proved to be to Rhodes. He formed the most favourable opinion of the Kaiser, in sharp contrast to the strong dislike he took to King Leopold a few days later. The out-come was the inclusion of German students in the scheme of scholarships provided for in his will. For the rest of his life Rhodes talked with enthusiasm of the Kaiser, both in private and public. Though a short-sighted view, it seemed to be amply vindicated a few years later by the German attitude to the Boer War.

By the end of 1900, more than fifty miles of telegraph had been constructed through German territory, thanks to Rhodes's agreement with the Kaiser. He found it much less easy to obtain satisfaction from the British Government over the extension of the telegraph into Uganda. Immediately after his visit to Berlin, he started pressing Lord Salisbury on the subject, and he was answered on 25 March 1899 that the Prime Minister would give it his immediate attention. But eighteen months later the nego-tiations were still hanging fire.[20] The truth was that Salisbury was not really interested in the Cape-to-Cairo dream although he had been claimed as its progenitor. His interest in Uganda was strategic: its function was to safeguard the Nile Valley, par-ticularly against advances from the west, such as General Mar-chand's march to Fashoda, which precipitated the great Anglo-French crisis of October 1898. Communications were naturally important to the security of Uganda, but the direction for them dictated by Salisbury's policy was not from north to south, as Rhodes desired, but from the interior to the coast. The orienta-tion of Salisbury's African policy was, so to speak, at right angles to that of Rhodes's. Rhodes's failure to appreciate the difference was to cost him severe headaches over the second line of com-munication which he had in mind, that of the railway.

The railway presented a more complex political problem than the telegraph, besides being much slower and more expensive to construct. In November 1897 it reached Bulawayo, and Salisbury two years later. It was not too soon to negotiate its future extension through Tanganyika, which required fresh capital as well as German consent. Rhodes set out to obtain both on the same visit to Europe at the beginning of 1899. He had broached the problem with Milner a year earlier, with a request for support in obtaining the Imperial Government's guarantee for a new loan. This need was the measure of the cost to the Chartered Company of the rebellion in Matabeleland. Milner advised Rhodes in March 1898 not to be too pressing, because it was not a good moment for Chamberlain to advocate schemes "involving risk and expenditure in Imperial expansion", and it was important not to discredit Chamberlain, because no other Colonial Secretary would be "so likely to back up big schemes of expansion and to damn Treasury objections to them". Rhodes replied with a humility which may have surprised Milner that he would do nothing to embarrass the Government. He even telegraphed to Kitchener on 9 April 1898 expressing the fear that Kitchener would reach Uganda first.[21] But he had no intention of giving up.

He wrote his first formal application to the Colonial Office for a guarantee of the proposed loan on 28 April 1898, in response to an invitation from Chamberlain to explain what he had in mind. The correspondence went on throughout 1898, with Rhodes becoming increasingly exasperated. He attacked Hicks-Beach, the Chancellor of the Exchequer, in particular, comparing him rather tastelessly with "the young man in the Bible with our Saviour when asked to part with his wealth". Milner also raised objections which helped to harden Hicks-Beach against Rhodes's proposals. Beit further annoyed him by questioning some of the facts and figures in Rhodes's own letters. Grey, however, led him to believe from the beginning that everything would turn out all right in the end, and Rhodes made the mistake of saying in public speeches that the Government was about to guarantee him support. He could not believe that Hicks-Beach would be so shortsighted as to refuse, since he was not asking for Treasury money but only for a guarantee which would enable him to raise the loan at a cheaper rate of interest. He set out from the Cape full of optimism on 28 December. But when he saw Hicks-Beach in London on 26 January 1899, the Chancellor's answer was a firm negative.[22]

Rhodes was not prepared to take No for an answer. He left London for his hurried trip to Cairo and the Continent, intending to return in the spring. Immediately before leaving, he was in communication with Kitchener about the point of junction of their respective lines, which remained to be settled. That was looking far ahead, but not too far for Rhodes. On the way back he raised the same question with the Kaiser over the railway as over the telegraph, but was unable to reach so quick a conclusion. There was a strong disposition in Germany to help Rhodes, the British Ambassador assured him. But a railway was a bigger commitment than a telegraph-line, and the Reichstag "was not yet permeated by an Imperial spirit". It was not until October 1899 that an agreement with the Germans on the railway project was signed; and Rhodes later expressed himself disappointed with it. King Leopold whom he saw in Brussels on his way from Berlin to London, was even more of a disappointment still. He was, if possible, worse than Hicks-Beach, whom Rhodes was preparing to confront with a new proposition in April.[23]

Rhodes's new plan had Chamberlain's enthusiastic support, but Hicks-Beach demolished it in a devastating memorandum dated 18 April 1899. The proposed duration of the loan was too long; the security offered was insufficient; the share in the profits offered to H.M.G. was exaggerated; the B.S.A. Company was notoriously living on its capital; there was no need for Treasury backing if Rhodes was right in claiming that he could raise the loan by himself; an initial commitment for the first section, which was all that was now asked, would inevitably commit H.M.G. to the entire project; and in any case the natural outlet for a railway from Lake Tanganyika was south-eastwards to the sea, not to the Cape. Hicks-Beach doubted even whether Rhodes had any faith in the scheme himself. Chamberlain, however, insisted that the matter must go to the Cabinet before refusal. He argued that the Chartered Company must not be allowed to fail; that Rhodes had expressly asked for a Cabinet decision—which surely should not have implied that he was entitled to have one—and that he had already "been led in the first instance to believe that his request would be entertained"—which was true, but attributable only to Chamberlain's own irresponsibility and Grey's indiscretions. The Cabinet duly rejected all Rhodes's propositions, but offered in turn a direct loan to the Bechuanaland Railway Company on a series of extremely restrictive conditions. Rhodes refused the offer, as Chamberlain expected: indeed, his only object in suggesting that the Cabinet should make this unacceptable offer was to shift the onus of the breakdown from himself to Rhodes.

Rhodes delivered himself savagely on the subject of Hicks-Beach's lack of imagination. Contemporaries agree that his temper was abominable at this time, and patience was easily lost with people who could not see what was obvious to him. He had indeed much to annoy him, besides the nagging sense that his health was breaking down. On top of the argument with Hicks-Beach he had a row with his fellow-directors of De Beers in April 1899. He wrote intemperately to the Company Secretary on 19 April outlining the shortcomings of the Board and the "enormous injury that the Company has suffered owing to their opposition to my proposals". He instanced their opposition to his purchase of the Wesselton mine, their frustration of his efforts to invest in assets other than diamonds, their premature sale of shares in the Chartered Company, and so on. He also wrote to Rothschild on 12 April, justifying his actions as a Life Governor, which had been under criticism from the Board. A long and polite reply, putting Rhodes unmistakably in the wrong by any normal standards, came from the Company on 26 April. But of course the last thing Rhodes wanted to put up with was any normal standard.[24]

There were consolations. One was the planning of his Will, which was actively in his mind at this time. He told Rosebery that the thought of his Will was the pleasantest companion he had: "when I find myself in uncongenial company, or when people are playing their games, or when I am alone in a railway carriage, I shut my eyes and think of my great idea." Rosebery, who was to be a Trustee, was one of his special confidants about the Will; and Rhodes's admiration for the former Prime Minister was now so great that he offered him £50,000, unconditionally, towards the Liberal election fund. He was even ready to enter politics at Westminster if Rosebery wanted him, in two years' time. Rosebery replied that he must come and stand for the City, to which Rhodes agreed.

Another consolation was his growing friendship and sense of partnership with Kitchener, whom he saw frequently in London in the summer of 1899. He had readily acceded, a few months before, to Kitchener's request for a contribution to the foundation of a new school at Khartoum: the combination of conquest with education showed that the General was a man after his own heart.[25] Together, he foresaw, Kitchener and he would now settle the destiny of Africa by driving their railways from either end to some still unknown meeting point. Meanwhile they rode in

Hyde Park together, and went together to Oxford to receive honorary degrees in June.

At Encaenia, Rhodes was delighted to be acclaimed even more enthusiastically than Kitchener. But even in his beloved Oxford there were pin-pricks of annoyance. A group of dons (including one, H. A. L. Fisher, who was later to become a Trustee of his Will) passed a resolution deploring the conferment of an honorary degree on the man who had been responsible for the Raid. The proctors threatened to veto the conferment of his degree, exercising an ancient prerogative which had long fallen into disuse. An undergraduate called to him out of the crowd not to look so bored. There were trying people everywhere, from the Chancellor of the Exchequer downwards, though he had a triumphant reception at a dinner given to him by his old College after the successive hurdles of Encaenia had been surmounted.

The dinner in Oriel College Hall that night was one of the most moving occasions in Rhodes's life. It happened to be the College's annual Gaudy night. Rhodes was well aware of the continuing sense of hostility to him, which even began to manifest itself again during the dinner. But a more friendly section of the guests insisted that he should speak, for which he had made no preparation—not that he ever did. One of the Fellows, A. G. Butler, who had befriended Rhodes in his undergraduate days and now sat next to him, described the effect in a letter to his sister a few days later:

> "He spoke admirably, pointing out the difference between an old and settled country, and that of a country in formation. He spoke also of what he had done, or striven to do, not denying his mistakes, but pleading very great difficulties and provocations. It was a striking and historical scene. His humility was quite as marked as his consciousness of great achievement."

As so often, Rhodes left behind him enemies and critics converted to friends. It was on the same occasion that he promised the College a legacy in his Will—a gesture which his enemies would have denounced with knowing sarcasm as an example of "squaring", but of which no one except Butler and the Provost knew at the time.

Rhodes returned from Oxford to London, elated by his success at the University but still depressed by his failure with the one man he could not "square", the Chancellor of the Exchequer. So far as Hicks-Beach was concerned, the only satisfaction Rhodes had in revenge was to be able to announce that a new issue of the Chartered Company's shares had been over-subscribed, and that the money for the railway to Uganda would be raised in spite of him. He addressed the Annual General Meeting of the Company's shareholders for the second year in succession on 2 May 1899, the day after he heard of the Cabinet's final refusal.[26] He told them that the railway had reached Salisbury on the previous day, and announced a series of new railway projects. Everyone was now agreed on one thing, he assured them, and that was England's expansion. Railways were to be the vehicle of that expansion in Africa: Harcourt had called his railway "a wildcat scheme", but the English people had proved him wrong. The long-suffering shareholders enthusiastically voted to go without a dividend for yet another year, nor did they receive one at all until the 1920's. Nor did Rhodes ever see his beloved railway join up with Kitchener's line south into the Sudan. Nor, of course, did anyone else.

Sources

Colvin, Ian: *The Life of Jameson*
Gann, L. H.: *The Birth of a Plural Society*
Garvin, J. L.: *The Life of Joseph Chamberlain*
Gelfand, Michael: *Northern Rhodesia in the Days of the Charter*
Hanna, A. J.: *The Story of the Rhodesias and Nyasaland*
Headlam, C.: *The Milner Papers*
Hicks-Beach, Lady V.: *The Life of Sir Michael Hicks-Beach*
Hofmeyr, J. H. & Reitz, F. W.: *The Life of Jan Hendrik Hofmeyr*
Innes, James Rose: *An Autobiography*
James, R. V. Rhodes: *Rosebery*
Stead, W. T.: *The Last Will and Testament of Cecil J. Rhodes*
Walker, E. A.: *W. P. Schreiner—A South African*

Notes

[1] Rhodes Papers, C. 2. 161 (Crewe); C. 2. 165 (Sprigg); C. 2. 166 (Fuller); Michell, II, 216.
[2] Rhodes Papers, A. 30 (to Grey); B. 334 (to Gardner Williams); B. 592 (to Stevens); C. 24. 50 (cost of Raid); B. 1060 (Hawksley).
[3] Stead, 98.
[4] Rhodes Papers, B. 510 (to Grey); B. 780 (to Stevens).
[5] Rhodes Papers, C. 17. 2.
[6] Rhodes Papers, B. 637 (Jameson to Lawley); B. 663 (Rhodes to Fuller); B. 646 (to Stevens); B. 682 (to Stevens).
[7] Rhodes Papers, C. 17. 1 (Hofmeyr); C. 17. 2 (Grey).
[8] Rhodes Papers, C. 17. 3 (Hofmeyr); C. 17. 8 (Chartered Company); C. 24. 53 (Wernher, Beit & Co.); B. 639 (to Stevens).
[9] Rhodes Papers, A. 77 (to Chartered Company); A. 78 (to Stevens); A. 201 (to Chartered Company).

10 Rhodes Papers, C. 1. 76.
11 Rhodes Papers, A. 16 (Moodies); A. 28 (missionary); B. 694 (native labour).
12 Rhodes Papers, B. 743.
13 Rhodes Papers, C. 11. 6 (Hawksley to Rhodes).
14 "Vindex", 678–706.
15 Rhodes Papers, C. 5. 1 and 12 (Stevens to Rhodes).
16 Rhodes Papers, A. 30 (to Grey); C. 5. 9 (to Chartered Company).
17 Rhodes Papers, A. 76.
18 Rhodes Papers, B. 819, 821 and 832 (Turner); A. 41 (Codrington); A. 76 (Lawley); A. 100 (elephants); B. 780 (Barotseland); A. 27 (police); A. 28 (to Grey on police); R.H.L. MSS. Afr. t. 10, f. 123 (copper-belt).

19 Rhodes Papers, B. 346 and 906 (to Chartered Company); C. 22. 12 and 12 (a) (Post Master General); C. 22. 15 (Cromer).
20 Rhodes Papers, C. 22. 21 (Salisbury); C. 4. 45.
21 Rhodes Papers, B. 911.
22 Rhodes Papers, C. 18. 4 (Chamberlain); A. 66 (Hicks-Beach); C. 18. 8 (a) (Milner); C. 20. 51 (Grey); B. 1190.
23 Rhodes Papers, C. 22. 13 and 14 (Kitchener); C. 22. 20 (Kaiser); Michell II, 251.
24 Rhodes Papers A. 124 (to De Beers); A. 125 (to Rothschild); C. 7. 210.
25 Rhodes Papers, C. 16. 56.
26 "Vindex", 708–41.

CHAPTER TWENTY-FOUR

LAST ASPIRATIONS

THE last major field of activity in which Rhodes was pursuing the same single-minded aim of the unification of southern Africa was that of Cape politics, which he re-entered for the election campaign in 1898. In the opinion of his friends, it was a belated return. He had been urged to come back in April 1896, for the session in which Merriman bitterly attacked him and the Charter, and in which Schreiner declared that his methods were "utterly wrong" but his motives were never "low or grovelling or sordid". At that time Rhodes was deeply engaged in the Matabele rebellion, which was a respite by comparison. He preferred the background again in 1897, when Milner described him as "powerfully but silently" supporting the Ministry, and hoping to rout the Bond at the General Election. But although Rhodes attended Parliament between his return from the Enquiry in London and his departure for the north in June, he took no prominent part in public affairs. It was the approach of general elections in 1898— first to the Legislative Council or upper house in March and then to the Legislative Assembly, of which he was still himself a member, in August—which compelled him to make his decision whether or not to return to public life.

His friends renewed their pressure on him in the latter part of 1897, and Dutch colonists flatteringly wrote to assure him that he alone could still unite the two white races. But political life at the Cape was unattractive compared to pioneering in Rhodesia and the simple life on the *veld*. On the *veld*, as his boon-companions said—Metcalfe, McDonald, Michell, Jameson, Grimmer and the secretaries—he really lived. Even when he was Prime Minister, he had managed to take off two or three months at a time to travel on horse and foot in the open: riding, shooting and walking for eight or ten hours a day in his invariable white trousers and slouch hat; establishing a camp at nightfall—always insisting on a "clean camp"—with his half-caste cook, Tony, to prepare a meal —he called it "a chop on the veld", but it was often a four-course dinner, and washed down by a gin-and-soda or champagne followed by his favourite kümmel; a good night's sleep in his Cape-cart, except when lions kept him awake; rising early to dress and

shave punctiliously—"I believe I should shave if I were dying",
he told his friends, and made them do the same—and then another such glorious day.

Correspondence was accumulated in hampers to be sorted out
at irregular opportunities, as rarely as his secretaries would allow.
Perhaps the favourite secretary was Grimmer, because he had
the least interest in his secretarial duties and treated Rhodes like a
schoolboy: Grimmer himself, after all, almost was a schoolboy
still in age, and his master still was one at heart. They quarrelled
and gambled and chaffed each other as if nothing else in life
mattered. It was only on the *veld* that Rhodes had "world enough
and time". But his friends were determined to recall him to what
they saw as his duty.

Perhaps the argument which finally decided him to return to the
Cape was one put forcibly by Stevens at the end of 1897. The
Transvaal Government, he telegraphed Rhodes on 29 December,
was intending to spend £50,000 on the forthcoming elections.[1]
There had often before been allegations of the use of the Secret
Vote by Kruger to influence elections in the Cape Colony, but
since the Jameson Raid the threat had become more serious.
Dutch colonists had in general gravitated away from their
former acceptance of assimilation with their British fellow-colon-
ists; they felt themselves again to be brothers with the Transvaalers; and the symbol of inter-racial fusion, which was Rhodes's
alliance with the Afrikander Bond under Hofmeyr, was destroyed. There was a real danger, as Rhodes saw it, that the Cape
Parliament would be captured by pro-Kruger Boer candidates,
who would take their orders from Pretoria.

Such a victory would be irreversible, because the constituencies
in the Cape Colony were already so drawn as to give an advantage
to the country districts, where Boers predominated, as against the
towns, which were predominantly British. The consequence
would then be that the Union of South Africa, when it came,
would be dominated by the Transvaal instead of the Cape, and
by Boers instead of the British. Rhodes saw it to be essential to
his plans not only that his supporters should win the Cape elections, but also that a redistribution of constituencies should be
carried out to ensure against a recurrence of the threat. In January 1898 he returned to the Cape and threw himself heart and soul
into the election campaign.

Political power was still evenly balanced in the Cape Parliament; or rather, it was evenly diffused, because the disruption of

alliances caused by the Raid had left few clear-cut divisions on party lines. The government of Sir Gordon Sprigg, who had succeeded Rhodes in January 1896 as he always did when there was no obvious alternative Prime Minister, had the character of a "caretaker" coalition, always seemingly about to be overthrown though in fact it survived for two and a half years. Although it contained three Bondsmen, and the Bond had broken with Rhodes, two out of the three were personally in sympathy with him. Individuals counted rather than parties, and Rhodes was incomparably the greatest individual of all. Sprigg was a nonentity by comparison, and everyone regarded Rhodes as his master.

The only other party comparable to the Bond, though less numerous and even more divided, was that of the Progressives. It was an amorphous body, founded in the early 1890's and never yet a powerful factor in Cape politics; but when Innes, one of its founders, resigned the leadership in 1897 the way was open for its conversion into a more dynamic force with a new character. To convert it into the spearhead of British influence at the Cape, and to make Rhodes its leader, was the task undertaken by a few energetic figures at the Cape, of whom Garrett, the editor of the *Cape Times*, was among the foremost.

Neither part of the task was easy, because in many of the Progressives a certain vague liberalism was ineradicable, whereas Rhodes still hankered after the affection of the Dutch. In course of time the Progressives split into two wings: the moderates, who still looked to Innes for their leadership, and the diehards, who were linked mainly by loyalty to Rhodes. The former were supported outside Parliament by the South African Political Association, the latter by a newly formed body, rabidly patriotic in a British sense, called the South African League. The latter was set upon winning Rhodes to its leadership. A deputation from it was received by him at Groote Schuur in February 1898, but it was not until April 1899 that he accepted their offer of the Presidency.[2] Meanwhile he burnt his boats so far as the Bond was concerned by attacking it in an interview with the *Cape Times* on 8 March, after which Garrett was able to claim him openly as a Progressive.

He spoke for the first time from a Progressive party platform on 12 March 1898. The speech had a curious medley of themes, as if Rhodes was still not quite sure what it meant to be a Progressive, but hostility to Krugerism and the unification of South Africa were naturally prominent.[3] Milner had made a historic speech ten days before at Graaff Reinet, warning the Cape Dutch against disloyalty to the Colony and the influence of the Transvaal. No doubt Rhodes's intention was to underline the High Commissioner's point and to represent him by implication as an electoral ally. The result was satisfactory: the Progressives won the upper house by a small majority.

But the campaign was only just beginning. What mattered was control of the lower house, the Legislative Assembly. Sprigg's support there was precarious, varying between one issue and another. His coalition could not endure indefinitely, and only a general election could crystallise a new and firmer balance between Government and Opposition. The issue which brought matters to a head was inevitably the proposal for a redistribution of constituencies, which Sprigg introduced in May. His Bill, which was certain to favour the Progressives by creating new urban seats, was given a second reading by 42 votes to 35 after a fierce debate on 20 June, but two days later the Government fell after a defeat by 41 votes to 36 on a motion of No Confidence. One of the issues on which the second vote turned was Sprigg's personal defence of Rhodes. As Milner had written to Chamberlain on 18 May, "the hostility of the two parties is increased by the furious controversy which ranges over the position of Mr. Rhodes". Rhodes meanwhile had made a flying visit to England between the elections, and returned spoiling for a fight.

Parliament was prorogued for the general election to the lower house on 28 June. Schreiner formed a new party for the struggle, called the South African Party, with the slogan of "true imperialism and true colonialism". Rhodes came out openly at the head of the Progressives, whose campaign he financed as liberally as Kruger was supposed to be financing his Dutch opponents. He was still an uneasy Progressive. When he first defined his party's programme, it consisted of pledges to remove the duty on butcher's meat, to reduce the wheat tax, to introduce a duty on brandy, and to veto the sale of liquor to natives; worthy causes all, but somewhat elusive as a statement of policy on the lips of Rhodes.

In fact his campaign developed into a series of personal attacks: on Kruger, whom he always carefully distinguished from the Dutch in general; on Schreiner, who had been prepared to go to war with him against Kruger over the Drifts crisis in 1895 and then deserted him after the Raid; on Merriman, who had encouraged the Reformers to revolution in Johannesburg and then also let him down; on Hofmeyr, "the Mole", burrowing underground and not daring to come out into the open; on Innes and the Moderates, whom he called "the Mugwumps", because they called themselves Progressives but voted with the Bond. Very little was said in the election about redistribution, which was the cause that had brought it about and the issue which it was being fought to settle.

Rhodes himself stood for his old constituency of Barkly West, but friends who feared that the large Dutch vote there would go against him also nominated him for Namaqualand. He was so confident of his personal success—rightly, as it turned out, for he was elected for both constituencies—that he devoted much of his energy to helping supporters elsewhere. He spoke frequently, sometimes two or three times a day, in August and September: at Barkly West, Longlands, Klipdam, Vryburg, Kimberley, Cape Town and many other places. Garrett was standing at Victoria East; Jameson had been persuaded to stand down, to Rhodes's regret, and was inclined to write bitterly of him at this time; Fuller and other friends were safely elected. Rhodes showed tact and generosity even in the heat of the fight.[4] To one supporter he wired offering to refrain from coming to speak for him if his name would be an embarrassment. To De Waal, a Bondsman but still a personal friend, he sent congratulations on his election, "as you are a warm opponent of mine"; but his secretary, confused by the paradoxical expression, wrote "supporter" instead of "opponent", and then had to correct the text. There was no doubt that Rhodes was enjoying the fight, and his speeches read vigorously and well. But contemporaries agreed that the bitterness between the two white races was unexampled, Rhodes and Schreiner each uninhibitedly laying it to the blame of the other. Rhodes's trees and animals in the grounds of Groote Schuur were deliberately destroyed by hostile gangs, though it would be unjust to suppose that such vandalism was encouraged or organised by the Bond.

The result was very close. The Progressives had a majority of electoral votes, but Schreiner's South African Party won a narrow majority of seats. Such a result obviously strengthened the case for redistribution. Rhodes tried to use it at first to keep Sprigg's government in power, which Milner refused to tolerate, and then to make sure that Schreiner, who took office on 14 October, should pass a Redistribution Bill in spite of his victory. Schreiner's first statement of policy on 17 October indicated that a modified measure would be introduced, which Rhodes bitterly

attacked as inadequate. With the help of De Waal, nominally
Schreiner's supporter, Rhodes contrived to force on the Government a postponement of the Bill and an inter-party conference to
produce an agreed measure. The conference was held between
Schreiner, Rhodes, Innes and a Bondsman, te Water, who had
been a member of Sprigg's government. A new compromise Bill
was drafted, creating eighteen new seats and rearranging some
boundaries, and it passed the House unopposed. Rhodes's object
of redistribution was thus to a modest degree achieved; but the
effect of it as a means of bringing about unification through Parliament was forestalled by the outbreak of the Boer War a year later.

Contemporaneously with his efforts at the Cape, Rhodes was
also trying to bring the sister-colony of Natal into line, so that
they could advance to union on parallel courses. Just as the
"customs clause" was his instrument of uniformity in the northern territories, so a "permissive federation" Bill was to be the instrument at the Cape and Pietermaritzburg. A customs union was
created by the Cape Colony, Natal and the Orange Free State in
April 1898, but Rhodes wished to carry it further, into a formal
federation. He even made over his property at Groote Schuur to
the future federal Government as the home of its future Prime
Minister. Escombe, the Prime Minister of Natal, was not at first
one of Rhodes's admirers, but gradually he was won over. The
rapprochement had begun before the Cape Assembly elections in
1898, and by the end of the year Escombe was a whole-hearted
ally, plotting with him how they might achieve their common
end. In 1899 Rhodes set about enlarging Escombe's vision by
inviting him to share a trip to the North, but the trip was delayed
and finally made impossible by the outbreak of the Boer War. So
this step also in Rhodes's advance to union was frustrated, and it
came about only after his death, in a very different form.[5]

To be the leader of a parliamentary Opposition was not Rhodes's
métier. Milner tried to educate him for the part, but in vain. Having forced the Redistribution Bill on Schreiner, his attention to
parliamentary business during the rest of 1898 was desultory. He
spoke in the House in November on his plans for developing the
North, and later in the month on the Meat Duties Bill, which he
had pledged the Progressives to fight. Early in December he attacked Schreiner for trying to rush through a Rhodesian Appellate
Jurisdiction Bill without having consulted him. In the middle of
the month he was again in conflict with Schreiner, this time over a
motion introduced by Rhodes himself on irrigation works. Soon

afterwards he left the Cape for Kimberley, where he addressed the Annual General Meeting of De Beers on 19 December, and then sailed for England before the end of the month to settle the business of his railways and telegraph in the North. The short-lived revival of his spark of interest in Cape politics was virtually extinguished.

* * *

Apart from the railway and the telegraph, which have been dealt with in the previous chapter, there was one other matter to be settled during Rhodes's visit to England: the Will. It had not been touched since 1893, which was about as long as any of his Wills had lasted. Six successive versions in 1877, 1882, 1888, 1891, 1892 and 1893 had gradually crystallised his "great idea" from a shapeless and even indefinable dream, leaving the details to Neville Pickering or Lord Rothschild or W. T. Stead or whoever struck his fancy for the moment, to a concrete reality. From first to last the intention was quite simply to remould the world, but that was easier said than done. A secret society seemed for a long time to be the answer, and this theme dominated the first five Wills: in 1888, indeed, Lord Rothschild was instructed in a covering letter to "take Constitution Jesuits if obtainable and insert 'English Empire' for 'Roman Catholic Religion'." A year later, however, he had met Stead and his ideas began to mature. The notion that education might be a more fruitful method than a pseudo-Jesuitical conspiracy found expression for the first time in the Will of 1892, which provided for a site near Cape Town and a legacy of £10,000 to South African College to establish a residential college "on or as near as may be the Oxford and Cambridge system". Lord Rothschild, Stead and Hawksley, however, were still to use the residue (after bequests to relations) for the old, vague, conspiratorial purposes. It was only after signing this fifth Will, according to Stead, that Rhodes one day, while travelling on the Red Sea to Africa, had the inspiration of scholarships.

Scholarships first appear in the sixth Will, that of 1893. They were then to total thirty-six in all, for "young colonials" from South Africa, Australia, Canada and New Zealand. In a covering letter to the Will, Rhodes expressed the hope "that the Colonies and the Mother Country may never separate". His thoughts had not yet extended beyond them to embrace the U.S.A., which entered into his scheme only in 1899; still less to Germany, which entered only in 1901. Indeed, at this date, to judge from his conversations with

Stead, the U.S.A. appeared in his eyes in the guise of a rival and
an enemy; he even foresaw a hundred years of commercial war
with the Americans before the Anglo-Saxon nations were re-
united, though at the same time he recognised advantages in the
American system of government over that of Westminster, because it did not burden legislators "with the responsibility of
cleaning the parish drains". The combination of jealousy and
rivalry with which he looked upon both the Americans and the
Germans no doubt contributed to his later decisions to include
them in his scholarship plan. As he said in the final codicil to his
final Will, "the object is that an understanding between the three
great powers will render war impossible and educational relations
make the strongest tie". No doubt the fact of a common racial
descent was also in his mind, for he had told Stead, prophetically,
that religion was waning as a cause of strife, its place being taken
by race.

Rhodes had always a passionate belief in education. He knew
that Oxford men were always to be found at the top of the tree;
he had determined to complete his own education even when he
was a rich man; he subscribed liberally to the promotion of education wherever the opportunity offered—even as far afield as
Khartoum, where he helped Kitchener to found a school. This
passion was well known to his friends. In the middle of 1895—
while the revolution in Johannesburg was being plotted, in fact—
Lord Grey, who was not yet involved in his Will, proposed to
Rhodes on his own initiative that he should found a prize at Oxford for "the best essay or Poem on some subject connected with
the growth of the Empire". The idea was to counteract the impression that Rhodes was "rather a self-interested Africander
than a disinterested Englishman". Nothing came of the proposal: the year of the Raid was a bad one for educational plans.
But in any case Grey's ideas, although they lay in the right field,
would have been too unambitious for Rhodes. He wanted to use
education to change the world; he did not even draw the line,
according to Stead, at annexing the planets.[6]

He discussed his plans with Rosebery too. In May 1898, during Rhodes's short visit to England, they had a long and agreeable conversation, which Rosebery recorded in his betting book,
and they discussed both the past and the future. It was on this
occasion that Rhodes told Rosebery something of the part played
by W. L. Jackson, the Chairman of the Select Committee, in
"editing" one or more of the telegrams presented at the Enquiry

into the Raid. They talked also of the Will and the plan for scholarships to be offered "to colleges of each colony and U.S.— this more doubtful—to pass 3 men through Oxford or Cambridge". Such is Rosebery's recollection of what was perhaps the only occasion when Rhodes seriously considered including Cambridge in the scheme, though he was urged by others to do so. He told Rosebery, too, that he had "brought Beit into the scheme", and dwelt on the fact that Beit was childless—as, of course, he was himself, but he feared that his own remote heirs would "probably dissipate his fortune in follies". It was to prevent this that he was proposing to create a trust; and he expected, according to Rosebery, to leave enough to provide an income of half a million pounds a year, which proved grossly over-optimistic in the event.

Such were the thoughts that had been maturing in Rhodes's mind when he undertook his last Will, in close consultation with Stead, during his visit to England in 1899. It was signed on 1 July. A number of personal provisions precede the great plan for the scholarships. He was to be buried in the Matopos, at the site he called the "View of the World", and a monument was to be erected there to the first Matabele War. No one else was to be buried there except by a decision of the Government of Rhodesia and the Federal Government of South Africa after union: a provision which was in due course fulfilled when Dr. Jameson lay at his side. His estate in England was to pass to his family, to the exclusion of his half-sister. Oriel College was to receive £100,000, with the proviso that they should consult trustees about the investment of the legacy, "as the College authorities live secluded from the world and so are like children as to commercial matters". Groote Schuur, together with a sum of £1,000 a year to maintain the estate and to provide a carriage, horses and stablemen, was left to the Federal Prime Minister when union should be achieved, until which date it was to be "a park for the people". Detailed provisions were also made for his various properties in Rhodesia, with emphasis upon all Rhodes's familiar themes: irrigation, popular instruction and amusement, afforestation, and even "a short railway from Bulawayo to Westacre so that the people of Bulawayo may enjoy the glory of the Matopos from Saturday to Monday". But these are no more than the preliminaries to the "great idea".

The clauses providing for the scholarships begin with a general explanation of Rhodes's intentions. He had noted that many South African students went to Edinburgh because of its excellent medical school, but he preferred Oxford because of the residential system; though he urged Oxford at the same time to improve its medical school—a hope which was eventually realised with the help of another great benefactor a generation later. He then expounded the value of a "union of the English-speaking peoples throughout the world", including the U.S.A. His aim in creating scholarships was that of "promoting an attachment to the country from which they have sprung but without I hope withdrawing them or their sympathies from the land of their birth". He listed the fifteen colonies from which sixty scholars of the British Empire were to be drawn, to whom were to be added two from each of the United States. The U.S.A. was thus to have a large preponderance of scholars, though the trustees were empowered to create new scholarships when their income grew. The silly legend that Rhodes thought there were still only thirteen American states has been exploded long since by Sir Francis Wylie.

He also listed the qualities required of his scholars and the proportions to be assigned to them; literary and scholastic to prevail with four points out of ten; manly sports, qualities of manhood (defined as "truth, courage, devotion to duty, sympathy for and protection of the weak, kindliness, unselfishness and fellowship") and moral force of character each to count two out of ten. In conversation with Stead, he used cruder language about these qualities: "smugness", "brutality" and "unctuous rectitude" replaced the first, second and fourth; so it is not surprising that a later codicil revised the proportions.

Two other peculiarities marked the scheme. One was the system of selection: the first qualification to be determined by examination, the second and third by ballot among the candidate's fellow-students, and the fourth by the headmaster of the candidate's school. This provision shows that Rhodes was not thinking in 1899, as he clearly was in the Will of 1893, of students coming to Oxford from universities and colleges, but at an earlier age, direct from school; and the provision has not been strictly observed by his trustees in practice. The second peculiarity, on the other hand, enabled his trustees to follow the letter of his Will in a way that is hardly likely to have been Rhodes's intention. He laid it down that "no student shall be qualified or disqualified for election to a Scholarship on account of his race or religious opinions". When Rhodes spoke of "race" in a South African context, he invariably meant the distinction between Dutch and British: if he meant to refer to the coloured races, he spoke invariably of "the native question" in distinction from "the race question". It must be considered doubtful whether he personally envisaged coloured students benefiting from his Will; but such has been the fortunate result of the words he used. The results of his ideas were often different from his intentions, both for better and for worse, and this is one of the occasions when they were better.

In a covering letter to his Will, he spoke of having been impelled by two motives which he distinguished as "the higher motive" and "the personal motive". The higher motive he identified with a phrase of Aristotle, which is today inscribed round the base of the dome in Rhodes House. He interpreted it in his own words to mean "the active working of the soul in pursuit of the highest object in a complete life", which is an abridged translation of the original: "a working of the soul in the way of excellence, or, if excellence admits of degrees, in the way of the best and most perfect excellence; and, we must add, in a complete life." It was Aristotle's definition of the Good of Man. Rhodes's verdict on his own achievement was that he had failed to fulfil it, "but the highest object has been to me the greatness of my country". The Greek philosopher would probably have been surprised by the identification. Less so, the Roman poet to whom Rhodes turned to identify "the personal motive". He explained that "owing to reading Horace when a boy at school I then determined that I would as far as possible attain the object expressed in the Ode beginning:

> "*Exegi monumentum aere perennius*
> *Regalique situ pyramidum altius.*"

The "great idea" had now taken its final shape.

But Rhodes abhorred finality, and continued to refine and perfect his dream until the end of his life. A series of codicils modified the details at several points: altering the trustees, for instance, and adjusting the proportions between the qualities required of his scholars. Only a few weeks after signing the Will, he wrote two letters to Hawksley while *en route* back to South Africa, to clarify his intentions still further.[7] One, which is dated July 1899 from the R.M.S. *Scot*, instructs Hawksley on the use of the surplus funds, on which his last will is exceptionally reticent:

"My idea as to the yearly income of the balance of funds in my estate after providing for present scholarships and
o

perhaps some more that the trustees may create. My idea is
that they should be spent on the maintenance and extension
of Imperial thought by a party, literature, etc. You could have
a large number in the House of Commons who whilst being
either liberal or Conservative would be above all things
Imperial, in fact make the Imperial idea paramount. You
might in time have a distinct Imperial party in the House of
Commons though the name might be distasteful to the
electors and therefore perhaps better avoided. You should
also select the best of the students and send them to different
parts of the world to maintain Imperial thought in the
colonies, they would be better unmarried as the consideration
of babies and other domestic agenda generally destroys
higher thought. Please understand I am in no sense a woman
hater but this particular business is better untrammelled
with material thought."

The second letter to Hawksley, undated but written from
Madeira, returns to the theme of the scholarships:

"I think I have hit the phrase

'in awarding the scholarships great consideration shall be
given to those who have shewn during school days that
they have instincts to lead and take an interest in their
schoolmates which attributes will be likely in after life to
guide them to esteem the performance of public duties as
their highest aim'

the last thing I want is a bookworm.

"I do not think you will beat the above the thought came
from the sea.

"The temporary nature of human life is very depressing, as
soon as you have drafted kindly post to me for signature, or
some hidden devil may whip me off before my worldly de-
positions are signed."

After the touching and characteristic second paragraph,
Rhodes returned to other, more mundane themes: a renewed
tirade against Hicks-Beach, the Chancellor of the Exchequer, who
"is not fit to be treasurer to a village council and yet is in charge of
the empire"; and the familiar theme of the Bechuanaland Protectorate, which he still could not believe the Colonial Office
would be so foolish as to deny ultimately to the Chartered Company. The common thread of every paragraph was the fear of

death, the need to put one's house in order in good time, the maddening frustrations imposed on great visions by little-minded men. But at least his investment in Oxford University would be secure—perhaps the only dream of Rhodes that was truly to stand the test of time.

* * *

Other preoccupations of his last years, besides the Will, had a common basis in his craving to live in the memory of mankind after his death. The Will, the name of Rhodesia, the choice of his burial site in the Matopos, the legacy of Groote Schuur to future prime ministers, and many smaller plans and projects, were all elements in the quest for personal immortality, the *monumentum aere perennius*. But the fact that a man craves a monument more enduring than brass need not mean dispensing with less durable monuments, and even brazen monuments themselves. So Rhodes submitted to innumerable portraits, a few of which he liked, some of which he regarded with undisguised indignation and even violence: Baker says that he put a knife through more than one; and he particularly disliked a portrait by Fildes, and gave others away in contempt. There are also five full-size statues of him in South Africa, as well as many busts in London, Oxford and elsewhere. Of these too he was a harsh judge. He objected particularly to a bust by Tweed, who later carved the panels for the memorial to Allan Wilson's last stand on the Shangani River, and he even stopped payments to the sculptor until Hawksley insisted, under the threat of litigation, that he must pay up.[8]

The most famous of all visible monuments to Rhodes was not originally intended to be connected with his name at all. It is G. F. Watts's statue, "Physical Energy", which now stands on Table Mountain just outside Cape Town. The two men had met, but had not taken to each other, though a painting of Rhodes was commissioned from Watts in 1898. The circumstances in which the famous statue became linked with Rhodes are described in a letter from Lord Grey dated 11 June 1898—the same letter, incidentally, in which Grey misled Rhodes into believing that the Government was certain to guarantee the loan needed for the railway through Northern Rhodesia. So far as the statue is concerned, it reads as follows:[9]

"... I breakfasted with Watts yesterday at 8 o'cl. but he did not show me his picture of you. He had got up that

morning at 3.30 and had commenced work in his studio at 4!
Pretty good for 81 . . . I had some talk of course with him
about your Portrait, hoped he wd be able to make your Portrait convey a suggestion of your life's work etc., and recognising the difficulty of doing this thro' the medium of
oils, suggested that it wd be most effectively done if his
Statue of Horse and Man—the apotheosis of 'Physical
Activity' cd be made to represent you—He took me to the
Statue and said following up our conversation 'Well, that is
Rhodes!' I hope he may decide to give the Head of the Rider
some resemblance to your features, so that the Statue may go
out to the world as his conception of your character. It will
be a far finer monument to you than any that can be painted
on canvas . . ."

Watts's statue, two poems by Kipling, a magnificent building
at Oxford by his favourite architect, Herbert Baker—these should
have been enough to give Rhodes the artistic embodiment of immortality which he desired in addition to the perpetuation of his
name in the scholarships, in Rhodesia and among the landed
gentry of his native land. Indeed, these things were enough. But
the truth is that he desired something more than immortality,
something that he could not explain himself and practically no
one could explain for him. W. T. Stead, whose posthumous
commentary on the Will is perhaps the most revealing thing ever
written about him, said that "so utterly incomprehensible was
the higher mystic side of Mr. Rhodes's character to those among
whom it was his fate to live and work, that after a few vain
efforts to explain his real drift he gave up the task in despair".[10]
No wonder that his trustees found it difficult to interpret his
wishes for the disposal of the surplus funds of his legacy; perhaps it was as well that there has never been much surplus to dispose of. He was still dreaming in his last years, as Stead makes
clear, of the conquest of the world by the English-speaking races,
nor did he draw the line at annexing the planets if it were possible.
How were the friends to whom he bequeathed his dreams to
carry out their task?

It was better that Rhodes's dreams should not become definite
and specific, because that would have defeated their object. He
was trying to burst out beyond the confines of time and space,
which were so oppressive to him, into the infinite. The limitations
of time had always weighed him down, even when he was not

expecting imminent death: in 1900 he told Stead that he expected to live fourteen years, but that was a ridiculously little span. The scholarships were to release him from it. The world, too, was pitifully small to contain his ambitions, and yet he could not impose himself effectively even on such an out-of-the-way corner of it as the Cape Colony. No wonder the triviality of Cape politics disgusted the aspiring empire-builder! Only the North offered him a release from its claustrophobia.

Rhodesia, by its very name, would assure him of posterity, though his insufferable secretary, Le Sueur, took delight in reminding him that a country could change its name, as had happened to Van Diemen's Land. Rhodesia, too, had virtually no geographical limits, provided his drive to the north were fast and bold enough. It meant to Rhodes what the frontier meant to nineteenth-century Americans, or the virgin lands to twentieth-century Russians. It was another way of escape from the stifling limits of here and now. The Will and the North were the two dreams of Rhodes's last frustrated years. He called each of them indiscriminately his "idea", his "thought"; and he took comfort in them from the bitterness and buffeting of daily life.

Sources

Clark, G. N.: *Cecil Rhodes and his College*
Headlam, C.: *The Milner Papers*
Innes, James Rose: *An Autobiography*
James, R. V. Rhodes: *Rosebery*
Kruger, Paul: *Memoirs*
Laurence, Sir Perceval: *The Life of John Xavier Merriman*
Stead, W. T.: *The Last Will and Testament of Cecil J. Rhodes*
Walker, E. A.: *W. P. Schreiner—A South African*
Wylie, Sir Francis: *The American Oxonian*, Vol. XXXI (1944)
Vol. XXXII (1945)

Notes

1 Rhodes Papers, C. 2. 174.
2 Rhodes Papers, A. 128.
3 "Vindex", 520–44.
4 Rhodes Papers, B. 1034 (to Abrahamson); B. 1047 (to De Waal).
5 Rhodes Papers, B. 928 (to Natal Assembly); C. 16. 57 and 58 (Escombe to Rhodes); B. 1203 and 1211 (Rhodes to Escombe); B. 1229 (to Jameson).
6 Rhodes Papers, C. 16. 56 (Kitchener); C. 3B. 251 (Grey to Harris).
7 R.H.L. Rhodes Wills, 20–1.
8 Rhodes Papers, C. 11. 5 and 7.
9 Rhodes Papers, C. 4. 5.
10 Stead, *op. cit.*, 56.

CHAPTER TWENTY-FIVE

THE BREAKDOWN OF PEACE

THE North, in Rhodes's later terminology, always included the Transvaal. If a real union of southern Africa were to be brought about, it would have to include the Transvaal; and the Transvaal would first have to be tamed and purged. There was little prospect of this so long as Kruger was alive. He was re-elected President in February 1898, for his fourth term at the age of 72, by a record majority. Jameson had exaggerated when he said that the old man would see them all buried, but he was at least destined to outlive Rhodes. The notion that Krugerism was something different from the general spirit of burgher nationalism, which Rhodes had so much stressed in his election speeches, appeared to be repudiated by the burghers themselves. In fact there was no way of cutting the Transvaal down to size after the Jameson Raid, so that it would fit comfortably into an equal union, except by coercion; and coercion meant war.

To Rhodes, sick and impatient as he now was, this fact cannot have been in much doubt. Yet in the years between the Raid and the Boer War he played little part in guiding policy or shaping events so far as they concerned relations between the Transvaal and the Cape Colony. For this fact the reason certainly did not lie in the accident that he held no office; that would never have been a justification for inactivity on Rhodes's part, as he showed in Rhodesia, Bechuanaland, Natal and the Cape Colony itself. There were, rather, two different reasons: firstly, the extreme suspicion with which he was regarded in the Transvaal, so that he wished to give no excuse for accusations of interference; and secondly, the alacrity with which Milner adopted towards the Transvaal the very policy that Rhodes would have wished, so that he needed no pushing in the right direction.

The first reason would not have been compelling without the second. Rhodes knew that his slightest gesture was liable to misinterpretation in Pretoria, where it was common gossip that as soon as the celebrations of Queen Victoria's Diamond Jubilee were over in 1897, he intended to seize the Transvaal. "Beware of Rhodes and keep your powder dry," was in effect the slogan of Kruger's election campaign in 1898. The foundation of a branch of the South African League in Johannesburg was attributed by Kruger to the direct and malevolent instigation of Rhodes. He was named as the arch-villain of the march to war by de Villiers, Chief Justice at the Cape, by Schreiner, his Prime Minister, by Innes and Merriman and Hofmeyr, his former friends—all of them in touch with Boer friends in the Orange Free State or the Transvaal. Even Milner shared these suspicions in his early months. Before he had left England, he wrote in March 1897 that "the Rhodesites are, as far as I can judge, itching to involve us in a quarrel" with the Transvaal. The military commander of the Cape Colony's garrison, General Sir William Butler, who deputised for Milner when he was in England at the end of 1898, blamed Rhodes still more emphatically for all the troubles between the Cape and the Transvaal. Leyds also reported Rhodes as having "consistently said", obviously not with disapproval, that Chamberlain intended to coerce the Transvaal into a Union. Little wonder then that Rhodes, who was sensitive to these accusations, was determined to keep his hands clean. "I keep aloof from the Transvaal crisis," he told McDonald in 1899, "so that no one will be able to say if things go wrong that Rhodes is in it again."

By 1899, however, Milner's own opinions had changed. Brilliant though he was intellectually and as an administrator, Milner had an impulsive and often eccentric judgment. He had shown it from the beginning by the way he leapt to conclusions about Rhodes before seeing anything of what he was trying to do in southern Africa. He showed it again, in a more startling form, with the suggestion that Garrett, the editor of the *Cape Times* and a fellow-disciple of Stead, should succeed Bower as Imperial Secretary in 1897. Chamberlain was taken aback at the idea, and refused vehemently. He appointed instead a member of his own staff at the Colonial Office, G. V. Fiddes, perhaps with the idea that a closer eye should be kept on his unpredictable pro-consul. But he was not so taken aback, at any rate at first, by the readiness with which Milner faced the prospect of war with the Transvaal. It was the rest of the Cabinet rather than Chamberlain that was shocked.

Milner wrote on 20 March 1897, before he had even sailed from England, that war might be inevitable, and he faced the prospect calmly. Again in early August he wrote to Chamberlain that the despatch of a naval squadron to Delagoa Bay and the reinforcement of the South African garrison, though obviously moves that risked war, had probably served to avert it. Such arguments appealed to Chamberlain, who was repeatedly pressing strong measures on the Cabinet. But as time passed, the interpretations which the Colonial Secretary and the High Commissioner put upon their strong measures began to diverge. Chamberlain believed that the threat of war would suffice to bring Kruger to heel. Milner gradually realised that no permanent solution could be achieved in this way. An actual outbreak of war, short and decisive, and an actual conquest of the Transvaal, were the only logical conclusions of the policy of firmness with the Transvaal.

Milner therefore needed no pushing forward by Rhodes. It was the restraining hand which Chamberlain was forced to lay upon him that Milner resented as the year 1898 went by. Chamberlain reminded him in March 1898 that "the principal object of H.M. Government in South Africa at present is peace"; yet even so Chamberlain was under criticism from the Liberal leaders a few months later for his readiness to risk a war. Milner first, and Chamberlain more reluctantly behind him, had gradually been convinced that there was "no way out of the political troubles of South Africa except reform in the Transvaal or war". Chamberlain still believed in reform, but Milner did not. It was a surprising change of front for a naturally cautious and fundamentally liberal High Commissioner, who had come to South Africa to reconcile the two white races and repair the damage of the Jameson Raid; and one who had even been shocked himself by the bellicose tone of Chamberlain's speech at a farewell dinner to him in London. But it is only fair to Rhodes to acquit him of all responsibility for converting Milner to a war policy towards the Transvaal, which was the work rather of Kruger and of Milner himself.

The stages in the march to war with the Transvaal, which belong only to the background of Rhodes's biography, may be briefly summarised. In March 1897 a treaty of mutual defence was concluded between the Transvaal and the Orange Free State, which Kruger called a direct consequence of the Jameson Raid. The following month, just before Milner left England, two despatches from Chamberlain were presented to Kruger, summing up the British case against the Transvaal on account of breaches of the London Convention of 1884 and demanding the repeal or suspension of discriminatory legislation against the *Uitlanders*. Kruger's first reaction was not entirely discouraging. The Aliens Immigration Act and the Aliens Expulsion Act were repealed;

journals which had been suppressed under the Press Law were allowed to reappear under new names; and an Industrial Commission was appointed to investigate the dynamite monopoly, one of the chief grievances of the *Uitlanders*. The celebration of the Queen's Diamond Jubilee in the summer promoted a genuine upsurge of good feeling in the Transvaal; and Dr. Leyds, Kruger's State Secretary, who was in London for the occasion, made an unexpectedly favourable impression on both Chamberlain and Selborne.

But there were new troubles boiling up, both internally and externally. Within the Transvaal, there was a long-smouldering dispute between Kruger and his Chief Justice, Kotzé, over the right of the courts to test the legislation of the *Volksraad* by the Constitution (*Grondwet*), which reached a first crisis in February 1897, and a second and more serious one a year later. Kruger's peremptory dismissal of Kotzé did more than any other single event to convince Milner that he was irredeemable and inaccessible to reason. Externally, the major issue between Kruger and the British Government was the President's claim to the right of arbitration by a foreign power in disputes between the two governments, which would imply that the Transvaal was an independent sovereign state. In other words, it would involve acceptance of Kruger's thesis that the British suzerainty written into the Pretoria Convention of 1881 had lapsed in the London Convention of 1884.

Milner and Chamberlain were at one in holding that suzerainty still prevailed, but the legal basis of their contention was slender; so the less it needed to be asserted, the better. Meanwhile Kruger's mood of co-operativeness soon passed. The report of the Industrial Commission on the dynamite monopoly, damning as it was to the Government and astonishingly satisfactory to the mining industry and the High Commissioner, was accepted by the Transvaal Government on paper and evaded in practice. The prospect of an improved franchise for the *Uitlanders* receded, and Milner decided in August 1897 that the time was not yet ripe to press for it. By the turn of the year, however, he was in a more aggressive mood. A despatch reasserting the claim to suzerainty was published in December, and naturally repudiated by the Transvaal Government. In March 1898 Milner made his celebrated speech at Graaff Reinet, attacking the Transvaal Government and warning the Cape Dutch against being seduced from their loyalty. All accounts agree that this speech marked a decisive watershed in South African history. Its effect, wrote Innes, was "to make Milner at once the real leader of the British section". A modern historian, J. S. Marais, calls it "a challenge to all South Africans to choose their side". Rhodes was delighted to see his work done for him. He knew now that "you could trust Milner".

Chamberlain was not so sure, and Salisbury was more uncertain still. Not for the first time, Chamberlain was being held back from a firm policy with the Transvaal, and having to hold back Milner in his turn. The speech at Graaff Reinet worried the British Government so much that both Chamberlain and Selborne wrote to Milner advising him to moderate his language and not to force the pace. Milner felt that he was being let down from behind, as men on the spot often feel. But like other men on the spot, he did not appreciate the impulses that were affecting Chamberlain most strongly in the middle of 1898. The Anglo-French crisis which culminated in the confrontation of Kitchener and Marchand at Fashoda in September was already in sight on the horizon. A final attempt to negotiate the purchase of Delagoa Bay from Portugal was also under way. The attitude of Germany to both problems was vital and uncertain. No risk could be run with the Transvaal, Germany's best friend in Africa, until Britain's problems with the European powers were resolved. In the event, the French withdrew before the threat of force at Fashoda; and the Germans frustrated the Anglo-Portuguese negotiations over Delagoa Bay. But Chamberlain gained some comfort even from the setback with the Portuguese, for an Anglo-German agreement was reached on the eventual, though hypothetical, disposal of the Portuguese territories in Africa, as part of which the Germans virtually disinterested themselves in the fate of the Transvaal. Chamberlain was operating on a larger canvas than Milner appreciated at the time.

So disappointed was Milner at the misunderstanding which he detected that as soon as the Cape elections were over and the new government installed in October 1898, he asked to return to England for consultations. Arriving in England in mid-November, he found his fears confirmed. The "no-war" policy was still in favour in the highest quarters, he wrote to his Imperial Secretary, Fiddes, on 25 November, but the Anglo-German agreement gave some cause for satisfaction. He was also reasonably satisfied with his success in explaining his views and policy to Chamberlain. While he was away from South Africa, however, things had begun to get worse. He had left behind him a Prime Minister,

W. P. Schreiner, who was resolutely opposed to hostilities or even firmness against the Transvaal; and what was worse, a Deputy High Commissioner, General Butler, who considered that South Africa needed a rest-cure, and refused to put in train the military preparations for which he was responsible as Commander-in-Chief. The murder of an *Uitlander* by a policeman in Johannesburg on Christmas Eve, and the refusal of General Butler to receive a petition to the Queen from the *Uitlanders*, had sharply exacerbated the situation. Milner, on his way back to the Cape, wrote to Selborne about "Butler's idiotic proceedings" and described him as "out-Krugering Kruger". Yet this was the man with whom he had to concert the defence of the Cape Colony until barely two months before war broke out.

In 1899 the pace of the march towards war accelerated. Early in March the Transvaal Government communicated a plan for a comprehensive settlement of the *Uitlanders'* grievances, which Milner regarded with cautious scepticism. Various such offers were made during the course of the year, both officially and unofficially, by the Transvaal Government; but the fact was that no compromise could conceivably be devised which would both satisfy the *Uitlanders* and preserve the Boer character, or even the ultimate independence, of the Republic. All their offers were therefore either inadequate or accompanied by unacceptable conditions, such as the right to take disputes between the British and Transvaal governments to arbitration by a third power. So the *Uitlanders* were encouraged by Milner to treat such overtures suspiciously. "Keep pegging away," was his advice to them, and they did so. They collected signatures to a new petition, 21,684 in all, which was forwarded to the Queen, not without some hesitation on Chamberlain's part. By May 1899 Milner was saying that war "might be the only way out", and expressing fears for Kimberley; but he could not persuade either his Prime Minister or his Commander-in-Chief to take adequate measures for its protection until it was almost too late. Schreiner more than once thought of resigning in despair, and Milner more than once thought of dismissing him; but both refrained, perhaps because both realised that the only alternative Prime Minister would be Rhodes. General Butler was equally hard to displace, and continued his policy of obstructive pacifism until August.

A last major effort to forestall war was made at a conference between Milner and Kruger in Bloemfontein at the end of May, to which the moderates on all sides—Hofmeyr and Schreiner at the Cape, Steyn and Fischer of the Orange Free State, and the young Attorney-General, Jan Smuts, in the Transvaal—attached the highest importance. But Kruger and Milner were equally stubborn; Milner refused to discuss anything else until the *Uitlander* franchise was settled, and Kruger argued that to enfranchise the *Uitlanders* meant surrendering his country to foreigners. Milner broke off the conference abruptly on 5 June, just before receiving a telegram from Chamberlain instructing him to persevere. From that day onwards the outbreak of war was only a matter of time. Chamberlain published a despatch from Milner in which the *Uitlanders* were compared to "helots" and the case for intervention was described as overwhelming. He declared that the "sands were running out" and drove the Cabinet hard into preparations for war. Each side was busy drafting its ultimatum in September, waiting only for the most favourable moment: on the Boer side, for the spring grass on the *veld* to feed their horses, on the British side for the arrival of reinforcements from India. On 11 October the war broke out, with the Orange Free State reluctantly following the Transvaal into hostilities and Natal no less reluctantly compelled by a Boer invasion to take sides with the Cape and the Imperial Government. Both sides expected a short war and an early victory.

*   *   *

In the melancholy sequence of events leading up to the Boer War, Rhodes played little part. During the first half of 1899 he was in Europe, apart from a flying visit to Egypt, preoccupied with other matters: the railway, the telegraph, the Will. When he sailed at last for the Cape on 1 July, he found that in addition to his current annoyances—Hicks-Beach, King Leopold, the directors of De Beers—he now had a new one aboard the ship: Princess Radziwill. She had been trying to re-enter his life for some time, though there is no trace of any correspondence on either side between April 1897 and April 1899. In the latter month she wrote to Rhodes asking for advice on investments. To her disappointment, all that she received in reply was advice on investments; but even that was something more than Rhodes usually gave his friends. Unfortunately, he added the casual postscript: "I hope I may see you on your return." Whether they met again in London or not—he was writing from the Burlington Hotel—there is no knowing, but the Princess contrived to travel to the Cape on the same ship as Rhodes. She pressed herself upon him during the voyage with an insistence which makes pathetic reading in Jourdan's memoirs. A bachelor, chiefly surrounded by bachelors, Rhodes was no match for the romantic adventuress. By the time they reached Cape Town, it had become impossible to shake her off.

On the first night at sea, she planted herself, by a well-contrived accident, at Rhodes's dinner-table, and remained there for the rest of the journey. Even Jourdan admitted at first that she was an acquisition: she was clever, witty, vivacious and charming, although she had the embarrassing habit, which Metcalfe told Jourdan was quite common among foreigners, of expressing herself "rather bluntly on delicate matters". At first Jourdan blushed, and so did Rhodes. So far as Jourdan was concerned, she recovered her standing by telling him heart-rending stories of the way her husband had treated her. Her voice was soft, trembling, hesitating and full of pathos and sadness, which stirred the blood in the young man's veins: "I felt as if I would kill the brutal Prince Radziwill if ever I met him." Jourdan, in fact, was a push-over: it is curious to find a telegram from him, dated over a year later, containing simply the question, "Who is Princess?"[1] Rhodes, on the other hand, was not quite so simple; and he was the main target. The Princess's solution to the problem was to faint in his arms one day while they were walking together on deck. Jourdan said he would "never forget the absolutely abject look of helplessness on his face". After that, Rhodes kept away from the main deck as much as he could, and even tried to avoid the Princess, joking contemptuously about her to conceal his embarrassment. But it was too late.

She had acquired a standing invitation to meals at Groote Schuur, which Rhodes bitterly regretted. "There was always a strained feeling when she was in the house," Jourdan writes, "and Mr. Rhodes appeared most uncomfortable." McDonald records that he had instructions never to leave Rhodes alone in a room with her. She used her contacts with Rhodes, and with Milner too, who was also a bachelor with inadequate resistance to her claws, for the promotion of her career as a political journalist. She sent articles to editors in Russia and England, including W. T. Stead, who regarded her highly, even after he had proved her a liar, and always warmly defended her to Rhodes. Her correspondence with Rhodes, from the Mount Nelson Hotel at Cape Town, begins within a few weeks of her arrival, and it suggests from the first an intimacy which was real but already beginning to be tiresome. She is feeling low and cannot come to lunch, she writes on 12 April: will he come and see her? Two days later, she says she has been warned against him. In September she again asks him to call on the 11th, and seeks a brief interview with him on the 30th. On the 17th she reports a complaint by the German Consul that he has been rude. On 5 October she apologises to Rhodes for having caused him to be upset. She has been worried about money, she explains, and also by her divorced husband. Such is the level and the trivial character of their early correspondence, at least on her side.[2]

Rhodes, who was always a reluctant letter-writer, seldom if ever replied. It is difficult to be sure how seldom, because there is doubt of the authenticity of the letters which the Princess later claimed, when she was in serious trouble in late 1901, to have received from Rhodes. A few weeks after Rhodes's death, she was convicted of forgery and sent to prison. The principal items in the indictment against her were charges of forging his signature to bills for various sums of money; but there were also included in the indictment two letters which she claimed to have received from him during 1901. These two forged letters naturally cast doubt on all the correspondence which the Princess said she had received from Rhodes, especially since none of the surviving letters purports to be an original. The matter is one of great perplexity, but it cannot be said for certain that all the Rhodes correspondence with the Princess is forged, since one of the surviving letters (that of April 1899) was admitted at her trial to be genuine.

In all, copies survive of twelve letters purporting to be from Rhodes to the Princess. There are seven in the Milner Papers at New College, Oxford, and five in the Radziwill Papers at Rhodes House: the texts will be found in Appendix B. They range in date from April 1899 to May 1901, and they are accompanied by other documents and letters attributed to Rhodes with equally suspect reliability. But it cannot be argued that because the Princess certainly forged some of them, therefore she forged all of them. She was undoubtedly a woman of fantastic imagination, and she succeeded in convincing the unlikeliest people of her *bone fides*; but just for that reason they may have committed some, though not all, of the indiscretions she attributed to them. Lord Salisbury, for instance, presumably did not make a habit of calling clandestinely at her rooms in London for confidential chats about the policy which his government was pursuing in South Africa, as her diary suggests. He did, however, on the evidence of one of his daughters and a daughter-in-law (later Lady Milner), almost certainly provide the Princess with a personal letter of introduction to Milner when she sailed for the Cape in 1899; for he had, after all, been liberally entertained at her husband's mansion in Berlin during the conference of 1878. The fact that she was a woman of brilliant talents, great social charm and *savoir faire*, as well as an incorrigibly romantic liar, makes it exceedingly hard to be sure where truth ends and fabrication begins in her story.

If the letters from Rhodes to the Princess were certainly genuine, they would throw an interesting light on his thoughts and policies in the last years of his life, particularly during the Boer War. Against their authenticity, it can be argued that a man who wrote few letters to anybody would hardly unburden himself so freely to a middle-aged female busybody whom he looked on with a mixture of amusement, contempt and exasperation. It is true, however, that these feelings only became acute in the later stages of their acquaintance: to begin with, he was impressed by the glamour of her wit and her aristocratic background. Against their authenticity can also be argued technical considerations. Some of the letters were typewritten, and according to Jourdan neither he nor Rhodes ever had a typewriter; but Jourdan was not Rhodes's only secretary, and he was a simple-minded young man who was certainly not privy to all Rhodes's secrets. Moreover, it was Rhodes's habit, as was noted by another former secretary, Currey, to keep his life in separate compartments and never to allow anyone to become intimate with him in more than one or two of them.

The most damaging consideration is, of course, that the Princess was a convicted forger; but the conviction in 1902 related to forgeries concerned mainly, if not entirely, with matters of finance (including letters about money) rather than politics. So far as the letters on political topics are concerned, it is noteworthy not only that they capture Rhodes's style and habit of thought with a skill amounting (if they are forged) to genius, but also that they interlock closely with contemporaneous events and Rhodes's reactions to those events, as known from other sources. The presumption is that if they were forged, they were forged at or very near the dates which the letters bear; and in the case of the earlier letters, this means from one to two years before the Princess attempted to make use of them in her hour of need. Since there was no reason in 1899 or 1900 to foresee the desperate straits in which she was to find herself at the end of 1901, it is hard to see why she should have constructed such a web of fabrication so long in advance, which no one but herself was to see at the time when she did it. On the other hand, webs of fabrication were part of her very existence.

No argument can be certain about the psychology of so extraordinary a woman, of whom W. T. Stead wrote in 1904: "I used to say that if it [her diary] were a fraud, Princess Radziwill possessed dramatic genius and imaginative talent much greater than that of any other human being that I had ever met." Stead then wryly added: "This, however, as the result proved, was the true explanation." Precisely there lies the crux of the problem. No one but a genius could have imitated Rhodes so perfectly—writing, moreover, in a foreign language—but the Princess was a genius in this particular way. On the whole, the evidence suggests that the earlier letters have a better chance of being genuine than the later. The earliest of all is in fact the only one that was admitted, on Rhodes's behalf, to be genuine at the Princess's trial: that was dated in April 1899. The second in the series, dated 10 September 1899, is a much more interesting letter than the first, because it indicates, if it is genuine, Rhodes's thoughts in the last few weeks before the outbreak of the Boer War. The later letters, which all fall within the period of the Boer War and lie under a progressively deeper shadow of suspicion, may be left for later consideration.[3]

The letter of 10 September (No. 2 in Appendix B) purports to answer a letter from the Princess about Rhodes's motives for withholding the "missing telegrams" from the Enquiry into the Raid. It gives familiar reasons, which the Princess could easily have picked up from general conversation, so that they are not conclusive indications of authenticity. There was the question of protecting the Queen's good name—because of assurances she had given to the Kaiser of the innocence of Chamberlain and the Colonial Office—an argument that Rhodes certainly used, or allowed to be used, though it was hardly decisive or soundly based. There was the need to safeguard the future of Rhodesia and "to obtain a free hand in South Africa", which would have been prejudiced by the production of the telegrams if they had led to the downfall of Chamberlain—a much more serious argument, which had in fact influenced Rhodes decisively.

It is interesting to see that the phrase about a "free hand in South Africa" practically echoes what George Wyndham wrote to Rhodes commenting on the Report of the Enquiry: "It has given a free hand to you in South Africa." [4] But the most interesting part of the letter concerns the prospect of a war with the Transvaal. "If Kruger does not climb down," the letter states, "the new year will see us masters of Pretoria." Several phrases echo the same thought: "A few weeks will see us masters of the Transvaal. As soon as troops arrive it will be a walk-over. . . . When my railway will be finished when our interests will have been established on a sound footing in the Transvaal then only will England be real mistress of the African continent."

Whether the letter is authentic or not, the Princess no doubt heard such phrases from Rhodes at the time. The contempt of Kruger and the Transvaal were characteristic of Rhodes's utterances in the last weeks of peace, which are confirmed from many sources. Indeed, such utterances were almost his only contribution to the preliminaries of the war. But whereas most other indications are that he did not, at least openly, expect a war to break out at all—in other words, he was sure that Kruger would "climb down"—here he appears to expect and welcome a war, assuming that it would be short and decisive. Whichever was his real thought, it is common ground between all reports of Rhodes's statements at the time about the quarrel with the Transvaal that it was a matter of "no importance whatever". According to the letter of 10 September, he told the Princess—and whether he wrote the letter or not, this is no doubt what he did tell many people—that "I don't understand how you can trouble yourself about the matter". He certainly did his best during the last weeks of peace to give substance to the implied attitude of total indifference to the Transvaal, by ostentatiously devoting himself to other, quite unrelated, interests in his public life.

One such interest was what he called the "native problem", on which his views, though they cannot be said to have radically changed, were evolving in a liberal direction. In his first speech on arrival at the Cape, on 18 July 1899, he re-stated and re-iterated his policy of "equal rights", this time in its maturer form: "equal rights for every civilised man south of the Zambesi." Among his few speeches in the Legislative Assembly during the following weeks were three in which he defended the natives' right to vote, against the attempts of Schreiner's government to disfranchise them. The passionate jeremiads of Olive Schreiner should not be allowed to obscure the fact that on this issue it was her enemy, Rhodes, whose views were progressive and her brother's that were reactionary.

Moreover, Rhodes sent an interesting telegram at this date to J. G. McDonald, defining his policy for distributing cattle in Rhodesia "to natives and white people that will work as I do not care about those who lie on their backs and sit in the sun all day". It was also at this date that he opposed the establishment of white police in Barotseland. The policy of treating Europeans and Africans on equal terms according to their abilities was now one which he not merely preached but practised. A year earlier he had declared that Africans were as much entitled to own land as Europeans in Rhodesia; and if that represented an ideal rather than a reality, it must nevertheless be counted as one in which Rhodes believed. It may be added to the reasons for his bitterness against Krugerism in the Transvaal, where both the practice and the theory were diametrically opposite.[5] The rest of Rhodes's political and parliamentary activities in the short interval before the war need little telling. They are for the most part consistent with his professed desire to stand aloof from the present great controversy, at least overtly. One may doubt whether his presentation of a lion to the Pretoria Zoo in September was intended as a gesture of conciliation or defiance; but Kruger at any rate had no doubts, and the director of the State Museum was instructed to return the animal, which he did with reluctance. Kruger was probably right in regarding the lion as Henry V regarded the Dauphin's tennis balls, but Rhodes's mischievous sense of humour was capable of combining two meanings in a single gesture: to taunt the detested President of the Transvaal with a symbol of British power, and to remind the Transvaal burghers that Englishman and Boer could still be friends.

Rhodes's contributions to public debate at this time were unprovocative. He spoke in the House on the Rhodesia Customs Bill on 26 July, and in the budget debate in August. It was the first budget to include provision for income tax, which Rhodes opposed; and he made his last speech in the House, attacking the Finance Bill, on 6 October, a week before Parliament was dismissed on the outbreak of war. The debates were acrimonious, Merriman and Schreiner in particular attacking Rhodes in violent terms. His friend Fuller noticed that he was by no means always quick to defend himself under such attacks, and so it was now. In a debate at the end of August, when Sprigg criticised the Government for allowing arms and ammunition to pass through the Cape Colony to the Orange Free State, Schreiner made a wholly irrelevant attack on Rhodes, to which (though he spoke in the debate) Rhodes left others to reply on his behalf. It later became known that the High Commissioner was himself aware of the transit of war supplies, and had not objected; and it is apparent from a note scribbled by Jourdan in the Gallery, which survives, that this information reached Rhodes during the debate.[6]

Only twice, when the Transvaal situation was the subject of debate, did he refer openly to it: once, on 22 August, when he predicted as usual that there would be no war; and once, on 30 August, when he alleged that his own opponent at Barkly West in the last election had been helped by funds from the Transvaal Secret Service. Otherwise he maintained his public position of aloofness from the quarrel. It needed no more help from him to force matters to a head.

His position is made clear in a letter to Stead, sent by Jourdan on Rhodes's behalf on 12 September, enclosing a satirical cartoon and comment on Kruger:[7]

"Mr. Rhodes desires me to forward the enclosed. He hopes your mind will not give way, rent between the Peace Conference and Sir Alfred Milner. He himself, though wholly quiescent on account of his past bad conduct in connection with the Transvaal, still wishes to place on record with you that he sides entirely with Sir Alfred Milner's views. He docs not advise him for the very good reason that Sir Alfred Milner takes only one person's advice and that is the advice of Sir Alfred Milner."

Although the last sentence has an ironical flavour, it is a truthful account of his policy of "leaving it to Milner". Rhodes's advice was unnecessary, because it was the same as Milner's.

But it is by no means certain that he did not make some contribution to the climax by his constant assertions that Kruger would never fight. His words can hardly have been without any effect. Two days after his return to the Cape, he declared in a speech that there was "not the slightest chance of war". Jameson, who had met him on arrival, repeated the same thing on the following day. A month later, Rhodes said in Parliament that there would be no bloodshed. "If Kruger is a sensible man, he will climb down in the end, and there will be a settlement." He wrote the same to Jameson on 6 September, and the same again to Milner on 13 September; and he repeated the refrain again and again to intimate friends, such as Michell and Beit. Even on the last day of September, although he admitted in a telegram to Heany at Bulawayo that the general opinion was that the Boers would fight, he added a saving clause which reserved his own opinion: "the matter will be settled one way or the other next week." Others, including Chamberlain and Milner, were long since convinced that war was certain.[8]

Some have suggested that Rhodes's apparently glaring error of judgment about the prospect of war was in fact deliberate. Innes recorded in his autobiography the conviction that "he was deliberately encouraging a policy which was bound to lead to war". He claimed to have indisputable private evidence of this belief. Innes is a sober and dependable witness, and the argument is plausible, though his source is not disclosed. For what it is worth, the purported letter of 10 September from Rhodes to Princess Radziwill supports the same interpretation. Schreiner had said in August that "the fundamental error which may yet embroil this sub-continent is the belief that when sufficient pressure is used Kruger will yield *everything*". It is known that many of the Boers were spoiling for a fight and feared only that Kruger might deprive them of it by concessions. Rhodes cannot have been oblivious of the possibility that a tough policy would lead to war rather than surrender, and that his own insistence on the certainty of Kruger's surrender would tend to promote the maintenance of just such a tough policy on the British side. Despite his professed determination to "keep aloof from the Transvaal crisis", he was certainly in touch with the Imperial South African Association in London, a body supported by George Wyndham, Rudyard Kipling and other Imperialists, which was actively preparing the public mind for war and doing so with Chamberlain's approval.

A letter to Rhodes of 22 July from C. W. Boyd, one of the organisers of the Association and also Rhodes's political secretary, gives a glimpse of what was going on:[9]

"Mr. Beit showed me your telegram dated Capetown 20 July beginning 'President Kruger etc.' The points indicated are being carefully taken up.

"I saw Mr. Chamberlain yesterday at the House of Commons for ¾ hour. The following summarises what he said—

(1) The Cabinet is quite united.

(2) It is extremely desirable to disarm the opposition and

doubtful people throughout the electorate by not seeming to refuse or discourage any concession of President Kruger.

(3) The Special Service Officers are being sent out as before and all the preparations continued, but while this is being done, quite openly as your cable recommends, the entire onus not only will lie upon President Kruger, but will be seen and admitted by all sections of opinion, to rest on him.

(4) There is such a thing as giving a man enough rope.

"Mr. C. seems very sensible of the discreet help, as he is good enough to call it, which is given him by your people. P.S. Dodd arrives tomorrow. He will be 'interviewed' for the *Daily News* (as a South African Radical in an English radical paper) in Monday's paper, and will talk to Massingham and others on *that* basis."

The letter from Boyd shows Rhodes to have been less aloof than he made out. The evidence is at least not inconsistent with Innes's allegation that he deliberately encouraged the belief in Kruger's eventual surrender in order to make sure that Kruger would be pushed to the uttermost limit. Then war would follow, and this time the problem of the Transvaal would be cleared up for good in the only possible way. Certainly he was ready for war himself when the moment came.

The reinforcement of Kimberley had begun in September, after a prolonged wrangle between Milner and Schreiner, and Lt. Col. Kekewich was appointed to take command there. Rhodes's intention to make for Kimberley as soon as war began was already well known. A telegram urging him not to do so was sent by the Mayor of Kimberley early in October, and many friends wrote to him to the same effect. But his mind was made up. He left Cape Town by train for Kimberley on 9 October, and arrived after hostilities began. Biographers have said that he never told his guests at Groote Schuur where he was going; but Lady Edward Cecil (later Viscountess Milner), who was one of them, suggested later that they too had known.[10] He was accompanied by Dr. Thomas Smartt (a medical man, like so many of his cronies, and later on a Minister under Jameson and Smuts); also by his secretary, Philip Jourdan, and his friend from Oxford days, Rochfort Maguire, with Mrs. Maguire. The craving for action which still animated him was to be satisfied again.

Sources

Butler, Sir W. F.: *An Autobiography*
Colvin, Ian: *The Life of Jameson*
Cook, E. T.: *Rights and Wrongs of the Transvaal War*
Fitzpatrick, Sir Percy: *The Transvaal from Within*
Garvin, J. L.: *The Life of Joseph Chamberlain*
Headlam, C.: *The Milner Papers*
Hofmeyr, J. H., & Reitz, F. W.: *The Life of Jan Hendrik Hofmeyr*
Innes, James Rose: *An Autobiography*
Kruger, Paul: *Memoirs*
Marais, J. S.: *The Fall of Kruger's Republic*

Notes

[1] Rhodes Papers, B. 1502.
[2] Radziwill Papers (Rhodes House).
[3] All quotations are from the Radziwill Papers (Rhodes House).
[4] Rhodes Papers, C. 27. 74.
[5] Rhodes Papers, B. 1327 (to Mc-Donald); B. 1241 (Barotseland); B. 1018 (property for natives).

[6] Rhodes Papers, C. 2. 176.
[7] R.H.L. Micr. Afr. 413, f. 26.
[8] Rhodes Papers, B. 1253 (to Milner); B. 1277 (to Heany).
[9] Rhodes Papers, C. 16. 60.
[10] Marginal note ("No-V.M.") in the London Library copy of Mc-Donald, p. 316.

CHAPTER TWENTY-SIX

THE BOER WAR

A STATE of war existed from 5 p.m. on 11 October, shortly before Rhodes's train arrived in Kimberley. It was delayed on the way by an accident, apparently not connected with the hostilities. The Boers crossed the frontiers, both from the Transvaal into the Cape Colony and more unexpectedly from the Orange Free State into Natal, almost immediately. Kimberley was cut off within two days. Mafeking, under the command of Rhodes's friend General Baden-Powell, and Ladysmith, where Jameson installed himself after declaring once more that the Boers would never be "foolish enough to begin shooting", were also invested almost immediately. But communications were never entirely severed.

Rhodes had made his own arrangements with efficiency. At his request, Fuller remained in Cape Town to act as an external link with De Beers, of which he was a director, while Rhodes himself took charge of the company's affairs in Kimberley. No doubt it was partly a concern for his first great enterprise in South Africa that took him to Kimberley at the critical moment. Although mining ceased, he was able to continue to conduct business from the besieged town, even to the point of completing the final stages of amalgamation by heliograph. Telegraphic traffic was sent to him through Reuter's office in Cape Town, addressed to Mrs. Maguire. This information is contained in the earliest surviving entry of Princess Radziwill's diary. Her comment on learning of the arrangement was: "Of course, I don't reply anything, but think a great deal." It is characteristic of the Princess's romantic imagination to imply a sinister secret behind a convenient arrangement, without being able to suggest what the secret might be.[1]

Rhodes's earliest communications from the besieged town show that he felt little cause for alarm, though the Boers knew from the first that he was there. With studied calm, he maintained a correspondence with his manager, McDonald, in Rhodesia: the first two letters dated from Kimberley on 12 October are concerned with the erection of fences on Rhodes's farms, a little gesture of bravado which it would have pleased him to have recorded.[2] "Business as usual" was to be the slogan. But within a few days the pace of the Boer advance became too hot for Rhodes's studied calm. One of the motives for his presence in Kimberley was probably a desire to make it imperative for the Imperial forces to save the town from enemy occupation.

There was not in fact much danger of the Boers capturing Kimberley at the beginning of the war, and that for several reasons: the defending force was considerable, the Boer commander-in-chief, General Joubert, was old and incompetent, and the commandoes were not equipped or trained for storming operations; and in any case they were convinced that they were marching south irresistibly to throw the British into the sea. But Rhodes did not know these things, and imagined that the danger to Kimberley was already great. On 17 October he telegraphed to Milner:[3]

> "You ought to send relief here and it is quite easy to get through from Orange River now with your present force but commandoes round us are increasing daily and getting more impudent owing to our helpless position. I feel it is useless pressing this on Cape military authority but wish to place fact on record."

Milner, who had not known of Rhodes's intention to go to Kimberley (as many others had, including his future wife, Lady Edward Cecil), wrote indignantly to Selborne the next day that Rhodes was sending him "panicky telegrams about immediate relief, which is impossible". His diary and letters record grave anxiety about the safety of Kimberley more than once in October and November 1899, though his anxiety was not extended to the person of Rhodes. But he would have preferred Rhodes away from Kimberley and even out of South Africa at this time. In December, according to Princess Radziwill, he tried to send an emissary to Rhodes to persuade him to go back to Europe.[4] Rhodes did not believe her story, but Milner's impatience with him at the time is evident from the Milner Papers.

Rhodes continued to send out his views on the military situation in all directions. On 30 October he wrote to Baden-Powell in Mafeking:[5]

> "Colonel Kekewich is worked off his legs and I am sending you a note as to information of your position. Let me know briefly for Cape Town how long your foodstuffs and forage

will last, the state of your health and water supply? How is
the shelling affecting you, and what are your losses to date?
What number of men is attacking you and who is in charge?
"As to ourselves here at Kimberley we can just hold our
own but cannot relieve you . . . I am rather afraid the military authorities at Cape Town think Kimberley and Mafeking
can hold out for ever and if it is otherwise with you, you
should pocket your pride and tell them the contrary."

The disrespect in which he held professional soldiers, with
honourable exceptions like Baden-Powell, is plain in this letter.
He regarded the military profession as a simple matter of common-
sense, which he could easily have mastered if he had chosen. The
same attitude towards the political authorities, subject to the
same exceptions, is shown in a telegram to Sprigg a few days
later.[6] If only Sprigg had been Prime Minister, Rhodes declared,
Kimberley would have been relieved.

As the attitude of the authorities continued to dissatisfy
Rhodes, he began to take the initiative himself. He could not
relieve Kimberley single-handed, but at least he knew how to
defend it, which was more than he could say for Kekewich.
The phrase he used to Baden-Powell about Kekewich being
"worked off his legs" was simply a euphemism addressed to a
fellow-soldier. What Rhodes really thought was that Kekewich
lacked drive and did not know his job. With characteristic direct-
ness, Rhodes began to teach him. Philip Jourdan, who was an
eye-witness, gives a good account of the activities which Rhodes
initiated. The most important military measures were the erection
of a fort near Kenilworth, on the outskirts of Kimberley, which
Kekewich thought unnecessary; and also the formation of a
cavalry unit of 800 horses. The manpower for both enterprises
was found from De Beers's employees. Rhodes was active, too,
on the side of the commissariat: ascertaining the supplies of coal
and mining materials, establishing a soup-kitchen under Mrs.
Maguire, supplying fruit to the troops and milk to the military
hospital from his own farm, and employing about 10,000 Africans
on public works, especially scavenging and making roads. The
last measure was particularly valuable, not only because it
brought permanent improvement to Kimberley but also because
it helped to avert trouble with a large unemployed population of
natives. According to a calculation made early in 1900, the
coloured population of Kimberley at this time was nearly double

that of the whites: 26,500 to 14,500. Rhodes also took the
initiative in asking the Mayor of Kimberley to form a committee
to look into hardships to the families of the killed and wounded,
and he made personal provision for the treatment of Boer
prisoners, of which Jourdan kept a meticulous record.[7]

Many other measures necessary to the defence of the town were
initiated by Rhodes with a disregard, which even sympathetic
biographers do not defend, for the authority of Kekewich. But
they were undeniably valuable, not only to physical security but
also to morale. A survivor of the siege, Mrs. Hickman, who knew
Rhodes well from her childhood, wrote many years afterwards
that he was responsible for persuading Kekewich to put search-
lights all round the town, in addition to barrage-balloons which
were already in use for artillery spotting.[8] She also records that
he tried unsuccessfully to persuade the military authorities to
camouflage red uniforms with sacks, and advised the relieving
force under General Methuen to abandon the square formation
and make use of ditches and rocks for cover. Like other witnesses,
she records his initiative in organising underground refuges in
the mines for women and children, as well as bomb-proof shelters
and a look-out system against the Boer artillery. When shelling
became a serious threat, one of Rhodes's mining engineers, the
American Labram, constructed a gun with which to retaliate.
Christened "Long Cecil", it first went into action on 19 January
1900.

There is justice in the claim that Rhodes was the life and soul
of the defence of Kimberley, and he was to some extent justified
in his contempt for the military authorities, whose performance in
the early weeks of the Boer War was notoriously inadequate.
After the "Black Week" of mid-December 1899, when British
reverses were reported daily from every front, the danger to the
besieged town became more immediate. Milner wrote to Chamberlain on 14 December that there seemed "little chance of
Methuen's being able to fight his way to Kimberley". But in
fact the tide was already on the point of turning. Lord Roberts,
with Kitchener as Chief of Staff, was appointed to relieve General
Butler as Commander-in-Chief in December 1899, and a new air of
efficiency soon entered into the operations. Rhodes, who had no
means of knowing that the tide was turning, nevertheless continued his feud with the military authorities unabated. He sent an
intemperate message to Roberts urging haste, which Kekewich
first refused to transmit; and when Roberts eventually received it

in mutilated form, he misinterpreted it as a threat that Kimberley would surrender.

The town was in fact relieved on 15 February 1900, when Rhodes entertained General French, in command of the relieving force, and misunderstandings were cleared up with due dignity. Roberts spoke warmly of Rhodes in his despatches; Rhodes undertook to see to the forage of Roberts's horses for the further advance; Methuen wrote a generous letter to Rhodes, deploring their earlier disagreements; and after Rhodes's death, his brother Frank received his campaign medal from the War Office (on behalf of "Colonel the Right Honourable Cecil Rhodes"—a rank which thus became authoritative), together with a letter conveying from Lord Roberts His Majesty's "high appreciation of the services rendered by the late Officer during the recent campaign". Only Kekewich was unforgiven for failing to support Rhodes's inspirations: an attack on him was published in *The Diamond Fields Advertiser*, which belonged to Rhodes, and a few weeks later Rhodes purported to have forgotten who he was—"You don't remember the man who cleans your boots."[9]

Before Rhodes left the relieved town towards the end of February 1900, he had many matters of unfinished business to attend to. There were addresses of thanks to be received from all the communities and groups of society that had shared the rigours of the siege with him: an impressive collection of testimonials to Rhodes's services to his fellow-citizens is published in Michell's biography. There were telegrams of congratulations to be answered: one from the Prime Minister of New Zealand, some of whose men had taken part in the relief: another from the Kaiser, who made no secret by this time of Germany's refusal to back the Boers. There were also the remaining problems of the war to be met, though no one expected it to last much longer now that Roberts and Kitchener were in control and advancing fast towards the Boer Republics. Rhodes's military appetite was whetted, and he was eager to lend a further hand. He made an offer to Milner that De Beers should buy guns for the future defence of Kimberley, and he sent instructions to De Beers on the help they should give for the relief of Mafeking: "Proper course ride over Barkly Ridge," he told them, confident in his newly acquired military experience. And there was next an Annual General Meeting of De Beers to be addressed, four days after the siege was raised.[10]

His speech to the shareholders gave Rhodes the first

opportunity for many months to reflect on the past and look to the future. The latter was what really interested him, as always, but he spoke of the past first in order to refute the notion that the war was one of aggression by the British. He spoke of "a long, long conspiracy of the neighbouring Republics to seize British South Africa", and quoted Theo Schreiner (the Prime Minister's brother) as having told him that seventeen years earlier old President Reitz, father of the author of *Commando*, had described his party's one aim as "to turn England out of Africa". (A few days later Rhodes received and acknowledged a friendly telegram from Theo Schreiner confirming the story.[11]) He next described the siege and his role in it in tones of jovial satisfaction. Everyone deserved congratulations, and in a peroration which later brought puritanical criticism on his head, he claimed that "we have done our best to preserve that which is the best commercial asset in the world, the protection of Her Majesty's flag". It was the kind of glimpse of truth to which Rhodes was addicted: he could not understand why his critics took exception to such simple revelations.

The most interesting aspect of his speech, however, lay in its reflections on the future. He reminded his hearers of the importance of co-existence with the Boers after the war. But he also laid stress on the other aspect of his racial policy: "equal rights for every civilised man south of the Zambesi." The phrase was repeated twice in his speech, and a few days later he wrote it out, at the request of representatives of the coloured community, characteristically on the edge of a scrap of newspaper. His words, which are reproduced in facsimile by Michell, included the following definition: "What is a civilised man? A man whether white or black who has sufficient education to write his name, has some property or works, in fact is not a loafer." That was the final formulation of Rhodes's motto for the future.[12]

But he was not allowed to confine his attention entirely to the future. The exasperating past raised its ugly head again on the day after his speech in Kimberley, when it was once more demanded in the House of Commons that the Enquiry into the Raid should be reopened. The occasion was furnished by the publication in a Brussels newspaper, *L'Indépendance Belge*, on 5 January of a number of documents stolen from Hawksley's office, evidently with the connivance of a pro-Boer Member of Parliament, Dr. Clarke, and the former State Secretary of the Transvaal, Dr. Leyds. These were not the "missing telegrams" but various communications between Hawksley and others connected with the Raid between May 1896 and August 1897. The English press, with few exceptions, ignored the documents, but Chamberlain's enemies in Parliament naturally did not miss the opportunity of arguing that they contained evidence of the Government's complicity in the Raid, as indeed by implication they did.

Chamberlain had little difficulty in resisting the demand for a fresh Enquiry. He used the occasion to elucidate his earlier defence of Rhodes as a "man of honour", on the ground that all allegations about sordid motives, pecuniary benefit and Stock Exchange speculations had been rebutted. But although the acrimonious debate in the House of Commons on 20 February 1900 led to no consequences, it did prompt Hawksley once more to press Rhodes, through Michell, to publish the "missing telegrams". Rhodes had already returned to Cape Town when Hawksley's letter arrived, and Michell's reply was that Hawksley should await his arrival in England. But Rhodes was not to be moved at this late date from his consistent resolve.

When he reached Cape Town at the end of February, he was soon joined by Jameson, fresh from Ladysmith where the siege was raised two weeks after Kimberley. Optimism was general by this time, both in London and South Africa. Overtures for peace from the Boers were therefore refused in mid-March. Chamberlain was already planning the annexation of the Republics and formulating the conditions of eventual federation; and he and Milner were debating, not altogether amicably, the policy to be adopted towards rebels (that is, those of Dutch descent who had joined the invading Boers) in the Cape Colony. Rhodes's mind was also on the post-war settlement.

His second speech since the siege was made in Cape Town early in March, to an audience of the South African League in the Town Hall. Eye-witnesses describe him gazing out of the window at Table Mountain "as if in a trance", while he told the startled patriots that it was not the Dutch but only Krugerism that they had defeated; and with the Dutch they must learn to live in amity again. McDonald reported him as believing that the war had actually helped to accelerate the approach to federation, much as he believed that the first Boer War had taught the British and the Dutch to respect each other. With these optimistic ideas in mind, he sailed from the Cape for England on 18 March 1900.

Herbert Baker, his architect, was with him, and heard him talking frequently of the duty of the rich to build and entertain lavishly. In keeping with his own doctrine, he had just planned the building of a little house in his own grounds, the Woolsack, which was to be the temporary home of Rudyard Kipling and other writers and artists when they came to the Cape. The rebuilt Groote Schuur was even more splendid than the old, and many guests were entertained there in his absence, including the new Prince and Princess of Wales on their way to New Zealand in 1901.

Rhodes's stay in London in 1900 was short: he arrived on 7 April, and left for the Cape again before the end of the month. He was restless and "far from well" according to Michell. The suddenness of his departure was the subject of comment. Princess Radziwill's diary, for instance, notes a paragraph about it in the *New York Times*.[13] No doubt the principal cause of his haste was the political situation in South Africa, where Schreiner's government was moving towards its fatal division and fall over the question of punishing the rebels and paying compensation to the loyalists in the Cape Colony. But during his short stay, one memorable event took place which sheds light on his state of mind.

On 10 April he had a long talk with Stead, whose attitude to the war was hostile to the British Government. Stead wrote a detailed account of their conversation on the following day, part of which was embodied in his book on *The Last Will and Testament of Cecil J. Rhodes* two years later, and the remainder was published half a century later as an Appendix to the revised edition of Mrs. Millin's biography of Rhodes. Stead was a good reporter, and his account is the best portrait that survives of Rhodes in his forty-eighth year. It shows all the familiar caprices and dreams and enthusiasms, and also the familiar pettiness and insensitivity. One thing only was momentarily lacking, and this was the sense that his own time was desperately short, for he was momentarily in a confident and ebullient mood.

His mind dwelt, as always, both on the past and the future, but they formed a continuous thread which shows through the disjointed dialogue. Looking to the past, he described his motives at the time of the Raid, particularly his fear of an "American-dominated anti-British Republic" in the Transvaal. The same thought, in another guise, troubled him about the future. "We shall have trouble in time to come with America," he told Stead: "Americans are our great danger." The Boers, too, could not be trusted; and here he failed for once to distinguish between Kruger and the rest. He had been mistaken in thinking Kruger "too clever to go to war", but he denied having called the Boers' power "an unpricked bubble". The trouble was the Dutch desire to dominate a united Republic; and he took an incidental swipe at Hofmeyr, for failing to support him at the 1898 election "as he promised", which would have averted the Boer War.

Here Rhodes showed how little he understood the fatal wound which he himself had dealt to Hofmeyr's faith in him in 1895. Stead chided him for having abandoned his old policy of friendship with the Dutch, and told him that he was "digging the grave of the British Empire in South Africa". Rhodes retorted with a striking argument that was never to be fulfilled: "In two years I shall be the best abused man in Africa by the British loyalist, for it will be my duty to stand up on behalf of the rights of the pastoral Dutch against the overbearing domination of our people." He was already meditating ways of trying to break down the distinction between the pastoral Dutch and the urban British.

Inevitably, the conversation moved at times off the mundane level towards the mystical ideas of imperialism which had first brought Rhodes and Stead together. Each complained that the other had departed from their common principles. Rhodes blamed Stead for his "insubordination" in attacking the British policy in South Africa, for which his own pupils, including Milner and Garrett, were largely responsible. How, he asked, could their "Society" succeed if its members would not submit to discipline? He had every confidence in Milner, though with some uneasiness about the influence of Princess Radziwill over him. Stead on his side claimed to have been "true to the real, aboriginal Cecil John Rhodes", as distinct from the impostor who was now using his name. Rhodes laughed and dismissed the subject. "The war is ending, and that is a past issue." But he left London dissatisfied with Stead, though not yet ready to remove his name from the list of Trustees of the Will.

One benefit, perhaps not unplanned, of Rhodes's early return to the Cape was that he escaped for the time being from the renewed attentions of Princess Radziwill. She had told him in March of her intention to go to England, and she was in fact on her way there when he set out in the opposite direction. By this time he was beginning to find her tiresome, as her own diary makes clear. Even while he was shut up in Kimberley, she had bombarded him with warnings against Milner, which he felt sure were unfounded; and she repeated the warnings as soon as she saw him again at Groote Schuur.[14] He had the utmost difficulty in shaking her off, together with two of her acolytes whom

Rhodes had also rashly befriended, Dr. Scholtz and his wife, Agnes. Later the Princess and the Scholtzes were to become bitter enemies, but in 1900 they appear to have attached themselves to Rhodes as a team. On four consecutive days in early March, the Princess's diary records that one or other of them saw Rhodes and she herself lunched or dined with him, by her own account, on three of them. Most of the entries in her diary record that Rhodes was in a furious temper. Later knowledge of the characters of his self-appointed companions makes this understandable.

In addition, the Princess had been engaged in a characteristic intrigue behind Rhodes's back with the leaders of the Bond, to bring about a reconciliation between them and Rhodes. Her theme was that they all had a common enemy in Milner. Hofmeyr and Sauer were naturally suspicious that such an extraordinary go-between should have been chosen, and dealt with her as much as possible through an intermediary of their own, Sonnenberg. The only outcome of the exchanges, which lasted from November 1899 to March 1900, if the Princess's diary is to be believed, was that Rhodes and Hofmeyr each refused to take any initiative until the other did so first. When Rhodes saw the draft programme of reconciliation which the Princess had prepared, her diary confesses that "he called me an idiot, and said that he had never read anything so stupid in all his life". Such candour predisposes one to believe that the account in her diary, trivial and futile as it appears, is not wholly imaginary.[15] But her own role, whatever her intentions, was purely that of a mischiefmaker, particularly between Milner and Rhodes. Both of them later independently realised that she was set upon antagonising them against each other. She told each of them in turn that her sole motive was to serve his interests. Her diary makes it clear that whereas this was a lie as regards Milner, it was in a pathetic sense true as regards Rhodes, for whom she had a real admiration and affection. But her novelettish intervention in his life did him only harm.

The danger of the woman lay in the fact that she had a powerful personality, a sharp intelligence at a superficial level, and an entrée wherever she wanted. Her role, as she saw it, was to become an indispensable intermediary and confidante of the great, and thus to influence them and dictate from behind the policy of the British Empire. Her imagination was boundlessly romantic, and not all of it was baseless. She had, after all, inter-

C. J. R. during the siege of Kimberley (with the Maguires and Dr. Smartt)

C. J. R. and Lord Kitchener after the relief of Kimberley in 1900

ested Salisbury and ingratiated herself with Rhodes, Milner, Hofmeyr and lesser figures in a remarkably short time. In London she had other conquests on a less exalted level: Moberly Bell, Stead, Labouchere, and even the sober Hawksley. Stead had implicit confidence in her at the time, as appears both from his correspondence and from reported conversations. Hawksley was the recipient of instalments of her diary while she was in London; and on 21 July 1900 he forwarded part of it in confidence to Michell at Cape Town, with a letter assuring him that the Princess was devoted to Rhodes's interests and her diary was an accurate record. All of them, nevertheless, recognised that from time to time she was an incorrigible liar. Their confidence in her ought not to have survived a perusal of her accounts of imaginary private conversations with Lord Salisbury, whom she reports more than once as having called on her clandestinely in her rooms in London. Lady Warwick told Stead that the Princess had never seen Lord Salisbury at all, but that was too much for him to believe; nor was it even true.[16]

She returned to South Africa in July 1900. When she reached the Cape, Rhodes was already out of the way. He had arrived back there himself on 8 May, as the crisis which brought about the fall of Schreiner's government was coming to a head, but he stayed only a week. Jameson met him at Groote Schuur, where they discussed the political situation, with much scorn directed at Schreiner's cabinet and warm expressions of admiration for Milner. Jameson described Milner early in May as "the really only satisfactory man out of all the authorities", and a few days later wrote of "Milner as sanguine and careful as he is strong, and most interesting". Jameson's views no doubt reflect his own renewed intention to enter politics. He achieved his first ambition in the following month, when he stood successfully at a by-election in Kimberley on the resignation of Rutherfoord Harris. His comments on Milner also reflect the views of Rhodes. It was Rhodes's firm policy to "leave everything to Milner", as he had told Stead in London, and to avoid embarrassing him by appearing ostentatiously as a candidate for office at the Cape. His very presence there was a reminder that there was no other conceivable Prime Minister, if he wanted the position and if Schreiner fell. It was in keeping with his policy of standing aloof, so that no one could blame him for whatever crisis occurred, that Rhodes left Cape Town again for the north on 15 May.

Not even the absence of Rhodes could save Schreiner's

P

government, which was irreparably divided on the issue of the treatment of rebels in the Cape Colony. At first the Cape cabinet wanted to grant a general amnesty, but that was vetoed by Chamberlain. Part of the cabinet, led by Merriman, then insisted on pressing for the amnesty while the rest, led by Schreiner, found it constitutionally improper to do so. The latter group therefore devised a compromise, on the basis of disfranchisement for five years as a uniform punishment for the rank and file, though they also agreed that the leaders would have to be more severely punished. The compromise was presented to the party caucus, which rejected it. Schreiner thereupon resigned on 13 June, and was succeeded by the perennial standby, Sir Gordon Sprigg, who introduced a Treason Bill based on Schreiner's compromise. It was successfully carried through the House in August by a small majority, with Schreiner's support. Innes, who introduced the Bill as Sprigg's Attorney-General, wrote in his reminiscences that if Schreiner had not resigned when he did, Milner would have dismissed him and summoned Rhodes to form a government. The same thought, or fear, was no doubt in everybody's mind.

Sources

Works mentioned under Chapter Twenty-five and additionally:
Amery, L. S.: *The Times History of the War in South Africa*, 1899–1902
Baker, Herbert: *Cecil Rhodes by his Architect*
Carrington, C. E.: *Rudyard Kipling*
Laurence, Sir Percival: *The Life of John Xavier Merriman*
Stead, W. T.: *The Last Will and Testament of Cecil J. Rhodes*

Notes

[1] Radziwill Diary (Rhodes House) 19 Oct. 1899.
[2] Rhodes Papers, A. 158 and 159.
[3] Rhodes Papers, B. 1294.
[4] Radziwill Diary (Rhodes House) 1 Dec. 1899.
[5] Rhodes Papers, A. 160.
[6] Rhodes Papers, B. 1229.
[7] Jourdan, 103–19; Rhodes Papers, C. 28; 69, enclosure (population); A. 161 and 162.
[8] R.H.L. MSS. Afr. t. 11, f. 21.
[9] Rhodes Papers, B. 1336 (to Chartered Company); letter in possession of Miss Georgia Rhodes (medal); C. 28. 69 (Kekewich).

[10] Rhodes Papers, A. 166 (to Seddon); B. 1319 (to Kaiser, etc., via Chartered Company); "Vindex", 825–38.
[11] Rhodes Papers, B. 1331.
[12] Michell, II. 276.
[13] Radziwill Diary (Rhodes House) 22 April 1900.
[14] Radziwill Diary (Rhodes House) 5 March 1900.
[15] Radziwill Diary (Rhodes House) 22 Nov. 1899 to 27 Feb. 1900.
[16] Radziwill Diary (Rhodes House) 20 May, 25 May, 8 June, 10 June, 12 June, 13–14 June 1900; Stead to Hawksley (Radziwill Papers) 18 June 1900.

CHAPTER TWENTY-SEVEN

ESSAYS IN RECONSTRUCTION

RHODES watched the political manoeuvres at the Cape with contemptuous indifference from a distance. He was back in his beloved Rhodesia when Schreiner fell, and there he spent nearly five months touring and relaxing and occasionally offering advice to Milner, while his agents kept him in touch with the petty politics of the Cape. McDonald and Jourdan give a pleasant picture of his activities: visiting the Matopos and the farm at Inyanga; gossiping with settlers, British and Dutch; riding about forty miles a day and often walking for seven or eight hours while shooting game; and talking endlessly with his cronies. The serious subjects of his talk, according to McDonald, were chiefly gold-mining, farming and the extension of the railway and telegraph; lucerne and ostriches as farm products also figure much in his correspondence. But another subject which now occupied the forefront of his mind was the plan to settle British and Colonial veterans of the war on the land, as a counter-weight to the "pastoral Dutch".

This was the matter that he put first when writing to Milner in May, as his reason for hoping that he would not be needed in Parliament or forced to return for a general election. He set out his views on the implementation of the scheme in two long letters, one to Milner on 7 May, while he was still at sea on the way from England to the Cape, and the other to Arnold-Foster (the Chairman of the Commission of Land Enquiry in South Africa, and later a Conservative Minister) on 6 November, after his return to the Cape from Rhodesia. The two letters contain two essentially separate but complementary schemes, one for irrigated farms and the other for dry farms.[1]

The earlier letter to Milner sets out proposals for giving grants of land and a bonus to men of "the Yeomanry and Colonials" after the war, in return for military service when called upon. Their services, he pointed out, would incidentally make it possible to reduce the size of the police force in Rhodesia. But similar plans would also be needed in the Transvaal and Orange Free State, in order to prevent *Uitlanders* from confining themselves to the towns, and thus to heal the division with the Dutch. In support of this policy, the letter quotes Rhodes's own successful experiment with English fruit farmers in the Paarl and Stellenbosch districts of the Cape Colony. Irrigation, he argued, must be provided by the Government, with the help of trained experts from India or Egypt.

From these details, Rhodes's mind soared to ideas of wider range, calculated to appeal to Milner's intellect. "My idea of an agricultural settlement is something on the basis of the Russian system so that the agricultural holding should belong to the individual but the grazing should be communal," he wrote, perhaps echoing some remembered conversation with the Princess; and again with what must have seemed to him, if not to Milner, an adroit subtlety of appeal:

"Your Excellency will remember this was the system adopted when the Spartan Commonwealth was divided into agricultural holdings. I forget whether the helots also received land but I do not think their case will arise when a proper government is established in the Transvaal."

He ended his letter with an estimate that 4,000 men would be needed to settle in the Transvaal, as against 25,000 Dutch families already there. The cost, he assured the High Commissioner, would not be exorbitant.

The second letter, to Arnold-Foster, expresses the results of further reflection during his extended tour of the north. It proposes that in addition to the scheme put forward in the first letter, ". . . it would be wise, in many parts of the Orange River Colony and the Transvaal, to purchase from the owners the very best land which consists chiefly of pastoral runs, and to make settlements of our people upon them." In order words, the Yeomanry and Colonials were to be encouraged to go in for cattle-raising as well as agriculture, to be keepers of sheep as well as tillers of the ground. Perhaps a reconciliation of Cain and Abel was consciously in Rhodes's mind, for Biblical analogies appealed to him almost as much as to Kruger. He went on:

". . . These settlements might be termed 'settlements on dry farms' and be additional to my original letter which suggested irrigation settlements and communal grazing. The two plans roughly will cost about twelve millions sterling—a mere bagatelle when compared with our daily war expenditure—and then we must remember that the twelve millions

will not be lost to us as in the case of money spent on the
war which disappears for ever, for there will be an asset in
the land and stock."

These two letters show Rhodes in his most constructive and
optimistic vein.

Closely related to the question of land settlement by British
and Colonials, at least in Milner's mind, was the problem of
finding sufficient labour of a low-grade type for menial tasks
both in the new territories and in the developing industries of the
Transvaal. African labour was in chronically short supply, and
the war had scared many Africans away from the white men's
areas. Even before the war, schemes had had to be devised to
attract Africans to settle in the areas where they were needed to
work for the Europeans. By 1900, when the task of post-war
reconstruction was already beginning, although prematurely as it
turned out, a serious crisis had become apparent. The solution
which was eventually associated with Milner's name, and did him
great harm, was the importation of indentured workers from
Asia, particularly Chinese. But that did not begin until 1904.
Meanwhile the problem impressed itself on Rhodes and Milner
almost daily with increasing seriousness. Rhodes received many
telegrams in July 1900 urging him to press for Chinese labour in
Rhodesia, but he repeatedly expressed himself as opposed to it.[2]
His own farm managers' experiences convinced him that Asiatic
labour, which had already been admitted on a small scale, would
be a failure. Milner, on the other hand, was eventually converted
to the plan for importing Chinese workers not, as he later pointed
out, as a substitute for white workers but as an essential basis on
which alone white settlement could be built up.

An enthusiastic supporter of Rhodes's plans for land settlement
was Abe Bailey, one of the new generation of mining millionaires
in Johannesburg, who had been a member of the Reform Committee in 1895 and later succeeded to Rhodes's seat in the Assembly at the Cape. A letter survives from him to Rhodes, dated
11 July 1900, proposing that he should make a trip to the north
to investigate the possibilities of buying land for such settlements,
and then to go on overland to Egypt. The letter is interesting
because of the suggestion it contains that Bailey should take with
him "someone who would be capable of writing up the country,
and giving in detail the beneficence to be derived by opening up
this huge country"—the man suggested for the assignment being

young Winston Churchill. Rhodes's reaction to Bailey's proposal does not survive, but Churchill's does.[3]

The only surviving exchange between the two great men was written on 12 July from the ship which was taking Churchill back to England:

My dear Mr. Rhodes,

Abe Bailey has spoken to me about a plan to send a small private expedition from Capetown to Cairo, and has suggested my coming with him. Of course I must think first of all of getting into the House of Commons, but I daresay the general election will be over before the expedition would start and were that the case I daresay I could get away.

I should personally like very much indeed to take part in such an interesting venture, and as I have to make my own living it would be a great advantage to me to do so, for what with a series of letters to a London newspaper and a good sized book to be published later, I should be able to earn a good deal of money.

Now it seems to me that this writing would help to attract public attention to the Cape to Cairo route and stimulate the interest taken in your railway scheme: so that perhaps you will think that our roads lie for some small distance in the same direction. If this be so and you would like me to go with this small expedition as Bailey's companion, will you write me— or have me written, for I know you have many things to occupy you—a letter on the subject. This should reach me in about two months time, and I will then give you a definite answer without delay, for by then I shall know what prospect there is of my be [sic] able to play at "the cup and ball trick" (to quote your expression) in the House of Commons.

I lunched and dined with Frankie at Groot Schurr [sic] and much admired your beautiful house. I am sorry not to have seen you in South Africa, but the Boers interfered with most people's arrangements.

Yours sincerely,
Winston S. Churchill.

Churchill's conception of the plan had run ahead of Bailey's, who was thinking primarily of the development of Rhodesia; but it had run ahead in a direction obviously congenial to Rhodes. Only a few weeks later Rhodes agreed to grant a unique favour to a young man with similar ideas, when he wrote a preface to

Grogan's *The Cape to Cairo*, an account of an expedition on foot along the still undeveloped route. Churchill was already a good deal more famous than Grogan, thanks both to his father—not that Rhodes ever liked Lord Randolph—and also to his own adventures, which included the battle of Omdurman and a legendary escape from captivity with the Boers.

The railway was still as much in Rhodes's mind as ever: he was already talking of carrying it across the Victoria Falls, so that the carriages would be splashed with the spray of the Zambesi. The territory north of the river was also in the forefront of his mind. In August he sent a message to Milner complaining about the boundary of Barotseland which was about to be settled; later in the same month he stressed to Stevens the importance of an out-let for the railway to the west from Northern Rhodesia; and negotiations were in active progress again for the passage of the telegraph line through Uganda.[4] The proposed expedition could be related to all these matters in Rhodes's mind, and Churchill was a young man who appealed to him. But Churchill was duly returned to the House of Commons in the "Khaki Election" in the autumn of 1900, and perhaps he found it less easy than he had imagined to combine the representation of his constituents with jaunts through central Africa. Nothing more was heard of the expedition, though Rhodes and Churchill were to meet in the future.

The trivialities of Cape politics were boring in comparison with Rhodes's magisterial vision of the future, but his agents would not let him forget them. Stevens wrote to him from Cape Town on 2 June to report the split in Schreiner's cabinet, and subsequent messages reached him asking for his views, to be conveyed to Milner. Fuller replied on Rhodes's behalf on 13 June that he would support whatever Milner wanted, though he doubted whether a government under Innes would succeed; but on the following day, when Innes was proposed instead as Attorney-General under Sprigg, Rhodes uttered his celebrated retort of acquiescence: "I can swallow a Mugwump if it will help the Governor." Two days later, on 16 June, Milner sent a message of thanks to Rhodes for his confidence; and Rhodes showed that he really meant it by telegraphing to two of his sup-porters to "do everything to help Governor". But he meant to have as little as possible to do with the daily round of politics in the Cape Colony. When Jameson made an election speech on 25 June, in which he included some indiscreet remarks about the

Raid, Stevens reported to Rhodes that Milner was embarrassed by it; but there is no trace of any comment or reply. Nor was he in any hurry to return to the Cape when pressed to do so by the South African League in September.[5]

He wrote to Milner that he would be coming south shortly on the League's business, but there was no sense of urgency in his explanation that he saw it as "a help to the first step that is the union of the States out here, that is of course when you feel they are ripe for it which all depends on the future conduct of the Dutch and whether we can get any considerable number of our people on the soil". He repeatedly postponed the meeting of the League Congress which he was due to address: in August proposing a date in September, and then 1 October; in mid-September promising to come south next week, and then postponing it again. On 18 September Stevens telegraphed urgently that Rhodes's return might break the Government. The following day he received a reply postponing the Congress once more. It was finally held on 10 October, two days after Rhodes's return. One of the first messages that greeted him was an unwelcome welcome from the Princess, dated 8 October: "I shall turn up for lunch tomorrow."[6]

The opinion was now general that the war was virtually over. Bloemfontein, Johannesburg and Pretoria were all in British hands; Kruger had fled to Europe, where he was well received by the French but cold-shouldered by the Kaiser; Milner had proclaimed the annexation of the Transvaal and Orange Free State. Rhodes telegraphed to the Chartered Company's Office on 7 September that "everything points to the war being not much longer prolonged". In his speech to the South African League on 10 October, he warned his audience against the spirit of jingoism in victory, and told them again that the battle had been with Krugerism and not with the Dutch. Lord Roberts committed himself to the view that the war actually was over early in October, and Milner made plans to move his residence to the north on being appointed Governor of the two new Colonies.

Chamberlain chose the same moment to persuade his Prime Minister to dissolve Parliament, but the general election only increased the Conservative majority by a handful of votes, from 128 to 134. By the end of October, Milner was writing to congratulate Chamberlain on having held the election "in the nick of time", for in another six weeks it might have been affected adversely by "the present discouraging phase of the war". As a note of caution, these words were to prove inadequate to the set-backs ahead. By mid-December Boer commandoes were again invading the Cape Colony. The war, in fact, was to outlast Rhodes's lifetime; but neither he nor anyone else would have dreamed in October 1900 that he had less than eighteen months to live and the war more than the same length of time to run. Nor could anyone have foreseen, when the Cape Parliament was pro-rogued on 15 October, that it would not meet again for nearly two years.

The inevitable questions raised by Rhodes's return to the Cape concerned his own political future. Milner saw him several times, but was pained to find him aloof and inscrutable. Did he want to be Prime Minister? Apparently not: he was content to support Sprigg. Nor did he want a general election, though Milner learned this only at second hand. Rhodes was unmoved even to be told that Salisbury would have welcomed his return to office, perhaps because this information reached him through Princess Radziwill. She reported his reactions to Hawksley in a number of foolish but revealing letters during October. When Rhodes avoided her, she told Hawksley that he was very childish, perhaps because he was in love; adding hastily that she herself was about to be married again, to a man with four children—who therefore could not have been Rhodes, but easily could have been a product of her fantasy. When she wrote to Rhodes on 26 October, having presumably failed to see him, that "Salisbury is more your friend than you think", his reaction was such that on the following day she told Hawksley he had been "very rude", and no one could manage him except Mrs. Scholtz.

A fortnight later she reported that Rhodes would take the Premiership if asked, and wrote twice on the same day to urge him to do so. Rhodes's reply, which does not survive, was evidently undecided: we know from Michell that he was ill at this time, and the Princess herself reports him in bad health. But she persevered again and again, assuring him that Milner as well as Salisbury wanted him back in office. She called on him on 27 November, having sent him in advance the draft of a letter which she proposed to send to Salisbury, for his comments; but she found him in an appalling temper, so she told Hawksley, smashing furniture and refusing to comment on her letter, which she was sending to Salisbury just the same. On 4 December she reported to Hawksley that they were not on speaking terms; but a week later Rhodes had shown kindness to her son, and by Christmas

Day the quarrel was made up. In London Stead, who had seen the correspondence with Hawksley, remarked that they had never before seen such a "vacillating" side to Rhodes's character. He already knew the Princess to be a liar in other connections, but he could not imagine that the whole story was fictitious.[7]

The evidence of Jourdan, who was with Rhodes at the time and hated and feared the Princess, shows that at least her own machinations were real. She was determined, he confirms, to make Rhodes Prime Minister of the Cape Colony again. "How she schemed and planned to gain her object!" She fabricated a record of an interview between herself and Salisbury, in which Salisbury spoke in favour of Rhodes's return to office; and Jourdan naïvely records that "she quite took me in", but Rhodes ascertained from Lady Edward Cecil that it was a fabrication. Similarly, her renewed efforts to bring about a reconciliation between Rhodes and the Bond a year later were genuine enough, and are accepted as such by Hofmeyr's biographers, but her practical achievements lay chiefly in her own imagination.

All her manoeuvres and combinations came to nothing, but that is not to say that they did not take place. On the contrary, unfortunately, they did; and much bad blood was created as a result. It was not until late in 1900 that Milner and Rhodes agreed in appreciating how much harm she was doing to their relations by her self-appointed role as a go-between. Milner wrote to Rhodes about her activities on 28 August, without naming her; and the editor of the Milner Papers, with even greater discretion, omitted the beginning of this letter, which in fact shows that Rhodes had been the first to approach Milner about the Princess. Rhodes replied to Milner's letter in September, expressing his gratitude for the return of confidence.[8] The strange fact is that nevertheless neither of them entirely broke his acquaintance with the scheming Princess. Milner said, in the same letter, that he "would be sorry to say a word against her personally". Rhodes continued to see her and even to give her financial assistance.

In the latter part of 1900, the Princess's main interest in life was to prod Rhodes into activity. There is a probability, which does not depend only on communications between the Princess and Stead, that she was acting on Stead's behalf. W. T. Stead was using all his influence to bring the Boer War to an end by negotiation, with the object of promoting a federation of self-governing territories in South Africa. Rhodes was his chosen candidate for the Premiership, and it was therefore essential to Stead's scheme to separate Rhodes from Milner, who was bent on total victory and the annexation of the Boer Republics. Rhodes sympathised with part of the scheme, but was evidently reluctant to undertake office or to act disloyally towards Milner. The Princess's efforts to promote antagonism between the two men are clear from her own diary; but they were unsuccessful. She was no more successful in trying to force Rhodes back into political office. Clearly she understood him very imperfectly; and this evident fact tends to give some credibility to the otherwise suspect letters purporting to have been written to her by Rhodes at the end of 1900 (Nos. 3 to 9 in Appendix B), since they repeatedly pour scorn on her ideas. They may or may not be genuine, but they probably reflect accurately what Rhodes had in mind.

He agreed with Stead in wanting a federal solution of the South African problem, though he thought it would take a long time to achieve. This view, together with his confidence in Milner who was totally opposed to federation, found expression in a letter of 4 December 1900, replying to an enquiry from General Brocklehurst (later Lord Ranksborough), who had commanded a cavalry brigade at Ladysmith, and was now Equerry to Queen Victoria:[9]

"You sent me a cable asking me my views as to federation out here. I told you, I believe, that we cannot think of it until the Transvaal settles down and I am afraid that will take several years. In the meantime the Transvaal and Free State should be governed by the Crown direct. I think there could be no better man than Sir Alfred Milner.

". . . Any hurried step to force federation would only end in failure. Even with Rhodesia we want time."

Federation, then, must wait: but it was the ultimate goal; and Rhodes may at times, under the prompting of Stead, have expressed himself more emphatically in favour of it, without the qualification about the necessary passage of time.

Stead, in any case, was an enthusiast who did not give up his pet ideas easily. He had found an ally in General Brocklehurst, who wrote to Rhodes under his influence on 14 December:

"I have been rubbing it into everyone that you are the only man who can save South Africa (beginning with the Queen) and I am surprised to find how many of your enemies agree. I told the Queen you and Gordon were the same

man, only with different methods. This fairly made her
jump, but she 'saw my point' as you would say.

"The Government I am sure would be only too thankful
for you to come out of your tent and give them a lead. I have
said you and Milner are on most cordial terms so that he
would approve—my line has been—you propose a Federal
Parliament right away (as Crown Colonies) yourself at the
head of it, compensation for both sides for all damage done
during the war and general amnesty—I've got rather hung
up in trying to work this out in detail, but that is where
Cecil Rhodes comes in, and it would mean peace, or at least
an alternative to the present policy of trying to sit on bayonets
which would probably be accepted by the Boer Leaders and
would bring peace.

"I've had a very sympathetic audience amongst all sorts
and conditions . . ."

Stead followed this up a week later with a letter of his own to
Rhodes on 22 December, reporting on a visit which he had
recently made to the Hague to meet Kruger, Leyds and other
Boer leaders who were now living there in exile. He wrote:

". . . I found them, with the exception of Leyds, quite
obdurate about you. I told them, except Kruger, who is
deaf and to whom I could only talk through an interpreter,
that you were the only Britisher in South Africa who had a
ghost of an idea of statesmanship, that you and you alone
were the real friend of the Dutch, and that you and you
alone could pull them out of their present hole, but they all
said that if the devil were to show them a short-cut to
Paradise, they would still decline his arm, and that no matter
what might be offered them by Chamberlain, you and
Milner, they could not rely upon any assurances that were
given them . . .

"I have had long talks with Dr. Jameson, who is as charming and delightful as ever, and with General Brocklehurst,
who seems to have a very clear appreciation of the necessities
of the situation. I have given Dr. Jameson an outline of the
scheme which I propounded to the Boer delegates, and
which they said might possibly form a basis for settlement if
it were put forward by anybody in whose word they had any
confidence; but if it were put forward by Chamberlain, they
were quite sure that the day after they laid down their arms,

he would discover loopholes through which he could escape
and break his word, as Roberts had done . . ."

Stead's letter then went on to outline his plan for peace, which
was to be carried out to Rhodes by Dr. Jameson.[10]
The plan recommended by Stead bears a remarkably close
resemblance to the contents of one of the letters purporting to
have been sent by Rhodes to Princess Radziwill on 2 December,
three weeks before Stead's letter (No. 5 in Appendix B). The
two texts have all essential point in common: a federation to be
imposed on the four territories (Cape Colony, Natal, the Transvaal and Orange Free State or Orange River Colony, as it was now
called since its annexation); the seven subjects to be reserved to
federal control, though given in a slightly different order; and the
provision that, apart from these, each territory was to enjoy a self-
government "as complete as that enjoyed by any Australian
Colony". There are other points of similarity in style and drafting
which show clearly that the two texts have a common origin, but
it is impossible to be sure whether Stead was adopting an idea of
Rhodes's or Rhodes an idea of Stead's. Rhodes's purported text
is the earlier in date, but its authenticity cannot be proved, and
it makes somewhat surprising reading within a few days of the
letter from Rhodes to General Brocklehurst, already quoted,
whose authenticity is undoubted. The most that can be said
is that, if the Princess was forging letters from Rhodes at this
date, she was forging them on the basis of an intimate knowledge of what was afoot—perhaps because Stead kept her fully
informed.
Whoever was the author of the plan, Stead was making the
running. Brocklehurst referred to it as Stead's plan in a letter
of 23 December, in which he told Stead that "Hawksley, the
Doctor, and I decided in solemn conclave on Friday night that
Rosebery was the man to give Salisbury a lead on your scheme".
Stead had also sent out an agent of his own called Armstrong to
help the Princess work upon Rhodes, though the choice proved a
bad one: he was a notorious drunkard and Rhodes took an instant
dislike to him. How far Rhodes allowed himself to be committed to Stead's plans remains difficult to establish, chiefly because the evidence consists mainly in the suspect letters which the
Princess later claimed to have received from him. If they are
genuine, they show him to have been in general accord with
Stead, at least in principle, and also to have been clandestinely in

touch with Louis Botha, the Boer general. Botha's name appears again in an undated memorandum (No. 1 in Appendix C) which is also ascribed to Rhodes, though again unfortunately only on the Princess's authority.

There is no corroboration from any other quarter of the remarkable suggestion that Rhodes was in touch with Botha, but if true it would not have been uncharacteristic. One of the letters to the Princess, dated 6 February 1901, names Dr. Scholtz as his intermediary to Botha. It would hardly have been possible to make a worse choice, but Rhodes more than once made bad choices, and he had a weakness for doctors, on the ground, so he said, that they were not so squeamish when a little blood-letting became necessary. The story of Rhodes's relations with the Cape Dutch and the Transvaal Boers which emerges from the Radziwill Papers is obscure and incomplete, but it is not wholly implausible, and it could be true in substance even if the letters between the Princess and himself were all forgeries. At the very least it must be conceded that if the Princess forged the letters, she achieved an astonishing consistency, both internally and in relation to other events. Yet her understanding of Rhodes's personality was in reality superficial.

The Princess imagined that he was becoming apathetic while in fact he was biding his time. She accused him of indifference in face of the renewed outbreak of fighting in December 1900, and planned a press campaign to stir him out of it; but in January she decided that his staying in Cape Town proved he had "something in view". She attributed his bad temper to ill health, and reported in the new year that they were on excellent terms and seeing each other frequently. It was true that his health was improving: Jourdan describes him as being "in a particularly happy frame of mind" in the early months of 1901, but tiring of his indolent life at the Cape. He toyed with various ideas. He bought his first motor-car; he wrote a long letter to Beit on post-war reconstruction, full of the familiar ideas about land settlement and the shortage of labour ("but we must do everything before we ever think of importing Chinese labour"); he offered to raise a new military force through De Beers; he proposed to Beit that they should undertake a world tour together; and he brooded on the Will.[11] Brooding on the Will was undoubtedly the most fruitful occupation.

It resulted in two decisions: firstly, to add German students to the beneficiaries of the scholarships; and secondly to remove Stead from the list of Trustees, on account of his "extraordinary eccentricity", which meant chiefly his refusal to follow Rhodes in trusting Milner. The idea then crossed his mind for the first time to make Milner a Trustee. The first hint of it appears in a letter to Milner in May, in which Rhodes wrote: "I would like . . . to talk the personal matter with you that may affect the world." It showed that he was still thinking of a vastly ambitious scheme, in which scholarships were only a part. Meanwhile he had decided on the creation of the first experimental scholarship, from the Diocesan College of Rondebosch to Oxford, for £250 a year, which was later increased to £300.

The Will was a satisfying occupation, but nothing could dissipate the feeling of being isolated from the stress of events. His advice to those who consulted him was to trust Milner, and to wait and see. Above all, the pace must not be forced. Federation would come when the Transvaal had settled down, and that might not be for several years: "even with Rhodesia we want time." The sense that he would not live to see the outcome was perhaps already on him. In March the Princess told Hawksley for the first time, that she feared Rhodes had not a long life before him. The intuition of an imaginative woman was not to be despised.

For want of occupation, and perhaps to escape from the Princess—who continued to write to him, sometimes asking for money—he left for the north with two favourite companions, Jameson and Metcalfe. The Princess wrote to Stead at this time that he was "surrounded with toadies", and her hatred of Jameson is apparent from the book she wrote after Rhodes's death. It was Jameson who evidently took the initiative in finding out that she had fabricated the stories of her conversations with Salisbury, for it was to him that Lady Edward Cecil wrote on 10 April that those parts of the Princess's diary were fictitious, and again in a separate letter on the same date that she was spoken of in Paris as a Boer agent. The Princess reported to Hawksley in the same month that Rhodes's "false friends" were keeping him in quarantine, and no doubt she had guessed correctly. While Rhodes was visiting Kimberley and Bulawayo, from which he did not return until early in July, the Princess's world of fantasy began to crumble.[12] Rhodes had been helping her financially, but not so much as she desired, particularly for the support of the periodical which she proposed to launch, under the title of *Greater Britain*. It lasted only from June to August 1901.

The first of many forgeries of Rhodes's name on promissory notes was detected, according to Jourdan, at this time, but hushed up before he returned to the Cape. The Princess's letters and diary begin to take on a hysterical and almost frantic note, and she quarrelled with her former crony, Mrs. Scholtz. She even began forging letters from Rhodes to herself: of those exposed as forgeries at her trial next year, the earliest was dated 20 May 1901, and purported to have been sent from Kimberley to tell her of his intention to go to Rhodesia, and later to London. Mrs. Scholtz also began writing to Rhodes, telling him not to believe the letters he was receiving, presumably from the Princess about herself. The Princess found herself in deeper and deeper water. On 30 May a cheque she signed for her rent was dishonoured. Within a few days a first warning had been sent to Rhodes by Michell, who received a curt reply from the farm in the Matopos on 5 June: "What do you mean?"[13]

Exasperated though Rhodes was with the Princess, he had not severed all contact with her. Whether or not he was still in correspondence with her depends on the verdict to be passed on the letters which the Princess had in her hands in the latter part of 1901. Two of those dated in May 1901 were declared at her trial to be forgeries, but a third, dated 30 May, the longest of all, was not. If forged, it was an astonishing *tour de force* (No. 12 in Appendix B). It speculates in characteristic fashion about the future of South Africa after Kruger's disappearance: Leyds may return to the political scene, and should be led on in hopes; the English will never match the Dutch as settlers on the soil, but they will "control the industry, without interfering with the Boer farmer"; and the time will come for Rhodes himself when he can "come into touch with the Dutch in the Transvaal", since he has no hope of winning back the Cape Dutch at present—"afterwards will be another matter". This is the last in the series of purported letters from Rhodes to the Princess, and like all of them it rings true in substance, even if the hand of Rhodes never penned it.

It must seem improbable at first sight that Rhodes should have unburdened himself so frankly, even recklessly, to an ageing foreign adventuress whom he had already learned to distrust. But it cannot be considered impossible that he, a bachelor surrounded by bachelors, should still be sufficiently credulous to believe that she might be useful, at least from a distance. There was still a chance that he might be recalled to office at the Cape, and the Princess was in touch with two men on whom this possibility largely depended: Hofmeyr, who was in Germany taking care of his health, and Milner.

It was in May 1901, the same month as the letter to the Princess, that Hofmeyr learned of the overtures which Rhodes had recently made to the Bond, through the connivance of the Princess, and which he advised the Bond for many reasons to reject. Nevertheless he still recognised Rhodes as a major force in the politics of the Cape. It was also in the same month that Milner wrote Rhodes a long letter on the political situation, to which Rhodes replied a few days later. The implication of their exchange is clear. Milner knew that Rhodes foresaw the possibility of his recall to power, and sought to tell him as tactfully as possible that it was impossible for the time being. Rhodes accepted the situation, and implied that his state of health disqualified him from any ambition except the big questions: "My heart is dicky and has given me more trouble the last bout than ever before, so you like to put your house in order."

Rhodes's letter, dated 13 May 1901, has been published by the editor of the Milner Papers. Milner's original letter of 8 May, not previously published, reads as follows in so far as it concerns Rhodes's future:[14]

"... There is ever such a pother here about supposed changes of Ministry and your coming in *vice* Sprigg. I don't think it is my business to mix myself up with Cape internal politics, but I just tell you, privately and *entre nous*, what strikes me. There is no doubt Sprigg is ageing and that a good many people fret for a more vigorous hand at the helm. I have also no doubt that they would all jump at you, if you wanted to come in. My own impression, derived from conversations with you, is *that you don't want to*, as long as things go decently well without, but want to reserve yourself for Rhodesia, for the larger S.A. questions, and for the future. And I think that, if it is practicable—of course it may not be —that is the wiser course in the long run. I am rather afraid of the effect of a change at the present moment—the outcry then would be about 'capitalistic intrigue' and all that old nonsense, *just now*. Of course all this may change, and as Parliament approaches, it may be found that your coming in is the only way of keeping things together.

"But I am strongly of opinion that the meeting of Parlt and

all that it may lead to—a fresh election etc.—should be deferred to the last possible moment.

"By October we may see our way much clearer and changes wh., if made now, would, I fear, cause an unnecessary and dangerous disturbance, might, if they are necessary, come about easily and naturally. At least so it strikes me as an outside observer . . ."

Milner was entitled to take such a professedly detached view of Cape politics, because he had now moved to Johannesburg to take over responsibility for the conquered Boer Republics, and he had been succeeded as Governor of the Cape Colony by Sir Walter Hely-Hutchinson, formerly the Governor of Natal. Milner's transfer was not only a promotion, followed as it shortly was by the conferment of a Barony and appointment to the Privy Council, but also an indication that Chamberlain was worried about him. In December 1900 Chamberlain described him as "overstrained and pessimistic", a judgment which his correspondence bears out. There continued to be many subjects on which they failed to see eye to eye, of which the most important during the last year of Rhodes's life was the question of the suspension of the Cape Colony's constitution.

An undertaking had been given at the beginning of the war that constitutional government would not be suspended, but Parliament did not in fact sit from October 1900 until August 1902, largely because of the difficulty of deciding what to do about the representation of the areas of large-scale rebellion. Sprigg was therefore governing without a parliament, and finance was authorised by the Governor's decree. The suggestion that the situation should be regularised by suspending the constitution instead of by recalling Parliament was made as early as 1900, and was generally attributed to Milner's initiative. Rhodes's views on the subject were sought for the first time, no doubt on Milner's behalf, by the Chartered Company on 8 June 1901. He did not yet commit himself in favour of the movement for suspension, of which he was later to become the figurehead.[15] In July, however, he wrote to Milner that although he did not want the Premiership, he was prepared, if called upon, to take office and govern without Parliament "until certain of a majority on a new register".

But if he was not going to be recalled to office, there was no point in wasting his time at the Cape; and in fact he spent only two or three days there during the last nine months of 1901. Almost all his real interests now lay in the North; and even those that did not could easily be dealt with from there. His few speeches show his mind concentrated on the future of the northern territories. On 15 June he laid the foundation-stone of a new Volunteer Drill Hall at Bulawayo, and told his audience that the unity of South Africa would come from the North: "This great dominant North—and I call it a dominant North—will dictate the federation." A week later he made the last reported speech of his life at St. John's School in Bulawayo, again dwelling on unification through the collaboration in common problems of the North and South. He talked of both parts of the future Union together, but it was from the North that he took his viewpoint.

It was for the development of Rhodesia that he argued with Sprigg at Cape Town over the right to tax brandy imported from the Cape Colony—though he warned the Administrator not to overtax it when the customs agreement lapsed.[16] In the same good cause he argued angrily with Kitchener about rolling-stock on the railways, which Kitchener wanted in order to win the war, and Rhodes wanted to open up the North.[17] The vexed question of importing Asiatic labour also continued to disquiet him: strong arguments were urged upon him both for and against it, but by the end of May he had committed himself so far as to enquire whether Milner would sanction it if asked. Indians, Arabs and Chinese were all suggested. But Milner was not ready for the fateful decision: he was about to return to England for leave and consultation. Rhodes thereupon loyally urged the South African League to take the opportunity of passing resolutions of confidence in him; and Rhodes himself was due to follow Milner to England soon afterwards.[18]

Sources

Works mentioned under Chapters Twenty-five and Twenty-six, and additionally:
Curtis, Lionel: *With Milner in South Africa*
Halpérin, Vladimir: *Lord Milner and the Empire*
Worsfold, W. B.: *The Union of South Africa*
Whyte, Frederic: *The Life of W. T. Stead*

Notes

[1] Rhodes Papers, A. 172 (to Milner); A. 208 (to Arnold-Foster).

[2] Rhodes Papers, C. 19. 11 (from Willoughby); C. 19. 12 (from Jameson); C. 19. 13 (from Heaney); B. 1483; B. 1490; B. 1491.

[3] Rhodes Papers, C. 16. 70 (Bailey); R.H.L. MSS. Afr. t. 5, f. 492 (Churchill).

[4] Rhodes Papers, A. 198 (to Grogan); B. 1419 (to Administrator, Bulawayo); B. 1448 (to Stevens); C. 4. 45 (J. F. Jones).

[5] Rhodes Papers, C. 2. 229 (a) (to Fuller); C. 2. 230(a) (Innes); C. 2. 231(a) (Milner to Rhodes); C. 2. 232 (to Smartt & Graham); C. 2. 234 (Stevens to Rhodes).

[6] Rhodes Papers, B. 1425; B. 1452; B. 1481; B. 1489; C. 2. 243; Radziwill Papers (Princess to Rhodes, 8 Oct. 1900).

[7] Radziwill Papers (Princess to Hawksley, 25 Sept.; 16 and 27 Oct.; 7, 13, 17, 21, 27 and 28 Nov.; 4, 11 and 25 Dec., 1900; Princess to Rhodes, 26 Oct.; 13, 23, 27 Nov., 1900; Stead to Hawksley, 29 Dec. 1900); Rhodes Papers, C. 27. 124 (Stead to Rhodes, 29 Dec. 1900).

[8] Rhodes Papers, C. 27. 115 (Milner to Rhodes, only partly quoted by Headlam, II. 102–3).

[9] Rhodes Papers, A. 216.

[10] Rhodes Papers, C. 27. 120 (Stead); C. 27. 123 (Brocklehurst).

[11] Radziwill Papers (Princess to Hawksley, 25 Dec. 1900; 8 and 17 Jan., 13 March 1901); Rhodes Papers, A. 212 (Rhodes to Beit); B. 1615 (to De Beers); C. 27. 129 (to Beit).

[12] Radziwill Papers (Princess to Hawksley, 13 March 1901; Violet Cecil to Jameson, 10 April 1901; Princess to Hawksley, 23 April 1901).

[13] Radziwill Papers (Princess to Hawksley, 2 April 1901; Mrs. Scholtz to Rhodes, 21 May 1901); *The Trial of Princess Radziwill* (reprinted from the *Cape Times*) pp. 3–6; Rhodes Papers, B. 1692 (Rhodes to Michell).

[14] Rhodes Papers, C. 27. 134.

[15] Rhodes Papers, C. 1. 266.

[16] Rhodes Papers, C. 251 (Sprigg to Rhodes); B. 1640 (Rhodes to Milton); B. 1643 (Rhodes to Smartt).

[17] Rhodes Papers, B. 1700 and 1707 (to Smartt); B. 1723 (to Armstrong).

[18] Rhodes Papers, B. 1625 (to Milton); C. 1. 155(a) (Milton to Rhodes); C. 14. 61 (McDonald); C. 1. 135 (Milton); C. 1. 141 (Shaw); C. 5. 28 (Chartered Company); B. 1679 (Rhodes to Chartered Company); B. 1644 (South African League).

CHAPTER TWENTY-EIGHT

THE FINAL CATASTROPHE

PASSING through Cape Town on the way to England, Rhodes and Jameson stayed only two nights at Groote Schuur. They did not see the Princess, but she sent Rhodes a farewell note and a book for the voyage. On the same day, 3 July 1901, she forged his signature on a bill for £4,500. Nemesis was now close upon her. In the second week of July frantic letters passed between her and Dr. Jameson about her desperate financial predicament, and on the 20th, the day of Rhodes's arrival in London, Hawksley wrote to her to ask for an explanation of "a promissory note for £6,300 drawn by you in favour of Mr. Rhodes and endorsed by him", payable on 20 June 1902 (that is to say, a year later). In August, when she received the letter from Hawksley, her protestations became hysterical.

On 14 August she wrote to Stead that he must help shield "the woman", presumably meaning Mrs. Scholtz, on whom she intended to throw the blame. The next day she forged two telegrams to herself from Hawksley, purporting to promise her supplies of money, and the following day she wrote to Hawksley that his suspicions were nonsensical, since she was not in need of money and had accepted the bills from an unnamed woman. So far there had been no occasion to worry Rhodes with the scandal. He had other matters to deal with on arrival in London, before travelling to Scotland, where he had taken a shooting lodge from the beginning of August.

Ten days in London were spent largely in the City, on the business of De Beers and the Chartered Company. Fuller recalled that he was in masterly form, but aware that he was not at all well. He saw Milner two or three times, which was more than he had done for many months at the Cape. They breakfasted together one morning with Grey; they met Beit together to discuss the problem of land settlement; together they were sworn of the Privy Council, Milner for the first time and Rhodes because there was a new sovereign, Edward VII, who had succeeded to the throne in January. The most important business, however, was to see a heart specialist. Rhodes knew from Jameson that his heart was critically weak: he insisted on hearing from him that heart failure would be a quick death, and Jameson lied in answer with tears in his eyes. The heart specialist told Rhodes that his condition was very serious, and recommended a long rest and constant change of surroundings. Scotland would do very well for a start. After that, a trip to Europe and Egypt was planned.

Rhodes was not despondent when he arrived at Rannoch Lodge in Scotland in early August, where a large party of friends joined him: Jameson, Metcalfe, the Maguires and Jourdan as a matter of course; and as guests, Beit and Grey, Lady Warwick, Gardner Williams and Robert Williams from his African enterprises, Abe Bailey and the new young friend he had introduced, Winston Churchill. "He is a young man who will go far if he doesn't overbalance," Rhodes remarked of Churchill. Sixty years later, after going far, Churchill recalled the holiday with pleasure: "We rode ponies and carried guns and engaged in various affairs, nominally sporting." He too thought highly of his host.[1]

The report on his heart naturally turned Rhodes's thoughts back to his Will. No fundamental changes were needed any longer in its structure and principles, but it needed improving and supplementing here and there. He was not sure that he had got the balance of qualifications for the scholarships quite right. Above all, he wanted to avoid "bookworms"; and after much thought in Scotland he altered the proportions to be allotted to the different qualifications, in a codicil dated 11 October 1901. A comparison of the marks to be assigned under the Will of 1899 and the codicil of 1901 shows how he brought the humaner qualifications up to parity with the intellectual:

	1899	1901
Literary and scholastic	4/10	3/10
Manly sports	2/10	2/10
Qualities of manhood	2/10	3/10
Moral force of character	2/10	2/10

The qualities of manhood were defined as "truth, courage, devotion to duty, sympathy for and protection of the weak, kindliness, unselfishness and fellowship". The charitable side of Rhodes's nature was growing in strength as his life ebbed.

It extended, too, to his family, few of whom had ever been very close to him. He was planning to buy a family property for his heirs, particularly for Frank and the children of his brother Ernest, and Hawksley was instructed to negotiate the purchase of an estate in Norfolk, Dalham Hall. He also planned more specific bequests to his relations, which were finally embodied in another codicil on 18 January 1902, together with a characteristic lecture on the duties of an expectant heir and a country landlord: he must live in dignity and comfort, but he must have a profession or business for at least ten years, provided it be not in the army, and above all he must not develop into "what I call a loafer".[2]

More important was the question of the Trustees, for there would be money to spare when all the bequests were met. This was "the personal matter that may affect the world", which Rhodes had told Milner he wished to discuss with him in May. While in Scotland he had made up his mind to add Milner to the list of Trustees, from which he had deleted Stead in January. Milner was flattered and enthusiastic, and took his responsibilities with the utmost seriousness. He wrote to Rhodes on 10 August, before his appointment was finally decided, in admiration of the scholarship scheme: "It is conceived in the most broad and munificent spirit and is calculated to produce an effect out of all proportion to the mere money outlay, enormous though that is." As to the wider purposes for which the residue of the money was to be used, Milner confessed that he did not entirely understand what Rhodes had in mind, and wished he would put some thoughts on paper for the general guidance of the Trustees, though without fettering their discretion by binding clauses in the Will. He was personally willing to serve or to stand down, but "being in complete sympathy with your broad ambitions for the race", he obviously hoped to be appointed; and he duly was.[3]

Grey, too, was thoroughly dependable. After he had left Rhodes's house party at Rannoch Lodge, a letter followed him in the last week of August:[4]

"You will find under the disposition of my will there will be a large yearly balance. For the Scholarships will not absorb more than £60,000 a year—I put no instructions in the will as to this but I suggest that you should dispose of the balances per annum.

(1) By creating a Reserve Fund for the Scholarships as the Diamond Mines cannot last for ever.
(2) You would assist after college the most promising of your youths in their professions in after life especially if they show indications of higher ideas and a desire to

undertake public duties—the paramount object instilled into them being the preservation and consolidation of the British Empire.

(3) If deemed advisable the assistance of the formation of a Parliamentary Party who without any desire for office will always give their vote to Imperial Purposes.

(4) The most dangerous portion of the Empire being Africa, the steady encouragement of emigration especially women and getting *our* people on the land.

"We shall never be safe in Africa until we occupy the soil equally with the Dutch."

Rhodes's third proposal seems to have emanated from discussion with Milner.

The letter shows, as one would expect, that the future of Africa was never far from his mind. Even on holiday in Scotland or on the Continent he continued planning and sending out advice and directives. His correspondence between August and December is full of letters on private and public problems in the Cape Colony and the North. There was still the question of Asiatic labour: Arabs were a failure, and McDonald was pressing for Indians or Chinese. There was the question of land settlement, on which Rhodes reported Milner's thoughts to Michell and published his own in the *Daily Telegraph*. There were important developments in Northern Rhodesia, with which the missionary Coillard and a cousin of Grey's kept him in touch. Stevens wrote to ask if Rhodes wanted to continue his subsidy to two periodicals at the Cape, one Dutch and one English. He heard with pleasure that the Prince and Princess of Wales had stayed at Groote Schuur. Michell kept him in touch with the political situation, reporting pessimistically on the war and urging Rhodes to return to the Cape. The High Commissioner would dismiss the Government if he did, said Michell; and Kipling confirmed that Milner was saying "Rhodes or suspension".[5]

Meanwhile Rhodes had left Scotland, obedient to the welcome injunction of "constant change". He spent a few days in London —long enough to deal with another matter resurrected from the past, the correspondence with Schnadhorst about his contribution to the Liberal Party in 1891, which showed clearly enough how Rhodes's unpolished style had betrayed him and misled Schnadhorst.[6] Then he set out for the Continent, travelling mainly by motor-car with his usual company of Jameson, Beit, Metcalfe and

Jourdan. They visited Paris, Lucerne, many towns in Italy, and finally sailed from Brindisi on 18 November for Egypt. Partly he was seeking health, but partly also new discoveries. He saw the northern end of his beloved railway advancing south, but failed to reach Khartoum owing to the heat; he found a drought-resisting maize for Mashonaland and bought more Egyptian donkeys; he was photographed at the newly rising Assouan dam. He wrote often to Michell: sometimes that he was fit, sometimes mentioning trouble with his heart, sometimes foreseeing death.[7] Unfortunately, the misdeeds of the Princess also played a large part in their correspondence.

After his brusque telegram to Michell on 5 June, Rhodes had taken no further interest in the Princess's forgeries until early September, when he referred to them in a letter to Michell. Jourdan assured Michell on 30 September that no compromising letters existed from Rhodes to the Princess; and a week later, in response to an enquiry from Michell, he explained that neither he nor Rhodes could type, an assurance which helped to destroy the authenticity of the two typewritten letters to the Princess supposedly signed by Rhodes. The development of the scandal at the Cape soon made it impossible for Rhodes to stand aloof. In August an advertisement in the *Cape Argus* warned the public against forged bills in the name of Rhodes. On 12 October the press reported a case brought by T. Louw against Rhodes and the Princess jointly, over a promissory note for £2,000 in Rhodes's name on which he had advanced £1,150 to the Princess. A verdict was given against the Princess, but the case against Rhodes was deferred as he denied signature.

Two weeks later Hawksley sent to Rhodes copies of the correspondence on the case which he had received from Michell. He reported that Michell was uneasy about the Scholtzes and wanted to get the Princess out of the country; but if the Princess were to be charged with forgery, evidence would have to be taken from Rhodes by a commission. Rhodes now began to take an active interest in the case. He wrote to Hawksley on 2 November instructing him to make sure of the truth about the Princess's purported visits to Hatfield, Lord Salisbury's home, in order to impugn her credibility. On the 20th of the same month Stevens informed him that the Princess had been arrested, and a week later that she had been released, presumably on bail. "The assumption is," he added, "a substantial remittance has arrived." Mr. Louw nevertheless was still out of pocket, and persisted with his case against Rhodes. On 3 December Rhodes wrote angrily to Michell from the Nile, complaining that he could not understand why Louw persisted since he knew the bills to be forged. The answer was surely simple: he wanted his money back.

Meanwhile the Princess had completely lost her head. Rumours fluttered round Cape Town, which she had started as a last desperate defence, that she possessed compromising letters from both Rhodes and Milner. The rumours reached Milner, who had been warily refusing to see the Princess for many months. On 6 November she wrote a hysterical letter to him, full of the same hints and scurrilous abuse of Rhodes, whose interests, nevertheless, she still professed to cherish. She assured Milner that Rhodes had indeed been helping her financially, but had stopped doing so because he disliked the policy she had pursued in *Greater Britain*. That was why he was now denying his signature on her bills, but he had offered to save her if she would hand over to him the letters from Milner which she had in her possession. Milner instituted discreet enquiries through his C.I.D. chief, Henry Widdowson, who visited the Princess on 11 November.

She gave Widdowson copies of what purported to be Rhodes's letters to her, alleging that "the originals were typewritten and were in the care of the German Consul at his residence at Newlands"; and a few days later she also gave him some more letters relating to Rhodes (but not by him) and two other documents purporting to have been written by Rhodes. All these are preserved in the Milner Papers, and the essential ones are reproduced in Appendices B and C. It is clear that the Princess was trying to make money by selling the documents, but they appear to have made little impression. The Milner Papers contain no comment on their authenticity, either by Milner or by anyone else. The series does not include the letters later denounced at the Princess's trial as forgeries, which are in the Radziwill Papers at Rhodes House. On the other hand, the originals alleged to be in the hands of the German Consul never turned up in public; nor did any letters from Milner himself to the Princess, though one or two, of a perfectly uncompromising character, are to be found in the Milner Papers.[8]

Milner also took another precautionary step which the Milner Papers reveal. Recalling the letter of introduction to himself which the Princess had brought out from Lord Salisbury two years earlier, he suggested to Hely-Hutchinson, his successor at the Cape, that he should enquire whether that too was a forgery. Hely-Hutchinson duly enquired, and replied on 24 December that Salisbury had no recollection of writing it. But many years afterwards Lady Milner (Salisbury's daughter-in-law by her first marriage) enquired about it from her sister-in-law, Lady Gwendolin Cecil, who replied that she thought the letter "undoubtedly genuine" though "not characteristic" of her father. Lady Milner wrote a note to this effect across Hely-Hutchinson's letter to Milner; but that was done, of course, long after the event and after Milner's death. His suspicions of the Princess at the time were easily understandable.[9]

In December the case began to take on a still more deplorable aspect. Hawksley was able to assure Rhodes, on Lord Robert Cecil's authority, that the Princess's diary was false throughout so far as references to Salisbury were concerned; but he also suggested for the first time that Rhodes might have to go to the Cape to give evidence. It was not yet certain: possibly an affidavit would suffice if he could not reach Cape Town by 1 February 1902, when Louw's case against him was to be heard. Early in January, however, this prospect disappeared, since the Princess had to be allowed to exercise the right of cross-examining Rhodes in the course of her prosecution. The best that Hawksley could do was to apply for a postponement of Louw's case until 8 April, which was not granted, and for a commission to take Rhodes's evidence against the Princess in London, which was forestalled by Rhodes's own decision to return to South Africa at once, regardless of his health.

Meanwhile the Princess was desperately trying to protect herself by ruining others. After appealing vainly to Mrs. Scholtz for financial help, she successfully sought to embroil Dr. Scholtz with a fellow-doctor, who thereupon reported him to the Medical Council for professional misconduct. Dr. Scholtz, who seems to have been something of a charlatan in any case—he included among his medical qualifications the description of "Fellow of the Balneological and Climatological Society, London"—was duly struck off the Medical Register. He collapsed and died a few weeks later. Mrs. Scholtz bombarded Rhodes with letters attacking the Princess in hysterical terms, and begging him to come to the Cape. The Princess returned as good as she got, describing Mrs. Scholtz as Rhodes's mistress and threatening to reveal compromising correspondence about the Raid if the case against herself were not stopped. To this ghastly imbroglio Rhodes decided on 14 January to return.

He had arrived back in London from Egypt on 2 January,

mainly to deal with family matters. The negotiations for the purchase of Dalham Hall were virtually complete, and he planned to visit it with Hawksley. The consequential amendment to his Will was prepared for signature on 18 January; and that was in fact his last day in England. He sailed that night from Southampton with Jameson for the last time, having refused to plead ill health as an excuse for fear of upsetting the stock market. He caught a severe cold at sea, and suffered a bad fall one night when he had chosen to sleep on a table in the hope of enjoying a cooler breeze across his cabin. By the time the ship reached the Cape, he was already in fact a dying man.

Few of his friends appear to have realised how desperately ill he was: Hawksley, for instance, wrote more than once after his departure hoping to see him back in a few weeks.[10] When he arrived at the Cape on 2 February, the day after Louw's case against him had been heard and dismissed, local politics began at once to embroil him again as if nothing had changed. The South African League urged him to take up the cause of suspension, to which he agreed. He met a group of its members on 17 February in Cape Town, and a petition to the Governor to suspend the constitution, signed by Rhodes and almost all the Progressive Members of the Legislative Assembly, was duly presented. Sprigg resisted it; Merriman opposed it; Milner wrote to Hely-Hutchinson to give it his blessing; but Rhodes's last bolt was already shot.[11]

Not even Milner knew how near the end was. He still looked on Rhodes as the only alternative Prime Minister. Ignoring the distasteful scandal of the Princess, he wrote a long letter on the political situation to welcome Rhodes on his arrival. The tone of the letter is again that of an elder statesman, detached from the turmoil at the Cape, to a politician who still, presumably, had a part to play there.[12] On land settlement, he reported that "we are *crawling* along in this matter, and, owing to the disturbed state of affairs, very little land has been obtainable". On the political position at Cape Town, he expressed delight that the meeting of Parliament had been put off, and hoped that it would not be summoned for at least six months, preferably not until there was an assured majority. He examined the various alternatives to suspension of the constitution, lamenting that they would need legislation at Westminster. He concluded:

"It is not for me to take a leading part in the matter. These are my *private* views, given to you in confidence, as I believe our objects are the same. But I disclaim any desire to dictate to Cape Colony, though I am prepared to back up any action the loyal party may decide to take."

It is not such a letter as Milner would have written to a man he knew to be dying. The truth is that he was now deeply under Rhodes's influence, and at last genuinely regarded him as indispensable for the future. The posthumous remarks on Rhodes in the Milner Papers are unmistakable in this sense.

Such a note of welcome from Milner was deeply gratifying to Rhodes, and it was to please Milner that he sponsored the movement for suspension of the constitution. But the rest of what awaited him at the Cape was tragic and bitter.[13] A letter from the Princess reached Jameson on the day after their arrival, 3 February, asking to see him; another came the next day; and on the same day a friend of the Princess also wrote to him to blacken the character of the Scholtzes. Evidently none of this campaign yielded any result. On 12 February the Princess wrote to Jameson again to tell him that she had repaid Louw and now intended to hit back at Rhodes. "Well, the woman will show she can bite," she wrote; and on the 21st she commenced an action against Rhodes for £1,400.

A week later, on the last day of February, Rhodes gave evidence to a commission, repudiating her forgeries. He drove into Cape Town for the purpose in a Cape-cart from his seaside cottage at Muizenberg, where he stayed every night for the sake of the cool breeze. Usually he went to and fro in his new Wolseley car, but for this last occasion he preferred the old-fashioned transport of his early days. He sat in court munching sandwiches while he gave evidence, just as he had done once before at Westminster, because he feared that friends would see how ill he was if he lunched at the Club. It was his last appearance in Cape Town. Jameson and other intimates knew, and Rhodes himself was soon to know, that his condition was desperate. The Princess, who had a cottage near his at Muizenberg, tried repeatedly to see him, but he always avoided her.

It was probably as early as 24 February that the end was seen, though not by Rhodes, to be certain. On that day Rhodes telegraphed his friend Grimmer not to come yet to the Cape; on the same day Le Sueur countermanded the instruction. Michell and Smartt were near at hand; Jameson and Metcalfe were constantly with him; McDonald was summoned from Bulawayo on 4 March.

Innes came of his own accord to visit the dying man, and described the scene long afterwards in his *Autobiography*:

"On the narrow *stoep* of that tin-roofed cottage (the thatch which now decks it was a later improvement) sat, mortally stricken and in sore need of spacious and airy surroundings, one of the most famous and wealthiest men in the British Empire."

None but the most intimate friends was allowed near him. Jameson forbade Merriman and Currey to come; Le Sueur told the Archbishop of Cape Town, who asked if Rhodes would welcome a visit, that he was disinclined to see anyone. Only such news as might cheer him up was allowed to reach him: a letter from Lady Ormonde reporting the Kaiser's delight at the progress of the transcontinental telegraph; a message from Kitchener that the Boers had asked for an armistice conference; a sympathetic telegram from Lord Rosebery and another from Hofmeyr; a special edition of the *Cape Argus*, faked for his benefit with an encouraging bulletin on his illness. It is not certain when Jameson finally declared that there was no hope, but he certainly telegraphed Hawksley to that effect on 10 March. Rhodes still fixed his mind on the future and his friends. On 12 March he made Jameson an executor of his Will; on the same day, through Jameson, he sent instructions appointing Rudd to be a Director of De Beers. Ten days later he ordered a passage to be booked for him on a ship sailing for England on 26 March. To placate him, the passage was booked and a cabin prepared.

He was already sinking, and he died on the day the ship sailed. In his last hours, those nearest to him heard more than one dying whisper. "So little done, so much to do," was a favourite version of his last words, heard by Michell a few hours before the end, but there were many other phrases on his lips. "Rhodes was talking to God," wrote Stead, "and not merely talking to God, but himself assuming both parts of the dialogue." It was not the easy death which he had forced Jameson to promise him. The death certificate was simply inscribed: "Heart disease". A postmortem confirmed the diagnosis, with macabre details.[14]

*   *   *

The funeral ceremonies were after Rhodes's own heart: "big and simple, barbaric, if you like." His body was moved the same night, in a coffin of Matabele teak, from Muizenberg to Groote

Schuur, where a woman friend laid two sprays of white flowers on it on behalf of his sisters and his aged friend, Mrs. Schreiner, still living, and of "loyal South African womanhood generally". The next day the Prime Minister announced a state funeral and national mourning. Rhodes's own train, recently designed to popularise the northern journey, was made ready to carry him to the Matopos, with the De Beers directors' private coach converted into a "*chapelle ardente*". From Saturday to Monday (Sunday, 30 March, being Easter Day) the body lay in state at Groote Schuur. On Wednesday, it was moved to Cape Town to lie in state in Parliament, and thence, on the following day, to the Cathedral, where a funeral service was conducted and the Archbishop delivered an address on the text: "Know ye not that there is a prince and a great man fallen this day in Israel?" From the Cathedral the coffin was carried to the train, which left by night for the north, loaded with flowers.

It passed through Kimberley in the early morning of Friday, 4 April, and thence to Vryburg and Mafeking, skirting the area where renewed hostilities were in progress and Methuen had just sustained a defeat. At every halt there were more flowers and more mourners: among them, at Kimberley, one of Lobengula's sons, an employee of De Beers. It was not until Tuesday, 8 April, that the train reached Bulawayo, where a second funeral service was held. The next day the coffin was carried up into the hills, where a grave had been dug on the site of the "View of the World." The burial took place on 10 April, more than a fortnight after Rhodes's death. The officiating clergyman preached a sermon on Rhodes's three ideas: imperialism based not on force but on freedom; the solidarity of humanity; and progress. A valedictory poem was read out by Rudyard Kipling, later to be inscribed on the memorial at Cape Town. The gravestone carried the simple inscription: "Here lie the remains of Cecil John Rhodes". Thousands of Matabele lined the route, and cried out their royal salute, "*Bayete*", which had never been given to any white man before. Three weeks later they held an *indaba* at the World's View, attended by Colonel Frank Rhodes, who committed his brother's grave to their care.

Milner had written on 20 March, when he was daily expecting the news of Rhodes's death, that "certainly there has never been a time since first I came to South Africa when I have wanted him more". The words were true in more than a conventional sense, for Milner was only then beginning to appreciate Rhodes's potentialities, having at last overcome his initial suspicions. The most serious problems that he had to face in South Africa were still before him. In the face of many of them wrong courses were taken, which might have been taken differently if Milner had had either Rhodes's advice to counter his own or Rhodes's support to endorse his own. The movement for the suspension of the constitution was defeated finally at an Imperial Conference in London. The Boers' surrender at Vereeniging in May 1902 was followed by a policy of clemency combined with assimilation into a unitary state, which was clean contrary to Rhodes's plan for federation. The disastrous decision was taken to admit Chinese labour, which contributed substantially to the fall of the Conservative Government in 1905. Not all was failure, of course, nor could Rhodes have set everything right. The faithful Jameson followed Rhodes's precepts, as Prime Minister of the Cape Colony from 1904, in seeking reconciliation with General Botha and promoting a customs union of the four colonies. Milner's administrative work in the period of reconstruction also deserved the highest praise. But two things are certain which might have been less certain if Rhodes had lived. The first is that the two European races in South Africa have never fused, but grown farther apart. The second is that sixty years afterwards, it was the successors of Kruger who could be seen to have won the Boer War.

In a curious way, it was the egregious Princess Radziwill, though she could hardly tell truth from fiction in her own mind, who best understood the failure of Milner and Rhodes to work together. Her case moved to its inevitable conclusion soon after Rhodes died. The trial, on twenty-four counts of forgery, began on 28 April and lasted three days. She was convicted and sentenced to two years' imprisonment. After her release, she tried to bring a case against the Rhodes Trustees for £400,000, but she bore no personal animosity against Rhodes. When she wrote her book, *Cecil Rhodes, Man and Empire-Maker*, in 1918 in a style of high-flown imperialism, some of her judgments of Rhodes and Milner were surprisingly just; and of the contemporaries who wrote about either, she has the distinction of being the only one who had an intuitive understanding based on personal acquaintance with both.

There is much that is ridiculous or reads ironically in her book, but little that is vindictive. She laments the intrigues that served to keep the two men apart, without mentioning her own lamentable contributions to them. She was at pains to deny that she

C. J. R. on horseback near the end of his life

Cartoon by Max Beerbohm of "The New Rhodes Scholar" (received by C. W. Boyd, first Secretary of the Rhodes Trust), dated 1907

was in love with either of them; but both were bachelors, and the thought of her powers of attraction did not displease her. She was right in guessing that Milner did not trust Rhodes, "but nevertheless, he would have liked Rhodes as a coadjutor"; and right in seeing that Rhodes would only help either Milner or the Bond if, in her crude terms, "they were willing to eat humble pie before him". Her judgment is also right that "had there existed any real intimacy between Groote Schuur and Government House at Cape Town, the whole course of South African politics might have been different". Both the Rhodes Papers and the Milner Papers bear her out; and the Radziwill Papers show how tireless, irresponsible and damaging were her own efforts to remedy the situation which she correctly divined. She was a fatal busybody, but she had her moments of penetrating perception.

Rhodes died at a bad moment for his reputation. The miserable fiasco of the Boer War, from which his name could not be dissociated, had still not reached its conclusion. Whenever his name was publicly mentioned in the last year of his life, it seemed to be in some unsavoury connection; and there were many of them. One occasion was a last attempt to force the publication of the "missing telegrams" in March 1901. Another was the allegation, in the *Spectator*, that the Liberals had let him down lightly at the Enquiry because of his contributions to the party funds; and this was followed by the publication of his correspondence with Schnadhorst in September. Then there was the autocratic attempt to suspend the constitution at Cape Town; and finally the scandal of Princess Radziwill. But in a way he was fortunate. If his reputation could hardly sink lower, it was bound to rise; and rise it did, in spectacular fashion, with the publication of his Will on 5 April 1902, followed a few weeks later by Stead's commentary on it and on his life, *The Last Will and Testament of Cecil John Rhodes*. "It is no exaggeration," wrote Sir Francis Wylie many years later, "to say that the publication of Rhodes's Will changed overnight the world's estimate of the man."

Every contemporary account confirms the verdict on the unique quality of Rhodes's Will, and the verdict has stood the test of time. In quantity, however, the estate proved less stupendous than the legends of his wealth had perhaps led people to expect. He was, of course, a very rich man, but for some years he had not been actively engaged in money-making—not so actively, at any rate, as he thought necessary for anyone really interested in money-making, which he considered a full-time job.

Q

He had remarked in his later speeches that politics and making money were incompatible activities, and that was true for anyone who wanted to put his whole heart and soul, as Rhodes did, into whatever he was doing. In his later years he had begun to be anxious whether he would even leave enough to pay for his beloved scholarships in addition to the other bequests. His intimates remarked on the growing caution and diminishing generosity of his later years, though characteristically he chose to sacrifice his own comforts first: for instance, the improvements needed to make his cottage at Muizenberg habitable, which were not completed even when he died there. He never had a very accurate idea how much he was worth, but he feared that it might not be enough.

When his estate was first valued on his death, the preliminary figure was £4,137,130. But since his ways with his current accounts—a necessary plural—were both casual and complex in the extreme, it was difficult to say how much there was to be paid in debts. By 1907, when the debts and the death duties and the smaller legacies had been paid, the estate was revalued at £3,383,691, and that was the total sum from which the Trustees had to carry out the main purposes of the Will. It was ample enough, and careful stewardship has since increased the capital. The tasks defined in the Will could comfortably be met, as the world knows they have been. But there was clearly insufficient margin for the undefined tasks which had been discussed with Stead in the early 1890's and which had given Milner and Hawksley so much anxiety towards the end. The Secret Society had fortunately disappeared from the text of the Will, though the idea had not disappeared from Rhodes's mind. He still hoped to the last that the Trustees would somehow carry out his plans for remoulding the world nearer to his heart's desire, and Milner at least would gladly have devoted his life to carrying out Rhodes's purpose. But in so far as power is money—and that was certainly Rhodes's definition of it—he left them virtually without the power to do so, except through the medium of the scholarships.

It is no small exception. That the scholarships have justified themselves is a commonplace. They are probably the only scholarships in the world which are widely known by the name of their founder, and whose purpose is broadly understood, outside the University where they are held. To what extent they have fulfilled their founder's purpose is still a moot point. If it was, as Jameson once said with characteristic impercipience, to produce another Rhodes, then clearly they have failed and are likely to continue to fail, and probably few would now want them to succeed. If it was, as Stead believed, to create a world-wide order of dedicated Imperialists destined to control mankind, then one can only be thankful that the failure has been total and decisive. If it was, as the Will itself declared, to promote international peace and avert war, then the fact that two world wars have occurred in the sixty years since Rhodes's death, in which his scholars have been ranged on opposite sides, is clearly neither here nor there in judging a purpose which would at best need several generations for its fulfilment.

There can be no final judgment, and Rhodes would have been pleased that it should be so. He was striving after a visionary ideal which he could not define himself; still less could he grasp it. No one else is likely to be able to define or grasp it for him. Much of what he brooded over, and talked about in his interminable monologues, has gone with the wind of change. In a sense it was fortunate that there was not too much money left over in his Will to be devoted to ill-defined and obsolete enthusiasms, which could only have brought Rhodes's name into posthumous ridicule and contempt. As it is, apart from the detractors who will never forget ancient wrongs, his memory is embodied today for most people in two symbols: the name of a country, which may still prove to be the first successful model of a multi-racial partnership, and the title of an educational trust. The latter at least is likely to survive when everything else that Rhodes hoped to be remembered for, and all the mud that his enemies threw at him, has disappeared and been forgotten. It may not be quite what he expected; but it is his *monumentum aere perennius*.

Sources

Works mentioned under Chapters Twenty-five and Twenty-six, and additionally:

Aydelotte, F.: *The Vision of Cecil Rhodes*
Elton, Lord: *The Rhodes Trust, 1903–1952*
Parkin, George: *The Rhodes Scholarships*
A Chronicle of the Funeral Ceremonies from Muizenberg to the Matopos March–April 1902
The Trial of the Princess Radziwill (reprinted from the *Cape Times*)

Notes

1 Personal reminiscence of Sir Winston Churchill on 8 March, 1961.
2 R.H.L. Rhodes's Wills, 6.
3 R.H.L. MSS. Afr. s. 8, f. 78.
4 R.H.L. MSS. Afr. t. 5, f. 506.
5 Rhodes Papers, A. 224 (Arabs); C. 14. 81 and 82 (McDonald to Rhodes); A. 225 (Rhodes to Michell); C. 1. 155 (Coillard); B. 1740 (Rhodes to Beit); C. 5. 42 (subsidies to periodicals); C. 11. 10 (Hawksley); C. 15. 65 (Michell); C. 28. 54 (Kipling).
6 Rhodes Papers, B. 1731 (to Rosebery); C. 27. 141 (to *Spectator*).
Rhodes Papers, A. 225, A. 227. A. 231; Radziwill Papers (Rhodes to Hawksley, 2 Nov. 1901; Stevens to Rhodes, 20 and 27 Nov. 1901).
8 Unpublished Milner Papers, vol. 48 (New College).
9 *Ibid.*, vol. 12, ff. 169A and 169B.
10 Rhodes Papers, C. 11. 11, 12 and 13 (Hawksley to Rhodes).
11 Rhodes Papers, C. 2. 276 and 281 (branches of South African League).
12 Rhodes Papers, C. 27. 140.
13 Radziwill Papers and Diary (Rhodes House).
14 Rhodes Papers, B. 1767 (Grimmer); A. 243 (Rudd); C. 28. 55 (Kaiser); R.H.L. MSS. Afr. t. 5, ff. 491a and 491b (death certificate and postmortem).

TELEGRAMS CONNECTED WITH THE JAMESON RAID

THE following are the texts, as received by Rhodes in Cape Town, of a number of telegrams sent from London in the months before the Jameson Raid. The first text (a "missing telegram" not previously published in full) is contained in a confirmatory letter, which is reproduced here. The deciphered version of it, from which the last four sentences (the only part previously published) have been torn off, is filed with the letter, folded up inside it.

The other four telegrams were all published (with some interesting discrepancies) in an Appendix to the Report of the Select Committee on the Raid. The diagonal lines indicate the division of the corresponding cipher-groups. The cipher-book used for these telegrams is preserved in the Central African Archives at Salisbury, Southern Rhodesia.

Articles on these five telegrams have been published in *History Today*, June and July 1962.

1. Rhodes Papers, C. 3B. 255
   H. Canning (British South Africa Company, London) to Rhodes

   2/8/95

   Dear Mr. Rhodes,

   We sent you today the following private wire, which I confirm. "Earl Grey and Dr. Harris saw Secretary of State for Colonies, he considers Crown Colony having been transferred to Cape Colony at moment entering office he has shown practical proof of sympathy with Mr. C. J. Rhodes' policy; but although he is friendly very, considers cession Protectorate at any near date utterly impossible. His attitude on this point without compromise and decisive. He states presence C. J. Rhodes England will not alter his mind; that C. J. Rhodes must leave him alone for the present. In his opinion he acceded to transfer Crown Colony in order to ensure immediate further Railway construction, and much upset that it was not the case because sale B. Ry. Co. to Cape Colony it had not taken place.

Dr. Harris explained Parliamentary position and Sauer's remarks to convince Secretary of State for Colonies no breach of faith on our part; but he still considers BSA Co. if finance is favourable is obligated to proceed at once with Railway towards Palapye. We decided therefore to inform Secretary of State for Colonies guardedly reason we wish to have base at Gaberones, and advisable our presence in Protectorate. Secretary of State for Colonies heartily in sympathy with C. J. Rhodes' policy but he would not on this account alter decision with regard to Protectorate, but offered as alternate, to justify residents of BSA Co. in Protectorate, to consider favourably at once application for large land grant in Protectorate in exchange for Railway extension north. It is now for Mr. C. J. Rhodes to decide whether large land grant with formation Township and sale of stands is practicable for October. This appears to be the only solution."

This was a somewhat long cable to code but I hope it came to you in a clear form. The time will come no doubt.

Believe me,

Yours faithfully,

Herbert Canning.

2. Rhodes Papers, C. 3B. 266

(i) Harris to Rhodes 4/11/95 (as decoded)

Mr. Chamberlain / he does not return / London / until / to morrow / we have / spoken / E. Fairfield / and / we have agreed to / if / Colonial Office / they will transfer / to us / balance / protectorate / with / police / 7th November / we will accept (agree to) / any liberal / native / reserve / for / Native Chiefs / also / remain / under / Imperial / rule / for a period / of / years / and / we do give up / railway / subsidy / £200,000 / last bargain / E. Fairfield / he does urge / if you cannot approve / let us know about this as soon as possible by telegram / we believe / E. Fairfield / he will carry out / Regret to inform you that / Mr. Chamberlain / he does continue / consult / Transvaal / with regard to / drifts

F. Rutherfoord Harris

(ii) Harris to Rhodes 4/11/95 (as decoded)

Registered / address / of / Earl Grey / is / Gothical / London / You must / with regard to / this / [undeciphered group] / only

F. Rutherfoord Harris

(iii) Harris to Rhodes 4/11/95 (as decoded)

Your telegram of 3rd received / E. Fairfield / we will / see him / and / explain / in return / for / transfer at once / Protectorate / with / police / we are / prepared / deal / liberally / land / we have offered already / if they give / now / police / and / balance / protectorate / we / will leave / native / reserves entirely / under / imperial / rule / for a period / of / years / it is / native chiefs / wish / more than / more / land / will you agree to it / have telegraphed / Earl Grey / must come / London / you have not selected / best / man / to arrange / with / Mr. Chamberlain / we have sent / already / Flora / to convince / Mr. Chamberlain / support of / Times / newspaper / and / if you can telegraph / course / you / wish / Times / to accept / now with regard to / Transvaal / Flora / will do so

F. Rutherfoord Harris

(iv) Harris to Rhodes 5/11/95 (as decoded)

We have seen / E. Fairfield / Hon. R. H. Meade / Col. Goold-Adams / and / we have agreed to / what / land / we do give / Native Chiefs / Secretary of State / holds an interview with us / tomorrow / afternoon / three o'clock / and after / Native Chiefs / if he is satisfied / and / they will be / present / Secretary of State / he will give / BSA Company / balance / Protectorate / with / police / We reported / your / letter / to / A. Beit / during the month / to / these / and / Flora / We have / these / solid

F. Rutherfoord Harris

LETTERS PURPORTING TO HAVE BEEN WRITTEN BY RHODES TO PRINCESS RADZIWILL

OF the following letters, which are printed in chronological order, Nos. 1, 2, 10, 11, 12 are to be found in the Radziwill Papers at Rhodes House, and Nos. 3, 4, 5, 6, 7, 8, 9 in the Milner Papers (Vol. 48) at New College, Oxford. No. 1 was admitted by Rhodes, or on his behalf, to be genuine; Nos. 10 and 11 were declared to be forgeries at the Princess's trial in April 1902. The remainder are in doubt.

1. April 1899 (from the Burlington Hotel, London)
Dear Princess,
   Excuse my delay but I have been very busy. It is always dangerous to advise in money matters to friends and I make a rule not to do so. In order to get a safe 5¼ per cent I think any-one might subscribe with safety to the Mashonaland Railway debentures a proposal for which is in the papers but I dislike business matters with friends.
Yours truly,
C. J. Rhodes
I hope I may see you on your return.

2. 10 September 1899
Dear Princess,
   I read your letter. With regard to your remarks I must refer you to our conversation on board the Scot. I could not produce the telegrams because it was impossible to drag the Queen's name into this matter. I know Chamberlain better than you imagine I do. I had to look to the future, about which I never felt misgivings. If Kruger does not climb down, the new year will see us masters of Pretoria. I dont understand how you can trouble yourself about the matter. You would not care if you heard there was a quarrel between your cook and her kitchen-maid. This business has no importance whatever. A few weeks will see us masters of the Transvaal. As soon as troops arrive it will be a walk-over. I shall then go home and get out of Chamberlain the price he agreed to pay for my scheme. I

dont see where Rhodesia would have come in had I produced the cables, it was necessary for my scheme to obtain a free hand in South Africa which I mean to have as soon as this business is over. When my railway will be finished when our interests will have been established on a sound footing in the Transvaal then only will England be real mistress of the African continent. Producing the cables at the time of the enquiry would have been a stupidity worthy of a schoolboy.

Yours,   C. J. Rhodes

3. 17 November 1900
Dear Princess,
    I will not see Armstrong, I will not receive messages from Hofmeyr—
Hofmeyr will not help me, I will not take office at present, perhaps later on if I am asked from all sides to do so. Why do you worry me, I will not be worried. I have got work to do in Rhodesia, I wont be annoyed with these silly small Cape Politics, my future is known to me, no man, woman or child will turn me from my path, I know what I have got to do, all those people can shout as much as they like, I know when I have got to assert my rights, don't worry me. I will not take pledges, and I will have nothing to do with Hofmeyr at present.
    Don't come to lunch tomorrow.

Yours,   C. J. Rhodes

4. 30 November 1900
Dear Princess,
    Sonnenberg has been to see me. I wish you would not meddle in matters you do not understand, and influence people to speak to me on subjects I dislike. Sprigg is quite capable of doing what is required at present.
    Your remark as to my proving myself a good Premier of Federated South Africa, by becoming, first, Premier of the Colony, is absurd.
    I know what I have got to do and must not spoil my future by taking part in local politics.

Yours   C. J. Rhodes

5. 2 December 1900
Dear Princess,
    I have sent Stead through Jamieson [sic] the outline of the scheme which I think represents what ought to be done in the

matter of the settlement. It is as follows. Declare at once South Africa is Federated and summon the Federal Parliament at Cape Town. Let Milner nominate the representatives of the Transvaal, and the Orange Free State, and do one's level best to get the very best Boers to accept seats in the Assembly. The Federal Parliament would control the following seven subjects,

1. Armaments
2. Minerals
3. Tariffs
4. Ways and Communications
5. Native Policy
6. Coolie Immigration
7. Franchise and Naturalisation

Excluding the seven reserved subjects, I would give the Republics immediately a self government as complete as that enjoyed by any Australian Colony. The formula to be that they have not to be British Subjects, but that they have to be citizens of a Federated Empire, enjoying Australian Independence, each Colony would have a right to its own flag together with the Union Jack. All damages done by the war in the shape of burned Farmhouses to be restored, and the farms restocked this to be a first charge upon the federated revenue.

You must persuade Stead to offer these conditions as a possible base of agreement without pledging me in any way whatever. I cannot take any pledges, as circumstances may force my hand, and Rhodesia's interests must remain paramount. Milner is to be told that the scheme is Stead's, and you must find out in a discreet way what he thinks about it. I have had a hint of this given to Botha some time ago, but he did not see his way to discuss the question, so at least I was told.

Yours   C. J. Rhodes

6. 7 January 1901 (in answer to a letter of 4 January complaining that Rhodes's conduct was incomprehensible and wanting in frankness towards Stead and herself)
Dear Princess,

Your letter amused me: you do not seem at all to understand the position. I cannot bind myself to Cape Politics nor allow people to put me into a position where I should have to do something which might be misconstrued.

I must not lose from view the future development of Rhodesia; it is an excellent country for Dutch settlers and besides the Cape Colony has no future before it. All the interests of South Africa will concentrate themselves in the Transvaal and Rhodesia. It is in the North that we will find ourselves confronted by the social problems of the future.

It is silly saying I deal in underhand intrigues. I cannot prevent my friends saying what they think and it is just as well the Burghers know I am not their enemy.

They like me at heart and I do not see why they should not be told I am in favour of self government being granted to them as soon as possible. On the other hand we must think of the compensation due to the loyalists, and I wish you would write to Milner and ascertain his views on the subject.

Yours,   C. J. Rhodes

7. 10 or 16 January 1901
Dear Princess,

Thanks for Stead's letter. I see he agrees with my scheme, except on one or two points. Of course his idea of Steyn becoming Prime Minister of the Orange River Colony is preposterous, but I do not see the necessity to discourage him in his hopes of a future political career.

A great deal has been said about Federation. Jameson and Stead have discussed the subject at length several times and I can only agree with what Jameson said.

Yours   C. J. Rhodes

8. 6 February 1901
Dear Princess,

I have read your letter. You do not understand the situation. You preach a reconciliation with H and bring once more Armstrong forward. Armstrong may be Stead's friend but he is not the man I can employ.

He is a confirmed drunkard they tell me. About H why make overtures to him! All these people will come to me of their own accord when I will offer them what they want.

Sauer and Merriman only care for seats in the Cabinet. Scholtz had no business to tell you anything about his conversation with Botha, you cannot understand what I mean to do, so do not mention the subject again.

Find out what Milner thinks and means to do, this is the important point for me. We must federate at once if only on a/c of Rhodesia. Now is the time for the Imperial Government to impose Federation, once it has become a fact we can easily manage the Dutch, we have got several years before us to do the work and we possess the means to keep the Liberals at Home out of office: Roseberry [*sic*] will join us, as for the others, they have been bought once and can be so once more. I repeat it. Federation must be reached quickly and Milner made to understand he has got to work it.

Come to lunch when you can.

Yours   C. J. Rhodes

9. 20 February 1901
  Dear Princess,

Thanks for Stead's letter, of course all he says about Sauer is rubbish. I know Sauer well, all this hatred of myself is assumed and there are anxious times connected with our past relations which must almost oblige him to work with us when the time comes.

Stead knows what to say to him. I hope only he will take care not to make any suggestions in my name. —will understand him quite well without it.

I don't believe Milner will do any good up there unless he agrees to immediate Federation.

The Military are fools this business ought to have been finished long ago, but what could one expect of Roberts' silly proclamations. The Boers must be made to feel that they are beaten. It is absurd to think I cannot go on with my railway on account of the stupidity of our staff. If Botha had common sense he would have listened to the messages which I had conveyed to him last winter.

I shall expect you tomorrow.

Yours   C. J. Rhodes

10. 14 May 1901 (from Kimberley)
  Dear Princess,

The contemporary is quite good, only too weak as regards Roberts. In your next please stand up more energetically for Milner. And the paper, when it is started, must oppose any idea of the suppression of the Constitution. Writing to Chamberlain by this next mail. I am all right: feel stronger than a month ago. How are money matters? Enclosed is a bill; if anything unpleasant happens you will always find a friend who will advance you money on it, as you refuse to take mine. Only don't put it in a bank, and don't write about it; no need for Jordain [*sic*] to know anything about it. Any friend will do it, Scholtz or another one. I should give you the money to pay it when I come back, sometime in October or November. Don't go further than a thousand for yourself, and again as much for the paper, if you split with Burdett-Coutts. But in that case, let the account be put in your and the manager's joint names in the bank. If you don't find a friend, Hawksley will settle it for you in London.

Yours,   C. J. Rhodes

11. 20 May 1901 (from Kimberley)
Dear Princess,
   Marriott is here; I think we shall come to terms. He is anxious to go to Johannesburg; quite useless. Had better come to Rhodesia. If his report is favourable, will go to London and settle matters myself. Don't mention this to Salisbury when you write; he need not know it a day sooner than he ought. How is the paper getting on? I am sure you will not come to terms with Coutts; he is an awful little beast. You will have to fall back on me. How is the boy? and yourself, any more heart attacks? I am better; Jameson objects to Rhodesia, but I am going nevertheless.

Yours,   C. J. Rhodes

12. 30 May 1901
Dear Princess,
   Thanks for communication received through Mrs Scholtz. I have also heard from Stead. I am not surprised to hear Leyds is the only Boer who might be led to listen to his overtures. Leyds wants to be allowed to return to Pretoria, where he has got interests; besides a man of his kind will never consent to disappear from the political scene. I have always held the opinion that he ought to be encouraged in any friendly feelings he may have. Things will change in many ways when Kruger disappears. We must not lose sight of the fact that we will never succeed to induce Englishmen to settle definitely on the soil as farmers. We must of course offer them every possible inducement to do so, if only to silence certain sections of the Press at Home, but the Dutch will always be the strong element in the rural population, and my policy would be to let them know in an indirect way, we shall put no obstacles in their path, and allow our people to control

the industry, without interfering with the Boer farmer. I do not believe that the present peace negotiations will lead to anything. Leyds will not allow them to be brought to an issue, until he gets the assurance that he will not be interfered with in his plans for the future. I do not see why the Government will not let him hope he may in time return to Pretoria. It is always easy to get out of such promises. For my part I should not hesitate to let him believe the thing could be managed, and I would help him to obtain it, without in the least meaning to do so.

You reproach me for not stepping forward—but what would be the use of doing so at present. My time will come when all others will have failed. I know I shall not succeed now in winning over the Dutch in the Cape Colony, afterwards it will be another matter. My present aim is to come into touch with the Dutch in the Transvaal: they hold the key to the situation, and they must find me ready to respond to their appeal when they make it. This will take time of course, and I am not sorry for it, as I must first get this Chartered Business over. We must either get fresh capital, or take our chance with the Imperial Government. By the way try and buy Chartered shares when I am in London, they are sure to go up, Maguire I believe means to get something out of them, it will help to buy Julia some new frocks. I hope the paper will be a success.

Yours,

(sgd) C. J. Rhodes

DOCUMENTS IN THE MILNER PAPERS (VOL. 48) ALLEGED BY PRINCESS RADZIWILL TO HAVE ORIGINATED FROM RHODES

1. Undated memorandum on a proposed settlement of the Boer War:

A speedy termination of the war is to be desired in the interests of the burghers themselves as well as of the leaders. It is certainly in the interest of the English Colonial Secretary to grant as soon as possible Self Government to the two new Colonies.

Men like Commandant Botha and de Wet will most certainly later on be called upon to fill important positions in the new Federal Parliament and possibly in the future Cabinet. It would therefore be to their advantage to try and influence the Burghers so as to put an end to the present struggle. If they give later on their support to Mr. Rhodes and used their influence to bring about Federation in as short a time as possible, they would find he would do all he could to extend as far as possible, and as much as would be compatible with the safety of the Empire, the privileges attached to Self-government—one could hint that in case of a prompt termination of hostilities, certain concessions would not be too closely enquired into, and urge on Commandant Botha that a demand on his part for Federation would be met with eagerness by the British Government—The Military Authorities must be kept out of these negotiations and of course all these points must be touched upon only verbally.

*   *   *

The Princess states the above to be a true copy of the original in her possession.

2. Copy of a paragraph handed to the Princess by Mr. C. J. Rhodes in February 1901 to be published in "Greater Britain" as soon as the news reached us of Messrs. Sauer and Merriman's return to the Cape:

Paragraph

Messrs. Sauer and Merriman have sailed from Southampton for the Cape. We know one house in Town where they will be warmly welcomed. The divinity which presides at the hospitable board at 23 Strand Street will no doubt receive them with open arms, the more so that she will be able to hear from her old friend (?) who faithful to his character as a mole worked in the dark at his marriage with a lady who was not Madame Koopmans de Wet.

In February 1900 on his return from Kimberley after the siege Mr. Rhodes tried to see Madame Koopmans de Wet in which through her to try and receive negotiations with the Dutch party.

The person to be sent to her with a message asking for an interview, was Mrs. Bairns Father.

Madame Koopmans declined, and declared nothing should induce her to see Mr. Rhodes.

The paragraph above, which I refused to insert, was a revenge.

INDEX

497

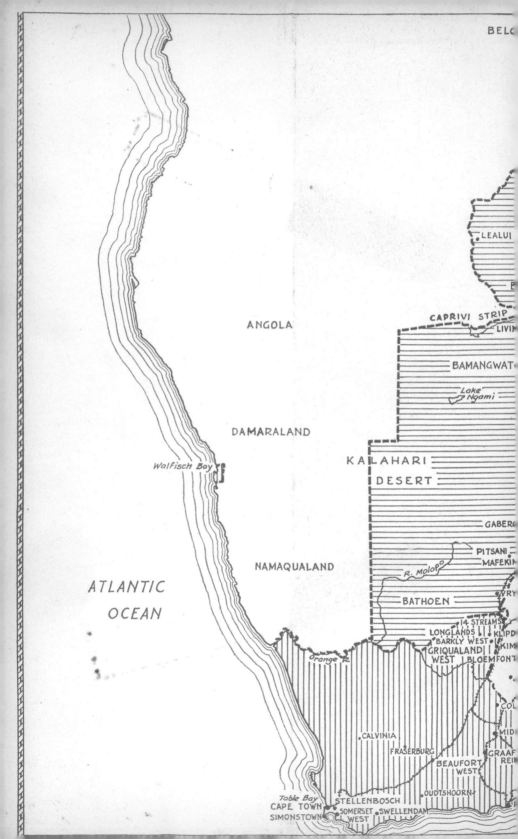

LEALUI

P

CAPRIVI STRIP

LIVIN

ANGOLA

BAMANGWAT

Lake
Ngami

DAMARALAND

KALAHARI

Walfisch Bay

DESERT

GABER

PITSANI

MAFEKIN

NAMAQUALAND

R. Molopo

ATLANTIC
OCEAN

BATHOEN

RY

14 STREAMS

LONGLANDS

KLIPD

BARKLY WEST

Orange R.

GRIQUALAND

KIM

WEST

BLOEMFONT

COL

MIDI

CALVINIA

GRAAF

FRASERBURG

REI

BEAUFORT
WEST

Table Bay

STELLENBOSCH

OUDTSHOORN

CAPE TOWN

SOMERSET

SIMONSTOWN

WEST

SWELLENDAM